American Legal Theory

The International Library of Essays in Law and Legal Theory
Series Editor: Tom D. Campbell

Schools

Natural Law, Vols I & II *John Finnis*
Justice *Thomas Morawetz*
Law and Economics, Vols I & II *Jules Coleman and Jeffrey Lange*
Critical Legal Studies *James Boyle*
Marxian Legal Theory *Csaba Varga*
Legal Reasoning, Vols I & II *Aulis Aarnio and Neil MacCormick*
Legal Positivism *Mario Jori*
American Legal Theory *Robert Summers*
Law and Language *Fred Schauer*
Sociological Theories of Law *Kahei Rokumoto*
Rights *Carlos Nino*
Law and Psychology *Martin Levine*
Feminist Legal Theory *Frances Olsen*
Law and Society *Werner Krawietz*

Areas

Criminal Law *Thomas Morawetz*
Tort Law *Ernest Weinrib*
Contract Law, Vols I & II *Larry Alexander*
Anti-Discrimination Law *Christopher McCrudden*
Consumer Law *Iain Ramsay*
International Law *Martti Koskenniemi*
Property Law, Vols I & II *Elizabeth Mensch and Alan Freeman*
Constitutional Law *Mark Tushnet*
Procedure *Denis Galligan*
Evidence and Proof *William Twining and Alex Stein*
Administrative Law *Denis Galligan*
Child Law *Harry Krause*
Family Law, Vols I & II *Harry Krause*
Welfare Law *Peter Robson*
Medicine and the Law *Bernard Dickens*
Commercial Law *Ross Cranston*
Communications Law *David Goldberg*
Environmental Law *Michael Blumm*
Conflict of Laws *Richard Fentiman*
Law and Religion *Wojciech Sadurski*
Human Rights Law *Philip Alston*
European Community Law, Vols I & II *Francis Snyder*

Legal Cultures

Comparative Legal Cultures *Csaba Varga*
Law and Anthropology *Peter Sack*
Hindu Law and Legal Theory *Ved Nanda*
Islamic Law and Legal Theory *Ian Edge*
Chinese Law and Legal Theory *Michael Palmer*
Socialist Law and Legal Theory *W. Butler*
Japanese Law and Legal Theory *Koichiro Fujikura*
Law and Development *Anthony Carty*
Jewish Law and Legal Theory *Martin Golding*
Legal Education *Martin Levine*

Future Volumes

Labour Law, Common Law and Legal Theory, Civil Law and Legal Theory, African Law and Legal Theory, Legal Ethics and Cumulative index.

American Legal Theory

Edited by

Robert Samuel Summers

McRoberts Research Professor of Law,
Cornell Law School
and
Arthur L. Goodhart Visiting Professor of Legal Science,
University of Cambridge, 1991–92

NEW YORK UNIVERSITY PRESS
REFERENCE COLLECTION

First published in the U.S.A. in 1992 by
NEW YORK UNIVERSITY PRESS
Washington Square
New York NY 10003

Library of Congress Cataloging-in-Publication Data
American legal theory / edited by Robert Samuel Summers.
p. cm. – (The International library of essays in law and legal theory. Schools)
Includes bibliographical references and index.
ISBN 0-8147-7951-4
1. Law–United States–Philosophy. I. Summers, Robert S. II. Series.
KF379.A45 1992
349.73'01–dc20
[347.3001] 91-4202
CIP

Contents

PART III CRITIQUE

Acknowledgements

The editor and publishers wish to thank the following for permission to use copyright material.

American Bar Association Journal for the essay: Herman Oliphant (1928), 'A Return to Stare Decisis', *American Bar Association Journal*, Vol. **14**, pp. 71–6, 107 and 159–62. Reprinted with permission from Vol. **14** of the 1928 issue of the *ABA Journal*, the Lawyers' Magazine published by the American Bar Association.

Columbia Law Review for essays: Karl N. Llewellyn (1930), 'A Realistic Jurisprudence – The Next Step', *Columbia Law Review*, **XXX**, No.4, pp. 431–65. Copyright © 1930 by the Directors of the Columbia Law Review Association, Inc. All Rights Reserved. This article originally appeared at **XXX** Colum. L. Rev. 431 (1930). Reprinted by permission, and Roscoe Pound (1908), 'Mechanical Jurisprudence', *Columbia Law Review*, Vol. **8**, pp. 605–23. Copyright © 1908 by the Directors of the Columbia Law Review Association, Inc. All Rights Reserved. This article originally appeared at **8** Colum. L. Rev. 605 (1908). Reprinted by permission.

Walter Wheeler Cook (1939), 'Williston on Contracts', *Illinois Law Review of Northwestern Univeristy*, Vol. **33**, pp. 497–516. Copyright © Walter Wheeler Cook. Reprinted by permission of the Northwestern University Law Review.

Cornell Law Review and Fred B. Rothman & Co. for essays: John Dewey (1925), 'Logical Method and Law', *The Cornell Law Quarterly*, Vol. **10**, pp. 17–27. © Copyright 1924 by Cornell University. All Rights Reserved, and Robert S. Summers (1981), 'Pragmatic Instrumentalism in Twentieth Century American Legal Thought – A Synthesis and Critique of Our Dominant General Theory About Law and Its Use', *Cornell Law Review*, Vol. **66**, pp. 861–948. © Copyright 1981 by Cornell University. All Rights Reserved.

Harvard Law Review for essays: Thomas Reed Powell (1924), 'The Judiciality of Minimum-wage Legislation', *Harvard Law Review*, Vol. **37**, pp. 545–73. Copyright © (1924) by the Harvard Law Review Association, and Oliver Wendell Holmes, Jr. (1897), 'The Path of the Law', *Harvard Law Review*, Vol. **X**, No. 8, pp. 457–78. Copyright © (1897) by The Harvard Law Review Association.

Michigan Law Review for the essay: Joseph W. Bingham (1912), 'What is the Law?', *Michigan Law Review*, Vol. **XI**, No. 1, pp. 1–25 and 109–21.

The Modern Law Review and Felix S. Cohen (1937), 'The Problems of a Functional Jurisprudence', *Modern Law Review*, Vol. **1**, pp. 5–26. Copyright © The Modern Law Review and Felix S. Cohen.

New York University Law Review for the essay: K.N. Llewellyn (1938), 'Through Title to Contract and a Bit Beyond', *New York University Law Quarterly Review*, Vol. **XV**, No. 2, pp. 159–209.

Roscoe Pound (1906), 'The Causes of Popular Dissatisfaction With the Administration of Justice', *American Law Review*, **40**, pp. 729–49; Roscoe Pound (1907), 'The Need of a Sociological Jurisprudence', *The Green Bag*, **19**, pp. 607–15, and Roscoe Pound (1940), 'The Possibility of a Measure of Values', *Contemporary Juristic Theory*, Chapter III, pp. 57–83.

The University of Chicago Press for the essay: John Dewey (1916), 'Force and Coercion', *International Journal of Ethics*, Vol. **26**, pp. 359–67. Copyright © The University of Chicago Press.

University of Pennsylvania Law Review and Fred B. Rothman & Co. for the essays: John Dickinson (1931) 'Legal Rules: Their Function in the Process of Decision', *University of Pennsylvania Law Review*, Vol. **79**, No. 7, pp. 833–68 and L.L. Fuller (1934), 'American Legal Realism', *University of Pennsylvania Law Review*, Vol. **82**, No. 5, pp. 429–62. Copyright © University of Pennsylvania Law Review.

The Yale Law Journal and Fred B. Rothman & Co. for essays: Walter Wheeler Cook (1924), 'The Logical and Legal Bases of the Conflict of Laws', *Yale Law Journal*, Vol. **XXXIII**, No. 5, pp. 457–88, Underhill Moore and Theodore S. Hope Jr. (1929), 'An Institutional Approach to the Law of Commercial Banking', *Yale Law Journal*, Vol. **XXXVIII**, No. 6, pp. 703–19, Hermann Kantorowicz (1934), 'Some Rationalism About Realism', *Yale Law Journal*, Vol. **43**, pp. 1240–52, and K.N. Llewellyn (1940), 'The Normative, The Legal and the Law-Jobs: The Problem of Juristic Method', *The Yale Law Journal*, Vol. **49**, No. 8, pp. 1355–1400. Reprinted by permission of The Yale Law Journal Company and Fred B. Rothman and Co.

Every effort has been made to trace all the copyright holders, but if any have been inadvertently overlooked the publishers will be pleased to make the necessary arrangement at the first opportunity.

Series Preface

The International Library of Law and Legal Theory is designed to provide important research materials in an accessible form. Each volume contains essays of central theoretical importance in its subject area. The series as a whole makes available an extensive range of valuable material which will be of considerable interest to those involved in the research, teaching and study of law.

The series has been divided into three sections. The Schools section is intended to represent the main distinctive approaches and topics of special concern to groups of scholars. The Areas section takes in the main branches of law with an emphasis on essays which present analytical and theoretical insights of broad application. The section on Legal Cultures makes available the distinctive legal theories of different legal traditions and takes up topics of general comparative and developmental concern.

I have been delighted and impressed by the way in which the editors of the individual volumes have set about the difficult task of selecting, ordering and presenting essays from the immense quantity of academic legal writing published in journals throughout the world. Editors were asked to pick out those essays from law, philosophy and social science journals which they consider to be fundamental for the understanding of law, as seen from the perspective of a particular approach or sphere of legal interest. This is not an easy task and many difficult decisions have had to be made in order to ensure that a representative sample of the best journal essays available takes account of the scope of each topic or school.

I should like to express my thanks to all the volume editors for their willing participation and scholarly judgement. The interest and enthusiasm which the project has generated is well illustrated by the fact that an original projection of 12 volumes drawn up in 1989 has now become a list of some 60 volumes. I must also acknowledge the vision, persistence and constant cheerfulness of John Irwin and the marvellous work done by Mrs Margaret O'Reilly and Mrs Sonia Bridgman.

TOM D. CAMPBELL
Series Editor
The Faculty of Law
The Australian National University

Editor's Note

This set of readings was selected from a vast wealth of periodical literature. No two scholars of the period would agree on the entire selection, though I am confident that there would be substantial agreement on most of the items I have selected for inclusion. Of course, it might have been desirable to include a larger total number of essays, but page limits for the book did not permit this.

I have received valuable advice in making this selection from my colleague Professor Roger Cramton. Professor Erik Jensen kindly and carefully prepared the biographical materials (in 1978–1979 while my research assistant), and I thank him, too. I am also grateful to my then secretary, Kathy Wimsatt, and my previous secretary, Harry Dutton, for valuable assistance.

Robert Samuel Summers
Goodhart Lodge, Cambridge
January, 1992

Introduction

The essays in this book consist, firstly, of various authentic and representative formulations and applications of the dominant general theory of law and its use in the United States during the middle decades of the 20th century. Secondly, this book includes major contributions critical of that theory.[1]

I use the phrase 'general theory of law and its use' to refer to a general set of tenets on several overlapping jurisprudential topics including the following: the very purpose of legal theorizing itself; the nature of law and of salient legal phenomena such as courts and legislatures; values, value theory and the law, including the relations between law and morals; the theory of law-making by legislatures, courts and other agencies; the theory of how valid law is to be identified; the methodology of interpretation and application of law (including precedent); law's basic techniques and implementative machinery; the nature and role of legal personnel; the place of force and coercion in law, and the appropriateness of scientific method and empiricism in the workings of law and in the study of law as a complex social reality. Thus, I interpret the phrase 'general theory of law' much more broadly than is frequently the case in European legal scholarship. In particular, I include important facets of what I call the 'law in use'.

During the first half of this century in the United States, there was a coalescence of philosophical pragmatism, sociological jurisprudence and the less extreme versions of legal realism. Although this body of legal theory was not worked out in detail, its leading tenets nevertheless became dominant in the US by the late 1930s, and many of those tenets continue to be highly influential there today.

For reasons that I will explain, I call this general theory of law and its use 'pragmatic instrumentalism'. It is important to remind readers, however, that the American version of this theory typified in the essays in this book represents only one possible interpretation. The theory of law of the English jurist Jeremy Bentham (1748–1832)[2] and that of the German jurist Rudolf von Jhering (1818–1892)[3] can be classified as theories of the same basic pragmatic instrumentalist type (though there are important variations in each case). In my view, theories of this general type comprise a fourth great branch of legal theory alongside analytical positivism, historical jurisprudence and natural law thought.

In America and to some extent in Germany (following the lead of von Jhering), there was also an important 'realist' wing or offshoot of instrumentalist legal theory.[4] I will have more to say about this later.

Before I introduce the main tenets of pragmatic instrumentalism as a general theory of law and its use, it would seem appropriate to identify the leading American pragmatic instrumentalists. Of course, representative writings of all of them could not be included in this book, but a list of possible classical figures would include: John Chipman Gray (1839–1915), Oliver Wendell Holmes, Jr (1841–1935), John Dewey (1859–1952), Roscoe Pound (1870–1964), Walter Wheeler Cook (1873–1943), Joseph W. Bingham (1878–1973), W. Underhill Moore (1879–1949), Herman Oliphant (1884–1939), Jerome Frank (1889–1957),

Karl N. Llewellyn (1893–1962) and Felix Cohen (1907–1953). Each of these scholars wrote various essays or books; since no single author drew all the tenets of pragmatic instrumentalist theory together in one place, however, more than the usual reconstruction is necessary. Two essays reproduced here, although written 40 years apart, each includes authentic formulations of most of the leading tenets: 'The Path of the Law' by Oliver Wendell Holmes Jr,[5] and 'The Problem of a Functional Jurisprudence' by Felix Cohen.[6]

The first main tenet of pragmatic instrumentalism is a conception of the essential purpose of theorizing about law. That purpose is to provide a body of concepts that will help make law more useful; in other words, help facilitate what many have called 'social engineering' through law.[7] I will not elaborate on the phrase 'social engineering' except to say that it contrasts sharply with other more academic conceptions of the essential purpose of legal theory, conceptions which stress the accumulation of general insight and understanding about law and legal phenomena for its own sake, either from the perspective of philosophical analysts, of social theorists, of scientists or still others.

Second, in this body of thought one encounters a broadly utilitarian theory of value.[8] Law is to be created in order to serve 'wants' or 'interests' external to law. 'Interest' is defined as the object of any desire. Holmes said: 'The first requirement of a sound body of law is, that it should correspond with the actual feelings and demands of the community, whether right or wrong.'[9] Wants or interests may conflict, and the law should resolve these conflicts so as to maximize the realization of all the wants or interests involved. This overall approach to value may be characterized as empiricist and pragmatic rather than ideological.

An instrumentalist conception of legal rules and other forms of law is the third basic tenet.[10] The law is viewed essentially as a body of social means designed to serve goals derived from underlying wants and interests. These means consist of an elaborate man-made set of tools – a kind of technology. In Llewellyn's words, this technology is a 'heterogeneous multitude of engines' – a vast and sophisticted apparatus that may be broken down into a variety of component parts.[11] Legal officials, 'social engineers', are to deploy the tools – the instrumentalities of the law – in the cause of social improvement. Officials thus necessarily play a large role in instrumentalist theory, a role often conceived as discretionary.

Fourth, the instrumentalists espoused a robust and optimistic theory of law–making. Judges as well as legislatures and administrative agencies were to draw extensively on social scientific knowledge and take full account of substantive, future–regarding considerations when making law.[12] Formalistic notions, including theories about the separation of powers, had obscured the true and proper role of judges. Judges could and should join with legislators in making the law. All law-makers were to draw heavily on the findings of the social sciences because it was said that the main issues in law-making could ultimately be reduced to questions of fact. Law-makers were also to draw on democratic processes and on rough-and-ready judicial judgments both in determining actual wants and interests and in formulating means–goal hypotheses to maximize them. Social phenomena, including legal precepts, processes and structures, were considered relatively malleable and could thus readily be adapted as legal means. The key ends of legal formalism – such as harmony, coherence and consistency with the rest of the system – were considered relatively unimportant when making new law. In law–making, choices should be made in light of the probable substantive effects of alternative means, and the extent to which these effects fulfil wants and interests. In this view, the entire law–making process was to be essentially scientific, consistent with, and indeed a means of implementing, the broadly utilitarian and therefore empiricist theory of value. Also, particular laws would be experiments which required constant monitoring. The general theory of law–making thus required an empirical science of law.

The influence of scientific versions of legal positivism is evident in the instrumentalists' official–oriented and largely source–based theory of what can constitute valid law within a legal system. According to this fifth basic tenet, a putative law cannot qualify as 'valid' law unless an appropriate court or other official body has acted upon it or laid it down as law.[13] In this view, the content of a putative precept (including its reasonableness and its moral quality) must be irrelevant to whether the precept is valid as law. Moreover, 'law in action' prevails over 'law in books'. Law is not mere words on paper. It consists essentially of behavioural regularities of officials, and it is those that must be scientifically catalogued and described. According to many of these theorists, lawyers were to *predict* the behavioural regularities of officials, particularly judges, when identifying valid law.

Sixth, judges and other administrators were to adopt and follow purposeful and goal–oriented methods when interpreting and applying valid law.[14] Judges were not to follow literalist 'plain meaning' methods, nor resort to conceptualist 'logic' or other 'formalistic' methods. Thus, forms of law were to be interpreted in light of authoritative goals and other purposes properly attributable to the law in question. Policy considerations were to inform interpretation and application. In deciding on the meaning of judicial precedents, lawyers were to consider not only what judges said they were doing, but also what the judges were actually doing. Lawyers must categorize and describe common-law holdings narrowly in terms of specific patterns of fact. Otherwise, they would overgeneralize, misstate and misapply the law. Judges and other officials should not pretend that the law was always determinate. Instead, they should frankly confront the necessity of choice and come to grips with all relevant extra–legal considerations in the decision–making process.

A seventh tenet, also positivistic, was that the law and non–law were to be sharply separated.[15] In particular, most of these theorists embraced a sharp separation between law and morals. Otherwise, or so they believed, there would be confusion and uncertainty about what the actual law was. It followed, too, that the validity of putative law should be determined solely by whether it was authoritatively laid down or acted upon, and not by reference to its content. If the content were made relevant to validity, this would invite confusion between law and morals. A sharp separation of law and morals was also thought to facilitate the pointed criticism of law.

Coercion, force and direct official action were considered characteristic of law, an eighth leading tenet of the theory.[16] The effectiveness of law in daily life ultimately derived largely from the state's monopoly on coercion, force and direct action. Felix Cohen said: 'Whatever cannot be...translated [into acts of state force] is functionally meaningless'.[17]

Finally, the success of uses of law was to be judged by the effects of those uses.[18] Put roughly, if the desired effects occurred, then a use of law had been successful. It was thought that determinations of the effectiveness of uses of law were essentially factual rather than evaluative, and relatively straightforward. In the face of social change, the uses of law were to be constantly monitored so that appropriate reforms and adjustments could be made.

I have said that along with the foregoing general tenets there was also a 'realist' wing or offshoot of the instrumenalist theory that became prominent during the middle decades of this century. In other words, the instrumentalist movement bifurcated into a 'mainstream' in which certain views (mainly of Holmes, Pound, Dewey, Gray and Llewellyn) became widely influential, and an extremist wing, characterized by certain realist views expressed most stridently in the 1930s. The special elements of this realist wing or offshoot included a cynical conception of the 'true' factors that influence judicial decisions (including gastronomic jurisprudence and the 'personality' of the judge), a virulent strain of scepticism about the primacy and even the very existence of legal rules, a radical moral scepticism bearing on the content of law, and a view that legal theory itself is entirely reducible to an empirical science. Despite the stridency with which such views were expressed, most of them did not, as I read the historical record, become very influential either in the world of law or in legal theory.

The readings in the first two parts of this book set forth and illustrate the central tenets of American pragmatic instrumentalism, and, to a much lesser extent, some tenets of its extreme realist wing. The central tenets and some of their realist offshoots are then subjected to criticism in the third part of the book.

Having sketched leading tenets of the general theory, I can now more meaningfully explain why I have chosen to call it 'pragmatic instrumentalism'. This is mainly because of the term's descriptive accuracy – various elements of this type of theory are both instrumentalist and pragmatic. Thus, the main task of legal theory is conceived to be that of providing an understanding of law that will make it more valuable as a practical tool in the hands of legal personnel. The varied instrumental facets of legal phenomena (including law's goals, law's means and their interactions) are the primary focus of study. Also, rules of law are viewed essentially as social instruments rather than as mere authoritative norms, expressions of reason, historical data or the like.

This type of theory is also pragmatic in ways not necessarily implied by the term 'instrumentalist'. For example, its adherents concentrate on the law *in use* – the 'law in action' as well as the 'law in books'. This focus extends beyond law's external effects and includes the internal workings of its processes. Such theories are also pragmatic in their conception of the relative malleability, for human use, of social and legal phenomena, including legal processes and institutional structures. Further, the law's means and goals are held to derive significantly from functional interrelations emergent in discrete social contexts – also a pragmatic notion. In addition, the theory of value of relevance to law making is utilitarian, and thus pragmatic rather than ideological.

I concede that the name 'legal realism' is already *sometimes* used to refer to the central tenets of the American version of the type of theory under study. In my judgement, there are many good reasons to cease this use of 'legal realism' and to adopt 'pragmatic instrumentalism' instead. The expression 'legal realism', as often used, is both under-inclusive and over-inclusive. On the one hand, as often used the phrase does not include Holmes, Pound, Dewey and Gray,[19] but refers rather to certain views of a group of younger thinkers writing mainly in the 1920s and 1930s such as Llewellyn, Frank and Cook. So used, the term is under-inclusive. To my mind, Holmes, Pound, Dewey and Gray should be grouped together with Llewellyn, Frank, Cook et al., since all participated in most of the same general directions of thought which had come to prevail by the middle decades of this century. Holmes, Pound, Dewey and Gray were not mere precursors; their work was seminal and highly influential on the younger thinkers who followed.

On the other hand, the expression 'legal realism' is over–inclusive in an important way. The expression is commonly used to encompass certain extreme tenets that did not, in my view, become part of our dominant instrumentalist philosophy of law. These include the cynical conception of various factors that influence judicial decisions (such as gastronomic jurisprudence and the personality of the judge), deep scepticism about the very existence or bearing of rules, radical moral scepticism, and the view that legal theory is essentially an empirical science. While the expression 'legal realism' is commonly understood today to encompass some or all of these extreme views, 'pragmatic instrumentalism' does not. Of course, one might legitimately refer to an 'extreme realist wing' of pragmatic instrumentalism. But even this formulation is misleading insofar as it signifies that this wing has been as influential as instrumentalist theory generally.

In addition, the term 'legal realism' has misleading philosophical connotations. Most instrumentalists were not realists in the traditional philosophical sense. They did not share the philosophical realist view that abstract words name entities that 'exist' outside the mind.[20] Nor did they generally subscribe to a version of scientific realism (in which, roughly speaking, all objects of knowledge are taken to exist independently of the knower).[21]

'Pragmatic instrumentalism' is thus a descriptively accurate term for the type of legal theory involved, whereas 'legal realism' is not. (Nor is 'sociological jurisprudence', with its narrow connotation.) 'Pragmatic instrumentalism' is the name I have given not only to the American version, but also to a general type of legal theory originating in the eighteenth century. As I have indicated, Bentham led an instrumentalist revolution in legal thought in Great Britain in the late eighteenth and early nineteenth centuries, followed by Rudolf von Jhering in Germany and Austria in the second half of the nineteenth and in the early twentieth century. It would seem highly desirable to have a common name for both the general type of theory and for the American version. The idiosyncratic American term, legal realism, is plainly inadequate for this purpose too.[22]

Notes

1 I have published a systematic book–length study of the thinkers represented here, with extensive bibliographical references. See Robert Samuel Summers (1982), *Instrumentalism and American Legal Theory*, Ithaca, New York: Cornell University Press. Earlier versions of this book appeared in Dutch and German. See *Het pragmatisch instrumentalisme,* Antwerp-Amsterdam: S.W.U. (1980; *Pragmatisher Instrumentalismus, und amerikanische Rechtstheorie*, Freiburg-München: Verlag Karl Alber (1982). For a critique of the reconstructive methodology of my book, and a rebuttal, see Moore (1984), 'The Need for a Theory of Legal Theories: Assessing Pragmatic Instrumentalism – A Review Essay of Instrumentalism and American Legal Theory, *Cornell Law Review*, **69**, 998 and Summers (1984), 'On Identifying and Reconstructing a General Legal Theory – Some Thoughts Prompted by Professor Moore's Critique', *Cornell Law Review*, **69**, 1014.

Further book–length studies on the general subject of this book include: Wilfred Rumble (1968), *American Legal Realism*, Ithaca: Cornell University Press; Edwin Garlan (1941), *Legal Realism and Justice*, New York: Columbia University Press; William Twining (1973), *Karl Llewellyn and the Realist Movement*, London: Willmer Bros.; Julius Paul (1959), *The Legal Realism of Jerome N. Frank*, The Hague: Nijhoff; Grant Gilmore (1977), *The Ages of American Law*, New Haven: Yale University Press.

2 See generally, J. Bentham (1843), *The Works of Jeremy Bentham*, edited by J. Bowring, Edinburgh.

3 See generally, R. Jhering (1913), *Law as a Means to an End* (trans. by I. Husik). On Bentham's

possible influence on Jhering, see Coing (1968), 'Bentham's Bedeutung für die Entwicklung der Interessenjurisprudenz und der allgemeinen Rechtslehre', *Archiv für Rechts– und Sozial–philosophie*, **54**, 69.
4 See especially the manifesto of the young Llewellyn (1931), 'Some Realism About Realism: Responding to Dean Pound', *Harvard Law Review*, **44**, 1222.
5 See herein Chapter 1.
6 See herein Chapter 11.
7 See, for instance, R. Pound (1922), *An Introduction to the Philosophy of Law*, New Haven: Yale University Press, 47.
8 See further herein Chapter 21 at pp. 534–42.
9 Oliver Wendell Holmes, Jr. (1881), *The Common Law*, Boston: Little Brown, 41.
10 See further herein Chapter 21 at pp. 542–9.
11 K. Llewellyn (1930), 'A Realistic Jurisprudence: The Next Step', *Columbia Law Review*, **30**, 432, 464.
12 See further herein Chapter 21 at pp. 549–56.
13 See further herein Chapter 21 at pp. 556–61.
14 See further herein Chapter 21 at pp. 568–73.
15 See further Robert Samuel Summers (1982), *Instrumentalism and American Legal Theory*, Ithaca, New York: Cornell University Press, Chapter 7.
16 See further herein Chapter 21 at pp. 588–93.
17 F. Cohen (1937), 'The Problems of a Functional Jurisprudence', *Modern Law Review*, **1**, 5, 8.
18 See further herein Chapter 21 at pp. 597–606.
19 Although Holmes, Pound and Dewey are represented in the readings in the present book, Gray is not. This is because his influential work took book form, and the readings here have to be from periodicals. See J.C. Gray (1921), *The Nature and Sources of the Law*, New York: Macmillan.
20 See, for instance, A.G.N. Flew (1979), *A Dictionary of Philosophy*, 228.
21 See generally Boyd (1983), 'On the Current Status of the Issue of Scientific Realism', *Erkenntnis*, **19**, 45.
22 There was also a rather different movement in Scandinavia called 'legal realism'. See Hart (1959), 'Scandinavian Realism', *Cambridge Law Journal*, **17**, 233.

Biographies of Authors in Part I

Oliver Wendell Holmes, Jr. (1841–1935)

Holmes was the most revered jurist of his time and a dominant figure in the American judiciary for 50 years. Following his graduation in 1861 from Harvard, he fought in the American Civil War and was thrice wounded. Upon discharge, he studied at the Harvard Law School, graduating in 1866. Son of the patrician poet, novelist and physician of the same name, Holmes regularly travelled abroad and pursued wide intellectual interests. From 1867 until 1873, he worked on a revision of Chancellor Kent's *Commentaries*. From 1870 until 1873, he served as co–editor of the *American Law Review*. A series of lectures given at Boston's Lowell Institute in 1880–81 became a classic – *The Common Law*. In the autumn of 1882, he became a professor at the Harvard Law School, but several months later was appointed to the Supreme Judicial Court of Massachusetts, becoming Chief Justice of that court in 1899. In 1902, at the age of 61, he became a Justice of the US Supreme Court, where he remained for 30 years. For a bibliography, see Harry C. Shriver (1978), *What Justice Holmes Wrote, and What Has Been Written About Him: A Bibliography 1866–1976*. Potomac, Md: Fox Hills Press.

John Dewey (1859–1952)

America's most influential philosopher, Dewey was born in Burlington (Vermont) and graduated from the University of Vermont. After several years teaching high school, he entered Johns Hopkins University, from which he received his doctorate in 1884. Except for one year at Minnesota, he taught at the University of Michigan until 1894, when he was drawn to the newly-founded University of Chicago. At Chicago he became chairman of an interdisciplinary department consisting of philosophy, psychology and education. As a philosopher he helped found what William James called the 'Chicago School' of pragmatic philosophy. He later moved to Columbia as professor of philosophy, with additional responsibilities in the Teacher's College – a position he maintained until his official retirement in 1930. He continued his scholarly writing and political involvement until his death. For a bibliography, see Milton H. Thomas (1962), *John Dewey: A Centennial Bibliography*, Chicago: The University of Chicago Press.

Roscoe Pound (1870–1964)

Pound was one of the two or three most influential American legal philosophers of the 20th century. He grew up in Lincoln (Nebraska) where he attended the University of Nebraska and earned a basic degree and a Ph.D. in botany. He also spent a year at the Harvard Law School, after which he was admitted to the Nebraska bar and began legal practice. In 1901 he was appointed an auxiliary judge of the Nebraska Supreme Court. In 1903 he began his academic career and served successively on the faculties of Nebraska, Northwestern, Chicago and Harvard. From 1916 until 1936 he was Dean of the Harvard Law School and thereafter became University Professor. For bibliographies, see Franklin C. Setaro (1942), *A Bibliography of the Writings of Roscoe Pound*, Cambridge: Harvard University Press; George A. Strait (1960), *A Bibliography of the Writings of Roscoe Pound: 1940–1960*, Cambridge, Mass.

Walter Bingham (1878–1973)

A 'pioneer of the realist movement', Bingham taught at the Stanford School of Law from 1907 until his retirement in 1944. After growing up in Chicago, Bingham graduated from the new University of Chicago (1902) and its even newer law school (1904). He practised in Chicago for one year, taught at Cornell Law School from 1905 until 1907, and then took up his Stanford position. Among his early colleagues on the Stanford faculty was Wesley Newcomb Hohfeld, and among his students was Lon L. Fuller. Bingham wrote widely on torts, property, conflict of laws, public international law and, of course, jurisprudence. His jurisprudential writing was motivated in part by a desire to elucidate the legal theory he used in his analysis of other legal topics. See (1965), 'A Preliminary Bibliography', *Stanford Law Review*, **17**, 1017.

Herman Oliphant (1884–1939)

Oliphant emphasized the analysis of judicial *decisions* as distinguished from judicial opinions.

He received undergraduate degrees both from Marion College (1907), where he also served as Professor of Language for three years, and from Indiana University (1909). After completing his legal studies at the University of Chicago (1914), he joined the Chicago faculty, teaching in various areas of commercial law. In 1921, he was drawn to the Columbia School of Law, where he became a noted legal educator. He served as president of the Association of American Law Schools in 1927–28. Discontented with the state of legal education, he joined the faculty of the new Johns Hopkins Institute of Law in 1929. Oliphant was attracted by the New Deal and became General Counsel of the Treasury Department, a position he retained until his death. For a bibliography, see Robert Samuel Summers (1982), *Instrumentalism and American Legal Theory*, Ithaca N.Y.: Cornell University Press, p.287.

Karl N. Llewellyn (1893–1962)

A master of many disciplines, Llewellyn combined emphasis on narrow factual issues with broad-gauged theorizing. After studying in Germany and France, Llewellyn graduated from Yale (1915) and its law school (LL.B. 1918, J.D. 1920). Among his law professors were Arthur Corbin, Wesley Newcomb Hohfeld and Walter Wheeler Cook. For two years he practised at Shearman & Sterling in New York City. He returned to Yale to teach (1922–25), but soon went to Columbia, where he remained until 1951 as Betts Professor of Jurisprudence. Throughout his Columbia tenure, he drafted legislation for the Conference of Commissioners on Uniform State Laws. From 1941, he was Chief Reporter for the Uniform Commercial Code. He had wide interests. He conducted anthropological research on the law-government of the Cheyenne Indians (*The Cheyenne Way*, 1941) and drafted legal codes for the Santa Ana and Santo Domingo Pueblos. In 1951, Llewellyn moved to the University of Chicago, where in his later period he concentrated on completing a major work on appellate judging. For a fine biography and a bibliography, see William Twining (1973), *Karl Llewellyn and the Realist Movement*, Birkenhead: Wilmer Brothers Ltd., Weidenfeld and Nicholson.

Felix Cohen (1907–1953)

Son of the philosopher Morris R. Cohen, Felix Cohen received his M.A. in 1927, completed his residency for the Ph.D. in 1928, entered Columbia Law School in the same year, received his Harvard Ph.D. in 1929 and received his Columbia LL.B. in 1931. After a year as a research assistant to a New York judge, Cohen entered private practice in 1932. With the coming of the New Deal, he became Assistant Solicitor in the Interior Department. In various capacities he remained there for 14 years, working on a broad range of problems and becoming an expert on American Indian law. Throughout his government career, he published widely on philosophical matters. In 1946 he began teaching a course in legislative drafting at the Yale Law School, a course he continued to teach when he re–entered private legal practice in 1948. See (1974), 'Bibliography of Felix S. Cohen', *Rutgers Law Review*, **9**, 351.

Part I
The 20th Century Instrumentalist Movement including its Realist Wing

[1]

HARVARD

LAW REVIEW.

VOL. X. MARCH 25, 1897. NO. 8.

THE PATH OF THE LAW.[1]

WHEN we study law we are not studying a mystery but a well known profession. We are studying what we shall want in order to appear before judges, or to advise people in such a way as to keep them out of court. The reason why it is a profession, why people will pay lawyers to argue for them or to advise them, is that in societies like ours the command of the public force is intrusted to the judges in certain cases, and the whole power of the state will be put forth, if necessary, to carry out their judgments and decrees. People want to know under what circumstances and how far they will run the risk of coming against what is so much stronger than themselves, and hence it becomes a business to find out when this danger is to be feared. The object of our study, then, is prediction, the prediction of the incidence of the public force through the instrumentality of the courts.

The means of the study are a body of reports, of treatises, and of statutes, in this country and in England, extending back for six hundred years, and now increasing annually by hundreds. In these sibylline leaves are gathered the scattered prophecies of the past upon the cases in which the axe will fall. These are what properly have been called the oracles of the law. Far the most important and pretty nearly the whole meaning of every new effort of legal thought is to make these prophecies more precise, and to

---

[1] An Address delivered by Mr. Justice Holmes, of the Supreme Judicial Court of Massachusetts, at the dedication of the new hall of the Boston University School of Law, on January 8, 1897.

generalize them into a thoroughly connected system. The process is one, from a lawyer's statement of a case, eliminating as it does all the dramatic elements with which his client's story has clothed it, and retaining only the facts of legal import, up to the final analyses and abstract universals of theoretic jurisprudence. The reason why a lawyer does not mention that his client wore a white hat when he made a contract, while Mrs. Quickly would be sure to dwell upon it along with the parcel gilt goblet and the sea-coal fire, is that he forsees that the public force will act in the same way whatever his client had upon his head. It is to make the prophecies easier to be remembered and to be understood that the teachings of the decisions of the past are put into general propositions and gathered into text-books, or that statutes are passed in a general form. The primary rights and duties with which jurisprudence busies itself again are nothing but prophecies. One of the many evil effects of the confusion between legal and moral ideas, about which I shall have something to say in a moment, is that theory is apt to get the cart before the horse, and to consider the right or the duty as something existing apart from and independent of the consequences of its breach, to which certain sanctions are added afterward. But, as I shall try to show, a legal duty so called is nothing but a prediction that if a man does or omits certain things he will be made to suffer in this or that way by judgment of the court; — and so of a legal right.

The number of our predictions when generalized and reduced to a system is not unmanageably large. They present themselves as a finite body of dogma which may be mastered within a reasonable time. It is a great mistake to be frightened by the ever increasing number of reports. The reports of a given jurisdiction in the course of a generation take up pretty much the whole body of the law, and restate it from the present point of view. We could reconstruct the corpus from them if all that went before were burned. The use of the earlier reports is mainly historical, a use about which I shall have something to say before I have finished.

I wish, if I can, to lay down some first principles for the study of this body of dogma or systematized prediction which we call the law, for men who want to use it as the instrument of their business to enable them to prophesy in their turn, and, as bearing upon the study, I wish to point out an ideal which as yet our law has not attained.

The first thing for a business-like understanding of the matter is to understand its limits, and therefore I think it desirable at once to point out and dispel a confusion between morality and law, which sometimes rises to the height of conscious theory, and more often and indeed constantly is making trouble in detail without reaching the point of consciousness. You can see very plainly that a bad man has as much reason as a good one for wishing to avoid an encounter with the public force, and therefore you can see the practical importance of the distinction between morality and law. A man who cares nothing for an ethical rule which is believed and practised by his neighbors is likely nevertheless to care a good deal to avoid being made to pay money, and will want to keep out of jail if he can.

I take it for granted that no hearer of mine will misinterpret what I have to say as the language of cynicism. The law is the witness and external deposit of our moral life. Its history is the history of the moral development of the race. The practice of it, in spite of popular jests, tends to make good citizens and good men. When I emphasize the difference between law and morals I do so with reference to a single end, that of learning and understanding the law. For that purpose you must definitely master its specific marks, and it is for that that I ask you for the moment to imagine yourselves indifferent to other and greater things.

I do not say that there is not a wider point of view from which the distinction between law and morals becomes of secondary or no importance, as all mathematical distinctions vanish in presence of the infinite. But I do say that that distinction is of the first importance for the object which we are here to consider, — a right study and mastery of the law as a business with well understood limits, a body of dogma enclosed within definite lines. I have just shown the practical reason for saying so. If you want to know the law and nothing else, you must look at it as a bad man, who cares only for the material consequences which such knowledge enables him to predict, not as a good one, who finds his reasons for conduct, whether inside the law or outside of it, in the vaguer sanctions of conscience. The theoretical importance of the distinction is no less, if you would reason on your subject aright. The law is full of phraseology drawn from morals, and by the mere force of language continually invites us to pass from one domain to the other without perceiving it, as we are sure to do unless we have the boundary constantly before our minds. The law talks about rights, and duties, and malice, and intent, and negligence, and so forth, and nothing is easier, or, I may say, more common in legal reasoning, than to take these words in their moral sense, at some stage of the argument, and so to drop into fallacy. For instance, when we speak of the rights of man in a moral sense, we mean to mark the limits of interference with individual freedom which we think are prescribed by conscience, or by our ideal, however reached. Yet it is certain that many laws have been enforced in the past, and it is likely that some are enforced now, which are condemned by the most enlightened opinion of the time, or which at all events pass the limit of interference as many consciences would draw it. Manifestly, therefore, nothing but confusion of thought can result from assuming that the rights of man in a moral sense are equally rights in the sense of the Constitution and the law. No doubt simple and extreme cases can be put of imaginable laws which the statute-making power would not dare to enact, even in the absence of written constitutional prohibitions, because the community would rise in rebellion and fight; and this gives some plausibility to the proposition that the law, if not a part of morality, is limited by it. But this limit of power is not coextensive with any system of morals. For the most part it falls far within the lines of any such system, and in some cases may extend beyond them, for reasons drawn from the habits of a particular people at a particular time. I once heard the late Professor Agassiz say that a German population would rise if you added two cents to the price of a glass of beer. A statute in such a case would be empty words, not because it was wrong, but because it could not be enforced. No one will deny that wrong statutes can be and are enforced, and we should not all agree as to which were the wrong ones.

The confusion with which I am dealing besets confessedly legal conceptions. Take the fundamental question, What constitutes the law? You will find some text writers telling you that it is something different from what is decided by the courts of Massachusetts or England, that it is a system of reason, that it is a deduction from principles of ethics or admitted axioms or what not, which may or may not coincide with the decisions. But if we take the view of our friend the bad man we shall find that he does not care two straws for the axioms or deductions, but that he does want to know what the Massachusetts or English courts are likely to do in fact. I am much of his mind. The prophecies of what the courts will do in fact, and nothing more pretentious, are what I mean by the law.

Take again a notion which as popularly understood is the widest conception which the law contains; — the notion of legal duty, to which already I have referred. We fill the word with all the content which we draw from morals. But what does it mean to a bad man? Mainly, and in the first place, a prophecy that if he does certain things he will be subjected to disagreeable consequences by way of imprisonment or compulsory payment of money. But from his point of view, what is the difference between being fined and being taxed a certain sum for doing a certain thing? That his point of view is the test of legal principles is shown by the many discussions which have arisen in the courts on the very question whether a given statutory liability is a penalty or a tax. On the answer to this question depends the decision whether conduct is legally wrong or right, and also whether a man is under compulsion or free. Leaving the criminal law on one side, what is the difference between the liability under the mill acts or statutes authorizing a taking by eminent domain and the liability for what we call a wrongful conversion of property where restoration is out of the question? In both cases the party taking another man's property has to pay its fair value as assessed by a jury, and no more. What significance is there in calling one taking right and another wrong from the point of view of the law? It does not matter, so far as the given consequence, the compulsory payment, is concerned, whether the act to which it is attached is described in terms of praise or in terms of blame, or whether the law purports to prohibit it or to allow it. If it matters at all, still speaking from the bad man's point of view, it must be because in one case and not in the other some further disadvantages, or at least some further consequences, are attached to the act by the law. The only other disadvantages thus attached to it which I ever have been able to think of are to be found in two somewhat insignificant legal doctrines, both of which might be abolished without much disturbance. One is, that a contract to do a prohibited act is unlawful, and the other, that, if one of two or more joint wrongdoers has to pay all the damages, he cannot recover contribution from his fellows. And that I believe is all. You see how the vague circumference of the notion of duty shrinks and at the same time grows more precise when we wash it with cynical acid and expel everything except the object of our study, the operations of the law.

Nowhere is the confusion between legal and moral ideas more manifest than in the law of contract. Among other things, here again the so called primary rights and duties are invested with a mystic significance beyond what can be assigned and explained. The duty to keep a contract at common law means a prediction that you must pay damages if you do not keep it,—and nothing else. If you commit a tort, you are liable to pay a compensatory sum. If you commit a contract, you are liable to pay a compensatory sum unless the promised event comes to pass, and that is all the difference. But such a mode of looking at the matter stinks in the nostrils of those who think it advantageous to get as much ethics into the law as they can. It was good enough for Lord Coke, however, and here, as in many other cases, I am content to abide with him. In Bromage *v.* Genning,[1] a prohibition was sought in the King's Bench against a suit in the marches of Wales for the specific performance of a covenant to grant a lease, and Coke said that it would subvert the intention of the covenantor, since he intends it to be at his election either to lose the damages or to make the lease. Sergeant Harris for the plaintiff confessed that he moved the matter against his conscience, and a prohibition was granted. This goes further than we should go now, but it shows what I venture to say has been the common law point of view from the beginning, although Mr. Harriman, in his very able little book upon Contracts has been misled, as I humbly think, to a different conclusion.

I have spoken only of the common law, because there are some cases in which a logical justification can be found for speaking of civil liabilities as imposing duties in an intelligible sense. These are the relatively few in which equity will grant an injunction, and will enforce it by putting the defendant in prison or otherwise punishing him unless he complies with the order of the court. But I hardly think it advisable to shape general theory from the exception, and I think it would be better to cease troubling ourselves about primary rights and sanctions altogether, than to

[1] 1 Roll. Rep. 368.

describe our prophecies concerning the liabilities commonly imposed by the law in those inappropriate terms.

I mentioned, as other examples of the use by the law of words drawn from morals, malice, intent, and negligence. It is enough to take malice as it is used in the law of civil liability for wrongs, — what we lawyers call the law of torts, — to show you that it means something different in law from what it means in morals, and also to show how the difference has been obscured by giving to principles which have little or nothing to do with each other the same name. Three hundred years ago a parson preached a sermon and told a story out of Fox's Book of Martyrs of a man who had assisted at the torture of one of the saints, and afterward died, suffering compensatory inward torment. It happened that Fox was wrong. The man was alive and chanced to hear the sermon, and thereupon he sued the parson. Chief Justice Wray instructed the jury that the defendant was not liable, because the story was told innocently, without malice. He took malice in the moral sense, as importing a malevolent motive. But nowadays no one doubts that a man may be liable, without any malevolent motive at all, for false statements manifestly calculated to inflict temporal damage. In stating the case in pleading, we still should call the defendant's conduct malicious; but, in my opinion at least, the word means nothing about motives, or even about the defendant's attitude toward the future, but only signifies that the tendency of his conduct under the known circumstances was very plainly to cause the plaintiff temporal harm.[1]

In the law of contract the use of moral phraseology has led to equal confusion, as I have shown in part already, but only in part. Morals deal with the actual internal state of the individual's mind, what he actually intends. From the time of the Romans down to now, this mode of dealing has affected the language of the law as to contract, and the language used has reacted upon the thought. We talk about a contract as a meeting of the minds of the parties, and thence it is inferred in various cases that there is no contract because their minds have not met; that is, because they have intended different things or because one party has not known of the assent of the other. Yet nothing is more certain than that parties may be bound by a contract to things which neither of them intended, and when one does not know of the other's assent. Sup-

[1] See Hanson v. Globe Newspaper Co., 159 Mass. 293, 302.

pose a contract is executed in due form and in writing to deliver a lecture, mentioning no time. One of the parties thinks that the promise will be construed to mean at once, within a week. The other thinks that it means when he is ready. The court says that it means within a reasonable time. The parties are bound by the contract as it is interpreted by the court, yet neither of them meant what the court declares that they have said. In my opinion no one will understand the true theory of contract or be able even to discuss some fundamental questions intelligently until he has understood that all contracts are formal, that the making of a contract depends not on the agreement of two minds in one intention, but on the agreement of two sets of external signs, — not on the parties' having *meant* the same thing but on their having *said* the same thing. Furthermore, as the signs may be addressed to one sense or another, — to sight or to hearing, — on the nature of the sign will depend the moment when the contract is made. If the sign is tangible, for instance, a letter, the contract is made when the letter of acceptance is delivered. If it is necessary that the minds of the parties meet, there will be no contract until the acceptance can be read, — none, for example, if the acceptance be snatched from the hand of the offerer by a third person.

This is not the time to work out a theory in detail, or to answer many obvious doubts and questions which are suggested by these general views. I know of none which are not easy to answer, but what I am trying to do now is only by a series of hints to throw some light on the narrow path of legal doctrine, and upon two pitfalls which, as it seems to me, lie perilously near to it. Of the first of these I have said enough. I hope that my illustrations have shown the danger, both to speculation and to practice, of confounding morality with law, and the trap which legal language lays for us on that side of our way. For my own part, I often doubt whether it would not be a gain if every word of moral significance could be banished from the law altogether, and other words adopted which should convey legal ideas uncolored by anything outside the law. We should lose the fossil records of a good deal of history and the majesty got from ethical associations, but by ridding ourselves of an unnecessary confusion we should gain very much in the clearness of our thought.

So much for the limits of the law. The next thing which I wish to consider is what are the forces which determine its content and its growth. You may assume, with Hobbes and Bentham and Austin, that all law emanates from the sovereign, even when the first human beings to enunciate it are the judges, or you may think that law is the voice of the Zeitgeist, or what you like. It is all one to my present purpose. Even if every decision required the sanction of an emperor with despotic power and a whimsical turn of mind, we should be interested none the less, still with a view to prediction, in discovering some order, some rational explanation, and some principle of growth for the rules which he laid down. In every system there are such explanations and principles to be found. It is with regard to them that a second fallacy comes in, which I think it important to expose.

The fallacy to which I refer is the notion that the only force at work in the development of the law is logic. In the broadest sense, indeed, that notion would be true. The postulate on which we think about the universe is that there is a fixed quantitative relation between every phenomenon and its antecedents and consequents. If there is such a thing as a phenomenon without these fixed quantitative relations, it is a miracle. It is outside the law of cause and effect, and as such transcends our power of thought, or at least is something to or from which we cannot reason. The condition of our thinking about the universe is that it is capable of being thought about rationally, or, in other words, that every part of it is effect and cause in the same sense in which those parts are with which we are most familiar. So in the broadest sense it is true that the law is a logical development, like everything else. The danger of which I speak is not the admission that the principles governing other phenomena also govern the law, but the notion that a given system, ours, for instance, can be worked out like mathematics from some general axioms of conduct. This is the natural error of the schools, but it is not confined to them. I once heard a very eminent judge say that he never let a decision go until he was absolutely sure that it was right. So judicial dissent often is blamed, as if it meant simply that one side or the other were not doing their sums right, and, if they would take more trouble, agreement inevitably would come.

This mode of thinking is entirely natural. The training of lawyers is a training in logic. The processes of analogy, discrimination, and deduction are those in which they are most at home. The language of judicial decision is mainly the language of logic.

And the logical method and form flatter that longing for certainty and for repose which is in every human mind. But certainty generally is illusion, and repose is not the destiny of man. Behind the logical form lies a judgment as to the relative worth and importance of competing legislative grounds, often an inarticulate and unconscious judgment, it is true, and yet the very root and nerve of the whole proceeding. You can give any conclusion a logical form. You always can imply a condition in a contract. But why do you imply it? It is because of some belief as to the practice of the community or of a class, or because of some opinion as to policy, or, in short, because of some attitude of yours upon a matter not capable of exact quantitative measurement, and therefore not capable of founding exact logical conclusions. Such matters really are battle grounds where the means do not exist for determinations that shall be good for all time, and where the decision can do no more than embody the preference of a given body in a given time and place. We do not realize how large a part of our law is open to reconsideration upon a slight change in the habit of the public mind. No concrete proposition is self-evident, no matter how ready we may be to accept it, not even Mr. Herbert Spencer's Every man has a right to do what he wills, provided he interferes not with a like right on the part of his neighbors.

Why is a false and injurious statement privileged, if it is made honestly in giving information about a servant? It is because it has been thought more important that information should be given freely, than that a man should be protected from what under other circumstances would be an actionable wrong. Why is a man at liberty to set up a business which he knows will ruin his neighbor? It is because the public good is supposed to be best subserved by free competition. Obviously such judgments of relative importance may vary in different times and places. Why does a judge instruct a jury that an employer is not liable to an employee for an injury received in the course of his employment unless he is negligent, and why do the jury generally find for the plaintiff if the case is allowed to go to them? It is because the traditional policy of our law is to confine liability to cases where a prudent man might have foreseen the injury, or at least the danger, while the inclination of a very large part of the community is to make certain classes of persons insure the safety of those with whom they deal. Since the last words were written, I have seen the requirement of such insurance put forth as part of the programme of one of the best known labor organizations. There is a concealed, half conscious battle on the question of legislative policy, and if any one thinks that it can be settled deductively, or once for all, I only can say that I think he is theoretically wrong, and that I am certain that his conclusion will not be accepted in practice *semper ubique et ab omnibus*.

Indeed, I think that even now our theory upon this matter is open to reconsideration, although I am not prepared to say how I should decide if a reconsideration were proposed. Our law of torts comes from the old days of isolated, ungeneralized wrongs, assaults, slanders, and the like, where the damages might be taken to lie where they fell by legal judgment. But the torts with which our courts are kept busy to-day are mainly the incidents of certain well known businesses. They are injuries to person or property by railroads, factories, and the like. The liability for them is estimated, and sooner or later goes into the price paid by the public. The public really pays the damages, and the question of liability, if pressed far enough, is really the question how far it is desirable that the public should insure the safety of those whose work it uses. It might be said that in such cases the chance of a jury finding for the defendant is merely a chance, once in a while rather arbitrarily interrupting the regular course of recovery, most likely in the case of an unusually conscientious plaintiff, and therefore better done away with. On the other hand, the economic value even of a life to the community can be estimated, and no recovery, it may be said, ought to go beyond that amount. It is conceivable that some day in certain cases we may find ourselves imitating, on a higher plane, the tariff for life and limb which we see in the Leges Barbarorum.

I think that the judges themselves have failed adequately to recognize their duty of weighing considerations of social advantage. The duty is inevitable, and the result of the often proclaimed judicial aversion to deal with such considerations is simply to leave the very ground and foundation of judgments inarticulate, and often unconscious, as I have said. When socialism first began to be talked about, the comfortable classes of the community were a good deal frightened. I suspect that this fear has influenced judicial action both here and in England, yet it is certain that it is not a conscious factor in the decisions to which I refer. I think that something similar has led people who no longer hope to control the legislatures to look to the courts as expounders of the Constitutions, and that in some courts new principles have been discovered outside the bodies of those instruments, which may be generalized into acceptance of the economic doctrines which prevailed about fifty years ago, and a wholesale prohibition of what a tribunal of lawyers does not think about right. I cannot but believe that if the training of lawyers led them habitually to consider more definitely and explicitly the social advantage on which the rule they lay down must be justified, they sometimes would hesitate where now they are confident, and see that really they were taking sides upon debatable and often burning questions.

So much for the fallacy of logical form. Now let us consider the present condition of the law as a subject for study, and the ideal toward which it tends. We still are far from the point of view which I desire to see reached. No one has reached it or can reach it as yet. We are only at the beginning of a philosophical reaction, and of a reconsideration of the worth of doctrines which for the most part still are taken for granted without any deliberate, conscious, and systematic questioning of their grounds. The development of our law has gone on for nearly a thousand years, like the development of a plant, each generation taking the inevitable next step, mind, like matter, simply obeying a law of spontaneous growth. It is perfectly natural and right that it should have been so. Imitation is a necessity of human nature, as has been illustrated by a remarkable French writer, M. Tarde, in an admirable book, "Les Lois de l'Imitation." Most of the things we do, we do for no better reason than that our fathers have done them or that our neighbors do them, and the same is true of a larger part than we suspect of what we think. The reason is a good one, because our short life gives us no time for a better, but it is not the best. It does not follow, because we all are compelled to take on faith at second hand most of the rules on which we base our action and our thought, that each of us may not try to set some corner of his world in the order of reason, or that all of us collectively should not aspire to carry reason as far as it will go throughout the whole domain. In regard to the law, it is true, no doubt, that an evolutionist will hesitate to affirm universal validity for his social ideals, or for the principles which he thinks should be embodied in legislation. He is content if he can prove them best for here and now. He may be ready to admit that he knows nothing about an absolute best in the cosmos, and even that he knows next to nothing about a permanent best for men. Still it is true that a body of law is more rational and more civilized when every rule it contains is referred articulately and definitely to an end which it subserves, and when the grounds for desiring that end are stated or are ready to be stated in words.

At present, in very many cases, if we want to know why a rule of law has taken its particular shape, and more or less if we want to know why it exists at all, we go to tradition. We follow it into the Year Books, and perhaps beyond them to the customs of the Salian Franks, and somewhere in the past, in the German forests, in the needs of Norman kings, in the assumptions of a dominant class, in the absence of generalized ideas, we find out the practical motive for what now best is justified by the mere fact of its acceptance and that men are accustomed to it. The rational study of law is still to a large extent the study of history. History must be a part of the study, because without it we cannot know the precise scope of rules which it is our business to know. It is a part of the rational study, because it is the first step toward an enlightened scepticism, that is, toward a deliberate reconsideration of the worth of those rules. When you get the dragon out of his cave on to the plain and in the daylight, you can count his teeth and claws, and see just what is his strength. But to get him out is only the first step. The next is either to kill him, or to tame him and make him a useful animal. For the rational study of the law the black-letter man may be the man of the present, but the man of the future is the man of statistics and the master of economics. It is revolting to have no better reason for a rule of law than that so it was laid down in the time of Henry IV. It is still more revolting if the grounds upon which it was laid down have vanished long since, and the rule simply persists from blind imitation of the past. I am thinking of the technical rule as to trespass *ab initio*, as it is called, which I attempted to explain in a recent Massachusetts case.[1]

Let me take an illustration, which can be stated in a few words, to show how the social end which is aimed at by a rule of law is obscured and only partially attained in consequence of the fact that the rule owes its form to a gradual historical development, instead of being reshaped as a whole, with conscious articulate reference to the end in view. We think it desirable to prevent one man's property being misappropriated by another, and so we

[1] Commonwealth *v.* Rubin, 165 Mass. 453.

make larceny a crime. The evil is the same whether the misappropriation is made by a man into whose hands the owner has put the property, or by one who wrongfully takes it away. But primitive law in its weakness did not get much beyond an effort to prevent violence, and very naturally made a wrongful taking, a trespass, part of its definition of the crime. In modern times the judges enlarged the definition a little by holding that, if the wrong-doer gets possession by a trick or device, the crime is committed. This really was giving up the requirement of a trespass, and it would have been more logical, as well as truer to the present object of the law, to abandon the requirement altogether. That, however, would have seemed too bold, and was left to statute. Statutes were passed making embezzlement a crime. But the force of tradition caused the crime of embezzlement to be regarded as so far distinct from larceny that to this day, in some jurisdictions at least, a slip corner is kept open for thieves to contend, if indicted for larceny, that they should have been indicted for embezzlement, and if indicted for embezzlement, that they should have been indicted for larceny, and to escape on that ground.

Far more fundamental questions still await a better answer than that we do as our fathers have done. What have we better than a blind guess to show that the criminal law in its present form does more good than harm? I do not stop to refer to the effect which it has had in degrading prisoners and in plunging them further into crime, or to the question whether fine and imprisonment do not fall more heavily on a criminal's wife and children than on himself. I have in mind more far-reaching questions. Does punishment deter? Do we deal with criminals on proper principles? A modern school of Continental criminalists plumes itself on the formula, first suggested, it is said, by Gall, that we must consider the criminal rather than the crime. The formula does not carry us very far, but the inquiries which have been started look toward an answer of my questions based on science for the first time. If the typical criminal is a degenerate, bound to swindle or to murder by as deep seated an organic necessity as that which makes the rattlesnake bite, it is idle to talk of deterring him by the classical method of imprisonment. He must be got rid of; he cannot be improved, or frightened out of his structural reaction. If, on the other hand, crime, like normal human conduct, is mainly a matter of imitation, punishment fairly may be expected to help to keep it out of fashion. The study of criminals has been thought by some well known men of science to sustain the former hypothesis. The statistics of the relative increase of crime in crowded places like large cities, where example has the greatest chance to work, and in less populated parts, where the contagion spreads more slowly, have been used with great force in favor of the latter view. But there is weighty authority for the belief that, however this may be, "not the nature of the crime, but the dangerousness of the criminal, constitutes the only reasonable legal criterion to guide the inevitable social reaction against the criminal."[1]

The impediments to rational generalization, which I illustrated from the law of larceny, are shown in the other branches of the law, as well as in that of crime. Take the law of tort or civil liability for damages apart from contract and the like. Is there any general theory of such liability, or are the cases in which it exists simply to be enumerated, and to be explained each on its special ground, as is easy to believe from the fact that the right of action for certain well known classes of wrongs like trespass or slander has its special history for each class? I think that there is a general theory to be discovered, although resting in tendency rather than established and accepted. I think that the law regards the infliction of temporal damage by a responsible person as actionable, if under the circumstances known to him the danger of his act is manifest according to common experience, or according to his own experience if it is more than common, except in cases where upon special grounds of policy the law refuses to protect the plaintiff or grants a privilege to the defendant.[2] I think that commonly malice, intent, and negligence mean only that the danger was manifest to a greater or less degree, under the circumstances known to the actor, although in some cases of privilege malice may mean an actual malevolent motive, and such a motive may take away a permission knowingly to inflict harm, which otherwise would be granted on this or that ground of dominant public good. But when I stated my view to a very eminent English judge the

---

[1] Havelock Ellis, "The Criminal," 41, citing Garofalo. See also Ferri, "Sociologie Criminelle," *passim*. Compare Tarde, "La Philosophie Pénale."

[2] An example of the law's refusing to protect the plaintiff is when he is interrupted by a stranger in the use of a valuable way, which he has travelled adversely for a week less than the period of prescription. A week later he will have gained a right, but now he is only a trespasser. Examples of privilege I have given already. One of the best is competition in business.

other day, he said: "You are discussing what the law ought to be; as the law is, you must show a right. A man is not liable for negligence unless he is subject to a duty." If our difference was more than a difference in words, or with regard to the proportion between the exceptions and the rule, then, in his opinion, liability for an act cannot be referred to the manifest tendency of the act to cause temporal damage in general as a sufficient explanation, but must be referred to the special nature of the damage, or must be derived from some special circumstances outside of the tendency of the act, for which no generalized explanation exists. I think that such a view is wrong, but it is familiar, and I dare say generally is accepted in England.

Everywhere the basis of principle is tradition, to such an extent that we even are in danger of making the rôle of history more important than it is. The other day Professor Ames wrote a learned article to show, among other things, that the common law did not recognize the defence of fraud in actions upon specialties, and the moral might seem to be that the personal character of that defence is due to its equitable origin. But if, as I have said, all contracts are formal, the difference is not merely historical, but theoretic, between defects of form which prevent a contract from being made, and mistaken motives which manifestly could not be considered in any system that we should call rational except against one who was privy to those motives. It is not confined to specialties, but is of universal application. I ought to add that I do not suppose that Mr. Ames would disagree with what I suggest.

However, if we consider the law of contract, we find it full of history. The distinctions between debt, covenant, and assumpsit are merely historical. The classification of certain obligations to pay money, imposed by the law irrespective of any bargain as quasi contracts, is merely historical. The doctrine of consideration is merely historical. The effect given to a seal is to be explained by history alone. — Consideration is a mere form. Is it a useful form? If so, why should it not be required in all contracts? A seal is a mere form, and is vanishing in the scroll and in enactments that a consideration must be given, seal or no seal. — Why should any merely historical distinction be allowed to affect the rights and obligations of business men?

Since I wrote this discourse I have come on a very good example of the way in which tradition not only overrides rational policy, but overrides it after first having been misunderstood and having been given a new and broader scope than it had when it had a meaning. It is the settled law of England that a material alteration of a written contract by a party avoids it as against him. The doctrine is contrary to the general tendency of the law. We do not tell a jury that if a man ever has lied in one particular he is to be presumed to lie in all. Even if a man has tried to defraud, it seems no sufficient reason for preventing him from proving the truth. Objections of like nature in general go to the weight, not to the admissibility, of evidence. Moreover, this rule is irrespective of fraud, and is not confined to evidence. It is not merely that you cannot use the writing, but that the contract is at an end. What does this mean? The existence of a written contract depends on the fact that the offerer and offeree have interchanged their written expressions, not on the continued existence of those expressions. But in the case of a bond the primitive notion was different. The contract was inseparable from the parchment. If a stranger destroyed it, or tore off the seal, or altered it, the obligee could not recover, however free from fault, because the defendant's contract, that is, the actual tangible bond which he had sealed, could not be produced in the form in which it bound him. About a hundred years ago Lord Kenyon undertook to use his reason on this tradition, as he sometimes did to the detriment of the law, and, not understanding it, said he could see no reason why what was true of a bond should not be true of other contracts. His decision happened to be right, as it concerned a promissory note, where again the common law regarded the contract as inseparable from the paper on which it was written, but the reasoning was general, and soon was extended to other written contracts, and various absurd and unreal grounds of policy were invented to account for the enlarged rule.

I trust that no one will understand me to be speaking with disrespect of the law, because I criticise it so freely. I venerate the law, and especially our system of law, as one of the vastest products of the human mind. No one knows better than I do the countless number of great intellects that have spent themselves in making some addition or improvement, the greatest of which is trifling when compared with the mighty whole. It has the final title to respect that it exists, that it is not a Hegelian dream, but a part of the lives of men. But one may criticise even what one reveres. Law is the business to which my life is devoted, and I should show less than devotion if I did not do what in me lies to improve it, and, when I perceive what seems to me the ideal of its future, if I hesitated to point it out and to press toward it with all my heart.

Perhaps I have said enough to show the part which the study of history necessarily plays in the intelligent study of the law as it is to-day. In the teaching of this school and at Cambridge it is in no danger of being undervalued. Mr. Bigelow here and Mr. Ames and Mr. Thayer there have made important contributions which will not be forgotten, and in England the recent history of early English law by Sir Frederick Pollock and Mr. Maitland has lent the subject an almost deceptive charm. We must beware of the pitfall of antiquarianism, and must remember that for our purposes our only interest in the past is for the light it throws upon the present. I look forward to a time when the part played by history in the explanation of dogma shall be very small, and instead of ingenious research we shall spend our energy on a study of the ends sought to be attained and the reasons for desiring them. As a step toward that ideal it seems to me that every lawyer ought to seek an understanding of economics. The present divorce between the schools of political economy and law seems to me an evidence of how much progress in philosophical study still remains to be made. In the present state of political economy, indeed, we come again upon history on a larger scale, but there we are called on to consider and weigh the ends of legislation, the means of attaining them, and the cost. We learn that for everything we have to give up something else, and we are taught to set the advantage we gain against the other advantage we lose, and to know what we are doing when we elect.

There is another study which sometimes is undervalued by the practical minded, for which I wish to say a good word, although I think a good deal of pretty poor stuff goes under that name. I mean the study of what is called jurisprudence. Jurisprudence, as I look at it, is simply law in its most generalized part. Every effort to reduce a case to a rule is an effort of jurisprudence, although the name as used in English is confined to the broadest rules and most fundamental conceptions. One mark of a great lawyer is that he sees the application of the broadest rules. There is a story of a Vermont justice of the peace before whom a suit was brought by one farmer against another for breaking a churn. The justice took time to consider, and then said that he had looked through the statutes and could find nothing about churns, and gave judgment for the defendant. The same state of mind is shown in all our common digests and text-books. Applications of rudimentary rules of contract or tort are tucked away under the head of Railroads or Telegraphs or go to swell treatises on historical subdivisions, such as Shipping or Equity, or are gathered under an arbitrary title which is thought likely to appeal to the practical mind, such as Mercantile Law. If a man goes into law it pays to be a master of it, and to be a master of it means to look straight through all the dramatic incidents and to discern the true basis for prophecy. Therefore, it is well to have an accurate notion of what you mean by law, by a right, by a duty, by malice, intent, and negligence, by ownership, by possession, and so forth. I have in my mind cases in which the highest courts seem to me to have floundered because they had no clear ideas on some of these themes. I have illustrated their importance already. If a further illustration is wished, it may be found by reading the Appendix to Sir James Stephen's Criminal Law on the subject of possession, and then turning to Pollock and Wright's enlightened book. Sir James Stephen is not the only writer whose attempts to analyze legal ideas have been confused by striving for a useless quintessence of all systems, instead of an accurate anatomy of one. The trouble with Austin was that he did not know enough English law. But still it is a practical advantage to master Austin, and his predecessors, Hobbes and Bentham, and his worthy successors, Holland and Pollock. Sir Frederick Pollock's recent little book is touched with the felicity which marks all his works, and is wholly free from the perverting influence of Roman models.

The advice of the elders to young men is very apt to be as unreal as a list of the hundred best books. At least in my day I had my share of such counsels, and high among the unrealities I place the recommendation to study the Roman law. I assume that such advice means more than collecting a few Latin maxims with which to ornament the discourse, — the purpose for which Lord Coke recommended Bracton. If that is all that is wanted, the title "De Regulis Juris Antiqui" can be read in an hour. I assume that, if it is well to study the Roman law, it is well to study it as a working system. That means mastering a set of technicalities more difficult and less understood than our own, and studying another course of history by which even more than our own the Roman law must be explained. If any one doubts me, let him read Keller's "Der Römische Zivil Prozess und die Aktionen," a treatise on the prætor's edict, Muirhead's most interesting "Historical Introduction to the Private Law of Rome," and, to give him the best chance possible, Sohm's admirable Institutes. No. The way to gain a liberal view of your subject is not to read something else, but to get to the bottom of the subject itself. The means of doing that are, in the first place, to follow the existing body of dogma into its highest generalizations by the help of jurisprudence; next, to discover from history how it has come to be what it is; and, finally, so far as you can, to consider the ends which the several rules seek to accomplish, the reasons why those ends are desired, what is given up to gain them, and whether they are worth the price.

We have too little theory in the law rather than too much, especially on this final branch of study. When I was speaking of history, I mentioned larceny as an example to show how the law suffered from not having embodied in a clear form a rule which will accomplish its manifest purpose. In that case the trouble was due to the survival of forms coming from a time when a more limited purpose was entertained. Let me now give an example to show the practical importance, for the decision of actual cases, of understanding the reasons of the law, by taking an example from rules which, so far as I know, never have been explained or theorized about in any adequate way. I refer to statutes of limitation and the law of prescription. The end of such rules is obvious, but what is the justification for depriving a man of his rights, a pure evil as far as it goes, in consequence of the lapse of time? Sometimes the loss of evidence is referred to, but that is a secondary matter. Sometimes the desirability of peace, but why is peace more desirable after twenty years than before? It is increasingly likely to come without the aid of legislation. Sometimes it is said that, if a man neglects to enforce his rights, he cannot complain if, after a while, the law follows his example. Now if this is all that can be said about it, you probably will decide a case I am going to put, for the plaintiff; if you take the view which I shall suggest, you possibly will decide it for the defendant. A man is sued for trespass upon land, and justifies under a right of way. He proves that he has used the way openly and adversely for twenty years, but it turns out that the plaintiff had granted a license to a person whom he reasonably supposed to be the defendant's agent, although not so in fact, and therefore had assumed that the use of the way was permissive, in which case no right would be gained. Has the defendant gained a right or not? If his gaining it stands on the fault and neglect of the landowner in the ordinary sense, as seems commonly to be supposed, there has been no such neglect, and the right of way has not been acquired. But if I were the defendant's counsel, I should suggest that the foundation of the acquisition of rights by lapse of time is to be looked for in the position of the person who gains them, not in that of the loser. Sir Henry Maine has made it fashionable to connect the archaic notion of property with prescription. But the connection is further back than the first recorded history. It is in the nature of man's mind. A thing which you have enjoyed and used as your own for a long time, whether property or an opinion, takes root in your being and cannot be torn away without your resenting the act and trying to defend yourself, however you came by it. The law can ask no better justification than the deepest instincts of man. It is only by way of reply to the suggestion that you are disappointing the former owner, that you refer to his neglect having allowed the gradual dissociation between himself and what he claims, and the gradual association of it with another. If he knows that another is doing acts which on their face show that he is on the way toward establishing such an association, I should argue that in justice to that other he was bound at his peril to find out whether the other was acting under his permission, to see that he was warned, and, if necessary, stopped.

I have been speaking about the study of the law, and I have said next to nothing of what commonly is talked about in that connection, — text-books and the case system, and all the machinery with which a student comes most immediately in contact. Nor shall I say anything about them Theory is my subject, not practical details. The modes of teaching have been improved since my time, no doubt, but ability and industry will master the raw material with any mode. Theory is the most important part of the dogma of the law, as the architect is the most important man who takes part in the building of a house. The most important improvements of the last twenty five years are improvements in theory. It is not to be feared as unpractical, for, to the competent, it simply means going to the bottom of the subject. For the incompetent, it sometimes is true, as has been said, that an interest in general ideas means an absence of particular knowledge. I remember in army days reading of a youth who, being examined for the lowest grade and being asked a question about squadron drill, answered that he never had considered the evolutions of less than ten thousand men. But the weak and foolish must be left to their folly. The danger is that the able and practical minded should look with indifference or distrust upon ideas the connection of which with their business is remote. I heard a story, the other day, of a man who had a valet to whom he paid high wages, subject to deduction for faults. One of his deductions was, "For lack of imagination, five dollars." The lack is not confined to valets. The object of ambition, power, generally presents itself nowadays in the form of money alone. Money is the most immediate form, and is a proper object of desire. "The fortune," said Rachel, "is the measure of the intelligence." That is a good text to waken people out of a fool's paradise. But, as Hegel says,[1] "It is in the end not the appetite, but the opinion, which has to be satisfied." To an imagination of any scope the most far-reaching form of power is not money, it is the command of ideas. If you want great examples read Mr. Leslie Stephen's "History of English Thought in the Eighteenth Century," and see how a hundred years after his death the abstract speculations of Descartes had become a practical force controlling the conduct of men. Read the works of the great German jurists, and see how much more the world is governed to-day by Kant than by Bonaparte. We cannot all be Descartes or Kant, but we all want happiness. And happiness, I am sure from having known many successful men, cannot be won simply by being counsel for great corporations and having an income of fifty thousand dollars. An intellect great enough to win the prize needs other food beside success. The remoter and more general aspects of the law are those which give it universal interest. It is through them that you not only become a great master in your calling, but connect your subject with the universe and catch an echo of the infinite, a glimpse of its unfathomable process, a hint of the universal law.

[1] Phil. des Rechts, § 190.

[2]

FORCE AND COERCION.

FORCE AND COERCION.

JOHN DEWEY.

THE empirical perplexities which attend the question of the relationship of force and law are many and genuine. The war brings home to us the question not only of the relation of force to international law, but the place of force in the economy of human life and progress. To what extent is organization of force in the multitude of ways required for the successful conduct of modern war a fair test of the work of a social organization? From another angle, the reform of our criminal law and our penal methods compels us to consider the significance of force. Are the Tolstoians right in holding that the state itself sets the great example of violence and furnishes the proof of the evils which result from violence? Or, from the other side, is not the essence of all law coercion? In the industrial domain, direct actionists lead us to inquire whether manifestation of force, threatening and veiled if not overt, is not, after all, the only efficacious method of bringing about any social change which is of serious import. Do not the usual phenomena attending strikes show us that the ordinary legal forms are just a kind of curtain drawn politely over the conflicts of force which alone are decisive? Are our effective legislative enactments anything more than registrations of results of battles previously fought out on the field of human endurance? In many social fields, reformers are now struggling for an extension of governmental activity by way of supervision and regulation. Does not such action always amount to an effort to extend the exercise of force on the part of some section of society, with a corresponding restriction of the forces employed by others? In spite of the fact that the political thinking of the seventeenth and eighteenth centuries is out of date, were not the thinkers of that period clearer headed than we are in acknowledging that all political questions are simply questions of the extension and restriction of exercise of power on the part of specific groups in the community? Has the recent introduction of an idealistic terminology about moral and common will, about juridical and moral personalities, done anything but muddle our minds about the hard fact that all our social questions at bottom concern the possession and use of force; and the equally hard fact that our political and legal arrangements are but dispositions of force to make more secure the other forms of its daily use?

In taking up the writings of the theorists it is not easy to persuade oneself that they are marked by much consistency. With a few notable exceptions, the doctrine that the state rests upon or is common will seems to turn out but a piece of phraseology to justify the uses actually made of force. Practices of coercion and constraint which would be intolerable if frankly labelled "Force" seem to become laudable when baptized with the name of Will, although they otherwise remain the same. Or, if this statement is extreme, there seems to be little doubt that the actual capacity of the state to bring force to bear is what has most impressed theorists, and that what they are after is some theoretical principle which will justify the exercise of force; so that in a great many cases such terms as common will, supreme will, supreme moral or juridical personality, are eulogistic phrases resorted to in behalf of such justification. The one thing that clearly stands out is that the use of force is felt to require explanation and sanction. To make force itself the ultimate principle is felt to be all one with proclaiming anarchy and issuing an invitation to men to settle all their difficulties by recourse to fighting it out to see which is the stronger. And yet what every political student is profoundly convinced of, is, I suppose, that at bottom every political struggle is a struggle for control, for power.

Although I have raised large questions, it is not my ambition to answer them. I have but outlined a large stage upon which to move about some quite minor figures.

In the first place, something can be done, I think, by clarifying certain of the ideas which enter into the discussion. We may I think profitably discriminate the three conceptions of power or energy, coercive force, and violence. Power or energy is either a neutral or an eulogistic term. It denotes effective means of operation; ability or capacity to execute, to realize ends. Granted an end which is worth while, and power or energy becomes an eulogistic term. It means nothing but the sum of conditions available for bringing the desirable end into existence. Any political or legal theory which will have nothing to do with power on the ground that all power is force and all force brutal and non-moral is obviously condemned to a purely sentimental, dreamy morals. It is force by which we excavate subways and build bridges and travel and manufacture; it is force which is utilized in spoken argument or published book. Not to depend upon and utilize force is simply to be without a foothold in the real world.

Energy becomes violence when it defeats or frustrates purpose instead or executing or realizing it. When the dynamite charge blows up human beings instead of rocks, when its outcome is waste instead of production, destruction instead of construction, we call it not energy or power but violence. Coercive force occupies, we may fairly say, a middle place between power as energy and power as violence. To turn to the right as an incident of locomotion is a case of power: of means deployed in behalf of an end. To run amuck in the street is a case of violence. To use energy to make a man observe the rule of the road is a case of coercive force. Immediately, or with respect to his activities, it is a case of violence; indirectly, when it is exercised to assure the means which are needed for the successful realization of ends, it is a case of constructive use of power. Constraint or coercion, in other words, is an incident of a situation under certain conditions—namely, where the means for the realization of an end are not naturally at hand, so that energy has to be spent in order to make some power into a means for the end in hand.

If we formulate the result, we have something of this kind. Law is a statement of the conditions of the organization of energies which, when unorganized, conflict and result in violence—that is, destruction or waste. We cannot substitute reason for force, but force becomes rational when it is an organized factor in an activity instead of operating in an isolated way or on its own hook. For the sake of brevity, I shall refer to the organization of force hereafter as efficiency, but I beg to remind you that the use of the term always implies an actual or potential conflict and resulting waste in the absence of some scheme for distributing the energies involved.

These generalities are, it will be objected, innocuous and meaningless. So they are in the abstract. Let us take the question of the justification of force in a strike. I do not claim, of course, that what has been said tells us whether the use of force is justified or not. But I hold that it suggests the way of finding out in a given case whether it is justifiable or not. It is, in substance, a question of efficiency (including economy) of means in the accomplishing of ends. If the social ends at stake can be more effectively subserved by the existing legal and economic machinery, resort to physical action of a more direct kind has no standing. If, however, they represent an ineffective organization of means for the ends in question, then recourse to extra-legal means may be indicated; provided it really serves the ends in question—a very large qualification be it noted. A recourse to direct force is a supplementation of existent deficient resources in effective energy under some circumstances.

Such a doctrine is doubtless unwelcome. It is easily interpreted so as to give encouragement to resorting to violence and threats of violence in industrial struggles. But there is a very large "if" involved—the "if" of greater relative economy and efficiency. And when so regarded, it at once occurs to mind that experience in the past has shown that it is not usually efficient for parties to be judges in their own cause: that an impartial umpire is an energy saver. It occurs to mind, also, that the existing legal machinery, whatever its defects, represents a contrivance which has been built up at great cost, and that the tendency to ignore its operation upon special provocation would so reduce the efficiency of the machinery in other situations that the local gain would easily be more than offset by widespread losses in energy available for other ends. In the third place, experience shows that there is general presumption on the side of indirect and refined agencies as against coarse and strikingly obvious methods of utilizing power. The fine mechanism which runs a watch is more efficient than the grosser one which heaves a brick. Thus the bias against any doctrine which seems under any circumstances to sanction resort to personal and primitive methods of using force against the more impersonal juridical contrivances of society turns out to be *prima facie* justified on the principle of efficiency in use of means.

Over and above this bare presumption, it must be admitted that our organized contrivances are still so ineffective that it is a delicate matter to tell how far a standing menace to resort to crude methods may be a necessary stimulus to the better working of the more refined methods. There is a general presumption in politics against doing anything till it is clearly necessary; and indication of potential force operates as a sign of necessity. In other words social reorganization is usually a response to a threatened conflict—witness the present "preparedness" agitation.

This conclusion that violence means recourse to means which are relatively wasteful may be strengthened by considering penal measures. Upon the whole, the opinion seems to be current that in such matters force is hallowed by the mere fact that it is the State which employs it, or by the fact that it is exercised in the interests of "justice" —retribution in the abstract, or what is politely called "vindicating the law." When the justification of force is sought in some kind of abstract consideration of this sort, no questions are to be raised about the efficiency of the force used, for it is not conceived as a specific means to a specific end. It is the sacrosanct character thus attributed to the State's use of force which gives pungency to the Tolstoian charge that the State is the arch-criminal, the person who has recourse to violence on the largest scale. I see no way out except to say that all depends upon the efficient adaptation of means to ends. The serious charge against the State is not that it uses force—nothing was ever accomplished without using force—but that it does not use it wisely or effectively. Our penal measures are still largely upon the level which would convince a man by knocking him down instead of by instructing him.

My treatment is of course very summary. But I hope that it suggests my main point. No ends are accomplished without the use of force. It is consequently no presumption against a measure, political, international, jural, economic, that it involves a use of force. Squeamishness about force is the mark not of idealistic but of moonstruck morals. But antecedent and abstract principles can not be assigned to justify the use of force. The criterion of value lies in the relative efficiency and economy of the expenditure of force as a means to an end. With advance of knowledge, refined, subtle and indirect use of force is always displacing coarse, obvious and direct methods of applying it. This is the explanation to the ordinary feeling against the use of force. What is thought of as brutal, violent, immoral, is a use of physical agencies which are gross, sensational and evident on their own account, in cases where it is possible to employ with greater economy and less waste means which are comparatively imperceptible and refined.

It follows from what has been said that the so called problem of "moralizing" force is in reality a problem of *intellectualizing* its use: a problem of employing so to say neural instead of gross muscular force as a means to accomplish ends. An immoral use of force is a stupid use. I sometimes hear apologies for war which proceed by pointing out how largely all social life is a disguised contest of hostile powers. Our economic life, so it is said, is but a struggle for bread where the endurance and even the lives of laborers are pitted against the resources of employers. Only lack of imagination fails to see the economic war, the industrial battlefield with its ammunition trains and human carnage. Let the point be admitted. What still remains true is that the decisive question is the level of efficiency and economy upon which the deploying of forces goes on. Our present economic methods may be so wasteful, so destructive, as compared with others which are humanly possible, as to be barbarous. Yet competitive commercial methods may represent an advance in the utilization of human and natural resources over methods of war. In so far as they involve greater indirection and complexity of means, the presumption is that they are an advance. Take, however, on the other extreme the gospel of non-resistance. Except upon a doctrine of quiescence more thorough-going than any St. Simon Stylites has ever adopted, the non-resistance doctrine can mean only that given certain conditions, passive resistance is a more *effective* means of resistance than overt resistance would be. Sarcasm may be more effective than a blow in subduing an adversary; a look more effective than sarcasm. Only upon such a principle of expediency can the doctrine of non-resistance be urged, without committing ourselves to the notion that all exercise of energy is inherently wrong—a sort of oriental absolutism which makes the world intrinsically evil. I can but think that if pacifists in war and in penal matters would change their tune from the intrinsic immorality of the use of coercive force to the comparative inefficiency and stupidity of existing methods of using force, their good intentions would be more fruitful.

As my object is rather to make a point clear than to convince anyone, let me take another example. In the labor struggle we sometimes hear a right of free labor and free choice appealed to as against the movement for a closed shop. Men like President Eliot are sincerely convinced that they are continuing the fight for human freedom. Perhaps they are. I do not pretend to pass upon the merits of the question. But *perhaps* they are only fighting in behalf of the retention of methods of waste against those of efficient organization. There was a time when our ancestors had the personal right of inflicting punishment upon offenders. When the movement set in to restrict this office to a limited number of designated officers and thereby to deprive the mass of their prior right, one wonders whether the spiritual ancestors of President Eliot did not protest against this invasion of sacred personal liberties. It is now clear enough that the surrender of the power was an incident of organization absolutely necessary to secure an efficient utilization of the resources entering into it. It may turn out in the future that the movement for the closed shop is an incident of an organization of labor which is itself in turn an incident in accomplishing a more efficient organization of human forces.

In other words, the question of the limits of individual powers, or liberties, or rights, is finally a question of the most efficient use of means for ends. That at a certain period liberty should have been set up as something antecedently sacred *per se* is natural enough. Such liberty represented an important factor which had been overlooked. But it is as an efficiency factor that its value must ultimately be assessed. Experience justifies the contention that liberty forms such a central element in efficiency that, for example, our present methods of capitalistic production are highly inefficient because, as respects the great body of laborers, they are so coercive. Efficiency requires methods which will enlist greater individual interest and attention, greater emotional and intellectual liberty. With respect to such a liberation of energies, older and coarser forms of liberty may be obstructive; efficiency may then require the use of coercive power to abrogate *their* exercise.

The propositions of this paper may then be summed up as follows: First, since the attainment of ends requires the use of means, law is essentially a formulation of the use of force. Secondly, the only question which can be raised about the justification of force is that of comparative efficiency and economy in its use. Thirdly, what is justly objected to as violence or undue coercion is a reliance upon wasteful and destructful means of accomplishing results. Fourthly, there is always a possibility that what passes as a legitimate use of force may be so wasteful as to be really a use of violence; and *per contra* that measures condemned as recourse to mere violence may, under the given circumstances, represent an intelligent utilization of energy. In no case, can antecedent or *a priori* principles be appealed to as more than presumptive: the point at issue is concrete utilization of means for ends.

John Dewey.

Columbia University.

[3]

Logical Method and Law

JOHN DEWEY†

Human conduct, broadly viewed, falls into two sorts: Particular cases overlap, but the difference is discernible on any large scale consideration of conduct. Sometimes human beings act with a minimum of foresight, without examination of what they are doing and of probable consequences. They act not upon deliberation but from routine, instinct, the direct pressure of appetite, or a blind 'hunch.' It would be a mistake to suppose that such behavior is always inefficient or unsuccessful. When we do not like it, we condemn it as capricious, arbitrary, careless, negligent. But in other cases, we praise the marvellous rectitude of instinct or intuition; we are inclined to accept the offhand appraisal of an expert in preference to elaborately calculated conclusions of a man who is ill-informed. There is the old story of the layman who was appointed to a position in India where he would have to pass in his official capacity on various matters in controversy between natives. Upon consulting a legal friend, he was told to use his common-sense and announce his decisions firmly; in the majority of cases his natural decision as to what was fair and reasonable would suffice. But, his friend added: "Never try to give reasons, for they will usually be wrong."

In the other sort of case, action follows upon a decision, and the decision is the outcome of inquiry, comparison of alternatives, weighing of facts; deliberation or thinking has intervened. Considerations which have weight in reaching the conclusion as to what is to be done, or which are employed to justify it when it is questioned, are called 'reasons.' If they are stated in sufficiently general terms they are 'principles.' When the operation is formulated in a compact way, the decision is called a conclusion, and the considerations which led up to it are called the premises. Decisions of the first type may be reasonable: that is, they may be adapted to good results; those of the second type are reasoned or rational, increasingly so, in the degree of care and thoroughness with which inquiry has been conducted and the order in which connections have been established between the considerations dealt with.

Now I define logical theory as an account of the procedures followed in reaching decisions of the second type, in those cases in which subse-

†Professor of Philosophy, Columbia University.

quent experience shows that they were the best which could have been used under the conditions. This definition would be questioned by many authorities, and it is only fair to say that it does not represent the orthodox or the prevailing view. But it is stated at the outset so that the reader may be aware of the conception of logic which underlies the following discussion. If we take an objection which will be brought against this conception by adherents of the traditional notion, it will serve to clarify its meaning. It will be said that the definition restricts thinking to the processes antecedent to making a decision or a deliberate choice; and, thereby, in confining logical procedure to practical matters, fails to take even a glance at those cases in which true logical method is best exemplified: namely, scientific, especially mathematical, subjects.

A partial answer to this objection is that the especial topic of our present discussion is logical method in legal reasoning and judicial decision, and that such cases at least are similar in general type to decisions made by engineers, merchants, physicians, bankers, etc., in the pursuit of their callings. In law we are certainly concerned with the necessity of settling upon a course of action to be pursued, giving judgment of one sort or another in favor of adoption of one mode of conduct and against another. But the scope of the position taken will appear more clearly if we do not content ourselves with this *ad hoc* reply.

If we consider the procedure of the mathematician or of any man of science, as it concretely occurs, instead of considering simply the relations of consistent implication which subsist between the propositions in which his finally approved conclusions are set forth, we find that he, as well as an intelligent farmer or business man or physician, is constantly engaged in making decisions; and that in order to make them wisely he summons before his mental gaze various considerations, and accepts and rejects them with a view to making his decision as rational as possible. The concrete subject with which he deals, the material he investigates, accepts, rejects, employs in reaching and justifying his decision, is different from that of farmer, lawyer, or merchant, but the course of the operation, the form of the procedure, is similar. The scientific man has the advantage of working under much more narrowly and exactly controlled conditions, with the aid of symbols artfully devised to protect his procedure. For that reason it is natural and proper that we should, in our formal treatises, take operations of this type as standards and models, and should treat ordinary 'practical' reasonings leading up to decisions as to what is to be done as only approximations. But every thinker, as an investigator, mathematician, or physicist as well as 'practical man,' thinks in order to determine *his* decisions and conduct—his conduct as a specialized agent working in a carefully delimited field.

It may be replied, of course, that this is an arbitrary notion of logic, and that in reality logic is an affair of the relations and orders of relations which subsist between propositions which constitute the accepted subject-matter of a science; that relations are independent of operations of inquiry and of reaching conclusions or decisions. I shall not stop to try to controvert this position, but shall use it to point the essential difference between it and the position taken in this article. According to the latter, logical systematization with a view to the utmost generality and consistency of propositions is indispensable but is not ultimate. It is an instrumentality, not an end. It is a means of improving, facilitating, clarifying the inquiry that leads up to concrete decisions; primarily that particular inquiry which has just been engaged in, but secondarily, and of greater ultimate importance, other inquiries directed at making other decisions in similar fields. And here at least I may fall back for confirmation upon the special theme of law. It is most important that rules of law should form as coherent generalized logical systems as possible. But these logical systematizations of law in any field, whether of crime, contracts, or torts, with their reduction of a multitude of decisions to a few general principles that are logically consistent with one another while it may be an end in itself for a particular student, is clearly in last resort subservient to the economical and effective reaching of decisions in particular cases.

It follows that logic is ultimately an empirical and concrete discipline. Men first employ certain ways of investigating, and of collecting, recording and using data in reaching conclusions, in making decisions; they draw inferences and make their checks and tests in various ways. These different ways constitute the empirical raw material of logical theory. The latter thus comes into existence without any conscious thought of logic, just as forms of speech take place without conscious reference to rules of syntax or of rhetorical propriety. But it is gradually learned that some methods which are used work better than others. Some yield conclusions that do not stand the test of further situations; they produce conflicts and confusion; decisions dependent upon them have to be retracted or revised. Other methods are found to yield conclusions which are available in subsequent inquiries as well as confirmed by them. There first occurs a kind of natural selection of the methods which afford the better type of conclusion, better for subsequent usage, just as happens in the development of rules for conducting any art. Afterwards the methods are themselves studied critically. Successful ones are not only selected and collated, but the causes of their effective operation are discovered. Thus logical theory becomes scientific.

The bearing of the conception of logic which is here advanced upon legal thinking and decisions may be brought out by examining the apparent disparity which exists between actual legal development and the strict requirements of logical theory. Justice Holmes has generalized the situation by saying that "the whole outline of the law is the resultant of a conflict at every point between logic and good sense—the one striving to work fiction out to consistent results, the other restraining and at last overcoming that effort when the results become too manifestly unjust."[1] This statement he substantiates by a thorough examination of the development of certain legal notions. Upon its surface, such a statement implies a different view of the nature of logic than that stated. It implies that logic is not the method *of* good sense, that it has as it were a substance and life of its own which conflicts with the requirements of good decisions with respect to concrete subject-matters. The difference, however, is largely verbal. What Justice Holmes terms logic is formal consistency, consistency of concepts with one another irrespective of the consequences of their application to concrete matters-of-fact. We might state the fact by saying that concepts once developed have a kind of intrinsic inertia on their own account; once developed the law of habit applies to them. It is practically economical to use a concept ready at hand rather than to take time and trouble and effort to change it or to devise a new one. The use of prior ready-made and familiar concepts also give rise to a sense of stability, of guarantee against sudden and arbitrary changes of the rules which determine the consequences which legally attend acts. It is the nature of any concept, as it is of any habit to change more slowly than do the concrete circumstances with reference to which it is employed. Experience shows that the relative fixity of concepts affords men with a specious sense of protection, of assurance against the troublesome flux of events. Thus Justice Holmes says, "The language of judicial decision is mainly the language of logic. And the logical method and form flatter that longing for certainty and for repose which is in every human mind. But certainty generally is an illusion."[2] From the view of logical method here set forth, however, the undoubted facts which Justice Holmes has in mind do not concern logic but rather certain tendencies

[1]Collected Legal Papers, p. 50.
[2]*Ibid.*, p. 181.

of the human creatures who use logic; tendencies which a sound logic will guard against. For they spring from the momentum of habit once forced, and express the effect of habit upon our feelings of ease and stability—feelings which have little to do with the actual facts of the case.

However this is only part of the story. The rest of the story is brought to light in some other passages of Justice Holmes. "The actual life of the law has not been logic: it has been experience. The felt necessities of the times, the prevalent moral and political theories, intuitions of public policy, avowed or unconscious, even the prejudices which judges share with their fellow-men, have had a good deal more to do than the syllogism in determining the rules by which men should be governed."[3] In other words, Justice Holmes is thinking of logic as equivalent with the syllogism, as he is quite entitled to do in accord with the orthodox tradition. From the standpoint of the syllogism as the logical model which was made current by scholasticism there *is* an antithesis between experience and logic, between logic and good sense. For the philosophy embodied in the formal theory of the syllogism asserted that thought or reason has fixed forms of its own, anterior to and independent of concrete subject-matters, and to which the latter have to be adapted whether or no. This defines the negative aspect of this discussion; and it shows by contrast the need of another kind of logic which shall reduce the influence of habit, and shall facilitate the use of good sense regarding matters of social consequence.

In other words, there are different logics in use. One of these, the one which has had greatest historic currency and exercised greatest influence on legal decisions, is that of the syllogism. To this logic the strictures of Justice Holmes apply in full force. For it purports to be a logic of rigid demonstration, not of search and discovery. It claims to be a logic of fixed forms, rather than of methods of reaching intelligent decisions in concrete situations, or of methods employed in adjusting disputed issues in behalf of the public and enduring interest. Those ignorant of formal logic, the logic of the abstract relations of ready-made conceptions to one another, have at least heard of the standard syllogism: All men are mortal; Scorates is a man; therefore, he is mortal. This is offered as the model of all proof or demonstration. It implies that what we need and must procure is first a fixed general *principle*, the so-called major premise, such as 'all men are mortal;' then in the second place, a fact which belongs intrinsically and obviously to a class of things to which the general

[3] The Common Law, p. 1.

principle applies: Socrates is a man. Then the conclusion automatically follows: Socrates is mortal. According to this model every demonstrative or strictly logical conclusion 'subsumes' a particular under an appropriate universal. It implies the prior and given existence of particulars and universals.

It thus implies that for every possible case which may arise, there is a fixed antecedent rule already at hand; that the case in question is either simple and unambiguous, or is resolvable by direct inspection into a collection of simple and indubitable facts, such as, 'Socrates is a man.' It thus tends, when it is accepted, to produce and confirm what Professor Pound has called mechanical jurisprudence; it flatters that longing for certainty of which Justice Holmes speaks; it reinforces those inert factors in human nature which make men hug as long as possible any idea which has once gained lodgment in the mind.

In a certain sense it is foolish to criticise the model supplied by the syllogism. The statements made about men and Socrates are obviously true, and the connection between them is undoubted. The trouble is that while the syllogism sets forth the *results* of thinking, it has nothing to do with the *operation* of thinking. Take the case of Socrates being tried before the Athenian citizens, and the thinking which had to be done to reach a decision. Certainly the issue was not whether Socrates was mortal; the point was whether this mortality would or should occur at a specified date and in a specified way. Now that is just what does not and cannot follow from a general principle or a major premise. Again to quote Justice Holmes, "General propositions do not decide concrete cases." No concrete proposition, that is to say one with material dated in time and placed in space, follows from any general statements or from any connection between them.

If we trust to an experimental logic, we find that general principles emerge as statements of generic ways in which it has been found helpful to treat concrete cases. The real force of the proposition that all men are mortal is found in the expectancy tables of insurance companies, which with their accompanying rates show how it is prudent and socially useful to deal with human mortality. The 'universal' stated in the major premise is not outside of and antecedent to particular cases; neither is it a selection of something found in a variety of cases. It is an indication of a single way of treating cases for certain purposes or consequences in spite of their diversity. Hence its meaning and worth are subject to inquiry and revision in view of what happens, what the consequences are, when it is used as a method of treatment.

As a matter of fact, men do not begin thinking with premises. They begin with some complicated and confused case, apparently admitting of alternative modes of treatment and solution. Premises only gradually emerge from analysis of the total situation. The problem is not to draw a conclusion from given premises; that can best be done by a piece of inanimate machinery by fingering a keyboard. The problem is to *find* statements, of general principle and of particular fact, which are worthy to serve as premises. As matter of actual fact, we generally begin with some vague anticipation of a conclusion (or at least of alternative conclusions), and then we look around for principles and data which will substantiate it or which will enable us to choose intelligently between rival conclusions. No lawyer ever thought out the case of a client in terms of the syllogism. He begins with a conclusion which he intends to reach, favorable to his client of course, and then analyzes the facts of the situation to find material out of which to construct a favorable statement of facts, to *form* a minor premise. At the same time he goes over recorded cases to find rules of law employed in cases which can be presented as similar, rules which will substantiate a certain way of looking at and interpreting the facts. And as his acquaintance with rules of law judged applicable widens, he probably alters perspective and emphasis in selection of the facts which are to form his evidential data. And as he learns more of the facts of the case he may modify his selection of rules of law upon which he bases his case.

I do not for a moment set up this procedure as a model of scientific method; it is too precommitted to the establishment of a particular and partisan conclusion to serve as such a model. But it does illustrate, in spite of this deficiency, the particular point which is being made here: namely, that thinking actually sets out from a more or less confused situation, which is vague and ambiguous with respect to the conclusion it indicates, and that the formation of both major premise and minor proceed tentatively and correlatively in the course of analysis of this situation and of prior rules. As soon as acceptable premises are given and of course the judge and jury have eventually to do with their becoming accepted—and the conclusion is also given. In strict logic, the conclusion does not follow from premises; conclusions and premises are two ways of stating the same thing. Thinking may be defined either as a development of premises or development of a conclusion; as far as it is one operation it is the other.

Courts not only reach decisions; they expound them, and the exposition must state justifying reasons. The mental operations therein involved are somewhat different from those involved in arriving at a conclusion. The logic of exposition is different from that of search and inquiry. In the latter, the situation as it exists is more or less doubtful, indeterminate, and problematic with respect to what it signifies. It unfolds itself gradually and is susceptible of dramatic surprise; at all events it has, for the time being, two sides. Exposition implies that a definitive solution is reached, that the situation is now determinate with respect to its legal implication. Its purpose is to set forth grounds for the decision reached so that it will not appear as an arbitrary dictum, and so that it will indicate a rule for dealing with similar cases in the future. It is highly probable that the need of justifying to others conclusions reached and decisions made has been the chief cause of the origin and development of logical operations in the precise sense; of abstraction, generalization, regard for consistency of implications. It is quite conceivable that if no one had ever had to account to others for his decisions, logical operations would never have developed, but men would use exclusively methods of inarticulate intuition and impression, feeling; so that only after considerable experience in accounting for their decisions to others who demanded a reason, or exculpation, and were not satisfied till they got it, did men begin to give an account to themselves of the process of reaching a conclusion in a justified way. However this may be, it is certain that in judicial decisions the only alternative to arbitrary dicta, accepted by the parties to a controversy only because of the authority or prestige of the judge, is a rational statement which formulates grounds and exposes connecting or logical links.

It is at this point that the chief stimulus and temptation to mechanical logic and abstract use of formal concepts come in. Just because the personal element cannot be wholly excluded, while at the same time the decision must assume as nearly as possible an impersonal, objective, rational form, the temptation is to surrender the vital logic which has actually yielded the conclusion and to substitute for it forms of speech which are rigorous in appearance and which give an illusion of certitude.

Another moving force is the undoubted need for the maximum possible of stability and regularity of expectation in determining courses of conduct. Men need to know the legal consequences which society through the courts will attach to their specific transactions, the liabilities they are assuming, the fruits they may count upon in entering upon a given course of action.

This is a legitimate requirement from the standpoint of the interests of the community and of particular individuals. Enormous confusion has resulted, however, from confusion of *theoretical* certainty and practical certainty. There is a wide gap separating the reasonable proposition that judicial decisions should possess the maximum possible regularity in order to enable persons in planning their conduct to foresee the legal import of their acts, and the absurd because impossible proposition that every decision should flow with formal logical necessity from antecedently known premises. To attain the former result there are required general principles of interpreting cases—rules of law—and procedures of pleading and trying cases which do not alter arbitrarily. But principles of interpretation do not signify rules so rigid that they can be stated once for all and then be literally and mechanically adhered to. For the situations to which they are to be applied do not literally repeat one another in all details, and questions of degree of this factor or that have the chief weight in determining which general rule will be employed to judge the situation in question. A large part of what has been asserted concerning the necessity of absolutely uniform and immutable antecedent rules of law is in effect an attempt to evade the really important issue of finding and employing rules of law, substantive and procedural, which will actually secure to the members of the community a reasonable measure of practical certainty of expectation in framing their courses of conduct. The mechanical ease of the court in disposing of cases and not the actual security of agents is the real cause, for example, of making rules of pleading hard and fast. The result introduces an unnecessary element of gamble into the behavior of those seeking settlement of disputes. while it affords to the judges only that factitious ease and simplicity which is supplied by any routine habit of action. It substitutes a mechanical procedure for the need of analytic thought.

There is of course every reason why rules of law should be as regular and as definite as possible. But the amount and kind of antecedent assurance which is actually attainable is a matter of fact, not of form. It is large wherever social conditions are pretty uniform, and when industry, commerce, transportation, etc., move in the channels of old customs. It is much less wherever invention is active and when new devices in business and communication bring about new forms of human relationship. Thus the use of power machinery radically modifies the old terms of association of master and servant and fellow servants; rapid transportation brings into general use commercial bills of lading; mass production engenders organization of laborers and collective bargaining; industrial conditions favor concentration of capital. In part legislation endeavors to reshape old rules of law to make them applicable to new conditions. But statutes have never kept up with the variety and subtlety of social change. They cannot at the very best avoid some ambiguity, which is due not only to carelessness but also to the intrinsic impossibility of foreseeing all possible circumstances, since without such foresight definitions must be vague and classifications indeterminate. Hence to claim that old forms are ready at hand that cover every case and that may be applied by formal syllogizing is to pretend to a certainty and regularity which cannot exist in fact. The effect of the pretension is to increase practical uncertainty and social instability. Just because circumstances are really novel and not covered by old rules, it is a gamble which old rule will be declared regulative of a particular case, so that shrewd and enterprising men are encouraged to sail close to the wind and trust to ingenious lawyers to find some rule under which they can get off scot free.

The facts involved in this discussion are commonplace and they are not offered as presenting anything original or novel. What we are concerned with is their bearing upon the logic of judicial decisions. For the implications are more revolutionary than they might at first seem to be. They indicate either that logic must be abandoned or that it must be a logic *relative to consequences rather than to antecedents*, a logic of prediction of probabilities rather than one of deduction of certainties. For the purposes of a logic of inquiry into probable consequences, general principles can only be tools justified by the work they do. They are means of intellectual survey, analysis, and insight into the factors of the situation to be dealt with. Like other tools they must be modified when they are applied to new conditions and new results have to be achieved. Here is where the great practical evil of the doctrine of immutable and necessary antecedent rules comes in. It sanctifies the old; adherence to it in practise constantly widens the gap between current social conditions and the principles used by the courts. The effect is to breed irritation, disrespect for law, together with virtual alliance between the judiciary and entrenched interests that correspond most nearly to the conditions under which the rules of law were previously laid down.

Failure to recognize that general legal rules and principles are working hypotheses, needing to be constantly tested by the way in which they work out in application to concrete situations, explains the otherwise paradoxical fact that the slogans of the liberalism of one period often become the bulwarks of reaction in a subsequent era.

There was a time in the eighteenth century when the great social need was emancipation of industry and trade from a multitude of restrictions which held over from the feudal estate of Europe. Adapted well enough to the localized and fixed conditions of that earlier age, they became hindrances and annoyances as the effects of methods, use of coal and steam, showed themselves. The movement of emancipation expressed itself in principles of liberty in use of property, and freedom of contract, which were embodied in a mass of legal decisions. But the absolutistic logic of rigid syllogistic forms infected these ideas. It was soon forgotten that they were relative to analysis of existing situations in order to secure orderly methods in behalf of economic social welfare. Thus these principles became in turn so rigid as to be almost as socially obstructive as "immutable" feudal laws had been in their day.

That the remarks which have been made, commonplace as they are in themselves, have a profound practical import may also be seen in the present reaction against the individualistic formulae of an older liberalism. The last thirty years has seen an intermittent tendency in the direction of legislation, and to a less extent of judicial decision, towards what is vaguely known as "social justice," toward formulae of a collectivistic character. Now it is quite possible that the newer rules may be needed and useful at a certain juncture, and yet that they may also become harmful and socially obstructive if they are hardened into absolute and fixed antecedent premises. But if they are conceived as tools to be adapted to the conditions in which they are employed rather than as absolute and intrinsic "principles," attention will go to the facts of social life, and the rules will not be allowed to engross attention and become absolute truths to be mantained intact at all costs. Otherwise we shall in the end merely have substituted one set of formally absolute and immutable syllogistic premises for another set.

If we recur then to our introductory conception that logic is really a theory about empirical phenomena, subject to growth and improvement like any other empirical discipline, we recur to it with an added conviction: namely, that the issue is not a purely speculative one, but implies consequences vastly significant for practise. I should indeed not hesitate to assert that the sanctification of ready-made antecedent universal principles as methods of thinking is the chief obstacle to the kind of thinking which is the indispensable prerequisite of steady, secure and intelligent social reforms in general and social advance by means of law in particular. If this be so infiltration into law of a more experimental and flexible logic is a social as well as an intellectual need.

[4]

THE NEED OF A SOCIOLOGICAL JURISPRUDENCE.

By Roscoe Pound.

If we may credit press reports, an eminent Canadian asserted recently in an address in London that "peace and order are more assured in Canada than in the United States." [1] I do not believe that this is so. But it is noteworthy that a conservative and experienced man of affairs should so believe, and that his statement made on an occasion of some importance should remain unchallenged. And it must be admitted that the law of the land has not the real hold upon the American people which law should have, and that there is a growing tendency to insist upon individual standards and to apply them in the teeth of the collective standard which is or ought to be expressed in the law. Illustrations of this tendency are abundant. From examination of the volumes in the National Reporter System, it appears that in 1906 over ninety new trials were directed by our highest courts of review in actions against employers for personal injuries because the verdicts were not sustained by evidence warranting a recovery. During the same year, over forty new trials were granted by these courts for the same reason in actions against railroad companies for personal injuries. How many verdicts were set aside by trial courts in such cases for the same reason, we do not know. Nor is there means of knowing in how many more such cases the verdicts returned would not have been rendered if the law had been zealously applied and enforced. But it is notorious that a crude and ill-defined sentiment that employers and great industrial enterprises should bear the cost of the human wear and tear incident to their operations, dictates more verdicts than the rules of law laid down in the charges of the courts. Many jurors who evade an irksome service by affirming scruples against capital punishment are doubtless shamming. Yet the fact remains that a large proportion of the veniremen summoned in all recent trials for murder have testified under oath that they could not be trusted to investigate and determine issues of fact as sworn jurymen in a court of justice because their views as to punishment differed from those of the law. In one of these trials a venireman told the court that where an act resulting in a murder was directed against society generally, there should be capital punishment, but that where only the citizen killed was the object of attack, such punishment could not be justified; and this theory was gravely discussed by the press without suggestion that there was anything amiss in refusal of a citizen to do his legal duty in the public administration of justice because he had thought out a new theory of punishment which the state did not recognize. The appeals to the so-called unwritten law, of which we have heard so much of late, are appeals from the clear and settled law to the individual feelings of the citizen, and no one seems to be deterred from following his own inclinations in such cases by the thought that it is his duty to subordinate those feelings to the general sense as formulated in the law.[1] Much of this individual self-assertion against the law is due, no doubt, to the lack of a settled social standard of justice during

[1] "Lord Strathcona in his address referred to the increase of American immigration into Canada, declaring that many American farmers know that in the Canadian Northwest prospects are better, and that peace and order are more assured in Canada than in the United States." Nelson B. C. *Times*, July 2, 1907.

[1] Since the foregoing was written, we have been afforded a good example in the Labor Day address of Mr. Gompers, in which, if correctly reported, he said "he would obey no injunction that deprived him of his rights." Chicago *Inter-Ocean*, September 3, 1907.

a period of transition. But a large part must be attributed to a wide-spread disrespect for law, to a general sentiment that unless the individual does so assert himself, he or those in whom he feels an interest will not be dealt with as justice requires. "*Neminem opportet esse sapientiorem legibus,*" says Coke, "no one out of his own private judgment ought to be wiser than the law."[1] When everyone out of his private judgment is wiser than the law, there is a condition in which the law is of no effect. The fault, when such a condition exists, may rest with the people or with the law. For my part, I believe that current disrespect for law is not, in intention at least, disrespect for justice, and that the fault must be laid largely to the law and to the manner in which law is taught and expounded.

Political and juridical development were necessary before industrial and social development. Government and law created the environment of peace and order and stability in which alone the industrial and social organization of to-day could grow. Hence legal theory and doctrine reached a degree of fixity before the conditions with which law must deal to-day had come into existence. And at this point where legal principles were taking a final shape the growing point in human progress began to shift to the natural and physical sciences and their applications in engineering, in the arts, and in scientific cultivation of the soil and development of its resources. Titius and Seius, who in their day had driven philosophy from the schools, are not unlikely to be driven out in turn. The changed order of things has been felt in legal science. Research of almost every other sort has been endowed. Laboratories are set up to investigate every other human interest. A flood of bulletins goes forth annually to spread far and wide the latest results in the application of natural and physical science to health and wealth, in the application of economic theory to our material well-being, in the application of sociological principles to problems of state and municipal life. In all these things the public shows an enduring interest. It ought to be someone's duty to advise the people of the progress of juridical science and to make its results public property. It ought to be someone's duty to gather and preserve statistics of the administration of justice and to apply thereto or deduce therefrom the proper principles of judicial administration. Law teachers ought to be making clear to the public what law is and why law is and what law does and why it does so. But no one can obtain statistics at all complete nor at all authoritative upon the most everyday points in judicial administration. No one is studying seriously or scientifically how to make our huge output of legislation effective. There are no endowments for juridical research. There are no laboratories dedicated to legal science whose bulletins shall make it possible for the scholar to obtain authoritative data and for the lay public to reach sound conclusions. No one thinks of establishing them. In state universities where one may be trained gratuitously in the most specialized applications of science, where an engineer may obtain his technical training without expense, students of law are charged a heavy tuition. The obvious reason is that the people do not feel that jurisprudence is doing anything for them. Legal science must first exhibit some practical results. It must show that it has something to offer before it may hope for public recognition. But it should not be suffered to remain stricken with sterility in face of the fruitful tasks that await it in this era of transition.

Legal science seems to begin everywhere in the attempt to distinguish cases superficially analogous and to establish "differences" or "diversities."[1] From this comparison of rules within the legal system,

[1] Co. Lit. 97*b*.

[1] Ihering, Geist des Römischen Rechts, III, 1, 11. In the period just before Coke the reports

it is but a step to compare with the rules of other legal systems and to compare systems themselves. This was the theory of the *Ius Gentium*, and doubtless to some extent the practice. It is to be seen in our own law at least as far back as Fortescue, and, though scorned by Coke, was well marked in the seventeenth and eighteenth centuries in the development of equity[1] and the rise of the law merchant.[2] The comparative tendency is followed by a philosophical tendency. Law is felt to be reason. It is not enough that a rule exist in one system or that it has its analogues in others. The rule must conform to reason, and if it does not, must be reshaped until it does, or must have reasons made for it. This was the dominant idea of the *Ius Naturale*. It is seen in continental Europe in the period after Grotius and in the *usus modernus*. In our law it is seen in the eighteenth and nineteenth centuries in the giving of "reasons" in which Blackstone and the lecturers on law who followed him in America were so prolific. To this philosophical tendency an analytical tendency succeeds by way of revolt. The validity of the so-called reasons is examined. Being for the most part *ex post facto* and, though specious, neither historically sound nor critically adequate, they fall to the ground, and often carry the rules with them. Hence the analytical period usually coincides with a critical tendency and an era of reform through legislation. Such a tendency in Roman law culminated in the legislation of Justinian.[3] In Germany it has overthrown the long-dominant Romanism and brought forth a German code. In our common-law system it brought about the reform movement, inaugurated by Bentham, the force of which is not yet wholly spent. Along with this analytical tendency, sometimes beginning before it, sometimes after but as another phase of the revolt from the philosophical, there is an historical tendency. How far we see something of this in the classical Roman law I need not inquire. It preceded the analytical tendency in Germany, it has followed that tendency in France. In England, it seems to have followed. In either event, it completes the exposure of the specious explanations of the preceding period and insures the overthrow of pseudo-philosophy. With the rise and growth of political, economic, and sociological science, the time is now ripe for a new tendency, and that tendency, which I have ventured heretofore to style the sociological tendency, is already well-marked in Continental Europe.[1]

With us, the profession, at least, is still for the most part under the domination of the methods and phrases of the second tendency, long after that tendency has spent its force. The practitioner is little, if at all, beyond Blackstone and his nineteenth-century imitators. Even a respectable law-school advertises that it teaches "the law and the reasons." These "reasons" of the eighteenth-century type are still found in text books in common use, and the books which students read are too often full of them. They are to be found in judicial decisions also.[2] Distinctions of substantive law which have their origin in forgotten niceties of practice are

were full of "putting differences" and "noting diversities." e. g. Keilwey. 50, 53, 57, Dyer, 111 *b*.

[1] Spence, Equitable Jurisdiction of the Court of Chancery, I, 413.

[2] Wooddesson, Elements of Jurisprudence, lxxix, in 1792 treats the law merchant as part of the law of nations.

[3] See, for instance, Code VII, 25, in which Justinian says of a classical distinction that it is "a mere puzzle" and "a vain and superfluous phrase."

[1] See Stammler, Wirthschaft und Recht (1906), Ehrlich, Soziologie und Jurisprudenz (1906), Gumplowicz, Allgemeines Staatsrecht (1907), Vaccaro, Les Bases Sociologiques du Droit et de l'État (1898), Grasserie, Les Principes Sociologiques du Droit Civil (1906).

[2] To take a striking example, if an old one, a court of high authority in explaining the rule

still solemnly explained by "reasons" that neither conform to historical fact nor satisfy any real sense of justice. Undoubtedly we have made some progress. The teachings of historical and analytical jurists are percolating through the schools into the profession. The type of "reason" that sets forth how this or that was "presumed" or was "implied" or was "constructive," which had been used to explain gradual changes in the law by covering them up with fiction, or to reconcile existing doctrines with *ex post facto* generalizations, is falling out of use. First teachers and then a few text writers began to insist upon more scientific treatment. To-day even an occasional court makes bold to speak of quasi-contract. But the books are still full of the old method, even in those matters in which progress is making. To take but one example. In a book widely cited, used during the past year in at least ten law schools, and read by the majority of those who prepare for the Bar in the offices of practitioners, we are told of a presumption of damage in trespass to lands, in the attempt to make our common law of trespass fit into a Romanized mold of *damnum* and *iniuria*[1] and we are advised that there is no quasi-contractual liability (as we should put it now) in the case of a certain act, because "we cannot suppose it would take place except as a wrongful act."[2] So long as students are set to read these "reasons" and are taught that this or that is "implied" or "presumed" contrary to common sense, or is "constructively" something other than what it obviously is, and so long as laymen listen to these explanations from the bench when they sit upon juries, or from counsel whom they consult as clients, or from the published opinions of the courts, the people are certain to be confirmed in the belief, popular in all circumstances, that law is an arbitrary mass of technicalities having no relation to reason or justice. To-day the reasons behind the law must be such as appeal to an intelligent and educated public. There must be reasons behind it, as there must be behind everything that is imposed upon the people of the present. And, if I may adapt a common-law terminology, they must be reasons in deed rather than in law.

Law is no longer anything sacred or mysterious. Judicial decisions are investigated and discussed freely by historians, economists, and sociologists. The doctrines announced by the courts are debated by the press, and have even been dealt with in political platforms. Laymen know full well that they may make laws, and that knowledge of the law is no necessary prerequisite of far-reaching legislation. The legislative steam roller levels the just rule with the unjust in the public anxiety to lay out a new road. The introduction of the doctrine of comparative negligence in employer's liability statutes and recent statutes leaving questions of negligence wholly to juries or, in other words, cutting off all assurance that like cases involving negligence will receive a like decision, afford interesting examples. The common-law doctrines, at least as explained to the people, did not commend themselves to the public intelligence. In such cases, something is to be done; and it is done too often with but little understanding of old law, mischief, or remedy. But we have no right to rail at such miscarriages. The public must move in such legal light as the luminaries of the law afford. Those who practice and those who teach the law should be in a position to command the popular ear. We must reinvestigate the theories of justice, of law, and of rights. We must seek

altered by Lord Campbell's Act tells us, following Grotius, that "the life of a freeman cannot be appraised, but that of a slave who might have been sold, may." Hyatt *v.* Davis, 16 Mich. 180, 191.

[1] Cooley, Torts, 63, 69.

[2] Cooley, Torts, 95.

the basis of doctrines, not in Blackstone's wisdom of our ancestors, not in the apocryphal reasons of the beginnings of legal science, not in their history, useful as that is in enabling us to appraise doctrines at their true value, but in a scientific apprehension of the relations of law to society and of the needs and interests and opinions of society of to-day.

Ample reason for the present condition of jurisprudence in America is to be found in the dominance of practitioners and of the ideas and ideals of practitioners in legal education. So long as the one object is to train practitioners who can make money at the Bar, and so long as schools are judged chiefly by their success in affording such training, we may expect nothing better. Yet this is an explanation rather than an excuse. The schools must teach the rules by which the courts decide cases. They cannot teach a different law from that which is recognized and enforced by the courts. But they are not bound to teach traditional legal pseudo-science. They are not bound to teach the practitioner's philosophy of law, however much he may think it involved in the very idea of a legal system. It is not long ago that a fictitious legal history was equally orthodox. Freeman tells us of a law-teacher who "required the candidates for degrees to say that William the Conqueror introduced the feudal system at the great Gemot of Salisbury in 1086,"[1] and when remonstrance was made by the historian, replied that he was examiner in law; that "facts might be found in chronicles, but law was to be found in Blackstone; it was to be found in Blackstone as an infallible source; what Blackstone said, he, as a law-examiner, could not dispute."[2] But courts and law books can no more make authoritative philosophy than they can make authoritative history.

I do not advocate the adding of any new course or new courses to our curricula. Doubtless the schools are offering now all the courses that students may take with profit. But law schools not only make tough law,[1] they make tough legal science, as the long postponement of the German code through dominance of the historical school, the persistence of eighteenth-century theories in American legal thought, long after they had been abandoned in all other fields, and the sturdy resistance of common-law individualism to the collectivist tendencies of modern thought abundantly witness. We must not make the mistake in American legal education of creating a permanent gulf between legal thought and popular thought. But we may commit this mistake not merely by teaching legal pseudo-science and obsolete philosophy but quite as much by the more prevalent method of saying nothing about these matters at all, leaving the student to pick up what he may here and there in the cases and texts, with no hint that there are other conceptions and other theories entertained by scholars of no small authority, and to go forth in the belief that he is completely trained.[2] I have little faith in abstract courses, even if our schools had room for any new courses. Instruction of the sort required must be concrete. It must lie in the point of view from which concrete legal problems are discussed, concrete doctrines are expounded, and actual decisions are investigated and criticized. The modern teacher of law should be a student of sociology, economics, and politics as well. He should know not only what the courts decide and the principles by which they decide, but quite

[1] It is interesting to note that this statement is still with us in law-teaching. Mordecai, Law Lectures, 24 (1907).

[2] Freeman, Methods of Historical Study, 73-74.

[1] Maitland, English Law and the Renaissance, 25.

[2] Complaint has been made in France to the same effect. Vareilles-Sommières, Principes Fondamentaux du Droit, preface.

as much the circumstances and conditions, social and economic, to which these principles are to be applied; he should know the state of popular thought and feeling which makes the environment in which the principles must operate in practice. Legal monks who pass their lives in an atmosphere of pure law, from which every worldly and human element is excluded, cannot shape practical principles to be applied to a restless world of flesh and blood. The most logical and skillfully reasoned rules may defeat the end of law in their practical administration because not adapted to the environment in which they are to be enforced.[1] It is, therefore, the duty of American teachers of law to investigate the sociological foundations, not of law alone, but of the common law and of the special topics in which they give instruction, and, while teaching the actual law by which courts decide, to give to their teaching the color which will fit new generations of lawyers to lead the people as they should, instead of giving up their legitimate hegemony in legislation and politics to engineers and naturalists and economists.

Without trenching upon points of controversy, it may be assumed that the practical end of the administration of justice according to law, is such adjustment of the relations of men to each other and to society as conforms to the moral sense of the community. In the past this adjustment has conformed to the general moral sense by proceeding along lines of strict individualism. The idea has been, so far as possible, to allow everyone to do and to acquire all that he can. The individualist conception of justice as the liberty of each limited only by the like liberties of all has been the legal conception. So completely has this been true that sociologists speak of this conception as "legal justice," and it is sometimes assumed that law must needs aim at a different kind of justice from what is commonly understood and regarded by the community. But this cannot be. Law is a means, not an end. Such a divergence cannot endure unless the law is in the hands of a progressive and enlightened caste whose conceptions are in advance of the public and whose leadership is bringing popular thought to a higher level.[1] When, instead, law is in the hands of a highly cautious and conservative profession, whose thought on such matters lags behind, the divergence provokes irritation at law and disregard of its mandates. To-day, while jurists in America are repeating individualist formulas of justice, sociologists are speaking rather of "the enforcement by society of an artificial equality in social conditions which are naturally unequal."[2] They are defining justice as the satisfaction of everyone's wants so far as they are not outweighed by others' wants.[3] That this is the direction of popular thought is shown by the unconscious drift of the law in the same direction. It is true we still harp upon the sacredness of property before the law. The leader of our profession tells us that a fundamental object is, "preservation of the rights of private property."[4] A text book used in more than one law school advises us that "the right of property is of divine origin

[1] See Brunner's comment upon the effect of the reception of Roman law in Germany on peasant possessions. Grundzuge der Deutschen Rechtsgeschichte, 216.

[1] An excellent example may be seen in the history of equity in England. Equity was unpopular, but it was in the right line of progress. The chancellors, however, developed doctrines of an ultra-ethical character which went beyond the requirements of common sense, and these refinements of equity have been largely swept away. For instances of this, the doctrine as to compensation of trustees, precatory trusts, and the rules as to clogging the equity of redemption may suffice.

[2] Ward, Applied Sociology, 23.

[3] Ward, Applied Sociology, 22-24, Willoughby, Social Justice, 20-25.

[4] Argument of Mr. Choate in the Income Tax Cases, 157 U. S. 429, 534.

derived by title-deed from the universal creator of all things and attested by universal intuition."[1] The highest court of one of the states tells us in eloquent words that the right to take property by will is an absolute and inherent right, not depending upon legislation.[2] But the steady progress of the law is in another direction. Ihering lays down this as the difference between the new and the old: "Formerly high valuing of property, lower valuing of the person; now, lower valuing of property, higher valuing of the person."[3] He says the line of legal growth of the future is "weakening of the sense of property, strengthening of the feeling of honor."[4] And that this is true for our law in America, the continual complaints that modern legislation deprives men of the power to regulate their own affairs and to manage their own property bear abundant witness.

The progress of law away from the older individualism is not confined to property rights. A passing of ultra-individualist phases of common-law doctrines on every hand, both through legislation and through judicial decision, is sufficiently obvious. Let us note a few cases. One of the so-called natural rights, which is still insisted upon, is freedom of contract, the right of each man to say for himself what engagements he will undertake and to settle the details thereof for himself. But modern legislation is constantly abridging this right by creating classes of persons and classes of subjects, with respect to which rights and obligations are defined by law "and made conclusive upon the parties, irrespective of stipulations attempting to set them aside;"[5] and such statutes are now held constitutional within wide limits. Nor is this tendency confined to legislation. The contract of insurance has been so dealt with by the courts that it is no longer an ordinary contract, to be judged as such, but the law of insurance has become a specialized body of doctrine.[1] The older decisions were extremely strict in insisting upon the right of a surety to make his own contract in every respect. The slightest deviations, which had the effect of varying in some degree the obligation for which he engaged to become answerable, sufficed to relieve him. He and he alone could determine for what he would bind himself, and he could do so as arbitrarily as he chose, for it was his affair.[2] But the advent of the surety company has already produced a change. It was felt that the right of every person to make his own contracts for himself must give way to a public demand for enforcement of contracts of insurance unless some substantial injury to the insurer appeared, and this feeling has led to a line of judicial decisions with respect to contracts of surety companies that cannot well be reconciled with the settled course of adjudication as to natural persons.[3] Professor Gray has noted a similar phenomenon in the matter of spendthrift trusts.[4] The common law insisted rigorously on individual responsibility. It was not possible for a debtor through any device to enjoy the whole substantial benefit of property free from claims of his creditors. The American decisions which permit such trusts are, as he points out, at clear variance with the spirit of the common law. They are another sign of the drift toward equality in the satisfac-

[1] Smith, Personal Property, Sec. 33.

[2] Nunnemacher *v.* State, 108 N. W. 627.

[3] Ihering, Scherz und Ernst in der Jurisprudenz (9 ed.) 418.

[4] Ihering, Scherz und Ernst in der Jurisprudenz (9 ed.) 429.

[5] Freund, Police Power, Sec. 503.

[1] Wambaugh, Cases on Insurance, preface.

[2] Hence if the king died, surety for the peace was released "for 'tis to observe his peace, and when he is dead, 'tis not his peace." Anonymous. Brook's New Cas. 172. A typical modern case is U. S. *v.* Boecker, 21 Wall. 652.

[3] See for instance, American Bonding Co. *v.* City of Ottumwa, 137 Fed. 572, Segari *v.* Mazzei (La.) 41 So. 245.

[4] Gray, Restraints on the Alienation of Property (2 ed.) viii–x.

tion of wants rather than equality in freedom of action as the standard of justice; and the decisions which Professor Gray justly stigmatizes as "snobbish"[1] are but crude attempts to apply this standard before it has been recognized clearly or has taken definite shape. Probably nowhere is the individualism of the common law expressed more characteristically than in the doctrines as to contributory negligence. Recent legislation with respect to employer's liability is almost wiping out those doctrines. It seems to be felt that nothing short of fraud, or disregard of life or limb so gross as to amount to fraud, should preclude recovery. No less characteristic is the view which the common law takes of industrial accidents. It insists that such accidents must be due either to wholly unpreventible conditions or to the negligence of some person. Either the employer, it holds, was negligent or the employee. That the business itself, and not the negligence of some person operating therein, may be responsible for the accident, is a situation which it cannot conceive of and for which it makes no provision beyond laying down that the employee assumes the incidental risks. But it is coming to be well understood by all who have studied the circumstances of modern industrial employment that the supposed contributory negligence of employees is in effect a result of the mechanical conditions imposed on them by the nature of their employment, and that by reason of these conditions the individual vigilance and responsibility contemplated by the common law are impossible in practice. Hence, while the common law insists upon the workman taking the ordinary risks of his occupation, requires him to show negligence on the part of his employer as a prerequisite of recovery, and holds him to account rigidly for negligence of his own contributing to the accident, the public has been coming more and more to think that the employer should take the risk of accidents to his men, as of accidents to his plant and machinery, and that contributory negligence — where there is no willful self-injury and no fraud — is one of these ordinary risks. As the President put it recently in his address at the Georgia Day celebration at the Jamestown Exposition: "It is neither just, expedient, nor humane; it is revolting to judgment and sentiment alike that the financial burden of accidents occurring because of the necessary exigencies of their daily occupation should be thrust upon those sufferers who are least able to bear it. . . . When the employer . . . starts in motion agencies which create risks for others, he should take all the ordinary and extraordinary risks involved." Juries have perceived this dimly for years and have rendered verdicts accordingly. Legislation is now fast introducing rules founded avowedly upon this theory. If this legislation is constructed and applied by men thoroughly imbued with the common-law doctrine and with common-law prejudices, the divergence between legal rules and popular thought, if it does not produce legislation still more radical, will add to existing disrespect for the law. But we must note here once more that higher regard for the person and regard for equality in the satisfaction of wants are the controlling elements in the newer doctrine.

Another noteworthy sign of the shifting from the standard of so-called legal justice to that of social justice is to be seen in the tendency of modern legislation to reintroduce *status* or something very like it. The conception that rights should belong or duties attach to a person of full age and natural capacity because of the position he occupies in society or of the occupation in which he is engaged, is repugnant to the spirit of the common law. Hence courts, imbued strongly with common-law notions of this matter, have tended to hold statutes which carry out this idea unconstitutional whenever possible. But the conception is perfectly reconcilable with, and indeed is

[1] Restraints on the Alienation of Property, xi.

demanded by the idea of social justice. When the standard is equality of freedom of action, all classes other than those few and simple ones, based on so-called natural incapacities, such as infancy and lunacy, are repugnant to the idea of justice. When the standard is equality in the satisfaction of wants, such classification and such return in part to the idea of *status* are inevitable.

Even more marked and of longer standing is the weakening of extreme doctrines of *fides est servanda* through the shifting to the idea of social justice. Here again the point of view of the common law was extremely individualist. It left the individual free to assume whatever obligation he chose and to determine its details for himself. But here, as elsewhere, it imposed a responsibility corresponding to this freedom. If he chose to assume an obligation, the common law held him to it jealously. He had weighed the risk and had taken it. As he was allowed to incur it like a man, he must bear its consequences like a man. Hence common-law judges were extremely reluctant to permit contract debtors to escape by availing themselves of the statute of limitations, and for a time very nearly nullified that statute so far as it applied to debts.[1] But to-day exemption, homestead, and appraisement statutes, not to speak of bankruptcy and insolvency laws, greatly restrict the power of the creditor to enforce the liability assumed.[2] There is a growing sentiment that the creditor who extends credit should assume a risk. The principle that promises must be kept yields to the demand that satisfaction of the reasonable wants of the debtor be first reasonably provided for.

In all cases of divergence between the standard of the common law and the standard of the public, it goes without saying that the latter will prevail in the end. Sooner or later what public opinion demands will be recognized and enforced by the courts. A Bench and Bar trained in individualist theories and firm in the persuasion that the so-called legal justice is an absolute and a necessary standard, from which there may be no departure without the destruction of the legal order, may retard but cannot prevent progress to the newer standard recognized by the sociologist. In this progress lawyers should be conscious factors, not unconscious followers of popular thought, not conscious obstructors of the course of legal development. To this end it is the duty of teachers of law, while they teach scrupulously the law that the courts administer, to teach it in the spirit and from the standpoint of the political, economic, and sociological learning of to-day. It is their task to create in this country a true sociological jurisprudence, to develop a thorough understanding between the people and the law, to insure that the common law remain, what its exponents have always insisted it is — the custom of the people, the expression of their habits of thought and action as to the relations of men with each other. And if in so doing they must often take issue with courts and practitioners and books of authority as to the nature of justice and of rights and the basis of current legal conceptions and of received principles, they may say as the naturalist to his more conservative colleagues: "*raisonniert so viel ihr wollt, aber fügt Euch in das wissenschaftlich unvermeidliche.*"[1]

LINCOLN, NEB. August, 1907.

---

[1] See an interesting discussion of this in Pritchard *v.* Howell, 1 Wis. 131.

[2] See also the recent attempt of the federal circuit court to force a scheme of reorganization upon reluctant creditors of a public service company in the Chicago Traction Cases. Whatever view may be taken of this decree, it is a sign of the times.

[1] Otto Kuntze, Revisio Generum Plantarum, III, fin.

[5]

MECHANICAL JURISPRUDENCE.[1]

"There is no way," says Sir Frederick Pollock, "by which modern law can escape from the scientific and artificial character imposed on it by the demand of modern societies for full, equal, and exact justice."[2] An Australian judge has stated the same proposition in these words: "The public is more interested than it knows in maintaining the highest scientific standard in the administration of justice."[3] Every lawyer feels this, and every thoughtful student of institutions must admit it. But what do we mean by the word "scientific" in this connection? What is scientific law? What constitutes science in the administration of justice? Sir Frederick Pollock gives us the clew when he defines the reasons that compel law to take on this scientific character as three: the demand for full justice, that is for solutions that go to the root of controversies; the demand for equal justice, that is a like adjustment of like relations under like conditions; and the demand for exact justice, that is for a justice whose operations, within reasonable limits, may be predicted in advance of action. In other words, the marks of a scientific law are, conformity to reason, uniformity, and certainty. Scientific law is a reasoned body of principles for the administration of justice, and its antithesis is a system of enforcing magisterial caprice, however honest, and however much disguised under the name of justice or equity or natural law. But this scientific character of law is a means,—a means toward the end of law, which is the administration of justice. Law is forced to take on this character in order to accomplish its end fully, equally, and exactly; and in so far as it fails to perform its function fully, equally and exactly, it fails in the end for which it exists. Law is scientific in order to eliminate so far as may be the personal equation in judicial administration, to preclude corruption and to limit the dangerous possibilities of magisterial ignorance. Law is not scientific for the sake of science. Being scientific as a means toward an end, it must be judged by the results it achieves, not by the niceties of its internal structure; it must be valued by the extent to which it meets its end, not by the beauty of its logical processes or the strictness with which its rules proceed from the dogmas it takes for its foundation.

[1]The substance of this paper was presented before the Bar Association of North Dakota, at its annual meeting, at Valley City, N. D., Sept. 25, 1908.

[2]A First Book of Jurisprudence, 56.

[3]Richmond, J., quoted in Clark, Australian Constitutional Law, 348.

Two dangers have to be guarded against in a scientific legal system, one of them in the direction of the effect of its scientific and artificial character upon the public, the other in the direction of its effect upon the courts and the legal profession. With respect to the first danger, it is well to remember that law must not become too scientific for the people to appreciate its workings.[4] Law has the practical function of adjusting every-day relations so as to meet current ideas of fair play. It must not become so completely artificial that the public is led to regard it as wholly arbitrary. No institution can stand upon such a basis to-day. Reverence for institutions of the past will not preserve, of itself, an institution that touches every-day life as profoundly as does the law. Legal theory can no more stand as a sacred tradition in the modern world than can political theory. It has been one of the great merits of English law that its votaries have always borne this in mind. When Lord Esher said, "the law of England is not a science," he meant to protest against a pseudo-science of technical rules existing for their own sake and subserving supposed ends of science, while defeating justice.[5] And it is the importance of the rôle of jurors in tempering the administration of justice with common-sense and preserving a due connection of the rules governing every-day relations with every-day needs of ordinary men that has atoned for the manifold and conspicuous defects of trial by jury and is keeping it alive. In Germany to-day one of the problems of law reform is how to achieve a similar tempering of the justice administered by highly trained specialists.[6]

In the other direction, the effect of a scientific legal system upon the courts and upon the legal profession is more subtle and far-reaching. The effect of all system is apt to be petrifaction of the subject systematized. Perfection of scientific system and exposition tends to cut off individual initiative in the future, to stifle independent consideration of new problems and of new phases of old problems, and to impose the ideas of one generation upon another. This is so in all departments of learning. One of the obstacles to advance in every science is the domination of the ghosts of departed masters. Their sound methods are forgotten,

[4] Cf. Lord Herschell's remark to Sir George Jessel: "Important as it was that people should get justice, it was even more important that they should be made to feel and see that they were getting it." Atlay, Victorian Chancellors, II., 460.

[5] See Manson, The Builders of our Law, 398.

[6] Sternberg, Kirchmann und seine Kritik der Rechtswissenschaft, xi.

while their unsound conclusions are held for gospel.[7] Legal science is not exempt from this tendency. Legal systems have their periods in which science degenerates, in which system decays into technicality, in which a scientific jurisprudence becomes a mechanical jurisprudence.

Roman law in its decadence furnishes a striking example. The Valentinian "law of citations" made a selection of jurisconsults of the past and allowed their writings only to be cited. It declared them, with the exception of Papinian, equal in authority. It confined the judge, when questions of law were in issue, to the purely mechanical task of counting and of determining the numerical preponderance of authority.[8] Principles were no longer resorted to in order to make rules to fit cases. The rules were at hand in a fixed and final form, and cases were to be fitted to the rules.[9] The classical jurisprudence of principles had developed, by the very weight of its authority, a jurisprudence of rules; and it is in the nature of rules to operate mechanically.

Undoubtedly one cause of the tendency of scientific law to become mechanical is to be found in the average man's admiration for the ingenious in any direction, his love of technicality as a manifestation of cleverness, his feeling that law, as a developed institution, ought to have a certain ballast of mysterious technicality. "Philosophy's queerest arguments," says James, "tickle agreeably our sense of subtlety and ingenuity."[10] Every practitioner has encountered the lay obsession as to invalidity of a signing with a lead pencil. Every law-teacher has had to combat the student obsession that notice, however cogent, may be disregarded unless it is "official." Lay hair-splitting over rules and regulations goes far beyond anything of which lawyers are capable. Experienced advocates have insisted that in argument to a jury, along with a just, common-sense theory of the merits, one ought to have a specious technicality for good measure. But apart from this general human tendency, there is the special tendency of the lawyer to regard artificiality in law as an end, to hold science something to be pursued for its own sake, to forget in this

[7]The reasons for this and the laws by which the process takes place are well set forth in Ross, Social Psychology, chaps. 12, 13, 14.

[8]Cod. Theod. I, 4, 3. Karlowa, Römische Rechtsgeschichte, I, 933.

[9]This is said to be the period at which the notion that application of law is a purely mechanical process arose. Gnaeus Flavius (Kantorowicz), Der Kampf um die Rechtswissenschaft, 7.

[10]Pragmatism, 5. Dernburg refers to this as an "innate sense for formalism." Pandekten, I, § 97.

pursuit the purpose of law and hence of scientific law, and to judge rules and doctrines by their conformity to a supposed science and not by the results to which they lead. In periods of growth and expansion, this tendency is repressed. In periods of maturity and stability, when the opportunity for constructive work is largely eliminated, it becomes very marked.

"I have known judges," said Chief Justice Erle, "bred in the world of legal studies, who delighted in nothing so much as in a strong decision. Now a strong decision is a decision opposed to common-sense and to common convenience. * * * A great part of the law made by judges consists of strong decisions, and as one strong decision is a precedent for another a little stronger, the law at last, on some matters, becomes such a nuisance that equity intervenes, or an Act of Parliament must be passed to sweep the whole away." [11]

The instance suggested in the conversation from which the foregoing extract is taken illustrates very well the development of a mechanical legal doctrine. Successive decisions upon the construction of wills had passed upon the meaning of particular words and phrases in particular wills. These decisions were used as guides in the construction of other wills. Presently rules grew up whereby it was settled that particular words and phrases had prescribed hard and fast meanings, and the construction of wills became so artificial, so scientific, that it defeated the very end of construction and compelled a series of sections in the Wills Act of 1836.

I have referred to mechanical jurisprudence as scientific because those who administer it believe it such. But in truth it is not science at all. We no longer hold anything scientific merely because it exhibits a rigid scheme of deductions from *a priori* conceptions. In the philosophy of to-day, theories are "instruments, not answers to enigmas, in which we can rest." [12] The idea of science as a system of deductions has become obsolete, and the revolution which has taken place in other sciences in this regard must take place and is taking place in jurisprudence also. This revolution in science at large was achieved in the middle of the nineteenth century. In the first half of that century, scientific method in every department of learning was dominated by the classical German philosophy. Men conceived that by dialectics and deduction from controlling conceptions they could construe the whole content of knowledge. Even in the natural sciences

[11] Senior, Conversations with Distinguished Persons (Ed. of 1880) 314.
[12] James, Pragmatism, 53.

this belief prevailed and had long dictated theories of nature and of natural phenomena. Linnaeus, for instance, lays down a proposition, *omne vivum ex ovo,* and from this fundamental conception deduces a theory of homologies between animal and vegetable organs.[13] He deemed no study of the organisms and the organs themselves necessary to reach or to sustain these conclusions. Yet, to-day, study of the organisms themselves has overthrown his fundamental proposition. The substitution of efficient for final causes as explanations of natural phenomena has been paralleled by a revolution in political thought. We do not base institutions upon deduction from assumed principles of human nature; we require them to exhibit practical utility, and we rest them upon a foundation of policy and established adaptation to human needs. It has been asserted that to no small extent the old mode of procedure was borrowed from the law. We are told that it involved a "fundamentally juristic conception of the world in which all kinds of action and every sort of judgment was expressed in legal phraseology." [14] We are told that "in the Middle Ages human welfare and even religion was conceived under the form of legality, and in the modern world this has given place to utility." [15] We have, then, the same task in jurisprudence that has been achieved in philosophy, in the natural sciences and in politics. We have to rid ourselves of this sort of legality and to attain a pragmatic, a sociological legal science.

"What is needed nowadays," it has been said, "is that as against an abstract and unreal theory of State omnipotence on the one hand, and an atomistic and artificial view of individual independence on the other, the facts of the world with its innumerable bonds of association and the naturalness of social authority should be generally recognized, and become the basis of our laws, as it is of our life." [16]

Herein is the task of the sociological jurist. Professor Small defines the sociological movement as "a frank endeavor to secure for the human factor in experience the central place which belongs to it in our whole scheme of thought and action." [17] The sociological movement in jurisprudence is a movement for pragmatism as a philosophy of law; for the adjustment of principles and doctrines to the human conditions they are to govern rather than

[13]Philosophia Botanica, aphorisms 134, *et seq.*
[14]Figgis, From Gerson to Grotius, 152.
[15]Ibid., 14.
[16]Ibid., 206.
[17]The Meaning of Sociology, 14 Am. Journ. Sociol. 13.

to assumed first principles; for putting the human factor in the central place and relegating logic to its true position as an instrument.

Jurisprudence is last in the march of the sciences away from the method of deduction from predetermined conceptions. On the continent of Europe, both the historical school of jurists and the philosophical school, which were dominant until at least the last quarter of the nineteenth century, proceeded in this way. The difference between them lay in the manner in which they arrived at their fundamental conceptions. The former derived them from the history of juristic speculation and the historical development of the Roman sources. The latter, through metaphysical inquiries, arrived at certain propositions as to human nature, and deduced a system from them. This was the philosophical theory behind the eighteenth-century movement for codification.[18] Ihering[19] was the pioneer in the work of superseding this jurisprudence of conceptions (*Begriffsjurisprudenz*) by a jurisprudence of results (*Wirklichkeitsjurisprudenz*).[20] He insisted that we should begin at the other end; that the first question should be, how will a rule or a decision operate in practice? For instance, if a rule of commercial law were in question, the search should be for the rule that best accords with and gives effect to sound business practice. In the Civil Law, the doctrine as to mistake in the formation of a contract affords an example of the working of the two methods. Savigny treated the subject according to the jurisprudence of conceptions. He worked out historically and analytically the conception of a contract and deduced therefrom the rules to govern cases of mistake. It followed, from his conception, that if *A* telegraphed *B* to *buy* shares and the telegram as delivered to *B* read *sell,* there was no contract between *A* and *B*, and hence no liability of *A* to *B;* and for a time it was so held. But this and some of the other resulting rules were so far from just in their practical operation that, following the lead of Ihering, they have been abandoned and the ordinary understanding of business men has been given effect.[21] And, in this same connection, the new Ger-

[18] See Code of Frederick the Great, part I, Book I, tit. 2, §§ 3, 4.

[19] Der Zweck im Recht (1878); Scherz und Ernst in der Jurisprudenz (1884) especially the two essays "Im juristischen Begriffshimmel" and "Wieder auf Erden."

[20] Sternberg, Allegemeine Rechtslehre, I, 188. See Brütt, Die Kunst der Rechtsanwendung, § 5.

[21] Bernhöft, Bürgerliches Recht (in Birkmeyer, Encyklopädie der Rechtswissenschaft) § 46. Cosack, Lehrbuch des Deutschen bürgerlichen Rechts, I, § 64 (3 Ed. pp. 213-214), BGB, §§ 120, 122.

man code has introduced, as a criterion of error in the content of an expression of the will, the question, what would be regarded as essential in the ordinary understanding of business.[22] Even better examples of the workings of a jurisprudence of conceptions, for our purposes, may be found in the manner in which common-law courts have dealt with points of mercantile law. For instance, the law of partnership is made difficult and often unjust by the insistence of the courts upon deducing its rules from a conception of joint ownership and joint obligation, instead of ascertaining and giving effect to the actual situation as understood and practiced by merchants. The legal theory does not affect the actual course of business an iota. But it leads to unfortunate results when that course of business, for some reason, comes before the courts.[23] Again, the refusal of Lord Holt to recognize the negotiability of promissory notes[24] proceeded upon a deduction from the conception of a chose in action. A jurisprudence of ends would have avoided each of these errors.

In periods of legal development through juristic speculation and judicial decision, we have a jurisprudence of ends in fact, even if in form it is a jurisprudence of conceptions.[25] The Roman *jus gentium* was worked out for concrete causes and the conceptions were later generalizations from its results. The *jus naturale* was a system of reaching reasonable ends by bringing philosophical theory into the scale against the hard and fast rules of antiquity. The development of equity in England was attained by a method of seeking results in concrete causes. The liberalizing of English law through the law merchant was brought about by substituting business practice for juridical conceptions. The development of the common law in America was a period of growth because the doctrine that the common law was received only so far as applicable led the courts, in adapting English case-law to American conditions, to study the conditions of application

[22]BGB, § 119, Saleilles, De la déclaration de la volonté, § 2. Leonhard, Der Irrtum als Ursache nichtiger Verträge (2 Ed.), II, 178.

[23]Lindley, Partnership (7 Ed.) 4.

[24]Buller *v.* Crips (1703) 6 Mod. 29. Compare modern decisions as to presentment of checks through a clearing house. Holmes *v.* Roe (1886) 62 Mich. 199; Edmiston *v.* Herpolsheimer (1901) 66 Neb. 94. In the former case we are told gravely that "the clearing house and the method of doing business through it had no bearing" on the case!

[25]See, for instance, Modestinus in Dig. I, 3, 25. As Stammler says: "It is notoriously a fundamental property of the classical Roman law to have shown itself exceedingly elastic in its substance, without thereby materially injuring the sharpness and certainty of its conceptions and rules." Wirthschaft und Recht (2 Ed.) 175.

as well as the conceptions and their logical consequences. Whenever such a period has come to an end, when its work has been done and its legal theories have come to maturity, the jurisprudence of conceptions tends to decay. Conceptions are fixed. The premises are no longer to be examined. Everything is reduced to simple deduction from them. Principles cease to have importance. The law becomes a body of rules. This is the condition against which sociologists now protest, and protest rightly.[26]

A period of legislative activity supervenes to supply, first new rules, then new premises, and finally a systematic body of principles as a fresh start for juristic development. But such periods hitherto have not been periods of growth. Usually legislative activity has not gone beyond the introduction of new rules or of new premises, and the chief result has been a summing up of the juristic accomplishment of the past in improved form. The further step, which is beginning to be taken in our present era of legal development through legislation, is in reality an awakening of juristic activity, as jurists perceive that they may effect results through the legislator as well as through the judge or the doctrinal writer. This step has yet to be taken outside of Germany. And in the first and second stages of a period of legislation the mechanical character of legal science is aggravated by the imperative theory, which is a concomitant of legislative activity. Austin's proposition that law is command so complete that even the unwritten law must be given this character, since whatever the sovereign permits he commands, was simply rediscovered during the legislative ferment of the reform-movement in English law. In the flowering-time of Papal legislation the canon law had already asserted it.[27] Moreover, a period of legislation and codification has brought German jurists to a like conclusion.[28] At such times, when law is felt to be positive, to be the command of the law-maker, a tendency to enact rules as such becomes manifest. Roman law, in its period of legislation, can furnish more than one example of the sort of law-making of which we complain to-day.[29]

[26] See Professor Henderson, 11 Am. Journ. Sociol. 847.

[27] c. I in Vito de Constitutionibus (I, 2).

[28] Czyhlarz, Institutionen, § 4.

[29] e. g. The legislation of Claudius, permitting marriage with a brother's daughter, Gaius, I, 61; imperial legislation as to testaments, Dig. XXIX, I, 1, pr., Code VI, 23; the *beneficium diuisionis* in suretyship, Dig. XLVI, I, 26-27, which has given so much trouble in modern law and is being rejected in recent codes. Dernburg, Lehrbuch des Preussischen Privatrechts, II, § 2466; Dernburg, Das bürgerliche Recht, III, § 162; Baudry-Lacantinerie, Traité de droit civil (2 Ed.), XXI, § 1053, *et seq.* Compare also the imperial legislation as to the making and revocation of gifts and Justinian's legislation as to revocation for ingratitude of the donee. Inst. II, 7, § 2; Cod. Theod. VIII, 12, 3, 5, and VIII, 12, 5; Code V, 12, 31; Code VIII, 54, 34; Code VIII, 56, 10.

Before the analytical school, which revived the imperative theory to meet the facts of an age of legislation, had become established, historical jurists led a revolt. But their jurisprudence is a jurisprudence of conceptions. Moreover, they have had little effect upon the actual course of Anglo-American law. The philosophical jurists have protested also and have appealed from purely legal considerations to considerations of reason and of natural law. But theirs, too, is a jurisprudence of conceptions, and their method, of itself, offers no relief. Their service has been in connection with the general sociological movement, in giving natural law a new and a modern aspect, and in promoting a general agreement among jurists on a sociological basis. In Europe, it is obvious that the different schools are coming together in a new sociological school that is to dominate juristic thought. Instead of seeking for an ideal universal law by metaphysical methods, the idea of all schools is to turn "the community of fact of mankind into a community of law in accord with the reasonable ordering of active life." [30] Hence they hold that "the less arbitrary the character of a rule and the more clearly it conforms to the nature of things, the more nearly does it approach to the norm of a perfect law." [31] The utilitarian theory of Bentham was a theory of legislation.[32] The sociological theory of the present is a theory of legal science. Probably the chief merit of the new German code lies in its conformity in so large a degree to this theory.[33] It lays down principles from which to deduce, not rules, but decisions; and decisions will indicate a rule only so long as the conditions to which they are applied cause them to express the principle. This, and not lax methods of equitable application,[34] into which American courts are falling so generally, is the true way to make rules fit cases instead of making cases fit rules.[35]

An efficient cause of the failure of much American legislation is that it is founded on an assumption that it is enough for the State to command. Legislation has not been the product of preliminary study of the conditions to which it was to apply. It has not expressed social standards accurately. It has not responded

[30] Jitta, La substance des obligations dans le droit international privé, I, 18.

[31] Baty, A Modern *Jus Gentium*, 20 Juridical Review, 109.

[32] This is pointed out very clearly by Maine, Early History of Institutions, Lect. xii.

[33] e. g. BGB, § 242.

[34] See my address, "Enforcement of Law," 20 Green Bag, 401.

[35] Lord Westbury had this idea. Atlay, Victorian Chancellors, II, 259.

accurately to social needs. Hence a large proportion has been nugatory in practice. But the difficulty is not, as some have assumed, that matters of private law are not within the legitimate scope of legislation.[36] It is rather that legislation has approached them upon a false theory. Judicial law-making also has acted upon an erroneous theory; and its results are often quite as much disregarded in practice as are statutes.[37] Judicial law-making, however, cannot escape, except within very narrow limits, until it is given a new starting point from without. Legislative law-making, on the contrary, may do so and is beginning to do so.

That our case law at its maturity has acquired the sterility of a fully developed system, may be shown by abundant examples of its failure to respond to vital needs of present-day life. Its inadequacy to deal with employers' liability;[38] the failure of the theory of "general jurisprudence" of the Supreme Court of the United States to give us a uniform commercial law; the failure of American courts, with centuries of discussion before them, to work out a reasonable or certain law of future interests in land; the breakdown of the common law in the matter of discrimination by public service companies because of inability to make procedure enforce its doctrines and rules; its breakdown in the attempt to adjust water rights in our newer states, where there was opportunity for free development;[39] its inability to hold promoters to their duty and to protect the interests of those who invest in corporate enterprises against mismanagement and breach of trust;[40] its

---

[36]Carter, Law, Its Origin, Growth and Function, 3.

[37]See my paper, "Common Law and Legislation," 21 Harv. Law Rev. 383, 406, note. The recent reversal by the House of Lords of a Scotch case (Toal *v.* North British R. Co. [1908] 16 Scot, L. T. 69) in which the Court of Session spoke "*ex cathedra* as to the right management of a railway train," assuming "an exhaustive knowledge of the whole art of train and railway-platform management," calls attention to a type of judicial law-making which endeavors to dictate rules for practical affairs by deduction from juristic conceptions. Legislation intended to turn questions of negligence over to juries for all purposes, now becoming somewhat common, is a crude attempt to counteract the same judicial tendency in our American law of torts.

[38]See a layman's view in the two articles of Mr. Hard, in "Everybody's" for September and October, 1908.

[39]See Long, Irrigation, § 99.

[40]For instance, compare Old Dominion Copper Mining and Smelting Co. *v.* Lewisohn (1908) 28 Sup. Ct. Rep. 634 with Old Dominion Copper Mining & Smelting Co. *v.* Bigelow (1905) 188 Mass. 315. In this connection note also the reactionary course of the courts in the matter of payment for shares. After starting out to deal with the matter on the ground of public policy, they came finally to treat it wholly from the standpoint of estoppel, and put the assets of a corporation in the same position as those of a natural person. Hospes *v.* Northwestern Mfg. Co. (1892) 48 Minn. 174; Clark *v.* Beaver (1890) 139 U. S. 96; Handley *v.* Stutz (1891) 139 U. S. 417; Fogg *v.* Blair (1890) 139 U. S. 118.

failure to work out a scheme of responsibility that will hold legal entities, or those who hide behind their skirts, to their duty to the public—all these failures, and many more might be adduced, speak for themselves. But compare these failures with the great achievements of the youth of our case-law, with Lord Mansfield's development of a law of quasi-contracts from the fictions of the common counts, with Lord Mansfield's development of mercantile law by judicial decision, with Kent's working out of equity for America from a handful of English decisions, with Marshall's work in giving us a living constitution by judicial interpretation. Now and then, at present, we see vigorous life in remote corners of our case law, as, for instance, in the newer decisions as to surface and underground waters. But judicial revolt from mechanical methods to-day is more likely to take the form of "officious kindness" and flabby equitable application of law.[41] Our judge-made law is losing its vitality, and it is a normal phenomenon that it should do so.

I have suggested some examples of the failure of our case law to rise to social and legal emergencies. Let me point to some phases of its active operation which lead to the same conclusion.[42]

The manner in which the Fourteenth Amendment is applied affords a striking instance of the workings to-day of a jurispru-

[41] See my address, "Enforcement of Law," 20 Green Bag, 401.

[42] Numerous examples from our private substantive law might easily be adduced, e. g., to take those that are first at hand, the curious inability of courts to reach a common-sense result, demanded also by principles of law, in cases of contributory negligence of one of several beneficiaries under Lord Campbell's Act, because of hard and fast procedural conceptions (see Wigmore, Contributory Negligence of the Beneficiary as a Bar to an Administrator's Action for Death, 2 Illinois Law Rev. 487); the narrow and unjust application of Lord Campbell's Act, in many of our State courts, where aliens are beneficiaries (Deni *v.* Pennsylvania R. Co. [1897] 181 Pa. St. 525; Brannigan *v.* Union Gold Mining Co. [1899] 93 Fed. Rep. 164; McMillan *v.* Spider Lake Saw Mill & Lumber Co. [1902] 115 Wis. 332; Roberts *v.* Great Northern R. Co. [1908] 161 Fed. Rep. 239), due for the most part to mechanical deduction from a conception of the universality of common-law doctrines and the necessity of strict construction of everything in derogation thereof, and the mechanical doctrine in New York as to jurisdiction over transitory actions between non-residents which accrued abroad (Collard *v.* Beach [1904] 81 App. Div. 582, 93 App. Div. 389) as compared with the just and flexible rule adopted in England (Logan *v.* Bank of Scotland [1906] 1 K. B. 141, 150).

Criminal procedure is full of instances that will occur to everyone. Not the least striking is our application of the rule as to double jeopardy in the form in which it arose when no appeal was allowed in criminal causes, so as to cut off appeal by the State after appeal by the accused had been allowed. In criminal law, an interesting example may be seen in the judicial demand that medical experts furnish "a definite account of the course of symptoms collectively constituting the disease" of insanity. Mercier, Criminal Responsibility, 88.

dence of conceptions. Starting with the conception that it was intended to incorporate Spencer's Social Statics in the fundamental law of the United States,[43] rules have been deduced that obstruct the way of social progress.[44] The conception of liberty of contract, in particular, has given rise to rules and decisions which, tested by their practical operation, defeat liberty.[45] As Mr. Olney says of the *Adair* Case,[46] "it is archaic, it is a long step into the past, to conceive of and deal with the relations between the employer in such industries and the employee, as if the parties were individuals."[47] The conception of freedom of contract is made the basis of a logical deduction. The court does not inquire what the effect of such a deduction will be, when applied to the actual situation. It does not observe that the result will be to produce a condition precisely the reverse of that which the conception originally contemplated.[48] Again, the Commerce Clause of the Federal Constitution has been taken by one judge, at least, to be a constitutional enactment of a conception of free trade among the states.[49] Deductions from this and like conceptions, assumed to express the meaning and the sole meaning of the clause, have given us rules which, when applied to the existing commercial and industrial situation, are wholly inadequate.[50]

---

[43]Holmes, J., in Lochner *v.* New York (1905) 198 U. S. 45, 75.

[44]See Professor Henderson in 11 Am. Journ. Sociol. 847.

[45]I have cited some of these in my paper, "Do we Need a Philosophy of Law?" 5 Columbia Law Rev. 339, 345. Cf., the dissenting opinion of Holmes, J., in Adair v. United States (1908) 208 U. S. 161.

[46](1908) 208 U. S. 161.

[47]42 Am. Law Rev. 164.

[48]One might cite in this connection the classical remarks of Maule, J., to the prisoner whom he was sentencing for bigamy. When he had explained to the prisoner how, after years of litigation and the expenditure of hundreds of pounds, he might have obtained a divorce (under the then law), he proceeded: "and if you ask me where you were to get all this money and tell me you never in your life had so many pennies at one time, I must remind you that it hath ever been the glory of the law of England not to have one law for the rich and another for the poor." See James, Curiosities of Law and Lawyers, 317.

[49]This conception appears very clearly in the opinions of the present Chief Justice from Leisy *v.* Hardin (1889) 135 U. S. 100, 109, down to the concurring opinion of Peckham, J., in which the Chief Justice joined, in Howard *v.* Illinois C. R. Co. (1908) 207 U. S. 463. In the latter, an opinion is indicated that Congress can not legislate upon the relation of master and servant involved in interstate traffic. Of course, this is a necessary deduction from the free-trade conception of the Commerce Clause.

[50]Compare the abstract and impracticable distinction between interstate and intrastate activities of employees of railways engaged in both species of commerce indiscriminately, upon which the court proceeds in Howard *v.* Illinois C. R. Co., *supra*, with the pragmatic view taken by Judge Amidon in his paper, "The Nation and the Constitution", Proc. Am. Bar Assn. xxi, 463, 474-5.

Procedure, with respect to which every thoughtful lawyer must feel that we are inexcusably behind the rest of the English-speaking world, suffers especially from mechanical jurisprudence. The conception of a theory of the case, developed by the common-law forms of action, has, in nearly half of our code jurisdictions, nullified the legislative intent and made the practice more rigid than at common law.[51] But this conception is regarded by many as fundamental. In deductions from this conception they lose sight of the end of procedure, they make scientific procedure an end of itself, and thus, in the result, make adjective law an agency for defeating or delaying substantive law and justice instead of one for enforcing and speeding them. Aristotle discusses a project of a Greek reformer for enabling tribunals to render what he called a divided judgment. At that time, the judgment had to be absolute one way or the other. If a plaintiff claimed twenty *minæ* when but eighteen were proved to be due him, there was no course but to find for the defendant. The proposal to correct this and to allow a finding for the eighteen *minæ* due did not meet with Aristotle's approval. He said:

"A juror who votes acquittal decides, not that the defendant owes nothing, but that he does not owe the twenty *minæ* claimed."[52]

We smile now at Aristotle's hard and fast deduction, in the face of a manifestly absurd result, from his conception of the trial of an issue. But at least half our jurisdictions do the same thing essentially in this matter of the theory of a plaintiff's case. That his pleadings and proofs disclose a case and a good case is not enough. The courts say they are not foreclosing that case; they are merely deciding upon the theory he has chosen to advance.

[51]Mescall *v.* Tully (1883) 91 Ind. 96; Carbondale Inv. Co. *v.* Burdick (1903) 67 Kan. 329; Maguire *v.* Vice (1855) 20 Mo. 429; Rust *v.* Brown (1890) 101 Mo. 586; Supervisors of Kewaunee County *v.* Decker (1872) 30 Wis. 624; Dessert Lumber Co. *v.* Wadleigh (1899) 103 Wis. 318. See Barnes *v.* Quigley (1874) 59 N. Y. 265; Goelet *v.* Asseler (1860) 22 N. Y. 225; Anderson *v.* Chilson (1895) 8 S. D. 64; Casey *v.* Mason (1899) 8 Okl. 665.

In Mescall *v.* Tully, the Court says: "It is an established rule of pleading that a plaintiff must proceed upon some definite theory, *and on that theory the plaintiff must succeed or not succeed at all.* * * * The theory upon which the complaint is constructed is that the parol agreement transformed the deed from an absolute conveyance into an instrument creating a trust, and as this theory is overthrown by the authorities, the entire complaint is foundationless. This theory is the foundation of the complaint, and, as that falls away, the whole pleading must go down." The plaintiff must now begin over again on another *theory* of the same facts.

As a consequence of such decisions, "the distinction between trover and assumpsit is to-day even more rigidly observed than under the common-law practice." W. B. Hornblower, quoted in 2 Andrews, American Law (2 Ed.) § 635, n. 29.

[52]Politics, ii, 8.

Again, in the practice as to parties, the common-law conception that there must be a joint interest or a joint liability, because there must be one controversy and joint parties are as one party, has seriously interfered with the liberal plan of the framers of the original Code of Civil Procedure. I can only cite some of the cases.[53] But let me compare with our American cases a recent English decision.[54] In that case two plaintiffs sued for an injunction against infringement of copyright and for an accounting of profits. Only one was owner of the copyright; the other was a mere licensee. But which one was owner was not clear. The court did not deem it necessary to take up this question and determine whether one only was owner and if so which, although a money recovery was to be had. So long as the plaintiffs were agreed among themselves and the defendant had wronged and owed money to one or the other of them, it affirmed a decree for an injunction and accounting. Although in strictness it might be that only *one* was entitled to judgment and so it would be necessary to determine *which* one, the court wasted no time on that question so long as nothing turned on it.[55] Here the court was conscious that procedure was a mere means. It strove to vindicate the substantive law. It was not set upon adhering with scrupulous exactness to logical deductions from a conception of adjective law at the expense of the merits the latter exists to give effect to.

---

[53] Voorhis *v.* Childs (1858) 17 N. Y. 354; Union Bank *v.* Mott (1863) 27 N. Y. 633; Borden *v.* Gilbert (1861) 13 Wis. 750; Phillips *v.* Flynn (1880) 71 Mo. 424; Setton *v.* Casseleggi (1883) 77 Mo. 397; Trowbridge *v.* Forepaugh (1869) 14 Minn. 133.

[54] Macmillan & Co. *v.* Dent [1907] 1 Ch. 107, 113.

[55] A like sensible conclusion was reached in Louisville N. A. & C. R. Co. *v.* Lange (1895) 13 Ind. App. 337. But see the usual treatment of this matter in America illustrated in Prestwood *v.* McGowin (1900) 128 Ala. 267; Glore *v.* Scroggins (1905) 124 Ga. 922; State *v.* Beasley (1894) 57 Mo. App. 570; Goodnight *v.* Goar (1868) 30 Ind. 418; McIntosh *v.* Zaring (1898) 150 Ind. 301; Blewett *v.* Hoyt (N. Y. 1907) 118 App. Div. 227. In the last case cited the court says the defect is fatal, "though somewhat technical." Even where a more liberal view is taken, the court must find out *which* is entitled, render judgment for him, and dismiss as to the other. Cf. Gillespie *v.* Gouley (Cal. 1908) 93 Pac. 856. Hence, in a case like Macmillan & Co. *v.* Dent, *supra,* if the trial court hit on the wrong one, a reversal would follow, though no harm was done.

Perhaps the acme of technicality was reached in Wisconsin. There a statute gave permission to courts, in their discretion, to render judgment *against* one or more defendants and allow the cause to proceed as to others. The court said: "The judgment appealed from it not *against* but in *favor* of, certain defendants, and therefore does not come within the statutory permission to vary from the general rule." Egaard *v.* Dahlke (1901) 109 Wis. 366, 369. Although there may be no case against these parties and the plaintiff may not be harmed in any way by terminating the cause as to them, the etiquette of justice requires them for the final judgment, and the plaintiff may reverse the judgment in their favor.

Trial procedure is full of mechanical jurisprudence born of deduction from conceptions. The decisions as to the effect of a view of the *locus* by a jury, in which judgments are reversed unless jurors are told, in the face of common-sense, not to use what they see as evidence, in order to vindicate a conception of the duty of a court of review;[56] the wilderness of decisions as to the province of court and jury, in which, carrying a conception of distinction between law and fact to extreme logical results, the courts at one moment assume that jurors are perfect and will absolutely follow an abstract instruction to its logical consequences, in the face of common-sense and the evidence, and at the next assume that they are fools and will be misled by anything not relevant that drops from the court;[57] and the practice of instructions, one way or the other, when doubtful points of law arise, a general verdict, and a new trial, if the court of review takes another view of the point, when the verdict could have been taken quite as well subject to the point of law reserved, and a new trial obviated,[58] illustrate forcibly the extent to which procedural conceptions, pursued for their own sake, may defeat the end of procedure and defeat the substance of the law. For delay of justice is denial of justice. Every time a party goes out of court on a mere point of practice, substantive law suffers an injury. The life of the law is in its enforcement.

[56]Chute *v.* State (1872) 19 Minn. 271; Close *v.* Samm (1869) 27 Ia. 503; Sasse *v.* State (1887) 68 Wis. 530; Machader *v.* Williams (1896) 54 Ohio St. 344; Neff *v.* Reed (1884) 98 Ind. 341. There is a strong tendency to get away from this rule at present. Compare Wright *v.* Carpenter (1875) 49 Cal. 607, with People *v.* Milner (1898) 122 Cal. 171.

[57]See Judge Thompson's observations in the Preface to his Law of Trials, xi.

[58]In the discussion of this matter at the meeting of the American Bar Association meeting at Seattle (August, 1908), many thought reservation of the point and judgment thereon, if required, in the court of review, involved subversion of trial by jury. Mr. Johnston seems also to have this idea. Law Notes, xii, 130. He can conceive no middle ground, where a question of the measure of damages arises, between requiring the trial judge to choose one of two theories and charge the jury accordingly, sending the cause back for a complete new trial, if the court of review chooses the other, and allowing the court of review to determine the *quantum* of damages for itself. To require the trial court to take a finding on each theory and choose in the final judgment seems to infringe upon the necessity of a decisive finding *in form* by the jury. This is mechanical jurisprudence indeed. But when one may solemnly argue that reversing the presumption of prejudice from errors of procedure will require assessment of damages by a court of review, and assume that a statute making such change must be applied in a mechanical fashion to defeat its end, it is evident that a deep-rooted professional obsession that mechanical procedure is fundamentally inherent in law has to be reckoned with.

Evidence also has been a prolific field for the unchecked jurisprudence of conceptions. But one example must suffice. The decisions by which in a majority of jurisdictions jurors are not permitted to learn directly the views of standard texts upon scientific and technical subjects, but must pass upon the conflicting opinions of experts without the aid of the impartial sources of information to which any common-sense man would resort in practice, carry out a conception of the competency of evidence at the expense of the end of evidence.[59] In one case,[60] the question was whether death had taken place from strangulation. The trial was held in a rural community, and the medical experts accessible had had no actual experience of cases of strangulation of the sort involved. But standard medical works did relate cases precisely in point, and, after proof that they were standard authorities, a physician was allowed to testify with respect to the symptoms disclosed in the light of the recorded experience of mankind. For this, the judgment was reversed.[61] To vindicate a juridical conception, the court shut out the best possible means of information, in the circumstances of the case in hand, and allowed an accused person to escape because of the inevitable limits of experience of a rural physician.

How far the mechanical jurisprudence, of which the example just given is an extreme case, forgets the end in the means, is made manifest by the stock objection to attempts at introducing a common-sense and business-like procedure. We are told that formal and technical procedure "makes better lawyers." [62] One might ask whether the making of good lawyers is the end of law. But what is a good lawyer? Let Ulpian answer:

"Ius est ars boni et æqui. Cuius merito quis nos sacerdotes appellet; iustitiam namque colimus et boni et æqui, notitiam profitemur, æquum ab iniquo separantes, licitum ab illicito discernentes, bonos non solum metu pœnarum, verum etiam præmiorum quoque exhortatione efficere cupientes veram, nisi fallor, philosophiam, non simulatam affectantes."[63]

The nadir of mechanical jurisprudence is reached when conceptions are used, not as premises from which to reason, but as

[59] See the excellent critical discussion in 3 Wigmore, Evidence, §§ 1690-1700.

[60] Boyle *v.* State (1883) 57 Wis. 472.

[61] This decision has received the approval of the United States Circuit Court of Appeals, Union P. R. Co. *v.* Yates (1897) 79 Fed. Rep. 584.

[62] Cf. also the remarks of Lord Halsbury in Clydesdale Bank *v.* Patton [1896] A. C. 381.

[63] Dig. I, 1, 1.

ultimate solutions. So used, they cease to be conceptions and become empty words. James has called attention to a like vice in philosophical thought:

"Metaphysics has usually followed a very primitive kind of quest. You know how men have always hankered after unlawful magic, and you know what a great part in magic *words* have always played. If you have his name, or the formula of incantation that binds him, you can control the spirit, genie, afrite, or whatever the power may be. * * * So the universe has always appeared to the natural mind as a kind of enigma of which the key must be sought in the shape of some illuminating or power-bringing word or name. That word names the universe's *principle,* and to possess it is after a fashion to possess the universe itself. 'God,' 'Matter,' 'Reason,' 'the Absolute,' 'Energy,' are so many solving names. You can rest when you have them. You are at the end of your metaphysical quest."[64]

Current decisions and discussions are full of such solving words: estoppel, malice, privity, implied, intention of the testator, vested and contingent,—when we arrive at these we are assumed to be at the end of our juristic search. Like Habib in the Arabian Nights, we wave aloft our scimitar and pronounce the talismanic word.

With legislative law-making in the grip of the imperative theory and its arbitrary results, and judicial decision in the grip of a jurisprudence of conceptions and its equally arbitrary results, whither are we to turn? Judicial law-making cannot serve us. As things are, the cure would be worse than the disease.[65] No court could hold such hearings as those had by legislative committees upon measures for the protection of operatives, described by Mrs. Kelley,[66] or that recently had before the Interstate Commerce Commission as to uniform bills of lading.[67] We must soon have a new starting-point that only legislation can afford. That we may put the sociological, the pragmatic theory behind legislation, is demonstrating every day. Legislative reference bureaus, the Comparative Law Bureau, the Conferences of Commissioners on Uniform State Laws, such hearings as the one before the Interstate Commerce Commission already referred to, hearings before legislative committees, such conferences as the one held recently

---

[64]Pragmatism, 52.

[65]Fortunately, even the layman recognizes this. Ross, Social Psychology, 333.

[66]Some Ethical Gains Through Legislation, 156.

[67]See Appendix to Report of Committee on Commercial Law at the Eighteenth Conference of Commissioners on Uniform State Laws.

with respect to the Sherman Anti-trust Law, bar-association discussions of reforms in procedure,—all these are furnishing abundant material for legislation of the best type. No such resources are open to the courts. Hence common-law lawyers will some day abandon their traditional attitude toward legislation; will welcome legislation and will make it what it should be. The part played by jurists in the best days of Roman legislation,[68] and the part they have taken in modern Continental legislation, should convince us, if need be, that juristic principles may be recognized and juristic speculation may be put into effect quite as well by legislation as by judicial decision.

Herein is a noble task for the legal scholars of America. To test the conceptions worked out in the common law by the requirements of the new juristic theory,[69] to lay sure foundations for the ultimate legislative restatement of the law, from which judicial decision shall start afresh,—this is as great an opportunity as has fallen to the jurists of any age.[70] The end of a period of development by judicial decision is marked by the prevalence of two types of judges; those who think it a great display of learning and of judicial independence to render what Chief Justice Erle called "strong decisions," and those who fix their gaze upon the raw equities of a cause and forage in the books for cases to sustain the desired result. But the task of a judge is to make a principle living, not by deducing from it rules, to be, like the Freshman's hero, "immortal for a great many years," but by achieving thoroughly the less ambitious but more useful labor of giving a fresh illustration of the intelligent application of the principle to a concrete cause, producing a workable and a just result. The real genius of our common law is in this, not in an eternal case-law.

---

[68]Hofmann, Kritische Studien im römischen Rechte, Essay I.

[69]One of the cardinal points of the doctrine of sociological jurists is that it is enough to work out such rules as may clearly govern particular facts or relations without being over-ambitious to lay down universal propositions. Jitta, op. cit. I, 20. Doubtless courts have been led into excess of zeal to lay down universal propositions by having to do in the past so much of the rightful work of legislatures. But at an earlier period, when conceptions were not so thoroughly worked out and rules were not so numerous, there was always before them the practical problem of devising new theories for a concrete cause. To-day the principles are hidden by the mass of rules deduced from them, and, as these rules are laid down as and taken to be universal, not mere expressions for the time being of the principles, we have an administration of justice by rules rather than by principles. Legislative superseding of this mass of rules by well-chosen and carefully formulated principles seems to offer the surest relief.

[70]The restating and rationalizing of our law of partnership upon which Professor Ames is engaged for the Commissioners on Uniform State Laws is a striking example.

Let the principles be formulated by whom or derived from whence you will. The Common Law will look to courts to develop and expound them, the Civil Law to doctrinal treatises. It is only a lip service to our common law that would condemn it to a perpetuity of mechanical jurisprudence through distrust of legislation.

ROSCOE POUND.

CHICAGO.

[6]

THE POSSIBILITY OF A MEASURE OF VALUES

III

PICTURE to yourselves a crowd at the box office of a movie theatre at the first performance of a new and much advertised film or a crowd trying to get in to see the crucial baseball game of an exciting race at the end of the season, where forty thousand try to get into a baseball park normally seating thirty thousand. Spontaneously as a matter of custom or else under the compulsion of a policeman, people line up and take their turn and are served rapidly with no pulling and hauling and no injury to anyone until all the seats are taken. Experience has taught us that this is the only practical way in which such situations can be handled and that experience has crystallized in the custom followed spontaneously or enforced upon refractory persons by the police. But suppose there was no such custom or no policeman to enforce against refractory individuals the rule indicated by experience. In that event no one could get in without a struggle in which many would be hurt and the struggle would take up so much time and involve so much injury that many would not try to get in and many more after pulling and hauling would give up the attempt. The ordered line-up insures that as many will be served as may be and that they will be served with a minimum of friction. So it is with life in a civilized society. As the saying is, we all want the earth. There are many of us, but there is only one earth. It is the problem of social control so to line us up and order our endeavors to satisfy our desires, so to rule our strivings to obtain the material goods of existence, that if there is not enough to go around, yet what there is may be made to go as far as possible with the least friction and waste.

At the end of the eighteenth century Kant saw that there was a problem of reconciling or ordering conflicting claims. But he thought of the problem in terms of the free individual will. Each of us was seeking to exert his will in the external world. When, however, we did exert our wills we clashed with others who were exerting their wills. Thus there had to be some systematic ordering of the exertions of free will whereby each would have the greatest freedom in this respect consistent with the like freedom of all. He put the matter, therefore, as one of bringing about a maximum of free individual self-assertion. Spencer also put it in terms of liberty, formulating his theory of social control in what he called the law of equal freedom: the liberty of each limited only by the like liberties of all so as to bring about a maximum of individual liberty. To Marx the problem seemed one of satisfying material wants, and he conceived of a social order so ruling the distribution of the material goods of existence as to give to each a maximum equal use of the means of satisfaction of those wants.

Let us pass by the philosophical and ethical and economic questions involved in these theories which held the ground in the last century and see exactly how the problem is presented to the jurist as a practical problem to be dealt with in a practical way. It is obvious that he cannot expect to secure every claim made or demand asserted by everybody or even a selected number of claims to their full extent. Nor can the selection be made arbitrarily. All experience has shown that unrecognized claims or demands will continually press for recognition until lawmakers or courts or administrative agencies or jurists find out what to do about them. First, therefore, there is the task of making an inventory of the wants, desires, claims or demands which men assert and call upon the legal order to satisfy or to enable them to satisfy, of which, therefore the legal order must take account. But an inventory of such magnitude is not usable unless it is classified. Hence as it is made it must be arranged systematically. There must be a classification of the claims pressing for recognition as well as of those already recognized with which the newly urged claims come into competition. Next must come selection out of the whole inventory of the claims which are to be recognized. But none of them can be recognized to their full extent in view of other recognized claims. Those which are recognized must be delimited. We must fix the limits within which they are to be given effect in view of others. Finally we have to devise legal institutions—rights, duties, liabilities, powers, liberties and privileges—whereby to give effect to the legally recognized claims or demands within the limits fixed upon.

At every step in this processs we encounter the problem of values. In the very first step after we have made our classified inventory we must ask why are we to admit this claim or demand to our scheme of recognized interests and not that one? Again we have to ask why do we limit our recognition of this claim or demand differently from that one? Why do we limit each as we do? Next we must ask why do we give effect to one by a legal right with correlative duty, to another by imposing a liability, to another by creating a power, to another by providing a privilege, and to another by leaving a whole field of activity untouched and recognizing a liberty? Why do we give effect to this one by punishment or by penal treatment, to that one by an action for damages, to another by an injunction, and to another by exempting certain occasions from the legal liability which generally attaches to actions of the sort? All of these things, and indeed, every step in the process just sketched, call for comparison of one claim or one set of claims with another which it overlaps or with which it comes in competition or in conflict and a giving of more weight or wider recognition or more effective securing to those which are held to have higher value.

Since Jhering showed us the difference between the legal institution we set up to secure a recognized claim or demand and the claim or demand itself, as it exists apart from the law, we have known the claim or demand by the name of interest. The term has occasioned some confusion because it has easily been confused with an idea of advantage; the more so since

Jhering's social utilitarianism made social advantage the criterion of value and treated it as something given, as something we know exactly as we know that a certain claim or demand exists *de facto* and is pressed upon lawmakers and courts for recognition. Everyone has an interest in, that is, makes a claim to the satisfaction of his desires. They are his interests as he sees it, and his view of the matter cannot be ignored by telling him it is not to his advantage to want what he feels he wants and insists he ought to have. Very likely we can't give him what he claims or all that he claims, but it is because we have to consider the conflicting or overlapping claims of others, not because we decide he does not want it. We must, therefore, as I have said, begin by ascertaining what are the claims or demands which press upon lawmakers and judges and administrative agencies for recognition and securing.

In the inventory with which we must begin it is convenient to classify the interests of which the legal order must take account as individual or public or social. All interests are those of individual human beings asserted by individuals. But some are claims or demands or desires involved in the individual life and asserted in title of that life. Others are claims or demands or desires involved in life in the politically organized society and asserted in title of that society. Others or the same in other aspects are claims or demands or desires involved in social life in civilized society and asserted in title of that life. Every claim does not necessarily go once and for all in one of these categories. The same claim may be asserted and may have to be looked at from different standpoints; it may be asserted in title of more than one aspect of life. Thus my claim to my watch may be asserted as an individual interest of substance when I sue someone, who walks off with it without my consent, either to recover possession of it or to obtain the money value as damages for converting it. But it may be looked at also as a social interest in the security of acquisitions and asserted as such when I persuade the district attorney to prosecute for larceny someone who has stolen it from me.

A mere sketch in broad lines of the scheme of interests which have pressed upon the legal order in the past will suffice for our purposes. Individual interests are interests of personality or interests in the domestic relations or interests of substance. Interests of personality are those involved in the individual physical and spiritual existence; in one's body and life, i.e. security of his physical person and his bodily health, in free exertion of one's will, i.e. freedom from coercion, and from deception as to what one is tricked into doing by false representations, in free choice of location, in one's reputation, in freedom to contract and of entering into relations with others, in free industry, i.e. in freely employing himself or gaining employment in any occupation or activity for which he is or is considered qualified, and in free individual belief and opinion. It is enough to point out in passing that the interests in freedom of contract and in freedom of industry overlap or come into competition with claims of laboring men asserted through trade unions and have raised typically difficult questions for the courts for a generation.

Like difficult questions are raised by individual interests in the domestic relations. It is obvious that husband and wife have each a claim or demand which they make against the whole world that outsiders shall not interfere with the relation. Yet on a weighing of all the interests involved California and many other states have been impelled to abrogate the action for alienation of affections by which that interest had been secured. The interest is still recognized but effective security is now denied. It is obvious too that the relation involves reciprocal claims or demands which each asserts against the other. The claims of the husband to the society of the wife and to her services for the benefit of the household, formerly well secured, are now deprived of all substantial security on a weighing in comparison with the individual interest of the wife in individual free self-assertion. But the claim or demand of the wife for support and maintenance is not only recognized but is secured in a variety of ways which make it one of the best secured interests known to the law. So it is with the interests involved in the relation of parent and child. Formerly the claims of the parent were given effect by privileges of correction, by control of the child's earnings, and by a wide authority of shaping the training and bringing up of the child in every phase. Everywhere today individual interests of the child and a social interest in dependents have been weighed against the claims of parents, and juvenile courts, courts of domestic relations, and family courts in our large cities have greatly changed the balance of these interests.

By interests of substance we mean the claims or demands asserted by individuals in title of the individual economic existence. Claims with respect to property involve too many questions to make it worth while to do more than mention them in the present connection. It will be more useful for our immediate purpose to look at a group of interests in economically advantageous relations with others. Such relations may be social or domestic or official or contractual. If a man is wrongfully and maliciously expelled from a social club the injury to his social standing in the community may have a serious economic effect upon him. Yet other claims have to be considered and the courts cannot compel the members of the club to associate with him if they persist in refusing to do so. In one case where the courts ordered the expelled member restored to membership the club reinstated him and then dissolved and formed a new club, leaving him out. We have noted already how claims of the husband to the services of the wife in the household are no longer effectively secured either against outside interference with the relation or against the wife's refusal to perform. As to official relations, public interests have to be weighed and the older conception of property in a profitable office has been given up. But the most significant questions have arisen with respect to contractual relations. If A has a contract with B he makes a claim against the whole world that third persons shall not interfere to induce B to break the contract. Yet the third person may assert claims which have to be taken account of in this connection, and some of the hardest questions in labor law have turned on recognition of claims of labor organizations to induce breaking of contracts of employment and what should be regarded as giving a privilege to interfere with such contracts.

As to public interests, it will be enough to instance one type of question where difficult problems of weighing have arisen. How far is the dignity of the political organization of society an interest to be taken into account? When the political organization was struggling with kin organization and religious organization for the primacy in social control, the dignity of the state was a very serious matter. Hence it was settled that the state could not be sued without its consent, that its debts could not be set off against its claims, that it was not estopped by what was done by its officials, and that its claims were not lost by official neglect to assert them nor barred by limitation. Other public interests, e.g. a claim to unimpaired efficiency of the political organization, entered into the reckoning. But the extent to which the rules just mentioned secure no more than the dignity of the state and the weight to be given to that interest today are controversial subjects in public law.

One could devote a whole lecture to a catalogue of social interests. First we may put the general security, including claims to peace and order, the first social interest to obtain legal recognition, the general safety, long recognized under the maxim that the public safety is the highest law, the general health, the security of acquisitions and the security of transactions. The two last afford an excellent example of the overlapping and conflict of recognized interests. From the standpoint of the security of acquisitions a thief or one who wrongfully holds another's property should not be able to transfer to a third person a better title than he has. But from the standpoint of the security of transactions, people generally who have no knowledge or notice of the owner's claim and, acting in good faith, part with value in a business transaction with one in possession of the property ought to be protected. Possession ought to give a power of business transactions as to the thing possessed and apparently owned. This question as to the limits of what is called negotiability has been coming up all over the world and recent legislation has been giving greater effect to the security of transactions in comparison with the security of acquisitions. Closely related, and scarcely less important is the social interest in the security of social institutions, domestic, religious, political, and economic. According as one gives the chief weight to the individual claims of husband and wife or to the social interest in marriage as a social institution, he arrives at different results on the vexed questions of divorce legislation. According as he gives more weight to individual interests in free belief and opinion or to the social interest in the security of political institutions, he will reach different results as to legislation against and prosecutions for sedition.

Other important social interests are an interest in the general morals, an interest in the use and conservation of social resources, and an interest in general progress, social, political, economic and cultural. Finally and by no means least there is the social interest in the individual life, the claim or demand asserted in title of social life in civilized society that each individual be secure in his freedom, have secured to him opportunities, political, social and economic, and be able to live at least a reasonably minimum human life in society. Here again all manner of overlappings and conflicts are continually encountered. But perhaps enough has been said to bring out that every item in the catalogue requires to be weighed with many others and that no one can be admitted to its full extent without impairing the scheme as a whole.

There is, moreover, a constant struggle to obtain a higher valuing of particular claims or demands. Thus, for example, the case pressed upon the legal order by organized labor is not that laborers and labor organizations were not treated as other litigants and litigant organizations, but that they were so treated, whereas they claimed a higher value than that accorded by legal formulas which put them on the same plane with other men and treated their disputes as ordinary controversies about trespass, breach of contract and interference with contracts and business relations. There are standing puzzles of the law about which lawmakers and jurists have debated and exercised their ingenuity since the time of Cicero which are no nearer satisfactory solution now than they were then.

Perhaps the best illustration is afforded by the case where one in good faith adds his labor to another's materials to make a new thing. Someone must be owner of the new thing and someone must be left to a claim for the value of his labor or materials as the case may be. The classical Roman jurists differed as between two solutions. Justinian chose a third. The modern codes have tried others and one of the greatest gave the matter up and left each case to the discretion of the judge in that case. The Anglo-American courts have not agreed and one of them added another possible solution which has been much followed.

From the Greek philosophers of the fifth century B.C. political philosophers and jurists have busied themselves in the quest of a measure of values for the problems of social control and the legal order. In its first stage of development the law aimed at nothing more than keeping the peace. It made no attempt at any general adjustment of relations and did not attempt to order conduct beyond putting an end to revenge and private war as the means of redressing injuries. A philosopher of an earlier date, quoted by Aristotle, considered that there were but three possible subjects of legal proceedings, namely, insult (which seems to have included injuries to the physical person), theft, and homicide. The burden of social control was carried by kin organization or religious organization rather than by political organization of society. Greek thought, directed to the phenomena of the developed city state, soon got beyond this primitive conception and put as the end of social control an orderly maintaining of the social *status quo*. The highest good was harmony, and harmony was to be assured by assigning each man to the groove for which he was fitted in the social order and keeping him there. The versatile man, so dear to the imagination of the American pioneer, was out of place in the Greek city. Roman jurists took over this idea and made it the theory of the legal order; and whatever had behind it the combined authority of Aristotle and of the Roman law was accepted as a matter of course by the later Middle Ages. A wholly different idea that the end of social control and so of the legal order is to bring about and maintain a maximum of individual free self-assertion begins to be urged after the Reformation, develops in the seventeenth and eighteenth centuries and culminates in the nineteenth century, although for juristic purposes it gets its classical formulation at the hands of Kant at the end of the eighteenth century. After the middle of the next century the Kantian idea of the end of law begins to be contested by an idea of a maximum satisfaction of material wants, putting material wants where Kant put free wills. Later this last idea merged in one of bringing about and maintaining a maximum of strength and efficiency in organized society, identifying the political organization of society with civilization.

But such ideas of the end of law have not so much given a measure of valuing interests as a starting point for legal reasoning, a criterion of interpretation, and a measure of the application of standards. For the practical purposes of recognizing, delimiting, and securing interests, lawyers have without formulating it worked out a practical measure which has been adapted to different ideas of the end of the legal order and yet has a distinct idea implicit in it.

Let us put some examples of practical problems with which courts have been wrestling recently. A woman falls in a fit or has a stroke in a bank. A surgeon who has just drawn some money is going out to keep an immediate appointment at a hospital where he is to perform an important operation. There are many bank employees about and many customers. What is his legal duty? A ship is tied up to a dock unloading. It has finished unloading and its license to remain tied up has expired when a severe windstorm comes up. It remains tied up and is pounded against the dock, injuring it. Granting it has a privilege in the emergency to remain tied up, which would otherwise be a trespass, does the privilege cover the damages to the dock or only the occupancy of the dock after the license to be there had expired? Waste matter from an oil refinery operated with all care is carried into the soil by rains and penetrates to percolating water so that it reaches a creek and poisons the stock of a farmer who uses the creek to water his animals. Is there liability? A passenger seeking to get on a moving train at a station is helped by a porter so carelessly that a parcel he is carrying drops on the rails and is run over. It contains explosives and the explosion which follows blows the weights off of scales on the platform and one flies to some distance and hits a woman who is waiting for another train. Is the railway company liable for the injury? Here we have the antinomy which runs all through the law as to liability for injuries. Is the emphasis to be put on culpability—no liability without fault—or on security? Or take the case of the sit-down strike. Are the claims of labor organizations to advance the cause of the working class to be given greater value than the general security? A novelist picks out the most unlikely name he can think of and attributes to a man of that name participation in flagrant municipal corruption in a city easily identified as one of the principal cities of the land. There had been prosecutions in that very city for corruption of the sort and, unknown to the author, a man of the very name used had been indicted in connection with this prosecution but it had been dismissed as to him. People generally who knew him would think this man was described, although the author had no idea of doing so. Again we have the question as between fault and security. As the law has stood if employees so carry on the course of their employment as to create a nuisance, although the employer uses all care to prevent their doing so, the employer is liable to a criminal prosecution because when the rule arose he had full control and could pick and discharge as he liked. What is to be the effect of a regime of collective bargaining upon this rule? We are told by philosophers today that these questions, put as questions of morals, cannot be answered with assurance. But the law must answer them and perhaps we may learn something by perceiving how it has gone about answering them in the light of experience in the past.

Generally experience has revealed practical adjustments of interests to competing interests. Sometimes however, it has taken a long time and a cautious process of trial and error or of inclusion and exclusion, with the inevitable errors involved in trial and error, to reveal the workable compromise or workable harmonizing. But the solutions arrived at in this way have pointed the way for analogous cases and reason acting upon experience has achieved much more than reason proceeding independently, which was relied upon in the era of natural law in the seventeenth and eighteenth centuries.

In the last century philosophical jurisprudence sought to solve the practical problems of law by a theory of natural rights. These rights, it was held, could be defined with precision as deductions from a fundamental idea of liberty. Every natural right was to be fully secured and as these rights had full and equal validity they could not conflict or overlap. What we now term social interests were put on a lower plane as mere policies guiding interpretation and application but not calling for securing in and of themselves. Thus the natural-rights theory put individual claims or demands, arranged in abstract categories, and thought of as having universal validity, above state and society. They could be secured but they must not be infringed. They did not admit of adjustment or compromise. They could only be recognized and given legal effect. But no one was ever equal to giving them the precise delimitation in detail which the theory demanded. The problems of the law in action lay at the periphery—in the undefined and undefinable uncharted ground between these rights. As to these the theory simply darkened counsel because it did not admit the validity of the adjustments and compromises which experience had shown to be necessary. Claims which had been traditionally recognized and were delimited by traditional legal precepts were postulated as beyond the reach of legislation. Claims which it was considered ought to be recognized and secured were confused with the legally delimited claims and the apparatus by which the law secured or sought to secure them. But all experience showed that recognized interests must be reconciled with each other in action by some sort of compromise; that no claim could be admitted to its full logical extent. The courts and lawmakers were left to do blunderingly and yet with much practical effectiveness what they had always been doing in the way of trial and error.

After interests have been recognized and delimited there still remains how to secure them and the problem of a measure of values is decisive here also. One way is to confer a legal right, that is a capacity of influencing others through invoking the force of politically organized society. My interest of substance is secured in one of its aspects by a legal right of possession of my watch. If someone takes it I can regain possession by an action in the courts. My interest of substance is secured in another of its aspects by a legal right of excluding others from my garden. All others are under a legal duty of keeping out and can be sued in court if they do not and are under a legal liability if in anything they do they cast an unreasonable risk of injury upon it and injury results. I can go into the courts and enforce that liability. Another way is to confer a legal power. A wife has an interest in support by the husband. If he does not provide her with necessaries, she can pledge his credit at the grocer's and he can be held by the grocer as if he had bought them himself. Again recognized interests may be secured legally by privileges. You have a recognized interest in the integrity of your physical person. I have a recognized interest in the exclusive enjoyment of my garden. If a lunatic chases you with a hatchet, the law confers on you a privilege in that emergency of running across my garden to safety. Or finally, recognized interests may be secured by a liberty, by a condition of legal hands off, as for instance what is called the right to pursue a lawful calling. The law leaves your natural liberty in that respect unrestrained. You may choose what calling you like. It will be seen that an adjustment of claims to a measure of values governs here as in every other step in the legal adjustment of relations and ordering of conduct.

There is still another matter to be taken into account before the task of adjusting competing interests is complete. There are limits to the possibility of securing some types of interest by the machinery of the legal order. If someone converts my watch to his own use the law can award me the value of the watch by way of damages and I can buy a new one just as good. If someone takes wrongful possession of my house I can have a judgment of recovery of possession and the sheriff can put him out and put me in again. But if a libeler injures my reputation I can't buy a new one with money damages nor if a malicious and unfounded prosecution for a detestable crime is brought against me can the judgment of a court wholly restore me to good esteem in the community. The books are full of proofs that pitch, even when wrongfully applied, will defile. The catalogue of cases in which any remedy which the legal order can apply is intrinsically inadequate is a long one. When the legal order seems to fall short of what is demanded by morals this must be borne in mind.

One more caution about juristic theories as to the adjustment of competing interests must be added. We must be careful to compare them upon the same plane. It is easy to answer our question in the way we put it. If we label one claim an individual interest and the other a social interest, that may afford a seeming answer although both claims could be put equally in either category. There has been too much of this in recent political and juristic arguing.

What then is the practical measure of values which the law has been using where theories have failed it? Put simply it has been and is to secure as much as possible of the scheme of interests as a whole as may be with the least friction and waste; to secure as much of the whole inventory of interests as may be with the least impairment of the inventory as a whole. No matter what theories of the end of law have prevailed, this is what the legal order has been doing, and as we look back we see has been doing remarkably well.

One of the hard problems of the law as to wrongs is that of causation. Just how close must be the connection between fault and injury so that responsibility for resulting damage should be thrown upon a careless actor? People must be secure so far as reasonably may be. But other people must be free to act so far as reasonably may be, and a margin of bad judgment has proved to be inherent in human behavior. It is significant that the Roman jurists, commenting on an old statute of the Roman republic about wrongful injury to property, put most of the hard questions of causation with which we in England and America have been wrestling for the past hundred years and dealt with them very much as courts have dealt with them independently in our common-law system in modern times. Our courts have had a sound instinct that it is not wise to carry responsibility for wrongs done by a servant or agent, or for carelessness where an unreasonable risk to others is not reasonably in sight, too far. It is not sound social engineering to carry the idea of security so far as to discourage individual enterprise by making it carry too heavy a burden.

Anyone who thinks that the whole of modern law may be thrown over and the legal order replaced by administrative absolutism, should look at the title *Ad Legem Aquiliam* in Justinian's Digest and see how perennial questions of intentional aggression upon others and injury to others through culpably casting upon them an unreasonable risk of injury have proved to be; how universal practically workable solutions of the questions raised by these aggressions and injuries have proved to be; how experience in every part of the world has led to and confirmed results reached on the basis of experience and reason by Roman jurisconsults two thousand years ago.

What are the substitutes proposed to take the place of the legal order—to take the place of adjustment of relations and ordering of conduct by a judicial process, employing an authoritative technique upon a body of authoritative precepts formulating experience of the administration of justice? One is a regime of free contractual determination of rights and duties by individuals whose claims come into competition. This was the program of philosophical anarchy a generation ago. It is out of fashion today because of its ultra-individualist presuppositions and in any event it is built on a faith in the efficacy of promises as intrinsically binding and self-enforcing which runs counter to the realist thought of today. Another, following Marx's doctrine of disappearance of law with the disappearances of classes, sees a regime of administrative absolutism. As one of the clearest exponents of the doctrine puts it, in the ideal society there will be no law, or rather only one rule of law, namely that there are no laws but only administrative ordinances and orders. Yet the country in which this was adopted as a policy and applied under every favorable condition after two decades is reverting to law. A third is what is called the corporative state, a state in which the unit is no longer the individual human being but instead the occupational group. In such a state, we are told, law will not be necessary. Controversies between members of the same group will be adjusted by a committee of the group and those between members of different groups by a general committee in which all groups are represented. The country in which this has been preached as the outcome of a totalitarian state has not as yet tried to put the program into practice. But legal history shows us that a somewhat similar regime in kin organized society simply led to the development of law.

Propositions not unlike that of the corporative state, involving off-hand disposition of cases by laymen applying their discretion to each case as something unique, are not uncommon in our own land in recent years. We have by no means outgrown the pioneer's faith in versatility. The pioneer had perforce to be versatile and he believed any man equal to anything. During the Civil War it took us some time to learn at much cost that a lawyer could not be made into a competent general by giving him a major general's commission. We were a long time learning that lay judges were not equal to administration of justice in a highly developed legal order. Lay healers still make good incomes where legislation does not exclude them. Any man appointed to a commission or board or bureau becomes an *ex officio* expert equal to regulating the most technical activities, the most highly developed enterprises, in the light of his good intentions and personal ideals, without the guidance of the law. If no measure of valuing competing interests is possible, this may be as good a way out as any. But the courts have in fact found and used one and formulated experience of using it in the law.

It is too much to expect that the results achieved by long experience of administering justice according to law can be achieved independently by even the wisest of men acting on single cases with nothing but their personal judgment to guide them. If a court in one of our large cities, with one hundred and fifty thousand cases a year before it, had to work out a balancing or harmonizing or adjustment of interests in each case, as something unique for the single case, there could not be judges enough provided to do the work. An architect may use formulas of the strength of materials although he could not work out one of them independently. A judge may use a formula of law, embodying long experience of deciding cases, although he personally has had little or none of the experience formulated and would not know how to reach the formula independently.

While philosophers are debating whether a scheme of values is possible, lawyers and courts have found a workable one which has proved as adequate to its tasks as any practical method is in any practical activity. Without putting it in that way they have treated the task of the legal order as an engineering task of achieving practical results with a minimum of friction and waste. We must not forget that law is not the only agency of social control. The household, the church, the school, voluntary organizations such as trade associations, professional associations, social clubs and fraternal organizations, each with their canons of conduct, do a greater or lesser part of the task of social engineering. But the brunt of the task falls on the legal order. The increasing secularization of social control, the disintegration of kin organization, loosening of the discipline of the household, loss of ground by the church and secularizing of education, have added immeasurably to what we expect of the law. It is the more idle to expect its task to be performed by some off-hand system of personal discretion applied to single cases as unique.

There is at any rate an engineering value in what serves to eliminate or minimize friction and waste. It may be that an ethical value may be found in what gives the most effect to human demand with the least sacrifice. At any rate William James thought so. It may be that this adjustment of competing interests with a minimum of waste makes for civilization and has a philosophical value.

I am not offering this idea of social engineering as a cure-all to be taken over by political and juristic theory and used to solve all the difficult problems of the science of law in the world of today. What I have set forth is no more than a description of how the legal order actually functions. It is a sketch of what courts do and jurists and judges have been doing since the Roman jurisconsults of the first century. In the whole development of modern law courts and lawmakers and law teachers, very likely with no clear theory of just what they were doing, have been at work finding practical adjustments and reconcilings, and if nothing more was possible, practical compromises of conflicting and overlapping interests.

Sometimes philosophy has moved ahead of the law, guiding its development. Sometimes the science of law has moved ahead of the practice, guiding the work of tribunals by criticizing and defining their ideals. But sometimes philosophy has come after legal development and done no more than organize what has been discovered in practice. So it was with the metaphysical jurisprudence of the historical school and with positivism and utilitarianism in the last half of the nineteenth century. They did no more than intrench the ideas of past eras of legal development and enable the established legal tradition to fight an obstinate rear-guard action for the first generation of the present century. Now for a season philosophy is neither leading nor organizing. It is telling us lawyers that we can't do what it is our job to do.

But jurists are perceiving what it is that the legal order has to do and has been doing, even if we have had no clear theory of it. It may be that we can expect no more than an organizing legal philosophy to give us a critique of what we now see we have been doing and of how we do it. Be this as it may, to the proposition that we can't arrive at a measure of values we may answer that we have found one, and a very workable one, whether we can prove its philosophical validity or not.

We may concede, if you will, that there is no absolute value; that value is relative to something. Perhaps value in jurisprudence is relative to civilization. Proximately it is relative to the task of the legal order, to the task of enabling men to live together in civilized society with a minimum of friction and a minimum of waste of the goods of existence. What accords with the jural postulates of the civilization of the time and place has juristic value. If it will work in adjusting relations and ordering conduct so as to eliminate or minimize friction and waste, it is a valuable measure for a practical activity.

But I am not giving up faith in philosophical jurisprudence because the fashionable philosophies of the moment despair of doing anything for law. In the Anglo-American political-legal polity questions of reasonableness have to be determined with respect to new types of social legislation. More and more in the ordering of conduct, especially the conduct of enterprises, the law relies today on standards rather than on rules. Also constitutional provisions, intended to maintain a balance of state and national government, have to be interpreted. Application of standards and interpretation are done with reference to received ideals, authoritative pictures of the social order which are as much a part of the law as rules and principles and conceptions and technique. It is here that most of what creates dissatisfaction with the work of American courts has its origin. If philosophy cannot give us a measure of values, it can give us a critique of the traditional ideals of the law. Our nineteenth century ideal was drawn from the society of economically self-sufficient neighborhoods of economically self-sufficient individuals in pioneer, rural, agricultural America. Certainly it is not a picture of American society of today. What the administration of justice in America needs is not a reversion to justice without law, a further development of absolutism, but a re-drawing of the authoritative picture of the society in which justice is administered.

It is bad social engineering to administer justice to a blue print of a society of the past as a means of maintaining the jural postulates of civilization in a different society of the present.

[7]

MICHIGAN

LAW REVIEW

Vol. XI. NOVEMBER, 1912 No. 1

WHAT IS THE LAW?

IT is intended that this title shall demand an analysis of the field of study in which the lawyer or jurist works and a determination of its essential and contributing elements. The purpose of the article is to sketch briefly a partial answer which will be instructive and helpful to the student who faces the problem as I faced it some ten years ago. I do not expect that anything new will be found in these ideas. I imagine that all of them must have been expressed many times before. Some of them are commonplace. None is esoteric. Probably the value of what I shall say will lie in focusing the attention on facts which commonly influence thought and action, but seldom are brought before the footlights of consciousness, comprehended, and properly correlated.

At the outset I wish to free my discussion from a cloud which would dim whatever clarity it might otherwise possess. In all philosophical debate there is much that is only a wrangle over language and its meanings. This is true of the literature of jurisprudence. It is not easy to keep a controversy concerning a hazy topic of substance from stumbling into the ditch of merely verbal disputes. It requires unprejudiced, receptive, and discriminating habits of thought to understand opposing statements as the maker understood them, to get fully and in proper relief his point of view, and then to criticise, not his expression, but his perception and comprehension of facts. The flexibility of language and the uncommonness of clear, adequate exposition increase the difficulty. It is comparatively easy to attach an unintended meaning to expression in honesty and with plausibility which will open it to criticism. The ensuing dispute frequently will rage interminably over matters of language without either party realizing that this is the only issue. Such differences between myself and my reader I hibernically desire to remove before they occur. It will be necessary in the course of this article to mention various legal meanings of the word "law;" but this definition of the word is only for the purpose of facilitating the communication of my ideas. Therefore I shall not quarrel with anyone who chooses to evolve different meanings or to object to some or all of mine. All I ask on this matter is that my language be interpreted in accordance with my discussion of its meanings. The reader may make mental reservations of his own definitions and usage. I do not regard such differences as important ones and I am not concerned to war over them. My purpose is not to define the word "law," but to focus your attention on each of several sorts of elements which exist in the field of legal study and their essential differences and correlations. My language and its definition are merely means to this end. Do not let your criticism of the means prevent the full accomplishment of the end.

Many attempts have been made to define the field of law. Perhaps the most familiar sort of result is typified by Blackstone's dictum: "Municipal law * * * is properly defined to be a rule of civil conduct, prescribed by the supreme power in a state, commanding what is right and prohibiting what is wrong."[1] John Austin similarly defined "the matter of jurisprudence" as "positive law; law, simply and strictly so called: or law set by political superiors to political inferiors" and "a law" as a "rule laid down for the guidance of an intelligent being by an intelligent being having power over him."[2] In the explanation and elaboration of this definition Austin, with his superior independence of mind and analytical power and the advantage of a more enlightened environment of thought, attacked Blackstone's exposition at various points; but criticised and critic and all who have followed similar lines display a common fault. They start with the idea of defining the *word "law"* as the proper avenue to the determination of the field of jurisprudence and they assume that its ordinary general meaning, "a rule," is an essential pervasive element of its technical meaning.[3] There is nothing which will tend to pervert critical investigation of a field of study or exposition of the results from its proper purpose more radically than the very common habit of entangling it at the outset in a mesh of carefully interwoven and finely distinguished technical terms. In any such work, the more we can keep language to its proper subordinate function of assisting thought and communication with efficiency and dispatch, the greater are our chances for success. It is

---

[1] 1 Bl. Com. 44.

[2] Austin's Jurisprudence, Vol. I, p. 86.

[3] See in addition to previous references:—Salmond on Jurisprudence (2nd ed.) pp. 9-10; Terry "The Common Law," pp. 1-2; Holland on Jurisprudence (10th ed.) pp. 1-52.

always best to realize external facts and distinctions and to make others see them with as little stress upon technical verbal definition as possible. Then the independent and subordinate matter of verbal labels may be discussed with less mental strain. We are not interested primarily in knowing the various discriminated uses of the word "law," but the various elements in the field of law and their interrelations.[4]

All the ambitious attempts to define this field which the student ordinarily will run across, agree that it consists of a system of rules and principles enforced by political authority. I believe that this idea is fundamentally erroneous and that it is a bar to a scientific understanding of our law and its particular problems. Therefore my first task will be to attempt to make clear its error. In order to establish my points efficiently, it is necessary that I recall to my readers some facts concerning knowledge and particularly concerning the nature and use of generalizations. The digression will be made as brief as is consistent with its purpose and will justify itself, I hope, by preventing doubt and misunderstanding later in the article.

[4] This is an essential error of Austin's work. It examines the paraphernalia of the field of law rather than its substance. He especially elaborated his ideas concerning the proper definition of certain technical terms and sought to evolve a harmonious and unified theory a priori from definition of the word "law." Consequently his theory is out of focus and his attempt to harmonize and unify led him into artificialities and the emphasizing of immaterial distinctions. Analysis and verbal definition often were confused by him and the emphasis was so strongly laid on definition that the work does not approach a scientific exposition of the field of law and its elements. Nevertheless it contains much careful analysis and clear discrimination and well repays attentive study.

Austin's Jurisprudence is not peculiar in its errors. Indeed the typical works on jurisprudence in English seem to comprise only a critical abstract discussion of the meanings of certain terms, such as, law, jurisprudence, sovereignty, right, duty, equity, legislation, possession, and contract, and fragmentary cursory comment on the purport and supposed influence upon the law of some of the denoted abstract ideas. Much acute intellectual ability, energy, and expository skill has been thus uneconomically spent in an attempt to distill from knowledge of a phase of governmental business a rarefied and sublimated science to be labeled "jurisprudence."

The law is essentially a practical matter. No theory or effort concerning it can command much attention and respect unless it is directed by an intelligent recognition of this fact. Various fields of investigation may be staked out and worked for the enrichment of utilitarian knowledge of this phase of government. Legal history is a field of great interest and importance and has several branches. Legal classification and terminology is a field of subordinate but considerable importance in which a great deal of good work has been done, but in which full development often has been hampered by mistaken ideas of its proper scope and relative importance and by dogmatic methods. If rightly directed, intelligent effort in this field should produce a harvest of economics in legal thinking and the communication of its processes and results. Legal philosophy is another field, legal psychology a fourth possible field, the art of legislation a fifth, comparative law a sixth; and others might be devised. Always, however, the focal work of jurisprudence should be the comprehension, exposition, sustaining, and amelioration of the concrete work of government, particularly in the administration of justice, although for the enlightenment of this work we may draw on all the sciences and philosophies which in any way concern human intercourse and social life.

In the development of any science, phenomena of certain sorts are studied to ascertain their causes and effects. A purpose common to all intelligent students of a science not purely historical, is the acquisition of an ability to predict that described effects will or will not follow from definite concrete conditions and forces. This is the practical end of their scientific inquiries.

I imagine that some of my readers may dispute the soundness of this last statement. "Science," they may say, "is organized, generalized knowledge. It does not consist of knowing the results which may be expected from a given concrete condition and operating forces. Often this sort of knowledge is merely empiric. The essence of scientific work is the extraction of the principles which govern sequences within the scope of a particular field and the utilization and systematization of such principles as already have been ascertained. Therefore any science consists of an organized mass of definitions, principles, rules, and formulae."

As a natural step to indicating my objections to the views outlined in the preceding paragraph I desire to combat especially the vague current idea that the purpose of scientific investigation is the extraction from their hiding places and the domestication of certain wild beasts of the jungle of ignorance known as principles and rules. We unconsciously are led by common speech to think of principles and rules as integral things existing outside of the human mind, which may be perceived by a gifted or trained intelligence and communicated to others. We speak of "grasping" a principle or a rule and of "transmitting" it to others. We speak of a principle as having been "discovered" at a certain time in history and used by men of succeeding generations. Regarded in any other than a metaphorical light, the conceptions of principles and rules indicated by such language are erroneous.

That which we label an idea is a concept or a group or combination of concepts. A rule or a principle is a connected series of concepts or associations or combinations of concepts. A concept is a psychological phenomenon. It does not exist outside of the mind entertaining it. Without discussing the possible physiological causes and processes of its occurrence, we may postulate as an axiom upon the basis of common knowledge that the idea of X cannot be literally the idea of Y. Figuratively speaking, X can transmit his idea to Y. What occurs, however, is not the passage of the idea to Y, but the formation of a similar one in Y's mind because of the expression which X uses as his means of communication. Principles and rules cannot exist outside of the mind. The external expression of them does; and, in the case of writing, it may endure from generation to generation; but the external expression consists only of signs and symbols, and the meaning thereof exists only in the mind of the speaker or writer as he makes it and in the mind of the interpreter when he interprets. A generation derives ideas from preceding ones, but they are the several ideas of the members of the later generation who entertain them, similar to those entertained at various times by the members of preceding generations. The principle that one man should not forcibly attack another is old in the common law. By that I mean that from generation to generation judges have entertained such a principle in deciding cases to which it is applicable; but the principle entertained to that effect by a certain judge in the 15th century is not the same principle as that similar one entertained by another judge in the same century or by any particular judge today. When we say that the principle is old, we are speaking figuratively. To conceive of these many similar strings of mental concepts as one enduring thing existing outside of the minds which have used them is a convenient and time-saving metaphor and is so much a part of our everyday mental equipment that we lose sight of the fact of its lack of literal truth. When we come to analyze the law, however, it is necessary to see naked realities if we are to escape being led into false theories.[5]

If we would think clearly, we must distinguish carefully three sorts of things. First, there are objective facts external to our thought, with which our thinking may be concerned; for instance we may think about a bit of scenery, or a picture, or the expression of the thought of another person, or a series of events constituting, perhaps, an experiment. Secondly, there are our mental processes concerning these facts. Thirdly, there is the expression of our consciousness.[6]

[5] I have dealt with this in some detail, because it is essential to comprehension of my argument that my readers see the nature of rules and principles. Now that I have made these points, however, I shall return to the use of that common time-saving metaphor which treats similar mental ideas, rules, and principles of the same or different persons as identical and continuously enduring. For instance I may speak of the existence of a rule against unexcusable assault without meaning to designate a particular rule existing in the mind of any ascertained individual. This is common and unexceptionable language, but we should bear in mind that it is figurative and does not literally express the truth.

[6] I hasten to make my peace with those whose philosophical predilections lead them to deny that anything substantial exists to be comprised in my first class. When they shall have finished their metaphysical disputations, I can only affirm my belief that if we could reduce our respective views to a common denominator of language we should find that an amazing portion of our apparent differences had vanished with the obliteration of our differences in terminology and points of outlook.

To obviate further and irrelevant analysis I intend to include in the third of these rough classes, the external signs, motions, and symbols by which communication is attempted and also the mental and physical processes through which they are used. It will include, therefore, the mental definition cf words and the mental formulation

Two points should be noticed with respect to the classes of things distinguished in the preceding paragraph. Substantially like chains of reasoning or other thinking may occur in various mental forms and may be expressed in various ways. The order, connection, and combination of concepts, the mental symbols and figures used and the words and sentence arrangements employed in the thinking and expression of two men concerning the same problem may differ greatly in details and still the reasoning and conclusions may be substantially similar. It is important to bear this point in mind when testing the theory that the field of law consists of a system of principles and rules.

The other point which should be noticed is that definition consists only in determining the meaning which shall be attached to certain labels such as words and phrases. In the bare act of defining we do not learn anything about the things to which we attach the labels. We must, however, have knowledge of the nature of things and the distinctions between them if we are to evolve a thorough and clearly-cut set of technical terms. Therefore the process of definition often forces us to clarify our conceptions of the things to which we apply our verbal labels, and this fact in turn tends in some cases to obscure the nature of definition and to induce the vague notion that it is essentially reasoning concerning the nature of things rather than concerning the meaning of words only.[7] As I indicated at the commencement of my article, this mistake has played havoc with the progress of philosophical thinking and particularly has been responsible for much bootless wrangling and much narrow work in the field of jurisprudence.

Now I am ready to state my objections to the theory that any science consists of a system of definitions, rules, principles, and formulæ. Every science has a practical bearing, either direct or indirect, immediate or more remote. It deals with sequences of concrete phenomena. The object of scientific inquiry is to obtain thorough knowledge of sequential causes and effects of sorts with-

of sentences for the purposes of communication. Definition and sentence formulation often are done, however, to clarify and further uncommunicated reasoning. Insofar as they are used for such purposes, these mental processes fall as subordinate tools into the second of our classes.

[7] This notion is encouraged by the similar fact that words defined by others—in a dictionary for instance—often are applicable to things of which we know little or nothing and of which we learn something substantial by reading or hearing the definition. The impartation of this knowledge through the expression which we hear or read is not abstractly part of the process of definition. Our acquisition of this knowledge is preliminary and prerequisite to understanding the definition; but the definition would be just as novel to us if we had possessed the substantial preliminary knowledge but had been unfamiliar with the word. In essence definition of language consists merely in indicating the range and limits of its application.

in a circumscribed field of study and to communicate this knowledge to others. The knowledge is obtained by observation, experiment, comparison, induction, deduction and other elements of learning and reasoning. Abstract concepts are used and principles and rules are formulated. They are mental processes and are not external things discovered and abstracted by the mind. Definitions are made of words, phrases, and other labels. Formulae are devised. Orderliness and systematization are aimed at throughout. All of these mental processes, however, are inspired by the purpose of acquiring, retaining, and communicating knowledge concerning concrete objective phenomena. For instance the purpose of the study of chemistry is the acquisition of ability to determine the potential causes and results of any of the possible concrete chemical combinations and disintegrations within its scope. Principles, rules, definitions and formulae are only tools for the acquisition, retention, and communication of such knowledge. I do not deny that these tools are necessities of a perfected science nor that they tend to assume a stereotyped form; but I insist that science is substantially thorough and efficient knowledge and that these mental tools are necessary only because such knowledge cannot be acquired, retained, used, and imparted without them. We should not confuse the content of knowledge with its form or with the mode of its expression, nor blur the proper relation between these things to such an extent as to think of science as in essence merely formally organized knowledge rather than broad and deep knowledge which is systematized and formulated as a means to effectuating economically the practical scientific ends.[8]

[8] It scarcely is necessary to say that I do not wish to enmesh myself in a discussion of the physiological and psychological aspects of knowledge or of the question whether it can exist independently of the particular form in which consciousness clothes or realizes it. At any rate our common experience will satisfy us that consciousness may grasp and wield the same detailed facts by various mental images, forms, and processes.

I do not wish to appear dogmatic about the proper meaning of the word science. In fact I do not pretend to define the word at all extensively. I seek only to clarify a rough practical distinction between knowledge content and knowledge forms and their relative values in fields of scientific work.

Let me add a protest against the view that a science becomes more perfected in proportion as its accepted generalizations become broader. Insofar as increasing the range of our mental forms tends to simplify the processes of memory, reasoning, and exposition without loss of clarity and definiteness, the change is an improvement. It economizes mental effort. Clarity and definiteness should never be sacrificed, however. A generalization is not laudable simply by virtue of its own form and relevancy. Efficiency is the criterion of its excellence. The more general we make our postulates, the vaguer they tend to become; and when their vagueness passes the limits of utility they should be discarded.

If as often happens in legal investigations and discussions, a problem is too complex for analysis into a few sweeping but accurately indicative generalizations, we should be satisfied with a more involved but adequate and clear summary. It in no way tends to increase the sum of knowledge concerning a subject to drape it in specious, wide,

In view of the very common mental haziness covering the points which I have been discussing, it is not logically a cause of wonderment that a theory of law should have been evolved which makes the essential subject matter of legal study a mass or system of principles and rules conceived as existing independently of the comprehension of any individual observer. If there were, as some of these theorists apparently would have us imagine, a system of co-ordinated rules and principles, developed by the experience of the race or evolved by inspired human reasoning from an enmeshment in the nature of things, which might be devoured and digested in all its ready made symmetry, and which infallibly and clearly would indicate through deductive processes all the concrete legal consequences that are being produced day after day by regular governmental action, and if none of these generalizations or sets of generalizations would fail correctly to indicate legal consequences within its scope until another had been substituted in its place by authoritative promulgation, there would be less cause to condemn this doctrine. Prudence and practical wisdom might satisfy themselves with mastering the import of the system. I venture to say, however, that no one who is not entangled in the mazes of a theory would assert that we have such a system.[9] If the law consists only of rules and principles, it does not exist outside of the minds which for the moment are using those rules and principles. For instance, a common law principle demanding consideration as a prerequisite to the validity of a simple contract does not exist literally at the present moment unless it is part of the active comprehension of some

flowing robes of abstract generalities and language, and they naturally obscure obvious particular facts. The literature of our law has been prolific of instances where superficial and partial analysis into a few vague and utterly misleading generalities has removed an important topic of law almost beyond the range of correct apprehension by one who is not ready to undertake an independent and thorough investigation. I have had to deal with several topics of this sort in the course of my teaching. Two of them I have discussed briefly in previous articles. ("Some Suggestions Concerning the Law of Fixtures" 7 Col. Law Rev. 1, and "Some Suggestions Concerning Legal Cause at Common Law," 9 Col. Law Rev. 16, 136.) A science grows towards perfection in proportion as the knowledge becomes more thorough, dependable, and economically usable and communicable. Its generalizations are but tools. Insofar as any one of them does not indicate and carry knowledge of particular facts clearly, definitely, and economically, it is a deficient tool, however alluringly simple it may be.

[9] "To us who have the disadyantage of living in a more sceptical age, it must seem the beginning of wisdom to recognize, frankly and unreservedly, that law never has been, and never will be, adequate to existing need. This must be so under the completest code that man could devise. The wisest legislator cannot foretell the future, or entirely comprehend the present."—W. Jethro Brown in an excursus appended to "The Austinian Theory of Law," p. 290.

"The narrow compass of human wisdom cannot take in all the cases which time may discover." Bacon, "De Augmentis" Lib. VIII; "Works," V, 90, 91.

"Be the law statute or judiciary, it cannot anticipate all the cases which may possibly arise in practice." Austin's Jurisprudence Vol. II, p. 664. (Lecture 39.)

person, although we may say figuratively that it exists because of the potentiality of its use when a problem shall arise to which it is applicable. The field of any science consists of sequences of concrete phenomena which are studied to determine their causes and effects, and, if the science is not purely historical, to predict concerning similar future sequences. The generalizations and definitions used are only mental implements manufactured by the mind and senses to aid in acquiring, retaining, and communicating knowledge of the objective phenomena within the scope of the science. I assume that no one will contradict that the field of law is part of the field of the science of government. What are the proper objects of comprehension within this field? Only or primarily rules, principles and definitions? No. The lawyer, as does the scientist, studies sequences of external phenomena and he studies them with a similar purpose—to determine their causes and effects and to acquire an ability to forecast sequences of the same sort.

I have stated that the field of law is part of the field of the science of government.[10] I delimit it further by saying that it includes only the organization of the institutions and agencies of authoritative government, their concrete operations and effects, and the causal facts which bring about those operations. These things constitute external sequences of phenomena which correspond to the working field of the scientist. Knowledge of such concrete governmental phenomena obtained by observation, report, inductive and deductive reasoning, and the other implements of scientific investigation, may be generalized into rules and principles. A technical vocabulary and stereotyped methods of phrasing may be developed with accompanying definitions. When thorough knowledge so obtained has been fully organized we shall have that which may with propriety be called a science of law.[11]

---

[10] The existence of the law as we know it is dependent on the existence of authoritative government. In a state of anarchy there is nothing closely analogous to the field of our profession because there is no continuity of authority and therefore no certainty concerning the governmental sequences of events.

[11] To assert that the law is an art and not a science does not obviate the difficulty, for no art consists of rules and principles only, although rules and principles may be employed in exercising it.

One sometimes hears in academic circles a discussion of whether law is a science or an art. Of course unless there is a preliminary definition of the words law, art, and science, the question is hopelessly vague and is productive of endless debates which careful definition would obviate. If we mean by the law the field of study which students of the law cultivate, by science, thorough, analyzed and systematized knowledge, and by an art, skill and applied knowledge directed towards production, the law is neither a science nor an art. It consists of external governmental phenomena and their concrete causes and effects. It is a field for scientific investigation and thorough systematized knowledge of the field may be called a science with propriety. On the other hand,

Though the entire range of the operations of authoritative government come within the scope of the lawyer's profession, he is usually concerned particularly with one sort of these operations—those of the law-determining bodies and their complementary and supplementary agencies. Of these, the courts are the most prominent in the view of the student of law, for in the great majority of cases where stubborn disputes over questions of law are fought out, those questions are ultimately determined by the courts. It will facilitate our discussion and not prejudice its soundness, I think, to confine it to law which has been or may be so determined.

To obviate as much as possible certain confusing facts which might prevent a clear perception of the argument which I am making, let us pause here a moment to determine the attitude from which we are to view the field of law. The judge, presiding over and deciding litigation, is engaged in the art of government. He is making law. The lawyer, who argues a case before judge, jury, or other law determining agency, is assisting in the law-making process. The legislator also indirectly influences similar future processes by the part which he plays in determining the existence and form of legislative expression, which authoritatively indicates what shall or shall not be done in concrete instances. These processes lie in the field of legal study. They are some of its objective phenomena. Therefore to view the field from the attitude of the judge at his official work, or of the lawyer in court, or of the legislator performing his function is, metaphorically, to attempt to see the field from a small spot inside it instead of from above and outside of it. If we are to view the law as a field of study analogous to that of any science, we must look at it from the position of the law teacher, the law student, the legal investigator, or the lawyer who is engaged in searching the authorities to determine "what the law is." These men are not directly acting as part of the machinery of government. Their study is not part of the external phenomena which compose the field of law. They are studying that field from without and therefore from the position which will give a wholly objective and the least confusing view. Let us continue our discussion from this external attitude.

To clarify the expression "external governmental (or legal) phenomena" which I shall use occasionally, imagine any case which passes through our courts of law to final judgment. The actual concrete facts on which the action is or might be based and defended

the skill and applied knowledge of judges or of practicing lawyers legitimately may be called an art. This academic debate therefore often resembles the dispute of the three blind men over the elephant.

are external and generally non-legal phenomena. When the suit is initiated, however, the string of legal consequences commences and continues until it finally is disposed of, by full execution of judgment or otherwise, and completion of the records. Such strings or combinations of interwoven strings of causal external facts and legal external consequences[12] constitute the laboratory material of the lawyer and jurist. In using such material, their purposes are, first, to learn by mental processes similar to those employed in scientific investigation, essential causal elements in the strings of occurrences producing certain of the legal consequences in those strings and, secondly, to base upon knowledge so obtained and other pertinent knowledge a forecast of the potential legal consequences of similar or analogous causal facts. Concrete occurrences to the lawyer are pregnant with potential sequences which threaten governmental action. His essential business is to predict these future sequences accurately and to induce the desired and guard against the undesired. The generalizations expressed in text-books, on the statute books, or in judicial opinions have no value to him—have no practical value to any man—except insofar as they affect such problems or aid in their solution. They are but means to an end.

What of it? The field of law is far wider and more complex than an imaginary system of promulgated or developed stereotyped rules and principles. It is a field for scientific study analogous to the field of any other science. Concrete sequences of facts and their legal consequences are the external phenomena for investigation and prediction. Knowledge of the causative interrelations of such sequences and of the causes, organization, and operation of the governmental machinery entering into them constitutes knowledge of law in one of the legal senses of the word. Rules and principles have been developed for use in this field and technical terms with definitions more or less stereotyped have been adopted. They are only mental tools which are used to classify, carry, and communicate economically the accumulated knowledge of the law similarly to the use of generalizations and definitions in other sciences.

Although I have said that it is not my purpose to define the word "law," it may contribute to my argument to point out some of its different legal senses. Therefore I shall pause occasionally in the course of my discussion to do so. At this place I call attention to the use of the word to indicate the field of the lawyer's study or,

[12] Including the facts of pertinent legislation, of course, and all other sorts of facts that produce strings of consequences which finally enter into the determination of litigation.

often, a part of that field. When it is used in this sense, the speaker or writer consciously or unconsciously indicates by it causal relations of occurrences external to the mind of the observer and their governmental consequences, past or potential.[13] The fact that the use is unconscious in the sense that the speaker or writer does not realize the nature of the thing he designates, and the fact that if he were asked to define his use he might repeat a variation of the Blackstonian[14] definition of law, do not affect the usage. A man may be mistaken both in his assumption of knowledge of the nature of things concerning which he converses and in the analysis of his thinking. In such cases his definitions are not likely to indicate the actual application of his terms.

Our field of law does not consist of rules and principles only. Similar fields existed before adequate rules and principles were developed to aid in comprehending them, just as the field of geology existed before the science of geology was developed. It would not be true, however, to say that the field of law exists independently of rules and principles as does that of geology. The objective phenomena of law include principally human actions and the legal sequences are brought about through voluntary action. The intelligent direction of human action necessarily involves the use of generalizations. Generalizations therefore have a causative force in producing legal effects, and that force must be estimated as carefully as any other operating within the field; but they are not the whole field. In order that we may appreciate the function of generalizations in producing legal sequences, let us spend a little time discussing judicial reasoning, judicial opinions, and especially the authoritative effect of judicial generalizations.

In the course of my studies in particular parts of the field of law, I have become convinced that there exists widespread a vague theory that the "unwritten" or "common" law finds its only authoritative expression in abstract pronouncements in judicial opinions and that the concrete determinations of cases do not constitute law, but normally are made "according to law" and "illustrate" law. That is to say, they are deduced from its application. In its older phase this theory denies that judges legislate in expressing legal rules and principles, and asserts that they only discover, announce, and apply them. In a newer phase, it admits that judges make the law, but still insists upon generality as an essential characteristic

[13] This use occurs when one speaks of studying "law," or "the law of property" or labels a described sequence of facts and their predicated legal consequences "law" or "the law."

[14] I apply this label for convenience only. I do not intend to imply that Blackstone was the originator of the theory.

of law. It has even been contended that nothing which can be called law legitimately exists concerning a class of legal questions until a generalization which covers them has been announced judicially or by legislation. I consider these ideas to be erroneous fundamentally, and prejudicial not only to understanding of our system of law, but also to progress towards the perfection of our administration of justice. An elemental error in the theory lies in the idea that the statement of a rule or a principle of law by the judges of a court as a material part of their reasoning in explanation of the decision of a case is normally a fundamental and essentially authoritative thing.[15] My attempt to disclose the fallacy of this view will be distributed into two themes. The next few pages will be devoted to clarifying our ideas of the nature and purposes of judicial reasoning, generalizations, and expression. Then I shall discuss briefly the causative potency of precedents in producing legal consequences. It will be necessary to encroach a little on the second theme in pursuing the first, but I wish to disentangle them as much as possible in the interests of clarity.

How do judges reason towards a determination of the cases before them? Insofar as valid legislative expression is deemed applicable, it is controlling. The validity, effective purport, and applicability of such expression is determined by the court. Concerning the causative potency of legislation in producing legal consequences, I shall make a few remarks later in this article. For the present we may facilitate understanding by excluding consideration of legislation entirely. Precedents are also given a weight in judicial reasoning which we shall discuss when we have finished the present theme. Within the bounds of the established jurisdiction and procedure of their courts, and excepting insofar as they are guided by legislative expression, precedents, and a tradition that any but the most gradual and conservative innovation is not a proper product of judicial functions, judges are free to give weight in their deliberations to all

[15] Some of those who believe that mandatory rules and principles are the essential subject matter of law admit that judicial generalizations are not dependable or necessarily authoritative. See for instances: Austin's Jurisprudence Vol. II pp. 620-639 (Lecture 37). Also see idem p. 661 (Lecture 39); Salmond Jurisprudence 2nd ed. pp. 9-22. To make this admission and not abandon their main theory requires some ingenious and fictitious reasoning which could be welded into logical coherence only by a belief that rules and principles are external things to be discovered and "applied" or by excluding a great number of judicial decisions from the scope of law. Austin choses neither horn of this dilemma. His analytical insight naturally would forbid acceptance of the first and he ingeniously but illogically avoids the second. Salmond boldly excludes judicial questions which cannot be brought within the scope of "pre-established and authoritative principle" from the realm of law and antithetically groups them with all other questions not "of law" under the omnibus label "questions of fact."

See also in this connection an excursus by W. Jethro Brown—"The Austinian Theory of Law" p. 288.

considerations of justice or policy logically applicable to their legal problems. Ordinarily they exercise this freedom to the varying degrees which might be expected from men who vary widely in intellectual ability, independence, and initiative. Cases are not decided by reference to some mysteriously and anciently evolved system of rules and principles of inherent authority and potency, nor do the mental processes of the judges commonly consist of using stereotyped generalities. The processes of decision are processes of intelligent reasoning, such as are operative in other fields of mental activity. Generalizations are used, but they are only the mental implements of those who use them. Impressions, beliefs, and conclusions concerning the facts of the case, concrete precedents, applicable customs, habits, common ideas, moral blameworthiness, and other logically pertinent considerations are consolidated and welded in generalizations. Some of these generalizations are constructed by a judge on the basis of data obtained by his investigation of preceding cases. Some are based on knowledge obtained from the evidence or from his general experience. Some, metaphorically, are adopted from the works of text writers or from the opinions in previous cases. These last, however, are used, as are the others, only because the judge accepts them as correct indications of facts and as considerations pertinent to the decision of his problem. The mental forms which considerations took in the judicial mind in previous cases and the language in which they were expressed are not abstractly of fundamental importance, but knowledge concerning all external facts which logically are relevant to a present legal problem, including knowledge of the relative weight given to each sort of fact in former adjudications, is important.[16] This last know-

[16] Let me illustrate. X inexcusably attacks Y. Y, in necessary self-defense, strikes X. We may generalize, somewhat indefinitely, to the effect that a personal assault without excuse or justification is legally actionable, but that necessary self-defense is a legally valid justification of a blow. Y, however, may never have formed this or any similar generalization and yet may have realized that his conduct was morally and legally justifiable. Likewise a judge might decide a controversy between X and Y arising over this incident without the aid of such generalization. The most elementary knowledge of human motives and affairs would lead to a condemnation of X's conduct and a justification of Y's, and on examination of previous concrete adjudications without consideration of formal general statements would endorse such a judgment. The particular facts that X was attacking Y when Y struck him and that Y's blow was necessarily self-defense are considerations which would control a court's decision independently of use of a formal generalization of the legal consequences of such conduct. That such a generalization has been made and expressed by other judges does not establish that this one decision resulted from use of a legal rule or was based upon a legal rule. If my argument is followed, it should be clear that even though such a rule was used, it was not an essential cause of the decision.

Similarly the potency of particular sorts of facts in producing legal consequences may be comprehended in various mental forms and expressed in various ways. In other words, a topic of law may be comprehended in any of various systems of rules

ledge is of peculiar pertinency because in our system of law precedents are potent arguments and the precedential facts considered include not only the concrete question and adjudication in a former case, but also, with lesser stress, the reasoning through which the adjudication was reached. I wish to discuss briefly the effect which precedents have in determining judicial decisions and its reasons a few pages further on. At present I insist only that the statements of rules and principles by judges in their opinions of previous cases are not commonly given an authoritative force analogous to that of valid legislative expression and that neither their language nor the particular mental forms which it communicates are binding logically on subsequent judicial reasoning Let me make my argument clearer by a more detailed exposition including some reiteration.

The field of law is the field of a practical science and of a practical art. As lawyers we endeavor to forecast potential legal consequences of particular causal facts and to influence the actual trend of concrete legal consequences. We evaluate things professionally in the light of their bearing upon these problems. External phenomena which are not implicated in our cases are not studied for themselves, but for the professional knowledge and skill which the study will bring. Judicial generalizations may have any of several bearings upon these problems.

First:—Often judicial generalizations summarize past concrete decisions or their reasons and many do not purport anything else. As historical summaries they are not often of great importance in the solution of a present legal problem. They may be accurate or inaccurate, adequate or inadequate, helpful in varying degrees or

---

and principles variously expressed. These different expressions and systems are not the same although the knowledge content is equivalent. Some of the rules, principles, and language may resemble those used by judges. Others may not. Those which do not, may be simpler and more convenient. Text writers frequently simplify the expression of the law by their labor and skill. If all the various expositions indicate with equal accuracy the concrete legal consequences within their scope, all equally express rules and principles of law. The simpler and more economical are preferable for use, whatever their origin, if their accuracy has been tested. Vague or misleading generalizations, whatever their origin, should be discarded.

It must be remembered that I am speakng throughout from the attitude of the legal investigator and not from that of the advocate. One who is arguing a case before a court, in the exercise of his art should so adapt his forms of reasoning and his manner of expression as to convince the judges as thoroughly and easily as possible. Therefore usually he will find it expedient to employ generalizations and language which are current in the profession and which may be paralleled by quotations from judicial opinions and from standard texts. It requires some mental effort to recognize substantially the same consideration in a new garb and to appreciate improvements in arrangements and associations of ideas. One cannot be sure that busy judges will vigorously master such innovations and improvements, and this risk must be carefully weighed before one departs from the beaten paths of legal thought and speech in advocacy, however defective, dark, and inadequate those paths may be.

useless. Always they can be checked by reference to reports of the phenomena on which they are based. These summaries have no logical authoritative force upon future decisions.

Secondly:—Judicial generalizations often, expressly or by implication, purport also to predict legal consequences. Sometimes they purport to dictate or authoritatively promise decisions of certain sorts. Let us leave this phase of judicial generalizing until we have discussed the third phase.

Thirdly:—Judicial generalizations may be considered as elements in the causal procession of events towards the decision of the court. In this aspect they must be weighed and analyzed with the other interrelated facts in order to determine their causal efficiency in inducing the decision. This analysis is very valuable to the lawyer. It is necessary to a full understanding of the case and a correct estimate of the decision. To know just what sort of facts will weigh with courts as considerations on particular points is most important, and to know the best form and language in which to present these considerations is also important to the advocate. Dependable knowledge of these matters can be obtained only by study and experience. Furthermore a judicial generalization in connection with the decision and facts of the case in which it occurs may have a precedential influence on the decision of subsequent cases. On the other hand it may not. It may even be criticised in later cases as faulty or wholly erroneous. This matter of the causal effects of judicial generalizations as precedents we shall consider later. At present we can easily note that in the third aspect past judicial generalizations have no intrinsic authoritative force on future decisions analogous to the force of valid legislative expression. The custom or principles giving logical weight to precedent, which we shall consider in a few moments, may stamp them with a reflection of authoritativeness; but it is only a reflection of the authority of the subsequent decisions which are based on their repeated use. I hope to make clear by my brief discussion of the effect of precedents, that courts follow precedents for reasons which do not include an authority in courts to dictate even within limits the disposal of future litigation.

Let us now discuss the second aspect of judicial generalizations which I mentioned a page or two back. There have been and are judges whose narrow intellectual horizon and lowly conception of the judicial function have led them to decide questions of common law by a process similar to the construction and application of a statute. Their doctrine, which apparently has an extensive vogue but actually is not commonly practiced in the decision of cases, is that the province of the judge is to search the authorities for general statements of considerations of law which seem to be applicable to his case, to determine which of these statements is sufficiently supported by authority to stand as "law," to interpret these established statements, and to decide the case by application of the interpretations. The old superstitions that law necessarily pre-exists, that it is something general and authoritative, and that judges have no power to make the law but can only interpret and apply it, are the philosophical tenets of these jurists.[17] They have been advanced or un-

[17] "In like manner the canon laws or decretal epistles of the popes, are all of them rescripts in the strictest sense. Contrary to all true forms of reasoning, they argue from particulars to generals." 1 Bl. Comm. 59.

Cf. II Austin's Jurisprudence 633-634 (Lecture 37).

See also:—"The Ideal and the Actual in Law," by J. C. Carter in 24 Am. Law Rev. 752; 3 Encyc. Brittanica (9th ed) pp. 800-802.

I am convinced that the theories which I criticise do not rest on analysis of the law, but are a manifestation of false fundamental notions of logic. The instinctive ideas which produce them are that something abstract and general always is the cause of concrete phenomena and that sound reasoning demands first an ascertainment of a proper cyclopedic rule and then its control of particular determinations. The syllogism is the Palladium of these thinkers. To trace their fallacy and its causes and effects through the history of thought would be an important study in historical psychology and philosophy. Its influence on the administration of justice in different countries and ages would not be the least interesting phase of such an investigation. Abstract ideas have been deified; independently of reason and validity they have exercised tremendous force upon the course of human events; they have been tyrants, builders, and destroyers; and they have made and broken rulers of men. It is but a step from religion, politics, and the tenets of social existence to the administration of justice. No one who has given the slightest interested attention to analytical history or to the common political thought of our own time should be surprised to discover the unreasoning power which abstract generalities have had on the law of communities in past ages or which they occasionally have today. (See in this connection Maine's Ancient Law, Pollock's ed. pp. 76-79; 405). I do not deny this power. I assert that inadequate generalities have been potent factors in shaping the law of the past and that sometimes they have become tyrants instead of tools. I also assert that especially in politics and sporadically in the law phenomena of the same sort occur in our own times. They are symptoms of the deficiencies of human intelligence. To admit the potency of this influence is not to justify the related fallacious legal and philosophical theories, however. I trust that the main text of this article has made sufficiently plain the logical fallacies of those theories.

This article is due to three actuating causes. The first is the purpose of contributing my mite towards overcoming the sporadic potency of invalid generalities in our law and towards making the ordinary analysis and expression of legal reasoning more direct, forceful and clear. The second is a desire to influence legal education in the same direction and against false hobbling theories of the law. The third is the fact that whenever I attempt an exposition of a complex legal topic, I face potential objections to my analysis based upon opposing stereotyped theories of the nature of law and the sanctity of judicial generalizations, which I cannot obviate effectually in a cursory and distracting digression from my theme. Therefore I have sketched briefly my views in these pages to which I can refer hereafter as occasion arises.

Naturally I am concerned especially with the effect which the common theories have upon the education of students in our law schools. No single step in methods of legal instruction has been as effectual in really educating the students as has the adoption of the case system in our more important schools. Nevertheless I believe that only a small proportion of teachers and students who work under that system comprehend its educative value fully. Many of them look upon the cases as only incidental things—transient

questioningly adopted by able men. Their wide-spread persistence in a profession which demands so much acuteness of perception and analytical power is marvelous. Undoubtedly much of the backwardness of the law has been due to their influence and the instances are many in our books where this theory and just such legal reasoning as I have indicated have produced unwise and criticised decisions. Indeed I venture to assert that the greater part o fthe persistent bad law mirrored in our case books for which unwise legislation or political theory is not responsible, is due to such narrow legal methods of applying common law precedents or legislation. Fortunately, however, the common practice does not verify the theory. The judicial function of courts[18] is not legislation but the orderly settlement of litigation between parties. Their adjudications concern only the concrete cases before them. Courts have refused to decide moot cases. Would it not be logically inconsistent to settle moot questions by dictatorial generalizations broader than the concrete case before them?[19] To assume to dictate what the decision shall be in a future case even similar to the case before the court would be to assume authority to decide a controversy not yet properly before the court and therefore not within its jurisdiction. If valid, this would be action indistinguishable in species from legislation, and in amending or overruling previous judicial statements and immediately basing a decision on the changes, judges would be legislating *ex post facto*. Courts do not legislate. In deciding a case the judges themselves

husks enclosing and partially revealing the fundamental principles and rules which must be dragged out and digested. As I have labored to explain in this article, cases past and potential are the essential substance of the field of law. Past cases are experimental guides to prognostications of future decisions. Rules and principles are only mental tools for handling knowledge concerning the governmental sequences which compose cases. Cases are external actualities of the sort which the law student should seek to comprehend. Rules and principles are only chosen media of comprehension. The tendency of many teachers and students is to lay the emphasis improperly on stereotyped abstractions and formal definitions as inherently fundamental and inviolable things. Proportionally less insistent discussion of the proper definition of technical terms, less memorization of formal expressions of "rules and principles" and their "proper applications," and less exercise in dialectics, however fascinating to immature minds it may be, and more thorough training in analysis of cases and generalization of the results and more freedom in choice of expression, will lead the student to a clearer view of the field in which he works and an earlier mastery of his mental apparatus. The methods which I criticise justify a familiar dictum of graduates that they have learned more law in a year of practice than they accumulated in a law school course.

[18] I use the qualifying adjective "judicial" in recognition of the fact that some functions vested in some courts or in their judges are not judicial in nature.

[19] "It is certain that the most experienced and the most learned and able of our judges, have commonly abstained the most scrupulously from throwing out general propositions which were not as proximate as possible to the case awaiting solution. * * * * I have heard Lord Eldon declare (more than once) that nothing should provoke him to decide more than the decision of the case in question absolutely required." Austin's Jurisprudence, Vol. II, p. 658 (Lecture 39.)

determine what non-legislative considerations shall weigh in the decisions and the result of balancing these considerations. They ordinarily do not make their determinations arbitrarily, but in accordance with the knowledge, the logic, the mental instincts, and the views of judicial custom and policy at their command. Novel cases constantly arise and cases similar to old ones are differently decided.[20] Although a generalization is used as a material step in the reasoning of a court towards a decision, it does not thereby become an accurate rule of law. The expression of an alleged rule may be reiterated in case after case and remain unreliable. Courts may reject previous concrete adjudications as authorities or may declare previous judicially announced rules wholly erroneous and refuse to use them.[21]

---

[20] If the concrete decision in a preceding case is disapproved, then, pro tanto, past law is disapproved.

[21] That courts are not bound by precedents although they give great weight to them see: Hart v. Burnett, 15 Cal. 530 at pp. 598 et seq.; Houghton v. Austin, 47 Cal. 646 at pp. 666 et seq.; Bright v. Hutton, 12 Eng. L. and Eq. at p. 15; Paul v. Davis, 100 Ind. at pp. 426 et seq.; Jasper Co. v. Allman, 142 Ind. 573 at pp. 591 et seq.; Cohens v. Vrginia, 6 Wheat. 264 at pp. 399-402; I Kent Comm. 477.

Of course it is too much to expect that judges will not commonly reflect in their language the tradition that they do not make the law, but only express it, and therefore in many cases where they exercise their liberty of departing from precedent we find them calling the decisions which they "overrule" departures from the law.

Deciding cases "on principle" or "according to rule" is advocated sometimes even at the expense of justice between parties. Insofar as legislation, or the reasonable force of settled precedents, or the effectiveness of some sound judicial policy, logically demand such a particular result, I should assent to the argument; but I do not agree that it is wise or defensible for courts to mete out injustice or to refuse justice merely to maintain the validity of a generalization or to satisfy a fancy for simplicity and symmetry in comprehension and expression of the law. That the accomplishment of a desirable decision would infringe some previously announced cherished non-legislative rule should never abstractly be a mental barrier. One who has studied carefully a complex legal topic historically through the cases, will need no exposition of the fact that courts do not commonly raise such a barrier unless the rule or principle in question has been so endorsed by a succession of cases as to call effectively into play a phase of the influence of precedents which I shall discuss later in this article.

See Maine's Ancient Law, Pollock's ed., pp. 72-73. I deem this cited passage from Maine a great tribute to the legal ability of the ancient Greeks. If justice is satisfactorily and efficiently administered by any system of law, that system justifies itself whether or not great legal analysts and codifiers are produced by the nation to comprehend accurately, classify compendiously, and express clearly and adequately the results of the system. It is difficult to devise a sound reason for placing subordinate implements of jurisprudence above accomplishment of the purposes of jurisprudence. Why should substance be sacrificed to form? Also it is difficult to agree that a refusal to follow inadequate generalities in administering justice prevents systematization of knowledge of the law any more than continual abandonment or amendment of old theories used in the comprehension and production of the external phenomena of physics or chemistry prevents improved systematization of the science. If adequate systematization of knowledge concerning any sort of external phenomena is lacking, it is due to the fact that sufficiently able men in the art have not been attracted to that particular field of labor. Great minds of Rome's days of supremacy interested themselves in the development and scientific comprehension of juridical events. The great analysts of ancient Greece were absorbed in other fields of abstract thought.

Especially because of the fact that adequate scientific systematization and expression

In addition to these conceded facts, a more common phenomenon prevents one from relying with intelligent assurance on expressions of judicial generalizations without thorough scrutiny, analysis, and corroboration. They frequently display defects which are inherent in any but the ablest reasoning. Human minds commonly reach determinations by instinctive processes as well as through conscious detailed and orderly argument. Therefore to comprehend and express accurately one's own "reasoning" toward a determination requires some power of psychological insight and analysis as well as discrimination in the use of ideas and words. Doubtlessly most of us have had the experience of easily reaching a tentative decision on an important problem which we felt could be justified by analysis, and of finding extremely difficult the work of thoroughly comprehending the facts which abstractly have influenced our conscious and subconscious mental processes towards that decision and of accurately expressing the results of this analysis. To perceive all the considerations logically applicable to a difficult and complicated problem of any sort, to balance them intelligently and reach a logical and satisfactory decision, and then to express tersely, accurately, and clearly that decision and the course of reasoning on which it rests, is a task requiring great ability, industry, care, and patience. Rarely is such a piece of work performed in a manner above criticism. When a lawyer, a text writer, or a judge attempts to generalize and express the results of his investigations of past concrete cases, he has the same sort of difficult problem to solve as has the scientist who seeks to analyze certain sequences and generalize the results of his experiments. The chains of causal facts and their actual legal effects are concrete phenomena in the external world analogous to the experimental phenomena of the scientist. The legal thinker, however, works at a disadvantage which is common in few scientific lines. He cannot at will initiate and carry through experiments to cover the whole field of his generalizing in detail, so as to insure at once breadth and accuracy. When he merely is generalizing past concrete decisions, he finds often that they are not numerous and varied enough for satisfactory abstraction and analysis.[22] When the lawyer or judge seeks to go beyond a mere analytical summary of past cases and to generalize concerning existing law—i. e., concerning potential

are such difficult and rare things, it is desirable to keep constantly and distinctly in mind the purposes and art of administering justice on the one hand and the comprehension and expression of the concrete results of the administration of justice and their causes on the other. The art of administering justice may be greatly aided by careful systematization of thorough knowledge of the law, but we should never permit the purposes of the art to be jeopardized by a pseudo-science.

[22] See in this connection Maine's Ancient Law, Pollock's ed., pp. 36 et seq. Also see idem pp. 32-36.

legal consequences of actual or postulated facts—this difficulty is increased and accentuated. He is now not merely examining and expressing ideas of past occurrences; he is predicting in abstract generalizations what would be decided in concrete cases falling within their scope. He often is in the position of an astronomer, who on the basis of scattered and incomplete data is forced to predict the time and nature of some celestial event; or of our much abused friend the weather man; or of a pilot who has trained skill, the experience of past work in his profession, and knowledge of the geography of the water which he is navigating, but no prophetic vision to assure him of the outcome of the particular effort in which he is engaged. Therefore we should not be surprised to find in judicial opinions, as we do elsewhere, indications of misapprehension and of misinterpretation of controlling ideas and impulses, and also inaccurate and misleading expression of meaning. To expect that judicial generalization and expression will not display these defects which are common in reasoning and language is to assume arbitrarily that our judges are all masters of human thought or to believe superstitiously that there is something in the judicial office which purifies and perfects the judge's reasoning. To insist that the expressions of judicial generalizations, which so often display these defects, are authoritative dictates analogous to statutes is to contend for a hamper upon the development of the law which would unfit our system of jurisprudence for its purposes.[23]

If the expression of a judicial rule or principle be examined crit-

[23] "But in the analogous process of induction, by which a rule of law is extracted from judicial decisions, that scrupulous attention to the language used by the legislating judge would commonly defeat the end for which the process is performed. As the general propositions which the decision contains are not commonly expressed with much premeditation, and as they must be taken in connection with all the peculiarities of the case, it follows that the very terms in which those propositions are clothed are not the main index to the ratio decidendi;—to the general rule or principle which that decision established, and which is the governing principle of the case awaiting solution.

"In short, a statute law is expressed in general or abstract terms which are parcel of the law itself. * * * * *

"But a rule of law established by judicial decision, exists nowhere in precise expressions, or in expressions which are parcel of the ratio decidendi. The terms or expressions employed by the judicial legislator, are rather faint traces from which the principle may be conjectured, than a guide to be followed inflexibly in case their obvious meaning be perfectly certain." (Austin's Jurisprudence Vol. II, p. 630. See also p. 622.)

I do not deny that statements of judicial generalizations are important facts in the train of legal sequences, which must be carefully studied and interpreted in the course of obtaining a correct estimate of the indicative value of the decision to which they lead; nor that such statements are potent precedential considerations in the determination of subsequent cases; nor that judges often have decided cases contrary to their judicial inclinations because of the existence of such precedents, and have done so sometimes under influence of an idea that these precedents were authoritative dictates. I contend, however, that the statements of rules and principles of law in judicial opinions logically have no force analogous to that of legislative expression and that the ordinary course of judicial reasoning and decision gives them no such force.

ically in connection with the facts and course of reasoning of the case in which it played a part, it may disclose, suggest, or imply some applicable and endorsable consideration and yet be condemnable as a guide for any of several reasons. It may display deficient analysis and comprehension of all the applicable considerations within its purported scope. The generalizing may have been clumsy or too broad. The expression may be vague, indefinite in some particular, or not clear.[24] For these reasons frequently the expressions of judicial generalizations are revised, amended, and discarded and new generalizations are constructed to aid in deciding controversies founded on infinitely varied combinations of facts. Language that has been repeated through scores of judicial opinions will be criticised rigidly for inaccuracy, vagueness, or the unwisdom of its import.

Are there then no such things as rules and principles of law? I have had this question put to me in protest against my analysis. Certainly there are rules and principles of law, as there are rules and principles of biology or of architecture or of any other science or art. They occur whenever legal problems are under process of solution. We find statements of them in text-books and in judicial opinions and elsewhere. They are mental things. A rule of law is a generalized abstract comprehension of how courts would decide concrete questions within its scope. A principle of law is an abstract comprehension of considerations which would weigh with courts in the decision of questions to which it is applicable. Any one with sufficient knowledge and mental ability can construct a principle or a rule of law. Courts and legislatures have not a monopoly in producing them. There is nothing authoritative in the existence of a rule or a principle. Courts produce concrete legal consequences. Legislation guides courts through their construction of it to the decision of cases within its range. Anyone of sufficient intelligence may investigate the authorities, predict concerning potential legal consequences within selected limits, and make his own generalizations to carry his knowledge. If these generalizations accurately indicate potential legal effects within their scope, or comprehend accurately considerations which would be given weight by courts in the decision of cases, they are valid rules or principles of law.[25]

---

[24] For another reason judicial opinions are untrustworthy guides. They are not automatic expressions of the reasoning by which a decision was reached. Often they are subsequent and formal things devised to bear critical scrutiny. Sometimes they are rather elaborate justifications of the decisions than genuine records of the actuating courses of reasoning. Especially when this is the case, one cannot rely on the opinion to indicate correctly the considerations which produced the decision.

[25] One may, if he prefers, call any attempted generalization of law a rule or principle of law, regardless of its accuracy. Under such a method of applying the terms we would have accurate and inaccurate, or erroneous, rules and principles of law.

The mental forms in which the same sort of potent facts have been grasped and considered in previous judicial opinions need not be copied. Abstractly they are not of essential importance to the investigator. Nor is the manner of statement of rules and principles in judicial opinions logically of any binding force. Such generalizations, however they are evolved, may be stated in any language the speaker chooses without impairing their validity. The usual purpose of statement is facilitation of thinking, memory, and exposition. Accomplishment of this purpose justifies any particular statement. These matters of mental processes and of language are matters for free intelligent choice. The building and statement of legal rules and principles is not a prerogative of the judge or of the legislator, and such statements as are made in judicial opinions are as subject to criticism for inaccuracy and other defects as are those of other lawyers. Substantially the same considerations or other facts may be stated in various ways. Although the statement of a rule of law may differ from any ever made in court, its validity is not thereby affected. Its validity is to be tested by ascertaining whether it accurately indicates potential concrete decisions within its scope. Likewise the validity of a statement of a principle of law is to be tested only by ascertaining whether the substance of the considerations which it includes would weigh with the courts, not necessarily in the form which the statement communicates, but in any form.[26]

Now we are ready for some other technical meanings of the word "law." It is often used to indicate a correct legal generalization. We say of such a generalization "That is law" or "That is a law." We mean that it indicates what we are to expect of the operation of governmental machinery upon cases within its scope. When a generalization is referred to as "a law," the use is analogous to uses of the word in non-legal connections in the sense of a rule or mental guide.[27]

---

[26] I risk criticism for redundancy in this repetition because I deem it very important that these statements be comprehended. It is not unusual to hear one commend a summary of the law on a certain topic as concise, clear, comprehensive, and a trustworthy guide, and then voice the doubt that it constitutes a statement of the law because the courts have never analyzed the problems and expressed their conclusions in a similar manner. If judicial reasoning were always analytically comprehensive and sound, and the expression of judicial opinions was always an accurate and clear indication of the reasoning, there would be less practical cause for dwelling on these truths. The frequent errors in judicial generalization and the common defects of judicial expression make it extremely important to perceive that in conceiving and stating rules and principles and thus conversing concerning hypothetical questions other than the particular concrete case within its jurisdiction, the judges of a court are doing what any lawyer may do for himself and their product is not immune from criticism and is not necessarily dependable as rules or principles of law.

[27] Some probably will take issue with me on this definition of the word "law" and will insist that no generalization rightly can be called "law" in a legal sense unless

One further point concerning the word "law" may be noted in this connection. It is used to denote not only legal generalizations, but also their external expression. Mental operations and the signs and symbols through which they are communicated are obviously different sorts of things; but they are commonly associated in the mind and often are not distinguished in language. Thus we use the word "law" to denote both a legal generalization and the writing or speech which expresses it, often without noticing that they are essentially different things. Similar transferences of terms from one type of thing to a thing of a different but mentally related type are frequent. A rapid examination of almost any page of a dictionary will disclose instances.

Before considering the nature of the force which precedents have on judicial decisions and the reasons for its existence, I wish to interpolate the little that I have to say in this article concerning legislation. The phenomena of legislation are familiar to the lawyer. Legislation consists in formal action by an official or an official body resulting in authoritative expression concerning government. Courts regard such expression as a dictate binding upon their decisions. Therefore valid legislative expression is a causal factor of prime importance in determining the adjudication of a case within its scope, and is an element which must be given the most careful consideration in predicting potential governmental consequences. Legislation is effective only insofar as it is obeyed voluntarily or is sanctioned through other governmental operations. The existence and effective concrete purport of legislative expression, insofar as it concerns controversies coming under the jurisdiction of the courts, is determinable by them. Legislative expression often does not indicate clearly and certainly the intended effects upon concrete events. Not uncommonly it is very vague. Sometimes it amounts to only a bare

it is announced by a court or through legislation. Such an argument would concern merely the use of the word "law" and therefore would be one concerning language only, except insofar as it would imply that judicially announced generalizations—or such as are not obiter dicta—have authoritative force analogous to valid legislation or that such generalizations have a precedential force which non-official generalizations lack. My answer to the first of these possible implications is indicated in what I have said already. The implication is not true. I agree with the second implication, but I think it constitutes no logical reason for refusing to apply the term "law" to all correct legal generalizations. To confine the term in this sense to legislative and judicial generalizations only, does not tend to emphasize properly the precedential force of judicial generalizations and does tend to confuse the precedential force of judicial geenralizations with the authoritative force of legislation. Furthermore logically the word "law" can be applied to non-official legal generalizations and their expression and is so applied in ordinary usage. Its use in this sense is analogous to its use in phrases such as "the laws of chemistry." However, insofar as the objection is one of language only, it is hardly worth discussion beyond clarification of the fact that this is its nature.

declaration of general policy. Sometimes it is awkward, defective, or even misleading unless read in connection with legal history or other extrinsic facts. In short it may be expected to contain any of the common defects of written formal communication concerning abstract thinking. Therefore the task of construction thrown upon the courts by litigation is one which varies greatly in difficulty and in the latitude of discretionary judgment entailed. The courts have even refused at times to give a literal interpretation to a statute because to do so would bring results which they believed the legislature could not have intended. Therefore the determination of the exact bearing of a statute upon a case which a lawyer has under consideration is not to be reached by inspection and study of the language of the statute alone. One must always examine carefully whatever decisions there are construing the statutes, and determining its concrete effects on past cases. Often also one must consider carefully all other facts of legal history logically applicable to the problem of the detailed meaning of the statute.[28]

Legislation is a collateral causal phenomenon which affects the sequences of facts and their legal consequences within its interpreted scope. It affects them because courts adjudge that legislation and its expression is binding on them in deciding cases, and interpret and "apply" it accordingly. The fact of ultimate and direct practical importance is not the literal meaning of the words and phrases, but the causal effects on governmental sequences of external phenomena which it may have. Legislative expression affects such sequences in the same general manner as other external facts which may enter into the deliberations of a court; but it differs from other such facts in the compelling authoritative force which it normally possesses.

Another variant legal use of the word "law" should be noted. Official legislative expression is called "law" or "a law." Also the non-official repetition of such expression may be called "law" or "a law." These uses of the word are similar to its use to denote the expression of non-legislative rules of law; but the things denoted by the use which I am discussing now, differ from judicial expression, its non-official repetition, and the expression of non-official generalizations in that legislative expression has peculiar authoritative force, and this dictatorial force gives an additional justification to the application of the term "law," because it brings into play its latent connotation of command.

[To be continued.]

JOSEPH W. BINGHAM.

LELAND STANFORD JR. UNIVERSITY.

[28] See Austin's Jurisprudence, Vol. II, pp. 989-1001.

WHAT IS THE LAW?

II

I shall now discuss briefly the nature of the causal effects of precedents upon judicial decisions and the justifications for those effects. One frequently hears laymen scoffing at the respect which courts pay to precedents and sometimes displaying a lamentable ignorance both of the nature of the influence which precedents have on the law and of the reasons for the existence of that influence. The influence of past example on human action pervades all human conduct and endeavor at all times. That influence is fundamental. It occurs through instinctive as well as intelligent processes and sometimes runs to unreasonable extents. This sort of influence, then, is not peculiar to the field of law. Men in business, in social matters, in religion, in scientific pursuits, and in play, follow precedents and learn from precedents. Progress would not continue and human life could not long exist if it were not for the influence which precedent has on thought and instinctive action.

Comprehending these facts, let us observe some of the reasons for the influence which precedent has had and does have on the decisions of our courts. Conservatism—human inertia against change —is one cause of this influence, but a cause which has a diminishing potency as the progress of civilization and knowledge goes on. Today its causal effects on judicial decisions, independently of political theory and the other causes of the influence of precedent, is not greater than on other governmental functions.

When I made an exception of political theory in the preceding paragraph, I had in mind the vague tradition that courts should not break from long and firmly established main courses of decision even to improve the law.[29] Political and philosophical history has induced the wide spread political theory that this sort of work is legislative and the courts have followed the theory although it has hampered progress. On some occasions judges have held themselves bound by its dictates when judicial wisdom and courage would have justified the initiation of needed partial reforms. A full discussion of the historical reasons for this conservative clog on progressive rectification of the law through judicial initiative would require far more time, study, and space than the design of this article permits. I therefore merely indicate it as one phase of the potency which our

[29] I use the phrase "the law" in the sense of sequences of external facts and their concrete legal consequences through the concrete operation of governmental machinery.

courts give to precedents. It is the only common phase logically open to criticism.[30]

The other reasons for the influence of precedents on judicial decisions appeal directly to logic. Knowledge that a particular sort of problem has been solved in a certain way by a court in the past or that facts of a particular sort have been given an ascertained weight in its solution has a natural influence with judges who have a similar problem before them. Not only is this an example to be carefully studied by the judges as offering a possible solution, but the fact that such a solution has been made by others throws some weight in favor of a similar decision. Judges would be extraordinary human beings if they were not influenced to some extent by the expert previous opinions of others who have faced like problems. In this phase, a precedent is of weight whether it is a decision by a court of the same jurisdiction or not. Its force should logically depend on the known ability of the judges who rendered it.

Another and stronger logical justification for the influence of precedents on judicial decisions is that the time of a court would not be used economically if questions like ones which have been decided by it before could be litigated in indefinite number and in full detail without final settlement of the law through the accumulation of previous decisions. Furthermore, although litigation is necessary, it is a drain economically on the parties and, through the use of the courts and other governmental agencies and indirectly in other ways, on the community. If precedents were not given great weight, encouragement to litigate questions of law would be afforded where now discouragement exists because of opposing precedents. As long as the law is unsettled, litigation will not diminish. For these reasons it is sound policy for a court to treat its previous decisions as controlling unless some stronger argument of justice or policy overweighs. The following associated reason is also potent. It is one of the great advantages of civilized judicial administration that people know what to expect from governmental action because of different sorts of conduct. If precedents on common law points and the construction of legislation were not followed, the certainty of predictions of potential concrete decisions of our courts would be greatly diminished. This last consideration varies in logical force with the nature of the problem involved. It is particularly strong in connection with points of property law and commercial law. Titles to

[30] Lord Mansfield's attempts to subvert the theory in practice are familiar to students of the history of our law. In spite of the prevalence of the theory, a vast amount of change and amelioration of the law has been accomplished by the courts—often by the use of legal fictions, and more especially through the extension and influence of equitable jurisdiction and principles. See Maine's Ancient Law, Chapters 2 and 3.

property should be reasonably certain and it should be possible to proceed in commercial matters with assurance concerning legal rights and duties. On some sorts of legal questions, however, this consideration has little logical force. Whenever the problem is such that the certainty of prediction of the potential legal consequences would rarely or never affect or facilitate human conduct, it has slight or no logical weight.

It is difficult to generalize satisfactorily concerning the exact measure of the influence which precedents exert on judicial decisions.[31] That influence varies with the intelligence, intellectual independence, and mental tendencies of the judges, with the nature of the problem before the court, with the clearness and the pertinency of the precedents considered, with the jurisdiction of the courts which rendered them and the legal reputations of their judges, with the repeated accumulated weight of the precedents, with the cogency of the opinions of the judges in the cases used as precedents, and with other matters which might be noticed and catalogued. It was not within my purposes to undertake any such task, but only to call to your attention that precedents individually are not authoritatively compelling on the deliberations of courts as is legislative expression and that they are so collectively only insofar as a somewhat vague political theory concerning the boundaries of legislative and judicial functions make them so. In order to do this, I mentioned the well known facts that courts do not always follow precedents even in their

[31] The antithesis of decision and obiter dictum in legal discussion often puzzles students. An irrelevant remark is easily distinguished from the pertinent reasoning of the opinion in a case, but some of the pertinent judicial generalizations may be limited in later cases and the rejected purport may be classed with obiter dicta. Here we meet again the common linguistic phenomena of ill-defined and shifting usage. The matter is sometimes anxiously argued as though it were of fundamental importance. As a matter of fact it is not. The question which a court faces in dealing with past cases is simply: "What force shall we give this precedent," whether the precedent is the concrete adjudication of a previous case, the ratio decidendi of that adjudication, or some of the broader general expressions of the opinion. A concrete adjudication in point is certainly a more weighty thing to consider than expressions of reasoning in the opinion. On the other hand it may be overruled. The ratio decidendi may be criticised and discarded. Irrelevant obiter dicta generally are not given much weight; but, on the other hand, a well conceived and well expressed generalization, although it was wholly aside from the questions litigated in the case in which it appears, sometimes has been of great influence in the decision of a later case. The exposition of a text writer frequently has a similar precedential force. In short, the problem of the lawyer in dealing with precedents as "authorities" is to determine accurately their potential argumentative influence, and this question can not be helped by a bare division of judicial expression into "obiter dicta" on the one side and "rationes decidendi" on the other, however these terms may be defined. The following matters are of great value in the solution of his problem: an analysis of the bare concrete facts, the questions litigated, the decisions of them, and the adjudication in a concrete case; a determination of the causative importance of the formal reasoning expressed in the opinion; and a critical examination of the inherent cogency of any particular expression concerning the law.

own jurisdictions and sometimes overrule a long line of decisions, and I have just finished indicating the reasons for the force given to precedents by the courts. I desire only to reiterate one more fact in this connection. Judicial reasoning in a previous case, insofar as it can be ascertained, has a precedential force similar to that of a concrete adjudication in point; but its force logically is not as great. Even when a previous decision in point is squarely based upon the statement of a rule or principle in the reported opinion, the generalization indicated by the statement may be criticised as erroneous and amended or entirely discarded. A generalization which has been repeated in many opinions finally may be discredited.[32]

[32] There is little need to contend with intelligent lawyers that judges do and must make law in the sense of determining by juridical processes other than interpretation of previous expressions, the governmental results of concrete events. Even the theorists who adhere to the Blackstonian description of law with variations admit that the law changes and grows under the multiplication of judicial decisions. Some even assert that judges "legislate"—a use of language which implies obscuration of the essential difference between ordinary legislation and the administration of justice between parties. (See: Maine's Ancient Law, 4th Am. Ed., pp. 24-32; note by Pollock idem p. 395; Austin's Jurisprudence, Vol. II, pp. 620-639, and Vol. I, pp. 218-219, Lecture 37 and note to Lecture 5; Holmes' The Common Law, pp. 35-36; Holland on Jurisprudence (10th ed.), pp. 62-67.)

It also should be clear to the trained lawyer that judicial generalizations are not inherently dependable, for the reasons which I indicate in the principal text. If a doubter with clarity of vision makes a careful historical study of the decisions on almost any topic he will be convinced of the fact. (Austin's Jurisprudence, Vol. II, pp. 655-658, Lecture 39.) There are many expressions of generalizations in judicial opinions which are admirable indications of the law. The analyses, the comprehension of related questions and considerations, and the statements are adequate. They are reliable, however, not because they have been judicially announced, but because they will stand the test of use. "In fine," says Austin in the passage cited above, "we can never be absolutely certain (so far as I know) that any judiciary rule is good or valid law, and will certainly be followed by future judges in cases resembling the case by which it has been introduced. Here then is a cause of uncertainty which seems to be of the essence of judiciary law. For I am not aware of any contrivance by which the inconvenience could be obviated."

Undoubtedly judicial decisions make law and their multiplication tends to simplify the prediction of potential adjudications and the definite and certain generalization of the results; but a court has no legislative power to enact expression which is binding in other litigation. Its essential juridical function is to hear, supervise, and determine particular concrete controversies brought within its jurisdiction. (Compare Austin's Jurisprudence, Vol. II, pp. 621, Lecture 37.)

One has only to recall to mind the history of the decisions concerning the rule against perpetuities, liability for consequences of a legal default, trade and labor contests, contractual consideration, riparian rights, percolating waters, or appropriation of water in the western states and a sane, unbiased judgment will assure him that courts develop and settle the law by the slow process of reasoning out determinations of successive concrete decisions and not by promulgation of broad generalizations. (Austin's Jurisprudence, Vol. II, pp. 620-639, 657-658, Lectures 37 and 39; Sir Samuel Romilly on Codification, 29 Edinburgh Review, p. 331; See also Excursus by W. Jethro Brown in "The Austinian Theory of Law," p. 288. They do not dismiss cases because they can find no previously announced rule or principle to apply nor even because they cannot devise a satisfactory rule. Sometimes judges confess their inability to generalize certainly beyond the settlement of the particular case under consideration. Frequently their rules are tentative, or are negatived by the course of later decisions, or are vague and indefinite. Over the devising of methods of adequately generalizing the law on some topics, jurists are still puzzled. For instance who will undertake to point out anywhere the expression of a system of accurate, definite, usable rules indicating the limitations set by the courts on liability for consequences of legal defaults? Certainly the make-shift broad generalities of the judges on this abstract question are not illuminating or dependable. Yet most of the cases are well determined and there is no extraordinary conflict or incoherency in the mass of concrete adjudications.

However, there is quite a strong political and academic prejudice against admitting that judges are or should be free in their law-making work, except insofar as legislation and the sound traditions and training of their profession control their reasoning. The theory of the threefold division of the powers of government in the fanciful form which allots to the legislature exclusively the power of making new authoritative governmental expression, to the courts only the power of determining and interpreting valid governmental expression, and to the executive the power of enforcing "the law," has emphasized and fortified this prejudice. It finds voice in the familiar dogma that a government should be one of laws and not of men. At its foundation lies, I believe, ignorance of the proper function of courts, of the nature, use, and difficulties of generalization, and of the limits of efficient abstraction and expression.

A government is necessarily composed of the concrete actions and conduct of men. Laws are only mental processes. Judges may follow precedent, tradition, legislation, custom, public opinion, their ideas of justice, or other considerations; but as long as courts are invested with the power to determine finally the disposition of cases within their jurisdictions, the judge's reasoning will determine the decisions and we cannot hope to devise a system of expressed rules and principles which will make this reasoning perfunctory and mechanical. (See 6 Har. Law Rev., pp. 32-33.) The infinite variety of circumstance and the continual readjustments of the forces and conditions of social life and of the particular purposes and ideals of its members discourage such a hope. No code has been devised which would dispense entirely with judicial discretion and turn the judge into an interpreter only. (Even Austin in his elaborate argument for codification admits this. See Jurisprudence, Vol. II, pp. 663-665, Lecture 39.)

Furthermore to require judicial reasoning to proceed always within the confines of promulgated rules and principles, will not prevent individual bias from affecting a decision. It could be demonstrated that judges are able to manipulate generalized expressions to suit their preferences as easily as they could plausibly justify the same decision by free reasoning. Indeed previous judicial and legislative expression may be misused as a plausible mask to conceal the real motives or the incapacity of the judge. On the other hand, if the judge and the people realize that within the barriers set by legislation he is law maker and not merely law interpreter, there is forced upon him the full dignity and the full responsibility of his position. No longer can he safely shirk. No longer can he hide incapacity behind the printed rules in the book upon which he uncertainly leans. He must justify his decision on grounds that appeal to the enlightened opinion of his profession or suffer criticism. He cannot shift the blame to the past utterance of fallacious generalities. He is not arbitrary because he must be reasonable or fail, and he will be directed by his training, and the ideals and traditions of his profession. Austin has well answered the usual distrustful objections to what he calls "judicial legislation" in Lecture 38 of his work on Jurisprudence, Vol. II, pp. 641-647.

Inconsistently with the prejudice of which I have spoken, society is demanding with increasing persistence and occasional scornful opprobrium that the legal profession exert its influence and energies for the betterment of the law and particularly that the judges adopt a theory and an attitude which will augment instead of retard its development to meet the changing demands of our social and economic organization. Easy as it is for the unintelligent and unprogressive minds of the profession to recline on the venerable fiction that judicial functions do not include innovation, but only determination, interpretation, and application of pre-existing rules and principles, neither the bar nor the bench can weather the rising storm on such a fragile raft. Courts cannot avoid making law in deciding cases. The people demand of them justice in litigation and they will blame the courts as the proximate cause if injustice is frequently meted out. If the unjust

If what I said concerning the authoritative force of judicial generalizations and the expression of them is comprehended it will become clear that abstract definitions of legal terms by judges are not of authoritative force. Definitions concern only the meanings of language. The definition given a word by a judge in his opinion tends to show the sense in which he uses it or in which he understands others to use it; and the definition is of force only for the purpose of interpreting what the author says and understanding his point of view. Sometimes the definition fails even to communicate accurately the author's use of a term. The denotations of some important common legal ideas are vaguely comprehended by most judges and lawyers and therefore their use of the terms employed to indicate these ideas are defined by them erroneously. In all cases any lawyer may define legal terms as he pleases for his purposes. As long as he makes himself easily, correctly, and economically understood in his use of them he is subject to no logical linguistic criticism. The usage of judges influences the common and accepted uses of words; but neither judges nor courts have any inherent authority over the abstract definition of legal terms. It may serve to obviate delay in the full acceptance of this statement to say that I do not intend to comprehend in it those processes of interpretive definition which judges undertake in order to pass upon the legal effects of a written instrument or of legislative expression involved in a suit before them.

Definitions of legal terms expressed through legislation are authoritative only insofar as it is expressed or implied that they are to be taken as guides in interpreting legislative expression or other external communication. The bare definition of a legal term by legislation without some such further provision expressed or implied, is of no inherent force.

There may be some who will contend against me that "the law" consists not of actual and potential governmental sequences nor of past judicial generalizations concerning such sequences, but of the accurate generalizations which may be induced to comprehend these sequences and therefore of rules and principles of law.[33] This

---

decisions cannot clearly be attributed to legislation, the censure of the people will not easily be escaped. The people are not interested in precedent. They have lost their primitive reverence for it. They are interested in justice, and a dogmatic adjudication that "this is the law as settled by precedent" will not tend to counteract a fast developing prejudice to judges as a class of public servants and to courts as institutions. Precedents have a logical limited weight as considerations in the administration of justice, but they should not be used to make or perpetuate bad law.

[33] "Judiciary law consists of rules, or it is merely a heap of particular decisions inapplicable to the solution of future cases. On the last supposition, it is not law at all: And the judges who apply decided cases to the resolution of other cases, are not resolving the latter by any determinate law, but are deciding them arbitrarily"—Austin's Jurisprudence, Vol. II, p. 664, Lecture 39.

definition of the phrase conveniently may be regarded as an amendment of Austin's probable conception of the subject matter of judiciary law. I think that approximately Austin's subject matter of judiciary law would include only actual and potential generalizations of past cases and the considerations exclusive of legislation which produced them.

I at once agree that "the law" in the sense of the *science of law* largely will consist of accurate rules and principles concerning actual and potential concrete governmental sequences that that science or any part of it legitimately may be called "the law" abbreviately. I emphasize, however, the following facts.

1. The term so used does not denote the field of the lawyer's profession, but systematized *knowledge concerning that field.* The term is thus used in an additional distinct sense to denote an indefinite totality of systematized actual and potential knowledge or a part of that totality.

2. "The law" in this sense does not exist actually except insofar as systematized accurate knowledge of law is existing presently in the minds of persons. It "exists" potentially, however,—i. e. fictitiously—insofar as there is a possibility of minds entertaining such knowledge.

3. Much of the field of our profession never has been comprehended thoroughly in accurate rules and principles. Indeed it is a

I doubt that Austin meant by this passage that a judicial decision which is not based on a comprehended rule is arbitrary. (See note 23 supra.) Probably he meant only that decisions which cannot be brought into accord with rules obtained by induction are arbitrary. Seldon's often quoted dictum concerning equity and the chancellor's foot exhibits more augmentative cleverness than sound judgment. A decision may be based upon particular facts in the case without the formation or use of formal broad rules and will not be arbitrary if the judge is guided by balancing these particular considerations without prejudice or bias. Austin in Lecture 38, Jurisprudence, Vol. II, pp. 641-647 states some reasons why we need not fear arbitrariness in a judge's decisions although admittedly he "legislates" with some freedom. Austin's theory of the nature of "judiciary law" seems to be as follows: Judicial generalities are not safe guides. They may not be followed in decisions. Law, however, cannot consist of a mass of concrete decisions. Such a mass could not be law by hypothesis, since "law" is definable properly as something general. Therefore judiciary as well as statutory law must consist of rules or the decisions are arbitrary. The rules of which judiciary law is composed are not necessarily expressed in opinions, but are those which may be extracted by comparison of the decisions and their rationes decidendi. (See Jurisprudence, Vol. II, pp. 663-666; 620 639.)

The common view that the law is something general doubtlessly is colored by the facts that "laws" of any sort are general rules, that order, which the law connotes, is ordinarily associated with system and therefore abstract and general ideas, that legislative expression, to which modern minds independently of legal training instinctively turn as a familiar and normal type of "a law," is usually general in terms, and that it is natural to jump to the conclusion that "the law" is simply a name for the totality of a mass of "laws." If we had had two different terms to denote "the law" and "a law" or rule of law, such as "jus" and "lex" of Roman jurisprudence, the misleading influence of language might have been obviated; but there are other co-operating causes of the common confusion which probably suffice to produce it. These causes are familiar to intelligent students of the history of law, government, and philosophy.

useful hyperbole to say that only a relatively small fragment of it has been. In other words, the science of our law is still undeveloped.

4. "The law" in this sense has no authoritative form and there is no exclusive authoritative mode of expressing it. It may vary in mental forms within the bounds of flexibility of accurate human abstract thinking and its accurate expression may vary within the bounds of possible methods of accurate communication.

5. The expression of judicial generalizations is not necessarily an accurate indication of such knowledge and is not authoritative for reasons stated in this article.

Valid legislative expression is authoritative in the sense that courts and other governmental agencies are constrained to construe and give effect to it, but it is not independently an authoritative or necessarily accurate expression of those effects. They may be generalized into any accurate efficient forms and expressed in any accurate and efficient manner and the results will compose part of the science of law and its expression.

Briefly, thinking and communication in the field of law should be as free of artificial fetters as are the thinking and communication concerning any field of thought.

Among other things external to the official machinery of government which have an elemental force in the determination of law—that is in the determination of what concrete legal sequences follow from concrete causal conduct and conditions—custom has a prominent place. A custom consists of similar habitual sequences of occurrences external to the mind of the observer. It is not a formal authoritative thing like legislation. Its existence is not a part of organized government unless it is a governmental custom. It may affect legal sequences, however, in the same general way as legislation. It affects lawyers' problems because its existence induces a consideration which will weigh, and weigh heavily, in the deliberations of courts in cases upon which it has a relevant bearing. The potency of its influence is illustrative of a fundamental principle of good government:—that when no stronger considerations conflict, the wheels of society should not be forced from a smoothly worn groove. In earlier stages of society custom has an almost tyrannical force in government. The opposition to innovation grows varyingly less as civilization and wide spread intelligence increase, and therefore the coercive unreasoning force of custom in moulding the law tends to disappear. But custom and usage, within reasonable limits, are of great social utility in all ages, and therefore they will always continue to have an influence within limits which appeal to intelligent ideas of justice and governmental policy. Often positive injustice would be done if courts did not consider customs or usages in deciding cases. Wherever customary ways of settling legal disputes out of court have been adopted by courts, we have a phenomenon which is closely related to the act of a court in following precedents.

It is not unusual to hear a certain custom spoken of not merely as a source of law, but as "the law." The explanation of this distinct application of the term is that the custom is a controlling consideration with the courts and therefore knowledge of the custom will enable us to predict future decisions within the scope of its influence. The custom guides the courts and guides us to foretell their action. For this reason it is labeled "law." In this respect this use of the word is similar to its use to designate rules of law. The two sorts of things indicated by these two uses are very different, however. A rule of law is a mental tool. Customs are similar habitual sequences of occurrences external to the mind of him who observes them and incapable of being entertained by his mind. They include mental operations of those who participate in the customary events, of course; but these mental operations are not part of the observer's process of deciding a legal problem. The custom guides directly through the judge giving weight to it as a controlling consideration and through our knowledge that he will do so. A rule of law guides through its use as an aid in thinking. This use of the word law must therefore be distinguished from the others which we have noticed.[34]

[34] See, however, and cf: Austin's Jurisprudence, Vol. I, p. 199; See also: Holland on Jurisprudence (10th ed.), pp. 54-61.

Another technical use of the word "law" should be perceived. I have noted its distinct uses to indicate the field of our professional study or a part thereof, a totality of thorough knowledge, actual and potential, of that field or a part of such a totality, a legal generalization, expression of such a generalization, legislative expression, its reiteration, and any custom which is potent as a consideration in the determination of cases. This other meaning sometimes attaches to the word in the antithetic phrases "questions of law" and "questions of fact."

If these phrases always had been used with comprehension and care, the division between the sorts of things denoted by them would be indicated by the following statement:

Questions which arise for solution by courts in litigation may be divided roughly into three general sorts. The first sort includes questions of what facts logically relevant to the litigation have occurred in the past and exist in the present and what pertinent consequences may be expected to flow from them in the future. The second sort includes questions of what concrete determinations concerning governmental consequences shall be made, and the weight and bearing of different considerations in the process of determination. The third sort includes questions concerning what procedure and routine shall be followed in the course of conducting the process of litigation before the court. The decision of questions of all three sorts is accomplished by human reasoning and therefore ordinarily through the use of abstractions and generalizations. Also the generalizations used with respect to a question of any of these sorts may or may not be of stereotyped, frequently used, and precedentially endorsed models. A clear and important technical distinction would be indicated by applying the phrase "questions of law" only to questions of the second and third sorts and the phrase "questions of fact" (and impliedly "but not of law") to questions of the first sort. Questions of the second and third sorts concern the concrete purposes, policies, procedure, and juridical actions of the governmental law determining bodies. Questions of the first sort ask the ascertainment, conjecture, prediction, or assumption of some of those facts which are deemed necessary by the court as a prerequisite to a satisfactory determination of questions of the second and third classes.

Although the use of these terms is a mere matter of language, the use often is associated with a need for discriminating carefully between these different sorts of things and a loose, unconsidered usage tends naturally to obscure proper distinctions and to emphasize immaterial ones. It is unfortunate, therefore, that usage has not always been guided by clear and comprehensive analysis. Sometimes it has been influenced by an idea that only questions resolvable by an authoritative legal generalization are properly called "questions of law." See Salmond Jurisprudence, 2nd ed., pp. 9-22, and compare Austin's Jurisprudence, Vol. II, p. 664. Sometimes the historical division of the functions of judge and jury in actions at common law has befogged the usage, and questions to be settled by the judge, of whatever nature, have been denominated "questions of law," and questions which are submitted to the jury, of whatever nature, "questions of fact."

Professor J. B. Thayer, in his "A Preliminary Treatise on Evidence at the Common Law," Chapter V, instructively treats of this vague and confusing use of the word "law." One cannot read comprehendingly any of the writings of this master scholar and analyst without admiration for his clearness of discrimination and exposition. I would venture less confidently to differ from him with regard to his restricted use of the word "law" in its legal sense and the implied conception of the nature of the subject matter of legal study, if he had ever made a thorough, independent analysis of the problem of which this article treats, similar to his studies of topics of the law of evidence. He makes no pretense to such an analysis in the chapter to which I have referred, but takes for granted a partial definition of the word for the purpose of discussing the particular topic of the chapter.

No doubt judges often have endorsed by their language the common theory that the law is a mass of generalities, just as they have endorsed the more discredited but still vigorous superstition that judges only interpret law. The course of their decisions, however, will support neither theory. Difficult debatable questions of the concrete detailed definition of particular rights, duties, liberties, and powers often are determined by judges instead of being submitted to the triers of fact although no definite rule is available for decision of them. For instance questions of "legal causation"—the delimitation of the scope of legal liability—are generally so decided whenever there is no preliminary "question of fact" of my first class to be settled.

Questions of "reasonable use," of "legal negligence," and many others on which it is impossible to generalize definitely and expeditiously, involve "questions of law" according to my indicated definition of those words. Whenever all such "questions of law" are clearly predetermined abstractly by the judges and are stated in definite generalizations, leaving nothing to be done by the jury except an ascertainment of facts of the first of my sorts and a non-discretionary comparison with the definite generalizations communicated to them by the judges, the judgment of the jury is confined to "questions of fact" of my first sort; but whenever a "rule" is indicated to the jury which is not comprehensive and definite for the purposes of their work—such, for instance as the familiar "rules" of "reasonable use," "reasonable time," "natural and proximate cause,"—and the deficiency in detailed definiteness is not otherwise supplied, the jury is left to decide substantial "questions of law" of the second of my sorts. They do not simply interpret language and use the resulting definite guides, but necessarily they exercise judicial discretion, and either reason out their answers as do judges when some vague legislative expression is being "construed" and "applied," or grope their way with less understanding to a result. See also a note discussing this matter partially and in somewhat fictional language in 9 Col. Law Rev. at p. 154.

I have not attempted to catalogue all the technical meanings of this much discussed word. The variations which I have indicated, should satisfy my readers, however, of the error of attempting a universal technical definition or of basing a theory of law on

This finishes the partial outline of the field of our law which I purposed to present. I do not intend it as a comprehensive catalogue of the features of the field nor as an adequate description of any of them. My purpose has been only to give a point of view and to clarify certain realities and distinctions which I usually have found blurred in the minds of my students and of others with whom I have conversed on legal topics or whose writings I have read. Blurring of this sort is prejudicial to clear thinking on complicated problems of law, and hinders progress towards betterment of our jurisprudence.

A movement which portends changes in our administration of justice is gathering momentum all over the country. If this movement is to be directed and controlled towards true and permanent progress, the work must not be attacked in ignorance of the machinery and forces with which we are dealing; and if accomplishment is to satisfy our needs, the work should be done under the leadership of men who realize that the law is not an easy field of endeavor, and that desirable results cannot be won by the untrained. There is no more dangerous fallacy rampant in the popular mind than that the law is complex unnecessarily and that if it were not for lawyers, legal controversies might be determined easily, speedily, and justly. No art is more difficult than the art of good government and at the foundation of permanent good government must be laid the unavoidably difficult and intricate science of the law.[35] If those who realize this are to lead, it is necessary that they clear their minds of befogging superstitions, mystifying dogmas, and the treadmills of inadequate generalities and sophistical reasoning. They should direct their lawmaking efforts by comprehension of the purposes of good government, the needs of our people, and the experience of the past,[36] and should not be divorced from these guides by

---

such an attempt. When we consider that the forms and the substance of government have varied completely in different stages of human civilization, the fallacy of the definition theorists becomes even more emphasized. (Maine's Ancient Law, Pollock's ed., pp. 1-19; 389-394.)

[35] "I am far from thinking, that the law can ever be so condensed and simplified, that any considerable portion of the community may know the whole or much of it." Austin's Jurisprudence, Vol. II, p. 653, Lecture 39. This quotation is from the works of an ardent advocate of codification.

"It is not possible, indeed, for any fully developed body of law to be such that he who runs may read it. Being, as it is, the reflection within courts of justice of the complex facts of civilized existence, a very considerable degree of elaboration is inevitable." Salmond, Jurisprudence, 2nd ed., p. 25.

"* * * for I am fully convinced that only from enlightened and experienced lawyers is any substantial improvement of the law to be hoped for" * * *. Austin's Jurisprudence, Vol. II, p. 681 (Lecture 39).

[36] "On the other hand, the conception of law as a means towards social ends, the doctrine that law exists to secure interests, social, public, and private, requires the jurist

a narrow interpretation of the learning of the books, heedlessness of popular judgment, or absorption in their private practices and pursuits. Progress in law reform is the work of the intelligent lawyer. If he shirks it, others will perform it less aptly and effectually. If he turns to it an open, inquiring mind and seeks the scientific thoroughness for which there is crying need, he will perform a great public service and rehabilitate his profession in the esteem of the people from which it is rapidly being divorced.[37]

Therefore I make this plea for greater emphasis on the thorough study of concrete facts of government, their causes, and their concrete effects and for subordination of generalization, definition, and verbal expression to their proper purposes. Widespread adequate understanding of the facts over which my argument has run would produce an increase in the efficiency of our legal education, a better comprehension of the high functions of the judicial office, and a consequent improvement of the administration of justice through more

to keep in touch with life. Wholly abstract considerations do not suffice to justify legal rules under such a theory. The function of legal history comes to be one of illustrating how rules and principles have met concrete situations in the past and of enabling us to judge how we may deal with such situations in the present, rather than one of furnishing self-sufficient premises from which rules are to be obtained by rigid deduction." Professor Roscoe Pound, 25 Harvard Law Rev., 146-147.

"* * * The lawyer who wishes to forecast the judicial interpretation of any problem that is not already covered by precise rule will be the more capable of doing so if he has learned to regard law, not as something existing in complete detachment from life, or as a mere beau chef d'oeuvre de logique, but rather as something which is being constantly reshaped by the facts of life, the thought and aspiration of men." * * * "The Austinian Theory of Law," W. Jethro Brown, pp. 376-377.

[37] To those who would raise the cry of "chaos" or "case-lawyer" or "judicial legislation" in protest against my theory I recommend careful cogitation over the following quotations:

"When we have escaped from the tyranny of mere forms, and have overcome the superstition that we must not regard things in their totality, when we have learned that, on the contrary, it is only when we so regard them we can hope to comprehend them, we shall find some place in legal theory for ideas which have already profoundly affected less conservative branches of learning. * * * It has been said of a great scientist that he closed the door of his laboratory before he entered the door of his church. The attitude is suggestive of the provisional order of things, since a theological theory which will not somehow square with the laboratory can afford no resting-place. Similarly a lawyer who leaves what he has learned from history and science behind him when he opens his Law Reports is merely postponing a difficulty. That difficulty will have to be met somehow. When it has been met, legal theory will not be the less, but the more, worthy of his homage." W. Jethro Brown, "The Austinian Theory of Law," p. 287.

"I by no means disapprove of what Mr. Bentham has chosen to call by the disrespectful, and therefore, as I conceive, injudicious, name of judge-made law. For I consider it injudicious to call by any name indicative of disrespect what appears to me highly beneficial and even absolutely necessary. I cannot understand how any person who has considered the subject can suppose that society could possibly have gone on if judges had not legislated, or that there is any danger whatever in allowing them that power which they have in fact exercised, to make up for the negligence or the incapacity of the avowed legislator. That part of the law of every country which was made by judges has been far better made than that part which consists of statutes enacted by the legislature." Austin's Jurisprudence, Vol. I, pp. 218-219.

uniformly enlightened and progressive decisions and careful, scientific legislation.[38]

JOSEPH W. BINGHAM.

LELAND STANFORD JR. UNIVERSITY.

---

[38] One cannot go far in a discussion of the law without meeting the terms "right" and "duty." I have avoided them in this article partly because I wished to free the tenor of my argument from as many bye topics as possible, and partly because of the exigency of space. An exposition of some of the things commonly denoted by these terms in legal communication may be of interest to those who desire some further indication of my analysis of the law, however. Therefore I shall append a supplementary note covering the topic "The Nature of Legal Rights, Liberties, Duties, and Powers," which will appear in a later number of this Review.

At the beginning of an article which I contributed to the Columbia Law Review almost three years ago ("Some Suggestions Concerning Legal Cause at Common Law," 9 Col. Law Rev., 16, at pp. 17-23), I gave a very brief indication in nearly orthodox and figurative language of some of the principal views of the law which I have tried to explain in this article. My purpose was to clear the minds of my readers for my main theme by emphasizing three facts: (1) that the law does not consist of generalizations, (2) that rules and principles of law are only mental tools used in discussing and deciding legal problems, and (3) that sequences of legal phenomena are always concrete. I did not wish to weary my readers before we reached the main subject of that article by a thorough discussion of my theories nor to shock them into opposition by an abrupt and not fully explained departure from the ordinary views and language. I therefore adopted as far as was consistent with my purpose the common phraseology, and stated that "the law consists of concrete governmental dictates." This language is figurative. If it is interpreted literally, it is open to the same objections as validly may be advanced against the Austinian theory of law with the exception that I denied the general nature of the dictates. What I meant by the figurative language was that sequences of legal phenomena are necessarily concrete. If we figuratively conceive of law as consisting of commands, therefore, to make our fictitious conception of law tally with the truth, we must make the fictitious dictates concrete and detailed for all the situations requiring them as they arise. Valid legal generalizations of all sorts we may then regard as abstract indicatory guides to these fictitious concrete dictates which compose the law. If any of my readers find themselves unable to consent to my views as announced in this article because of a predilection for the Austinian theory of law, I commend to them the attempted adaptation of my views to that theory which I advanced in the article cited above. It will at least save him from the confusing error of conceiving of the law as a system of rules and principles.

This article has been written for common lawyers and the emphases and distinctions have been calculated for the needs of those who are professionally interested in the system of jurisprudence which prevails in most English speaking parts of the world. I do not feel competent to analyze and discuss fields of law in other countries even as sketchily and partially as I have our own. Some things, however, I can say with confidence on the basis of the slight knowledge which I have:

The matter of use of the word law in English or of partially analogous terms in other tongues is one only of language. The uses of these partially analogous words in other languages are not individually co-extensive with the legal uses of our word law, and to force any partially analogous words in different languages into exactly co-extensive meanings will necessarily result in arbitrary and useless definitions. Things of the nature of the different elements which I have described as existing in our field of law will be found under all advanced systems of law. My scheme of analysis with adaptations will answer for all such systems. We may find, however, for instance, that the courts of some countries do not weigh preceding cases as heavily as do ours or do not weigh them at all theoretically, and that they give to certain private texts a greater authority than is given by our courts to any similar writings. These facts, however, do not alter the nature of the things which I have mentioned, and my analysis in this respect could be copied in describing these other systems.

[8]

A RETURN TO STARE DECISIS

We Are Well on Our Way Toward a Shift from Following Decisions to Following Principles and This Shift Has Far-Reaching and Important Consequences for Art of Judicial Government and Science of Law—First Meaning of Stare Decisis—How Retreat Began and What Was Lost By It in Fields of Government and Legal Scholarship—How to Regain Lost Ground*

By HERMAN OLIPHANT

Professor of Law, Columbia University; President, 1927, Association of American Law Schools

Introduction

THE practice of those who have preceded me at this post and your tolerance as auditors seem to have fastened upon you the annual duty of listening, with such patience as you can command, to some remarks by the president. Thus entrenched, I speak.

A study of former presidential addresses discloses among many more important things, the interesting fact that the lot of them is divided, Gallic fashion, into three parts; those addresses which point with pride, those which view with alarm, and those offering a certain salvation.

And future presidents of this Association may well again and again point with pride to its accomplishment in the improvement of legal education and the elevation of the quality of the bar. The progress made has been substantial. Repeated reviews of it cannot minimize its extent. They are always a source of zeal for new effort and at times a merited comfort when plans fail.

Presidential addresses which have viewed with alarm have been numerous and this for the encouraging reason that members of the Association have been constantly restive under the short-comings they have found in law schools and law practice, an impatience with short-comings motivating such progress as we have already made. The present faults in our work, corrected tomorrow, will be followed by those of another day considered equally grave. We may as confidently expect as we do earnestly hope that critics shall be with us, perennial as the poor.

Plans for improvement in legal education, varying widely in ambition and utility, have been laid before you in presidential addresses of the past. More are to come. The innovation of today becomes the anachronism of tomorrow and the end is not yet.

This part which you have given me the honor to play in this performance seems to admit of no other lines. You are doomed to be praised, scolded, or advised, world without end. All this being so, it is not easy to find in the fields of the immediate interests of this group unthreshed straw which promises much grain. Hence I venture to look a bit more widely.

A number of current happenings show that some very fundamental changes in things legal may be in the making. Renewed popular criticisms of the law and its administration, the multiplication of legislation, the truly impressive movement to restate the law, and reports of experiments in legal education suggest at least the possibility that these and other things are merely the minor movements of parts of a whole army on the march. If so, it is worth while to neglect for a moment matters of tactics in legal education and to consider some phase of the broad strategy which may be shaping all of these movements seemingly so diverse. Let me anticipate criticism for attempting anything so ambitious by reminding you that it is at least the privilege though not the duty of any petty officer concerned with such prosy business as finding billets for a company to speculate at times about the possible plans and purposes of headquarters.

This Association of law teachers, students, and writers, as a group, occupies a position more potent in determining the future trend of legal thought than that of any other like number of persons in the country. As the teachers of future lawyers and judges, the potency of our present position, among the factors which can alter men's thinking and action on legal matters, is outstanding. But it is as those who are training the law teachers of tomorrow that we are the responsible part of a circle most vicious in perpetuating and multiplying the vices in our present thinking or most beneficent in propagating its virtues. The long hoped for day when the better law schools should have their say in fixing the direction of the law's advance is come. A misplaced modesty at the present time might easily conceal from us a part of the opportunity which this affords and much of the responsibility which it entails.

That the law schools have come into this new estate is shown by many events. It will suffice to mention but a few. There is an increased frequency of reference in judicial opinions to the treatises written by law teachers and to our law review literature. The personnel chosen to draft our uniform state legislation and to formulate the law's restatement together with the reception which both of these projects are receiving at the hands of the bench, the bar and the public, is most significant. Current progress in the effort to raise the standards for admission to the bar advances a project at which the law schools of this Association have long labored and marks an increasing acceptance of the ideals for which they have stood. These are not formal matters. They mark a change of substance in our relations to the profession and to the public and as yet we have no adequate measure of the extent and potentialities of this change.

Thesis Stated

Our part in shaping the future of legal scholarship thus recognized makes this an appropriate time and gathering to consider what seems to be a most profound change which has been slowly and imperceptibly creep-

*Presidential Address delivered at Annual Meeting of Association of American Law Schools held at Chicago, December 29, 30 and 31, 1927.

ing into our treatment of problems in Anglo-American law, a fundamental change which merits careful study in order that we may recognize its presence, measure its extent, and judge its consequences. Let me anticipate my conclusions by asserting that we are well on our way toward a shift from following decisions to following so-called principles, from *stare decisis* to what I shall call *stare dictis;* by saying that this shift has far-reaching and unfortunate consequence for both the art of judicial government and the science of law and by proposing a return toward the ancient doctrine of *stare decisis.*

Stare Decisis Analyzed

Support for this position will be found by examining that doctrine. It asserts not one thing, but two. For one thing, it asserts that prior decisions are to be followed, not disregarded. But it also asserts that we are to follow the prior decisions and not something else.

The First Meaning of the Doctrine

Most discussions of the doctrine of *stare decisis* have emphasized the first of these two assertions. In those we are told of the advantages and disadvantages of the doctrine. It has been pointed out how, on the one hand, it makes the law applicable to future transactions certain and the future decisions of judges predictable: and again, how it gives us justice according to law and not according to the whims of men. On the other hand, it has been shown that to follow it gives us a measure of inflexibility in our law resisting changes needed to meet changing conditions. We are all familiar with these and other broad implications of this branch of the doctrine and have considered the necessary choice between conflicting advantages which its acceptance or rejection involves. The vigor of this branch of the ancient doctrine has been weakened but little. Something in the cases is being followed. This whole aspect of the matter is mentioned here only to be set to one side.

The Second Meaning of the Doctrine

The drift in our methods of dealing with legal problems which is upon us and is the subject of this discussion, concerns more intimately the second branch of the rule dealing with what it is in prior decisions which is to be followed. It is to be carefully noted that, when *stare decisis* is hereinafter mentioned, only this branch of the doctrine is referred to. It is in this quarter that innovation has been at work and is carrying us farther and farther toward treating this ancient doctrine as if it were *stare dictis* instead of *stare decisis.*

There seems to have been little critical study of this phase of the doctrine,—of just what it is in prior decisions which is to be followed. General statements that the decision is to be looked for, that dicta are of slight weight and offer no certain guide can be turned to at many places in the books and are familiar to all. Students beginning their law study are told these things in a general way and then are left to an apprenticeship among the cases to discover largely for themselves their fuller meaning. Yet this matter is the one most vital and difficult factor conditioning the soundness of their scholarship. It is because the word *decision* may mean any one of many things that it is perilous to leave the matter thus unarticulated.

What Does a Case Decide?

In the first place, a court, in deciding a case, may throw out a statement as to how it would decide some other case. Now if that statement is a statement of another case which is as narrow and specific as the actual case before the court, it is easily recognized as dictum and given its proper weight as such. In the second place the court may throw out a broader statement, covering a whole group of cases. But so long as that statement does not cover the case before the court, it is readily recognized as being not a decision, much less the decision of the case. It is dictum, so labeled and appraised. But in the third place, a court may make a statement broad enough to dispose of the case in hand as well as to cover also a few or many other states of fact. Statements of this third sort may cover a number of fact situations ranging from one other to legion. Such a statement is sometimes called the *decision* of the case. Thereby the whole ambiguity of that word is introduced and the whole difficulty presented.

If a more careful usage limits the word *decision* to the *action* taken by the court in the specific case before it, *i. e.*, to the naked judgment or order entered, the difficulty is not met: it is merely shifted. *Stare decisis* thus understood becomes useless for no decision in that limited sense can ever be followed. No identical case can arise. All other cases will differ in some circumstance,—in time, if in no other, and most of them will have differences which are not trivial. *Decision* in the sense meant in *stare decisis* must, therefore, refer to a proposition of law covering a group of fact situations of a group as a minimum, the fact situation of the instant case and at least one other.

To bring together into one class even this minimum of two fact situations however similar they may be, always has required and always will require[1] an abstraction. If Paul and Peter are to be thought of together at all, they must both be apostles or be thought of as having some other attribute in common. Classification is abstraction. An element or elements common to the two fact situations put into one class must be drawn out from each to become the content of the category and the subject of the proposition of law which is thus applied to the two cases.

But such a grouping may include multitudes of fact situations so long as a single attribute common to them all can be found. Between these two extremes lies a gradation of groups of fact situations each with its corresponding proposition of law, ranging from a grouping subtending but two situations to those covering hosts of them. This series of groupings of fact situations gives us a parallel series of corresponding propositions of law, each more and more generalized as we recede farther and farther from the instant state of facts and include more and more fact situations in the successive groupings. It is a mounting and widening structure, each proposition including all that has gone before and becoming more general by embracing new states of fact. For example, A's father induces her not to marry B as she promised to do. On a holding that the father is not liable to B for so doing, a gradation of widening propositions can be built, a very few of which are:

1. Fathers are privileged to induce daughters to break promises to marry.
2. Parents are so privileged.
3. Parents are so privileged as to both daughters and sons.

1. This needs emphasis to avoid any impression that abstractions and generalizations are thought to have no useful part to play. They are always and everywhere indispensable.

4. All persons are so privileged as to promises to marry.
5. Parents are so privileged as to all promises made by their children.
6. All persons are so privileged as to all promises made by anyone.

There can be erected upon the action taken by a court in any case such a gradation of generalizations and this is commonly done in the opinion. Sometimes it is built up to dizzy heights by the court itself and at times, by law teacher and writers, it is reared to those lofty summits of the absolute and the infinite.

Where on that gradation of propositions are we to take our stand and say "This proposition is the decision of this case within the meaning of the doctrine of *stare decisis?*" Can a proposition of law of this third type ever become so broad that, as to any of the cases it would cover, it is mere dictum?

A Question of Double Difficulty

That would be difficult enough if it ended there. But just as one and the same apple can be thrown into any one of many groups of barrels according to its size, color, shape, etc., so also there stretches up and away from every single case in the books, not one possible gradation of widening generalizations, but many. Multitudes of radii shoot out from it, each pair enclosing one of an indefinite number of these gradations of broader and broader generalizations. For example, a contract for wages contains a stipulation that it shall be non-assignable by the employee. A court holds that the laborer can assign any way and that his assignee can sue the employer for the wages regardless of the stipulation. This holding can serve as the apex of many triangles of generalizations. At the base of one will be a broad generalization treating the claim as property and asserting the alienability of property; at the base of another will be an equally broad generalization having to do with contractual stipulations opposed to public policy and the base of a third will be similarly wide generalization concerning the liquidation of claims in the labor market. Others could be enumerated and other cases similarly analyzed. That is not needed, for we all know of at least one case appearing in the casebooks of more than one subject upon which securely rests more than one inverted pyramid of favorite theory.

A student is told to seek the "doctrine" or "principle" of a case, but which of its welter of stairs shall he ascend and how high up shall he go? Is there some one step on some one stair which is *the* decision of the case within the meaning of the mandate *stare decisis?* That is the double difficulty. Each precedent considered by a judge and each case studied by a student rests at the center of a vast and empty stadium. The angle and distance from which that case is to be viewed involves the choice of a seat. Which shall be chosen? Neither judge nor student can escape the fact that he can and must choose. To realize how wide the possibilities and significant the consequences of that choice are is elementary to an understanding of *stare decisis.* To ask whether there exists a coercion of some logic to make that choice either inevitable or beneficent, searches the significance of *stare decisis* in judicial government and the soundness of scholarship in law. This question is real and insistent. It is one which should be asked explicitly and faced squarely.

An attempt to answer this question will be made later. When an answer is looked for, it will be well to consider whether the answer must of necessity be a statement. There may be some gratuity in assuming that the answers to all questions are inevitably so. The answer to some questions, including this one, may be, not a statement, but an attitude, a matter not of affirmation but of method. If our attitude on this question be that of approximating the experimentalism of an earlier *stare decisis,* and if our method of dealing with cases be one of increasing objectivity and precision, such may well constitute a full answer for us in our work here and now, both as students and judges. It has been pointed out that one can embrace skeptical empiricism as a method of work without embracing it as a philosophy of life.

What Stare Decisis Once Meant

But to support the assertion that there is a drift both marked and unfortunate away from the ancient doctrine of *stare decisis,* it is not needed at this time to attempt a full answer to the question as to the angle and distance of the view of a precedent. It is enough to find out from what angles and at what distances courts and students formerly viewed a precedent as compared with the angle and remoteness of our present points of view.

In earlier English law there were many writs, each writ having many forms and each form being quite specific. Each would cover only a relatively few human situations and those so covered were relatively well defined. Recall such random examples as *de homine replegiando, rationabilibus estoveriis,* and *parco fracto* out of scores which could be mentioned. Contrast such actions as these with that of trover in its later stages. The old actions divided and minutely subdivided the transaction of life for legal treatment. Speaking of the place occupied by trespass in a Register of Writs belonging to the 14th century when the scheme of writs was about fully developed and required some hundreds of large pages when later printed, Maitland says: "There has been (up to this time) no generalization; the imaginary defendant is charged in different precedents with every kind of unlawful force, with the breach of every imaginable boundary, with the asportation of all that is asportable, while the new well-known writs against the shoeing smith who lames the horse, the hirer who rides the horse to death, the unskilled surgeon, the careless innkeeper creep in slowly amid the writs which describe wilful and malicious mischief, how a cat was put into a dove-cote, how a rural dean was made to ride face to tail, and other ingenious sports."[2]

Then, too, pleading was more discriminating. In earlier law there was a wealth of well differentiated pleas. Pleas to the jurisdiction, to the person, to the court, to the writ, to the action of the writ, and pleas in bar, were each divided into many kinds, each kind covering some specific set of facts or question of law. As to pleas in bar, there was, for example, no omnibus general issue such as that which later developed in assumpsit, for example. The general issue in each action covered a limited number of fact situations enumerated in the old books. Special traverses were numerous and the learning as to special issues, *i. e.,* pleas in confession and avoidance, constituted the largest part of ancient books on pleading.

The result of both this great multitude of writs and this greater definiteness of pleading was much greater particularity and minuteness in the classification of human transactions for legal treatment than prevailed

2. Maitland, The History of The Register of Original Writs, 3 Harvard Law Review, 212, 225 (1889).

later. The judges were, by the particularity of the actions and the pleadings, brought and held closer to the actual transactions before them, whatever they may have said in their opinions. The result was that *stare decisis* meant something decidedly different at that time, being more specific and definite. It was operated in terms of abstractions no wider than the propositions of law covering the several classes of this more specific classification of human transactions. The abstractions were, therefore, relatively narrower. When principles were enunciated, though stated too broadly, they related, and were applied, only to these narrow categories of fact situations.

Then too *stare decisis* in actual operation meant something different at that time for the further reason that the phases of human life regulated in the King's Courts were those of a simpler life and time. Judges and lawyers could then more nearly acquire an adequate understanding of those phases of life by merely growing up and living in the society of the time. Transactions were simpler and more nearly homogeneous. Then, again, the courts of Westminster did not have cognizance of all phases of English life. Other tribunals and agencies were then operating.

For yet another and most important reason, *stare decisis* operated in earlier times with greater effectiveness. The abstractions made to correspond to the categories into which the more definite procedure of the time had grouped the human transactions of that simpler economy were quite contemporary. Considered absolutely many of them were old, but relatively they were recent. For great stretches of time there were few fundamental changes in the structure and operation of English domestic, industrial, and political life. Abstractions once made fitted longer. Corresponding rules of law asserting this or that about them, however abstract in phrasing, related, in actual operation, to fact situations to which they had not become alien. The resulting social control better fitted current needs. We in the field of law are far from having finished drawing all the implications of the fact that the last two hundred years have brought more changes in the circumstances of men living together than the previous two thousand years had done.

For these reasons and others no doubt, the empiricism of *stare decisis* proved a most effective and secure way of handling legal problems. What courts then did, as opposed to what they said, shaped itself to the life affected because the problems treated were less numerous and complex, their treatment of these legal problems was more particularistic, and their closer view of them was from the side on which men in life worked and worried with them. The method of *stare decisis* was preeminently empiric and so close and contemporary was the point of view that it might well be called a radical empiricism.

How the Retreat Began

But fundamental changes ensued. The phases of life regulated by the Courts of Westminster were multiplied. A whole society began to stir. A tide of change set in. The business of living together became more and more complex as man's activities became more and more diversified. There was the early rise of English trade with profound changes in rural living. There was later the Industrial Revolution. Problems of life requiring legal treatment multiplied in kind and complexity.

How did the legal thought of the time try to meet this situation? Was it done by increasing the number of actions and by elaborating pleading, *i. e.*, by improving the only machinery available for sorting and simplifying the situations of life for legal treatment? On the contrary, the number of actions became greatly reduced. Those retained were broadened to include both the situations covered by those abandoned and also a flood of wholly new situations. In addition, pleading lost much of its power to discriminate between differing fact situations. Some pleas were abandoned, others were broadened. The attempt to cope with the situation by thus dulling the tools for producing the discrimination necessary for intimacy of treatment is the over-towering fact in Anglo-American legal history of recent centuries. Take but one item in it. The debauching of the general issue in some of the most important actions, had many profound effects on the art of judicial government and the science of law. That Anglo-Saxon empiricism we know as *stare decisis*, which was evolved to deal with human problems as particulars, had thrust upon it the staggering task of dealing with them wholesale. Small wonder that judges and scholars have since gone off in search of help from strange and alien gods.

Reduction in the number of actions and pleas and the broadening of those that remained, with no substituting machinery of classification, resulted in wider and wider groupings of multiform states of fact. In order to subtend the hosts of fact situations thus fortuitously grouped into broader and broader classes, old abstractions had to be made more and more tenuous. The attempt to find new categories carved along lines other than procedural ones and calculated to bring the courts nearer in time and closer in detail to current life was slight and unsystematic. Instead, largely by fictions, old categories of facts were expanded to include diverse states of fact with the result that the very devices designed to bring and keep the courts close to the issues of life before them operated to remove them to positions more and more remote from the life which they regulated, with the result that they regulated it with an ever-decreasing feeling for its realities.

This process of widening generalizations was carried farther than was dictated by the falling away of procedural distinctions. A wave of continental learning swept over England, leaving a thick deposit of its obscurant abstractions, and much of it still remains. When the history of this period is fully written, we may find that the breakdown of procedure was partly an effect as well as a cause of this orgy of overgeneralization.

While the law was thus grouping the transactions of life into larger and larger piles, held together by common attributes more and more accidental, life rolled on, always concrete, always specific, but becoming more and more diversified with ominous speed.

The Movement in America

In this country, the presence of the frontier kept life simple for a while and there was a breathing spell which ended near the middle of the last century. How did we then go about meeting the situation? We did not meet it. We, too, ran away from it. We, too, first tried broadening our forms of actions and our pleas. Finally in most states, we executed a grand strategic retreat by reducing all forms of action to one, by making the general issues all but universal, and by abandoning all pleadings subsequent to the answer or the replication. Then abstraction and generalization ran riot. Courts and scholars began to talk less and less about what prior courts had actually done in ordering men's affairs and more and more about the universals they had promulgated. Great cargoes of continental speculations were imported and thrown in to make the dikes of the old abstractions hold. A whole new breed of law books sprang up,—encyclopediæ and corpora juris hastily made by stringing together judicial generalities usually innocuous and frequently inconsistent and by peppering them with cast citations either to the number of recent minimum or with the abundance of an undiscriminated deluge. Lawyers began to buy these books, first sparingly, then by wholesale, and courts began to quote their weighty findings.

Its Later Stages

In other quarters the retreat has been more orderly, but not less marked. The last quarter of the 19th century ushered in the university law school. In them a truly conscientious labor of excellent workmanship has been carried on patiently and persistently for the last forty or fifty years. During the first half of that period, there was a renewal of historical study. The old and recent cases were re-examined, not with a view, however, to finding new groupings of human transactions with their corresponding abstractions fitting more closely into current needs, but with a view to reconciling the welter of conflicts and exceptions which the mass of our law displayed when looked at through the peepholes of the old points of view. The old abstractions were modified and, as was inevitable, greatly expanded.

The second half of that period has been devoted largely to the process of logical elaboration. Absolutes and universals begin to replace mere generalizations. Broad principles begin to spring from few cases. If there be only one case in point and that be in conflict with some implication of our favorite universals, it is wrong—wrong on principle. This search becomes partly one for mere word patterns. Statements, if all inclusive so long as not self-contradictory, are enunciated as authoritative. This work in form and flavor is nearer to the work of continental theorists than that of the patient particularists who were our laws' early judges and scholars. The spirit of the common law may still reside in the day to day work of our judges who face realities as they decide cases, but it has all but departed the body of their opinions and the writing of scholars.

But life has been rolling on, always specific, always concrete, and in a broadening stream which, until it is charted, must seem like a flood. It rolls on, finding new ways around new and old obstructions, sometimes because of the law, often in spite of it. And it will keep on.

The Classificatory Function of Pleading

No return to the ancient procedural machine is advocated. The present classification of human situations of procedural origin may be sufficiently detailed and recent to serve in handling those situations as law suits in matters of pleading and practice. The wide scope of trover may be no serious disadvantage to a pleader. It may be an advantage. But it is a grave error to assume that a classification adequate for that purpose is either detailed or recent enough for the treatment of substantive rights by even the judge much less the scholar. Confusion follows if we overlook the fact that actions and pleading have had, and still have, in our law a classificatory function as well as a procedural one,[3] and if we overlook the further fact that the requirements of their procedural function have made the product of their taxonomic function over generalized and obsolete and hence inadequate for current needs.

What Was Lost by the Retreat

But what has this general retreat in legal thinking toward supergeneralized and outworn abstractions meant for the doctrine of *stare decisis?* It is just this retreat which I characterize as the shift from *stare decisis* towards *stare dictis*. Not that courts have ceased to be motivated dominantly by an intuition born of their experience and to respond to the stimulus of the facts in the concrete cases before them rather than to the stimulus of over-general and outworn abstractions in opinions and treatises. It is something to know that judges will continue to be men and that we shall always have some measure of that safeguard. But the effects of this shift, both on the art of judicial government and on legal science, are profound and unfortunate.

Losses in the Field of Government

The political virtues of *stare decisis* are difficult to exaggerate. It has two active qualities, one affording us the counsel of experience: the other, the latitude of trial and error. The first element of its strength and security is its unalterable refusal to indulge in broad speculation, and its untiring patience to keep attention pinned to the immediate problem in order that a wise solution for it may be found. It stoutly refuses to answer future questions, prudently awaiting the time when they enter the field of immediate vision and become issues of reality in order that to their solution may be brought the illumination which only immediacy affords and the judiciousness which reality alone can induce. It is indifferent to broad generalizations or is made apprehensive by them. It accepts few generalizations, narrow or broad, until they have been transmuted into the wisdom of experience by experimentation. It uses generaliaztions to suggest and to orient that experimentation but not to replace it. The second element in the strength and security of *stare decisis* is but another aspect of the constant immediacy of its ends. It leads us forward over untried ground, a step at a time, no step being taken until it is judged wise, and the stages of its advance are so short that the direction of march can be quickly shifted as experience dictates.

This tremendous political significance of *stare decisis* in the art of judicial government should not be overlooked and it should be seen as but one aspect of the political empiricism of English speaking peoples. The grace to drudge away on today's problem and the refusal to foreclose tomorrow's issues run all through our political endeavors. This sagacious opportunism in government has reared many of our most valuable institutions. In English statesmanship and diplomacy it made the British Empire and still holds together that structure which seems fragile only to those who do not know how it was wrought. It built the English Constitution and has shaped the evolving parts of our own. It abides in the very genius of our people and

3. To distribute transactions under the headings assumpsit, trespass detinue and replevin may be adequate for procedural purposes but it is inadequate as a classification of substantive law.

is our most important contribution to the art of modern government.[4]

Of all those political fabrics which Anglo-Saxon opportunism has woven, that, threaded together by *stare decisis* into our common law, shows richest with the work of patience and fine skill. Its methods can be improved, but we shall find no craftsmanship more worthy. A better informed public might well inquire, "Who are these innovators among us so active even further to undermine that time-tried and priceless institution?"

Losses in the Field of Legal Scholarship

The gradual and widespread drift away from the rigorous kind of work necessitated by the particularity and realism of *stare decisis* in its earlier application has had unfortunate consequences in the field of scholarship as well as in courts of justice. Scholarship has been drifting into a way of dealing with fact situations collected wholesale into groupings becoming more and more antiquated by the shift in the patterns of life. This drift has changed the very fiber of our work.

Of course, complete particularity in our treatment of legal problems is not possible. If states of fact are not grouped at all, no decision can be followed since no two cases are identical. Some abstraction and generalization is unavoidable if *stare decisis* is to operate so as to make law certain and impersonal. Some distance from the case in hand to give some perspective of view is unavoidable, and considerable distance is desirable. If we are to see and to judge the play, others must carry the ball. The shift from *stare decisis* has not been from absolute particularity to absolute generality but from greater particularity to greater generality. But the difference, though one of degree, has been great enough to alter the very texture of our work even though the outlines of its design seem still unchanged. Moreover, perfect modernity in the laws' treatment of life's problems is not desirable were it possible. This factor concerns not the distance, but the angle of our view of those problems. That angle should not shift with each move of the play. Unless the common law is to be capricious, it must lag a bit. It must lag enough for the fitful actions of men to disclose trends of customary practice.

But all this granted, there has been such a shift in our work on cases from particularity to generality of treatment and such a shift of life from the grooves of our present long-standing abstractions, that our scholarship becomes loose and unreal. No longer coerced to think in exact procedural moulds, and few substitute devices to compel particularity in thinking having been set up, our minds are free to wander. The former discipline of a more rigorous *stare decisis* is replaced by the current license of *stare dictis*. Our categories of thought have become unreal by life having left them behind and no alert sense of actuality checks our reveries in theory.

The effect of these two things is to cause most of our students to remain intellectual infants with toothless gums too soft except for munching elastic generalities with sophomoric serenity. The law's present classification of human activities, compels us to sit in places where life's game is no longer played. In pondering many of our long prized abstractions, we study dead bodies from which the life we would know has departed. When the unreality of it all is sensed, that reality is sought elsewhere. Generalized abstractions are called "principles" and these are endowed with a reality of their own. Generalized statements, when broad enough and old enough, transcend the world of time, place, and circumstance to dwell in realms of universal reality.

We use much of our scholarly resources to erect on sands thus doubly uncertain ambitious structures of pure reason expecting them to house all the activities of the whole work-a-day world, and then we seek to hold them together by the bare strength of combined professional authority.

If such be a science of law, it is unique. Law purports to be not a pure science, but an applied science. All other applied sciences have both a rational and an empirical branch. The work of observing and testing reality goes hand in hand with that of elaborating theory and explanation. Law approximates the unearthy perfection of pure reason. The products of a legal science which neglects its empirical branch share some of the futility of the findings of a cloistered biologist whose mind ponders only such specimens as his cat may chance to bring in.

Those are but some of the losses strewing the field of legal scholarship in the wake of the retreat from *stare decisis* toward *stare dictis*.

Evidence of these Losses

So severe an estimate may well be challenged; but what is some of the evidence? We are often told that, because of the overwhelming multiplication and conflict of cases, authoritative generalization must replace individualized treatment of cases. In the first place, it should be well marked and most soberly considered that this judgment is made when only pennies have ever been spent by any of our universities on particularized or objective research in law. In the second place, a science of law cannot be built on experimentation. Like geology, its rational branch must rest on testing by observation. If our main business as legal scientists is to predict the behavior of courts in deciding future cases, then, when we complain that there are too many cases—cases of observed judicial behavior—we take the position of a geologist complaining that too many observations of the earth's crust are being made. In the third place, there would be no conflicts among the cases if they were not grouped at all under any generalizations. This suggests the possibility that, as to many of the exceptions and conflicts of which we complain, the difficulty may be with parts of our classification and not with the results actually reached by the courts. That classification being based on abstractions which changes in life have made obsolete, it would not be surprising if we should find that judges, responding to the needs of current life, had frequently departed from the confines of that classification though still stating and justifying their results in terms of it.

We have been drifting from observation of judicial action to an excess of concern about judicial utterances. More and more we have been taking abstractions of the past,—many going back to medieval scholasticism—and tracing them down, not through the holdings of the cases, but through the opinions to see how they have fared in those essays of rationalization. There has been little but lip service to the discipline of seeking the exact holdings of cases, as opposed to their generalized pronouncements, except when the cases happen to lie near the rim of some

(Continued on page 167)

4. This does not, of course, carry any implication that there is no need for forethought in the scheme of things.

A Return to Stare Decisis

(Continued from page 76)

favorite theory whose precise border we want to mark out. There has been little genuine re-examination of the holdings of those cases which lie at the center of that theory in order to test the utility of the whole generalization.

We have heard much complaint of the more highly commercialized type of law books. In them a summary statement of the whole law is attempted in a relatively few volumes and some courts are citing them with increasing frequency. They and sound scholarship stand at antipodes. But consider the demand for them. Their sales have been mounting while those of truly critical text books have languished. Have we paused to consider that our drift toward more generalized statements of aging abstractions may have been helping to create that demand? If they be an evil,—and that has been widely asserted,— is the way to meet that evil to surrender to it by adopting their approach and methods. An era of scholarship whose end product is the erection of a law of ruling cases composed of word patterns largely detached from life, broad enough to be all inclusive, vague enough to be self-consistent, leaves so much to be desired that no general silence, whether timorous or reverential, can long conceal it.

All this must be an end product marking the close of an era of legal scholarship, rather than the opening of a new one, for what promise of rich fields for truly productive scholarship does it hold out? Certainly the prospect of some generations of energy being spent in glossing the text of authoritative general statements is not inviting. And there is some reason for one to fear that, unless one does not expect them to be accepted as authoritative. The prospect of lengthy discussions of just why "a" instead of "the" was used in the black letter of a horn book does not fire the imagination. Nor is there escape in the proposal continually to restate these statements if that be carried on along present lines. Such further restatements will be made necessary by exceptions and conflicts which appear from time to time. They can be reduced and subtended only by expanding present generalizations into yet larger bubbles of unreality. Nothing new and nothing vital lies in this direction. This path inevitably leads to viewpoints more and more remote from life, more and more obsolescent. Ahead are the mirages of an intellectual dreamland. No new era of sound scholarship can have for its principal business the further logical elaboration of present abstractions. Pursuit of them through the opinions drives thought down no constraining channels so that its courses can be mapped.

(Concluded in March issue)

STARE DECISIS—CONTINUED*

By Herman Oliphant

Professor of Law, Columbia University; President Association American Law Schools, 1927

The Essence of Stare Decisis and of a Science of Law

But there is a constant factor in the cases which is susceptible of sound and satisfying study. The predictable element in it all is what courts have done in response to the stimuli of the facts of the concrete cases before them. Not the judges' opinions, but which way they decide cases will be the dominant subject matter of any truly scientific study of law. This is the field for scholarly work worthy of best talents because the work to be done is not the study of vague and shifting rationalizations but the study of such tough things as the accumulated wisdom of men taught by immediate experience in contemporary life,—the battered experiences of judges among brutal facts. The response of their intuition of experience to the stimulus of human situations is the subject-matter having that constancy and objectivity necessary for truly scientific study. When we pin our attention to this, we may more freely criticize what courts have said but we shall more cautiously criticize what they have done realizing, as we shall, that they were exposed to the impact of more of the facts than we.

This surer thing for scholarly purpose is also the inner secret of what is soundest in the enfeebled *stare decisis* in judicial government of today. With eyes cleared of the old and broad abstractions which curtain our vision, we come to recognize more and more the eminent good sense in what courts are wont to do about disputes before them. Judges are men and men respond to human situations. When the facts stimulating them to the action taken are studied from a particular and current point of view, which our present classification prevents, we acquire a new faith in *stare decisis*. From this viewpoint we see that courts are dominantly coerced, not by the essays of their predecessors[5] but by a surer thing,—by an intuition of fitness of solution to problem,—and a renewed confidence in judicial government is engendered. To state the matter more concretely, the decision of a particular case by a thoughtful scholar is to be preferred to that by a poorly trained judge, but the decision of such a judge in a particular case is infinitely to be preferred to a decision of it preordained by some broad "principle" laid down by the scholar when this and a host of other concrete cases had never even occurred to him.

One sampling of this proposed subject-matter of a real science of law must suffice. There are two lines of old cases involving the validity of promises not to compete. They are considered in square conflict. But when the opinions are ignored and the facts re-examined all the cases holding the promises invalid are found to be cases of employees' promises not to compete with their employers after a term of employment. Contemporary guild regulations not noticed in the opinions made their holding eminently sound. All the cases[6] holding the promises valid were cases of promises by those selling a business and promising not to compete with the purchasers. Contemporary economic reality made these holdings also eminently sound. This distinction between these two lines of cases is not even hinted at in any of the opinions but the courts' intuition of experience led them to follow it with amazing sureness and the law resulting fitted life. That is a sample of the stuff capable of scientific study.

How the Ground Lost May Be Regained

Because our law students are to be the scholars, advocates, counselors, and judges of tomorrow, their training is the area of supreme strategic importance in this whole situation. That is our opportunity and responsibility. Regaining the values lost to judical government by the retreat from *stare decisis* and making law more a science of realities and less a theology of doctrines require a radical reorganization of legal education. The remainder of this discussion will be devoted to three large undertakings considered basic for any such reorganization.

Study of the Social Structure Needed

Law teachers should have and law students should get either before or after they come to the law school a comprehensive knowledge of the whole social structure. This should not consist of theories as to domestic, economic and political life nor of unrelated description of disjoined social phenomona. The whole life which law affects should be viewed comprehensively as an interrelation of processes. This understanding cannot be got today by a hit and miss apprenticeship in life any more than living in our bodies can teach us its structure and functioning. Systematized study, deliberately focused toward getting an adequate knowledge of the entire social structure as a functioning and changing but coherent mechanism, is a basic prerequisite.

Only by such organized and thorough study can we get an understanding of social reality equal to that of the judges and scholars who merely grew up in the earlier and simpler social environment. The realism of *stare decisis* cannot equal its realism in that earlier time until that knowledge is brought to bear in deciding cases. Something more than the layman's knowl-

*Continued from February issue. Presidential Address delivered at Annual Meeting of Association of American Law Schools held at Chicago, December 29, 30 and 31, 1927.

5. The thesis is that facts are the only stimuli capable of scientific study as a basis of prediction. Prior rationalizations are rejected *for this purpose* because the facts prevail when they diverge from the prior generalizations and for each rationalization indicating one result, a contradictory one indicating the opposite result can usually be found. The utility of prior rationalizations in the study of judicial forensics is not being discussed at this time.

6. In one case it did not appear which situation was involved.

edge of the social structure is not overambitious as a part of the equipment of a legal scholar.

A Reclassification of Law Is Proposed

The second undertaking proposed is a radical reclassification of most of law in terms of the human relations affected by it. The catogories of that reclassification emerge from the suggested study of the whole social structure.

Our procedural set up will not provide this reclassification. Marks of its former fine discrimination are still visible and their significance is not to be neglected. Students of procedure can help in checking the present validity of old procedural groupings and the significance of the new procedural groupings which we are getting from the organization of specialized courts, commissions and administrative agencies. (Such students some times complain that their colleagues attach no importance to procedure except for the light it throws on substantive law. This complaint can hardly convict of sin so long as only a beginning has been made in exhausting the possibilities of that position.)

This task of reclassification cannot be left to the publishers of digests. Judges do not have the leisure or freedom to do it. It is not suited to be done by town meetings of judges, lawyers and scholars. It is the job of the American Law School in its capacity as part of a university.

The double ideal of this new classification should be an ever greater and greater particularity and recency of view. *Stare decisis* has been sapped of much of the spirit of the common law, and legal scholarship approaches an architecture of castles in the thin air of pure theory because of the breadth and antiquation of present groupings of human situations for legal treatment. Such a reclassification will help to send us about our proper business of raising the walls within which men must work and live by just laying one brick upon another, letting a keener awareness of the needs of the life and labor which they are to house guide our hands.

No reclassification can get us as near to a case as the judge who decides it, yet, about it lies a considerable field across which its currents can be felt. Each human situation has many aspects, yet somewhere in its field are points of opposite polarity charged with human concern. It is between these poles that the currents of our time flow and these currents are the prime stimuli of nonvocal judicial behavior. Our classification should bring us close to them for truly scientific observation.

We cannot come close to them without leaving many of our present remote points of view and without abandoning many present groupings of material which are sterile except for logical purposes and often confusing even for those. In our present classification, problems of getting laws observed, *i. e.*, problems of law administration, are intermingled with problems as to what conduct is desired. The illegality of a contract of sale, though raising a question as to the use of the disability to sue on the contract as an indirect deterrent of the illegal conduct in question, is treated as one of substantive law and discussed in terms of some such barren and ambiguous abstraction as title. These two widely different kinds of questions are now confused because we have only two groupings, substantive law and adjective law, the latter being too narrow to embrace broad areas of law administration. Human relations as diverse as political relations, familial relations, and business relations are hopelessly mixed and confused in such broad and outworn categories as property, trusts, torts, and contracts. Problems as to leaseholds of dwellings and of railroads are grouped together so that practical differences are obscured. A contract to marry is grouped with a speculative contract to purchase stocks and their differences considered as relatively minor. Again, in those areas where only political relations are treated, no consistent grouping and subgrouping of greater current significance are attempted. Constitutional law embraces categories with wide practical divergencies because the exigencies and accidents of post revolutionary government happened to get them mentioned in a single document. Where we segregate a fraction of familial relations and call it domestic relations, the subgrouping is in terms of such nonfunctional concepts as contract, property, and tort. When chance brings some business problem together for treatment, as happens in sales, divergent questions as to marketing, finance, and risk are confused under such labels as "passage of title."

Practical Attitude and Objective Methods Are Needed

These two undertakings, *viz.*, a study of the social structure and a reclassification of the law in the light of that study would accomplish the return to *stare decisis* proposed. But are we not ready to plan for more? There is a third undertaking which will improve on the hard practicability of *stare decisis* oi earlier times. For us to attempt some improvement in some centuries cannot seem precipitate. And this further undertaking is necessary if we are to begin to build a science of law by exploiting non-vocal judicial behavior. In recent times the world of scientific thought has been turning dark places into light. We now can see that the choice between the legal principles competing to control the new human situations involved in the cases we pass upon is not dictated by logic. Neither deduction nor induction can do more than suggest the competing analogies and to indicate promising directions for trial and error testing. Neither the astuteness of legal scholarship nor the authority of judicial position can transcend these limitations inherent in logic. The final choice of analogy can be made only in reliance upon practical considerations or upon pure chance. Rejecting sheer guess as a basis of sound judicial action and of worthwhile scholarship, then discovering and marshalling decisive practical considerations inevitably constitute the essence of both an improved judicial process and of a more useful scholarly effort. A return to the sounder empiricism of *stare decisis* of former times should reckon with the recent advances in scientific thought referred to. That ancient empiricism was intuitive. It worked well because judges sat close to problems and viewed them as current problems. It would have worked better still had it been conscious and methodical. Remembering always that the final choice for both judge and scholar in deciding a case or criticizing a decision is always a practical one, whether consciously or unconsciously so, the problem, how a more conscious and methodical process can be substituted for an intuitive empiricism in making that choice, transcends in importance all other problems of legal education. Until its solution is attempted, a socialized jurisprudence will continue a mere aspiration and social engineering will be the profession of many but the occupation of none.

The Nature of the Problem

An examination of some of the presuppositions of intuitive empiricism as a method of deciding cases and evaluating decisions may shed some light on the solution of that problem. Good as it has been, it assumes that we know social reality and shape our actions to it merely because we live in it. It presupposes that the affairs of life cannot be more wisely controlled than by men of affairs. But none of us knows social reality merely because we live in it. The experience of any man, however broad, is limited largely to one period of time. The future he cannot know and the past is reported to him by men of equally limited experience. The social experience of most of us is limited largely to one people, yet social reality encircles the globe. Our social experience is limited to one class of people though we must govern all classes. Indeed, it is limited to but one occupation and the part often most decisive in determining our attitudes is the experience of but a single family group. Complete reliance upon an intuition of fitness of solution to problems was better placed when used in the solution of the legal problems emerging from the simpler life of early England. Some parts of current social life are no more complex now than then, but great areas of it—and the areas of most frequent dispute—are most complex, being knit together by a social and mechanical technology which only experts can hope to understand. Complete reliance upon an intuition of such a limited experience is a policy of doubtful wisdom.

But more can be said. If our individual experience were as broad as the life whose problems we work on, still our intuition of experience would be no certain guide. Not all of our experience goes to make up that intuition. Individual temperament and our self-interest cause us, in the most subjective fashion, to select from the totality of our experience that which satisfies our temperament, and fortifies our interest. Thus but a small fraction of total social reality forms our attitudes and grounds our intuition of experience. To distill a guide from so little of the immense and complex social reality about us is a procedure for which the modern scientific thought must offer some better substitute. Such an unconscious empiricism, such a common-sense pragmatism can be improved upon by borrowings from the accumulated wisdom of the sciences.

Making that improvement is a problem first of attitude and second of method.

Attitude Toward Matters of Method

The attitude required is complete and constant self-consciousness as to methods of thought and procedure. That means an active awareness that these matters are not solely the concern of the philosophical theory of a few, but are things of immediate practical importance to all in day to day observation and thinking. The required attitude involves keeping in the forefront of the mind a complete understanding of the limitations and dangers of deduction, of over-generalized induction, and of common-sense pragmatism. If in our return toward *stare decisis* we could do no more than attain this attitude, the gain would be tremendous. If as law teachers we could do no more than to make students and, through them, lawyers and judges realize that judgments on new questions must, in the last analysis, be either fortuitous or practical, and to realize the perils of an unconscious empiricism in complex situations, that would be taking a long step forward. Much is accomplished by having merely the consciousness that there resides in the human mind no benevolent predestination of logical necessity and no intuition of universal experiences to shape our solutions of the practical problems of law in life. That consciousness alone induces an attitude of wholesome caution and fruitful eagerness more carefully to weigh the little objective evidence at hand.

Projects Relating to Objective Methods

The third undertaking envisages not merely a conscious empiricism, but also a methodical one. Our minds permeated with the attitude just described and oriented by a comprehensive knowledge of the makeup and operation of the whole social structure should begin the quest for greater objectivity in methods employed in study and decision. So far as may be, the operation of *stare decisis* in deciding cases and our evaluation of decisions should be impersonalized by the use of methods of marshalling and judging practical considerations which have as great a degree of objectivity as may be.

Under the head of finding and using objective methods, two large projects stand out:

Our case material is a gold mine for scientific work. It has not been scientifically exploited. The science of mechanics was built up by experimentation, but geology, for example, has had to rely almost solely upon observation. In law we cannot institute suits to test judicial behavior, as the physicists make experiments to test the behavior of matter. But each case is a record of judicial behavior. And there is a wealth of such records equaling that to which geology, for instance, has had access and the individual records are not more fractional or otherwise imperfect. A sufficient number of recorded experiments, all of whose factors are not known but with the unknown factors varying, may be quite as illuminating as a limited number of controlled experiments. Why has not our study of cases in the past yielded the results now sought? The attempt has been made to show that this is largely due to the fact that we have focused our attention too largely on the *vocal behavior* of judges in deciding cases. A study with more stress on their *non-vocal behavior, i. e.*, what the judges actually do when stimulated by the facts of the case before them, is the approach indispensable to exploiting scientifically the wealth of material in the cases. Economists may well congratulate themselves that they have the statistical method to add objectivity to their results. The case method when used scientifically will be found to be a method fully as significant for law as statistics is for economics. It is outstanding as an objective method.

The second project is this: We should critically examine all the methods now used in any of the social sciences and having any useful degree of objectivity. Their possibilities for law should be studied and their use attempted.

General Considerations as to Methods

In this connection, two general considerations should be kept in mind. It is common for those despairing of the widespread application of scientific methods in legal study to assume that a method having the objectivity and precision of that of mathematical physics is prerequisite in order for us to have any scientific method in the study of law. Reflection reveals that objective methods having great utility in such areas as biology and geology differ widely from the methods of mathematical physics with respect to their precision and objectivity.

The word "objective" in the term "objective method" is itself pragmatic. A very gross measurement of an object may be sufficiently accurate for the purposes of a rough carpenter and hence for his purposes "true" while hopelessly inaccurate for the purposes of a physicist working upon the expansion coefficient of a metal. The personal equation and subective elements bulk large in the first measurement. but for the purposes of a carpenter, they are unimportant. They are, of course, present in the measurements of a physicist. All that he can hope to do is reduce them to a minimum, and how far he needs to reduce them depends upon the particular purpose for which he is making a particular measurement. When this fact is fully appreciated by legal scholarship its hope for truly scientific methods may be found to be nearer to realization than it is now thought to be. Other social scientists are certainly making substantial progress in developing objective methods in many of their fields.

Conclusion

Such is the double task before us: first to work out a truly contemporary and detailed reclassification of human situations for legal treatment: and second, to develop that understanding of the social structure which will make possible a gradual return to that particularity of problem and awareness of reality which will make the opportunism of *stare decisis* an effective and enlightened tool for ordering human affairs: thus inaugurating a return to *stare decisis*, that greatest contribution of our common law and of our people to the art of human government: to *stare decisis*, a doctrine all of whose political wisdom cannot be caught into a sentence, but whose spirit, thoughtful about consequences, is cautious to consider only immediate problems and careful to illuminate them from the glow of the prudence and insight which its own experimentation patiently forges. To those high aims should be added the yet higher one of improving on the intuitive prudence of *stare decisis* by inaugurating a methodical empiricism.

Those are the tasks and that the call,—such a return to *stare decisis*. Pride of authorship should not hamper nor institutional jealousies retard. Many experiments should be made. One new classification should be tried in one place while some new methods of research are being tested elsewhere.

The most vital thing which this Association could set itself to do during the next decade is to serve as a stimulus to such widespread experimentation, as a clearing house for its results, and a forum for their discussion.

A return to a more rigorous and enlightened empiricism in the study and making of law is our most urgent need. We must work our way toward it. There is no short and certain way. It means to leave the Egypt of easy abstraction and generality and to face again the hardships of uncharted paths into the desert. Those marches already beginning will be many and trying. While those of riper years help with sympathy and understanding, younger shoulders must carry most of the loads. If we could but make something of a common task of these great labors, we might well hope soon to reach much of the promise of this common good.

[9]

COLUMBIA LAW REVIEW

VOL. XXX APRIL, 1930 NO. 4

A REALISTIC JURISPRUDENCE—THE NEXT STEP*

The problem of defining law; focus versus confines

The difficulty in framing any concept of "law" is that there are so many things to be included, and the things to be included are so unbelievably different from each other. Perhaps it is possible to get them all under one verbal roof. But I do not see what you have accomplished if you do. For a concept, as I understand it, is built for a purpose. It is a thinking tool. It is to make your data more manageable in doing something, in getting somewhere with them. And I have not yet met the job, or heard of it, to which all the data that associate themselves with this loosest of suggestive symbols, "law," are relevant at once. We do and have too many disparate things and thinkings to which we like to attach that name. For instance, legislators pass "a law," by which we mean that they officially put a new form of words on the statute books. That calls up associations with regard to attorneys and judges, and to suits being brought "under the statute." But it also calls up associations with regard to those sets of practices and expectations and people which we call political parties and machines and lobbies. The former we should want, in some way, to include under the head "law," I suspect. If we did not, we ought to stop defining and think a little further. The latter—the parties and lobbies—we might have more doubt about, even if we did stop and think. Again, it seems fairly clear that there has been something we could not well dissociate from our symbol "law" in places and times when there was no legislature and even no state—indeed when there was no organization we can call "political" that was distinct from any other organization. You cannot study the simpler forms of society nor "the law" of such forms without looking into the mechanisms of organized control at such times and places; but today you will be likely to distinguish such types of control as *non-legal*. Of course, you would not disregard them, if you wanted to

* The substance of this paper was presented at the Round Table on Current Trends in Political and Legal Thought of the American Association of Political Science, December, 1929, under the title *Modern Concepts of Law*.

know anything about "law" that was worth knowing. But you would regard them as background, or foreground, or underground, to your center of interest. They would be something that you would compare and contrast with "law," I suspect, in the present order of society. And yet I also suspect you would have your hands full if you set about to draw the line between "the two." Or again, there are gentlemen who spend a good deal of time discussing "the ends of law," or "what law ought to be." Are they talking about "law"? Certainly their postulates and conclusions, in gross and in detail, have no need to look like anything any judge ever did; and at times some of those gentlemen seem to avail themselves of that freedom; but it would be a case-hardened person who denied that what they are dealing with is closely connected with this same loose suggestive symbol. What interests me about that is when a judge is working in a "well-settled field" he is likely to pay no attention to what such gentlemen say, and to call it irrelevant speculation; whereas when he is working in an "unsettled field" he seems to pay a lot of attention to their ideas, or to ideas of much the same order. This I take to mean that *for some purposes* they are talking something very close to "law," under any definition; and for *other* purposes, they are talking something whose connection with "law" as just used is fairly remote. And this problem of the word calling up wide-scattered and disparate references, *according to the circumstance,* seems to me vital.

So that I am not going to attempt a definition of law. Not anybody's definition; much less my own. A definition both excludes and includes. It marks out a field. It makes some matters fall inside the field; it makes some fall outside. And the exclusion is almost always rather arbitrary. I have no desire to exclude anything from matters legal. In one aspect law is as broad as life, and for some purposes one will have to follow life pretty far to get the bearings of the legal matters one is examining. I say again, therefore, that I shall not attempt a definition. I shall not describe a periphery, a stopping place, a barrier. I shall instead devote my attention to the *focus* of matters legal. I shall try to discuss a *point of reference*; a point of reference to which I believe all matters legal can most usefully be referred, if they are to be seen with intelligence and with appreciation of their bearings. A focus, a core, a center—with the bearings and boundaries outward unlimited. Pardon my saying it so often; but I find it very hard to make people understand that I am not talking about putting or pushing anything *out of* the field or concept of law. People are so much used to definitions—although definitions have not always been of so much use to people. I am, therefore, going to talk about substituting a somewhat unfamiliar, but more exciting and more useful focus, for the focus that most thinking about law in the past has had.

Two references to the course that thought has taken will help to set the perspective: one, to the tenets of the nineteenth century schools of jurisprudence; one, to the development of the concepts of rights and of interests.

For the nineteenth century schools I am content to accept one of Pound's summaries.[1] It fits with what reading in the field I have done; it is based upon vastly more reading in the field than I shall ever do. With regard to the analytical jurists, Pound stresses their interest in a body of established precepts whereby a definite legal result is supposed to be fitted to a definite set of facts; he stresses the centering of their definition upon the "aggregate of authoritative legal precepts applied by tribunals as such in a given time and place," and their presupposition of a state to make precepts and tribunals authoritative. The historical jurists, on the other hand, he finds making little distinction between law and other forms of social control; with them customary precepts, irrespective of whether they originate in the organs of politically organized societies, come in for heavy attention; central in their picture of law are the traditional techniques of decision and the traditional or customary notions of rightness. (All this, it may be added, without any too close analysis as to what is meant by "custom.") For the philosophical jurists, finally, Pound finds that "philosophical, political and ethical ideas as to the end of law and as to what legal precepts should be in view thereof" occupy the center of the stage.

I have no wish to put the tenets of these schools to the test, nor to pursue them further. Their value here is limited, but great within its limits: taken together, they hammer home the complexity of law. Each school was reaching for a single definition of all that was significant about law. Each school wound up with a definition which stressed some phases and either overlooked or greatly under-stressed others. Each had a definition with which, for its purposes, and especially in the hands of its creative thinkers, it made striking headway. But too close attention to any one of the definitions—in its exclusion aspects—for too long, would have meant ultimate barrenness. And I gather that one lesson Pound has drawn from his study of these and other schools has been to insist rather on what goes into the idea of law than on what is to be kept out of it.

---

[1] LAW AND MORALS (1924), 25 *et seq.*

Precepts as the Heart and Core of Most Thinking About Law

Moreover, you will have noted running through his summary of their views the word "precepts." This is traditional. When men talk or think about law, they talk and think about *rules*. "Precepts" as used by Pound, for instance, I take to be roughly synonymous with rules and principles, the principles being wider in scope and proportionately vaguer in connotation, with a tendency toward idealization of some portion of the *status quo* at any given time. And I think you will find as you read Pound that the precepts are *central* to his thinking about law. Along with rules and principles—along with precepts proper, may I say?—he stresses for instance "standards" as a part of the subject matter of law. These standards seem to be those vague but useful pictures with which one approaches a wide and varied field of conduct to measure the rights of a particular situation: a conception of what a reasonable man would do in the circumstances, or of what good faith requires, and similar pictures. They differ from rules, though not from principles, partly in their vagueness; they differ from both in being not propositions in themselves, but normative approaches to working out the application of some one *term* in a major proposition. The principle, let us say, would read: a man must answer for what good faith requires. But a standard (like a concept; like any class-term, loose or sharp) functions chiefly or exclusively as *part* of a precept. Consequently, it belongs in much the same world. It, too, *centers* on precepts. But Pound mentions more as law than precepts and standards. Along with the standards he stresses also ideals as to "the end" of law. These I take to be in substance standards on a peculiarly vague and majestic scale; standards, perhaps, to be applied to rules rather than to individual transactions.[2] Finally, he stresses—and we meet here a very different order of phenomena—"the traditional techniques of developing and applying" precepts. Only a man gifted with insight would have added to the verbal formulae and verbalized (though vague) conceptual pictures thus far catalogued, such an element *of practices,* of habits and techniques of action, of *behavior*. But only a man partially caught in the traditional precept-thinking of an age that is passing would have focussed that behavior on, have given it a major reference to, have belittled its importance by dealing with it as a phase of, those merely verbal formulae: precepts. I have no wish to argue the point. It will appeal, or it will not, and argument will be of little service.

[2] Not only ideals, but standards, not only standards, but concepts, not only concepts, but rules, involve of course generalized mental pictures which play a part in shaping both rules and the actions of courts. But as traditionally dealt with, this ideal element, even where observed, is promptly related in the first instance to rules.

But not only this particular bit of phrasing (which might be accidental), but the use made in Pound's writings of the idea, brings out vigorously the limitations of rules, of precepts, of *words*, when made the focus, the *center of reference*, in thinking about law.[3]

Remedies, Rights and Interests: A Developing Insight

Indeed, those limitations appear throughout the current analysis of law in terms of interests, rights and remedies. The growth of that analysis requires a short digression, but one that I believe worth making. It has to do with the *subject matter* of the rules and pre-

[3] Pound's work in this aspect is as striking in its values as in its limitations. It is full to bursting of magnificent insight. It is to Pound we owe the suggestion of "the limits of effective legal action" (worked out in terms of *court* decisions). It is to Pound we owe the contrast of law-in-books and law-in-action (the latter limited again, in his working out of it, to what *courts* do; though in other places he insists upon *administrative* organs as the present center of legal growth). It is to Pound we owe the formulation "individualization of treatment of an offender," and the reference to the proceedings of the Conference on Charities and Corrections to see what the criminal law is really doing. And so it goes. I am not concerned here with whether prior writers may have contributed to, or anticipated, some or all of these ideas. Pound saw them, he formulated them, he drove them home. But these brilliant buddings have in the main not come to fruition. No one thinks them through in their relation either to each other or to the bulk of received jurisprudence. "Balancing of interests" remains with no indication of how to tell an interest when you see one, much less with any study of how they are or should be balanced. "Sociological jurisprudence" remains bare of most that is significant in sociology. "Law-in-action" is left as a suggestion, while further discussion of "the law" centers on "precept." "The limits of effective legal action" —a formulation that fairly shrieks for study of the habit and control set-up of society (that *complex*, industrialized, [partially] urban, indirect-cooperation society he has given us words for)—is left without study of the society to which law is supposed to have relation. The more one learns, the more one studies, the more light and stimulus Pound's writings give. But always peculiarly on a fringe of insight which fails to penetrate at all to the more systematic set-up of the material. One is tempted to see in the thinking of the one man and of the American school of sociological jurisprudence a parallel to the development of case law as a whole: accepting in the main what has been handed down; systematizing compartment-wise; innovating where need shows, powerfully and surely—but *ad hoc* only, with little drive toward or interest in incorporating the innovation into or aligning it with the mass of the material as received.

Critical reading of Pound's work, it may be noted in passing, and especially the phrasing of any concrete criticism, are embarrassed by the constant indeterminacy of the level of his discourse. At times the work purports clearly to travel on the level of considered and buttressed scholarly discussion; at times on the level of bed-time stories for the tired bar; at times on an intermediate level, that of the thoughtful but unproved essay. Most often, it is impossible to tell the intended level of any chapter or passage, and the writing seems to pass without notice from one to another. Now it is obvious that three successive, mutually inconsistent generalizations, though no one of them sustainable as the deliberate propositions of a scholar, may all be illuminating and indeed all true at once—on the level of the after-dinner speech, or even of the thought-provoking essay. All of which gags the critic at the same time that it perhaps stimulates his critical faculties. There is value in this. There is value, even, in the legal bed-time story. But there is greater value to be had. What would one not give for the actual appearance of the long-awaited *Sociological Jurisprudence*, if its author would integrate it in terms of those pioneering thoughts of his which thus far have been waiting to be called together in a Constituent Assembly?

cepts of which men regarded the legal system as made up. Both with us and in the Roman system that subject matter has in the course of time undergone striking changes.

In the earlier stages the rules were thought of almost exclusively as rules of remedies.[4] Remedies were few and specific. There were a few certain ways to lug a man into court and a few certain things that you or the court could do with him when you got him there. We are concerned here not with why that was (why "can" a court of law give no injunctive relief today?) but only with *that* it was. The question for the man of that day took this shape: on what facts could one man make use of any specific one of the specific ways of making the court bother another man? And the rules of law were rules about that. They clustered around each remedy. In those terms people thought.[5] They thought about what they could see and do. Their crude minds dealt only with what they could observe. What they observed, they described.

---

[4] I am presupposing the presence of "rules of law," *i.e.*, at least assuming law as a semi-specialized activity of control distinguished from other mechanisms of control; and also presupposing generalization to have set in. Just how far this first assumption reaches I am sure I do not know; I should be inclined to regard any special assembly held for the purpose of adjusting disputes, by say village elders otherwise without official position or authority (*cf.* GUTMAN, DAS RECHT DER DSCHAGGA, DER SPRUCHRASEN), as one instance of its presence. The second assumption presupposes that prior decision has begun to be dealt with as precedent; that *Themis* is not merely an oracle, but marks a norm. But I am insisting that it be a norm *of law*. Vinogradoff cogently points out that Maine's *Themis* is not a pure creation of the judgment maker; before the *Themis* was a societal life in which norms were both explicit and implicit. I hesitate, however, to call the *implicit* norms either "rules" or "legal," and see nothing but confusion to be had from so doing. I see only *practices*, more or less definite, more or less conscious, plus a generalized attitude that whatever is practice is right, and whatever varies widely enough is wrong. Certainly the process of making the implicit norm express calls for difficult creative work (two pieces of gold as the reward, on the shield of Achilles!) though any man can *recognize* the result once arrived at *as* right, if it is right (the crowd will award the gold!). Certainly also the "explicit-making" permits a twisting. Finally, once the judgment is made, it is both clearer to see, firmer in outline, more rigid, and perhaps more authoritative than it was before. If authoritative at all *because of who made it*, or the circumstances of its making, moreover, it has certainly begun the differentiation out of the general social matrix into the specific character of legality. (Malinowski's analysis in *Crime and Custom in Savage Society* (1926) is somewhat similar: but it moves in terms of dominant authoritativeness of the norm, not of the functionary. If, *when appealed to*, a norm will prevail over an inconsistent norm or common practice, he thinks of it as legal. An illuminating discrimination.)

[5] Here and in the following I am talking about the thinking of what my friend T. R. Powell calls the "postmortemizers," those who hash over events that are past, and write books about them, or build taught law. Such persons typically show a wider range of thought than the practical man of similar ability, but a greater naiveté. The practical man seems to think in two water-tight compartments. One half of his mind grinds out the ideology of the day, as gospel, over pippins and cheese or from the rostrum; that half belongs to the postmortemizers. The other half deals cannily with existing institutions, of whatever holiness, to shape (at times it verges on twisting) them to the needs of the practical man or of

To later writers this seemed primitive. The later thinkers find a different kind of order in the field of law. Remedies seem to them to have a *purpose,* to be protections of something else. They could imagine these somethings and give them a name: *rights,* substantive rights. Thus the important, the substantial rules of law become rules defining rights. Remedies are relegated to the periphery of attention. They are "adjective law" merely—devices more or less imperfect for giving effect to the important things, the substantive rights which make up the substance of the law. The relation of rights to rules is fairly clear: the two are aspects of the same thing. When a rule runs in favor of a person, he has a right, as measured by the rule. Or, if he has a right, that can be phrased by setting out a rule ascribing to him and persons in like situation with him the benefits connoted by the rights. Rights are thus precise counterparts of rules, when the rights are ascribed generally to all persons in a class in given circumstances; and this is the typical postmortemizer's line of discourse. Or rights, when ascribed to particular individuals in specific circumstances, are deductions which presuppose the rule; the major premise is the general rule on rights; the minor is the proposition hooking up this individual and these circumstances with that general rule. Rights and rules are therefore for present purposes pretty much interchangeable; the right is a shorthand symbol for the rule.[6]

Substantive rights and rules are spoken of as prevailing between people, laymen: one has, *e.g.,* a right to the performance of a contract. It is a heresy when Coke or Holmes speaks of a man having liberty under the law to perform his contract, or pay damages, at his option. It would likewise be a heresy to argue that the vital real evidence of this supposed "right" lies in an action for damages, and that the right could rather more accurately be phrased somewhat as follows: if the other party does not perform as agreed, you can sue, and *if* you have a fair lawyer, and nothing goes wrong with your witnesses or the jury, *and* you give up four or five days of time and some ten to thirty percent of

---

his client. This side of the practical man's mind must have been at work in every legal system from the days of the most formal rigidity. (Compare the whole preparation and sequence of the lawsuit in Dasent's *Njals-Saga.*) And some persons—conscious creators—must have taken thought of the relation of interest and remedy since there has been law. (Compare the protection of the Church in the old English laws.) But the tone and ideas of the postmortemizers have changed from age to age, and while not altering the basic attitudes of the practical man, have changed his words and his stock of ideas, his tools, seemingly with powerful effects on his results.

[6] For present purposes the dubious distinction taken by the German thinkers: "objective *Recht*" (rather "law" than "right") and "subjective *Recht*" (close to our pre-Hohfeldian "right") can be disregarded. It fits the discussion in that the subjective *Recht* is viewed first of all as a deduction from the rule of law, and then as an independent something.

the proceeds, and wait two to twenty months, you will *probably* get a judgment for a sum considerably less than what the performance would have been worth—which, if the other party is solvent and has not secreted his assets, you can in further due course collect with six percent interest for delay. To argue thus would be to confuse the remedy (which you can see) with the substantive right (which you cannot see, but which you know is there—somewhere; people tell you so). The substantive right in this body of thought has a shape and scope independent of the accidents of remedies. And herein lies the scientific advance involved in the concept. You are freed of any necessity of observing what courts do, and of limiting your discussion to that. You get back into the ultimate realities behind their doing. Obviously you can think more clearly among those ultimate realities. They are not so much obscured by inconsistency and divergence of detail. They are not answerable to fact.

Most lay thinking, it may be noted in passing, is on this level today. Typical is the current acceptance of a paper rule or statute as meaning something simply because it has paper authority—indeed, as meaning all it says, or all it is supposed to have been intended to say, simply because it has paper authority.

Far be it from me to dispute that the concepts of substantive rights and of rules of substantive law have had great value.[7] They moved definitely and sharply toward fixing the attention of thinkers on the idea that procedure, remedies, existed not merely because they existed, nor because they had value in themselves, but because they had a purpose. From which follows immediate inquiry into what the purpose is, and criticism, if the means to its accomplishment be poor. They moved, moreover, to some extent, toward sizing up the law by situations, instead of under the categories of historically conditioned, often archaic remedy-law: a new base for a new synthesis; a base for law reform.

The Ambiguities in the Concepts of Rules and Rights

But that should not obscure the price that was paid for the advance. A price first, as already described, of moving discussion away from the checkup of fact. To a legal reformer in his campaigning, in his getting of new views across, this may have value, if "the fact" in question be existing positive law. He may move more comfortably if he can keep people from observing that his moves mean change. To a scientist, observing, or to a reformer engaged not in selling his reform,

[7] Neither would I be understood to deny practical consequences to this mode of thinking, in our case results, in constitutional law, limitation of actions, etc., or to urge that describing the remedy describes the whole situation, today. It *does* describe the most important, and a much neglected aspect of the situation.

in propaganding, in putting ideas over, but in inquiring what is before him, where he wants to get, and how to get there, this obfuscation of the facts is another matter.

Secondly, a price was paid, of ambiguity—indeed of multiguity. "Rules" is a term sufficiently ambiguous. A rule may be prescriptive: "this is what *ought* to be; what the judges *ought* to do in such cases." Or it may be descriptive: "this is what *is;* what the judges *actually* do in such cases." Or it may be both at once: "this is *both* what they do *and* what they ought to do."[7a] And when theorists discuss, they will move from one of these meanings into another without notice, and with all and any gradations of connotations. In the particular case of rules "of law" a further ambiguity affects the word "rule": whether descriptive or prescriptive, there is little effort to make out *whose* action and *what* action is prescribed or described. The statement "this is the rule" typically means: "I find this formula of words in authoritative books."[8] Does this connote: *Courts are actually proceeding* according to this formula"; or *"Courts* always *rehearse* this formula in this connection?" Does it connote: *"People* are conducting themselves in the light of this formula"; or even "People are conducting themselves as this formula suggests that they ought to." The theorist will rarely trouble to tell you how many (if any) of these connotations are implicit in his statement: "this is the rule." But he will reason, on the next page, from some one of such implications. Which means: confusion, profuse and inevitable.[9]

The confusion is stirred blacker with the concept "right" poured in. "Right" adds nothing to descriptive power. But it gives a specious

[7a] Put another way, prescriptive rules are rules *for* doing something; descriptive rules are so-called rules *of* doing something—statements of observed regularity. But "rules *of*" in common speech includes both aspects at once, and "rules *for*" as often as not connotes the presence of a corresponding practice. I shall limit my term "rules" to "rules for," and shall not *imply* any such connotation.

[8] I omit from discussion here one other troublesome confusion: whenever rules are discussed in their prescriptive aspect, it is frequently difficult to tell whether a writer is giving *his own view* of what ought to be, or, on the other hand, a view sanctioned by authority—the prevailingly accepted prescriptive rules. In this last case the *prevalence* of a given prescriptive rule is a fact capable of description (or misdescription); but it always remains to be noted whether that prevailing prescriptive rule has any counterpart in *practice,* or remains in the paper or lip-service stage.

[9] Refinement of terms goes some distance to avoid this confusion. "Rule" is well confined to the *pre*scriptive sphere. "Paper rule" is a fair name for a rule to which no counterpart in practice is ascribed. "Working rule" indicates a rule with counterpart in practice, or else a practice *consciously* normatized. *Cf. supra* note 4. "Practice" indicates an observable course of action, with no necessary ascription of conscious normatizing about it. In an earlier paper (15 AM. EC. REV. 671) I failed to make this last distinction; it seems obvious, however, that it refines one's descriptive and reasoning technique in an important detail. Consider, *e.g.,* the double value Ehrlich's work would have had, if his stock of terms had served to keep such distinctions clear, and to let his magnificent thinking work itself out free of confusion.

appearance of substance to prescriptive rules. They seem to be *about* some *thing*. So that to clothe one's statement about what rules of law are in terms of rights, is to double the tendency to disregard the limitations actually put on rules or rights by practice and by remedies. At the vital core of thought about law, at the very place where one thought impinges on another, or where one part of law impinges on another, one sees the impingement in terms of idealized somethings which may not, which mostly *do* not, reflect men's actions. In terms of words, and not in terms of conduct; in terms of what *apparently* is understandable *without* checking up in life. So that one makes the assumption—without the urge to inquiry—that one is dealing with reality when he talks of rights, and proceeds to use these unchecked words for further building.

There is another confusion, found in dealing with rules, and strengthened by the associated idea of rights, within the field of doctrine itself. Having come to regard words as sound bases for further thinking, the tendency is well nigh inevitable to simplify the formulations more and more: to rub out of the formulations even the discrepancies in paper doctrine which any growing system of law contains in heaping measure; doubly so because the word "rights" introduces *sub rosa* at this point the additional notion of "rightness" (in the sense of what ought to be)—before which unwanted discrepancies must fall. I am speaking here of the effects of the idea of rightness on the rejection of some of the existent purely doctrinal materials in favor of other equally doctrinal materials, the case of conflicts in and within legal doctrine—a matter of vast concern to a lawyer, though perhaps of no great moment to a political scientist.

But the same tendency carries over quite as well into the confusion of legal with non-legal materials, where it concerns political scientist and lawyer in common; and here the idea of "rights" seems to be the heavy tool of confusion, with no help at all from the idea of "rules." "Right" eternally suggests its connotation of inherent "rightness"—social, political, economic, and especially moral. It takes more careful self-analysis than most have been interested in giving to keep the *non-legal* "right" (which was a reason for claiming or striving toward or awarding a legal right) distinguished from the "legal right" which was conceived, I take it, as something not quite a mere description of an available remedy, but at least an official recognition that some kind of remedy could be had. The threat of ambiguous middle is obvious.[9a] The natural rights theorists did little to make it less.

[9a] Wherever the plaintiff has a [legal] right to recover, he can recover at law. This plaintiff has a [social, moral, economic] right to recover. Therefore this plaintiff can recover in this action at law. This may improve the law. It has. It is not, for that, any the better thinking for a scientist *to use*.

Interests

This third confusion (but, be it noted, neither the second nor the first) was cleared up by the controversy that centered about Ihering. Since that controversy we take some care to limit our term "rights" to legal rights ("substantive," if nothing more be said), and are thereby aided in keeping the legal separate from the social factors at work in a situation. The term *interests,* on the other hand, comes in to focus attention on the presence of social factors, and to urge that substantive rights themselves, like remedies, exits only for a purpose. Their purpose is now perceived to be the protection of the interests. To be sure, we do not know what interests are. Hence, behind substantive rights (which we need not check against anything courts *do*) we now have interests (which we need not check against anything at all, and about whose presence, extent, nature and importance, whether the interests be taken absolutely or taken relatively one to another, no two of us seem to be able to agree). The scientific advance should again be obvious. Complete subjectivity has been achieved.

At this stage of the development, then, one arrives at a double chain of purposes. One starts with the interest. That is a social fact or factor of some kind, existing dependent of the law.[9b] And it has value independent of the law. Indeed, its protection is the purpose of substantive legal rights, of legal rules, of precepts of substantive law. "Security of transactions" is such an interest. The rules and rights of contract law exist to protect and effectuate it. The rules and rights are not ends, but means. But they are means which in another aspect (like most means) themselves become ends: remedies exist as means to effectuate the substantive rights, to realize the substantive rules. Obviously the means may be inadequate, badly chosen, wasteful, even self-defeating, at either stage. They may be so, cumulatively, at both stages. The rule that consideration is necessary to make an offer irrevocable for three days, even when the offer is fully intended, business like, signed, in writing, and expressed to be irrevocable for three days, may be thought not adapted to further security of transactions. The rule that certain oral and essential terms of an agreement are without force, if the balance of the agreement has been committed to writing, and looks on its face to be complete, raises considerable doubts as to its furtherance of security of transactions—sufficiently so as to have made our rules on the subject rather intricate and uncertain, and our judicial practices at times highly uncertain.

[9b] This is an overstatement. Past law may have contributed much to the present existence of an interest, and to its shape and extent.

The rules standardizing the remedies in contracts for the sale of goods, limiting the remedy to a suit before a jury, and for damages, and measuring the damages in the great body of cases by arbitrary standards which presuppose a frictionless market, may be thought to give inadequate remedy, even if the basis of supposed substantive rules and rights be thought wholly adequate to *its* purposes. The means, I say, may be inadequate; but the analysis invites discovery of the inadequacy. Hence, whatever one thinks of the sufficiency in the large of the analysis in the threefold terms of interests, substantive rights and rules, and remedies, one can but pay homage to the sureness with which it forces law on the attention as something man-made, something capable of criticism, of change, of reform—and capable of criticism, change, and reform not only according to standards found inside law itself (inner harmony, logical consistence of rules, parts and tendencies, *elegantia juris*) but also according to standards vastly more vital found *outside* law itself, in the society law purports both to govern *and to serve.*

On the other hand, the set-up in these terms has carried over its full measure of confusion, as I have tried to indicate above. And the confusion thus carried over is not—like the virtues of the analysis—familiar, well understood, and regularly taken account of. Which brings me again to the suggestion made above, that the use of precepts, or rules, or of rights which are logical counterparts of rules—of *words,* in a word—as the *center* of reference in thinking about law, is a block to clear thinking about matters legal. I want again to make sure that I am not misunderstood. (1) I am not arguing that "rules of substantive law" are without importance. (2) I am not arguing that it is not humanly *possible* to use the interests-rights and rules-remedies analysis and still think clearly and usefully about law. (3) Least of all, am I attempting to urge the exclusion of substantive rights and rules from the field of "law." Instead of these things, I am arguing (1) that rules of substantive law are of far less importance than most legal theorizers have assumed in most of their thinking and writing, and that they are *not* the most useful center of reference for discussion of law; (2) that the presence of the term "rights and rules" in the interest set-up (a) has persistent tendency to misfocus attention on that term; (b) that the avoidance of that tendency is a great gain in clarity; and (c) that to both attempt such avoidance and retain the term is to cumber all discussion with embarrassing and quite unnecessary baggage; (3) that substantive rights and rules should be removed from their present position at the *focal point* of legal discussion, in favor the *area of contact* between judicial (or official) *behavior* and the *behavior* of laymen; that the substantive rights and rules should be studied not as self-existent, nor as a major point of reference, but themselves with constant reference to that area of behavior-contacts. Let me take up the second and third of these positions together, and turn then to the first.

The Interests-Rights-Remedies Analysis: Words v. Practice

I see no value to be gained from the interests-rights and rules-remedies set up except to bring out, to underscore, that law is not all, nor yet the major part of, society; and to force attention to the relations and interactions of law and the rest of society; and as a matter of method, to provide words which keep legal and non-legal aspects of the situation and the interactions distinct. And it would seem to go without demonstration that *the most significant* (I do *not* say the *only* significant) aspects of the relations of law and society lie in the field of behavior, and that words take on importance either because and insofar as they are behavior, or because and insofar as they demonstrably reflect or influence other behavior. This statement seems not worth making. Its truth is absurdly apparent. For all that, it reverses, it upsets, the whole traditional approach to law. It turns accepted theory on its head. The traditional approach is in terms of words; it centers on words; it has the utmost difficulty in getting beyond words. If nothing be said about behavior, the *tacit* assumption is that the words do reflect behavior, and if they be the words of rules of law, do influence behavior, even influence behavior effectively and precisely to conform completely to those words. Here lies the key to the muddle. The "rules" are laid down; in the type-case they are "ought" rules, prescriptive rules: the writer's prescriptions, the writer's oughts, individually proclaimed oughts—the true rule is that judges should give judgment for the plaintiff on these facts.[10] From this we jump without necessary notice into equivalent oughts as *accepted* in the legal system under discussion: prevailing oughts—the authorities agree that judges should give judgment for the plaintiff on these facts. Here, again without notice and without inquiry, we *assume* that *practice* of the judges conforms to the accepted oughts on the books; that the verbal formulations of oughts *describe* precisely the is-es of practice; that they *do* give such judgment on such facts. A toothed bird of a situation, in law or any other walk of life. Where is men's ideology about their doing, about what is good prac-

---

[10] How joyously sharp, under this addressing of the rule to the judge becomes the distinction between a rule telling him what to *do*, himself, and one telling him how to instruct a jury!

tice—where is that ideology or has it ever been an adequate description of their *working* practice?

This is the first tacit imputation of factuality to the rules of ought. A second such imputation follows forthwith—again without explicitness, again without inquiry, again (save in odd instances) without challenge or suggestion or doubt. The paper rule of ought which has now been *assumed* to *describe* the judges' *working* rule of ought (*i.e.*, to correspond with the judges' practice of decision) is now further assumed to *control* the practice of the interested laymen, to *govern* people's conduct. Pray for the storm-tossed mariner on a night like this! What hope is there for clarity of reasoning with such a waste of billowing to build on?

Do I suggest that (to cut in at one crucial point) the "accepted rules," the rules the judges say that they apply, are without influence upon their actual behavior? I do not. I do not even say that, *sometimes*, these "accepted rules" may not be a very accurate description of the judges' actual behavior. What I say is that such accuracy of description is rare. The question is how, and how much, and in what direction, do the accepted rule and the practice of decision diverge? More: how, and how much, *in each case?* You cannot generalize on this, *without investigation*. Your guesses may be worth something, in the large. *They are worth nothing at all, in the particular.* The one thing we know now for certain is, that different rules have totally different relations to the behavior of judges, of other officials, and of the particular persons "governed" (optimistic word!) by those different rules. The approach here argued for admits, then, out of hand, *some* relation between *any* accepted rule and judicial behavior; and then proceeds to deny that that admission involves anything but a problem for investigation in the case in hand; and to argue that the significance of the particular rule will appear only *after* the investigation of the vital, focal, phenomenon: the behavior. And if an empirical *science* of law is to have any realistic basis, any responsibility to the facts, I see no escape from moving to this position. Thus, and only thus, is the real gain sought by the interests-rights and rules-remedies analysis to be made tangible. I do not deny, be it noted, that those who have cast their thinking in that set-up are from time to time aware of the importance of what is here urged. "Law-in-books and law-in-action." Indeed, whenever challenged on the point, any one of them will proceed to remodel his emphasis *ad hoc;* he will, for a moment, fix his stress on the remedy, even on the effects of the remedy, as used, in life. *But* it is an *ad hoc* remodelling. It is forgotten when the immediate issue is passed. It is no part of the standard equipment of investigation, discussion, synthesis; it is a part only of the equipment of defense. When used apart from combat, as a result of a worker's own curiosity or of some sudden fact-stimulus from outside, it flares like a shooting star, and disappears. Always the night of words will close again in beauty over the wild, streaked disturbance.

Interests: What Are They?

This emphasis on behavior, on the observable, on *attempts* at objective cross-check on the data under discussion, on *attempts* to find words which describe and do not misdescribe those data, ought to bear fruit in the discussion of interests, as well. The attribution of "interest" quality to anything of necessity involves a value-judgment over and above those value-judgments inherent in any scientific inquiry.[11] At that point the behavior approach ceases to promise objective agreement, except in tnis—that isolation of the value-judgement, in presentation, from the observed phenomena on which it in part rests, would clarify much discussion. Above all, such an approach to interests would move in terms of *demonstrating the existence of groupings* of behavior claimed to be significant, as the part of scientific decency when any "interest" is set up for discussion. The present approach tends instead to set up the broadest of formulae about interests, and to attribute them to situations in magisterial unconcern for the specific facts. I have paid my respects briefly above to some aspects of "security of transactions." I would not be understood thereby to deny that those three words are highly useful, or that they refer to very significant aspects of our life. But I am very eager to be understood as questioning how much is accomplished, for any given specific problem, by resting merely on the magic of those words. I think my friend Patterson has wisely described the interest-concept, in its present stage of development, as merely a red flag to *challenge investigation* in certain general directions—as leaving in any concrete situation most of the fact gathering and most of the fact weighing still to be done. "Security of transactions," in the contract cases I have put above would, to him, mean the most useful raising of a query: what kind of transactions is involved? Better, what *kinds* of transactions are involved? How many? What results, at present? What disappointments? What effects would any proposed change have? What possible undesired effects, in the hands of interested parties? And

[11] As, *e.g.*, that it is worth while finding out; that it is worth while checking conclusions constantly by facts; and striving to state conclusions which stay within the observed facts; probably also that it is worth while to publish such conclusions for discussion irrespective of what prejudices they may affront, or what accepted values they may disturb.

so on. "Security of transactions" would settle nothing. It would, as facts become clear, suggest one line of policy which has come in many phases of the law to be regarded as important; but it would leave the importance of that line of policy in any case to be illumined by the facts relevant to the situation in that instant case. No elimination of the subjective value-judgment, then; but an illumination by objective data of the basis and bearings of a subjective value-judgment. Insofar, a comparison of *facts* with *facts,* and not of *words* with *words.* Not a comparison of a mere formula of words about an interest with a formula of words said to be a "rule of law," a precept with no man knows what unexamined meaning in life. Nay, rather the objective data, the *specific* data, *claimed* to represent an interest, compared with the *actual doings* of the judges and the *actual effects* of their doings *on the data claimed to represent an interest.* If the judges' *sayings* have *demonstrable* effects, add those to the comparison. What else is relevant? Better: is anything else anything like *so* relevant?

I have said above that this can be done under the more cumbersome three-fold analytical set-up.[12] I have said that it semi-occasionlly

[12] Throughout this paper I am speaking primarily from the viewpoint of the postmortemizer, the observer, the orderer, the scientist. But in passing let me pay my respects to four other lines of legal thinking in which the utility of the suggested approach seems equally striking. (a) That of the practicing lawyer. In his moments of action, in his actual handling of a case or situation, the measure of his success is the measure in which he actually uses this approach. (The question of how far he uses it consciously, how far intuitively, is immaterial.) His job is either to guide a specific client through the difficulties of action in a concrete situation, or to bring the personnel of a specific tribunal to a specific result. The desired results, and not formulae, are his focus, and he uses formulae as he uses his knowledge of both judicial tradition and individual peculiarity: as tools to reach his desired result. He can be more effective, as any other practical man or artist can, if his technique be consciously studied. This is not to say that all that goes to make up his technique can be laid down or be consciously imparted. Still less is it to urge that he is himself a trustworthy reporter of his own technique.

(b) That of the legislator. Here is a man who wants results. How can one doubt the added utility to be derived from his wrestling with the observable facts of official action and lay action as those facts exist? Indeed, the successful practitioner and the successful politician are precisely the men whose grasp of the realities of law puts the word-beclouded theorist to shame.

(c) That of the philosopher of law—on the side of the "ends of law" and social values. He takes his data for philosophizing from somewhere. The worthwhileness of his philosophy is to a considerable degree conditioned on those data. If they be data of life, his problems become more real, his check-up easier, his basis of thinking more actual. This means at least, when he comes to the application of his chosen values to the criticism of "positive law," that he would bridge to the law-in-action of his day, not merely to the books. If he be a pure mystic, this may be immaterial; otherwise the gain seems inevitable.

For the devotee of formal logic in the law the picture is somewhat different. He will be concerned with words, with propositions. Probably almost wholly with propositions which move within the realm of ought—of doctrine—presumably the accepted doctrine of the system. Once he has his propositions, he runs free of the

has been done. I have said that it is rarely done, and that the definite tendency of that set-up is to block off the doing of it. I venture to predict that without the shift of emphasis, of focus, to behavior, that tendency will continue cheerfully in evidence.

Meaning of Rules and Rights Under the Behavior Analysis

What now, is the place of rules and rights, under such an approach? To attempt their excision from the field of law would be to fly in the face of fact. I should like to begin by distinguishing real "rules" and rights from paper rules and rights. The former

approach here discussed. He meets that approach in two places: the first, when he puts concrete content into his symbols, to start with. He will be no more accurate a logician, but a more useful one, if he reaches into observed fact, not merely into paper words, for that life content. And again, when the logical process is over, and he wishes to compare his results with something, to see whether he would not prefer another line of systematizing, he can use the behavior-area effectively for his comparison.

But what I have said of the logician suggests the making express of a matter implicit throughout the paper. To say that the area of behavior contact is the most useful point of reference for all matters legal is *not* to say that a specialist may not do the most useful of work, conceivably, without even reaching to that point of reference. A careful study of the formal logic of judicial opinions would be a useful study. But I would urge that even its usefulness would be hugely increased by an equally careful study of the instrumentalism, the pragmatic and socio-psychological decision elements in the same cases. And that an equally geometric increase in illumination would follow a further careful study of the effects on the society concerned of the same cases. Under the present "words" and "rules" appproach, all the tendency would be to stop with, or slightly modify, the first of these hypothetical studies. Under the behavior-contact approach each would be welcome, but the insistent drive would be toward completing the last before the significance of the others would be thought even measurably understood.

(d) That of the judge. His approach as one member of a bench to his colleagues does not seem to me to differ significantly for the present purpose from that of the practicing lawyer. His approach *for himself* involves (as does the approach of the philosopher) his forming a value-judgment on the case in hand, in addition to observation and predicition. How his value-judgment can fail of higher utility if he sees his problem not as the mere making of an abstract paper formula, but as the devising of a *way of working* in court *which will in due course affect people* is hard for me to see. The latter approach will certainly force him toward using all facilities he has available to *visualize* in advance the effects of the decision. Such visualization has been thought—and, I conceive, rightly—to be the essence of case-law wisdom-in-action. The approach described should make this wisdom-in-action a reality in a higher percentage of cases. I have developed elsewhere that whereas the net effect is undoubtedly an expansion of the traditional field of discretion and judicial law-making, yet this should give even a conservative no cause for alarm: first, because even when expanded, that field remains amazingly narrow, taken in relation to law as a whole, or to the movement of law—only cumulative changes over decades being in the main of much note; second, because it involves the introduction of no technique of change not already hallowed by conservative tradition, but only a reorganization, for conscious utilization, of techniques accepted for centuries as good; third (this an article of faith, not a matter capable as yet of proof) because the type of change produced under these circumstances is change which moves official action more into keeping with current needs; and another type of change, now constantly occurring, though hidden, tends to be eliminated: change by way of over-simplification of verbal formulae and over-"application" of such formulae to cases they never had before been applied to, and do not fit. DAS AMERIKANISCHE PRÄJUDIZIENRECHT (in preparation).

are conceived in terms of behavior; they are but other names, convenient shorthand symbols, for the remedies, the actions of the courts. They are descriptive, not prescriptive, except in so far as there may occasionally be implied that courts *ought to* continue in their practices.[13] "Real rules," then, if I had my way with words, would by legal scientists be called the practices of the courts, and not "rules" at all. And statements of "rights" would be statements of likelihood that in a given situation a certain type of court action loomed in the offing. Factual terms. No more. This use of "rights," at least, has already considerable standing among the followers of Hohfeld. This concept of "real rule" has been gaining favor since it was first put into clarity by Holmes. "Paper rules" are what have been treated, traditionally, as rules of law: the accepted *doctrine* of the time and place—what the books there say "the law" is. The "real rules" and rights—"what the courts will do in a given case, and nothing more pretentious"—are then predictions. They are, I repeat, on the level of isness and not of oughtness; they seek earnestly to go no whit, in their suggestion, beyond the remedy actually available. Like all shorthand symbols, they are dangerous in connotation, when applied to situations which are not all quite alike. But their intent and effort is to describe. And one can borrow for them Max Weber's magnificent formulation in terms of probability: a right (or practice, or "real rule") exists *to the extent that* a likelihood exists that *A* can induce a court to squeeze, out of *B*, *A*'s damages; more: *to the extent that* the likely collections will cover *A's* damage. In this aspect *substantive* rights and "rules," as distinct from adjective, simply disappear—on the descriptive level. The measure of a "rule," the measure of a right, becomes what can be done about the situation. *Accurate* statement of a "real rule" or of a right includes all procedural limitations on what can be done about the situation. What is left, in the realm of *description*, are at the one end the facts, the groupings of conduct (and demonstrable expectations) which may be claimed to constitute an interest; and on the other the practices of courts in their effects upon the conduct and expectations of the laymen in question. Facts, in the world of isness, to be compared directly with other facts, also in the world of isness.

A reversion, do you say, to the crude and out-moded thinking of rules in terms of remedies only, to confining legal thinking to the vagaries of tradition-bound procedure? Not quite. It is a reversion

---

[13] Eliminating such an implication would to my mind be pure gain. The question of desirability of continuing a given practice, when it comes up for discussion at all, is better made express.

to the realism of that primitive point of view. But a sophisticated reversion to a sophisticated realism. Gone is the ancient assumption that law is because law is; there has come since, and remains, the inquiry into the purpose of what courts are doing, the criticism in terms of searching out purposes and criticizing means. Here value-judgments reenter the picture, and should. Observing particular, concrete facts of conduct and of expectation which suggest the presence of "an interest," one arrives at his value conclusion that something in those facts calls for protection at the hands of state officials. What protection is called for, and called for in terms of what *action* of the state officials? Again a matter of judgment—but a matter of judgment which at least foots on reality and comes to results in terms of action. With that hypothetical action, the actual conduct of those officials can be directly compared. Room for error, in plenty, in diagnosing interests, and in imagining the forms of official conduct suited to their protection. But realism in discussion; realism at each end of the comparison; a narrowing as far as the present state of knowledge will permit, of the field for obstructing eyes with words that masquerade as things without a check-up.

The Place and Treatment of Paper Rules

Are "rules of law" in the accepted sense eliminated in such a course of thought? Somewhat obviously not. Whether they be pure paper rules, or are the accepted patter of the law officials, they remain present, and their presence remains an actuality—an actuality of importance—but an actuality whose *precise* importance, whose bearing and influence become clear. First of all they appear as what they are: rules of authoritative ought, addressed *to* officials, telling *officials* what the *officials* ought to do.[14] To which telling the officials either pay no heed at all (the pure paper rule; the dead-letter statute; the obsolete case) or listen partly (the rule "construed" out of recognition; the rule to which lip-service only is paid, while practice runs another course) or listen with all care (the rule with which the official practice pretty accurately coincides). I think that every such official precept-on-the-books (statute, doctrine laid down in the decision of a court, administrative regulation) tacitly contains an element of pseudo-

[14] This I think holds true of *all* official ought-rules, irrespective of their form. I speak of their effects, not of their purposes. And the rights of laymen result through the screen of the official's practice, by a kind of social reflex. Ehrlich described the phenomenon cogently, so far as concerned the rules governing the set-up of the state governmental machine. A legal philosopher or a normatizer, with his mind fixed on the purpose of rules to ultimately affect the conduct of the "governed," will quarrel with this. A sociologist is content to see and describe what happens—and *compare* that with what is purposed.

description along with its statement of what officials ought to do; a tacit statement that officials do act according to the tenor of the rule; a tacit prediction that officials will act according to its tenor. Neither statement nor prediction is often true *in toto*. And the first point of the approach here made is skepticism as to the truth of either in the case in hand. Yet it is an accepted convention to act and talk as if this statement and prediction were most solemn truth: a tradition marked peculiarly among the legal profession when engaged officially. It is indeed of first importance to remember that such a tradition contains a tendency to verify itself.[15] But no more so than to remember that such a tendency is no more powerful than its opposite: that other tendency to move quietly into falsifying the prediction in fact, while laying on an ointment of conventional words to soothe such as wish to believe the prediction has worked out.

Thus the problem of official formulations of rules and rights becomes complex. First, as to formulations already present, already existent: the accepted doctrine. There, I repeat, one lifts an eye canny and skeptical as to whether judicial behavior is in fact what the paper rule purports (implicitly) to state. One seeks the real practice on the subject, by study of how the cases do in fact eventuate. One seeks to determine how far the paper rule is real, how far *merely* paper.[16] One seeks an understanding of *actual* judicial behavior, in that comparison of rule with practice; one follows also the use made of the paper rule in argument by judges and by counsel, and the apparent influence of its official presence on decisions. One seeks to determine when it is stated, but ignored; when it is stated and followed; when and why it is *expressly* narrowed or extended or modified, so that a new paper rule is created. One observes the level of *silent* application or modification or escape, in the "interpretation" of the facts of a case, in contrast to that other and quite distinct level of express wrestling with the language of the paper rule. One observes how strongly ingrained is the tradition of requiring a good paper justification, in terms of officially accepted paper rules, before any decision, however appealing on the facts, can be regarded as likely of acceptance. And by the same token, one observes the importance of the

[15] Ehrlich, again, brings this out beautifully.

[16] And on moving into the further fields of contact between judicial or official behavior and lay behavior, one gets into much deeper water: how does the paper rule work out (*i.e.*, have a reflection or a counterpart in behavior) in lower court cases, unappealed? How often does it have any influence? What influence on administrative officials? On transactions between laymen which never reach any officials? All signs point to this being vastly more important than the set-up of doctrine, or even than the actual practices of higher courts. What is documented takes on a specious appearance of value, as against the unexplored.

official formulae as tools of argument and persuasion; one observes both the stimuli to be derived from, and the limitations set by, their language. Very rapidly, too, one perceives that neither are all official formulae alike in these regards, nor are all courts, nor are all times and circumstances for the same formula in the same court. The *handling* of the official formulae to influence court behavior then comes to appear as an art, capable only to a limited extent of routinization or (to date) of accurate and satisfying description. And the discrepancy, great or small, between the official formula and what actually results, obtains the limelight attention it deserves.

Paper Rules and New Control

I am tempted, however, to regard the *new* formulation of official rules as even more vitally affected by the approach here suggested than is the dealing with existing formulations. For such new formulation is always with a purpose.[17] The effectuation of this purpose (one recalls "the protection of an interest," *supra*) *must be sought by means of verbal formulation.* In part the need is based on our legal tradition: our officials move to a great extent on the stimulus of and in the light of verbally formulated rules.[18] In part, moreover, verbal formulations, and especially those in regard to *new, planned* change in action, are an inherently essential tool of communication in a complex society; they are peculiarly important in a society which depends in good part upon written records to maintain continuity of practice between successive incumbents of an office, and between suc-

[17] This hopelessly over-simplifies. There may be as many divergent purposes as there are participants. Almost regularly the formulator's purpose and the purpose he publicly assigns are in part disparate.

[18] This factor has by no means the exclusive importance the devotees of paper rules tend to attribute to it. The keener observers constantly stress this: what other meaning has the emphasis on the traditional techniques "for developing and applying precepts"; the *practice* of the office, or of the Constitution, which shift emphases, and often create or abrogate whole institutions; the "interpreting away" of a rule; the importance of experience in the office, of the "trained" incumbent. And so forth.

On the other hand the factor of verbally formulated rules has enough importance to explain why they have so long been considered the core of even the substance of law. They are not the sole machinery for *producing* regularity. Habit, practice, unverbalized experience and tradition, are vital to regularity. But they are *a* factor in *producing* it—to the extent that officials react to words, and read words, alike. They are, moreover, the main device for *checking* regularity, for letting outsiders get an idea that officials are staying within the due limits of discretion. And they are, as indicated, a most vital element in introducing change in regularity. Where official behavior occurs *without* regularity, the older views tend to deny it the character of law (the assumed irregularity or caprice of cadi-justice, and the like). On this I differ. I should of course stress as the more perfect illustration of the concept *regular* official behavior; but I regard the behavior as more vital than the regularity, and the mere paper expression of desired regularity—save so far as it expresses an ideal—well, as paper.

cessive generations. But since the ultimate effectuation of a purpose is in terms of action, of behavior, the verbal formulation, to be an efficient tool, must be such as will produce the behavior[19] desired. *This turns on the relevant prevailing practices and attitudes of the relevant persons.* In one familiar doctrinal illustration, language used in a statute "will be read" in the light both of the existing common law, and of prior judicial construction of that language. But that is a matter of the top, the most superficial, level. Below that are the more vital practices prevalent as to *handling* official rules, described roughly above; practices, *i.e.,* of courts and of lawyers.

But in regard to the new (and especially the statutory) formulation, the behavior problem goes much deeper than such practices of the legal elect. The ways of appellate courts in handling existing official rules presuppose the cracking of the toughest nut the statutory draftsman has to crack: the case is already in court; someone is already making an appeal to the official formula. Whereas one of the statutory draftsman's major problems is to look into existent behavior beforehand, to make sure that his formula, when it becomes an official rule, will not merely bask in the sun upon the books. He must so shape it as to *induce its application* (with all the discrepancies that may entail) or else (for any purpose save that of pacifying clamorous constituents content with words) his blow is spent in air.[20]

Only as a second job does he have to wrestle with making his formula so impinge upon judicial tradition that the results in action will be those desired *if* a case gets into court. Again there is little to be gained by laboring the point. It seems patent that only a gain in realism and effectiveness of thinking can come from consistently (not occasionally) regarding the official formulation as a tool, not as a thing of value in itself; as a means without meaning save in terms of its workings, and of meaning in its workings only when these last are compared with the results desired. In the terms used above: as *prima facie* pure paper until the contrary is demonstrated; and as at best a new piece of an established but moving environment, one single element in a complex of practices, ideas and institutions without whose study the one element

---

[19] I have not attempted in this paper to define conduct, action, behavior. I have no desire to exclude such things as the arousing and disappointment of expectations, the creation of hopes and fears, etc. The approach advocated would, however, go vigorously to inquiring into the grounds for claiming the arousing or disappointment of expectations in any given case,—as also to inquiring into what expectations, and whose. So, too, for example, with the thought processes of judges, the influence of ideology on judges and laymen, etc. *Cf.* 15 AM. EC. REV. 670, n. 17, 675, n. 32.

[20] Other aspects are developed in PROCEEDINGS OF CONFERENCE OF SOCIAL WORK (1928), at 129 *et seq.*

means nothing. Hence: not the elimination of rules, but the setting of words and paper in perspective.

The Place and Treatment of Concepts

Like rules, concepts are not to be eliminated; it cannot be done. Behavior is too heterogeneous to be dealt with except after some artificial ordering. The sense impressions which make up what we call observation are useless unless gathered into some arrangement. Nor can thought go on without categories.

A realistic approach would, however, put forward two suggestions on the making of such categories. The first of them rests primarily upon the knowledge that to classify is to disturb. It is to build emphases, to create stresses, which obscure some of the data under observation and give fictitious value to others—a process which can be excused only insofar as it is necessary to the accomplishing of a purpose. The data to be singled out in reference to that purpose are obviously those which appear most relevant. But true relevancy can be determined only as the inquiry advances. For this reason a realistic approach to any new problem would begin by scepticism as to the adequacy of the *received* categories for ordering the phenomena effectively toward a solution of the new problem. It is quite possible that the received categories as they already stand are perfect for the purpose. It is, however, altogether unlikely. The suggestion then comes to this: that with the new purpose in mind one approach the data afresh, taking them in as raw a condition as possible, and discovering how far and how well the available traditional categories really cover the most relevant of the raw data. And that before proceeding one undertake such modifications in the categories as may be necessary or look promising. In view of the tendency toward over-generalization in the past this is likely to mean the making of smaller categories—which may be either sub-groupings inside the received categories, or may cut across them.

The other suggestion of a realistic approach rests on the observation that categories and concepts, once formulated and once they have entered into thought processes, tend to take on an appearance of solidity, reality and inherent value which has no foundation in experience. More than this: although orginally formulated on the model of at least some observed data, they tend, once they have entered into the organization of thinking, both to suggest the presence of corresponding data when these data are not in fact present, and to twist any fresh observation of data into conformity with the terms of the categories. This has been discussed above in its application to rules; it holds true, however, of any concept. It is peculiarly troublesome in regard to legal concepts, because of the tendency of the crystallized legal concept to persist after the fact model from which the concept was once derived has disappeared or changed out of recognition. A simple but striking instance is the resistance opposed by the "master-servant" concept to each readjustment along the lines of a new industrial labor situation. The counsel of the realistic approach here, then, would be the constant back-checking of the category against the data, to see whether the data are still present *in the form suggested by the category-name*. This slows up thinking. But it makes for results which means something when one gets them.

Background of the Behavior Approach

All this is nothing new in social science. It is of a piece with the work of the modern ethnographer. He substitutes painstaking objective description of practice, for local *report* of what the practice is, or for (what is worse) a report either of local practice or of local ideology pleasantly distorted by the observor's own home-grown conventions. It is of a piece with the development of objective method in psychology. It fits into the pragmatic and instrumental developments in logic.[21] It seeks to capitalize the methodological worries that have been working through in these latter years to new approaches in sociology, economics, political science. The only novel feature is the application to that most conventionalized and fiction-ridden of disciplines, the law. In essence the historical school of jurists from the one side, and Bentham and later Ihering from the other, were approaching the lines of theorizing here put forth. Holmes' mind had travelled most of the road two generations back. What has been done in the last decades that has some touch of novelty, is for theorizers to go beyond theorizing, to move, along such lines as these, into the gathering and interpretation of facts about legal behavior: Ehrlich, Nussbaum, Hedemann, Brandeis, Frankfurter, Moore, Clark, Douglas, Moley, Yntema, Klaus, Handler, Lambert[22]—I name only enough to show that neither a single country nor a

---

[21] Mortimer Adler suggests to me that the operational approach to modern physics is a classic analogue and precursor.

[22] The work of the different men moves in somewhat different fields, and is uneven in value. The same holds often of different work of the same man. And an exhaustive bibliography of all that has been done along the lines discussed would be long. Probably most titles would fall in the useful but less advanced field of discovering the appellate courts' real practice as distinct from the paper pattern of courts or writers. The names listed were chosen with reference to work at the next stage beyond: facts as to lower court operations, and the beginnings of inquiry into the contact-area between official and layman's conduct. EHRLICH (Czernowitz), GRUNDLEGUNG EINER SOZIOLOGIE DES RECHTS, and see PAGE, PRO. ASSN. AM. L. S. (1914), 46. Unfortunately most of the findings of his investigations into "living law" are inaccessible. NUSSBAUM (Berlin), in his RECHTSTATSACHEN-FORSCHUNG; HEDEMANN (Jena), REICHSGERICHT UND WIRTSCHAFSRECHT; Brandeis, the brief in *Muller v. Oregon*, and his opinions, repeatedly; FRANKFURTER

single school is involved, and to make clear that the point of view has moved beyond the stage of chatter and has proved itself in operation. That out of the way, I should like to glance at a few further implications of the approach.

Administrative Action as Law

Three of them appear together. First, to focus on the area of contact between judicial behavior and the behavior of the "governed" is to stress *interactions.* Second, central as are the judges' actions in disputed cases, there is a vast body of other officials whose actions are of no less importance; quantitatively their actions are of vastly greater importance, though it may well be that the judge's position gives him a leverage of peculiar power. In what has preceded I have somewhat lightly argued as if judge and court were the be-all and end-all of the legal focus. It is time to reformulate, to grow at once more accurate and more inclusive.[23] The actions of these other officials touch the interested layman more often than do those of the judge; increasingly so, and apparently increasing at a rising rate of increase as the administrative machine gains in force and function. More often than not, administrative action is, *to the layman affected,* the last expression of the law on the case. In such a situation, I think it highly useful to regard it as the law of the case. I see no gain whatever, and much loss, from setting up a fictitious unity in the law, when some officials do one thing, some another, and the courts now and again a third. Realistically, the law is then not one, but at least three, and by no means three-in-one. If what the courts do ultimately prevails *and is translated into* administrative practice, that is that. If such an event is predictable in advance, I find it vastly more useful to think of that event as the emerging unity of the law, which until it happens may be an ought, and is already an opportunity (at a price) for him with gumption and money to reach for it, but is not *yet* the probable law for the ordinary case. What—more

and Landis (Harvard), The Business of the Supreme Court (1928); Frankfurter and Green, The Labor Injunction (1930); Underhill Moore (Yale), mimeographed and MS. materials on banking in relation to the law of banking; Moore and Shamos, *Interest on the Balances of Checking Accounts* (1927) 27 Columbia Law Rev. 633; C. E. Clark (Yale), MS. materials on the actual practice of litigation in Connecticut and New York; partial results appear in the Conn. Bar J. for July, 1928, April and July, 1929, and the W. Va. L. J. for Dec. 1929; Wm. Douglas (Yale), study in bankruptcy and insolvency practice, still under way; Moley (Columbia), the crime surveys, generally; Yntema and Theo. Hope (Johns Hopkins), pending investigations into the use of federal jurisdiction and into the actual course of litigation in state courts; Klaus (Columbia), *Sale, Agency and Price Maintenance* (1928) 28 Columbia Law Rev. 312, 441; Handler (Columbia), *False and Misleading Advertising* (1929) 39 Yale L. J. 22; Ihigahi, Le Droit Corporatif International de la Vente de Soils (1928); and Klaus' excellent review (1928) 28 Columbia Law Rev. 991.

[23] The reformulation would complicate the preceding argument, but would not essentially change it. Except insofar as the argument would thereby gain cogency.

than one law, on a single point, in a single jurisdiction, according to the whim or practice of an official, or according to the funds or temperament or political complexion of the layman affected? Just that. What else expresses the facts? Why blink and squint because the paper tradition is annoyed? As long as there are words to describe the court rule which will ultimately prevail (in a case where it will!), and to describe the situation differently before and after the victory, what is gained in a *science of observation* by using the same words to describe both conditions—except a sure confusion?[24]

Hence I argue that the focus, the center of law, is not merely what the judge does, in the impact of that doing on the interested layman, but what *any* state official does, officially.[25] Lawyers are curious. As to a *court* of first instance, though it be a justice's court, they would have no difficulty seeing this. They could even see that a wrong decision below, appealed from and reversed, would be part of the troubles of a litigant, would reduce his effective rights—how often do they jockey the case to bring about a settlement, by trading on just such friction-factors! But to say that the decision of the eighteen hundred dollar clerk in Bureau *B* that certain expenses are not deductible from my income tax return *is* the law in my case, gives a lawyer's ideology the same shock that it gives to a political scientist to urge that for purposes of that decision, that official *is* the State. One needs again to wash the matter down with Holmes' "cynical acid" and see what is left. In the same manner, if the official's decision is adverse and erroneous, I should include as a subtraction from my effective rights, if I proceeded to get a reversal, the ill-will and subsequent trouble I might incur at the hands of that official; as a part of the law, if I won; and its predictability as a determining part of the law, if I decided not to fight.

[24] On the *normative* side of law no confusion or doubt would exist in this case. The "right rule" would be the same all along. But that is no reason for obscuring the divergence in the results, on the level of description and prediction. We need, precisely for such purposes, to sever the normative from the descriptive aspects of law. Moreover, results affect norms, quite as much as norms affect results. If the outcome were going to be the overthrow of the judicial by the administrative practice, in the case put, the norm would pending outcome be in considerable doubt. And one of the (quite incidental) advantages of the approach contended for is to make explicit, understandable, *and non-shocking* the fact and realm of occurrence of such doubts as to norm.

[25] If we were dealing with a society which lacked political organization, this obviously would be a bad terminology. But another of the futilities of overgeneralization in the law has been the attempt to find *one* set of terms to cover the institutions of disparate societies. Before political organization we find control, and often specialized or semi-specialized control institutions. But in describing a politically organized society it is exceedingly convenient to limit the term to the official Big Stick. A convenient term for the closely similar "law" of the subgroup in such a society is "by-law." Sociologically the two are often more similar than dissimilar. *Cf.* MAX WEBER, WIRTSCHAFT U. GESELLSCHAFT, 16, 17, 27 etc.; and 15 AM. EC. REV. 672 *et seq.*

Laymen's Behavior as a Part of Law

Interactions between official behavior and laymen's behavior, first; and second, the recognition of official behavior of all officials as part of the core of law. Third, and an immediate part of both, the recognition of what Nicholas Spykman so strongly and properly stresses: that the word "official" tacitly presupposes, connotes, reaches out to include, all those patterns of action (ordering, initiative) and obedience (including passivity) on the part both of the official and of all laymen affected which *make up* the official's position and authority as such. Something of this sort is the idea underlying "consent of the governed," "ultimate dependence upon public opinion," and the like; but these older phrasings have no neatness of outline; they do not even suggest the need of sharp-edged drawing, which I take to be the reason why they act as a soporific, while the Spykman formulation acts as a stimulant to the curiosity and imagination. In a passing it is well to note that here, too, Max Weber's method of formulation becomes classic: the official exists as such precisely *insofar as* such patterns of action and obedience prevail.[26] I agree whole-heartedly that these patterns are an essential part of any phenomena we call law. The more whole-heartedly because Spykman's formulation brings out with fresh emphasis the difference between paper rules and resultant behavior, and the extent to which the behavior which results (if any) from the official formulation of a rule depends on the patterns of thought and action of the persons whose behavior is in question.

The Need for Narrower, More Concrete Study

How far these patterns can be presupposed, how far they require specific examination, depends on the individual case. Here as throughout we run into the need for reexamining the majestic categories of the romantic period of jurisprudence. The old categories are imposing in their purple, but they are all too big to handle. They hold too many heterogeneous items to be of any use. What is true of some law simply will not hold of other law. What is true of some persons as to some law will not hold of other persons, even as to the same or similar law.[27] I care not how reclassification be made, so long as it is in terms of observation and of organizing the data usably, *and* with back-check to the facts. But reclassification is called for. From another angle, what we

---

[26] In the same way (borrowing Spykman again) *to the extent that* the official's behavior plays into these interlocking patterns of action it becomes "official" rather than personal behavior, and so of direct interest here. "Purely" personal behavior of an official approaches inconceivability; but substantially personal behavior may take up a great bulk of a given official's time.

[27] *Cf.* PRO. CONF. SOCIAL WORK (1928), 129, 131. *et seq.*

need is patience to look and see what is there; and to do that we must become less ambitious as to how much we are going to look at all at once.

An illustration may make the point clearer. Some "rules" are aimed at controlling and affecting the behavior of persons whose whole set and interest is opposed to making the adjustment desired; others are aimed at affecting behavior of persons who are not only willing to adjust, but have an existing effective machinery for accomplishing the adjustment. A type of the first is almost any phase of professional crime; a type of the second, perhaps, would be some change in the law affecting city real estate transactions which happens to be desired by the dealers. Most cases are compounded of both elements. If city real estate alone is involved, much might be said at first blush for law reform being peculiarly easy and quick, because the practice is firmly entrenched of never entering a real estate deal without consulting a lawyer. But other practices are also entrenched, such as relying upon first mortgage finance from a particular type of, concern which in turn insists upon a title policy which in turn is under control of companies whose interest runs counter to certain types of law reform. The troubles of Torrens titles in New York City are an instance. They are substantially unmarketable; no mortgage company will loan on them because no title company will insure them.[28] That is, however, an instance of attempted "helpful-device" legal innovation. It is a different problem from the "ordering-and-forbidding" legal innovation. Barring questions of constitutionality, and barring the political question of how far legislation running counter to the desires of a well organized and powerful group can be achieved at all, it is obvious that enforcement of a new prescribed style of doing business upon New York City title companies would be *prima facie* a promising problem of legal engineering, precisely because their business is localized, well organized, and run by relatively few business units. Unlike the professional criminal, they could not dive underground and survive. The problem of detection would therefore be one of detecting not persons, but infractions by known units; and their deals could almost certainly be forced into the open. The major policing problem would therefore in all likelihood become one of anticipating and barring out in advance "evasions" undertaken by changing the methods of business under advice of counsel: *i.e.*, a problem of initially or subsequently so framing the official formulae of ordering and forbidding that transactions could not be accomplished (at a profit, after deducting fines, etc.) except along lines of the general purposes of the legislation. True.

[28] Thus one Torrens title to one lot in a block makes the block unavailable for large scale improvement. R. R. B. Powell tells me that Torrens titles have even on occasion been de-registered, in order to gain access to mortgage money.

unless the engineering were so successful that a somewhat comparably profitable new turn to the business developed, the legislator would have to reckon not only with initial, but with persistent and highly skilled resistance—which might even take the line it once did with the railroads, of seeking to capture the governmental machine. And it is of course this type of resistance which would in fact (contrary to our hypothesis) keep the constitutional issue in the forefront of the fight. The parallels and the divergencies from regulation or prohibition of liquor traffic would be instructive. As one moves to bank robberies or jewelry thefts the parallels begin to fade out and the divergencies to sharpen. I have purposely chosen an illustration from a field in which I am blankly ignorant, in order to bring out the lines of thought and inquiry which open, under the approach, *even before the gathering of data is begun.* It is obvious that the set or attitude of those affected or sought to be affected by any piece of "law" is at the heart of the problem of control; it should be equally obvious that the style of organization of those persons, their group ways of action—whether among themselves or with regard to society at large—is equally vital. Behavior effects depend upon present behavior conditions.

The Narrow Application of Most Rules—and Its Implications

This leads directly into the next point: most pieces of law affect only a *relatively* small number of persons ever or at all, with any directness—or are intended to. Where that is the case, the *organization, attitude, present and probable behavior of the persons sought to be affected* is what needs major consideration, from the angle of getting results (or of understanding results). Indeed, the very *identification* of those persons may be a precondition calling for much study. Which is a somewhat absurdly roundabout way of saying that unless those matters are studied, the rules drawn, and the administrative behavior adapted to the persons in question, results will be an accident. *"To the persons in question,"* and, indeed, "to those persons *under the conditions in question.*" It cannot be too strongly insisted that our attitude toward "rules" of law, treating them as universal in *application,* involves a persistent twisting of observation. "Rules" in the realm of action *mean* what rules *do;* "rules" in the realm of action *are* what they do. The *possible* application and applicability are not without importance, but the *actual* application and applicability are of controlling importance. To think of rules as universals—especially, to think of them as being applicable to "all persons who bring themselves within their terms"—is to muffle one's eyes in a constitutional fiction before beginning a survey of the scene. To be sure, constitutions purport to require rules of law to be "equal and general."[29] But most rules, however general as to the few they cover, are highly special, when viewed from the angle of how many citizens there are. And most rules "applying" to "all who come within their terms" (all those who set up barber shops, or are tempted to commit murder, or to bribe officials, or to embezzle from banks or certify checks without the drawer having funds, or to adopt a child, or run a manufacturing establishment employing five or more persons) do not and will not, realistically considered, ever be "applicable" in any meaningful sense of the term, to *most* people in the community. Such rules are indeed open. Persons do move in and out of the sphere of their applicability. But that sphere is much more clearly seen, when viewed (as compared with the community) as narrow, as special, as peculiar. Obviously even more special is the sphere of *real* application: of official *behavior* with reference to application. (And is it not clear that this most special sphere is the one of greatest consequence to the persons on whose behavior any results depend: the objects of the "regulation?")[30]

I know of no consequence of the approach here contended for—the approach in terms of organized behavior interacting with organized behavior—no consequence more illuminating than this immediate opening up for study of the sub-group and institutional structure both of "governors" and of "governed." Its opening up for study as a first essential to any understanding at all, as making the study of law a study in first instance of particularized situations and what happens in or can be done about them.[31]

---

[29] In practice this comes to: "*equable* in the choice of the very limited class to be affected." *Equality* of rule is impossible in a specialized society. It is true that some few of the lines of discrimination which are under our system excluded from consideration, are suggested by the word "equality." But it is not particularly significant, save historically.

[30] I have stressed elsewhere that the vital problem in such cases is that of creating in the conduct of the relevant persons new *practices* (folkways) which conform to the purposes sought *via* the new legal rules. PROC. CONF. SOC. WORK (1928), at 132 *et seq.* And that the effectiveness of legal rules, old or new, is not to be measured simply by how often officials act in accordance with them. *Ibid.*, and 15 AM. EC. REV. 682. Indeed the ideal effectiveness is not achieved until officials do not have to act at all. But if the rules are of the kind which coincide roughly with ancient, established lay practice *(mores)* it becomes a serious problem how far we have in such cases effectiveness of the *legal rule*, or of the occasional official behavior with reference to the rule. Contrast the extreme opposite case: an entire organized line of activity all units of which are prepared to move or not to move along lines newly prescribed, according to the outcome in court of a deliberately chosen test case. It is behavior of officials *alone*, but behavior of officials in its *interaction* with that of the relevant laymen.

[31] What is wanted in the way of generalization must come from a resynthesis of such particularized studies, when we have them. Meantime, we have our common sense and tradition-given understanding of *some* of the regularities of official behavior, and sufficient traditional skills in predicting, influencing, managing official or other behavior to get on after a fashion, in practice, while we learn more.

Realism as to "Society"

"What can be done," and by whom? I have spoken of law as a means: *whose* means, to *whose* end? Discussions of law, like discussions of "social control," tend a little lightly to assume "*a* society" and to assume the antecedent discovery of "social" objectives. Either is hard to find in any sense which corresponds with the facts of control. Where is the unity, the single coherent group? Where is the demonstrable objective which is social, and not opposed by groups well nigh as important as those which support it? And law in particular presents over most, if not all of its bulk, the phenomenon of clashing interests, of antagonistic persons or groups, with officials stepping in to favor some as against some others. Either to line up the dissenter in the interests of his own group; that is one broad phase. Or to regulate the relations between two groups, or to alter the terms of the struggle (competitive or other) between them. Hence the eternal fight for the control of the machinery of law, and of law making, whereby the highly interested *A*s can hope partially to force their will upon the equally but adversely interested *B*s, and to put behind that control the passive approval and support of the great body of *C*s—who happen to be disinterested, or, what is equally to the point, uninterested. To the truth of this observation it makes little difference whether the ends of the *A*s are material or idealistic whether wholly selfish, or dedicated most altruistically to some concept of the welfare of the whole. And while this welter with regard to change in law may, if you will, be thought of as political, the presence of the welter raises problems in defining "interests." One must also recur to the fact that it is on the same welter that official behavior is expected to be brought to bear when the new "rule" has been proclaimed.[32] Thus raising all the problems raised above, with this addition: the possibility, not there mentioned, of a group of laymen pushing to help the official program through.

One matter does need mention here, however: the eternal dilemma of the law, indeed of society; and of the law because the law purports peculiarly among our institutions to "represent" the whole. There is, amid the welter of self-serving groups, clamoring and struggling over this machine that will give power over others, the recurrent emergence of some wholeness, some sense of responsibility which outruns enlightened self-interest, and results in action apparently headed (often purposefully) for the common good. To affirm this is to confess no Hege-

[32] Not quite the same. The fight and victory may have somewhat changed the picture. And the enactment of a new formula has some consequences in itself: among others, that the formula chosen imposes temporary (though sometimes wide) limits upon what the officials can do, whereas the prior struggle is typically in terms of policies, not measures.

lian mysticism of the State. It leaves quite open any question of the existence of some "life principle" in a society. It merely notes that, lacking such a self-sanation in terms of the whole, the whole would not indefinitely continue as a whole. And to deny that would be folly. It would be to carry emancipation from the idle ideology of "representation of the whole" into blindness to the half-truth around which that once-precious ideology was built. But to deny the emancipation, to worship the half truth without dire and specific concern for the details of the welter, would be a folly quite as great.[33]

What Law is Thought to Be: Folk-Law

In all the emphasis placed upon behavior I may have created the impression that a "realistic" approach would make itself unrealistic by disregarding what people *think* law is. Not so. But a realistic approach would cut at once into analysis and subdivision of the terms "people," "think," and "law" in such a phrase. For the great mass of persons not particularly concerned, I suspect that "law" in this aspect, *so far as* it concerns themselves, means "what I ought to do" and is not much distinguished from those selective slight idealizations of current practice we think of as morals. At times the issue certainly gets closer: "I want this contract to stick"—and doubtless I will then think of putting it in writing, and will meditate on reciting a formula I saw somewhere (in a deed, was it?): "for one dollar and other good and valuable considerations"; I may get a witness to the signing, too. In the field of private law we know singularly little of this folk-law-in-action. In that of criminal law we can suspect a very rough coincidence of folk-law-in-action with folk-morality-in-action,[34] except that here and there the thought of cop

[33] It is along the same line that I feel strongly the unwisdom, when turning the spotlight on behavior, of throwing overboard emphasis on rules, concepts, ideology, and ideological stereotypes or patterns. These last are, by themselves, confusing, misleading, inadequate to describe or explain. But a jurisprudence which was practically workable could not have been built in terms of them, if they had not contained a goodly core of truth and sense. To be sure, it was not the precept-ideology of jurisprudence, but the practice that jurisprudence only partly mirrored, which actually worked. But one thing sociological study ought to do for the advance of science is to school the advocates of new insight no longer to junk wholesale the old insight against which they are rebelling. The rebelling indicates inadequacy in the old. It does not indicate that the old did not have much solid basis. The bare fact that the old exists, could come into existence and persist, evidences that it had. If we can examine it for what it has, and carry that with us into a new alignment, we shall do much to reduce the well-known pendulum swing from exaggeration to exaggeration. This is of less moment in the early stages of a new movement. The innovator carries over willy-nilly the virtues of the same training against which he is in intellectual revolt. But those newly trained in the new school will be half-trained unsound exaggerators, if the original innovators fail to incorporate *in their doctrine as in their practice* the life-power of the older school, even while attacking the latter's false emphases and implications.

[34] May I insist again at this point that "folk morality" really means at least as many important varieties in specific details as there are sub-groups within the main group?

and jail will work deterrently when plain external and internal non-official social sanctions might not wholly click; we can suspect further that over considerable fields criminal law is too new and too specialized to have much background or counterpart in folk-morality; and, finally, that some fairly wide bodies of non-moral (or not yet moral) criminal law aspects will have percolated into folk-law: I think of traffic law (as known to the traffickers) as distinctly in advance in most places of traffic morality, and of similar discrepancies in regard to liquor, gambling, and sex matters, as to some portions of a population with variant morals. Now clearly what people think law to be, as regards themselves, has some effect at times upon their action. My guess is, however, the effect on the side of forbidding is much slighter than the lawyer is likely to imagine, whenever any important pressure of self-interest is present, except for a relatively small minority, or over relatively small areas of action for any particular person. On the other hand, my guess is that in the field in which law provides "helpful devices"—the attempt to use which presupposes concurrent self-interest—folk-law has very considerable influence in shaping conduct. The problem calls for exploration, from the realist's angle, by cautious study of detail. Even more important, I suspect, is the problem of what law is supposed to be with regard to others than the supposer. But important in accounting less for action than for inaction. For it seems likely that in this aspect law is mainly conceived simply as being all right, without concern for detail; and that this aspect of folk-law is close to the heart of the grand-scale passive cooperation of the uninterested which makes control of the political machinery a prize.

Ideals as to What Law Ought to Be

No less important than what people think law is, is what people conceive that law should be. Any change in law is in good part a reflection of someone's desire to produce a difference. And just as attitudes and expectations must be taken into account along with overt behavior, so must purposes and the ideal pictures toward which purposes drive. Thus far, even from the angle of a purely descriptive science.

Into another aspect of ideals as to what law ought to be this paper does not attempt to go. I make no effort here to indicate either the proper rule, or the proper action on any legal subject. I do, however, argue, and with some vigor, that as soon as one turns from the *formulation* of ideals to their *realization,* the approach here indicated is vital to his making headway. It is only in terms of a sound descriptive science of law (or of what is roughly equivalent, a soundly built working art, which takes equal account of conditions) that ideals move beyond the stage of dreams. Moreover, as has so often been pointed out, both the feasibility of accomplishing a policy and the cost of its accomplishment are in a world of limited possibilities vital elements in arriving at a judgment of the worthwhileness of the policy itself.

Conclusion

In conclusion, then, may I repeat that I have been concerned not at all with marking a periphery of law, with defining "it," with *excluding* anything at all from its field. I have argued that the trend of the most fruitful thinking about law has run steadily toward regarding law as an engine (a heterogenous multitude of engines) having purposes, not values in itself; and that the clearer visualization of the problems involved moves toward ever-decreasing emphasis on words, and ever-increasing emphasis on observable behavior (in which any demonstrably probable attitudes and thought-patterns should be included). Indeed that the focus of study, the point of reference for all things legal has been shifting, and should now be consciously shifted to the area of contact, of interaction, between official regulatory behavior and the behavior of those affecting or affected by official regulatory behavior; and that the rules and precepts and principles which have hitherto tended to keep the limelight should be displaced, and treated with severe reference to their bearing upon that area of contact—in order that paper rules may be revealed for what they are, and rules with real behavior correspondences come into due importance. That the complex phenomena which are lumped under the term "law" have been too broadly treated in the past, and that a realistic understanding, possible only in terms of observable behavior, is again possible only in terms of study of the way in which persons and institutions are organized in our society, and of the cross-bearings of any particular *part* of law and of any particular *part* of the social of the social organization.

Included in the field of law under such an approach is everything currently included, and a vast deal more. At the very heart, I suspect, is the behavior of judges, peculiarly, that part of their behavior which marks them as judges—those practices which establish the continuity of their office with their predecessors and successors, and which make their official contacts with other persons; but that suspicion on my part may be a relic of the case law tradition in which we American lawyers have been raised. Close around it on the one hand lies the behavior of other government officials. On the other, the sets of accepted formulae which judges recite, seek light from, try to follow. Distinguishing here the formulae with close behavior-correspondences from others; those of frequent application from those of infrequent. Close around these again, lie various persons' ideas of what the law is; and especially their views of what it or some part of it ought to accomplish. At first hand contact with officials' behavior, from another angle, lies the social set-up where the official's acts impinge directly on it; and behind that the social set-up which resists or furthers or reflects the impingement of his acts. Farther from the center lies legal and social philosophy—approaching that center more directly in proportion as the materials with which it deals are taken directly from the center. Part of law, in many aspects, is all of society, and all of man in society. But that is a question of periphery and not of center, of the reach of a specific problem in hand, not of a general discussion. As to the overlapping of the field as thus sketched with that of other social sciences, I should be sorry if no overlapping were observable. The social sciences are not staked out like real estate. Even in law the sanctions for harmless trespass are not heavy.

KARL N. LLEWELLYN

COLUMBIA LAW SCHOOL

[10]

THE YALE LAW JOURNAL

VOLUME 49 JUNE, 1940 NUMBER 8

THE NORMATIVE, THE LEGAL, AND THE LAW-JOBS: THE PROBLEM OF JURISTIC METHOD*

By K. N. LLEWELLYN†

PEOPLE who get interested in "sociology" "of law," whatever they prove to mean by either term, seem to find themselves caught in a tidal current that runs toward the troubled waters of a *Grundlegung*, an "Introduction," a "Foundations," a "What it will be about when I get around to really dealing with it." Max Weber, Ehrlich, Timasheff, de la Grasserie and the strange Jerusalem have all found their published efforts expended on introducing their subject, and only in Weber do the lines of the actual prospective building become at all clear. In part, at least, this is because Law is commonly conceived as a discipline whose very subject-matter is made up of norms for conduct, or imperatives, or rules for conduct, or correct dogmatic propositions, whereas sociology as a pre-science is a discipline which involves as its essential subject-matter sequences and

* The substance of this paper began in the summer of 1927, as a manuscript on Mechanisms of Group-Control, annotated chiefly with sociological material and material from American law. The analysis there detailed, however, had blurred the distinctions between intra-group and inter-group relations and reactions, which was fortunately discovered in time to keep it from publication. A second version became a major portion of my Leipzig lectures on Sociology of Law in 1931-32. It was annotated especially to, and tested against, materials from German law and legal history. A third reworking, this time with special attention to the fuller monographs on primitive law, became the theoretical framework for E. Adamson Hoebel's field studies on the law-ways of the Comanche and Shoshone Indians (1933-1934), and, finally, for his field work (1935-1936), in which in 1935 I had the luck to share, on the exciting law-ways and juristic method of the Cheyenne. The results of this last are presented in LLEWELLYN AND HOEBEL, LAW-WAYS AND THE CHEYENNE (in press). Meantime, other bodies of material involving the testing of the ideas, or of ideas closely similar, in particular areas have been published: my own PRÄJUDIZIENRECHT, my study on divorce, a succession of studies on contract, the bar, the growth of Sales law, Hall's THEFT, LAW AND SOCIETY, Goebel's FELONY AND MISDEMEANOR, Harper's THE ENGLISH NAVIGATION LAWS. And I have had the benefit of the manuscript of Malcolm Mason's lovely book on the struggles among rival legal buddings in Tudor England, and of numerous suggestions from my colleague Patterson. The one superb publication directly on the whole field is of course Max Weber's RECHTSSOZIOLOGIE, which few seem to read, and none to use.

The constructs I use are *sociological* constructs, aimed at clarifying happenings and problems in the world of behavior. So, for instance, "authority" does not refer to any orderings of actual behavior. The two realms of thought and discourse mix no more comfortably than oil and water; and efforts at *Grundlegung* are a fairly necessary result.

This is another of them. But it will give up in advance any effort to get at any sociology "of Law." The lines of attack of a social pre-science of human behavior are adapted, so far as I can discover, only to dealing with human behavior. So that in attempting to bridge between sociology and the legal, it is human behavior in the realm or in the aspects which we regard as legal with which I am concerned, and with those patternings of semi-recurrent behavior we know as legal institutions: courts, the office of judge and the like. This particular *Grundlegung* is a little one, with a narrow ultimate objective. It heads up in the sociological reasons for, underpinnings of, and nature of *juristic method;* it being my firm belief that one has to explore the behavior-situation, its needs, and its quirks, before one can build really satisfactory doctrine or practices to deal with those quirks, those needs, or — to any satisfaction — with that situation. Our doctrine and practices rest on past exploration of this sort, exploration long past, and currently renewed only case by case as one case after another arises. Betterment of the doctrine and practices will rest on re-

---

efflux of a "normative system," but to the basic situation which exists when Jones says "Go," and Smith goes, as distinct from that in which Smith does not go; and the drive of de facto authority of this sort to provide itself with felt "rightness" or rightfulness is regarded, again, as a behavior-drive observable among men-in-groups.

Two further points probably need mention. The one is that certain major points at which philosophy and ethics impinge upon the picture have been noted; and that one service which the analysis aims at is to clarify both the bearings of that impingement and the tool-stuff and working conditions of juristic work in furtherance of ideals.

The second is that such words as "drive" and "urge" are used in the paper as descriptive of observable behavior phenomena, not as indicating underlying "forces" which "explain" it. I have not been particularly careful to cast the analysis in terms conforming to the modern metaphysics of physics, nor in terms of the better work in semantics, nor in terms of the sound perception that behavior is wisely seen always as an interaction in a moving situation. I have tried to bear in mind the lessons properly derived from all of these; but the linguistic outlay required to express the material of this paper in terms at all accurate under those approaches seems to me like the outlay required to work up by way of five-decimal logarithms alleged "figures" which are trustworthy not even in the first decimal. The discipline has progressed to the place where one can wisely use any available technique to further objectivity of seeing and of statement; but we do not yet *know* enough about what we are looking at to warrant the more painfully elaborate expression of our inaccuracies. I have tried to keep the thinking of the paper abreast of the better level of working thought in the social disciplines, and of the better level of working thought in matters legal. I have tried to keep its terms a little clearer and its organization a little tighter than our knowledge of the data justifies, because constructs should not only organize what seems to be known but should also open leads for inquiry. But I have tried also to keep doubts live to be felt and to keep vaguenesses from being masked by words of simple-seeming solidity on the one hand or of an objective-sounding terminology which runs too far beyond the data, on the other.

† Betts Professor of Jurisprudence, Columbia Law School.

exploration undertaken in more sustained and cumulative fashion — it being also my firm belief that in these last few decades American juristic method has been subjected to an ever-increasing load, without equivalent study of how the method might be tuned up to better carry the load.

I have also been restless at the curious blankness with which men from other social disciplines face any legal matter or any talk of law. Of all the social disciplines it stands most isolated. My own guess is that that is because the law-men mainly think doctrine and talk a language which runs in terms largely of correct doctrine — which is to exclude communication and contact with any premises except the premises of correct doctrine. But underneath all doctrines there lie problems, and those problems seem to me a proper study for all men of the social disciplines, and an illuminating one. They extend through all group-living, in any type of group. They are a meeting-ground on which *exchange* of ideas and knowledge is possible between the men of law and the men of the social disciplines. And that, if true, also warrants its bit of *Grundlegung*. So do what I conceive to be certain inherently recurrent aspects of men's ways of going at some of those problems. For the store of record, of knowledge, and of light which the law-men have heaped up has no business to be kept locked away from the other social disciplines. Traffic in ideas, like traffic in goods, runs best when there are return-loadings. And just as anthropology has recently begun to discover that it can not only contribute to, but can learn from, the other social disciplines, so the social disciplines are due to discover that modern work in the legal field is not only a market for their product but a rich productive area. One thinks of ancient mines, once worked and valued, since lost, now relocated — and waiting.

On Certain Words: Especially Law-Ways and Law-Stuff

The legal discipline has, I repeat, always been focused on Law, or Rules of Law and the like, and its current vocabulary makes discussion of behavior difficult to carry on without inviting misinterpretation. This paper touches only incidentally on Rules of Law; its focus is upon certain ways in which people in groups behave. I have therefore been driven to invention of some words which will, I hope, serve to avoid confusion. Most of these — such as "law-job" — are explained at appropriate places in the text. Two, however, run throughout, and need a word of explanation in advance. "Law-ways" is used to indicate any behavior or practices distinctively legal in character, flavor, connotation, or effect: procedures for cleaning up trouble-cases, the use of tribunals, the enactment of legislation, the practice of policing. The having and using of formulated rules of law is a law-way, too. The having and using of a formal Code is a law-way which we do not have. A Rule of Law is not a law-way, not behavior, but a formulation with meaning and authority. Whereas using such a Rule, thinking in terms of such a Rule, observing it, applying it, construing it: those are law-ways. One needs, however, the wherewithal not only to distinguish the behavior aspects (along with the relevant attitudes) from the Rules of Law, but the wherewithal to lump the two, and to include in the reference such other things as tribunals, or specialized law-personnel. For the broad inclusive term I have chosen "law-stuff," and have used it to mean any phenomena in the culture which relate discernably to the legal; it includes rules of law, legal institutions of any kind, the presence and activity of lawyers, judges, jailors, law libraries and their use, courts, "habits" of obedience, a federal system: in short, to repeat, anything in the culture whose reference is discernibly legal, when that anything is being viewed under that discernibly legal reference. "Law-stuff" is used also to include anything which is discernibly *incipient* as law-stuff. What keeps this from being as meaninglessly broad as all outdoors is the orientation. "East," for instance, is also as broad as all outdoors, but it is not for that reason a meaningless or unusable concept.

Thus far there has been no effort here to indicate a meaning for "legal." And I wish it were possible to avoid such indication; but it is not. For "legal" is in common usage set not only against "economic, political, social, industrial-technological" — which is the general bearing of the use of the term in this paper — but it is also in common usage set against "illegal," so as to mean "lawfully according to law"; and it is also set against "moral," so as to mean "according to law, but not really 'right' "; and it is also set against "equitable," with the familiar connotations. Now if Law and all the relevant vocabulary were not a fighting matter as well as a confused one, it would be possible to make one's own definitions, stick to them, and still hope for understanding. But it is a fighting matter.

Let me therefore put "legal," and keep it, *in quotes* when the reference is to that phase of life and problem and behavior of men in groups which is set against the economic or religious or recreational. Let me *capitalize* it, as Legal, when the reference may be to the content or system or correct consequences of our high Rules of Law. This will not wholly do my work, for much of the time I shall be dealing with incipient or half-way material which is beginning to be distinctively "legal," but has not yet taken on all the attributes which things "legal" strain to acquire. I shall use some coinages to refer to one or another of the major incipient or part-way areas. For instance, in regard to the bare skeleton of authority and enforcement, where regularity and right are largely lacking, I shall speak of the "skelegal"; and where felt right is present in a penumbra between recognizable Law and clear morality or etiquette or decency, I shall speak of the "jurid." And where an incipient practice is yet unpredictable in detail, and is interrupted, as is our own judicial practice of distinguishing a precedent which needs to be distinguished, which our judges waver between doing and not doing, I shall speak of "law-wavers" which might be in process of becoming real law-ways. All of this part-way material, this penumbral stuff which does not answer to yes-or-no, but only to a how-much of intensity or regularity or clarity, I can then lump as the "legaloid," and many things will be much easier to say clearly, and briefly, and without misconstruction.

"Normative" is here used in the ethical sense, as indicating an expressed judgment of rightness. "Norm" I have avoided where possible; where used, it is used not in the statistical sense or in the sense of the "normal," but as an equivalent of "normatization" or "correct standard." As will be seen, I find it necessary to distinguish sharply the ethical or moral, or the individual's felt rightness, from the *imperative* of a "legal" system (whether it be "skelegal" or right legal); a matter which becomes of peculiar importance when the "Or else!" of a "legal" system has passed through a stage of threat of *some* consequence to a stage of specific and limited threat. To that I beg attention, because so much discussion of "rules of law" has run (to my mind very loosely) in terms of "norms and the normative" that one seeking to distinguish "You must, or else! . . ." from "You should, really . . ." needs to make such a purpose explicit.[1]

NORMATIVE GENERALIZATION

To see that something is *right,* or that something is *a* right, is to generalize. There is no practicable way, in ordinary life, to get at the notion of rightness without having, somewhere in your mind, a *general* picture or pattern which the case in hand fits into and fits under. You do not have to put the standard into words; you do not have to see it and know it as being a standard; it can be as vague as "somehow." But it is there: the *sensation,* if that be all it is, that somehow "cases like this ought to be dealt with this way," or that action like this is out of line with what action ought to be *in general.* Even to see a thing as right "simply" because you want it so, rests on a more general tacit proposition that what you want has extra claim to be considered.

Now setting up normative generalizations is creative action. To "see" a pattern is to make a pattern, and to make it a "right" pattern is to project it into the on-coming future. Being creative action, this normative generalizing can fasten on *anything* for its base, and can move from that base in any range and any direction. Even a fairy story — a single fairy story — can call up a normative generalization about the right behavior of mice and pumpkins, and of fairy godmothers and princes

1. The word "custom" is nowhere used; it is too blunt and confused to serve in careful analysis.

who have been experienced only in a newly created imaginary environment. The possibilities of normative generalization are limitless; the idiosyncratic actualities are almost so. The history of minority parties, freak sects, social and political dreamers, and paranoia, suggest the range. Some relatively few of these actual normative generalizations acquire peculiar social significance. They become accepted in a group, and by it. They prevail. They control behavior. People who are found at odds with them have trouble with that group, be it a family or a nation.

One factor urging powerfully in the direction of such socially significant normative generalization may be thought of as *quantitative.* If interlocking behavior gets patterned in fact, with a resulting back-and-forth of adjusted action and adjusted expectation, deviations will bother; generalizable pictures of rightness and of rights are pretty well bound to result. This does not depend on anybody wanting such patterns to develop, or planning them, or preaching them, though any or all of these things may happen. It does not even depend on people knowing that they have fallen into behaving along such patterned, interlocking lines, or that they have fallen into patterns of action and attitude which "strain" toward some particular line of normatizing. Often enough it takes a trouble-case to crystallize perception that the right pattern is there, in actuality or inescapably foreshadowed, when you come to think about it. This type of socially significant normative generalization is in original and eternal process of emergence from the mere living of any group, whether the case be one of a newly-wed's first failure to get home in ample time for dinner, or be one of a police force discovering that it will not be allowed to strike. Such interlocking behavior, however it comes into being, sets up originally, and eternally keeps setting up, *one line* of normative generalization, and does so in significant quantity (as to frequency, as to regularity, as to likeness among various relevant persons) so that it acquires a significant chance for acceptance by the relevant Entirety. I shall speak of this as direct, primitive normation, based on direct, primitive sense of justice.[2]

A second factor urging in the direction of socially significant normative generalization may be thought of, in contrast, as *qualitative.* The stress, the spectacular and memorable drama, the brain-sweat, of a trouble-case, though it be an utterly unique one, drives by its whole quality toward generalization; and this doubly, if the trouble-case becomes, as many do, the *occasion* for awakening to, and voicing, normative drives which have been building unnoticed. You can see this hypothetically if you will imagine that there never before has been a corrupt judge and one judge is suddenly discovered as corrupt. The theretofore unthinkable instance will crystallize a now conscious norm against corruption in judicial office;

2. By "primitive" I mean without need for organs of expression or for careful deliberation; I do *not* mean outmoded or displaced in any modern or sophisticated culture.

and if anything is done about it, the doing will become "the" procedure. History bears the marks of the phenomenon wherever some one baffling case of outrage has produced a "general" statute which no man passing it expected ever to see really needed. Our concern with this is threefold. First, trouble-cases must be seen as having peculiar power to become jumping-off points for socially significant normative generalization. They are "naturals" for precedent-production. Second, and by the same token, they are cases in which a uniqueness which may be accident or misfortune (or may be planned or prophetic) is yet hard to keep from being mixed into the basis of the normative *generalization*. And this means that occasional individuals concerned in trouble-cases may acquire a shaping power over their society. For a basic problem of juristic method is the disentangling of long-range policy-issues from the person, from the circumstance — and indeed from the particular issue-drawing and the particular lines of advocacy — which happen to accompany the emergence of the matter into group attention. Achievement of such disentanglement is rare. If accomplished, the accomplisher has set his mark on his society.

The third matter in this connection is that the trouble-cases form a line which may become, which *tends* to become, a line apart. If they ever come to stand on their own footing, memorable and so relatively unchanging, known in clear outline and so remembered, perhaps even a special object of the peculiar lore of specialists in trouble-cases — then the lines of normative generalization which they bring forth will have a likely chance to come into divergence from those of the direct, primitive normation which moulds ever freshly on whatever come to be the practices of life. In such case, the trouble-case stuff will offer a further and independent germ of the "legal"; this time as distinct not only from any other aspect of the culture but as distinct also from the primitively and directly just.

But one is not done with socially significant normative generalization by merely examining its two most frequent and most inevitable bases or foundations in life-stuff. For, as we have seen, such generalization is a *creation*. It is creative in its selection of life-stuff to work with and from; it is creative in what it does with the selection. Here are three farmers each of whom has borrowed to finance his working season and met with pest or drought, and each of whom has given as security his car, furniture, leasehold, and prospective crop. One lender takes the car and furniture, and turns out the farmer; one gives his farmer time; one forgives the debt. You can generalize and normatize from any of these, or you can imagine something fourth or fifth, and further, and generalize from that. Your generalizing normation will be creative also in the direction and scope, in the *range*, you give to the generalization: will it deal with "cotton-farmers," with "debtors," with "persons making contractual engagements," with "failure of crop," or with "unforeseen difficulty"? Will you introduce other limitations or extensions: "tenant-farmers," "white tenant-farmers with more than six minor children who have occupied the premises at least three successive years"? In these same illustrations I have sought to bring out what one may call color or flavor of available normative generalizations, and direction as well as scope. The lines of choosing significant factors can, in our instance, drive in the direction of permanency of relation, or peaceableness, or celibacy, or agricultural development, or race-selection. What concerns us is to hammer home two things. The first is that every normative generalization contains *some* quantum of idealization, of projection beyond the actual. The idealization may run only to the desirability of unchanged persistence of some particular variety of given condition; it may run to change so great that what results is empty crying in the wilderness. No matter: an ideal is set up. The second thing is that normative generalizations do not make themselves. Some*body* makes them. With luck or skill, he may indeed voice just what everybody feels. Again no matter: some-*body* had to voice it, before everybody could effectively feel it, for action.

Which brings us to the somebody who — in action or in speech — does this voicing. For in the voicing he gives form, shape, color, range, direction, to a normative generalization, as, so to speak, he throws its hat into the ring. The spokesman either hits or muddles what he is trying to communicate. He either lays an issue on the nose of the need or fills the woods with dragged red herring. He either has prestige of birth, wealth, position, or he has not. He may hold a key to more ready acceptance by voicing what most feel, or by the luck of events which focus interest on him. This gets complex to say, but it is not complex to see. The man either has skill or he has not. A good cause can be lost, or a bad one won, by the manner of issue drawing and of advocacy; and a cause which wins tends to put over for the future the very shape and color of the particular normation which it has come in the course of the struggle to embody. Not for nothing, in our modern law-life, do counsel search for the "favorable" or "advantageous" test-case to carry up; not for nothing do they delay here, settle there, while the "right" case is being found, and made ready, and pressed. Let me sum up these aspects of the individual's direct effect as those of his skill and his desire and his luck.

These processes of normative generalization — always in some degree wishful, idealizing — I hold to be part of man-in-culture. Together with them, and informing them with fuel and content, go two other urges each of which I hold to be always present in enough individuals to have impact on the Entirety. The one is the urge to use available social machinery to serve personal, sub-group or other ends which are ends at odds with interests of some other members of the Entirety. As applied to normative generalization, this means the persistent production of generalizations selected for their basis, and shaped for their content, color, and direction, to serve *some*, and against *others*. This may take vicious lines, in the view of right-minded men. Or the serving of some against others may appear as a device to "restore" balance and serve social health, as is urged on behalf of the rightness of relieving respectively the taxpayer and the unemployed. The "against others" may be quite direct, as in a dispute over boundaries or water rights, or a shift in the terms and advantages of a competitive struggle, or it may go less directly, as by reduction of the available pie by capture of one slice for Jones.

The contrasting urge can be roughly indicated as an urge to seek the welfare of the Entirety concerned. I refer here not to any net effect "as if by an invisible hand," nor to the mouthings of the hypocrite. I refer to the persistent recurrence in every culture of persons consciously and actively concerned about the common-weal. For these too bring forth normative generalizations; and those which they bring forth play on and against the products of the others.

Thus far we have looked into certain processes of normative generalization, their nature, and something of the bases and machinery of the ones most likely to become socially significant. These processes exist, persist, recur, whether or not there is anything in the culture of the group which can be spotted as distinctively "legal" in character. They are part of the living of man-in-groups. They are part of what generates the "legal." They affect the work of the "legal." They help effect change in it. And we have noted the persistent drive of interest in the use or twisting of institutions to individual or sub-group advantage; and the recurrent drive also, for the common-weal.

We turn now to something of the *form* which things "legal" tend to take, of those formal aspects which, when they have once developed into recognizability, enter thenceforward into the workings of men-in-groups in quite peculiar ways. When those have been examined, we shall come to what I see as the *law-jobs* common to all groups and cultures; those jobs around whose doing, those functions around whose fulfillment, one finds the most significant organization of normative generalization, of other law-stuff, such as procedures, and of the legal crafts and all the work and personnel of law.[3]

3. It is of course vital to clarity that the level and context of discourse be kept clear. I shall therefore attempt, when a complex great-group (a "society") is in question, to distinguish the specific Law and Law-stuff of the Whole from the specific by-law and by-law-stuff of any designated sub-grouping within the whole. It is in light of the functional similarity that the institutional differences and the conflicts gain clarity. The uncapitalized phrasings, "legal" and "law-job" and "law-way," I reserve for general applicability to the functional aspects common to groups of all kinds and sizes.

THE "LEGAL"

Normative generalization is part of what goes to generate and to make up the "legal"; it is not the whole. The generalization must also be somehow accepted, it must be somehow effective on men's behavior or consonant with men's behavior. It must be more; it reaches beyond the ***normation*** of oughtness into the *imperative* of mustness. The "legal" has to do with ways and standards which will prevail in the pinch of challenge, with rights and the acquisition of rights which have teeth, with liberties and powers whose exercise can be made to stand up under attack. Let there be no doubt about this: you can have law-stuff, undeniable law-stuff, which is neither right nor just; when you are put to the choice, you will know the "legal" from the right or just because the "legal," when insisted on, is what prevails, and the right or just will have to suffer accordingly.

But the "legal" is not brute power exercised at odds with, or without reference to the going order. That exercise of power which is to be "*legal*" (not necessarily "lawful") is exercise of power as part of an *order,* and as part of a *system* which is recognized by or in the Entirety concerned. The minimal *normative* generalization which suffices is that, as the order or system stands, exercise of power as part of or flowing from the system ought to be recognized as authoritative or conclusive; which is a different thing from right, or even from rightful under the Law. In our system, the wrong order or judgment of the court is the classic example. Other systems a-plenty hold the same of executive action.

Now this statement will not satisfy the moralist or any of half a dozen varieties of legal philosopher; but most of the matters such thinkers have in mind we shall be dealing with in due course. Here it is vital to see the possibility of the emergence of a "legal" structure (at need, "skelegal") which makes its own claim to *its own variety* of oughtness, regardless of the "inherent" rightness or justice of its any part or of its net weight: its claim to observance, obedience, authority, effectiveness because, but merely because, it is the effective expression of the ***recognized going order*** of the Entirety concerned.

And it is vital to see, second, and as a corollary, that wherever there is no single, unified, clearly perceived and recognized and centered structure making such a claim and making it effectively, then we shall be faced with rival lines and structures of the "legal," each one budding or semi-developed, and all in competition or at war for ultimate expansion and dominance. For the "legal" (like the Legal which is a phase of it) persists in driving toward exclusivity, toward systematization, toward integration. It must. Of its nature, it purports to be final and conclusive. Rival finalities drive toward some type of working integration, within any *felt* Entirety. Coke's war on the prerogative courts, the war of King's

Court law on local law, the struggle between federal control and states' rights, or between Reichsrecht, Landrecht, Stadtrecht — these are not only struggles over patronage and power, they are also instances of drives inherent in "legal" stuff.

In this, as in general, a drive need not of course mean accomplishment, or full accomplishment; in which aspect it becomes quite intelligible that a judgment may be and is "law" for the parties even when it is a wrong judgment "under The Law"; even a wrong and out of kilter detail takes its dominant color from the System to which it belongs. So also the System itself may be slow to work out observable integration: consider the technical difficulties still met in describing our own American Legal system as a Legal unity, or the problem of governmental departments working "uncoordinated." Indeed, once a society has become both really complex and at all mobile, a truly full integration of its legal stuff, even when one strips the "legal" down to the bare "official-Legal," becomes impossible. The *concept* of a coherent and ordered unity does serve as an ideal to unchain constant effort; it serves also as a fictional frame of discourse within which particular partial reconciliations and hierarchical integrations are constantly worked out, in appellate courts, the lawmen *talking* always, while they handle this conflict or that one, as if there could be but one right answer, and as if that one single right answer had already been in some manner predetermined by the system. This talk is fiction. The unity which a legal system has (in a mobile and complex society) is not an intellectual or intellectualized unity of actually prevailing doctrine. The doctrine at hand is always somewhat pluralistic, instinct with diverse and warring premises of growth. The unity which exists is like the unity of an organism — it is as real as is the unity of a society, that net working something which makes the society observable *as* a society; its unity is also of that same nature, with blurred spots and welters, with semi-disorganizations sometimes perhaps just barely held in check, but whose net balance yet yields a Whole. Any legal controversy is worked out not only against a dim ideal picture of a Whole, but also (to the extent that the tribunal is permitted to act *for* the Whole) as if that Whole were, so far as affects the case in hand, also a rationally intellectualized and systematic whole of doctrine. Thus the ideal, and the fictional frame of discourse, daily serve their purpose; for it is by means of them that the pluralistic, vari-tendencied system is kept at work on the digestion or assimilation of the constant in-flow of new law-stuff and new trendings into it from the readjusting areas of the culture. If the "legal" did not in some degree manage to unleash and channel such drives for internal tidiness, the influx of new stuff from the living world around it would prove overwhelming. And a main present problem of our own system — I refer here to our system on the strictly official-

Legal side — is that it has come to limp increasingly under a rate of absorption and digestion long fallen below its rate of intake.

Now things distinctively and recognizably "legal," — law-stuff, law-personnel — rarely appear in any group or culture full-blown and at one stroke. Even when six Americans gather together and promptly frame a written "constitution" for their new group, it is rare for that "constitution" to have much living connection with what comes to be the group's going law-stuff. Certainly in the simpler cultures a society possesses first of all just "what is being done," a general matrix; the pearl of the "legaloid," and then of Law, is secreted slowly, around some irritation. The major lines which may be hit upon seem to include the line of slowly specializing personnel and the line of slowly specializing procedures to handle grievance or dispute. But whether one approaches the matter with his eye primarily on effective practices (or semi-practices) which avoid conflict, or primarily on effective norms (or semi-norms) which guide non-litigious conduct, or primarily on trouble-case procedures (or semi-procedures) and results, or primarily on authoritative (or semi-authoritative) personnel who handle trouble (judges, *e.g.*) or declare or create either norms (prophets) or imperatives (kings)— in any case he must expect to find law-stuff beginning in *instances* of behavior, or of speech (which, incidentally, is also behavior), or of effort at normative generalization whose expression is behavior. Such instances are instances before they can be made practices, they are one-man stuff before they can become accepted, they are experiments and indeed deviations before they can even tend to become standard and institutional. *One germ* of law-stuff, then, precedes the phase or feature of *regularity.* It does not concern me whether, until some regularity is achieved, some one may prefer to see the stuff as *pre*-legal. What does concern me is that the student of the "legal" must wrestle with how the "legal" comes into recognizable being as a something discernibly different from just what is going on, in general. If one cannot distinguish the "legal" from what goes on, in general, one puts his finger on no law-stuff which he can know to be such: incipient *institutional specialization* is a pre-condition to study.

One line of such specialization centers, as we have seen, on the emergence of *authority* in *persons.* Another line centers on the emergence of *authority* in *patterns* of behavior and of norms for behavior; and especially around the trouble-case. Each line has to make its way into recognizability. And nature offers man no compulsion to take either road, first, or either road, alone.

But these are attributes to be looked for and seen in terms not of yes-or-no, but of more-or-less, of significant enoughness. "Regularity," *e.g.*, means not one hundred percent regularity; it means, as a minimum, enough of regularity to allow of prediction which is more than coin-flipping, plus some drive (which may be checked or counter-balanced) for more of regularity to develop. And "the legal" under immediate discussion is a very bare-bones kind of legal stuff; pre-law ways, if you will; law-ways, in any event, which may be very far from the finished and polished product of the jurist's art in a developed modern state. Yet even such crude law-stuff is complex enough in its clustered constitution.

Authority in Personnel or Action or Imperative

There follows an attribute or cluster of attributes which can be lumped as an element of *authority* (the "skelegal"), but which it helps clarity to treat as a cluster, and to break down:

(a) There is a necessary element of *effectiveness* or existence in and as a part of the Entirety concerned: some quantum of de facto obedience to or acquiescence in a mandate or ukase, or in a disposition of a trouble-case. If a recognizable system has emerged, this calls only for effectiveness, in some quantum, of its mandates or dispositions in general, despite some tolerance for individual cases of ineffectiveness. Though the jurisdiction of the Supreme Court over controversies between States lay long in a sort of penumbra here, controversies were submitted, and the judgments took color also from effective enforcement of other judgments.

(b) There is an element of *supremacy*: in the pinch the "legal" must prevail as against any competing standard or authority. More accurately, the *system* of which it is a part must be prevailing; for occasional doubt or even pitched-battle defeat of the "legal," in detail, is well within the concept's range of tolerance.

(c) There is an element of *enforcement,* of sanction, of perceptible teeth to call into play against the challenger. This goes to the heart of things. But here, too, tolerance is wide. Three-quarters of the offenders may go scatheless, if all have fear, or are driven into secrecy. Brandy smuggling in England during the blockade against Napoleon met real public support; but when the King's men rode, the caught smuggler suffered: a fine instance of the partial character enforcement can have without losing its meaning. And would any man argue that "nullification" of the capital penalty in larceny cases at the same period meant "no law"?

(d) There is an element of recognition that what is done or commanded or set as imperative or as norm is part of the going order of the Entirety concerned; not merely acceptance, but an attitude about the *why* of this acceptance: an element of *officialdom.* The attitude toward "why" need not go to approval; but it must go to recognition of the existence of a going system. This, as has been indicated, distinguishes legal outrage (wrong, biased, "technical"; perhaps colored as if rightly lawful) from *il*legal (contra-legal) outrage, legal tyranny from brute power, a corrupt administration from an Al Capone (the City or State being taken as the unit of discourse); or taking a smaller unit of discourse, it is what distinguishes an Al Capone felt as semi-permanent (say, as The True Big Shot within the relevant group) from a momentarily successful muscler-in.

Now if the "legal" ("skelegal") developed in a group or culture contains something of these elements but no more; and especially if there is developed the authority-cluster without the regularity-cluster to be next discussed, then pro tanto there would be presented the legal régime we know as *tyranny* (benevolent or otherwise); for it would then be using authoritative personnel, uncontrolled.

REGULARITY OF PATTERN

But equally insistent in their drive toward emergence are a cluster of attributes we can term *regularity*. Again the cluster is better broken down: first, into three types of de facto regularity of behavior (law-ways *or* "law-wavers"); and second, into the attachment of obligatory quality to imagined and projected regularity in each such type of behavior, (moving through the "jurid" up to the imperative). The imperative may creep in upon behavior already largely regular in fact, or it may jump far ahead of behavior, as a means to lining behavior up, or the two may mix.

(a) Behavior Aspect. There is, first, then, some degree of regularity in what we may follow Vinogradoff in thinking of as non-litigious behavior, especially in what Malinowski has stressed as conflict-laden situations. The degree of regularity needed is: enough to be perceived, so that it can be adjusted to — so that it can both found expectations and lay a basis for their recognition: call it *going expectations*.

(a) Imperative Aspect. There is the relevant imperative generalization about the obligatory character of behavior according to the relevant pattern (be the latter derived from life, or projected). I am not at this point concerned with what the reader is likely to be thinking of: Jellinek's "the normative power of the actual." Such regularity as is described under "((a)—Behavior Aspect)" will indeed produce normative generalization, sense of rightness, claim of right. That is one germ of law-stuff, original and eternal; and I have no intention of forgetting it. It may, it often will, coincide exactly with, and lead into, the *imperative* generalization I have here in mind. But when such highly desirable coincidence fails, then it is the imperative mustness, not the normative oughtness, which is the subject-matter here. The latter is commonly enough the fuel and the directive; the former is the machinery which not only furthers, but *limits*. What we are dealing with, therefore, is: "This is what you do, or else! . . ." And again: "This, it is safe to do. . . ."

(b) Behavior Aspect. There is a similar element of regularity in the ways of getting at a grievance or dispute, in the manner of articulating a rebuke, and the like: a quantum of *procedure*.

(b) Imperative Aspect (1). Companioning this (or running ahead of it) may be a relevant imperative generalization. This matter may grow quite complex, with available alternatives at odds one with another, and little clarity as to preference, in either the law-stuff or the ethics, with a resulting competition of *devices* which resembles somewhat the competition between rival *authorities*. Consider in our own history the decline of debt, as against *indebitatus assumpsit*.

(b) Imperative Aspect (2). This line of imperative generalization takes on a phase and flavor of peculiar importance if it binds not only the litigant, or his self-help representative, but also any official in authority. The question of degree is of course vital. Thus Pound uses as a favorite example of justiciation "without law" that kadi who is nonetheless "bound," *inter alia*, by the Koran, and, though remotely, by his superior. But it needs note here, as also in regard to scope of remedy, that the "imperative" addressed to the official, while more than merely normative, remains commonly in a "jurid" state far less sharp of sanction than that addressed to the "law-consumer."

(c) Behavior Aspect. There is, finally, an element of regularity — as to kind, as to minimum, as to maximum — in the ultimate outcome of adjustment of a grievance or dispute of some particular character; a regularity which is, in the main, slower to emerge than is some recurrent patterning of grievance-procedure, but is also one persistent in its emergent drive. Call it a quantum of *certainty of the scope of remedy*.

(c) Imperative Aspect (1) and (2). Here, too, imperative generalization appears, and here too it reaches peculiar importance if it lays its control also upon any relevant official in authority; at which point the Legal (by which I mean here to include much more than formulated Legal doctrine) completes its magnificent bridge into the political.

If these regularity-factors add themselves to a régime of authoritative personnel, they substitute pro tanto a régime of "government controlled by Law" for one of "tyranny" or benevolent "despotism." I say "pro tanto" because the occurrence in life of either of these ideal-types, in purity, verges on the inconceivable.

If no authoritative personnel is present, the aggrieved serving for instance as a self-redressor, then the "legal" becomes clearly recognizable in the culture to the degree that ways and imperatives of the kind described take on themselves the aspects of authority by legitimizing and limiting legitimate action toward redress.

On the other hand, if the regularity-elements not only gain the upper hand, but get out of hand, there results the wooden, externalized, graceless and cumbersome inadequacy summed up as legalism. That the "legal" may yield effectiveness, as we shall see, it is well-nigh indispensable for a culture to develop some type of personnel for the purpose. That it may yield bearable legality instead of legalism, or what will be felt as acceptable, rather than as arbitrary, requires that to the elements of pure form thus far discussed there be added *certain minimum matters of substance.*

(a) The content and substance of the norms and activities of the imperative System, as a whole, must be felt by the Entirety concerned to serve that Entirety reasonably well: a quantum of *general satisfaction.* The tolerances here are huge, but they have limits.

(b) The manner and substance of working out particular matters must remain somewhat understandable, as a proper part of a reasonably proper system, to the persons interested directly or in sympathy or as observers.

Legality thus seems to me marked by one type of *result* of the working of things "legal" when those things contain some quantum of the elements of regularity; that type of result is the result which gives moderate satisfaction. Legalism is marked by unsatisfactory results, by wooden arbitrariness, as compared to the tyrant's arbitrariness of whimsy or temper. A primitive with much time, much patience, much fatalism, and no comparative study of alternative possibilities may find results satisfactory with which an observer rooted in a legally more artistic culture may grow impatient. But however subjective the judgment of what distinguishes legalism from legality, three objective phenomena remain which make the terms worth saving. One is that when men feel the imperative system to be too much and too persistently out of gear with what they want from it, they hold back, they even kick up. Another is that in all cultures judgment frequently diverges widely about the system as a whole, which may be taken as blessed with proper legality, and about particular details, which may yet be seen as "technical," "legalistic," and, briefly, outrage. The third, as the curious and lovely Cheyenne material makes clear, is that when juristic art and method happen to be abreast of their function, there is no need for legalism, in anybody's definition of that term, to raise its head.

Philosophical Caveat and Excursus

With this I close the immediate discussion of the "legal," having touched hardly at all upon components of rightness or justice. That calls for a word in justification. I think the function of justice better seen and served by getting the bare "legal" thus set off. Many feel otherwise.

The cynically minded have always seen government and law as humanly given institutional devices by use of which some persons proceeded to get more of what they wanted. The idealistically minded have always seen Government and Law as imperfect means, humanly conditioned, but always driving, and always to be driven, toward a finer life for the Entirety and its almost-every member. Both have been rather obviously right. Every term used in connection with things legal reflects, in its common use, both views, both facts. At the one end, Law is flavored with what prevails, and even courts are courts "of law, and not of justice." A retroactive confiscatory decree inflicting penalty and visiting wholesale declassification of status, say for accidents of birth, is law, and that is that; but even such a decree is carefully made general, is put forth and administered in regular form, is "Justice under Law" as the books define the term, and is promulgated in the name of the public good. At the other end, Justice-in-result itself is flavored by the long-range view, and is contrasted with softheaded sentimentality; and the "political" criminal may be accorded admiration and a tear, but must be put out of circulation for mistakes in his procedure of attempted restoration of a commonwealth to its finest purposes. For the most part, the Legal System As Is, or any part of it, and The Purpose of a Legal System, or of any part of it, vary from each other within limits of tolerance, of endurance, of possible reform. Readjustment may be relatively imperceptible as it occurs, as in the gradual judicial rekiltering in unobserved places which has been so busily at work in our highest state courts over a generation; or it may be by similar processes which happen to be more carefully observed, as in the Supreme Court's taxation decisions of recent years; or it may be by way of political struggle and legislation and administrative policy; or it may take the ultimate form of war or revolution.

In all of this there are two major lines of approach for him who is concerned for his society, two major lines which seem in the heat of any controversy to be at odds. They are not at odds, in purpose. They may be at odds, at times, on means.

The one line, for purposes of reform, readjustment and health, seeks to make capital of the law-man's feeling and the layman's feeling that nothing is *True* Law which is not Just; and seeks thereby to deprive unjust Law or any part of it of the color and cover which it, and action "under" it, lay claim to as being a part, still, of the Legal System. This holds on the regularity side of the legal, in attacks on legalism, and it holds again, in attacks on what are seen as arbitrary or unjust decrees or regulations or administrative practices. It holds, on the authority side, in addition, as to particular acts of governing personnel, or irregularly introduced regulations or practices or decrees. The line of approach is to fuse and confuse, either deliberately or unconsciously, justice with law, regularity with right, and so to war on the unjust as unlawful, on the irregular as wrong. This line (if you do not like it) represents a capitulation to the inertia of the mind of lawman and of laymen, or (if you like it) a capitalization of that inertia, throwing the weight of the appeal of the felt just and right into the balance, to make the Law As Is (or as most think it is) *become* the Law That Should Be, the merely "legal" become the rightly Legal. Let me call this the line of legitimate fusion and confusion. I see the adoption of it as a politically dictated choice, a classification of ideas and terms adopted for purposes of more immediate persuasiveness. Its philosophical foundation lies in a belief that to discuss Law at all is to move any reader in favor of what is discussed as being Law, so that there rests on a thinker an obligation to put forward as being Law — even for purposes of discussion — only that which he would urge and approve. There is much to be said for the pragmatic force of this position.

It is not, however, my position, and I want to make that fact very clear. My faith is a different faith. I proceed upon the assumption that clear seeing and clear statement, to the extent to which it can be achieved, is a long-range greater gain. I hold the hard authority-aspect of the legal imperative, and the hard regularity-aspect, to be worth isolating for work and note, that they may be seen sharply as Not Enough for any decent system to rest content with. I deny, flat, any inherent tendency of hard seeing to drown the drive for the good and for the better. I hold the responsibility for working toward the Right and the Just within the hard legal frame to be better pinned on the official if it becomes common knowledge that to be Legal is not enough. I hold the jurists' job to remain undone until we can discover and make clear how far our officials *can* be controlled, and how far not, and, until we then devise means to control them effectively where they can be controlled, to be to give them some guidance in the remaining area, and to help them distinguish the arbitrary from the wise. The most fruitful angle of approach to accomplishing this task which I can see, is to *de*fuse and *de*-confuse the merely authoritative, the merely regular, the merely incidental to the accepted System, from the Just or the Right, and to get into spotlighted pillory so much of Law as has no business to be Law, so much of the Legal as should be made Unlawful, so much of Jumble as should be made into clear, guidesome Leads. I have no quarrel with any who may find the other road the wiser one, for their own efforts. But I hold the hard eye to be one most effective, though not the only, servant of the jurist's conscience and ideals; and I hold the dulling of conscience and ideals among too many men of law to be a result not of hardening of the eye, but, in good part, of a confused tradition that if it is Legal, it is *therefore* Right enough.

Nor can I find any way for getting into clarity the issues of policy about Law which emerge out of events at home and abroad over these latter years, save by recanvassing the work and material and function of things legal afresh and from the barest bed-rock upwards.

THE LAW-JOBS

The formal legal, the law-stuff and the law-ways, travel paths of their own, once they specialize out into recognizability. Upon them, in conflicting service of particular parts and of the whole, play human interests and normative generalizations which are thrown and followed into the ring by men. All of this takes meaning, takes shape, takes body under the eye, if it be set against those law-jobs whose sufficient doing goes to the very continued existence of a society as a society, of a group as a group.

The law-jobs are in their bare bones fundamental, they are eternal. Perhaps they can all be summed up in a single formulation: such arrangement and adjustment of people's behavior that the society (or the group) remains a society (or a group) and gets enough energy unleashed and coordinated to keep on with its job as a society (or a group). But if the matter is put in that inclusive way, it sounds like mere tautology — almost as if one were saying that to be a group you just must be a group. Whereas what is being said is that to *stay* a group, you must manage to deal with centrifugal tendencies, when they break out, and you must manage, preventively, to keep them from breaking out. And that you must *effect* organization, and that you must *keep* it effective. And that you must do all this by means which do not choke off, but elicit, your necessary flow of human energy.

Thus, for purposes of study, it is wiser to break down The Law-Job into lesser phases — doubly so, because to a very considerable extent the major lines of institutional machinery which men have hit upon for getting "the" job done have proved to focus interestingly around certain of the particular phases. Of these there are four around which matters legal group themselves rather illuminatingly:

I. The disposition of trouble-cases.
II. The preventive channeling and the reorientation of conduct and expectations so as to avoid trouble.
III. The allocation of authority and the arrangement of procedures which legitimatize action as being authoritative.
IV. The net organization of the group or society *as a whole* so as to provide direction and incentive.

There are two preliminary matters. The first is to make unmistakeable that the law-jobs hold, as basic functions, for *every* human group, from a group of two persons on up. They are implicit in the concept of "groupness." In any community or society which may be taken as a larger unit, the law-jobs therefore appear at least doubly: once for the big unit, and again for every sub-unit within the big one; and again, of course, for every sub-sub-unit within a sub-unit, "etc. ad inf." This requires to be made explicit, because the "Law"-concept of modern thought goes only to that great unit called the State or to such other *political* whole as may come in question. But in a functional view a newly wedded couple, a newly formed partnership, a two-child casual play-group, have each, *qua* group, the problems to deal with which are here our concern; and the aspects which those problems take on in the modern State are clarified and not obscured by observing them within such simpler groupings, taken as each, for the moment, a *unit* of observation. To put simple examples: with the arrival of a first child at talking age, certain portions of family by-law are simply forced into facing the juristic problems of *verbal* form; and the problems of "construction," "distinction," "true meaning," "underlying principle," and relation to the accepted general rightnesses, come promptly into being, nor can any arbitrary telling of the child to hold his tongue take them out of being. Or again, in any modern family in which graver matters are put up to father, or "told" to him, a three person group suffices to produce the differentiation and the conflict between a formal Legal system of the Whole Three, and the far-ramified by-legal system, of lesser and local jurisdiction, of the mother-child sub-unit. Father's precedents on the occasional matters put up to him raise promptly the control-problems of a distinctive "superior" set of imperatives. So that law-jobs and law-ways, I repeat, go to the essence of *any* group; and the presence of a larger and more inclusive one does not at all displace their functioning within sub-units. It may of course importantly condition problems within sub-units: under The Law of our modern State, wife-beating is no longer privileged and wife-desertion may have consequences visited upon it. But such alteration of conditions no more does away with fundamental family by-law problems than the condition of embarrassing war between neighbors does away with the internal problems of a neutral "sovereign" state. Indeed, it is when one marks out sharply *what group-unit* one is dealing with as being the Entirety concerned, that such a concept as "social control" loses its amorphousness and becomes manageable. Pick up any discussion of that topic and observe the sharpness which emerges if one carries in mind persistently such queries as "Control *of* whom, *by* whom, *for* what and in the context of what Entirety? Is this an intra-group case or an inter-group case? If the latter, how well organized a larger Entirety is there in the picture?"

The second preliminary matter is another which runs through all our law-jobs. Each alone, and all together, present first of all a basic aspect, one of pure survival, a bare-bones. The job must get done *enough* to keep the group going. This is a struggle for continued existence. It is order, in the pinch, at whatever expense to justice. Beyond this, there is to each job a double aspect which we may call the questing-aspect, a betterment aspect, a question so to speak of surplus and its employment. On the one side, this questing aspect looks to more adequate doing of the job, just as a doing: economy, efficiency, smoothness: at the peak, esthetically satisfying grace in the doing of it. On the other side, the questing aspect looks to the ideal values: justice, finer justice, such organization and such ideals of justice as tend toward fuller, richer life. It no more does to forget the bare bones over these latter things than it does to forget these things over the bare bones.

The Trouble-Case

I. The phase of the law-jobs which repays study first and fastest is the *adjustment of the trouble-case*: offense, grievance, dispute. Roughly described, this is garage-repair work on the general order of the group when that general order misses fire, or grinds gears, or even threatens total break-down. Around this aspect law-stuff becomes most easily, most quickly and most unmistakably observable; in the handling of this job lies also the testing of whether methods and manners of "control" which may have been thought to be law-stuff are or are not such. Finally, in any group or culture, the doing of this job gives off eternally, as by-product, new material for the doing of the other law-jobs. As to the *general order* of a group or society, it is just conceivable that adjustment of trouble cases might be purely repair work, and nothing more (though I have not yet met such a situation), but as to the *law-stuff* of the group or society, such adjustment of trouble-cases is a continuously creative feeder.

Typically, the trouble is minor trouble, "individual" trouble; in itself and case by case, bearable trouble. Typically, it would disrupt continuance of group-life only if sufficiently multiplied, sufficiently cumulative. This holds, even, of most homicides. The tighter the group, the more there is in its order of the traditionally accepted or of intensity of emotional binder, the tougher is its resistance to disruption from this quarter; yet picking up one's marbles and going home remains a symbol of factional strife which may mean bolt, divorce, or civil war. So that while adjustment of the trouble-case has a surface appearance not of life-saving so much as of life-easing, yet the elimination of conflict and grievance which has broken out remains a significant basic *line* of need and of activity, whether the individual instance correspond to bruised finger or to emergency operation. For enough unhealed breaches between members break the group, and tensions, left alone, build up potential toward explosion.

The bare-bones aspect of this law-job is plain enough: get enough of it done to leave the group a group. One or another member or faction can be cut down or cut off, and the group be still "the" group; bitterness can seethe; the line of adjustment may prove to be merely that what Big Fist wants, he gets. But if the group stays a group and neither explodes nor dribbles into disintegration, then this bare-bones survival-need is met. The questing aspects of the matter, on the other hand, run into reaches which few societies have penetrated in their High Law save in the person of some occasional transcendent judge. To adjust trouble cases with speed, smoothness, deep permanency, minimum outlay of effort and disruption of other activities — and, on points of fact, with accuracy — this is still a quest. Nor is it less a quest, still, to reach felt immediate justice in the settlement, or to reach in or via the settlement the line of long-range social health, or to combine either of these with a modicum of speed and economy.

Of this law-job, especially in its interaction with the second, more hereinafter. Here, let me point out merely its peculiar importance for the study of any but the most developed legal cultures, and its corrective importance for the study even of those; for when Rules branch and spread to form a quasi-world of their own, it is the trouble-case which tests which are the Rules that prevail in lawyers' lives instead of lawyers' legend.

Channeling

II. *Preventive channeling and shift of orientation.* The second phase centers on the effective channeling, preventively and in advance, of people's conduct — and attitudes — toward one another. Its importance lies peculiarly in areas of patent or of latent conflict of interest: in the arrangement of participation in the scarce and desirable, from physical things on through to power and prestige. This — as in marriage, and property-rights — has always been easy to see. But no less important is the avoidance of hitches in the coordination of life and work; for in any organized action, a slip of expected performance, a break of rhythmed timing, can produce conflict by its mere disruptive disturbance. In general, the job is that of producing and maintaining a going order instead of a disordered series of collisions; it is this order on which the first job does garage-repair work. The function includes, to repeat, not only the channeling of overt behavior but the channeling of expectations, norms and claims. It includes too the provision of such clarity as a culture affords as to what free play and leeway is permitted, or is not only permitted but actively protected — for the range and kind (and direction of urge) of free play and leeway in a set of structured ways, legal or other, is of as much significance as is the structure.

We meet in this channeling task a matter which is curiously easy to feel accurately in the particular but which taxes the ingenuity to state accurately in the general. It is this: that patently, as one must remember, the "legal" cannot exhaust the whole nature of a culture: the lines of factory-operation under industrial technology are, for instance, in one aspect technological, and insofar not "legal." Those same ways also involve governance, and can be studied with profit from that angle alone. They relate to education; they relate to the use of leisure. In somewhat the same way, however, there is almost no part of culture which is not *also* "legal" in nature (whatever else it is as well), in that a failure of any person to perform or to hold still *as and when expected* will be an occasion for grievance and conflict — as is forthwith made plain by any slip-up or slow-down or sit-down in the operation of the factory referred to, under the same machine technology. This is all quite apart from rights to division of the product. The intellectual task is to get stated the aspect and quantum of the "legal" that lies in those phases of culture which, so long as they present no hitch or trouble, seem to the observer wholly something else than "legal." And the "legal" aspect may well be conceived as lying in, almost confined to, so much of the patterning of behavior, attitude and expectation, as *prevents conflict* — conflict about anything: not, therefore, in the ways of making shoes or bottles or books, but in the ways of keeping some of the makers off others' toes and necks and tempers while such things are being made. Plainly, this means that the "legal" ("legaloid") fairly infests the culture. So it does, indeed; for some "legal" aspect is mixed into any coordinated action.[4]

The next difficulty is even more perplexing. Side by side with preventive channeling of behavior in men's life and work together goes creative, organizatory *re*channeling of such behavior. The child grows up, and starts to work. A man and woman marry. Some one is promoted, or elected to an office. A command is given. A contract is made, or there is death and succession. So long as such rechanneling is relatively rare in incidence upon a life; so long as the new patterns entered on are themselves clear, and largely understood, relatively permanent, prepared in fair part by anticipation; so long, rechanneling amounts only to the other side of the same coin, and is conveniently grouped, as it is grouped here, along with channeling *ab initio*. If it be true that *re*-orientation of behavior and expectations brings the "legal" aspect peculiarly to the fore, that only makes it easier to see: thus, the new is a bit more likely to meet challenge, expectant heirs may readily conflict, and the like; the as yet unhabituated is more likely to produce knocks and bumps, as the

4. But, as indicated, any other basic aspect of culture will be found, no less, to have a similar infesting quality: the economic, or the phase of governance, for example.

new man gets "broken in"; if the shift is at all individuated to desire, the lines of advance individuation are likely to fail of provision for one or another trouble-making contingency.

Our difficulty comes when we are dealing with a culture both complex and mobile of relations. If the possible lines of re-orientation are highly diversified, there is call for the specialist, to advise. If in addition the possible lines are capable of shrewd tailoring to particular desire, then the problems flood upon the specialist: there are techniques (contract, conveyancing), but there are also limits to their use; there are contingencies of which or in the handling of which only the specialists' lore accumulates accessible knowledge (corporate indenture forms and experience); and contingencies to be guarded against mean contingencies to be so guarded against that, in the eventual pinch, the guarding will *work*. In such a culture, the interest, the attention *and the building of tool-stuffs* by the legal specialists will concentrate upon the side of *shift* of orientation of relations, rather than upon any "normalities" of relation. The color of the culture derives in one main part from the degree and kind of mobility, variety and individuation of the working relations. Indeed, the preconditions of such a culture (commerce, market, industry, finance) set up so huge a variety of "normalities" according to the diverse types of specialized effort that little is left to be "normal" for everybody: with us, today, for instance, "public utilities" have trouble getting into activity, and trouble, once in, in getting out; but the ordering of any such line of activity is a whole field of its own whose technicians, managers and financiers live among legal stuff as foreign as Tibet to most of us. It is symptomatic that in the curriculum now in vogue to train our Legal specialists the relations which a person is born into are dwarfed by the concentration upon those which look toward being created by continuing shifts of orientation: contracts and all their sub-specialties: sales, negotiable instruments, insurance, vendor and purchaser, suretyship; trusts, wills, property arrangements, mortgages; corporations, corporate finance, reorganization, trade; labor relations.

Hence if one were setting up an analysis for study peculiarly of *modern* cultures-as-wholes, shift of orientation would loom as large, as a law-job, as does general channeling; and for the specialist in the modern Legal it would loom larger. A general and basic functional analysis does indeed bring light to the phenomena of modern official Law, reminding us, for instance, that the more articulately elaborate the recorded machinery of The Law gets to be, the more essential to health of the system is the careful provision, as part of the system, of a penumbra of those legally recognizable, but not yet clearly "recognized" lines of normation which I have called the "jurid"; and reminding us that if we try (as we do) to provide such a penumbra by way of a dozen different make-shift *and quite uncoordinated* devices (from admission of usage in commercial cases on up) we shall then find it working only sometimes, and missing often enough when it is most needed. But despite all such suggestion from the basic, there is no obscuring the fact that quite peculiar problems open as soon as the mere *quantitative* aspect of legal tool-stuffs turns them into a semi-independent world of their own, with upwards of a hundred thousand and a half of lawyer-specialists, and other hundreds of thousands of semi-specialists at work in office-forces, governmental administration, police departments; and with authoritative books enough to outrun the eye and drown the mind. Thus no analysis which is capable of general use for all groups can, unmodified, get into perspective all the official Law phases of a developed modern society. That once admitted, however, I yet insist that no quantity of modern technical complexity alters the nature of the basic functional problems, nor does it cause them to disappear. I insist, indeed, that the restatement of them in bald form helps more to organize the modern technical welter for seeing and for study than can any organization which takes our modern institutional forms as its major foci. But that, as Kipling taught, "is another story."[5]

Let me sum up this second law-job, then, (or, for developed and mobile Law-systems, these two "second" law-jobs) as that of *preventive channeling and of shift of orientation,* of behavior, attitude and expectation.[6] The bare bones and the double questing aspects speak here largely for themselves, save in this: that high efficiency in preventive channeling ("discipline," if you like it; "regimentation," if you do not) competes, as an ideal, with large leeways ("license"; "liberty") and creative use thereof ("captain of industry"; "industrial pirate").

5. Still another story, which does require mention, but which I cannot here develop, is this: the *upkeep* aspect of group-organization on which an analysis of the "legal" centers (including the established leeways) is that very heart and focus of social mechanisms in which "social organization, disorganization, reorganization," "social statics and dynamics," "social tradition and social change" meet to work in common ways on common ground, the differences being in first instance differences in the net resulting unbalance or balance, and the available corrective procedures being only adaptations and see-saw-ridings of the always continuing identical processes. *The "legal" is thus the needed keystone to integration of fundamental sociological theory.* "Old mines, once worked and valued. . . ."

6. Be it noted that the emphasis here is primarily upon the channeling and shift among smaller units—the individual, or the sub-group, in their relations to other individuals or other sub-groups; the emphasis is on the life-career of person or enterprise or transaction, seen from its own end; not on the net organizatory efforts of a whole complex society when taken as a whole. The distinction is artificial enough, but it is still worth making; for enterprises or individuals can learn to keep off one another's toes, and still leave such things as a continuing or cyclical depression which raises problems of a wholly different order or level of organization or reorganization. To use J. M. Clark's neat illustration: an enterprise can meet certain problems of labor overhead by simple, and quite peaceful, lay-off; not so, a nation.

This approach to law-stuff and law-ways via the law-jobs sets certain venerable problems in interesting perspective. When the official imperatives for behavior (say fresh-baked legislation which is meeting resistance) are proving inadequate as channeling devices, but are yet serving as effective standards for the official disposition of trouble-cases; or when they are channeling well for one section of the population, but not for another; or when "bargain-days" (prohibition in our courts) or deliberately evasive "enforcement" (the petty capital felonies in England about 1800) are substituting different, "off-the-record," standards in most of the official disposition of trouble-cases — such conditions yield readily, under such an approach, to analysis and description. It becomes easy to state that a given officially announced imperative or body of imperatives are indeed "Law" for the handling of trouble-cases, but are not serving their channeling purpose as to laymen well, or at all. It becomes easy to state that they are not serving their channeling purpose even as to the official staff, yet are still "Law" whenever the spotlight may pick out some particular trouble-case before an official tribunal. It becomes feasible also to find words for some of the halfway stations beyond which so many efforts at control by official Law never get. It should not be possible, in these post-Max Weber days, to forget that when official law-stuff becomes a conscious device for innovation (instead of a semi-"automatic" starching of patterns of conduct already given in tradition) it then operates in terms of a variegated interplay between its aspect merely as a part of something (The Law; That Man's Policies) which colors it, and occasional direct judgments on its own particular wisdom, and the *seeming likelihood* that, as new Law-stuff, it will bite any relevant person who may be tempted to disregard its promise or its threat.

Weber's development of such ideas suffers somewhat from the multiguity of his usage of "rational," but the results are clear enough, and they do need remembering because they come closer than has any other analytical framework to linking intelligibly the background of general tradition, the sharper-edged calculative thinking which works so remorselessly into a money-economy (or indeed, into any mobile society), the fixity of doctrine (in dogmatic discourse), the change of doctrine (which occurs in actual process of argument and decision), and the engineering problems of new channeling of behavior by way of official Law.

One cannot boil down writings which are themselves a distillate; but one can pick three aspects for emphasis:

(1) The new statute or regulation, these days, has to communicate itself largely by way of words. Words are at least *central* to the communication, even to an official staff.

(2) Along with communication, there goes a problem of persuasion, of energy-unleashing, and one of coordinating such unleashing. "The

official staff," these days, are themselves almost as hydra-headed as a public. And "the" likelihood that the new regulation will take hold as having teeth, or indeed on the side of persuasion of relevant laymen, depends in good part on its producing an effective similarity of reaction within "the" official staff. Again, "the" official staff itself is split fifty ways, in function and organization (from courts through to field inspectors), and in desire — to say nothing of skill. Companioning this, goes the divergent relative pulling power of the new regulation in its aspect simply as being part of The Legal System (or of somebody's Program; or of something enforced by persons toward whom there is a clearly built-up attitude: Cossacks). For some (perhaps most for judges) membership in The Legal System lends per se a tremendous power. Pound has noted the attempts of early law-making to borrow the flavor of the immemorially or supernaturally sacred Source and System for innovating measures, so as to first move and then hold "the" public; and our own Constitution and Founders have had their share of novelties fathered upon them. To others, these days, and at the opposite extreme, others who have seen enough of Law-as-an-Imperative to think overly much in terms of Law-*merely*-as-an-Imperative, of government as an interferer, and of own urge or income as a clear good, while The Whole is hid behind The Politicians or The Cops — to such, the matter can shape up in terms of what the chance can be held down to, that the new regulation will show teeth. It can appear simply as a bother, to be avoided or evaded or wangled out of or endured. What is of peculiar importance, in this many-tendencied modern society in which sight of the Whole gets lost, is that those who respond to mere traditional presumption in favor of a measure are likely to be the passive ones. They count, but they seldom count actively. Whereas those most likely to move on the calculative basis — not Holmes' "bad" men, but just sophisticated persons who have seen enough of Law's Personnel to doubt their sanctity — are the very persons whose channeling is the crux.

(3) From this there results a perception not only that the new regulation has its way to make, in terms of accomplishing an effective channeling of conduct; but that its way is a complex way, and begins *inside* the official staff; and it becomes materially easier to see, to foresee, and to both describe and plan to counter its possible undercutting.

But above all, Weber's approach makes clear what goes to the essence of sound analysis: the jobs to be done are jobs to be done; modern complexity of institution serves merely to highlight processes which require to be gone through, in some fashion, in any group. *The jobs, therefore, get themselves done after some fashion* always — or the group simply is no more. Hence if the officially announced imperatives fail to put themselves over, one must look elsewhere for the doing of the jobs. Consider the family in which father keeps announcing rules and then forgetting them. Hence to see a Legal regulation which is not working is promptly to face a problem of further inquiry: what *is* working? and how?

If all the machinery happens to run in coincidence, so to speak in parallel hook-up, then the normative and the imperative drive together. But when the various portions of the machinery diverge, the matter becomes difficult. We have various familiar formulations which hint at this: Law must not diverge too far from Custom, or from The Folkways, or from Morals; obedience to Law is best learned in the Home; and the like. And the sociologists and psychologists bring the scene into somewhat sharper focus when they look into divergent pulls and patterns at work in the individual's formative years, or thereafter. What we need to see in approaching our modern and complex society is that Custom, Morals, Folkways, the ways of The Home and the like, are not, with us, each a unit; nor are backgrounds in general a unit, nor the normative patternings and strains generated by living in the various backgrounds (*e.g.*, city white-collar, city work-shirt, farm). What this comes to in the matter of delinquency and predatory crime is one problem which opens; and it is complex enough, in all conscience. But unless I am much mistaken, even that problem gains its by-product of light from an attempt to move beyond it and to examine what the situation is in the *non*-criminal field when the machineries for channeling conduct diverge.

For, first of all, divergent patterns not only stir prejudice and enmities, as various We-groups draw together and, in the ancient manner of the primitive human tribe, misconceive, slander, fear and hate the Others-groups, *and typify them by their worst examples;* but divergent patterns also stir in some folk a comparison, an intellectualization about received tradition, and an increase of that "rational" type of direction of conduct which when we think it fine we call wisdom, when we think it skilful we call intelligent and resourceful, and when we think it unaccompanied by sound objectives we call merely expedient following of the main chance. The only voice of the Whole, in the welter, is the voice of the prophet (who has neither authority nor hall-mark) or that of The Law; and both mass and detail of The Law are too complex to understand, and often quite dubious as to their Whole-serving, if understood. I do not think criminologists have paid adequate attention to the strain which unfamiliarity with law puts upon the faith of the simple in The Law, nor to the strain which over-familiarity with it puts upon the self-restraint of the shrewd. In any event, with power organized behind the official-Legal, official imperatives become for anybody with a purpose, high or low, a force to get channelled to his aid. And when the multiple lines of the normative diverge among themselves, and most of them therefore diverge of necessity from the official imperatives, normation which candidates for acceptance and mint-mark as officially imperative is anybody's business, in the service of his desires — be they high or low. Protagonists of divergent normations then struggle to capture the backing of the *system* of imperatives; and that is a struggle for power, and by way of power and strategy. The protagonists struggle also to persuade relevant persons that such capture will serve the commonweal; that is both a tactic for capture and a tactic for more effective operation after capture. But its very basis is a reinforcement of our observation that the official imperatives in any system at all developed are themselves to be viewed always as means, not as ends. The "rule" of the legal philosopher, the "code" of the sociologist, remain, as applied to things legal, *imperative* and *limited* in nature, and remain in service always of normations derived from outside themselves. Except, of course, as *some* order (almost *any* order) continues to be the bare bones essential of group life.

The task which opens here is, plainly, not merely that of channeling behavior, but of selecting the lines along which it is to be channeled — a task chosen as part of our fourth focus for seeing the law-jobs. The logical over-lap is apparent. But so is the value, I hope, of the difference in emphasis. What concerns me here is to make explicit, before leaving the focus of channeling (especially, but by no means exclusively, that of channeling into *new* ways), a matter not unimportant merely because it is obvious: to wit, that the lines the channeling is to take will in part condition the effectiveness of the channeling.

The Say

III. The third phase which it seems convenient to mark off for special treatment centers on allocation and exercise of authority or jurisdiction, within a group, and of legitimatizing action as being authoritative; let me call it the job of *arranging the say, and its saying*. There occur doubts as to what to do, in drought, or war, or petty crisis; there occur disputes as to what to do, and as to whose say is to go. To get these matters settled in advance, and to get settled also what procedures must be gone through in order to legitimatize a decision and give it standing, and what the limits are on any person's authority — this is a matter of peculiar importance. It differs from ordinary channeling of conduct in looking to allocation rather of powers than of rights, to indication of the person and the procedure rather than the substance.

As the first job finds centered around its doing such institutional devices as tribunals, legal procedure, advocacy, peace-makers and jails; as the second finds centered about its doing such institutional devices as rules of substantive law, statute books, law publishing houses, sanitary inspection departments, traffic lights, preventive policing generally — and most of usage, and much of education; so this third task or function finds centered on its doing the "constitutions" of states and of minor interest-groups, and in general the institutional devices for allocating authority to persons or bodies *and* for fixing the time or manner or procedure whereby their say, when said, is to gain standing as being *the* say: the legislature must be "in session" (though with the clock turned back); the two houses must concur, by vote, and with a quorum; the bill must have been "read" the proper number of times.

Now choosing what the say shall be, and many phases of putting into operation a decision when made, are matters commonly and rightly thought to be matters rather of governance than of law; the case is clearest when no one has any idea whose say is to go, and both what we think of as law and what we think of as governance appear only in embryo, as in primitively emergent leadership. The legal gets into the picture here, to the degree of advance regulation. It gets in, further, to the degree to which forms, procedures, ideologies, limit, or even direct, the exercise of authority. Both substantive law and the liberties of the subject are indeed "secreted in the interstices of procedure," insofar as procedure limits the exercise of authority. The legend of the vase of Clovis makes a double point: a simple soldier could defy the King when the King sought to abrogate the ancient Law by singling out his own prospective share of the booty; but the King on the next inspection could find that particular simple soldier's equipment "untidy" enough to warrant spearing without mercy — and to pay off the grudge. A King who has to wait for an inspection, however, is a limited King; add an independent tribunal to determine the facts and he becomes a limited King, indeed. These are commonplaces. But there is a third line of limiting that King. It is no less real and it ought also to become a commonplace. That is by a tradition of what kind of action or exercise of authority is "kingly," and of what kind is unworthy of the kingly *office*. Such traditions are law-stuff, though they be not written; there is another legend, of an argument of one Nathan before one David, which makes that point; and our own society knows a standard phrased as "conduct unbecoming an officer and a gentleman." Form, procedure, occasion, tradition of the office, authoritative materials — none alone, nor all together, suffice to make the saying independent of the sayer; but insofar as any or all of such regulatory ways and/or norms reduce the idiosyncratic factor, insofar as they raise the effective character of the office and lower the effective influence of the office-holder, they increase the element of the "legal," and reduce that of governance-apart-from-the legal.

Let me recur now to a feature, especially of the tradition of the office, which is very hard to state but is real with a reality whose conception is the glory of the "legal," as its misconception is the terror. It is this: the "legal" which surrounds and affects the expression of the "say" drives to prop up inexperience and ignorance, to check stupidity, to thwart personal waywardness, to choke off corruption. This is accomplishable, in part, by forms which control and limit and by authoritative base-lines which control and guide. But in no skilfully built legal structure is the factor of movement, and of need for movement, or the factor of justice in effect, and of need for justice in effect, disregarded. That is simple enough to see. What is not so simple to see, what is more vital, what is the very sap, is this: that whereas a leeway of the holders of authority to *be* right is of necessity within a legal structure a leeway to *be* wrong, yet a leeway to *do* right is *not* a leeway to *do* wrong. The matter is clear if one will look to the *job* in hand, and see, beside its bare bones, its questing aspect. The heart of it is, that blindness and woodenness and red tape and sheer stupidity are desperately bad; and the reason is, because they *cut our institutions down, in effectiveness, to those institutions' own structured measure* by depriving us of the salvaging guidance which the men-in-office ought always to be *adding* to the best we have been able to build in the way of *explicitly structured* (as distinct from implicit and *unspoken*) institutional framework. But malevolence, distortion to wrong ends, abuse for profit or favor: these, though within the leeways left open by the institutional structure, are what theology might liken to sins against the Ghost of the Law; they take the very salvage-leeway itself and turn it to disruption.

Somewhere in every "legal" structure — big or little, crude or developed — there is implicit, not necessarily a spirit moving in these terms, but a claim to hold such a spirit, and a recognition of duty to make good thereon. This goes not to detail, nor, at a pinch, even to sometimes wide special areas. But it does go to the Whole of the system in net effect and especially in net intent. It is at this point that an imperative system and the net effect and intent of its authoritative staff make necessary contact with justification of themselves. And if there were no other reason, that would be enough to warrant singling out arrangement of the say and of the manner of its saying as a separate focus.

This I put forward here not as an ethical demand upon the system (though it is that); I put it forward in this context as a sociological fact, not negated by the most cynical egocentric who ever ran a "skelegal" system on fear and "arbitrary" force. If you prefer, I can rephrase and put it forward as a construct, as an element conceived to be always and strongly present in urge, even though in some few particular situations it may be so countered by other factors as not to appear overtly. But what I mean is that I believe that construct to reflect the facts with accuracy. I hold this to be one of some few drives and urges in behavior (among them, the drive toward habit and toward precedent) which are so almost universally observable as to put solidity under a belief that where not overt they are not absent, but only countered and drowned from overt appearance in the individual instance.

The overlap of this say-focus upon trouble-disposition and upon channeling is obvious enough. The trouble may be about who has the say, as has happened from time to time among our own States as to who "was" the Government, and as is still happening in regard to jurisdiction to tax. On the other hand, the disposition of trouble-cases via official personnel is an employment of say-allocation and of say-procedure. And, as has been mentioned, the very regularization of the who and the partial regularization of the how and when of the say, are channeling devices for trouble-avoidance — though they have always been sanctified as Constitution. But the test of the value of the focus must come from whether using it turns up cross-lightings of material which promise hope of developing what one may call not common sense, but less-common sense, a more ordered and effective body of sense, *un*common sense, about the problems concerned.

This "legal" problem runs throughout the society; and through all manner of groups. The allocation of authority in enterprises will serve to illustrate, or the conflict between the AFL and the CIO, or indeed jurisdictional union disputes. The question is one of de facto authority, first of all. It will of course not do to fail to recognize the vast differences between "proper" and "improper," "lawful" and "unlawful" de facto allocation of say. But neither will it do to see these as resting in any such dichotomy as being a dichotomy with sharp-drawn lines: the "king's favorite" may, for instance, stand in a recognized status which tomorrow will be that of "prime minister," or may occupy a spotlight of public scandal, or may be anywhere in a twilight between.

Let us then sum up this particular law-job, thus: advance allocation (certainly de facto; preferably, and always in urge, also de jure) to say the say which will go, in case of doubt or emergency; together with any fixing of procedures which legitimatize the say, and any explicit or tacit limitations (or guidances) which cut down authority's effective leeway: as that a judge must decide after due trial and under the law. But we must be remembering that in this area, of all areas, flux is the essence of history, that today's usurpation is often enough tomorrow's constitution while today's renewed exercise of indubitable ancient constitution is often enough the signal for explosion. In no area of law-stuff is power more likely to run at partial odds with right. In none is legality more likely to run at partial odds with wise ultimate policy, or with the immediately decent, on the one hand; or with the arbitrary, or, again, with the immediately personal and political, on the other. In none is a possible precedent as big with consequence if it does become a precedent. While the scope of matters in this area varies from the national or tribal down into those of the single family, all of these things hold good, as concerns whatever may be the particular unit, the particular Entirety, which may be concerned.[7]

Net Drive

IV. *Integration, incentive, direction, net.* The fourth focus of law-jobs goes to the whole net effect of the other three, as performed. The reason for choosing it as a distinct focus is that to do so brings out into an emphasis otherwise too easy to let drift away, the *positive,* the constructive, side of the "legal": the net organization around something, toward something: the Whither of the net Totality. It is doubly necessary to bring that into emphasis, because it is presupposed by the pervading, though implicit, drive of Law-officials (and indeed of political movements) for something felt, dimly or clearly, as Balance in the Total Legal, as well as for something felt as Health. Planning of the Whole has been too much for us, but tinkering is both furthered and fought, always, under the tug and torsion of some *feeling* for the Whole.

So that we can well take as a fourth focus the organization of the Entirety into some type of coordination which also unleashes enough incentive to get that enterprise carried on, and leaves the group-members sound enough to carry it on; along with which one must put the net shaping of direction of the enterprise toward one Whither rather than another.

However loose and vague such a description may appear, however joyous of infinite leeway and infinite variety, eluding all grasp, it nonetheless says something; as the seemingly tautologous statement of the total law-job said something; and as the statement that a society, or a Legal System, has its own variety of living unity says something. And I conceive it as peculiarly a *law*-job focus because the legal system of a group (not its Legal doctrine, merely, but its going whole) seems to me to be inescapably one place, and the main place, in which men face group-responsibility for shift in direction, and rekilter to achieve a readjusted net result or recapture of balance. The prophet labors also in this matter, and the blinder upshot of individual efforts, unplanned as a totality, sets conditions which may be too yeasty for conscious "legal" effort to handle. But, in the first place, modern techniques of organization, communication and striking power have made clear that the *possible* effective reshaping power of conscious "legal" effort reaches far beyond what a Savigny, a Carter or a Sumner believed. Sumner's favorite illus-

7. No Constitutional question of jurisdiction was ever more delicate or puzzling than that presented when Christmas is at Grandma's, and Grandma has said the lid is off, and Father thinks the children are getting out of hand, and Grandma is not Father's mother.

On the self-legitimatizing drive of de facto power, and its corrective drive, see p. 1394 *infra.*

tration of the abortive reforms of Joseph II can be seen more clearly, today, as involving a piece of defective technique rather than, necessarily, an impossible objective; for some reason, the normally hardheaded and hardeyed Sumner did not meditate upon Chaka and the Zulu, nor upon Ignatius Loyola's amazingly effective devices for the reshaping of personality and creation of a tightly integrated organization. One can no longer throw important social reorganization out of the window as being a job not doable by conscious revision of the "legal" system; one can today only challenge whether such reorganization is worth the price, or raise doubts as to whether other and unforeseen evils may not in the long run attend its doing. But the would-be sociologist of the "legal" must see as a law-job that coordination, direction and incentive-unleashing which it has been demonstrated that the "legal" *can* vitally effect, and must therefore see as a law-*choice,* at the least as a law-*way,* the leaving of such matters largely to other devices.

This, too, is of course not new, but old insight, merely forgotten over the laissez-faire ideology. Consider mercantilist policy, or Jonathan Swift's scorn for a system of law-stuff which failed to include the phase of incentive as well as that of regimentation and deterrence.

To give the topic perspective: on the bare-bones side, one remembers that if there be not adequate integration and efficiency in the doing of the other law-jobs, the costs rise too high for tolerability or the results drop too low. We are told that villages by the hundred were simply "lost" in the wars of the Thirty and the Hundred Years. And order laid on with too heavy a hand threatens to crush out life — one thinks of the later Roman agricultural enterprises. Our imagination faces similar possibilities, today, as to the international law-job.

The second matter of perspective goes to the questing aspects, and raises particularly the question of whether provision of direction is not a matter rather of leadership, governance, and the man, than in any reasonable sense a *law*-job. As always, the individual feeds his work into the scheme, as the scheme feeds itself into his work. But if the achievements of governing (or of other leadership) are to serve beyond the man's life; indeed, if they are to handle, even during a life-time, a group big enough to call for large-scale *delegation* to subordinates — then it is not only other *men* which they call for, but it is also law-stuff into which they must be incorporated. They call for what Alexander accomplished more effectively in his army than in his civil administration. Adjudication is familiar to any case-lawyer as showing the mark of the man, and familiar to him also as building law-stuff. But the same holds of the policy shaping of any governing persons; and never has a grander symphony been written on the theme than what I cannot help thinking of as Maitland's Pollock and Maitland, in regard to the effects on English King's law of particular English kings. It is a *culture's* law-job to get such law-stuff built and rebuilt workably and well, and to fuller ends: to make and to place and to support the necessary men.

And it is here, it seems to me, that one key-inquiry lies as to the interaction of "man," the individual, and "culture," the surrounding super-individual structure and welter of behavior and ideological tradition of his fellows. For I grow as clear that some individuals in key-position and at key-moments have tremendous shaping power as I do that mass-reactions of the "growth"-sort may have their own lines of semi-irresistibility. The reason why the "legal" may prove of peculiar general importance is that the "legal" shows a higher general likelihood of key-position than do most other phases of culture, other than political leadership. And I cannot avoid the conclusion that the reason why key-position effect has been now over-stressed (the "Great Man theory") and now almost denied ("Volksgeist" and its successors) has lain in a desire to see as a constant process what is better seen in terms of a greater or less degree of *likelihood* of significant shaping of the Whole from some key-position. The same holds of the likelihood of law-stuff finding itself in key-position: *most* law-stuff, in a complex culture, of course washes down-stream like salmon-spawn; but what of that?

If it be true, however, that law-stuff "drives" for key-position, and that political leadership "drives" also for key-position, then in this aspect of general coordination and direction, the two must be found driving toward coalescence. That seems to me well-nigh inherent in two aspects of a culture each of which, willy-nilly, comes under persistent urge to purport to speak for the Entirety, and, in some measure, to make the purport real.

This, again, is not to be taken as exclusive. De facto leadership may depart from the official-political, wandering underground to the boss in the back-room, or wandering wholly elsewhere, until we meet "figure-head government." For, as indicated above, the law-jobs get themselves done; but the official-Legal and official-Political need not be the mechanisms of their doing. One can note, indeed, in this coordination matter as in the matter of justice, that the provision of a twilight, of a flux and an overlap between the official and The Rest accords with social lubrication (as it accords also with a democrat's view of social health): if the jobs are too sharply in official hands, things creak as loudly (though in different key) as they do when the jobs have slipped through the fingers of the *roi fainéant*. But, above all, as one observes any line of going social institution, one observes also, first, that it participates in performance of a huge body of functions other than the one or ones primarily attributed to it in common thinking; and second, that "its" functions are in process of being helped into performance by many other going social institutions. It was astounding to me, for instance, in a canvass of Contract, to discover how much governmental work Contract was doing, and how much of the commonly supposed work of Contract was being done by such "other" institutions as association, property, industrial technology, and accounting — to pick a few. An analysis of the work of marriage-and-the-immediate-family brings out similar results. So that the "law"-job of coordination, direction and incentive (could we lump these as the "Net Drive"?) is being worked at also by religion, and by prevailing folk-philosophy, and by "economic organization," and by "education," and by "patriotism." But so long as it be clear how peculiarly the job in question *partakes* of the "legal," and *how much* of it, for purposes of the study of man-in-culture, must be dealt with together with other matters "legal," the overlaps with "other" phases of culture do not disturb.

On the contrary, they illumine. For save in quite extraordinary instances conscious production of Net Drive has been too big a job for man to handle with full success on a large scale; and the major effective device, whether for conscious creation or without it, seems to me to have been the throwing of large — though vaguish — blocs of desired Net Drive into ideal pictures accompanied each by an emotionally stirring symbol. Whether the symbol be a personality-model (Lincoln) or an emblem (the Cross, the Flag) or a slogan with some more or less intellectualized content (*"salus populi suprema lex; quid principi placuit legis habet vigorem; sic semper tyrannis"* make a nice interacting trio), in any event the bloc of Net Drive symbolized is an expression of *one phase* of actual life in the society, heavily idealized, heavily charged with a philosophy of felt rightness and heavily charged with emotional incentive. How vague or how clear, how far capable of the wilder forms of manipulation, how broad or how narrow in the range of person, class, or profession on whom its pull is effective — this differs.

But what is of immediate moment to us is, first, that such a symbolized bloc of Net Drive always takes in *something* from outside the immediately Legal (though it be nothing but the blinder esthetic and formal urges which substitute a Parke "strong opinion" for true elegantia juris); and second, that it is especially by way of such symbolized blocs that the men of law rework their structure and reshape it in direction, coordination, and incentive. It is true that those jurists whose eye has been on the decision of cases, on right doctrinal casuistry, or on cleanly intellectualized systematics, have grown properly impatient with maxims, brocards, and other outflowing and edgeless policy expressions; especially impatient, I suspect, because the nice and accurate mind can be driven wild by muddy and untrammelled slinging of such maxims as excuses for decisions not thought through. But their uselessness as effective major premises for syllogistic determination of the correct precise answer on the authorities does not mean that they lack driving power or lack even considerable *guiding* power; it is such conceptions as that the intention of the parties must control, or that this is a Christian country, or that taxation is a "necessary evil" rather than "the price of civilization" which mediate their quantum of general coordination to our Legal System, even as the law-men mediate the Legal System to the people. It is quite beside the point whether you do or you do not like any particular big or little bloc of Net Drive which is thus made to spread its strength and flavor. The point is that it is by way of these emotionally charged ideological configurations that the job is chiefly done. They run from such partly Legal ideas as Contract, Trust and Due Process, through those expressions of Legal Principle which are also expressions of antepenultimate social policy, on into such vague, pervasive, but forceful pictures as The Business Man as a sort of embodiment of the *vir justus et honestus* of America, or of Government as somehow different from and vastly better than any official. They are of course self-inconsistent in their working; in two hands the same one may produce differences which startle. It is that same Nazi legal ideology which in many points of confiscation, declassing, criminal trial, etc., has set our teeth on edge, which in the hands of Heinrich Lange could produce a reworking of contract doctrine which is probably the most enlightening job of the century in that field. That is the way of emotionally charged symbols whose intellectual content, in any particular context, is so vague as to call for the user to *ad lib.* And it reinforces the occasional crucial character of the individual who happens to hold key-position for The Law in any situation in which The Law happens to be occupying key-position for the culture: *i.e.,* when *his* normative generalizations *become imperatives* and those imperatives prove then to be imperatives which *count.*

There is one matter for final mention, in the interest of perspective: it is under this Net Drive focus that one can most readily pick out that phase of the Justice ideal which looks to long-range welfare of the Entirety. There is also Justice as even-handedness under Law, a conception looking toward impartiality and disregard of power, friendship, political influence, favor and the like; this, when one does not like it, is thought of as dry legality or even legalism. There is Justice as "fair" and wise individuation of the handling of the case — the ideal of the juvenile court — which is maudlin, or kadi-justice, if you do not like it. There is the many-flavored Justice, compounded of all of the above in thus far quite unreckonable mixtures, which is the "Justice under Law" our courts aim to afford. There is social Justice, which is the reformer's desire to see the worse-off be helped. Only the first of these is the Justice ideal appropriate to the context of this Net Drive job: level-headed, far-visioned, thinking for the whole — with *each* of all other phases of Justice coming in for, but held down to, its due share of influence.

JURISTIC METHOD: THE FIFTH LAW-JOB

If what has been written above had been written with adequacy, there would be no point in continuing. Put it together, and the problem of juristic method is set. Men deviate from the anticipated, or anticipate what others do not think they have business to anticipate, or clash otherwise, and there are cases of trouble. In furtherance of desire or interest, in the service of self or group or the Entirety concerned, to gain backing or to avoid pressure, men put forth normative generalizations which rest always in part on something in the culture, and move always to suppression or neglect of some other things in the culture. Decisions are reached, and some of those decisions become determinative of what can be expected. Out of them, out of action which they stimulate, out of the work of any specialists who emerge as men of trouble-settlement or of governing, régimes of authority bud and grow, tending into some working unity. The pressure toward regularity, and the pressure of the anticipable to be felt as right, is steady. The law-jobs of trouble-handling, of channeling, of say-allocation, of the Net Drive, all need doing, and they all drive toward the emergence of some type of institutional machinery (ways *and* personnel *and* ideology about both) which can be seen as different from just who is there and just what is done and what is thought or felt, in general. With the emergence of the perceptibly "legal," as a body of ways, people and ideology, there emerges at once the problem raised by any institution and its staff: the problem of keeping the institution and its staff in hand and on their jobs. Institutional ways and ideology tend to grow hard, wooden, tend to crystallize upon their own premises, tend to be patterned in further operation on their own past rather than on their living function; or they tend to be turned to service of their staff rather than of the people. Exactly comparable tendencies bud in the staff, the personnel. In the main, machinery "legal" in character, and personnel "official" in character, have best potentiality for accomplishing the "law-jobs." But rarely, in any culture, and never in a culture both developed and mobile, can official "legal" machinery and personnel accomplish the whole of those jobs. What is wanted is an on-going optimum balance, keeping in the hands of the official "legal" machinery and personnel, and well-handled by them, so much as they can best handle. This problem, seen as reaching over all the law-job foci, or seen if you will as one phase of the play of the fourth upon the first three, I take in any event to be worth isolation for study. I shall call it the problem of *juristic method,* that of the *ways* of handling "legal" tools to law-job ends, and of the on-going upkeep and improvement of both ways and tools. The bare-bones aspect carries one just far enough to scrape along, and that not in the individual case, but in the large. The law-suit which followed the burning of Njal not only broke into battle, but had been foreseen as likely to; yet the battle itself took place with friends of the rightful litigants standing by to "stop the fighting when you have slain as many as you can pay for." Iceland at the turn of the first millenium shows juristic method, here, with not too much spare meat on the bare bones.

"Juristic method" is likely, to a modern, to connote the task, or the ways of doing the task, of determining disputed questions of Law under the relevant prevailing authorities: the task peculiarly of the appellate court, reviewing on "The Law," or of the jurist at work on the elaboration of his dogmatics. And the work of the appellate court is indeed one point on which such an analysis as the present ought properly to focus, and together with the trial court's work, it is close to the center of my own interest. The general job of juristic method, however, as here conceived, does not presuppose of necessity the existence of any tribunal at all; it is illuminated by such an institutional figure as that queer Ifugao cross between a hired advocate and a mediator, the *monunkalon,* with his persuasion, his browbeating, his swellings of claims and driving of adjustment bargains. On the other hand, juristic method as here conceived extends over into reform legislation and especially into the still largely unspoken skills and multiform traditions of the official craftsmen of the Law. In a society with little "legal" differentiation, the task of juristic method and its ways of doing tend to be hidden in the mere handling of the trouble-cases. In a society with high differentiation inside the Legal, the specialization of some craftsmen or bodies on one or another phase which seems peculiarly one of juristic method threatens to hide the fact that each last part of the work of law continues to have its share in the problem. Thus primitive legal institutions, with the extreme difficulty they commonly encounter over problems of fact, ought to remind us that solution of such problems is a tough law-job, and that solution of them to satisfaction calls for juristic method and art; when we then recur to our own conditions, with legislative findings of fact, the jury, and the administrative semi-tribunal, for instance, or with a jury verdict in capital cases reviewable on the facts by the Court of Appeals, and the Court of Appeals by a pardoning governor, we ought to find that with us, no less, juristic method goes still to questions of fact.

So also it does to questions of grievance-adjustment, though both Law and fact may happen to be clear. I may say that in whole cultures (as distinct from formative groups within a culture), it is the grievance-case (as distinct from fact-dispute which is rarish in a close-knit face-to-face community, or from trouble over what is right, or is Law) which shows every sign of being, along with emergent leadership, the major matrix of the "legal." The institutions, as they first shape, much more commonly than not are cast in the mould of devices for *grievance*-handling; disputed matters of fact can lie over, almost indefinitely, with little institutional attention or can develop their own, independent lines of handling; disputed points of right, which, once determined, tend to be points of Law, seem most commonly attended to first as a sort of by-product of the grievance-handling machinery. But let a *tribunal* come into recognized existence, and the three types of trouble tend to merge in the doing of its business; and, once merged, they seem to be hard indeed to disentangle. And, of course, as tradition builds, the aspect of what is Law moves steadily into the forefront of attention — until it gets too close to the eye to let the rest be seen.

The first problem as to juristic method has to do with its available leeway for error. And here one has two phenomena to note which are puzzling to describe. The first is the extraordinary degree to which a System colors and covers its own blobs. Unless the case comes as the cumulation of a whole line of prior error or abuse, or unless circumstances (commonly political, and sometimes adventitious) have flavored it *as if* it presented such a cumulation, the leeway for error, abuse, even outrage in the individual case would be alarming if one conceived of it as available for deliberate exploitation. The test of this is in the cumulative effect of the work of a strong and long-lived judge (Mansfield) or of strong and skilful picking and pressing of selected cases by a particular interest (the old Anti-Boycott Association) or of strong and sustained executive pressure (the English kings and the Capetians). The other side of the same picture lies, however, in the no less extraordinary degree to which a System, on its regularity side, drives to cure its own past abuses by regularizing them. First, it tends to make them not only Legal, but right: the brute might or fraud or corruption which yields present outrage can generate not only the imperative of Law; but it can, and it drives to, generate future "right" as to its results, and often even as to its manner: by power first, but then by recognition, repetition, expectation — and so into tradition, until authority is backed by morality. At the same time, and under the same processes, the legitimatized is being driven toward the limited: legal, yes, right, yes, but legal and right only so far, and only when done in such a way. This double process of absorption and sanation of abuse and outrage, once they have been accomplished, is one of the major stumbling-blocks in communication between the world of Law and the world of sociology; for the world of Law-as-doctrine can and must encompass at any given instant of time only a very limited quantum of the process. A limited quantum it must encompass, for doctrine is not to stand stock still; but that quantum is very limited, for Law's office while it is still Law is to hold within due bounds even action which is pregnant with future Law.

The second boundary of leeway for juristic method, that of tolerance for *cumulative* misdoing of the job, may be very wide indeed, if the cumulative process goes by inches, but is likely to shoal off suddenly if the cumulation begins to attract attention from those who count *and if* an organizing spearhead appears. But the more important aspect of it seems to me to be the powerful tendency never to let error in juristic method carry the legal system down to the bare-bones level, but to react first by "turning the rascals out," or attempting some type of system-reform, or both.

Specialists

The case for the value of developing specialists to handle "legal" stuff, and so to handle juristic method, is quickly made on the basis of primitive culture. Grievance-adjustment, if left to the aggrieved, is hard to hold down to adjustment, in contrast to counter-grievance. The on-going cumulation of the blood-feud is the favorite instance of the writers; this, even when enough balance between the contesting "clans" is presupposed for the matter to work out as a feud. Over-balance of power on the side of the aggrieved, moreover, may mean no limit to "redress" in vengeance-form; over-balance on the side of the aggressor may mean no redress at all. Thus, even in the matter of articulating and directing pressure upon the breaker-over, the grievance-causer, the device of leaving the matter to the aggrieved to handle lacks adequacy. And labor disputes among us pointed this up for decades, and to some extent do still. But more especially does leaving control in the aggrieved lack adequacy on the side of *admeasuring* the adjustment. For admeasurement is a problem of exceeding toughness. Only in terms of the lack of graded extra-pressures to reach the horny-hided can one understand the way in which primitive peoples will simply tolerate aggressive, ruthless abusers of all decencies—until the time comes when a straw or a new bale breaks the back of public patience and an offender moves into a new and awful status, that of him-who-can-no-longer-be-borne; and the group shortly then — as is reported from the Eskimo, the Shoshone, etc. — goes on one man shy. Our own polity knows the problem still, when a family faces the dissolute son or daughter, holding off the only remaining and ultimate step of turning out a child. Admeasurement is a difficult problem, indeed.

No less difficult is *articulation* of pressure when there is no person or group clearly and peculiarly aggrieved or none recognized as so aggrieved. Not only does inertia stand in the way, but "face" stands in the way, and fear. "Face," because no man likes to be officious; what man wants to stick his neck out — to "assume" to be the man "called" to act? Fear, because to touch off group-resentment lightly leads further mob-wise than any man would care to go in cool blood; and a group can turn upon the person who has thus misled them. Malinowski gives a case in point: a young man who called attention to the breach of a formal "incest"-tabu by a girl he loved, with penalties not to be winked at, once the thing got into the spoken open; the girl, by protest-suicide, then threw the onus of outrage done back upon the informer. The case shows, as any study of group-life will, one social device for articulation of pressure in the general interest; the pulling forward into "voicing" of someone who for some other reason — old grudge, jealousy, envy, political rivalry, general dislike — is glad to seize on any opportunity to jump the particular culprit without personal risk. But that machinery is neither adequate nor is it over-satisfactory. Most cultures do manage one or another standard way of channeling gossip as a pressure, in praise and blame, as the women's: "David hath slain his thousands"; the Eskimo song-duel institutionalizes the same song of ridicule which Iceland made it a crime to publish. But some cases call for more than even this.

As if by raised lightning-rod, *any political authority* which develops in group or culture thus attracts to itself the two tasks of *articulation* and *admeasurement* of rebuke. The question here is of coalescence — by urge not so much of function as of mechanism. Political authority means power, and power is the refuge of the weak aggrieved. Political authority has rivals for power, and rebuke for good cause is a welcome tool against such rivals. Political authority speaks for the whole, and has standing so to speak — and who will then be better qualified to articulate a general, though unfocused grievance, or have so much to gain, so little to lose, by taking the initiative? Political authority must be concerned with the interest of the whole, and so of peace, and so of guiding adjustment, even by the aggrieved, into channels which reduce the chance of counter-grievance. Indeed, if the specialization of personnel into this law-job of the trouble-case take any of the alternative roads — that over the wise old man, the peace-maker, or over the judge, or over the priest, or over the Ifugao combination of advocate and mediator, or over the sorcerer — then such personnel must in turn be regarded as carrying latent germs of ultimate political power. Coalescence of the doing of law-jobs with the work of governing, while not inevitable, is thus nonetheless "natural," not only in function but in process. And I remind of another reason for a persistent urge toward such coalescence. What we think of as political authority is authority tending in fact and in recognized right to be supreme. But what we think of as the legal shows the same characteristics. If there is but a single standard against which to measure rights and rightness, or but a single authority to turn to, it is that single way or standard or authority which we shall have to take as all that the group has in the way of law for the trouble-case — as, in Felix Cohen's term, representing pro tanto "the most fundamental or most effectively organized set of conduct-imperatives." But if, as is much more frequently the case, there are available a variety of alternative procedures or authorities, and there is some range and variety of standards of right and rightness, then it is hard to escape choosing as the "legal" that one which serves as a last resort when others fail, and which, if appealed to before passing through the others, is recognized as proper to prevail in the pinch. Which means, as stated, that what we think of as "political authority" and the "legal" drive toward generating each the other. But which also makes clear the *points* at which they tend most strongly to coalesce: to wit, the point at which the "legal" takes the shape of *action by authoritative personnel* (the judge, the king, the council, the captain; and on a lesser level: the old peace-maker, the mediator-on-more-than-one-occasion, the skilled-in-law and the like); and the point at which the standard or norm recognized takes the form of one *pronounced by authoritative personnel.* Whereas that line of legal which moves by way of *accepted procedures* not only may emerge independently of political authority, but, as has been noted, tends to become a major device for holding political authority within bounds — "under law." Neither among child-groups nor in primitive cultures nor in formative groups in our own culture nor in the legal history of developed systems do we find evidence that law-stuff shows any preference in emerging into recognition by the route over redress-patterns as distinct from that over the actions of personnel or vice versa. Rather does each tendency seem to be latent always; in the Cheyenne material alone one can follow, in interplay, everything (save sorcery) from vengeance-killing and sudden lynching through to a High Council of extraordinary constitution called into conclave on an unprecedented case.

The Clash of Rival Lay-Normations

The effective articulation and admeasurement of rebuke, however, will not go unchallenged. It needs no rule of law, formulated and accompanied (to hold down officials who might get out of hand) by a régime of *nulla poena sine lege,* nor does it need the presence of a lawyer-tribe skilled in technical defense — it needs none of these things to produce in a human being a feeling that he is entitled not only to be guilty, but to be *found* guilty; that he is entitled to whatever due procedure may be; that he has a right to be afflicted no more than others have been afflicted in like case. There may be no machinery to make his feeling effective, but it is there. Out of predictive observation of what has been done in trouble-cases plus man's interest in his skin, his convenience, his goods, his honor and his vested hates, comes vigorous normative generalization: first, as to "legal" rights to repetition in "like" trouble-cases; and second, as to "legal" rights that there shall be no other and no more than repetition. The presence of law-men may intensify, articulate, give body to such lines of thought, as the tradition of the law-men also will, and as the cumulation of available written records will, again. The ingenuity of law-men can bring forth rules, fictions, lines of application and practice as tortured in shape as a Japanese stunted tree, as artificial, as slow and stubborn to produce. But it is the monopoly of the lore, of the material, it is trade-specialization in the use of it, which makes such things the peculiar product of the counsellor and advocate. The *lines of thought* are the lines of thought of his client. The lines of thought are found indeed in very little boys who are hurt thrice as badly by a spanking without a hearing when guilty, as by a spanking when innocent if only a fair hearing has gone against them. Literalness where there is a letter, formalism where there is a form, are of the essence of word-magic, and of other magic, and word and other magic are lay, not law-stuff.

Legalism, then, as a drive, must be seen as present wherever and as soon as law-stuff is recognizable as such. It must be seen as in first instance litigant's stuff: it is spawned by litigants and their counsellors, then by transactors and their counsellors, to get the backing of The System to their ends. It is one line of *legal* method; but it becomes *juristic* method only when *accepted* by the solvers who speak for the Whole. In part, perhaps, the litigants themselves come to it by sheer woodenness and ritualism, as modern laymen bind themselves in free will by Emily Post's pronouncements; but ever and again the litigant *shapes* things into woodenness and ritualism under the drive of interest. Lawyers, I repeat, can do all this more delicately and can hang it on a slimmer peg; but they can do it no more stubbornly than laymen. And ambiguous law-stuff can be read and normatized by laymen too in stiff-necked clashing ways.

Against this, and at the other extreme, as soon as the practices of life have begun to slip an inch away from the remembered law-stuff, there emerges normatization on the level of direct, primitive justice: the right, as felt out of the practices of life — duly extended. This also is eternal. And it reaches of course much further than "morals"; it need not be general, it need not be old, it need not be anything beyond what seems, in the light of interest, to be the implication of tendencies *felt* as present in what is *felt* as practice. It will appear under the name of Justice; and how it shapes up for argument, in contrast to the legalistic line, has never been better presented than in Aristotle's *Rhetoric*. But again, it is not juristic method; it is another, a competing line of legal method. And like the other, it is a line which is not only litigant's art but is the form also in which what often is a litigant's deep need is clothed.

Primitive normation needs no machinery, though it can use a spokesman. It rests on desire — a *will* aspect; it rests on need — a *mercy* aspect; it rests on directly felt life-practice — a *justice* aspect. Legalistic normation is by necessity a touch more sophisticated. It rests on life and right not directly, but indirectly, as right may have lain under the prior expression of authority. But it has its own sophisticated claims to being just. There is a type of right and justice which consists in the order of abiding by the old-and-known. There is a type of right and justice in the fairness of treating even formally similar cases in similar fashion.

There is a type of justice in sustaining expectations built (with *or* without "action in reliance") on either of the foregoing.

The conflicts which emerge, even on grievance matters, and *a fortiori* on matters involving questions of what is right, and then, what is the imperative, and then, what is the Legal answer — these conflicts open the fascinating tasks of juristic method. For juristic method has as its task the use of the available law-stuff, or the creation of new, to choose between conflicting needs, to choose between good needs to fill and worse ones, to invent as well as to choose — and to do all this, somehow, in tune with the net requirements of the Entirety, as those requirements shape up in terms of getting the law-jobs done and their questing aspects furthered. Between the claim for favor (often, as juvenile court work will remind, highly legitimate) or for rule-disregarding individuation of the case, and the claim for primitive justice (the absentee evictor) on the one hand, and the claim for the literal pound of flesh on the other, there lies no simple choosing, but a wide field in which there is no easy chart. Where is right legality in place, respecting form in the main with care, yet keeping the substance ever from defeat by form? Where is long-range Justice, the most sophisticated of all lines of normation, to outweigh the claims both of legality and of the immediate justice of the case? Where is strict formalism needed, for security? Where is the case in hand the major matter?

The object of the paper has been to get these lines of problem into their setting, to get clear the complex stuff which goes into them, in their very simplest form, and which is in them still, however heavily they come to us laden with technical machinery or technical camouflage. Under the analysis, for example, it becomes relatively easy to see and to state that the relation of our Legal System to our judges is strikingly different from its relation to persons not entrusted by office with use of juristic method. As to any person in his lay behavior, the System as a body of imperatives is clear, save on its edges, and is limited, even on its edges, and the normatives which accompany it are normatives of purpose: the "or else" imperative aspect has become a separate engineering problem for specialized attention, after the "should" has been spotted, has been decided on, has been phrased for communication. But as to the appellate judge (whom I choose here merely as the classic example of official entrusted with use of juristic method) the *imperatives* of our Legal System, though not absent, are poorly organized, and inexplicit; they are confused and imprecise in application, apart from a few gross matters such as corruption. Reversal, though important, is at most both indirect and a semi-sanction. Effective *control* (whether needing no sanction, or provided with one) by the Rules of Law has a range curiously more constricted than we commonly assume. Effective control by the tradition of the craft and office, on the other hand, has hardly been studied; that it is there, we know, but we know not its degree, nor its mechanisms, nor its certainty of operation on each chance-met individual officer. The semi-imperative lies thus, at the heart of the System's operation, in an unanalyzed colloidal mixture with the normative; and the problems of juristic method, posed above, not only have no machinery for answer offered by the System, but are not even clearly posed by its working machinery as calling for answer. For the polite convention of legal discourse is still that The Rules of Law, of themselves, not only guide but control. In a culture or group sufficiently unified to keep each officer of juristic method in reasonable fashion abreast, in both knowledge and feeling, of both the Entirety and each of its conflicting parts, this may do. In ours, intelligence and rational study toward guidance are needed, to aid. Our judges' intuition of their duty to Justice has aided much but it still cross-purposes itself. Yet juristic method, while never capable of mechanization, is nonetheless capable of such organization as to somewhat communicate both skills and guidances: what to do with the Rules of Law, and how, when they are judge-made, best to make them? That is the type of problem — one type, only — which the paper has aimed to get into better focus against the welter of normative generalizations and of law-stuff, with the law-jobs of the Entirety pulsing under all.

If one wants to startle himself with light on how little explicit effective direction or guidance Our Legal System offers the judges (taken as a group, to any one of whom a case may come, and from *any* one of whom the answer would, in ideal, be the same) let him look at the judges, for a moment, not as entrusted with the application of the Rules of Law, but as entrusted with the application of juristic method *to* the Rules of Law and *with* them. It is a truer picture.

And may it not be suggested in closing, that if our polity attempted once to go too far in separating and so simplifying the problems of juristic method by depriving our courts of law-making power, yet the judges' tacit correction by way of merely continuing case-law, old style, was an over-correction? The Cheyenne Indians found ways of keeping the individual needs of the individual case from troubling a policy-decision, while yet letting the issues of the individual case inform that policy-decision. For that reason, they were able to do with relative frequency what an American high court finds it is most puzzling to do: to keep the skilled advocate's use of the *atmosphere* of the particular controversy from foisting an unwise general ruling on the community. And the *Sunburst Oil* case makes it clear that some experimentation with such procedure would be constitutional in the courts of these United States.

[11]

THE PROBLEMS OF A FUNCTIONAL JURISPRUDENCE

IN the lists of jurisprudence, the champion of a new theory is generally expected to prove the virtue of the lady for whom he fights by splitting the skulls of those who champion other ladies. Yet despite the struggle of schools that has been waged for the last forty years in our law reviews,[1] it is possible, I think, to defend the functional approach in jurisprudence without attacking the doctrines or the achievements of any other school.

In jurisprudence as in other fields of thought, we are more likely to reach a just appraisal of a new school by asking not, "What thesis does it defend?" but rather, "What question does it put?" The most significant advances in intellectual history are characterised by the focusing of critical attention upon facts and issues which were formerly considered unimportant, indecent, or self-evident.

Modern physics begins when Galileo and his fellow workers first formulate such problems as, "How fast does a falling body fall?" Galileo is distinguished from his predecessors not because they differed in their answers to such questions, but rather because Galileo thought such questions were worth answering while earlier "natural philosophers" had considered such questions trivial as compared with theological or teleological questions concerning "perfect motion" and the "proper place" of things in the world-scheme.

The remarkable intellectual advance achieved during the past century in formal logic is very largely based upon the initiative of such mathematicians as Lobachewsky and Riemann, who,

[1] See Holmes, "The Path of the Law" (1897), 10 *Harvard Law Review*, 457, *Collected Legal Papers* (1920), 167; Pound, "Law in Books and Law in Action" (1910), 44 *American Law Review*, 12; Pound, "Mechanical Jurisprudence" (1908), 8 *Columbia Law Review*, 605; M. R. Cohen, "The Process of Judicial Legislation" (1914), 48 *American Law Review*, 161; *Law and the Social Order* (1933), 112; Cook, "Logical and Legal Bases of the Conflict of Laws" (1924), 33 *Yale Law Journal*, 457; Oliphant, "A Return to *Stare Decisis*" (1928), 6 *American Law School Review*, 215; Llewellyn, "A Realistic Jurisprudence—The Next Step" (1930), 30 *Columbia Law Review*, 431; Pound, "The Call for a Realist Jurisprudence" (1931), 44 *Harvard Law Review*, 697; Llewellyn, "Some Realism about Realism—Responding to Dean Pound" (1931), 44 *Harvard Law Review*; Kantorowicz, "Some Rationalism about Realism" (1934), 43 *Yale Law Journal*, 1240; John C. H. Wu, "Realistic Analysis of Legal Concepts: A Study in the Legal Method of Mr. Justice Holmes" (1932), 5 *China Law Review*, 1, 2; Yntema, "The Rational Basis of Legal Science" (1931), 31 *Columbia Law Review*, 925; M. R. Cohen, "Philosophy and Legal Science" (1932), 32 *Columbia Law Review*, 1103, *Law and the Social Order* (1933), 219; F. S. Cohen, "Transcendental Nonsense and the Functional Approach" (1935), 35 *Columbia Law Review*, 809.

challenging the "self-evidence" of Euclid's parallel postulate, asked: "What consequences will follow from geometric assumptions other than those of Euclid?" The result of such investigations was not to "disprove" Euclidean geometry, but rather to show it in its true perspective as one logical system within a matrix of systems, all of which have possible applications to the actual world.

If history-writing is on a more realistic plane to-day than it was a century ago, this is certainly due very largely to the work of Karl Marx. Non-socialist historians may reject entirely the thesis of the class struggle, and even the general doctrine of social evolution, but they cannot reject or forget the insistent questions that Marx put, "How is this or that event related to the system of production and distribution that prevails at the time and place?" Certainly the persistent reiteration of this question in fields of social organisation, politics, morality, and law is the first characteristic that distinguishes modern history-writing from the pre-Marxian histories that ascribe most historical events to the character of the sovereign, the fortunes of warfare, or the spirit of peoples.

Similarly it might be shown that in fields of biology, economics, psychology, and philosophy, to mention no others, the enduring contributions of new schools of thought have been not the new theories they have defended, which have more often than not turned out to be erroneous, but the new questions they have put.

Let us then survey the role of functionalism in legal science not as a refutation of past theories of law nor even as an improvement in our present methods of legal research, but rather as an insistence on certain questions that until recently have been generally ignored in legal studies. Specifically, the functional method poses such questions as: How do rules of law work? Are certain rules of law, so-called, merely ritual observances which have no verifiable relation to the decisions of judges who recite them? To what extent are laws actually obeyed? What are the limits of effective law enforcement? What are the social mechanisms and institutions that make certain rules of law effective and leave others dead letters? When rules of law are obeyed or disobeyed, what consequences actually follow from such conduct?

More generally, these questions may be compressed in the formula, "What is the human meaning of the law?" This is a very different question from the question, "How has law developed?" which historical jurists have asked and answered. It is very different from the question, "What is the nature or structure of law?" with which analytical jurists have been concerned. It is very different from the question, "What is the purpose of law?" which writers on justice and natural rights have pressed.

Precisely because it is a very different question from these questions that have occupied so large a part of traditional jurisprudence, the question of the human significance of law must be posed as a supplement to established lines of inquiry in legal science rather than as a substitute for them. Indeed, there is an intimate and mutual interdependence among these lines of inquiry, historical, analytical, ethical, and functional.

The law of the present is a tenuous abstraction hovering between legal history and legal prophecy. The functionalist cannot describe the present significance of any rule of law without reference to historical elements. It is equally true that the historical jurist cannot reconstruct the past unless he grasps the meaning of the present.

The functionalist must have recourse to the logical instruments that analytical jurisprudence furnishes. Analytical jurisprudence, in turn, may develop more fruitful modes of analysis with a better understanding of the law-in-action.

Functional description of the workings of a legal rule will be indispensable to one who seeks to pass ethical judgments on law. The functionalist, however, is likely to be lost in an infinite maze of trivialities unless he is able to concentrate on the *important* consequences of a legal rule and ignore the *unimportant* consequences, a distinction which can be made only in terms of an ethical theory.

Recognising then, that functional jurisprudence is not a new set of answers to the traditional problems of jurisprudence, nor even a new method of getting such answers, but rather a new set of problems, let us examine the issues which are thus brought to the forefront of legal consciousness. In general, these issues may be considered under two headings: the analysis of law as a function of judicial behaviour; and the appraisal of law as a determinant of human behaviour.

Functionalism, as a philosophy, may be defined as the view that a thing does not have a "nature" or "essence" or "reality" underlying its manifestations and effects and apart from its relations with other things; that the nature, essence, or reality of a thing *is* its manifestations, its effects, and its relations with other things; and that, apart from these, "it" is nothing, or at most a point in logical space, a possibility of something happening.

To defend this philosophical viewpoint,[2] or even to canvas the applications of this viewpoint in modern science[3] would take us beyond the assigned limits of this paper. We shall concern ourselves not with the truth or falsity of a doctrine but with the significance of functionalism as a methodologic principle. Functionalism as a method may be summed up in the directive. If you want to understand something observe it in action.

Applied within the field of law itself, this approach leads to a definition of legal concepts, rules, and institutions in terms of judicial decisions or other acts of state-force Whatever cannot be so translated is functionally meaningless.[4] Applied to the larger field of general human behaviour, this same approach leads to an appraisal of law in terms of conduct of human beings who are affected by law. In the former field, the outcome of the functional approach is generally designated as "realistic jurisprudence." In the latter field, the outcome of the functional approach is usually called "sociological jurisprudence." There is, however, no well-recognised definition of these schools of thought,[5] and I think it is fair to say that "realistic" and "sociological"

[2] The viewpoint is something common to logical positivism, pragmatism, operationalism, and Whitehead's "method of extensive abstraction." See C S. Peirce, *Chance, Love and Logic* (1923); *Collected Papers* (1931–34), especially vol. 5; James, *Pragmatism* (1908); *Essays in Radical Empiricism* (1912); Dewey, "Appearing and Appearance," in *Philosophy and Civilisation* (1931), 51; Russell, *Our Knowledge of the External World as a Field for Scientific Method in Philosophy* (1914); *Mysticism and Logic* (1918); Whitehead, *The Principles of Natural Knowledge* (1919); *The Concept of Nature* (1920); C. I. Lewis, *Mind and the World-Order* (1929); C. D. Broad, *Scientific Thought* (1923); Wittgenstein, *Tractatus Logico-Philosophicus* (1922); Carnap, "Ueberwindung der Metaphysik durch logische Analyse der Sprache" (1932), 2 *Erkenntnis*, No. 4; J. E. Boodin, "Functional Realism" (1934), 43 *Philosophical Review*, 147.

[3] See, for applications of a similar approach—

In mathematics: Russell, *Introduction to Mathematical Philosophy* (1919).

In psychology: W. James, *Essays in Radical Empiricism* (1912).

In religion: Max Weber, *The Protestant Ethic and the Spirit of Capitalism* (trans. by Parsons, 1930); R. H. Tawney, *Religion and the Rise of Capitalism* (1926); James, *The Varieties of Religious Experience* (1902); Kaplan, *Judaism as a Civilisation* (1934), c. 26 ("Functional Method of Interpretation").

In anthropology: Boas, *Primitive Art* (1927); Boas, "The Social Organisation and the Secret Societies of the Kwakiutl Indians" (1895), *Report of United States National Museum*, at 315; Malinowski, *The Family among the Australian Aborigines* (1913); Lowie, *Primitive Society* (1920); Goldenweiser, *History, Psychology and Culture* (1933), Part III (Totemism); Malinowski, *Crime and Custom in Savage Society* (1926); Hogbin, *Law and Order in Polynesia* (1934).

In political science: W. J. Shephard, "Democracy in Transition" (1935), 29 *American Political Science Review*, 1; cf. H. J. Laski, *Grammar of Politics* (2nd edition, 1929); W. Y. Elliott, *The Pragmatic Revolt in Politics* (1928).

[4] Cf. F. S. Cohen, "Transcendental Nonsense and the Functional Approach" (1935), 35 *Columbia Law Review*, 809.

[5] There is a good deal of overlapping, for instance, in the programme of sociological jurisprudence offered by Dean Pound, and the programme of realistic jurisprudence outlined by Llewellyn. Cf. Pound, "Scope and Purpose of Sociological Jurisprudence" (1912), 25 *Harvard Law Review*, 489, 512–515; and Llewellyn, "Some Realism about Realism—Responding to Dean Pound (1931), 44 *Harvard Law Review*, 1222, 1236–1255.

jurisprudence are in part complementary and in part overlapping, but in no way antithetical, and that both spring from a common sceptical, scientific, anti-supernatural, functional outlook.

Law as a Function of Judicial Decisions

Perhaps one reason why jurisprudence has been so slow in discovering the social content of legal rules and legal concepts is that jural facts, unlike the facts of physics or biology, generally purport to be self-explanatory. It has generally been considered an impertinence verging on political blasphemy to question the adequacy of these explanations. The statute carries on its face its intended effects; the decision of a court, if important, is generally accompanied by a rationale in the form of a judicial opinion; most of the acts of subordinate legal officials are surrounded by explanatory words and ritual. To take these explanations at their face value is at once a mark of political decorum and a release from arduous tasks of research.

The trends of modern jurisprudence that we call functional are inaugurated by sceptics who refuse to take these explanations at their face value and demand hard coin of social fact in place of paper legalities. Some of these sceptics have suggested that the words of a statute often have only the most superficial resemblance to the workings of the statute. A good deal of statute law turns out under investigation to be without any force—law-in-books rather than law-in-action; other parts of the statute law have been given new meanings in judicial, administrative, and popular construction—meanings that could never have been deduced from the words of the legislature. In either case, study of the statutes fails to provide a realistic picture of functioning law Again, this sceptical spirit has been applied to the official discourses in which judges set forth the reasons for their decisions. Judicial opinions have been viewed as no more and no less reliable than the statements in which octogenarians, golf champions, or successful bankers explain their achievements. In place of judicial introspection, or at least as a corrective for its deficiencies. we are invited to examine unmentioned factors leading to a given decision. These factors may range from weakness of intellect or digestive disturbances to political beliefs or economic backgrounds.

Under this sceptical gaze, a good many of the revered rules and principles of the law turn out to be pious frauds, contradicted by the actual holdings in decided cases, others turn out to be so ambiguous that they have no predictive or scientific value, and still others turn out to be disguised tautologies, similar to the doctrine established by Molière's physician, that opium puts men to sleep because it contains a dormitive principle.

The actual course of judicial decisions, conceived as a field of historical events rather than as a branch of geometry, reveals a much larger degree of uncertainty in the law than traditional jurisprudence has recognised. One of the most learned of living judges confesses to

> "a mounting sense of wonder that with all our centuries of common law development, with all our multitudinous courts, and still more multitudinous decisions, there are so many questions, elementary in the sense of being primary and basic, that remain unsettled even now. . . . One wonders how one has attained maturity without getting oneself in trouble when one has been so uncertain all along of the things that one might do in affairs of primary concern. Take such fundamental privileges or claims of privilege as these—the privilege to employ force against another who threatens one with bodily harm; the privilege to employ force to effect a recaption of chattels taken from one's custody; the privilege to employ force to effect an entry upon land. It is astonishing how obscure and confused are the pronouncements upon these fundamental claims of right."[6]

The extent of actual uncertainty in the body of the law is obscured by the legal fiction that courts do not make law but merely declare the law that already exists.[7] It is further obscured by linguistic conventions that give the appearance of certainty where there is no certainty.

> "Lawyers use what the layman describes as 'weasel words,' so-called 'safety-valve concepts,' such as 'prudent,' 'negligence,' 'freedom of contract,' 'good faith,' 'ought to know,' 'due care,' 'due process,'—terms with the vaguest meaning—as if these vague words had a precise and clear definition; they thereby create an appearance of continuity, uniformity and definiteness which does not in fact exist."[8]

Again the appearance of certainty is served by the verbal convention that established principles of law are never "refuted" but only "distinguished." Legal principles have a habit of running

[6] Cardozo, *Paradoxes of Legal Science* (1927), pp. 76–77.

[7] "The fiction that judges do not legislate has long since been abandoned by all who care for a conscious and realistic jurisprudence." H. J. Laski, "Judicial Review of Social Policy in England, A Study of *Roberts* v. *Hopwood et al.*" (1926), 39 *Harvard Law Review*, 832. Cf. M. R. Cohen, "The Process of Judicial Legislation," *supra*, note 1.

[8] Jerome Frank, *Law and the Modern Mind* (1930), p. 27.

in pairs, a plaintiff principle and a defendant principle.[9] As in the domain of popular proverbs one appeals with equanimity to the caution, "Look before you leap," or to its opposite, "He who hesitates is lost," depending upon which course of action he prefers, so in the law one generally has a choice between opposite "principles." Writers of legal treatises have no compunction about setting the two principles side by side, with only a "but" or "however" between them for the sake of decency. But in the actual decision of cases the choice between conflicting principles is likely to depend on unstated considerations. Mr. Justice Holmes was one of the first to take judicial notice of the inconclusiveness of legal principles.

> "The language of judicial decision is mainly the language of logic. And the logical method and form flatter that longing for certainty and for repose which is in every human mind. But certainty generally is illusion, and repose is not the destiny of man. Behind the logical form lies a judgment as to the relative worth and importance of competing legislative grounds, often an inarticulate and unconscious judgment, it is true, and yet the very root and nerve of the whole proceeding. You can give any conclusion a logical form. You always can imply a condition in a contract. But why do you imply it? It is because of some belief as to the practice of the community, or of a class, or because of some opinion as to policy, or, in short, because of some attitude of yours upon a matter not capable of exact quantitative measurement, and therefore not capable of founding exact logical conclusions. . . .
>
> "I think that the judges themselves have failed adequately to recognise their duty of weighing considerations of social advantage. The duty is inevitable, and the result of the often proclaimed judicial aversion to deal with such considerations is simply to leave the very ground and foundation of judgments inarticulate, and often unconscious, as I have said. When socialism first began to be talked about, the comfortable classes of the community were a good deal frightened. I suspect that this fear has influenced judicial action both here and in England, yet it is certain that it is not a conscious factor in the decisions to which I refer. . . . I cannot but believe that if the training of lawyers led them habitually to consider more definitely and explicitly the social advantage on which the rule they lay down must be justified, they sometimes would hesitate where now they are confident, and see

[9] Yntema, "The Hornbook Method and the Conflict of Laws" (1928), 37 *Yale Law Journal*, 468.

that they were taking sides upon debatable and often burning questions."[10]

To recognise this element of choice in the judicial process is to make the study of social factors that determine the course of judicial decision an essential part of the lawyer's outfitting if he is to predict with accuracy the probable legal course of his client's plans. To quote from Mr. Justice Cardozo's revealing study of the judicial process:

> "The spirit of the age, as it is revealed to each of us, is too often only the spirit of the group in which the accidents of birth or education or occupation or fellowship have given us a place. No effort or revolution of the mind will overthrow utterly and at all times the empires of these subconscious loyalties."[11]

Professor Laski has recently observed, in somewhat the same vein:

> ". . . no true science of law is possible unless its assumptions are built on a philosophy of history that enables us to predict the large consequences of the system in which we are involved."
>
> ". . . Once we realise that the legal relations of society are, broadly speaking, the expressions of class relations, once we recognise in the state supreme coercive power held at the disposal of those who own the instruments of production, the processes of law begin to clarify themselves in a fundamental way."[12]

Undoubtedly Professor Laski and Justice Cardozo would differ profoundly in analysing the social determinants of law. What is significant is that, despite these differences of social viewpoint, there is agreement on the direction of research required if one would understand the course of judicial decisions. Such understanding cannot be achieved within the confines of legal science traditionally conceived.

Fifty years ago Langdell wrote, "Law is a science, and all the available materials of that science are contained in printed books."[13] To-day we are disposed to recognise that judges are human beings, and that not all the forces which motivate judicial behaviour are words in printed books. There is, of course, wide difference of opinion as to the comparative importance of different

[10] Holmes, "The Path of the Law," *supra*, note 1, pp. 181, 184.
[11] Cardozo, *The Nature of the Judicial Process* (1921), pp. 174–175.
[12] Harold J. Laski, Book Review (1936), 46 *Yale Law Journal*, 951, 952.
[13] 3 *Law Quarterly Review*, 123–124.

fields of knowledge in helping us to predict judicial behaviour. Some are searching in fields of psychology and psychoanalysis,[14] without, I think, reaching any very significant results. Other students of the law have made illuminating studies of the social, economic, and political backgrounds of judges and decisions.[15] Equally useful studies are being made in the field of social institutional pressures that influence legislation.[16]

All this is of significance not merely to the legal philosopher but to the practising lawyer. The client who wants to know whether to organize a partnership or a corporation or whether to include a particular sort of renewal clause in his lease is not particularly interested in the present state of the law. He wants to know how the courts are likely to deal with the transaction some years hence. The solicitor who advises him must know more than words in law books if he is to give intelligent advice. There is need even in these narrow questions for social vision, knowledge, judgment, and the ability to weigh available evidence. Much more obvious is the need when the legal question presented involved the development of an important economic institution, social organization, or political instrumentality. The functional conception of legal science thus dictates a new vision of the scope of legal education. The student of law must be familiar not only with statutes and cases but with the social realities on which the statutes and cases impinge, and with the social realities that, in turn, impinge on courts and legislatures as determinants in the development of the law.[17] It is forty years, now, since Mr. Justice Holmes wrote:

"For the rational study of the law the black letter man

[14] Frank, "Law and the Modern Mind" (1930), c. 12–13; T. Schroeder, "The Psychological Study of Judicial Opinions" (1918), 6 *California Law Review*, 89; H. D. Lasswell, "Self-Analysis and Judicial Thinking" (1930), 40 *International Journal of Ethics*, 354; Hutcheson, "The Judgment Intuitive: The Function of the 'Hunch' in Judicial Decisions" (1929), 14 *Cornell Law Quarterly*, 274; Hutcheson, "Lawyer's Law and the Little, Small Dice" (1932), 7 *Tulane Law Review*, 1.

[15] See: Jerome Hall, *Theft, Law and Society* (1935), Appendix; Brooks Adams, "Law Under Inequality"; "Monopoly" in *Centralisation and the Law* (1906), Lecture 2; Boudin, *Government by Judiciary* (1932); Gustavus Myers, *History of the Supreme Court* (1912); W. Hamilton, "The Ancient Doctrine *Caveat Emptor*" (1932), 40 *Yale Law Journal*, 1133; Nelles, "The First American Labor Case" (1931), 41 *Yale Law Journal*, 165; Max Lerner, "The Supreme Court and American Capitalism" (1933), 42 *Yale Law Journal*, 668; C. G. Haines, "General Observations on the Effects of Personal, Political and Economic Influence in the Decisions of Judges" (1922), 17 *Illinois Law Review*, 96; R. A. Brown, "Police Power—Legislation for Health and Personal Safety" (1929), 42 *Harvard Law Review*, 866; M. Finkelstein, "Judicial Self-Limitation" (1924), 37 *Harvard Law Review*, 338.

[16] See, for example, Child: *Labor and Capital in National Politics* (1930).

[17] See Leon Keyserling: "Social Objectives in Legal Education" (1933), 33 *Columbia Law Review*, 437.

may be the man of the present, but the man of the future is the man of statistics and the master of economics."[18]

Pervading the realistic analysis of legal rules and concepts there is implicit a definition of law in terms of empirical realities This definition has been most trenchantly formulated by Mr. Justice Holmes:

> "If you want to know the law and nothing else, you must look at it as a bad man, who cares only for the material consequences which such knowledge enables him to predict, not as a good one, who finds his reasons for conduct, whether inside the law or outside of it, in the vaguer sanctions of conscience. . . . Take the fundamental question, What constitutes the law? You will find some text writers telling you that it is something different from what is decided by the courts of Massachusetts or England, that it is a system of reason, that it is a deduction from principles of ethics, or admitted axioms or what not, which may or may not coincide with the decisions. But if we take the view of our friend the bad man we shall find that he does not care two straws for the axioms or deductions, but that he does want to know what the Massachusetts or English courts are likely to do in fact. I am much of his mind. The prophecies of what the courts will do in fact, and nothing more pretentious, are what I mean by the law."[19]

Alternative functional definitions of law have been offered,[20] but all these definitions attempt to anchor the concept of law on a solid bottom of empirical fact. Perhaps the most important thing about these definitions is that they get away from the Blackstonian confusion that vitiates so much of traditional jurisprudence. Blackstone attempted to superimpose the picture of law as the perfection of reason[21] drawn by the tender-minded hypocrite, Coke, upon the picture of law as force[22] executed by the tough-minded cynic, Hobbes. The Blackstonian definition of law as a "rule of civil conduct prescribed by the supreme power in a State commanding what is right[23] and prohibiting what is

[18] "The Path of the Law," *supra*, note 1, 187.

[19] *Ibid.*, 171–173.

[20] See: Cardozo, *The Growth of the Law* (1924), 44, 52; C. J. Keyser, "On the Study of Legal Science" (1929), 38 *Yale Law Journal*, 413.

[21] Co. Litt. *976.

[22] "In matters of government, when nothing else is turned up, clubs are trumps." Hobbes, *Dialogue between a Philosopher and a Student of the Common Laws of England* (1681), "Of Punishments."

[23] That "right" and "wrong" are used in this definition as ethical, rather than strictly legal, terms is made clear in Blackstone's own exegesis upon his definition. *Comm.** 54–55.

wrong" provides a fertile source of confusion, which many important legal scholars since Blackstone have found about as useful in legal polemics as the ink with which a cuttlefish befuddles its enemies.

Those jurists who adhere to the Blackstonian definition of law are able to spin legal theories to the heart's content without fear of refutation. If legislatures or courts disagree with the writer's theory of "right" and "wrong" it is a simple matter to show that this disagreement is unjust, unreasonable, monstrous, and therefore, not "sound law." On the other hand, the intruding moralist who objects to a legal doctrine on the ground that it is unjust and undesirable can be told to go back to the realm of morality he came from, since the law is the command of the sovereign and not a matter of moral theory. Perhaps the chief usefulness of the Blackstonian theory is the gag it places upon legal criticism. If, by definition, the law is something that commands what is right and prohibits what is wrong, it is impossible to argue about the goodness or badness of any rule of law. And any definition that deters people from criticism of the law will prove very useful to legal apologists for the existing order of society. As a modern authority on legal reasoning declares:

> "Thus all things made legal are at the same time legally ethical because it is law, and the law must be deemed ethical or the system itself must perish."[24]

If the functionalists are correct, the meaning of a definition is found in its consequences. The definition of a general term like "law" is significant only because it affects all our definitions of specific legal concepts.

The consequence of defining law as a function of judicial decisions is that we may proceed to define such concepts as "contract," "property," "title," "corporate personality," "right," and "duty" similarly as functions of judicial decisions.[25]

The consequence of defining law as a hodge-podge of political force and ethical value ambiguously amalgamated is that every legal concept, rule or question will present a similar ambiguity.

Consider, for example, the elementary legal question: "Is there a contract?"

[24] Brumbaugh, *Legal Reasoning and Briefing* (1917), 7.

[25] See: M. R. Cohen, "Property and Sovereignty" in *Law and the Social Order* (1933), 41; R. L. Hale, "Coercion and Distribution in a Supposedly Non-coercive State" (1923), 38 *Political Science Quarterly*, 470; R. L. Hale, "Rate Making and the Revision of the Property Concept" (1922), 22 *Columbia Law Review*, 209; Llewellyn, *Cases and Materials on the Law of Sales* (1930); Oliphant, "Mutuality of Obligation in Bilateral Contracts at Law" (1929), 25 *Columbia Law Review*, 705; (1928), 28 *Columbia Law Review*, 997; Cook, "Logical and Legal Bases of the Conflict of Laws" (1924), 33 *Yale Law Journal*, 457.

When the realist asks this question, he is concerned with the actual behaviour of courts. For the realist, the contractual relationship, like law in general, is a function of legal decisions. The question of what courts *ought* to do is irrelevant here. When there is a promise that will be legally enforced there is a contract. So conceived, any answer to the question, "Is there a contract?" must be in the nature of a prophecy, based, like other prophecies, upon past and present facts. So conceived, the question, "Is there a contract?" or for that matter any other legal question, may be broken up into a number of subordinate questions, each of which refers to the actual behaviour of courts: (1) What courts are likely to pass upon a given transaction and its consequences? (2) What elements in this transaction will be viewed as relevant and important by these courts? (3) How have these courts dealt with transactions in the past which are *similar* to the given transaction, that is, *identical in those respects which the court will regard as important?* (4) What forces will tend to compel judicial conformity to the precedents that appear to be in point (e.g. inertia, conservatism, knowledge of the past, or intelligence sufficient to acquire such knowledge, respect for predecessors, superiors or brothers on the bench, a habit of deference to the established expectations of the bar or the public) and how strong are these forces? (5) What factors will tend to evoke new judicial treatment for the transaction in question (e.g. changing public opinion, judicial idiosyncrasies and prejudices, newly accepted theories of law, society or economics, or the changing social context of the case) and how powerful are these factors?

These are the questions which a successful practical lawyer faces and answers in any case. The law, as the realistic lawyer uses the term, is the body of answers to such questions. The task of prediction involves, in itself, no judgment of ethical value. Of course, even the most cynical practitioner will recognise that the positively existing ethical beliefs of judges are material facts in any case because they determine what facts the judge will view as important and what past rules he will regard as reasonable or unreasonable and worthy of being extended or restricted. But judicial beliefs about the values of life and the ideals of society are facts, just as the religious beliefs of the Andaman Islanders are facts, and the truth or falsity of such moral beliefs is a matter of complete unconcern to the practical lawyer, as to the scientific observer.

Washed in cynical acid,[26] every legal problem can thus be

[26] ". . . the vague circumference of the notion of duty shrinks and at the same time grows more precise when we wash it with cynical acid and expel everything except the object of our study, the operations of the law." Holmes, "The Path of the Law" (1897), *Harvard Law Review*, 457, 462.

interpreted as a question concerning the positive behaviour of judges.

There is a second and radically different meaning which can be given to our type question, "Is there a contract?" When a judge puts this question, in the course of writing his opinion, he is not attempting to predict his own behaviour. He is in effect raising the question, in an obscure way, of whether or not liability *should* be attached to certain acts. This is inescapably an ethical question. What a judge ought to do in a given case is quite as much a moral issue as any of the traditional problems of Sunday School morality.[27]

It is the great disservice of the classical conception of law that it hides from judicial eyes the ethical character of every judicial question, and thus serves to perpetuate class prejudices and uncritical moral assumptions which could not survive the sunlight of free ethical controversy.

The Blackstonian conception of law as half-mortal and half-divine gives us a mythical conception of contract. When the masters of classical jurisprudence ask the question, "Is there a contract?" they have in mind neither the question of scientific prediction which the practical lawyer faces, nor the question of values which the conscientious judge faces. If they had in mind the former question their studies would no doubt reveal the extent to which courts actually enforce various types of agreements.[28] Conclusions would be in terms of probability and statistics. On the other hand if our classical jurists were interested in the ethical aspects of contractual liability they would undoubtedly offer a significant account of the human values and social costs involved in different types of agreements and in the means of their enforcement. In fact, discussion will oscillate between a theory of what courts actually do and a theory of what courts ought to do, without coming to rest either on the existential plane of practice or on the ethical plane of values long enough to come to grips with significant problems. This confused wandering between the world of fact and the world of justice vitiates every argument and every analysis.

Intellectual clarity requires that we carefully distinguish

[27] Cf. F. S. Cohen, "Modern Ethics and the Law" (1934), 4 *Brooklyn Law Review*, 33.

[28] So hallowed is the juristic tradition of ignoring the actual facts of cases that a distinguished jurist, Professor Goodhart, can argue in all seriousness that the practice adopted by some American law libraries of putting the records of cases on file is very dangerous. Students might be distracted from the official *ratio decidendi* of the case, and try to discover what the actual facts of the case were, which would be a death-blow to traditional jurisprudence. See Goodhart "Determining the Ratio Decidendi of a Case" (1930), 40 *Yale Law Journal*, 161, 172.

between the two problems of objective description and critical judgment, which classical jurisprudence lumps under the same phrase. Such a distinction functional jurisprudence offers with the double-barrelled thesis: (1) that every legal rule or concept is simply a function of judicial decisions which may be described without reference to values, and (2) that the problem before the judge is not whether a legal rule or concept actually exists, but whether it *ought* to exist. Clarity on two fronts is the result. Description of legal facts becomes more objective, and legal criticism becomes more critical.[29]

Law as a Determinant of Human Behaviour

It is ancient wisdom that the human significance of law is found in the impact of law upon human behaviour. *Scire leges non hoc est verba earum tenere, sed vim et potestatem.*[30] Yet actual investigation of the effects of law upon conduct still has an air of novelty about it. One of the great protagonists of sociological jurisprudence, Professor Kantorowicz, puts the case in striking fashion. When the lawyer or law student reads a code of laws (or for that matter a legal treatise, a statute, or a collection of decisions),

> "Let him ask himself with respect to each statement . . . what harms would social life undergo if instead of this statement the opposite were enacted. And then let him turn to all textbooks, commentaries, monographs, and reports of decisions and see how many questions of this sort he will find answered and how many he will find even put."[31]

The problem of the effects of law upon human beings, which is central to legal science, is a problem which classical jurists of many schools have found it convenient to ignore. Ignoring this problem has been particularly easy in view of the hallowed legal conventions that everybody is presumed to know the law and that prudent men, the majority of mankind no doubt, obey the law. In that kind of world, all one needs to do in order to know the effects of a given rule is to read the rule and to appreciate its purpose.

Unfortunately, in the real world, most of us are vastly ignorant of the law, and are continually violating or disregarding the law. The question, then, of how much actual observance is given to any

29 F. S. Cohen, "Transcendental Nonsense and the Functional Approach" 1935), 35 *Columbia Law Review*, 809, 838–841.
30 *Dig.* 1.3.17 (Celsus).
31 *Rechtswissenschaft und Sociologie* (1911), 8.

legal rule is an empirical question that cannot be answered on *a priori* grounds.

Again one turns to Professor Kantorowicz for a striking portrayal of the disdain of facts by traditional legal theory:

> "This fiction (that every one knows the whole law of a state) contradicts the facts in the grossest manner. The truth is that nobody knows the whole law in its unsurveyable compass, that a few people know a portion of it, that most know nothing of it. So true is this that if a private citizen has acquired a thorough knowledge of the law of the state he will usually belong to a class of shady gentlemen. The usurer, the criminal apprentice, the yellow journalist, the fraudulent promoter know the rules which interest them accurately enough; the wholesale merchant, the artist, the statesman, the husband have only a sporadic acquaintance with even the paragraphs of the sales, copyright, public, international, or family law, without being disturbed in their activities by this ignorance. The traveller in a foreign country makes himself familiar with the language, the history, the art, the customs of the people—not even in a dream does it occur to any one to so much as open its statute books."[32]

It is certain that law does not secure obedience except in so far as it is known. Thus an important problem in determining the human significance of any rule or law is the problem of discovering the extent to which people theoretically affected by the rule are actually aware of it. From the point of view of the legislator, the problem takes a special form: In order to make this or that legislation effective, how can knowledge of it be conveyed to those who are concerned, including those who are expected to enforce it? The influence of newspapers, public trials, law treatises, and other instruments of education or propaganda, upon popular legal beliefs presents a fascinating problem for the sociological jurist, and the results to be achieved in such investigations may prove of considerable practical value.

The functional approach suggests that instead of tracing the effects of a decision along celestial lines of logical force we may look rather to the actual process of learning, or understanding and misunderstanding, which governs the interpretation that will be put upon a statute or a decision by laymen, by administrative officers, and even by successive judges.

The existence of this empirical problem has been somewhat

[32] Kantorowicz (*sub pseud.* Gnaeus Flavius), *Der Kampf um die Rechtswissenschaft* (1906), 13-14.

obscured by the traditional notion that legal rules may be deduced from decisions and that these rules "bind" future judges. As a matter of fact, no number of decisions can logically provide a rule of law, for the simple reason that a universal proposition can never be validly inferred from any number of particular propositions. A decision is a particular proposition, and a rule of law is a universal proposition.

The search for a logical formula that will determine precisely what rule each decision implies[33] is a wild goose chase starting from a logical confusion. The functional approach substitutes a wholly empirical question: "What influence is a legal decision likely to have on future cases?" This is not always a simple question to answer, as competing counsel in most cases will recognise. There is a vocabulary and a technique for restricting decisions to the particular facts of the case, that is to say for distinguishing any new case and thus destroying the precedent value of the old case. There is another vocabulary and another technique for drawing wider and wider morals from a decision, and applying these morals to cases more and more distantly removed. In selecting and compromising between these techniques, courts make choices which cannot be blamed on logic. To describe these choices as they occur is the objective of a functional theory of legal precedents.[34]

The problem of interpreting past decisions is not a problem restricted to the field of judicial action. A similar problem exists in the field of public administration and in the field of popular legal opinion. Here again there is need of patient study to show how people actually do interpret and misinterpret laws and cases. The results of such study may make it easier for judges and legislators alike to foresee the consequences of action.

The study of mental reactions to rules and decisions, while essential, is not sufficient to determine their full effects. Beyond this task is the task of determining how the incentives to obedience and disobedience will mould reactions to law.

The scope of this latter task is underestimated by those who deny that law consists of commands and point out that most legal propositions, at least outside the field of criminal law, are declaratory rather than imperative. What this criticism overlooks is that legal propositions which are declaratory in form owe their legal force to threats of state action.

[33] For examples of this search see Goodhart, "Determining the *Ratio Decidendi* of a Case" (1930), 40 *Yale Law Journal*, 161.

[34] K. N. Llewellyn, *The Bramble Bush* (1930), 47, 61–66. Oliphant, "A Return to *Store Decisis*" (1928), 6 *American Law School Review*, 215, 217, 218. F. S. Cohen, *Ethical Systems and Legal Ideals* (1933), 33–37.

> "An order does not cease to be a command because it contains an explanation of what it is that is commanded. Nor is a law permitting a man to do something at his option, e.g. to dispose of his property by testament, any less a part of the system of imperatives, in this case of what we call the law of property. It certainly is an imperative to the children or other heirs, who when the will is properly made, must yield certain goods to legatees or devisees."[35]

The human significance of any rule of law thus depends upon the extent to which it secures obedience. This, in turn, will depend upon the strength of the organised desire for which the rule provides an enforcing instrument, as compared with the strength of the organised desire which the rule is intended to frustrate. The failure to recognise this persistent struggle that underlies all law enforcement is written large in the history of social reform legislation. Again and again idealists have succeeded in writing their hopes on the statute books, only to discover in dismay that laws are not self-executing. Out of the past century's experience with social reform legislation certain elementary facts are beginning to emerge—for instance, that a law designed to help the weaker of two parties to a bargain will be useless if it is possible to "contract out," and that legislation designed to protect an oppressed class will not be effectively enforced unless it sets up some independent agency capable of representing the interests of that class in securing enforcement of the legislation.[36]

Every legal problem, viewed functionally, involves a conflict of interests. The stability of any solution will depend, at least in part, upon a correct appraisal of the desires that will be effectuated or frustrated by the solution.[37]

The problem of weighing incentives to obedience and disobedience leads finally to the problem of weighing social forces. What the law ought to accomplish in any given situation cannot be determined without determining what the law *can* accomplish. This latter question leads us inevitably to seek some measurement of the organised force that can be brought to bear on any legal issue. The force of law depends partly, to be sure, on the death-dealing equipment of the state; it depends also upon the essential human services which the state controls; it depends at the same time upon the organisational loyalties without which armies,

[35] M. R. Cohen, *Law and the Social Order* (1933), 206.

[36] See W. F. Dodd, *Administration of Workmen's Compensation* (1936), pp. 16–26, 70–99. Cf. E. A. Parry, *The Law and the Poor* (1914).

[37] See, for a significant application of this approach to the law of larceny, J. Hall, *Theft, Law and Society* (1935), chap. 6.

police forces, and all social institutions disintegrate. The effectiveness of the opposition to law, at any point in the legal order, will likewise be proportionate to the physical, economic, and emotional power which can be mustered to oppose a given objective affirmed by the law. Recent history in Italy, Germany, Austria, and Spain, reveals the tenuousness of traditional analyses of democracy in terms of constitutional rights and procedures. From a realistic point of view, democracy is gone when the theoretical power of the majority to govern ceases to correspond to an actual power to compel obedience. From this point of view the question of whether a democracy can tolerate vast concentrations of financial power assumes critical significance. In constitutional as well as in private law, the stuff of which living law is made is not concepts in logical arrangement but conflicting interests diversely organised and pitted against each other in an ever shifting battle line. A realistic appraisal of the human meaning of any legal rule involves us in a measurement of human desires and human powers in every domain of life.

The question of the proper scope of law has been argued back and forth for a good many centuries, and nearly all of the argument has been in *a priori* terms. From the functional standpoint, the problem takes a form in which empirical evidence becomes relevant. The central question is that of the effectiveness of various possible legal rules and arrangements. From this standpoint, if modern history shows a progress of the law in social control it is significant to ask whether this progress is not primarily ascribable to an increase in the realm of jurisdiction dominated by the state through its increased physical force rather than to any progress in legal wisdom or the moral qualities of humanity. In the modern centralised nation the monopoly of internal power by the sovereign, based upon centralising developments in the technology of industry, communication, and warfare, has made it possible to exercise effective legal control over many relationships that were once outside the realm of effective control. If legal development has not made full use of new opportunities, this is partly due to the heritage of thinking from an age in which the state could not undertake certain tasks of social control for lack of power, and in which it accordingly became the accepted duty of the moralist to prove that those things were not worth doing. A state which cannot secure obedience from those who control its industry may at least save face by issuing the unbreakable commandment, "Do as you please."[38] Unfortunately, the

[38] Cf. F. S. Cohen, "The Socialisation of Morality," in Hook and Kallen, *American Philosophy To-day and To-morrow* (1935), 83, 87.

fact tends to be viewed as an ideal. In political theory, at least, conservatism may be defined as the idealization of yesterday's misfortunes.

If the temporal variation of state power offers a useful key to the understanding of legal history, the varying degrees of state power in different fields of human conduct offer an equally useful key to the understanding of the law of a given epoch. The law is one among many "control" institutions. The direction of its powers is largely determined by a process of competition with organised religion, organised education, the family, professional and mercantile agencies of control, and various other social institutions, each with its own "inner order" and its own sanctions.[39] The disruption of any of these agencies throws new tasks upon the law; their development relieves the legal order of old responsibilities.

In this competition with other organisations of social force, the law realises the limitations of its machinery. Operating through courts, it is required by dictates of social economy to concentrate its attention upon facts readily verifiable. Laws against adultery are notoriously unenforceable. The fact that land cannot be concealed gives point to the peculiarly rich development of legal control over real property. The public events of birth, marriage, and death furnish stable fulcrums for legal leverage. The organisation of men into permanent groups offers new pressure points for the activity of the law.[40]

To describe law-in-action is to describe the inter-relationships between judicial decisions and all the other events of the social scene. The meaning of law depends not only upon the factors already noted, which determine how far it will be observed, but on all the social facts that give law-observance and law-breaking their human significance. In writing the life-history of a legal rule one does not reach the end of the story when the rule is obeyed or disobeyed. There remains to be told the meaning of obedience or disobedience, in terms of social institutions and customs, in terms of the material things over which law gives control, in terms of human habits, modes of thought, fears, hopes, pleasures and pains.[41]

The problems raised in the search for the human meaning of legal rules, decisions, concepts and institutions are problems to which the literature of functional jurisprudence gives, perhaps, only faltering and partial answers. To have lifted these problems

[39] See Ehrlich, *Fundamental Principles of the Sociology of Law* (translated by Moll; 1936), chaps. 2–3.

[40] F. S. Cohen, *Ethical Systems and Legal Ideals*, 269, 270.

[41] *Ibid.*, 271–285.

to the level of conscious formulation is itself an achievement. What remains is for the future.

A functional jurisprudence, in facing this task of tracing the human significance of law, will draw upon the results of scientific study in many related fields. Already first attempts have been made to trace the human consequences of specific rules and decisions.[42] There is a growing literature that analyses, from the legal standpoint, the fields of conduct to which law is applied.[43] More important, perhaps, than any of these published studies is the incorporation of social investigation into the process of law administration. The growing practice of including economic materials in legal briefs, the increased use of economists and statisticians by administrative bodies, and of psychiatrists and social workers by courts, the growing utilisation of social research in legislative hearings and investigations, all testify to the contemporary significance of the functional approach and its promise for the future.

Function and Value

The normative use of definitions is one of the most prevalent sources of confusion in legal criticism.

Those who define law as an outpouring of the *Volksgeist* are prone to argue that law which shows their theory to be false, e.g. code law, is undesirable. Those who define law as the will of the sovereign are apt to conclude that judge-made rules which ignore or defy the will of the sovereign are bad law. Those who define law as a body of authoritative principles recognised by the courts are likely to condemn as evil any course of judicial decisions that violates these assumed principles.[44]

It is one of the serious dangers of the functional approach that those who invoke it for the purpose of description may without

[42] See, for instance: McCracken, *Strike Injunctions in the New South* (1931).

[43] In addition to the vast modern literature on criminology, there is a growing corpus of legally oriented material on such subjects as corporate practice, banking practice, the organisation and functioning of trade unions, the disposition of decedents' estates, industrial accidents, automobile accidents, contracts of employment, and the psychology of the witness.

[44] Bertrand Russell points to a similar fallacy in the realm of philosophy:

"The philosopher first invents a false theory as to the nature of things, and then deduces that wicked actions are those which show that his theory is false. To begin with the traditional Christian: he argues that, since everything always obeys the will of God, wickedness consists in disobedience to the will of God. We then come on to the Hegelian, who argues that the universe consists of parts which harmonise in a perfect organism, and therefore wickedness consists of behaviour which diminishes the harmony—though it is difficult to see how such behaviour is possible, since complete harmony is metaphysically necessary. . . . These examples have, I hope, made it plain that a metaphysic can never have ethical consequences except in virtue of its falsehood; if it were true, the acts which it defines as sin would be impossible." *Sceptical Essays* (1928), ch. 7 ("Behaviourism and Values"), p. 91.

further thought utilise it as a criterion of value. It is important for the jurist to remember that when he has described the human significance of a rule he has not thereby justified its existence. The task of valuation remains to be faced.

Caution against normative use of a functional definition of law is particularly pertinent because of the ambiguity of the word "function." When one says, for instance, that it is the function of the judge to apply pre-existing law to the facts of a case, one may mean that this is what a judge *ought* to do or simply that this is what judges *actually* do. A statement of the latter type is purely descriptive. A statement of the former type assumes a standard of values, and is, in effect, an ethical judgment.

It is to be emphasised that functional analysis of a legal rule or decision is purely a descriptive process. On the other hand, an intelligent value judgment upon any legal rule or decision presupposes such descriptive functional analysis, but also involves an ethical premise.

It was Bentham's great and enduring contribution to legal criticism to insist that the value of a legal rule depends upon its human consequences. In the field of legal criticism, or normative jurisprudence, functionalism is simply a development of utilitarianism. It is a development, however, which seeks to overcome certain weaknesses in the philosophy and method of Bentham and his immediate successors.

In the first place, Bentham failed to distinguish between his general theory of value, i.e. that the value of any act depends upon its consequences, and his theory of the good, i.e. that pleasure or happiness is the only good. The latter theory is one that many reasonable people reject, and although I happen to believe that all the objections thus far levelled against Bentham's hedonism are inconclusive,[45] I should agree that one may adopt alternative standards of ultimate value without getting into logical self-contradiction.

But no matter what other standards of value one may adopt, the essential basis of utilitarianism remains.[46]

Bentham's doctrine that the value of any legal rule depends upon its consequences was met with the philosophical challenge: Why should we assume that the value of anything depends upon its consequences? Functionalism exposes the emptiness of this challenge, by showing that the distinction between law and its consequences is purely arbitrary. The meaning of a legal rule is

[45] F. S. Cohen, *Ethical Systems and Legal Ideals* (1933), pp. 185–220.

[46] This is recognised by so vigorous a critic of hedonism as G. E. Moore. *Ethics* (1912), chaps. 1–3; *Principia Ethica* (1903), chaps. 1–2.

not action commanded but action caused. One cannot evaluate a legal rule or institution intelligently without knowing the action caused which constitutes the human meaning of the rule or institution. The challenge to Bentham's general theory of value turns out to be only a verbal confusion.

A further weakness in Bentham's utilitarianism springs from the general state of the social sciences at the time Bentham wrote. While insisting that the value of law depends upon the effect of law on human conduct, Bentham himself was unable to utilise any scientific study of such effects, for the simple reason that no scientific study of such effects had ever been made. The bare materials for such a study—judicial statistics, general social statistics, and social case studies—were lacking. Bentham therefore had to rely entirely upon common observation in making his own calculations of the effects of various legal rules and institutions. To-day jurisprudence can draw upon a wealth of material, scientifically collected and organised, in tracing the effects of law in human society.

In the field of legal criticism the functional method may thus be conceived as essentially a reorientation of utilitarianism to a wider philosophical perspective and to a broader horizon of relevant knowledge in the fields of psychology, economics, criminology, and general sociology.

FELIX S. COHEN*

* Assistant Solicitor, U.S. Interior Department, Washington, D.C.

Part II
Some Illustrative Applications

[12]

THE CAUSES OF POPULAR DISSATISFACTION WITH THE ADMINISTRATION OF JUSTICE.[1]

Dissatisfaction with the administration of justice is as old as law. Not to go outside of our own legal system, discontent has an ancient and unbroken pedigree. The Anglo-Saxon laws continually direct that justice is to be done equally to rich and to poor,[2] and the king exhorts that the peace be kept better than has been wont,[3] and that "men of every order readily submit * * * each to that law which is appropriate to him."[4] The author of the apocryphal Mirror of Justices gives a list of 155 abuses in legal administration, and names it as one of the chief abuses of the degenerate times in which he lived that executions of judges for corrupt or illegal decisions had ceased.[5] Wyclif complains that "lawyers make process by subtlety and cavilations of law civil, that is much heathen men's law, and do not accept the form of the gospel, as if the gospel were not so good as pagan's law."[6] Starkey, in the reign of Henry VIII, says: "Everyone that can color reason maketh a stop to the best law that is beforetime devised."[7] James I reminded his judges that "the law was founded upon reason, and that he and others had reason as well as the judges."[8] In the eighteenth century, it was complained that the bench was occupied by "legal monks, utterly ignorant of human nature and of the affairs of men."[9] In the nineteenth century the vehement criticism of the period of the Reform Movement needs only to be mentioned. In other words, as

[1] A paper by Roscoe Pound, read before the American Bar Association, August 29, 1906.

[2] *E. g.* Secular Ordinance of Edgar, Cap. 1; Secular Ordinance of Cnut, 2; Laws of Ethelred, VI, 1; Laws of Edward, preface.

[3] Laws of Athelston, IV; Laws of Edward, 4.

[4] Laws of Ethelred, V, 4.

[5] Mirror, Chap. V, sec. 1.

[6] See Maitland, English Law and the Renaissance, 53.

[7] Id. 42.

[8] Conference between King James I and the Judges of England, 12 Rep. 63.

[9] Lord Campbell, Lives of the Chief Justices (3 Ed.), IV, 119.

long as there have been laws and lawyers, conscientious and well-meaning men have believed that laws were mere arbitrary technicalities, and that the attempt to regulate the relations of mankind in accordance with them resulted largely in injustice. But we must not be deceived by this innocuous and inevitable discontent with all law into overlooking or underrating the real and serious dissatisfaction with courts and lack of respect for law which exists in the United States today.

In spite of the violent opposition which the doctrine of judicial power over unconstitutional legislation at first encountered, the tendency to give the fullest scope to the common-law doctrine of supremacy of law and to tie down administration by common-law liabilities and judicial review, was, until recently, very marked. Today, the contrary tendency is no less marked. Courts are distrusted, and executive boards and commissions with summary and plenary powers, freed, so far as constitutions will permit, from judicial review, have become the fashion. It will be assumed, then, that there is more than the normal amount of dissatisfaction with the present-day administration of justice in America. Assuming this, the first step must be diagnosis; and diagnosis will be the sole purpose of this paper. It will attempt only to discover and to point out the causes of current popular dissatisfaction. The inquiry will be limited, moreover, to civil justice. For while the criminal law attracts more notice, and punishment seems to have greater interest for the lay mind than the civil remedies of prevention and compensation, the true interest of the modern community is in the civil administration of justice. Revenge and its modern outgrowth, punishment, belong to the past of legal history. The rules which define those invisible boundaries within which each may act without conflict with the activities of his fellows in a busy and crowded world, upon which invester, promoter, buyer, seller, employer and employee must rely consciously or subconsciously in their every-day transactions, are conditions precedent of modern social and industrial organization.

With the scope of inquiry so limited, the causes of dissatisfaction with the administration of justice may be grouped under four main heads: (1) Causes for dissatisfaction with *any* legal system, (2) causes lying in the peculiarities of our Anglo-American legal system, (3) causes lying in our American judicial organization and procedure and (4) causes lying in the environment of our judicial administration.

It needs but a superficial acquaintance with literature to show that all legal systems among all peoples have given rise to the same complaints. Even the wonderful mechanism of modern German judicial administration is said to be distrusted by the people on the time-worn ground that there is one law for the rich and another for the poor.[10] It is obvious, therefore, that there must be some cause or causes inherent in all law and in all legal systems in order to produce this universal and invariable effect. These causes of dissatisfaction with any system of law I believe to be the following: (1) the necessarily mechanical operation of rules, and hence of laws, (2) the inevitable difference in rate of progress between law and public opinion, (3) the general popular assumption that the administration of justice is an easy task, to which anyone is competent, and (4) popular impatience of restraint.

The most important and most constant cause of dissatisfaction with all law at all times is to be found in the necessarily mechanical operation of legal rules. This is one of the penalties of uniformity. Legal history shows an oscillation between wide judicial discretion on the one hand and strict confinement of the magistrate by minute and detailed rules upon the other hand. From time to time more or less reversion to justice without law becomes necessary in order to bring the public administration of justice into touch with changed moral, social, or political conditions. But such periods of reversion result only in new rules or changed rules. In time the modes of exercising discretion become fixed, the course of judicial action becomes stable and uni-

[10] Dr. v. Liszt, Professor at Berlin, delivered an address in the Rathaus in Berlin on this very subject, recently, if we may credit press accounts.

form, and the new element, whether custom or equity or natural law, becomes as rigid and mechanical as the old. This mechanical action of the law may be minimized, but it cannot be obviated. Laws are general rules; and the process of making them general involves elimination of the immaterial elements of particular controversies. If all controversies were alike or if the degree in which actual controversies approximate to the recognized types could be calculated with precision, this would not matter. The difficulty is that in practice they approximate to these types in infinite gradations. When we eliminate immaterial factors to reach a general rule, we can never entirely avoid eliminating factors which will be more or less material in some particular controversy. If to meet this inherent difficulty in administering justice according to law we introduce a judicial dispensing power, the result is uncertainty and an intolerable scope for the personal equation of the magistrate. If we turn to the other extreme and pile up exceptions and qualifications and provisos, the legal system becomes cumbrous and unworkable. Hence the law has always ended in a compromise, in a middle course between wide discretion and over-minute legislation. In reaching this middle ground, some sacrifice of flexibility of application to particular cases is inevitable. In consequence, the adjustment of the relations of man and man according to these rules will of necessity appear more or less arbitrary and more or less in conflict with the ethical notions of individuals.

In periods of absolute or generally received moral systems, the contrast between legal results and strict ethical requirements will appeal only to individuals. In periods of free individual thought in morals and ethics, and especially in an age of social and industrial transition, this contrast is greatly intensified and appeals to large classes of society. Justice, which is the end of law, is the ideal compromise between the activities of each and the activities of all in a crowded world. The law seeks to harmonize these activities and to adjust the relations of every man with his fellows so as to accord with the moral sense of the community. When the community is at one in its ideas of justice, this is possible. When the community is divided and diversified, and groups and classes and interests, understanding each other none too well, have conflicting ideas of justice, the task is extremely difficult. It is impossible that legal and ethical ideas should be in entire accord in such a society. The individual looks at cases one by one and measures them by his individual sense of right and wrong. The lawyer must look at cases in gross, and must measure them largely by an artificial standard. He must apply the ethics of the community, not his own. If discretion is given him, his view will be that of the class from which he comes. If his hands are tied by law, he must apply the ethics of the past as formulated in common law and legislation. In either event, judicial and individual ethical standards will diverge. And this divergence between the ethical and the legal, as each individual sees it, makes him say with Luther, "good jurist, bad Christian."[11]

A closely related cause of dissatisfaction with the administration of justice according to law is to be found in the inevitable difference in rate of progress between law and public opinion. In order to preclude corruption, to exclude the personal prejudices of magistrates, and to minimize individual incompetency, law formulates the moral sentiments of the community in rules to which the judgments of tribunals must conform. These rules, being formulations of public opinion, can not exist until public opinion has become fixed and settled and can not change until a change of public opinion has become complete. It follows that this difficulty in the judicial administration of justice, like the preceding, may be minimized, but not obviated. In a rude age, the Teutonic moots in which every free man took a hand might be possible. But these tribunals broke down under pressure of business and bcame ordinary courts with permanent judges. The Athenians conceived that the people themselves should decide each case. But the Athenian dikastery, in which controversies were submitted to blocks of several hundred citzens by way of reaching the

[11] Courtney Kenny, Bonus Jurista Malus Christa, 19 Law Quart. Rev. 326.

will of the democracy, proved to register its caprice for the moment rather than its permanent will. Modern experience with juries, especially in commercial causes, does not warrant us in hoping much from any form of judicial referendum. Public opinion must affect the administration of justice through the rules by which justice is administered rather than the direct administration. All interference with the uniform and automatic application of these rules, when actual controversies arise, introduces an anti-legal element which becomes intolerable. But, as public opinion affects tribunals through the rules by which they decide and these rules, once made, stand till abrogated or altered, any system of law will be made up of successive strata of rules and doctrines representing successive and often widely divergent periods of public opinion. In this sense, law is often in very truth a government of the living by the dead.[12] The unconscious changes of judicial law-making and the direct alterations of legislation and codification operate to make this government by the dead reasonably tolerable. But here again we must pay a price for certainty and uniformity. The law does not respond quickly to new conditions. It does not change until ill effects are felt; often not until they are felt acutely. The moral or intellectual or economic change must come first. While it is coming, and until it is so complete as to affect the law and formulate itself therein, friction must ensue. In an age of rapid moral, intellectual and economic changes, often crossing one another and producing numerous minor resultants, this friction can not fail to be in excess.

A third perennial source of popular dissatisfaction with the administration of justice according to law may be found in the popular assumption that the administration of justice is an easy task to which any one is competent. Laws may be compared to the formulas of engineers. They sum up the experience of many courts with many cases and enable the magistrate to apply that experience subconsciously. So, the formula enables the engineer to make use of the accumulated experience of past builders, even though he could not work out a step in its evolution by himself. A layman

[12] Spencer, Principles of Sociology, II, 514.

is no more competent to construct or to apply the one formula than the other. Each requires special knowledge and special prepartion. None the less, the notion that anyone is competent to adjudicate the intricate controversies of a modern community contributes to the unsatisfactory administration of justice in many parts of the United States. The older states have generally outgrown it. But it is felt in extravagant powers of juries, lay judges of probate, and legislative[13] or judicial law-making against *stare decisis,* in most of the commonwealths of the South and West. The public seldom realizes how much it is interested in maintaining the highest scientific standard in the administration of justice. There is no more certain protection against corruption, prejudice, class-feeling, or incompetence. Publicity will avail something. But the daily criticism of trained minds, the knowledge that nothing which does not conform to the principles and received doctrines of scientific jurisprudence will escape notice, does more than any other agency for the every-day purity and efficiency of courts of justice.

Another necessary source of dissatisfaction with judicial administration of justice is to be found in popular impatience of restraint. Law involves restraint and regulation, with the sheriff and his posse in the background to enforce it. But, however necessary and salutary this restraint, men have never been reconciled to it entirely. The very fact that it is a compromise between the individual and his fellows makes the individual, who must abate some part of his activities in the interest of his fellows, more or less restive. In an age of absolute theories, monarchial or democratic, this restiveness is acute. A conspicuous example is to be seen in the contest between the king and the common-law courts in the seventeenth century. An equally conspicuous example is to be seen in the attitude of the frontiersman toward state-imposed justice. "The unthinking sons of the sage-brush," says Owen Wister, "ill tolerate anything which stands for discipline, good order, and obedience; and the men who lets another command him, they despise. I can

[13] See an instance in the address of Mr. Justice Brown, Rep. Am. Bar Ass'n 1889, 282.

think of no threat more evil for our democracy, for it is a fine thing diseased and perverted—namely, the spirit of independence gone drunk."[14] This is an extreme case. But in a lesser degree the feeling that each individual, as an organ of the sovereign democracy, is above the law he helps to make, fosters everywhere a disrespect for legal methods and institutions and a spirit of resistence to them. It is "the reason of this our artificial man the commonwealth," says Hobbes, "and his command that maketh law."[15] This man, however, is abstract. The concrete man in the street or the concrete mob is much more obvious; and it is no wonder that individuals and even classes of individuals fail to draw the distinction.

A considerable portion of current dissatisfaction with the administration of justice must be attributed to the universal causes just considered. Conceding this, we have next to recognize that there are potent causes in operation of a character entirely different.

Under the second main head, causes lying in our peculiar legal system, I should enumerate five: (1) the individualist spirit of our common law, which agrees ill with a collectivist age, (2) the common-law doctrine of contentious procedure, which turns litigation into a game, (3) political jealousy, due to the strain put upon our legal system by the doctrine of supremacy of law, (4) the lack of general ideas or legal philosophy, so characteristic of Anglo-American law, which gives us petty tinkering where comprehensive reform is needed, and (5) defects of form due to the circumstance that the bulk of our legal system is still case-law.

The first of these, conflict between the individualist spirit of the common law and the collectivist spirit of the present age, has been treated of on another occasion.[16] What was said then need not be repeated. Suffice it to point out two examples. From the beginning, the main reliance of our common-law system has been individual initiative. The

[14] Quoted in Ross, Foundations of Sociology, 388.

[15] Leviathan, Chap. 26.

[16] Do We Need a Philosophy of Law? 5 Columbia Law Rev. 339; The Spirit of the Common Law, Green Bag, January, 1906.

main security for the peace at common law is private prosecution of offenders. The chief security for the efficiency and honesty of public officers is mandamus or injunction by a tax-payer to prevent waste of the proceeds of taxation. The reliance for keeping public-service companies to their duty in treating all alike at reasonable price, is an action to recover damages. Moreover, the individual is supposed at common law to be able to look out for himself and to need no administrative protection. If he is injured through contributory negligence, no theory of comparative negligence comes to his relief; if he hires as an employee, he assumes the risk of the employment; if he buys goods, the rule is *caveat emptor*. In our modern industrial society, this whole scheme of individual initiative is breaking down. Private prosecution has become obsolete. Mandamus and injunction have failed to prevent rings and bosses from plundering public funds. Private suits against carriers for damages have proved no preventive of discrimination and extortionate rates. The doctrine of assumption of risk becomes brutal under modern conditions of employment. An action for damages is no comfort to us when we are sold diseased beef or poisonous canned goods. At all these points, and they are points of every-day contact with the most vital public interests, common-law methods of relief have failed. The courts have not been able to do the work which the common-law doctrine of supremacy of law imposed on them. A wide-spread feeling that the courts are inefficient has been a necessary result. But, along with this, another phase of the individualism of the common law has served to increase public irritation. At the very time the courts have appeared powerless themselves to give relief, they have seemed to obstruct public efforts to get relief by legislation. The chief concern of the common law is to secure and protect individual rights. "The public good," says Blackstone, "is in nothing more essentially interested than in the protection of every individual's private rights."[17] Such, it goes without saying, is not the popular view today.

[17] 1 Bl. Comm. 139.

Today we look to society for protection against individuals, natural or artificial, and we resent doctrines that protect these individuals against society for fear society will oppress us. But the common-law guaranties of individual rights are established in our constitutions, state and federal. So that, while in England these common-law dogmas have had to give way to modern legislation, in America they stand continually between the people, or large classes of the people, and legislation they desire. In consequence, the courts have been put in a false position of doing nothing and obstructing everything, which it is impossible for the layman to interpret aright.

A no less potent source of irritation lies in our American exagerations of the common-law contentious procedure. The sporting theory of justice, the "instinct of giving the game fair play,"[18] as Professor Wigmore has put it, is so rooted in the profession in America that most of us take it for a fundamental legal tenet. But it is probably only a survival of the days when a lawsuit was a fight between two clans in which change of venue had been taken to the forum. So far from being a fundamental fact of jurisprudence, it is peculiar to Anglo-American law; and it has been strongly curbed in modern English practice. With us, it is not merely in full acceptance, it has been developed and its collateral possibilities have been cultivated to the furthest extent. Hence in America we take it as a matter of course that a judge should be a mere umpire, to pass upon objections and hold counsel to the rules of the game, and that the parties should fight out their own game in their own way without judicial interference. We resent such interference as unfair, even when in the interests of justice. The idea that procedure must of necessity be wholly contentious disfigures our judicial administration at every point. It leads the most conscientious judge to feel that he is merely to decide the contest, as counsel present it according to the rules of the game, not to search independently for truth and justice. It leads counsel to forget that they are officers of the court and to deal with the rules of law and procedure exactly as the professional foot-ball coach with the

[18] I Wigmore, Evidence, 127.

rules of the sport. It leads to exertion to "get error into the record," rather than to dispose of the controversy finally and upon its merits. It turns witnesses, and especially expert witnesses, into partisans pure and simple. It leads to sensational cross-examinations "to affect credit," which have made the witness stand "the slaughter house of reputations."[19] It prevents the trial court from restraining the bullying of witnesses, and creates a general dislike, if not fear, of the witness-function, which impairs the administration of justice. It keeps alive the unfortunate Exchequer-rule, dead in the country of its origin, according to which errors in the admission or rejection of evidence are presumed to be prejudicial and hence demand a new trial. It grants new trials because by inability to procure a bill of exceptions a party has lost the chance to play another inning in the game of justice.[20] It creates vested rights in errors of procedure, of the benefit whereof parties are not to be deprived.[21] The inquiry is not, what do substantive law and justice require? Instead, the inquiry is, have the rules of the game been carried out strictly? If any material infraction is discovered, just as the foot-ball rules put back the offending team five or ten or fifteen yards, as the case may be, our sporting theory of justice awards new trials, or reverses judgments, or sustains demurrers in the interest of regular play.

The effect of our exaggerated contentious procedure is not only to irritate parties, witnesses and jurors, in particular cases, but to give to the whole community a false notion of the purpose and end of law. Hence comes, in large measure, the modern American race to beat the law. If the law is a mere game, neither the players who take part in it nor the public who witness it can be expected to yield to its spirit when their interests are served by evading it. And this is doubly true in a time which requires all institutions to be economically efficient and socially useful. We need not wonder that one part of the community strain their oaths in the jury-box and find verdicts against unpopular litigants in the teeth of law and evidence, while another

[19] 2 Wigmore, Evidence, 1112.

[20] Holland v. Chicago, B. & Q. R. Co., 52 Nebr. 100.

[21] DeGraw v. Elmore, 50 N. Y. 1.

part retain lawyers by the year to advise how to evade what to them are unintelligent and unreasonable restrictions upon necessary modes of doing business. Thus the courts, instituted to administer justice according to law, are made agents or abettors of lawlessness.

Another source of irritation at our American courts is political jealousy due to the strain put upon our legal system by the doctrine of the supremacy of law. By virtue of this doctrine, which has become fundamental in our polity, the law restrains, not individuals alone, but a whole people. The people so restrained would be likely in any event to be jealous of the visible agents of restraint. Even more is this true in that the subjects which our constitutional polity commits to the courts are largely matters of economics, politics, and sociology, upon which a democracy is peculiarly sensitive. Not only are these matters made into legal questions, but they are tried as incidents of private litigation. This phase of the common-law doctrine was felt as a grievance in the seventeenth century. "I tell you plainly," said Bacon as attorney-general, in arguing a question of prerogative to the judges—"I tell you plainly it is little better than a by-let or crooked creek to try whether the king hath power to erect this office in an assize between Brownlow and Michell."[22] King Demos must feel much the same at seeing the constitutionality of the Missouri Compromise tried in an action of trespass, at seeing the validity of the legal tender laws tried on pleas of payment in private litgation, at seeing the power of the federal government to carry on the Civil War tried judicially in admiralty, at seeing the income-tax overthrown in a stockholder's bill to enjoin waste of corporate assets, and at seeing the important political questions in the Insular Cases disposed of in forfeiture proceedings against a few trifling imports. Nor is this the only phase of the common-law doctrine of supremacy of law which produces political jealousy of the courts. Even more must the layman be struck with the spectacle of law paralyzing administration which our polity so frequently presents. The difficulties with writs of habeas corpus which the federal government encountered during the Civil War

[22] Collectanea Juridica, I, 173.

and the recent case of the income-tax will occur to you at once. In my own state, in a few years we have seen a freight-rate law suspended by decree of a court and have seen the collection of taxes from railroad companies, needed for the every-day conduct of public business, tied up by an injunction. The strain put upon judicial institutions by such litigation is obviously very great.

Lack of general ideas and absence of any philosophy of law, which has been characteristic of our law from the beginning and has been a point of pride at least since the time of Coke,[23] contributes its mite also toward the causes of dissatisfaction with courts. For one thing, it keeps us in the thrall of a fiction. There is a strong aversion to straightforward change of any important legal doctrine. The cry is, *interpret it.* But such interpretation is spurious. It is legislation. And to interpret an obnoxious rule out of existence rather than to meet it fairly and squarely by legislation is a fruitful source of confusion. Yet the bar are trained to it as an ancient common-law doctrine, and it has a great hold upon the public. Hence if the law does not work well, says Bentham, with fine sarcasm, "it is never the law itself that is in the wrong; it is always some wicked interpreter of the law that has corrupted and abused it."[24] Thus another unnecessary strain is imposed upon our judicial system, and courts are held for what should be the work of the legislature.

The defects of form inherent in our system of case-law have been the subject of discussion and controversy too often to require extended consideration. Suffice it to say that the want of certainty, confusion, and incompleteness inherent in all case-law, and the waste of labor entailed by the prodigious bulk to which ours has attained, appeal strongly to the layman. The compensating advantages of this system, as seen by the lawyer and by the scientific investigator, are not apparent to him. What he sees is another phase of the great game; a citation match between counsel, with a certainty that diligence can rake up a decision *somewhere* in support of any conceivable proposition.

[23] Co. Lit. Preface.

[24] Fragment on Government, XVII.

Passing to the third head, causes lying in our judicial organization and procedure, we come upon the most efficient causes of dissatisfaction with the present administration of justice in America. For I venture to say that our system of courts is archaic and our procedure behind the times. Uncertainty, delay and expense, and above all the injustice of deciding cases upon points of practice, which are the mere etiquette of justice, direct results of the organization of our courts and the backwardness of our procedure, have created a deep-seated desire to keep out of court, right or wrong, on the part of every sensible business man in the community.

Our system of courts is archaic in three respects: (1) in its multiplicity of courts, (2) in preserving concurrent jurisdictions, (3) in the waste of judical power which it involves. The judicial organizations of the several states exhibit many differences of detail. But they agree in these three respects. Multiplicity of courts is characteristic of archaic law. In Anglo-Saxon law, one might apply to the Hundred, the Shire, the Witan, or the king in person. Until Edward I broke up private jurisdictions, there were the king's superior courts of law, the itinerant justices, the county courts, the local or communal courts and the private courts of lordships; besides which one might always apply to the king or to the Great Council for extraordinary relief. When later the royal courts had superseded all others, there were the concurrent jurisdictions of King's Bench, Common Pleas, and Exchequer, all doing the same work, while appellate jurisdiction was divided by King's Bench, Exchequer Chamber and Parliament. In the Fourth Institute, Coke enumerates seventy-four courts. Of these, seventeen did the work that is now done by three, the County Courts, the Supreme Court of Judicature, and the House of Lords. At the time of the reorganization by the Judicature Act of 1873, five appellate courts and eight courts of first instance were consolidated into the one Supreme Court of Judicature. It was the intention of those who devised the plan of the Judicature Act to extend the principle of unity of jurisdiction by cutting off the appellate jurisdiction of the House of Lords and by incorporating the County Courts in the newly formed Supreme Court as branches thereof.[25] The recommendation as to the County Courts was not adopted, and the appellate jurisdiction of the House of Lords was restored in 1875. In this way the unity and simplicity of the original design were impaired. But the plan, although adopted in part only, deserves the careful study of American lawyers as a model modern judicial organization. Its chief features were (1), to set up a single court, complete in itself, embracing all superior courts and jurisdictions, (2) to include in this one court, as a branch thereof, a single court of final appeal. In the one branch, the court of first instance, all original jurisdiction at law, in equity, in admiralty, in bankruptcy, in probate and in divorce was to be consolidated; in the other branch, the court of appeal, the whole reviewing jurisdiction was to be established. This idea of unification, although not carried out completely, has proved most effective. Indeed, its advantages are self-evident. Where the appellate tribunal and the court of first instance are branches of one court, all expense of transfer of record, of transcripts, bills of exceptions, writs of error and citations is wiped out. The records are the records of the court, of which each tribunal is but a branch. The court and each branch thereof knows its own records, and no duplication and certification is required. Again, all appellate practice, with its attendant pitfalls, and all waste of judicial time in ascertaining how or whether a case has been brought into the court of review is done away with. One may search the recent English reports in vain for a case where an appeal has miscarried on a point of practice. Cases on appellate procedure are wanting. In effect there is no such thing. The whole attention of the court and of counsel is concentrated upon the cause. On the other hand, our American reports bristle with fine points of appellate procedure. More than four per cent of the digest paragraphs of the last ten volumes of the American Digest have to do with Appeal and Error. In ten volumes of the

[25] Report of Judicature Commission, 1869, p. 13.

[26] Lord Elden's Commission, 1826; Royal Commission, 1829, 1830, 1832; Commission on Pleading and Practice in Courts of Common Law, 1851, 1853, 1860; Chancery Commissioners, 1852, 1854, 1856; Judicature Commissioners, 1869-1874.

Federal Reporter, namely, volumes 129 to 139, covering decisions of the Circuit Courts of Appeals from 1903 till the present, there is an average of ten decisions upon points of appellate practice to the volume. Two cases to the volume, on the average, turn wholly upon appellate procedure. In the ten volumes there are six civil cases turning upon the question whether error or appeal was the proper mode of review, and in two civil cases the question was whether the Circuit Court of Appeals was the proper tribunal. I have referred to these reports because they represent courts in which only causes of importance may be brought. The state reports exhibit the same condition. In ten volumes of the Southwestern Reporter, the decisions of the Supreme Court and Courts of Appeals of Missouri show that nearly twenty per cent involve points of appellate procedure. In volume 87, of 53 decisions of the Supreme Court and 97 of the Courts of Appeals, 28 are taken up in whole or in part with the mere technics of obtaining a review. All of this is sheer waste which a modern judicial organization would obviate.

Even more archaic is our system of concurrent jurisdiction of state and federal courts in causes involving diversity of citizenship; a system by virtue of which causes continually hang in the air between two courts, or, if they do stick in one court or the other, are liable to an ultimate overturning because they stuck in the wrong court. A few statistics on this point may be worth while. In the ten volumes of the Federal Reporter referred to, the decisions of the Circuit Courts of Appeals in civil cases average 76 to the volume. Of these, on the average, between four and five in a volume are decided on points of federal jurisdiction. In a little more than one to each volume, judgments of Circuit Courts are reversed on points of jurisdiction. The same volumes contain on the average 73 decisions of Circuit Courts in civil cases to each volume. Of these, six, on the average, are upon motions to remand to the state courts, and between eight and nine are upon other points of federal jurisdiction. Moreover, twelve cases in the ten volumes were remanded on the *form* of the petition for removal. In other words, in 19.3 per cent of the reported decisions of the Circuit Courts the question was whether those courts had jurisdiction at all; and in seven per cent of these that question depended on the form of the pleadings. A system that permits this and reverses four judgments a year because the cause was brought in or removed to the wrong tribunal, is out of place in a modern business community. All original jurisdiction should be concentrated. It ought to be impossible for a cause to fail because brought in the wrong place. A simple order of transfer from one docket to another in the same court ought to be enough. There should be no need of new papers, no transcripts, no bandying of cases from one court to another on orders of removal and of remand, no beginnings again with new process.

Judicial power may be wasted in three ways: (1) by rigid districts or courts or jurisdictions, so that business may be congested in one court while judges in another are idle, (2) by consuming the time of courts with points of pure practice, when they ought to be investigating substantial controversies, and (3) by nullifying the results of judicial action by unnecessary retrials. American judicial systems are defective in all three respects. The federal Circuit Courts and Circuit Courts of Appeals are conspicuous exceptions in the first respect, affording a model of flexible judicial organization. But in nearly all of the states rigid districts and hard and fast lines between courts operate to delay business in one court while judges in another have ample leisure. In the second respect, waste of judicial time upon points of practice, the intricacies of federal jurisdiction and the survival of the obsolete Chinese wall between law and equity in procedure, make our federal courts no less conspicuous sinners. In the ten volumes of the Federal Reporter examined, of an average of 76 decisions of the Circuit Courts of Appeals in each volume, two turn upon the distinction between law and equity in procedure and not quite one judgment to each volume is reversed on this distinction. In an average of 73 decisions a volume by the Circuit Courts, more than three in each volume involve this same distinction, and not quite two in each volume turn upon it. But many states that are supposed to have reformed procedure scarcely make a better showing.

Each state has to a great extent its own procedure. But it is not too much to say that all of them are behind the times. We struck one great stroke in 1848 and have rested complacently or contented ourselves with patchwork amendment ever since. The leading ideas of the New York Code of Civil Procedure marked a long step forward. But the work was done too hurriedly and the plan of a rigid code, going into minute detail, was clearly wrong. A modern practice act lays down the general principles of practice and leaves details to rules of court. The New York Code Commission was appointed in 1847 and reported in 1848. If we except the Connecticut Practice Act of 1878, which shows English influence, American reform in procedure has stopped substantially where that commission left it. In England, beginning with 1826 and ending with 1874, *five* commissions have put forth *nine* reports upon this subject. As a consequence, we have nothing in America to compare with the radical treatment of pleading in the English Judicature Act and the orders based thereon. We still try the *record,* not the *case.* We are still reversing judgments for nonjoinder and misjoinder. The English practice of joinder of parties against whom relief is claimed in the alternative, rendering judgment against any that the proof shows to be liable and dismissing the rest, makes an American lawyer rub his eyes. We are still reversing judgments for variance. We still reverse them because the recovery is in excess of the prayer, though sustained by the evidence.[27]

But the worst feature of American procedure is the lavish granting of new trials. In the ten volumes of the Federal Reporter referred to, there are, on the average, 25 writs of error in civil cases to the volume. New trials are awarded on the average in eight cases a volume, or nearly 29 per cent. In the state courts, the proportion of new trials to causes reviewed, as ascertained from investigation of the five last volumes of each series of the National Reporter System runs over forty per cent. In the three last volumes of the New

[27] Brought *v.* Cherokee Nation (C. C. A.), 129 Fed. 192.

York Reports (180-182), covering the period from December 6, 1904, to October 24, 1905, forty-five new trials are awarded. Nor is this all. In one case in my own state[28] an action for personal injuries was tried six times, and one for breach cf contract[29] was tried three times and was four times in the Supreme Court. When with this we compare the statistics of the English Court of Appeal, which does not grant to exceed twelve new trials a year, or new trials in about three per cent of the cases reviewed, it is evident that our methods of trial and of review are out of date.

A comparison of the volume of business disposed of by English and by American Courts will illustrate the waste and delay caused by archaic judicial organization and obsolete procedure. In England there are twenty-three judges of the High Court, who dispose on the average of 5,600 contested cases and have before them, in one form or another, some 80,000 cases, each year. In Nebraska there are twenty-eight district judges, who have no original probate jurisdiction and no jurisdiction in bankruptcy or admiralty, and they had upon their dockets last year 4,320 cases, of which they disposed of about seventy per cent. England and Wales, with a population in 1900 of 32,000,000 employ for their whole civil litigation 95 judges, that is 37 in the Supreme Court and House of Lords, and 58 county judges. Nebraska, with a population in 1900 of 1,066,000, employs for the same purpose 129. But these 129 are organized on an antiquated system and their time is frittered away on mere points of legal etiquette.

Finally, under the fourth and last head, causes lying in the environment of our judicial administration, we may distinguish six: (1) popular lack of interest in justice, which makes jury service a bore and the vindication of right and law secondary to the trouble and expense involved, (2) the strain put upon law in that it has today to do the work of morals also, (3) the effect of transition to a period of legislation, (4) the putting of our courts into politics, (5) the making the legal profession into a trade, and (6) pub-

[28] Omaha St. R. Co. *v.* Bocsen, 95 N. W. 617 Cf. Mutual Life Ins. Co. *v.* Hillmon (C. C. A.), 107 Fed. 834 (tried six times).

[29] Wittenberg *v.* Molyneaux, 60 Nebr. 107.

lic ignorance of the real workings of courts due to ignorant and sensational reports in the press. Each of these deserves consideration, but a few points only may be noticed. Law is the skeleton of social order. It must be "clothed upon by the flesh and blood of morality."[30] The present is a time of transition in the very foundations of belief and of conduct. Absolute theories of morals and supernatural sanctions have lost their hold. Conscience and individual responsibilty are relaxed. In other words the law is strained to do double duty, and more is expected of it than in a time when morals as a regulating agency are more efficacious. Another strain upon our judicial system results from the crude and unorganized character of American legislation in a period when the growing point of law has drifted to legislation. When, in consequence, laws fail to produce the anticipated effects, judicial administration shares the blame. Worse than this is the effect of laws not intended to be enforced. These parodies, like the common-law branding of felons, in which a piece of bacon used to be interposed between the branding-iron and the criminal's skin,[31] breed disrespect for law. Putting courts into politics and compelling judges to become politicians, in many jurisdictions has almost destroyed the traditional respect for the bench. Finally, the ignorant and sensational reports of judicial proceedings, from which alone a great part of the public may judge of the daily work of the courts, completes the impression that the administration of justice is but a game. There are honorable exceptions, but the average press reports distract attention from the real proceeding to petty tilts of counsel, encounters with witnesses and sensational by-incidents. In Nebraska, not many years since, the federal court enjoined the execution of an act to regulate insurance companies.[32] In press accounts of the proceeding, the conspiracy clause of the bill was copied *in extenso* under the headline "Conspiracy Charged," and it was made to appear that the ground of the injunction was a conspiracy between the state officers and some persons unknown. It cannot be expected that

[30] Sidgwick, Methods of Ethics, 6 Ed. 457.

[31] Bentham, Theory of Legislation (tr. by Hildreth), 401.

[32] Niagara Fire Ins. Co. v. Cornell, 110 Fed. 816.

the public shall form any just estimate of our courts of justice from such data.

Reviewing the several causes for dissatisfaction with the administration of justice which have been touched upon, it will have been observed that some inhere in all law and are the penalty we pay for uniformity; that some inhere in our political institutions and are the penalty we pay for local self-government and independence from bureaucratic control; that some inhere in the circumstances of an age of transition and are the penalty we pay for individual freedom of thought and universal education. These will take care of themselves. But too much of the current dissatisfaction has a just origin in our judicial organization and procedure. The causes that lie here must be heeded. Our administration of justice is not decadent. It is simply behind the times. Political judges were known in England down to the last century. Lord Kenyon as Master of the Rolls sat in Parliament and took as active a part in political squabbles in the House of Commons as our state judges today in party conventions.[33] Dodson and Fogg and Sergeant Buzzfuz wrought in an atmosphere of contentious procedure. Bentham tells us that in 1797 out of 550 pending writs of error, 543 were shams or vexatious contrivances for delay.[34] Jarndyce and Jarndyce dragged out its weary course in chancery only half a century ago. We are simply stationary in that period of legal history. With law schools that are rivaling the achievements of Bologna and of Bourges to promote scientific study of the law, with active bar associations in every state to revive professional feeling and throw off the yoke of commercialism, with the passing of the doctrine that politics too is a mere game to be played for its own sake, we may look forward confidently to deliverance from the sporting theory of justice; we may look forward to a near future when our courts will be swift and certain agents of justice, whose decisions will be acquiesced in and respected by all.

[33] Lord Campbell, Lives of the Chief Justices (3 Ed.) IV, 70-73.

[34] Works, VII, 214.

[13]

THE JUDICIALITY OF MINIMUM-WAGE LEGISLATION

MINIMUM-WAGE legislation has been of two main kinds. One is the Massachusetts variety which vests a commission with power to make inquiries and publish results.[1] Employers are exposed to public knowledge of the wages paid and are thereby subjected to public censure or public praise. Sentiments of decency or of vanity may move the niggardly to mend their ways, but the recalcitrant are left free to bargain as they can and will. The other type of legislation adds physical to moral force. A commission is authorized to discover and to declare the minimum cost of decent subsistence and on this basis to prescribe the minimum wage that may be paid to women and minors. Employment at less than the prescribed wage subjects the employer to punishment. While the variations in the wages fixed by various boards for various employments indicate that the cost of living is not always the sole criterion of the boards' determinations, there has been no judicial adjudication that their prescriptions have exceeded the cost of decent living. The constitutional issue raised by such compulsory legislation is therefore whether an employer may be compelled to pay the cost of maintaining the employee whose full services he voluntarily uses in the conduct of his enterprise.

This constitutional question finds no answer in the Constitution. While the legislation, like substantially all legislation and all law, involves a deprivation of liberty or property, such deprivation is constitutionally innocuous unless it is "without due process of law." The Constitution does not define due process of law. The task of definition is committed to the judges. They have recognized that definition is impossible. They have told us that instead of definition they will employ a process of "judicial inclusion and exclusion," and give us the reasons.[2] These reasons can not come from the Constitution. They come from

[1] This is described in Holcombe *v.* Creamer, 231 Mass. 99, 120 N. E. 354 (1918).

[2] Mr. Justice Miller, in Davidson *v.* New Orleans, 96 U. S. 97, 104 (1877).

the judges. The law of constitutional due process is therefore as much judge-made law as any common law is judge-made law. Until some due-process issue is authoritatively settled, one who would make a constitutional prophecy or a constitutional argument should be familiar with the outlook and the temper of the judges by whom the issue is to be decided. In cases of any considerable novelty, few reasons can be so compelling as to meet with universal acceptation. The determination of closely-controverted constitutional issues depends, therefore, in large part upon the composition of the court of last resort at the particular time when the issue comes before it.

Nowhere does this analysis find firmer confirmation than in the history of judicial decisions on the constitutionality of minimum-wage legislation. The question first came before the Oregon court in 1914, and in two decisions seven judges declared themselves in favor of the legislation and none was opposed.[3] The Oregon case went to the Supreme Court of the United States, and in 1917 the decree of the state court was sustained by a vote of four to four.[4] Mr. Justice Brandeis, having been of counsel, did not sit. His general outlook on what is called social legislation is so well known that there can be no doubt that, had he not been of counsel, he would have voted in favor of the law. In that event, the consequent five-to-four vote almost certainly would have established the constitutionality of such legislation against subsequent attack in the federal courts. Though conceivably a favorable decision might later have been overruled by a differently composed Supreme Court, the experience is that police issues of this general character are finally settled by such favorable decision. A four-to-four vote, however, settles nothing, except that the particular decision below is not reversed. After this tie vote, the constitutional issue still remained an open one. A prophet would be confident that if the same Supreme Court

[3] Stettler *v.* O'Hara, 69 Ore. 519, 139 Pac. 743 (1914); Simpson *v.* O'Hara, 70 Ore. 261, 141 Pac. 158 (1914).

[4] Stettler *v.* O'Hara, 243 U. S. 629 (1917). This case was first argued in the Supreme Court on December 16 and 17, 1914. It was restored to the docket for reargument on June 12, 1916, reargued January 18 and 19, 1917, and decided on April 9, 1917. The *per curiam* opinion reads as follows: "Judgments affirmed with costs by an equally divided court. (Mr. Justice Brandeis took no part in the consideration and decision of these cases.)"

bench had the question to decide in a case in which Mr. Justice Brandeis should sit, the answer would be in favor of the legislation. By reason of this confidence, he might add to it the further confidence that the objectors to the legislation would not again bring the issue to the Supreme Court until its personnel had changed. Such turned out to be the fact. Four changes in the Supreme Court had taken place before the issue again came before it.

In the meantime four other courts had passed upon the question. Two decisions of the Minnesota Supreme Court in 1917 and 1920 record six judges in favor of the legislation and none opposed.[5] An Arkansas decision of 1917[6] sustained the legislation by a vote of four to one, though one of the majority refrained from dissent only because he thought that the legislation was entitled to the benefit of the Supreme Court tie until it was broken. Two decisions of the Supreme Court of Washington in 1918 and 1920 add eleven judges to those in favor of the legislation and none to those opposed.[7] Thus the compulsory minimum-wage legislation of the states of Oregon, Minnesota, Arkansas, and Washington was thought constitutional by twenty-seven judges of the courts of those states and unconstitutional by only two judges, three of the four courts being unanimously in favor of the statutes.

Then came the anomalous somersault in the case before the Court of Appeals of the District of Columbia. This involved the act of Congress applicable to the District. On the first hearing Mr. Justice Robb was unable to sit because of illness. Under statutory authority the other two Justices designated Mr. Justice Stafford of the Supreme Court of the District to sit in his place. The decision, on June 6, 1921, was two to one in favor of the statute.[8] Chief Justice Smyth and Mr. Justice Stafford were in favor; Mr. Justice Van Orsdel was opposed. Motions for a re-

[5] Williams *v.* Evans, 139 Minn. 32, 165 N. W. 495 (1917); Miller Telephone Co. *v.* Minimum Wage Commission, 145 Minn. 262, 177 N. W. 341 (1920).

[6] State *v.* Crowe, 130 Ark. 273, 197 S. W. 4 (1917).

[7] Larsen *v.* Rice, 100 Wash. 642, 171 Pac. 1037 (1918); Spokane Hotel Co. *v.* Younger, 113 Wash. 359, 194 Pac. 595 (1920).

[8] This fact and the recital which follows in the text are found in the dissenting opinion of Chief Justice Smyth in the decision after the rehearing, cited in note 9, *infra*.

hearing were denied on June 22 of the same year. Three days later, Mr. Justice Robb, who had now recovered, wrote the Chief Justice that he was considering an application for a rehearing. On July 1 he wrote that he had decided to vote for a rehearing and had so notified counsel and Mr. Justice Van Orsdel. Later Justices Robb and Van Orsdel instructed the clerk to enter an order granting a rehearing. The Chief Justice dissented. The case was reargued on February 14, 1921, and decided on November 6, 1922. The vote was two to one against the statute.[9] Chief Justice Smyth in dissenting severely scored the method by which a rehearing was obtained.[10] Thus those who sat in the two hearings in the District Court of Appeals were divided two to two. Summarizing the votes outside of the United States Supreme Court, we have twenty-nine judges thinking compulsory minimum-wage legislation not wanting in due process as against four judges thinking the contrary.

The District of Columbia adverse decision was appealed to the United States Supreme Court where it was argued on March 14, 1923, and decided on April 9, 1923, in *Adkins* v. *Children's Hospital*.[11] The dates of the several proceedings in the District of Columbia case from its initiation to its final disposition in the Supreme Court are significant, for, as will later appear, the unconstitutionality of minimum-wage legislation has been dictated by the calendar rather than by the Constitution. The Supreme Court decision annulled the act of Congress by a vote of five to three. Mr. Justice Brandeis, *ex majore cautela*, from which Mr. Justice Robb was immune, did not sit, notwithstanding the fact that technically he was eligible since his disqualification was confined to the Oregon litigation in which he had been of counsel. The opinion of the Court was written by Mr. Justice Sutherland and concurred in by Justices McKenna, Van Devanter, McReynolds and Butler. Chief Justice Taft wrote

[9] Children's Hospital *v.* Adkins, 284 Fed. 613 (D. C., C. A., 1922).

[10] "It would seem from the foregoing that the appellants, finding themselves defeated, sought a justice who had not sat in the case, but who, they believed, would be favorable to them, and induced him, by an appeal directed to him personally, to assume jurisdiction and join with the dissenting justice in an attempt to overrule the decisions of the court. I shall not characterize such practice; let such facts speak for themselves." *Supra*, at p. 624 *et seq.*

[11] 261 U. S. 525.

a dissenting opinion in which Mr. Justice Sanford concurred. Mr. Justice Holmes wrote an additional dissenting opinion. Adding these Supreme Court votes to the votes in the lower courts, we have a total of thirty-two judges voting in favor of the constitutionality of minimum-wage legislation and nine judges voting against it.

Now for the importance of the time when the question reached the Supreme Court. Three of the five Justices who voted against the legislation in 1923 were on the bench in 1917 when the Supreme Court was divided four to four. These were Justices McKenna, Van Devanter, and McReynolds. We may be confident, therefore, that they gave three of the four votes against the law in 1917. The other Justices sitting in 1917 were Chief Justice White and Justices Holmes, Day, Pitney, and Clarke. Since Mr. Justice Holmes dissented in 1923, we know that he voted for the law in 1917. Followers of Supreme Court divisions can be certain also that Mr. Justice Clarke was on the same side. This confines the surmise as to the fourth Justice against the law in 1917 to Chief Justice White and Justices Day and Pitney. The evidence of other divisions of opinion points almost conclusively to Chief Justice White as the fourth in opposition. He had been more consistently with Justices Van Devanter and McReynolds against extensions of the police power than had either Mr. Justice Day or Mr. Justice Pitney.[12] In writing the opinion sustaining the constitutionality of the Adamson Law, he made a distinction between prescribing wages after the parties have failed to agree and prescribing wages in conjunction with forbidding or restricting an agreement, thus carefully differentiating minimum-wage legislation from the Adamson Law.[13] Mr. Rome G. Brown, one of the

[12] Most significant is the fact that Chief Justice White and Justices Van Devanter and McReynolds were the three dissentients in Bunting *v.* Oregon, 243 U. S. 426 (1917), which sustained the Oregon ten-hour law. They, with Mr. Justice McKenna, were the four opposed to the Washington Compulsory Insurance Act sustained in Mountain Timber Co. *v.* Washington, 243 U. S. 219 (1917). This same four constituted the minority in Block *v.* Hirsh, 256 U. S. 135 (1921), which sustained the laws regulating rents. Chief Justice White and Justices Van Devanter and McReynolds were the three opposed to the statute restricting the use of natural gas for making carbon, which was sustained in Walls *v.* Midland Carbon Co., 254 U. S. 300 (1920).

[13] Wilson *v.* New, 243 U. S. 332 (1917). This distinction is relied on by Mr. Justice Sutherland in the Minimum Wage Case where in speaking of

counsel before the Supreme Court in the first minimum-wage case, picks Chief Justice White as one of the four opposed to the legislation.[14] It seems, therefore, as safe a guess as any guess can be, that in 1917 Chief Justice White voted against minimum-wage legislation and Justices Day and Pitney voted in favor of it. Certainly three of these four Justices were in favor of the legislation and only one opposed, so that these votes added to the others already counted make a judicial majority of thirty-five to ten in favor, with the participating Supreme Court Justices divided six to six and a non-participating Justice known to be in favor.

The bench sitting in 1917 continued until the end of the October term of 1920. During the October term of 1921 the only change was that of Chief Justice Taft in place of Chief Justice White. If our guess as to Chief Justice White is correct, the Supreme Court from October, 1921, to June, 1922, contained six Justices who thought minimum-wage legislation constitutional. One of these was Mr. Justice Brandeis who doubtless would have refrained from sitting then as he did in 1923. The others were Chief Justice Taft and Justices Holmes, Day, Pitney and Clarke. If, therefore, any state case or the District of Columbia case had been argued before and decided by the Supreme Court between November, 1921, and June, 1922, the decision would, in all probability, have been five to three in favor of minimum-wage legislation. Even if the surmise as to Chief Justice White were incorrect, and either Mr. Justice Day or Mr. Justice Pitney were opposed to the legislation, the vote would have been four to four, with Chief Justice Taft, Justices Holmes and Clarke, and either Mr. Justice Day or Mr. Justice Pitney in favor. This would have sustained the state decisions and the first District of Columbia decision had Mr. Justice Robb not intervened to bring about a rehearing. That intervention, be it noted, set aside a decision rendered on June 6, 1921, and postponed the ultimate decision in the District of Columbia Court of Appeals until

the wage provision of the Adamson Law he says: "This feature of the law was sustained principally because the parties for the time being, could not or would not agree. Here they are forbidden to agree." Adkins *v.* Children's Hospital, *supra,* at p. 551.

[14] See Rome G. Brown, "Oregon Minimum Wage Cases," 1 MINN. L. REV. 471, 484, 485.

November 6, 1922. The appeal from this decision reached the Supreme Court for argument in March, 1923, and was decided less than a month later. Thus the earlier 1921 District of Columbia decision might have reached the Supreme Court for adjudication some time before June, 1922. If, therefore, Mr. Justice Robb had sat at the first hearing and the decision had then been against the act of Congress, the appeal might have been decided by the Supreme Court before June, 1922, when there were certainly only four Justices of the Supreme Court opposed to the legislation and, in all probability, only three opposed to it. Thus the state laws would surely have been saved for the time from annulment, and almost certainly both state and national legislation would have been sustained by a decision that would have been accepted as settling the issue forever. So, for a second time, the course of constitutional principles was changed by circumstances peculiar to an individual judge: first, because Mr. Justice Brandeis chanced to have been of counsel at an earlier stage of the Oregon case; and, secondly, because Mr. Justice Robb of the District of Columbia Court of Appeals was indisposed when the act of Congress first came before that court for consideration.

Before the District of Columbia case came on for argument before the Supreme Court, there had intervened three further changes in the composition of that body, all due to resignations of sitting Justices. Mr. Justice Clarke was succeeded by Mr. Justice Sutherland; Mr. Justice Day, by Mr. Justice Butler; and Mr. Justice Pitney, by Mr. Justice Sanford. By these changes either a possible tie vote of four to four or, more probably, a five-to-three vote in favor of minimum-wage legislation was turned into a five-to-three vote against it. It would, of course, be idle to speculate as to whether the new appointees to the bench would have been the same had the resigning Justices been different or had their resignations been in a different order. It can, however, hardly be attributed to anything but chance that the resignations after June, 1922, were of two or three Justices favoring minimum-wage legislation and that the new appointments added two Justices opposing it. It can not well be attributed to any assumed leanings of the appointing authority, since the four new Justices appointed by President Harding were evenly divided on the issue.

The political complexion of the bench at the time is of no significance. It is doubtless idle, too, to speculate as to whether Justices Sutherland and Butler might have voted differently had the question not come before them until they were further away from their days of legislation and of advocacy, and therefore perhaps more impregnated with the professed traditions of judicial tolerance in passing upon the constitutionality of legislation under the amorphous caution of the due-process clauses. Suffice it to say that minimum-wage legislation is now unconstitutional, not because the Constitution makes it so, not because its economic results or its economic propensities would move a majority of judges to think it so, but because it chanced not to come before a particular Supreme Court bench which could not muster a majority against it and chanced to be presented at the succeeding term when the requisite, but no more than requisite, majority was sitting. In the words of the poet, it was not the Constitution but " a measureless malfeasance which obscurely willed it thus " — the malfeasance of chance and of the calendar.

Such is the only possible realistic account of the reason why minimum-wage legislation is unconstitutional. Literary interpretation of the Constitution has nothing whatever to do with it. Neither legal learning nor economic exposition can explain it. Arguments *pro* and arguments *contra* have no compelling inherent power. The issue was determined not by the arguments but by the arbiters. The majority of the arbiters on the state courts favored the legislation, but under our constitutional system the majority of the arbiters on the Supreme Court have the determining voice. The unanimous vote of the electors of a state through solemn amendment of the constitution of the state could not reverse the vote of five members of the Supreme Court of the United States. This can be done only by the Supreme Court itself or by amendment of the Constitution of the United States.

While the decision under review was confined to the act of Congress for the District of Columbia, the interpretation of the due-process clause of the Fifth Amendment is a precedent for the interpretation of the same words in the Fourteenth Amendment, and the judicial aversion to the federal law would necessarily invalidate similar laws. There would, it is true, be a possible distinction by reason of the decisions of the state courts sustaining the state laws. The Supreme Court often professes to give weight to the sanction given by state judges to state laws. Such professions of respect are, however, honored in the breach as well as in the observance. In all substance there was as much reason to respect the state decisions in passing upon the issue which was the same as that presented by the state laws, as there would have been if a state law had been directly involved in the litigation. If, at some later time, a state law is sustained by the Supreme Court it will be either because one or more of the annulling five Justices has repented of his action in the *Adkins* case or because he has yielded his place on the bench to a successor of different temper or outlook. When the personnel of the Supreme Court changes sufficiently, the constitutionality *vel non* of minimum-wage legislation will again be an open question. Practitioners who take seriously the saying of Mr. Justice Holmes that law is a prophecy of what courts will do in fact will then have to consider the attitudes and dispositions of the new members of the Court, for those attitudes and dispositions will be the determining factors in the re-solution of the constitutional issue.

This perhaps may make it worth while to seek for the attitude and the disposition which underlay the action of the majority in the present case. It makes us eager to know why ten judges had this attitude and disposition when thirty-five judges did not, but such a quest would be too baffling to undertake. We should be fortunate if we could have any confidence in our estimate of what attitude and what disposition animated the five Justices whose action invites our inquiry. The published opinion of one of them cannot be taken as, in all details, the exact embodiment of the major and minor elements in the thought and the outlook of the others. Indeed the reasons which any individual gives for his own decisions may not be the reasons which moved him to make them. Many passages in judicial opinions are quite patently argumentative justifications rather than inducing reasons. The talk in the consultation chamber must often be very different from the talk in the published opinion. Yet to these arcana the uninitiated are not admitted. We must take the opinion as it is given to us and do our best with this imperfect explanation of the judgment.

Mr. Justice Sutherland starts with an analysis of the statute and a statement of the facts in the case before the Court.[15] He then announces that "the judicial duty of passing upon the constitutionality of an act of Congress is one of great gravity and delicacy"[16] and that the determination of the legislative branch in favor of its validity "must be given great weight."[17] From professions of duty he turns to professions of fact. He says:

> "This Court, by an unbroken line of decisions from Chief Justice Marshall to the present day, has steadily adhered to the rule that every possible presumption is in favor of the validity of an act of Congress until overcome beyond rational doubt."[18]

This seems to be the prelude either to a decision sustaining the statute or to an insult to the "rationality" of the thirty-five judges whose votes we have recorded. It turns out not to be the former. It is followed by the adversative that, "if by clear and indisputable demonstration a statute be opposed to the Constitution, we have no choice but to say so."[19] This by implication calls what is to follow a "clear and indisputable demonstration" of unconstitutionality and invites it, therefore, to be judged by that standard.

The next step in the opinion is to point out that minimum-wage legislation abridges liberty of contract and therefore must pass the test of due process. However questionable this might once have been,[20] it is no longer disputed.[21] It is, however, true also,

[15] These include allegations in one of the complaints that the plaintiff hotel company "had agreed upon rates of wages and compensation satisfactory to such employees," and in the other complaint that the plaintiff employee was anxious to continue her work at a wage less than that fixed by statute and that "she did not earn more." From the opinion in the court below it appeared that after her discharge the hospital hired a man to take her place as elevator operator.

[16] At p. 544.

[17] *Ibid.*

[18] *Ibid.*

[19] *Ibid.*

[20] See Charles E. Shattuck, "The True Meaning of the Term 'Liberty' in Those Clauses in the Federal and State Constitutions which Protect 'Life, Liberty, and Property,'" 4 HARV. L. REV. 365; Roscoe Pound, "Liberty of Contract," 18 YALE L. J. 454.

[21] Mr. Justice Holmes, however, helps to bring the concept down to earth by saying in his dissenting opinion in the Adkins case, at p. 568:

as Mr. Justice Sutherland goes on to say, that " there is, of course, no such thing as absolute freedom of contract." [22] As he recognizes, " it is subject to a great variety of restraints." [23] So far, well and good. Then follows, however, an announcement which gives us a clue to the major line of cleavage between the proponents of regulatory legislation and the objectors thereto. From somewhere or other Mr. Justice Sutherland derives the constitutional doctrine which he puts as follows:

> " But freedom of contract is, nevertheless, the general rule and restraint the exception, and the exercise of legislative authority to abridge it can be justified only by the existence of exceptional circumstances." [24]

No such doctrine is stated in the Constitution. As a statement of fact, it is unsupported by the balance on the ledger of Supreme Court decisions, for the catalogue shows that the Court has sustained many more regulatory statutes than it has annulled. If we may trust the annual addresses of presidents of bar associations, regulation has long since become the rule, and freedom the exception. Whence, then, comes the rule that Mr. Justice Sutherland reveals? Needless to say, it comes from Mr. Justice Sutherland. It represents his personal views of desirable governmental policy. Those views are shared by many others, but

" But in the present instance the only objection that can be urged is found within the vague contours of the Fifth Amendment, prohibiting the depriving any person of liberty or property without due process of law. To that I turn.

" The earlier decisions upon the same words in the Fourteenth Amendment began within our memory and went no farther than an unpretentious assertion of the liberty to follow the ordinary callings. Later that innocuous generality was expanded into the dogma, Liberty of Contract. Contract is not especially mentioned in the text that we have to construe. It is merely an example of doing what you want to do, embodied in the word liberty. But pretty much all law consists in forbidding men to do some things that they want to do, and contract is no more exempt from law than other acts."

Doubtless these are the remarks which prompted Chief Justice Taft to say in his separate dissent, at p. 567: " But for my inability to agree with some general observations in the forcible opinion of Mr. Justice Holmes, who follows me, I should be silent and merely record my concurrence in what he says."

[22] At p. 546.

[23] *Ibid.*

[24] *Ibid.*

they are not written into the Constitution of the United States except as judges from time to time have inscribed them there. For every such inscription we may find a corresponding erasure. Against this presumption in favor of individual freedom from legislative restraint, we may set the presumption in favor of legislative freedom from judicial restraint to which, a little earlier, Mr. Justice Sutherland paid tribute.

With his presumption against legislative interference with contract as his background, Mr. Justice Sutherland then goes on to consider whether the cases in which interference has been sanctioned are precedents in support of the interference under consideration. A negative answer can show at most that the legislation is novel, and its novelty does not make it unconstitutional. Practically every law is in some respects dissimilar from every other law. It does not get us far to expose these dissimilarities one by one, for side by side with the dissimilarities are similarities and analogies. The similarities may have a cumulative effect which no one would have if standing alone. Mr. Justice Sutherland's method of exposing particular differences makes his task too easy. It makes it easier still because he neglects to notice one of the strongest analogies pointed out in the brief supporting the legislation.

Three of Mr. Justice Sutherland's comparisons may be dealt with briefly. (1) Minimum-wage legislation differs from regulation of the rates of public utilities. (2) General minimum-wage legislation differs from regulation confined to labor in the performance of public work. (3) It differs, too, from prescriptions of the character, methods, and time for payment of wages. Such prescriptions still leave the parties free to bargain as to the amount to be paid. Yet such prescriptions, with their judicial sanctions, establish that the wage relation is a subject of public concern and that, therefore, the field in which minimum-wage legislation operates is a proper field of governmental activity. Nor is it substantially correct to say that such prescriptions do not affect "the heart of the contract."[25] The parties legally may be free to contract for a lower rate of wages after anti-screen laws, anti-scrip laws, and monthly or bi-weekly payment laws,

[25] See passage cited in note 51, *infra*.

but without doubt the practices thereby prohibited had affected the *quantum* of wages, and their abandonment was pecuniarily advantageous to employees. Mr. Justice Sutherland goes too far when he says of these prescriptions that " in no sense can they be said to be, or to furnish a precedent for, wage-fixing statutes." [26]

The opinion next turns to statutes fixing the hours of labor and finds that the sanction accorded to them is no precedent in favor of minimum-wage laws. It is pointed out that none of them applied to all occupations as does the minimum-wage law, and that the ground on which they were sustained was that long hours of labor in particular employments are dangerous to health. Mr. Justice Sutherland quotes five paragraphs from the opinion of Mr. Justice Peckham in the *Lochner* case [27] and then asserts that " subsequent cases in this Court have been distinguished from that decision, but the principles therein stated have never been disapproved." [28] If all he means is that liberty of contract may still claim constitutional protection, he is correct. If he means that the flavor of the *Lochner* opinion has persisted as the flavor of Supreme Court decision and Supreme Court doctrine, he is in error. As Chief Justice Taft points out in dissenting, the *Bunting* case [29] sustained a ten-hour law of broader application than the ten-hour law annulled in the *Lochner* case and made no mention of its much-criticised predecessor. Mr. Justice Sutherland refers to the *Bunting* case and says that the law there involved " was attacked on the ground that it constituted an attempt to fix wages, but that contention was rejected and the law sustained as a reasonable regulation of hours of service." [30] The wage provision in that law was a requirement of a higher

---

[26] At p. 547.

[27] Lochner *v.* New York, 198 U. S. 45 (1905). Mr. Justice Sutherland quotes that part of Mr. Justice Peckham's opinion which says that " Statutes of the nature of that under review, limiting the hours in which grown and intelligent men may labor to earn their living, are mere meddlesome interferences with the rights of the individual . . ." He does not quote two earlier sentences, one of which is: " We do not believe in the soundness of the views which uphold this law;" and the other of which is: " This is not a question of substituting the judgment of the court for that of the legislature."

[28] At p. 550.

[29] Bunting *v.* Oregon, *supra*, note 12.

[30] At p. 550.

hourly rate for work in excess of ten hours in emergencies. As Chief Justice Taft says in dissenting,

"this was sustained as a mild penalty imposed on the employer to enforce the limitation as to hours; but it necessarily curtailed the employee's freedom to contract to work for the wages he saw fit to accept during those three hours." [31]

The cases sanctioning limitation of the hours of labor for women are dismissed by Mr. Justice Sutherland as inapposite for the added reason that they were decided before women had the vote.[32] He recognizes that the vote has not affected women physi-

---

[31] At p. 565.

[32] His statement in full is as follows (at p. 552):

"In the Muller Case the validity of an Oregon statute, forbidding the employment of any female in certain industries more than ten hours during any one day was upheld. The decision proceeded upon the theory that the difference between the sexes may justify a different rule respecting hours of labor in the case of women than in the case of men. It is pointed out that these consist in differences of physical structure, especially in respect of the maternal functions, and also in the fact that historically woman has always been dependent upon man, who has established his control by superior physical strength. The cases of Riley, Miller and Bosley follow in this respect the Muller Case. But the ancient inequality of the sexes, otherwise than physical, as suggested in the Muller Case (208 U. S. 421) has continued 'with diminishing intensity.' In view of the great — not to say revolutionary — changes which have taken place since that utterance, in the contractual, political and civil status of women, culminating in the Nineteenth Amendment, it is not unreasonable to say that these differences have now come almost, if not quite, to the vanishing point. In this aspect of the matter, while the physical differences must be recognized in appropriate cases, and legislation fixing hours or conditions of work may properly take them into account, we cannot accept the doctrine that women of mature age, *sui juris*, require or may be subjected to restrictions upon their liberty of contract which could not lawfully be imposed in the case of men under similar circumstances. To do so would be to ignore all the implications to be drawn from the present-day trend of legislation, as well as that of common thought and usage, by which woman is accorded emancipation from the old doctrine that she must be given special protection or be subjected to special restraint in her contractual and civil relationships. In passing, it may be noted that the instant statute applies in the case of a woman employer contracting with a woman employee as it does when the former is a man."

The absurdity of all this is tersely pointed out by Professor Barbara N. Grimes:

"Will the learned justices of the majority be pardoned for overlooking the cardinal fact that minimum-wage legislation is not and never was predicated upon political, contractual or civil inequalities of women? It is predicated rather upon evils to society, resulting from the exploitation of women in industry,

cally, but he thinks that it signalizes the culmination of a movement which has in other ways put them upon an equality with men and has therefore made laws affecting them subject to the same constitutional limitations as laws affecting men. Just how the Nineteenth Amendment affects the civil, political, or any other status of women in the District of Columbia, it is hard to see. Equally vexing is the implication that legislation confined to women can be less constitutional when women can vote for it than when they cannot. This seems to find some distinction between legislation that is a gracious bounty from a male electorate and legislation in the making of which women have participated with the aid of means more effective than mere mendicancy. Such an attitude invites an excursion into fields of psychology, but it may be sufficient here to point out that, whatever the psychological explanation or significance of Mr. Justice Sutherland's elucidation of the meaning of the " diminishing intensity " of the " ancient inequality of the sexes," the dominance of such an attitude in a Justice of the Supreme Court threatens the further constitutional security of some previously established standards of legislation. Those who apprehend new perils from further constitutional amendments supplementing the Nineteenth are justified in their fears, however foolish might be the adverse judicial judgments premised on new conceptions of " equality."

In connection with hours-of-labor legislation, Mr. Justice Sutherland discusses the Adamson Law and distinguishes it from minimum-wage legislation on three grounds. It involved the regulation of a business charged with a public interest; it was a temporary measure passed to meet an emergency; and it established a wage for a situation in which the parties could not or would not agree and it therefore did not, as does the minimum-wage law, forbid agreements in contravention of its standards. The third distinction is not convincing. The Adamson Law made the employer pay more wages than he would bargain to pay, and it thereby interfered with his freedom of contract quite effectively. So, too, the presence of an emergency inducing the Adamson Law should not be significant if in the case of minimum-wage

who *as a class labor under a tremendous economic handicap*. The problem is one of economic fact, not of political, contractual or civil status." See 11 CAL. L. REV. 353, 357

legislation we have a situation which is continually baneful. The fact that the burden of the Adamson Law fell primarily on enterprises subject to a restricted limitation of their net earnings is a sounder basis of distinction, but it means no more than that some corresponding justification must be found for subjecting all employers to a corresponding burden.

This concludes Mr. Justice Sutherland's discussion of the exceptional circumstances which have been held sufficient to justify restraints on freedom of contract. It shows, at most, that minimum-wage legislation presents a novel constitutional issue not settled by any precedents. It does not in any way establish that minimum-wage legislation is unconstitutional. That must be established independently. This is the concern of the remainder of the opinion, which now passes to positive reasons against the statute under review. These positive reasons are unaccompanied by any citation of precedents. Not a decision is cited in the opinion after it passes from dismissal of the precedents urged on behalf of the legislation. All that follows is the economic analysis and views of social policy of Mr. Justice Sutherland. Thus the annulment of the legislation is without support, not only from the Constitution, but also from previous interpretations thereof, except as the abstract denunciation of interference with liberty is to be taken as constitutional interpretation.

The central point of Mr. Justice Sutherland's economic and ethical objections to minimum-wage legislation is that it fixes a wage in disregard of the value of the services rendered or the benefit obtained therefrom, and therefore,

> "to the extent that the sum fixed exceeds the fair value of the services rendered, it amounts to a compulsory exaction from the employer for the support of a partially indigent person, for whose condition there rests upon him no peculiar responsibility, and therefore, in effect, arbitrarily shifts to his shoulders a burden which, if it belongs to anybody, belongs to society as a whole." [33]

Throughout the argument it is assumed that the statute, in so far as it operates at all, compels the employer to choose between charity or the abandonment of his enterprise. The option of the

---

[33] At p. 557.

employer is described as "generously leaving him, of course, the privilege of abandoning his business as an alternative for going on at a loss." [34] No mention is made of the third possibility that the employer may secure male employees not subject to the act, though this, in fact, is what the employer did in the case at bar. There is no suggestion that it would be unconstitutional to force the employer to choose between abandoning his business or paying labor what it was really worth, so that the lack of any saving grace in the option to abandon is predicated wholly on the denial of the opportunity to secure labor at a wage not in excess of its value. The choice that cannot constitutionally be forced upon the employer is that between going out of business or giving alms to those for whom he has no peculiar responsibility.

This analysis assumes some standard of what labor is worth, which may be less than what it costs some one to enable the laborer to furnish it. Nowhere does Mr. Justice Sutherland specify this standard or indicate how it is to be ascertained. Nowhere does he affirm that the value of the employee's contribution is the lowest wage that the employer could bargain for if unrestrained by law. We know that some economists, by a cycle of abstractions, have established to their own satisfaction that under "free bargaining" a laborer gets what he is worth and is worth what he gets. The proof is fascinating in its ingenuity and intricacy, but all it shows is that under free bargaining the wages paid are the wages that labor is able to get. It gives us nothing but a statement of results under given conditions. If Mr. Justice Sutherland insisted upon this as the exact measure of the contribution of labor to the joint enterprise in which it is engaged, it might be worth while to elaborate the deficiencies of the conception. It is quite plain, however, that he has something else in mind, for he says that "a statute requiring an employer . . . to pay the value of the services rendered, even to pay with fair relation to the extent of the benefit obtained from the service, would be understandable." [35] He could not, of course, suggest such a statute if he thought it merely declaratory of the *status quo* in the absence of any statute. He, therefore, must have in mind some standard of the "fair equivalent of the service ren-

---

[34] *Ibid.*

[35] At p. 559.

dered " which may be higher than the level determined by higgling and lower than the level of the cost of decent subsistence.

Further recognition that the wages received at any given time do not measure the exact contribution of the laborer is to be inferred from the qualified approval accorded to the efforts of trade organizations to raise wages.[36] It cannot seriously be thought that increase by this method is inevitably accompanied by corresponding increase in the physical quantity of the product of the factory in which the increase obtains. Lament to the contrary is abundant. Any tendency to increase the price obtainable for that product would find a counterpart in increase of wages by legislation. By implication Mr. Justice Sutherland seeks to differentiate increase by organization from increase by legislation, when he says that the latter method assumes that the employer is bound at all events to furnish it, and that it ignores the moral requirement that the wage and the work bear to each other some relation of just equivalence. In both cases, however, the employer is free to refrain from hiring; in neither case is there secured any just equivalence between wage and service except as the employer by hiring on the terms obtainable indicates that he prefers the particular bargain to none at all. The only difference is that, when the law fixes no minimum, the employer has still the possibility of securing labor from the ranks of those who may prefer to work for wages less than the cost of living rather than to continue the struggle to get something better. Minimum-wage legislation curbs the employer in the use of his bargaining power, and therefore it raises wages above the level that would be fixed by bargaining, but the bargaining and the prescription of the cost-of-living standard are alike in not being premised on " the value of the services rendered."

The invalidity of minimum-wage legislation is thus predicated

[36] " The ethical right of every worker, man or woman, to a living wage may be conceded. One of the declared and important purposes of trade organizations is to secure it. And with that principle and with every legitimate effort to realize it in fact, no one can quarrel; but the fallacy of the proposed method of attaining it is that it assumes that every employer is bound at all events to furnish it. The moral requirement implicit in every contract of employment, *viz.*, that the amount to be paid and the service to be rendered shall bear to each other some relation of just equivalence, is completely ignored." 261 U. S. 525, 558.

on its disregard of a standard that is wholly mythical. Mr. Justice Sutherland honors the myth by reiterated invocation, but he shirks completely the obvious obligation of translating the myth into something comprehensible or ascertainable. He does not contend that the cost-of-living standard necessarily exceeds his value-of-services standard, but merely that it may do so and that to the extent to which it does do so it is an arbitrary exaction. Under the precedents involving rate regulation this should invalidate only what is in excess of the assumed constitutional standard. The failure thus to draw the line may perhaps be ascribed to unconscious recognition that no such line is drawable. Though the opinion says that legislation requiring wages to correspond to the value of the services rendered would be " understandable," the decision annulling the price-regulation provisions of the Lever Act indicates that the Supreme Court would rightly hold it void for indefiniteness.[37]

Coupled with this argument that the standard of the cost of

[37] United States *v.* Cohen Grocery Co., 255 U. S. 81 (1921). See also International Harvester Co. *v.* Kentucky, 234 U. S. 216 (1914); Collins *v.* Kentucky, 234 U. S. 634 (1914); United States *v.* Pennsylvania R. R. Co., 242 U. S. 208, 237, 238 (1916). To these may be added Mr. Justice Sutherland's condemnation of the indefiniteness of the standard of the cost of living when he says, at p. 555:

" The standard furnished by the statute for the guidance of the board is so vague as to be impossible of practical application with any reasonable degree of accuracy. What is sufficient to supply the necessary cost of living for a woman worker and maintain her in good health and protect her morals is obviously not a precise or unvarying sum — not even approximately so. The amount will depend upon a variety of circumstances: the individual temperament, habits of thrift, care, ability to buy necessaries intelligently, and whether the woman live alone or with her family. To those who practice economy, a given sum will afford comfort, while to those of contrary habit the same sum will be wholly inadequate."

This complaint is not that the statute is void for failure definitely to inform the employer what he must pay, but that it is void for setting a standard so indefinite that it amounts to a delegation of legislative power to the administrative board whose findings may, in individual cases, exceed the cost of individual support. Since these are minor peccadilloes which do not go to the root of all possible minimum-wage legislation, it is sufficient to point out that they have not seemed unconstitutional to the great majority of the judges who have considered them. The significant point to make here is that the standard of the cost of living is many degrees nearer to definiteness than the standard of the value of the employee's services or the benefits derived therefrom, for disregard of which the standard of the cost of living is declared to impose a compulsory exaction upon the employer.

living may exceed the standard of the value of the services is the further assertion that the need of the employee to live in health is no concern of the employer. This assumed excess is a "compulsory exaction from the employer for the support of a partially indigent person, for whose condition there rests upon him no peculiar responsibility. . . ."[38] The basis of the standard is the "extraneous circumstance that the employee needs to get a prescribed sum of money to insure her subsistence, health and morals."[39] The "necessities of the employee . . . arise outside of the employment."[40] The statute prescribes payment "solely with relation to circumstances apart from the contract of employment."[41] There is no more justification for compelling an employer to pay on the basis of the needs of the employee than to compel a grocer to sell on the basis of the needs of the housewife. "In principle, there can be no difference between the case of selling labor and the case of selling goods."[42]

Differences in fact are obvious. A housewife who buys a can of peas from a grocer does not thereby devote to his enterprise the whole of her working hours. The nexus between grocer and customer is casual and spasmodic. Grocers are in no such position to drive hard bargains with customers as are employers to

---

[38] At p. 557.
[39] At p. 558.
[40] *Ibid.*
[41] At p. 559.
[42] At p. 558. This is followed by the elaboration:

"If one goes to the butcher, the baker or grocer to buy food, he is morally entitled to obtain the worth of his money but he is not entitled to more. If what he gets is worth what he pays he is not justified in demanding more simply because he needs more; and the shopkeeper, having dealt fairly and honestly in that transaction, is not concerned in any peculiar sense with the question of his customer's necessities. Should a statute undertake to vest in a commission power to determine the quantity of food necessary for individual support and require the shopkeeper, if he sell to the individual at all, to furnish that quantity at not more than a fixed maximum, it would undoubtedly fall before the constitutional test. The fallacy of any argument in support of the validity of such a statute would be quickly exposed. The argument in support of that now being considered is equally fallacious, though the weakness of it may not be so plain."

All that follows to make it plainer is the renewed characterization of the minimum-wage statute as one that prescribes payment without regard to the value of the services rendered and solely with relation to circumstances apart from the contract of employment.

drive hard bargains with women employees. The effect of high prices for groceries tends to bring prices down more quickly than the effect of low prices for labor tends to raise them. Only a crass legalistic formalism could fail to see the far-reaching practical differences between compelling a grocer to keep prices down to the financial capacities of some class of desiring purchasers and compelling an employer to pay employees enough to enable them to continue the labor which he desires to use. If a construction company took workmen to a remote place where the only shelter, food, and clothing were what the company would furnish, there can be little doubt that a court would sustain a statute requiring that such supplies should be adequate to decent human requirements. Under different conditions the minimum-wage law says substantially the same thing. It commands industry to be self-supporting. It predicates a vital difference between the sale of labor and the sale of goods, — a difference that cannot be obliterated by a judicial declaration that "in principle" it does not exist.

The conception that the need of the employee to live in health is "extraneous" to the employment is sufficiently answered by pointing out that only by living in health can she furnish the labor which he chooses to use. Somewhat earlier the opinion criticised the cost-of-living standard because, "while it has no other basis than the assumed necessities of the employees, it takes no account of any independent resources she may have."[43] This possibility of support from others seems much more "extraneous" to the employment than does the "assumed" necessity of the employee to live in health. Yet the idea of the opinion seems to be that somehow the Constitution entitles the employer to such benefits as he may derive from the independent resources of possible women employees. There is something sacred in his opportunity to secure all women workers for less than it costs them to live because some of them are so situated that they can continue to live and to give their full working time for a wage that is less than what such living costs. This need to live in health does, it is true, "arise outside of the employment," but it becomes a need of the employment while the employment continues. To

[43] At p. 555.

say that the responsibility of the employer is in no sense "peculiar" overlooks the fact that he alone is making use of the labor of the employee. Under a régime of slavery the master must support the slave or suffer from the ineffectiveness of his labor. The Thirteenth Amendment ended this régime; the Fourteenth Amendment seems to have substituted for it a régime in which the employer must be free from legislative restraint in getting labor for less than the cost of producing it.

To his employee-grocer analogy Mr. Justice Sutherland adds another when he says that "the power to fix high wages connotes, by like course of reasoning, the power to fix low wages." [44] Chief Justice Taft declares this to be a *non sequitur*,[45] as of course it is. Surely a little calm reflection would instill in Mr. Justice Sutherland a confidence that an approval of the minimum-wage law would not incapacitate him from distinguishing between it and a maximum-wage law. He must know that the power to limit hours of daily labor to ten does not connote, by like course of reasoning, the power to limit them to six. He himself points out that the power to fix wages on railroads does not connote the power to fix them elsewhere, and that the power to regulate rents in an emergency does not connote a general price-fixing power. This shows that he is not unaware of the Supreme Court's capacity to make distinctions of degree and to apply the test of practical results and thereby to refrain from pushing any logic or any principle beyond the limits deemed wise. How can he be sincerely apprehensive that a sanction of legislative wage-fixing according to a standard of the cost of living would compel a court to sanction a standard of twice that or of half that? A parade of the imaginary horribles of the maximum-wage law and

[44] At p. 560.

[45] "With deference to the very able opinion of the Court and my brethren who concur in it, it appears to me to exaggerate the importance of the wage term of the contract of employment as more inviolate than its other terms. Its conclusion seems influenced by the fear that the concession of the power to impose a minimum wage must carry with it a concession of the power to fix a maximum wage. This, I submit, is a *non sequitur*. A line of distinction like the one under discussion in this case is, as the opinion elsewhere admits, a matter of degree and practical experience and not of pure logic. Certainly the wide difference between prescribing a minimum wage and a maximum wage could as a matter of degree and experience be easily affirmed." 261 U. S. 525, 564.

the price-fixed grocer may be diverting, but it will leave most of the spectators quite unterrified.

Strangely enough Mr. Justice Sutherland touches but lightly upon the most serious theoretical doubts as to the wisdom of minimum-wage legislation. This is its effect on the women who cannot find employment at the statutory wage. The opinion mentions that Miss Lyons lost her job, and it declares that the reports of general good results from the operation of the statute are " interesting, but only mildly persuasive " since the improved conditions " may be, and quite probably are, due to other causes." [46] The real test " will come in periods of depression and struggle for employment when the efficient will be employed at the minimum rate while the less capable may not be employed at all." [47] The wage provision without the establishment of a corresponding standard of efficiency " must lead to ultimate failure, in accordance with the inexorable law that no one can continue indefinitely to take out more than he puts in without ultimately exhausting the supply." [48] Perhaps, too, it was the welfare of employees which prompted the statement that " the employer by paying a fair equivalent for the service rendered, though not sufficient to support the employee, has neither caused nor contributed to her poverty," but " on the contrary, to the extent of what he pays he has relieved it." [49] These, however, seem to be the only objections raised by Mr. Justice Sutherland on behalf of the interests of employees, and they are but briefly mentioned, notwithstanding the fact that the plaintiff in one of the cases was a discharged employee.

Most of these objections depend upon the unwarranted assumption of a determinable fair value of the service rendered. It is not true that no one can continue indefinitely to take out more than he puts in without ultimately exhausting the supply, even if we could determine the precise part that each puts in. All that is true is that not all can continue thus indefinitely. Wages equal to the cost of living may cause a redistribution of the several shares from a joint product without making the combined shares exceed the product. Whether one division or the other results in the extraction by one factor or another of more

[46] At p. 560.

[47] *Ibid.*

[48] At p. 557.

[49] At p. 558.

than it puts in, must remain indeterminable. Granting whatever weight should be accorded to Mr. Justice Sutherland's prophecies of inexorable ultimates, the imaginary mobility on which they are predicated takes time to realize itself in the finite, and in the meantime the minimum-wage law may avert or alleviate more evil than its long-run tendencies may promote. The theoretical possibility of injurious effects on the interests of the laboring class is not to be taken too seriously in view of the line of cleavage between those who favor and those who oppose minimum-wage legislation. Its proponents are those who are not callous toward the interest of the employees whom it affects and who are not unfamiliar with the experience under the minimum-wage laws in operation. Similar theoretical possibilities of a worm in the bud were necessarily adjudged not controlling when the Supreme Court sustained the Rent Laws.

Of course minimum-wage laws may induce a better sifting of employees, and the less efficient may suffer therefrom. If this is an evil, it is to be compared with the evil of permitting the less efficient and those with independent resources to depress the wages of others. Most minimum-wage laws make exceptions for those in some way incapacitated, and no law covers all possible remunerated toil. Concededly there are what Mr. Justice Holmes calls " interstitial detriments " in the operation of minimum-wage laws to offset some of the gains. Experience, however, may find added ways of decreasing the detriments, and always there is the possibility of legislative modification or repeal. Emergencies of business depressions should not set the standard of constitutionality but should be left for legislative treatment. It should not be necessary to establish that minimum-wage legislation is all blessing and no bane in order to save it from the condemnation of due process. According to one of Mr. Justice Sutherland's tenets, every presumption is in its favor until removed beyond a rational doubt. This has prompted, if it has not justified, the major attention here devoted to the effort to suggest rational doubts of the validity of the arguments advanced by Mr. Justice Sutherland against the presumption.

Turning to more direct argument in favor of the constitutionality of minimum-wage legislation, we find two significant analogies which Mr. Justice Sutherland overlooked in his dismissal of the precedents invoked on behalf of the statute before him. These are usury laws and statutes forbidding contracts and combinations in restraint of trade. These laws directly or indirectly restrain the bargaining power of the powerful in order to prevent them from enjoying its full economic potency. They are premised on the same need to control bargaining and competition that underlies minimum-wage legislation. Chief Justice Taft puts this analogy in the forefront of his opinion when he refers to the evils of the "sweating system," and the peculiar subjection of certain classes of employees "to the overreaching of the harsh and greedy employer."[50] This is the actual situation with which minimum-wage legislation deals. The majority do not mention it. We are left in doubt as to whether they are ignorant of it or merely emotionally obtuse to it. They dwell upon the possible harshness of the proposed remedy in compelling employers to pay employees on some basis other than the unascertainable one of the "value of the services," but they do not compare this harshness with that of leaving the situation as it stands. Their omission of the two most significant analogies in making their selected list of those to be distinguished is an oversight that seriously detracts from any confidence which their opinions or their judgment might otherwise command.

---

[50] "Legislatures in limiting freedom of contract between employee and employer by a minimum wage proceed on the assumption that employees, in the class receiving least pay, are not upon a full level of equality of choice with their employer and in their necessitous circumstances are prone to accept pretty much anything that is offered. They are peculiarly subject to the overreaching of the harsh and greedy employer. The evils of the sweating system and of the long hours and low wages which are characteristic of it are well known. Now, I agree that it is a disputable question in the field of political economy how far a statutory requirement of maximum hours or minimum wages may be a useful remedy for these evils, and whether it may not make the case of the oppressed employee worse than it was before. But it is not the function of this Court to hold congressional acts invalid simply because they are passed to carry out economic views which the Court believes to be unwise or unsound.

"Legislatures which adopt a requirement of maximum hours or minimum wages may be presumed to believe that when sweating employers are prevented from paying unduly low wages by positive law they will continue their business, abating that part of their profits, which were wrung from the necessities of their employees, and will concede the better terms required by the law; and that while in individual cases hardship may result, the restriction will enure to the benefit of the general class of employees in whose interest the law is passed and so to that of the community at large." 261 U. S. 525, 562.

The distinction between laws fixing maximum hours and laws fixing a minimum-wage, on which the majority insist,[51] is rejected by the minority.[52] Without doubt, Mr. Justice Sutherland exaggerates the importance to the employer of legal freedom to contract for lower wages after the working day is shortened. The maximum-hour law decreases the number of laboring hours without increasing the number of laborers. Manifestly the employers need at least as many laborers after the law as before. The law is not likely to make any change in the supply or demand which

---

[51] "The essential characteristics of the statute now under consideration, which differentiate it from the laws fixing hours of labor, will be made to appear as we proceed. It is sufficient now to point out that the latter, as well as the statutes mentioned under paragraph (3) [those 'prescribing the character, methods, and time for payment of wages'], deal with incidents of the employment having no necessary effect upon the heart of the contract, that is, the amount of wages to be paid and received. A law forbidding work to continue beyond a given number of hours leaves the parties free to contract about wages and thereby equalize whatever additional burdens may be imposed upon the employer as a result of the restrictions as to hours, by an adjustment in respect of the amount of wages." 261 U. S. 525, 553.

[52] Chief Justice Taft says, at p. 564:

"I regret to be at variance with the Court as to the substance of this distinction. In absolute freedom of contract the one term is as important as the other, for both enter equally into the consideration given and received, a restriction as to one is not any greater in essence than the other, and is of the same kind. One is the multiplier and the other the multiplicand.

"If it be said that long hours of labor have a more direct effect upon the health of the employee than the low wage, there is very respectable authority from close observers, disclosed in the record and in the literature of the subject quoted at length in the briefs, that they are equally harmful in this regard. Congress took this view and we cannot say it was not warranted in so doing."

To this Mr. Justice Holmes adds, at p. 569:

"I confess that I do not understand the principle on which the power to fix a minimum for the wages of women can be denied by those who admit the power to fix a maximum for their hours of work. I fully assent to the proposition that here as elsewhere the distinctions of the law are distinctions of degree, but I perceive no difference in the kind or degree of interference with liberty, the only matter with which we have any concern, between the one case and the other. The bargain is equally affected whichever half you regulate. Muller *v.* Oregon, I take it, is as good law today as it was in 1908. It will need more than the Nineteenth Amendment to convince me that there are no differences between men and women, or that legislation cannot take those differences into account. I should not hesitate to take them into account if I thought it necessary to sustain this Act. Quong Wing *v.* Kirkendall, 223 U. S. 59, 63. But after Bunting *v.* Oregon, 243 U. S. 426, I had supposed that it was not necessary, and that Lochner *v.* New York, 198 U. S. 45, would be allowed a deserved repose."

would improve the bargaining power of the employer. Without straining such analysis too far it is safe to say that hours-of-labor legislation has not been rendered painless to employers by a compensating reduction in wages. This is true also of laws affecting methods of wage payment. The cumulative effect of the precedents sustaining such legislation and the laws regulating usury and the methods of competition goes far enough to make it difficult to call minimum-wage laws an extreme further step. One can hardly doubt that a living wage is a legitimate object of legislative endeavor. The only debatable question can be the propriety of putting the burden on the employer. Mr. Justice Sutherland's efforts to dissociate the employer from the situation can hardly be called satisfactory beyond a rational doubt. It is an essential condition of industry that employees be maintained in health. To put upon industry the legal duty to pay a living wage is only to put upon it the duty of being self-sustaining. The fact that the obligation is imposed by law and not by necessity does not differentiate this obligation from any of the others that have the sheriff behind them.

As we have seen, Mr. Justice Sutherland dismisses testimony as to the good results from minimum-wage legislation by the assertion that those results are probably due to other causes. He dismisses opinion in favor of it by saying:

> "We have also been furnished with a large number of printed opinions approving the policy of the minimum wage, and our own reading has disclosed a large number to the contrary. These are all proper enough for the consideration of the lawmaking bodies, since their tendency is to establish the desirability or undesirability of the legislation; but they reflect no legitimate light upon the question of its validity, and that is what we are called upon to decide. The elucidation of that question cannot be aided by counting heads."[53]

This cannot pass without a gentle challenge. Is it not clear that the difference between Congress and Mr. Justice Sutherland is a difference of opinion as to the desirability or undesirability of minimum-wage legislation? Congress thought it so desirable that it enacted it. Thirty-five of forty-five judges who have been

53 At p. 559.

called upon to consider it thought it at least not so undesirable as to warrant the interposition of a judicial veto. Mr. Justice Sutherland and four of his colleagues on the Supreme Court are of different opinion. The importance of their opinion is that under our system of government it has, for a time at least, the casting vote. This vote was determined by the capacity for economic analysis and the views of public policy of five individuals. It is their preference which has rendered minimum-wage legislation invalid. It is not wholly true that the elucidation of the question of its validity cannot be aided by counting heads. Only because in the final vote some heads rather than others are the ones to be counted is minimum-wage legislation invalid.[54]

This determining count of five heads is duly sanctioned by our existing constitutional system. We have chosen to subject state and national legislation to the judgment of the Justices of the Supreme Court with no further advice than that they must exercise their judgment. They have from time to time laid down rules and precedents for the guidance of their judgment, but these rules and precedents they remain free to disregard. They are the arbiters. The judgments they give are their judgments; the reasons they give are their reasons. Their judgments may differ from those of the great majority of judges; their reasons may be palpably absurd. As a flagrant instance of insufficient reasons and of a judgment widely regarded as an indefensible judgment, the minimum-wage decision has few, if any, rivals. While many may doubt the long-run wisdom of minimum-wage legislation, few have been heard to approve the authoritative declaration of its constitutional invalidity. The decision has evoked a more nearly unanimous chorus of disapproval than any other decision in years. Such a chorus was to be anticipated from the preponderant judicial opinion which the decision opposed. The self-confidence which enabled five Justices of the Supreme Court to disregard that preponderant opinion is quite as significant as the economic

---

[54] Happily the rejection of Mr. Justice Sutherland's *dictum* about counting heads finds support in the observations of that wise and learned lawyer, John Selden, when under the caption of "Council" he says:

"They talk (but blasphemously enough) that the Holy Ghost is President of their General Councils, when the Truth is, the odd Man is still the Holy Ghost." SELDEN, TABLE-TALK, 141.

objections which they advance. This is why in explaining the determination of constitutional issues we must take account of the temper, as well as of the outlook, of the judges before whom the issues chance to come.

Thomas Reed Powell.

School of Jurisprudence, Univ. of California.

[14]

YALE
LAW JOURNAL

Vol. XXXVIII APRIL, 1929 No. 6

AN INSTITUTIONAL APPROACH TO THE LAW OF COMMERCIAL BANKING

UNDERHILL MOORE AND THEODORE S. HOPE, JR.

The central problem of the lawyer is the prediction of judicial and administrative decisions of government officers. For its solution he has looked to the cases recording the decisions of such officers in the past, and has made no systematic study of other data. In adopting this course, he has postulated that study of the relation between the decisions and "the facts" of recorded cases would be sufficient to enable him to formulate laws, from which he could predict future judicial and administrative behavior. His method has been in part induction, in part hypothesis and verification. He has compared the cases and attempted to classify them, in accord with similarities and dissimilarities in their facts, to abstract the common element of each class, and to correlate this common element with the decisions. Finally, the results of such correlations have been generalized into laws of judicial and administrative behavior, from which it is supposed that, if "the facts of the case" are known, future behavior of a particular judge in a particular case may be predicted.

This supposition has not been verified in experience. In a case of any novelty whatever, the lawyer in predicting judicial behavior is compelled to rely not on logical application of those laws but on an intuitional judgment based on an experience only a small part of which is those laws. In part, the character of the problem accounts for his predicament. The problem is to predict the judicial behavior of a particular judge at a particular time and place in an uncontrolled environment. If the judicial behavior of every judge in the past had been correlated with every significant element in the situation including his behavior, and had the procedure netted very precise applicable laws, yet a prediction as probable as that of the physicist predicting the result of a time-worn experiment would not be possible. For in the experiment every element not present in the prior observations is painstakingly excluded. Such exclusion is not possible in the actual behavior situations of every-day life, including that in which the particular judge is to act. This difficulty of the lawyer, it should be noted, is not the result of his not employing an experimental technique. If it were possible to observe judicial behavior under conditions which excluded all elements not at the time under observation, by the experimental method of natural science, and as a result formulate laws of judicial behavior, the lawyer would certainly be no more able to predict the reaction of a particular judge in a particular situation not under experimental control than the natural scientist is able to predict whether a particular wild perennial will bloom next year.[1]

In greater part, however, the lawyer's limited success in formulating laws of judicial behavior is probably to be accounted for by his failure to attempt to correlate judicial behavior with any events except the "facts of the case." His persistent pursuit of his laws in the "facts of the case" may be explained by the fact that the judges and administrators themselves in their opinions began quite irrelevantly and ambiguously to say that their behavior was the necessary consequence of these laws. From necessary logical deduction to necessary behavior was an easy step, and the transformation of scientific generalizations into Law was complete. Whether this new and puissant being was the daughter of God, of nature, or of the state, her will had been ascertained by correlating judicial behavior with the facts of the case, and should therefore continue to be so ascertained.

There are innumerable other facts with which official behavior

[1] "The scientist is able to determine a limited number of *laws*—that under given conditions given results will invariably follow. He is not, however, able to give a *complete* causal explanation of any phenomenon. He cannot, for example, explain completely why a certain wild rose bloomed under a certain hedge at a certain moment. In order to do this it would be necessary to begin with the formation of the material world, determine every force and measure every influence in the universe in the order of their reciprocal actions down to the present moment.

"The complete determination of the causation of any act of human behavior would be a task not less impossible than this." THOMAS AND THOMAS, THE CHILD IN AMERICA (1928) 553.

might be correlated. The lawyer's colleagues in the other sciences of human behavior have attempted to correlate behavior with "racial" traits, structure, physiological processes, psychological adjustment, "personality," intelligence, and co-existent culture. The lawyer's single-mindedness has saved us thus far from a racial jurisprudence, a neurotic jurisprudence, etc., but it has unfortunately deprived him of worthwhile scientific experience. It is proposed that he begin acquiring that experience.

It is proposed that the field of the lawyer's attention be extended to include not only the relation between judicial behavior and "the facts of the case," but also the relation between judicial behavior and institutional (frequent, repeated, usual) ways of behaving (*e.g.*, doing business) in the contemporary culture of the place where the facts happened and the decision was made. If such a relation is found to be significant, a step towards more reliable prediction will have been made. The step will have been a short step, however. What is found to be true of the culture and decisions of today may not be true of the changed culture of tomorrow. What is found to be true of the group of cases examined may not be true of any other group of cases.

"The facts" of the recorded cases classified in the traditional "legal" categories are a small, and very probably non-representative, sample of all behavior, atypical as well as typical. The cases are distinguished by dissimilarity rather than similarity one to another. Thus in order that the "legal" categories might be multitudinous of individual cases, it was necessary that their differentiating concepts be exclusive of few individual cases. In consequence, the "legal" categories are inadequate for classification, and the "legal" abstractions (which were formulated with reference to those categories) are inadequate for manipulation of conduct typical and atypical. In a study such as that proposed, therefore, it will unfortunately be necessary to disregard the "laws of judicial behavior" stated in opinions since they are formulated in terms of "legal" categories. For a like reason it will also be necessary, in a study such as that proposed, to employ a method of procedure in detail quite dissimilar to the lawyers' traditional method of procedure. There follows an elaboration of such a methodology.

I

The subject of the proposed study is human behavior. The study proposed is a systematic study. A necessary step in such a study is the differentiation and organization of fields of investigation—the choice and logical elaboration of categories and sub-categories. The behavior constituting any such field includes only one aspect of mere fragments of observed behavior. This choice of a single aspect is inescapably the process of classification. The process of classification includes the selection of organizing common factors. The field of investigation and its subdivisions are defined by the organizing common factors selected.

The object of the proposed study is the relation between the decision in a particular case and the type and degree of deviation of the behavior followed by that decision ("the facts in the case") from institutional behavior. A necessary step is comparison of the behavior followed by the decision with institutional behavior. The making of such a comparison necessitates the formulation of abstractions through the manipulation of which comparison may be made. This formulation is independent of observation within any field of investigation; the abstractions formulated presuppose the definition and selection of some field of investigation, but not the definition and selection of any particular field of investigation.

The subject-matter of any field of investigation may be considered as a class of entities possessing the common factors by which the field is defined. The subject-matter of a field of investigation whose subject-matter is behavior may be considered as a class of segments of behavior possessing the common factors by which the field is defined. A segment of behavior is a succession of events of behavior. A segment of behavior which is an entity is a succession of events of behavior in some relation with each other. The relation chosen to determine the events constituting such a segment of human behavior might have been, but was not, solely a space-time relation (*e.g.*, all events occurring *today* in *this room*). The relation chosen was rather that often crudely referred to as the relation of cause and effect, or the causal relation.[2] The greatest segment of human behavior in causal relation and possessing the common factors by which the field is defined will be referred to as a *transaction-series*. The least segment of behavior in causal relation and possessing the

---

[2] A particular event E may be said to be in causal relation with another particular event e if the likelihood that event E will be succeeded by events e, e_1, e_2, e_3, etc., at particular intervals of space and time is greater than the likelihood that it will be succeeded by other particular events.

The likelihood referred to is not an *a priori* mathematical probability. That cannot be computed since the equally likely cases cannot be enumerated. It is not an *a posteriori* statistical probability. That has not been observed. It cannot too strongly be intimated that the judgment as to likelihood which is here supposed is a qualitative subjective judgment, and not a quantitative objective judgment. The word likelihood is used in this same sense hereafter. It refers neither to the result of a mathematical inference nor to the result of a statistical observation.

common factors by which the field is defined will be referred to as a *transaction.* A transaction-series is obviously a succession of one or more transactions in causal relations with each other.

A less segment of behavior than a transaction, because more concise than a transaction, might be, for some purposes, more conveniently dealt with than a transaction. One such segment of behavior, which will be referred to as a *term in a transaction,* is defined as follows: a term in a transaction is that segment of behavior in a transaction, during which one at least of the individuals, who was an actor in the transaction at the commencement of the term, continues (without the intervention of another actor) to be an actor in the transaction. A transaction is obviously a succession of one or more terms in causal relation.

Classes of transactions may also be organized with reference to descriptive similarity (looking alike, rather than having like consequences). Such classes are defined by a generalized description of the transactions of which the class is composed. An hypothetical transaction corresponding point for point with such a generalized description is, if the class of transactions which is defined by that description is sufficiently large, referred to as a sequence. An actual transaction which would, if hypothetical, be a sequence, is referred to as a *sequential transaction.* An actual transaction-series constituted of sequential transactions is referred to as a *sequential transaction-series.*

Institutional behavior (*i.e.*, behavior which frequently, repeatedly, usually occurs) may thus be defined as a class of sequential transactions. Actually, transactions are preceded, accompanied, and followed by other transactions. Some sequential transactions may frequently succeed certain series of sequential transactions. The relation of frequently following—frequently preceding is referred to as the institutional relation. The class of transactions which satisfies the condition of being sequential transactions in institutional relation is referred to as the institution.[3] Sequences in institutional relation are referred to at as *institutional sequences.*

The institutional analogue to a transaction-series is referred to as a *sequence-series.*

Any actual transaction which does not satisfy the condition of being a sequential transaction in institutional relation is referred to as a *deviational transaction.*

The problem of comparison may now be restated as a problem

[3] Within any particular field of observed behavior the institution is found, as well as may be, by the most available means for ethnologizing a particular present day culture: interviews and observation, questionnaires, letters, reports, books, and insight.

of comparing with comparable sequence-series actual transaction-series followed by judicial behavior (*i.e.*, in causal relation with succeeding judicial behavior). It is apparent that the initial deviational transaction and succeeding transactions—which by definition are also deviational—may in any transaction-series number one, two, three, etc. It will be convenient to formulate first a method of comparison of a transaction-series which is concluded by an initial deviational transaction.

That fragment of a transaction-series which precedes the initial deviation is most comparable, since it is institutional, with an identical fragment of a sequence-series. The entire transaction-series is thus to be compared with the institutional fragment of itself plus a sequence in institutional relation therewith. That comparison will be made transaction by transaction, since it is inconvenient (if not impossible) to compare a transaction-series with a sequence-series. But such comparison need only be made between a deviational transaction and its comparable sequence. It is necessary to select a basis for choice of such a particular sequence.

An actual transaction, it will be recalled, which does not satisfy the condition of being a sequential transaction in institutional relation, is a deviational transaction. A transaction has been defined as the least segment of behavior in causal relation and possessing the common factors by which the field is defined. The deviational transaction is comparable to any sequence possessing any one of the common factors. If the deviational transaction possesses more than one common factor the sequence chosen as comparable depends upon its possessing the common factor differentiating the subdivision of the field within which the transaction for the time being is under observation.

It will now be possible to formulate a method of comparison of a transaction-series which includes two deviational transactions.

The rule for choice of a sequence comparable to any initial deviational transaction is identically the rule for choice of a sequence comparable to a single deviational transaction. The rule for choice of a sequence comparable to a second deviational transaction is in part identically the rule for choice of a sequence comparable to any initial deviational comparison. One comparison is made with a sequence chosen in accordance with that rule. A second comparison is also made. This second comparison is made with a sequence in institutional relation with the sequence comparable to the initial deviational transaction preceded by the institutional fragment of the transaction-series. In making this comparison the sequence comparable to the initial deviational transaction is substituted for that transaction in the transaction-series.[4]

The method of comparison of an initial or any succeeding deviational transaction with its comparable sequence is to observe (1) the degree by which the prior terms in the deviational transaction deviate from the correlative terms in the comparable sequence, and (2) the degree by which the concluding terms in the deviational transaction deviate from the correlative terms of the comparable sequence.

The degree by which the prior terms in the deviational transaction deviate from the correlative terms of the comparable sequence is observed by supposing the concluding terms of the deviational transaction to be the same as the concluding terms of the comparable sequence. In this way it is hoped that it will be possible to compare a deviational transaction and its comparable sequence as possibly alternative devices for obtaining the same result.

The degree by which the concluding terms in the deviational transaction deviate from the correlative terms of the comparable sequence is observed by supposing the prior terms in the deviational transaction to be the same as the correlative terms in the comparable sequence. By this assumption it is intended to confine this second comparison to a comparison of ends, in the same way as the first comparison was confined to a comparison of means.

II

It is now pertinent to define the particular field of investigation in which it is proposed that this method should be applied, and exemplify its application in that field. The field can best be defined by stating the common factors which differentiate from other behavior the behavior constituting the field of investigation, and describing the behavior so differentiated.

Implicit in the choice of the common factors is the concept of

[4] This rule for comparison of a second deviational transaction with two possibly different sequences results from an hypothesis that it is to the highest degree likely that the judicial behavior following the transaction-series will be either the same as it would have been if instead of the initial deviational transaction an institutional transaction had occurred; or the same as it would have been if instead of the initial deviational transaction nothing had occurred; and that whether it is the one or the other may depend in large measure upon the degree of deviation of the initial deviational transaction.

An obvious extension of this hypothesis to the case of a third deviational transaction requires comparison of such a transaction with four possibly different sequences; of an nth deviational transaction with 2^{n-1} possibly different sequences. Fortunately all the possibilities of difference are seldom realized.

deposit currency. This concept is derived from certain transactions between a commercial bank and some other individual or group of individuals.

Deposit currency is but one among many forms of commercial bank credit; it is credit on the current checking account. Deposit currency of a particular bank in favor of a particular customer exists in the amount of the balance of the current checking account of that customer with that bank. The term balance is here used in a special sense, to refer to the *amount of deposit currency of a particular customer.* The balance may be described as the limiting amount up to which checks are likely to be drawn by the customer and honored by the bank. This description is obviously incomplete; nevertheless, it sufficiently approximates a description which to be exhaustive would of necessity enumerate many other sorts of behavior.

Deposit currency of a particular customer is created when the balance of that customer increases. Deposit currency of a particular customer is extinguished when the balance of that customer decreases. Deposit currency of a particular customer is transferred when the balance of that customer decreases and the balance of another customer (the transferee) of the same or another bank increases. Accounts between, for example, buyers and sellers are liquidated when it becomes unlikely that thereafter payment will be either demanded or offered.

The field of investigation is constituted of transactions which have either resulted in the creation of deposit currency, the extinguishment of deposit currency, the transfer of deposit currency, the liquidation of accounts by means of transfer of deposit currency, or which have created a likelihood that one or another such result would follow but, without any such result, have terminated by its becoming no longer likely.

The field of investigation is divided into four main subdivisions. A transaction may fall within more than one subdivision. As between some subdivisions this is obviously true; it could readily be shown to be true as among any subdivisions. If a particular transaction falls in more than one subdivision, in each of those subdivisions particular attention is paid only to that aspect of the transaction which brings it within that subdivision.

(a) The first subdivision includes transactions which have resulted in the creation of deposit currency, or which have created a likelihood that deposit currency would be created but, without its being created, have terminated by its becoming no longer likely that deposit currency would be created.

(b) The second subdivision includes transactions which have resulted in the extinguishment of deposit currency, or which have created a likelihood that deposit currency would be extinguished but, without its being extinguished, have terminated by its becoming no longer likely that deposit currency would be extinguished.

(c) The third subdivision includes transactions which have resulted in the transfer of deposit currency, or which have created a likelihood that deposit currency would be transferred but, without its being so transferred, have terminated by its becoming no longer likely that deposit currency would be transferred.

(d) The fourth subdivision includes transactions which have resulted in the liquidation of accounts by means of the transfer of deposit currency, or which have created a likelihood that accounts would so be liquidated but, without their being so liquidated, have terminated by its becoming no longer likely that accounts would be so liquidated.

Application of the method of comparison will be exemplified for some of these subdivisions.

Consider the following transaction-series:

(1) Let it be assumed that the *A* corporation, a customer of the *B* bank, has a balance of $10,000 with that bank.[5] Behavior occurs on the part of appropriate officers of the customer and appropriate bank officials which may be synopsised as follows: the *A* corporation and the *B* bank agree that upon the happening of a named contingency the *A* corporation shall offer and the *B* bank accept for discount at six per cent the *A* corporation's ninety-day note for $10,000 secured by mortgage on its fixtures and stock-in-trade, and that its account shall thereupon be credited with the proceeds of the discount. Upon the happening of the contingency the *A* corporation tenders its note and mortgage; the bank rejects the tender and the *A* corporation is compelled to borrow in the open market at the then market rate of nine per cent. The *A* corporation now sues the bank for $75, three-fourths of one per cent of $10,000.

(2) Let it be assumed that *A*, a customer of the *B* bank, has a balance of $10,000 with that bank. Behavior occurs on the part of the customer and appropriate bank officials which may be synopsised as follows: *A* signs ten instruments in form promissory notes payable to the order of the *B* bank, each in the amount of $1,000, with the space for the date left blank, and hands them to the appropriate bank officials; it is agreed that if a check of *A* is presented for payment for an amount in

[5] This form of statement is obviously elliptical. When it is said that *A*'s balance is $10,000, nothing is said about the order or amount of the past transactions between *A* and his bank. What is said is that whatever they may have been they have been in institutional relation with each other, and that the drawing and honoring of a check for $10,000 would be in institutional relation with the last of them.

excess of his then balance as it appears on the books of the bank, the check shall not be dishonored, but the then date shall be inserted in one of these notes, it shall forthwith be discounted at the rate of six per cent, and the proceeds credited to *A*'s account. *A* then draws his check for $10,500 payable to *C*'s order and hands it to *C*, who indorses it and deposits it to the credit of his account with the *D* bank of which he is a customer. The *D* bank presents the check to the *B* bank through the clearing-house. The *B* bank sends it back marked "insufficient funds." *A* now sues the bank for damages for the dishonor of this check.

(3) Let it be assumed that *A*, a customer of the *B* bank, has a balance of $10,000 with that bank. At the bank offices and during banking hours he orally requests of the paying teller that he pay him the sum of $500. The paying teller refuses to comply with the request, and *A* sues the *B* bank for the amount of $500.

(4) Let it be assumed that *A*, a customer of the *B* bank, has a balance of $10,000 with that bank. He draws his check for $1,000 payable to the order of *C*, who indorses it and deposits it to the credit of his account with the *D* bank, of which he is a customer. The *D* bank presents the check to the *B* bank through the clearing house. The *B* bank sends it back marked "insufficient funds." The *D* bank now sues the *B* bank for $1,000, the amount of the check.

As to each of these transaction-series, it has already been assumed that that part of the series symbolized in the words "Balance $10,000" has been institutional. As to each of these series let it also be assumed that succeeding transactions are deviational.

In making the comparison, the following notational system will be employed:

Double lines (||, //) to indicate the end of a transaction or sequence. Vertical double lines (||) to indicate the end of a sequential transaction in institutional relation, or of an institutional sequence. Oblique double lines (//) to indicate the end of a deviational transaction. A vertical single line (|) to indicate the end of a term in a transaction or sequence.

(1) The assumed transaction-series numbered (1) may, in symbolic notation, be expressed as follows:

ᵀBal. $10,000 || Agreement to lend $10,000 | Note for $10,000 offered for discount | Rejected //

It will be observed that the series is concluded by an initial deviational transaction. That transaction is within the field of investigation, and within the first main subdivision of that field (the "creation subdivision") ; initially, it became likely that deposit currency would be created by subsequent discount of the customer's note; when the note was refused to be discounted that likelihood ceased.

The transaction, then, is comparable to a sequence in institutional relation with the transactions symbolized by "Balance $10,000" and chosen from the "creation" subdivision of the field of investigation. There may be many such sequences. Among them may be, for example, the deposit of currency, the offering for discount of the customer's note and its refusal, the offering for discount of the customer's note and its acceptance for discount. If these be assumed to be such sequences, and it be further assumed that "agreements to lend" such as the one assumed for this transaction-series, performed as well as unperformed, are in this particular community deviational, the particular sequence for comparison may be chosen from among these three sequences. The particular sequence chosen for comparison is the last of these three sequences. Implicit in this choice is the judgment that the sequence chosen is more similar to the transaction than other possible sequences; in other words, that the transaction to be compared is most nearly identical with the transactions typified by the sequence chosen for comparison in respect of likely following transactions.

It will be recalled that the first comparison is made by substituting for the concluding terms of the transaction the correlative terms of the comparable sequence. The transaction, so modified, and its comparable sequence are, in symbolic notation, expressed as follows:

IA { ^{T}Bal. $10,000 || Agreement to lend $10,000 | Note for $10,000 offered for discount | Accepted //
^{S}Bal. $10,000 || Note for $10,000 offered for discount | Accepted ||

The degree of deviation should be measured in accordance with the rules hereafter stated.

It will also be recalled that second comparison is made by substituting for the prior terms of the transaction the correlative terms of the comparable sequence. The transaction, so modified, and the comparable sequence are, in symbolic notation, expressed as follows:

IB { ^{S}Bal. $10,000 || Note for $10,000 offered for discount | Accepted ||
^{T}Bal. $10,000 || Note for $10,000 offered for discount | Rejected //

No rules for measurement of the degree of deviation of the concluding terms of a deviational transaction from the correlative terms of its comparable sequence have as yet been formulated. The concluding terms of the deviational transactions in this and the succeeding exemplary comparisons seem to be either identical with, or logically opposite to, the correlative terms of the comparable sequence. Apparently the statement that they are either identical or logically opposite is itself a measurement of the degree of deviation.

(2) The assumed transaction-series numbered (2) may, in symbolic notation, be expressed as follows:

^{T}Bal. $10,000 || Offer of "overdraft agreement" for $10,000 with notes of customer | Accepted // Check for $10,500 to payee | Payee to his bank | Presented through clearing-house | Dishonored //

It will be observed that the initial deviational transaction is followed by a second deviational transaction.

The initial deviational transaction is within the "creation" subdivision of the field of investigation. It is comparable to the sequence which is expressed in symbolic notation as follows:

^{S}Bal. $10,000 || Note for $10,000 offered for discount | Accepted ||

It will be recalled that two comparisons of a transaction with a comparable sequence are made.

The first comparison of the initial deviational transaction is made by substituting for the concluding terms of the transaction the correlative terms of the comparable sequence. The transaction, in this instance, remains unmodified after such substitution. The transaction and its comparable sequence are, in symbolic notation, expressed as follows:

IA	^{T}Bal. $10,000 ||	Offer of "overdraft agreement" for $10,000 with notes of customer	| Accepted //
	^{S}Bal. $10,000 ||	Note for $10,000 offered for discount	| Accepted ||

The degree of deviation should be measured in accordance with the rules hereafter stated.

The second comparison of the initial deviational transaction is made by substituting for the prior terms of the transaction, the correlative terms of the comparable sequence. The transaction, so modified, and the comparable sequence are, in symbolic notation expressed as follows:

IB	^{T}Bal. $10,000 || Note for $10,000 offered for discount | Accepted //
	^{S}Bal. $10,000 || Note for $10,000 offered for discount | Accepted ||

The second deviational transaction is to be compared successively with two comparable sequences. It will be recalled that the first comparison was to be made with a sequence chosen by identically the rule by which a sequence comparable to an initial deviation is chosen. The comparable sequence, chosen by that rule, is, in symbolic notation:

[S]Bal. $10,0000 ||	**Check for $10,000 to payee |**	**Payee to his bank |**	**Presented through clearing-house |**	**Paid ||**

The first comparison of the second deviational transaction with its first comparable sequence is made by substituting for the concluding terms of the transaction the correlative terms of the comparable sequence. The transaction, so modified, and its comparable sequence are, in symbolic notation, expressed as follows:

II A	[T]Bal. $10,000 ||	Check for $10,500 to payee |	Payee to his bank |	Presented through clearing-house |	Paid //
	[S]Bal. $10,000 ||	Check for $10,000 to payee |	Payee to his bank |	Presented through clearing-house |	Paid ||

The degree of deviation should be measured in accordance with the rules hereafter stated.

The second comparison of the second deviational transaction with its first comparable sequence is made by substituting for the prior terms of the transaction the correlative terms of the comparable sequence. The transaction, so modified, and its comparable sequence are, in symbolic notation, expressed as follows:

II B	[T]Bal. $10,000 ||	Check for $10,000 to payee |	Payee to his bank |	Presented through clearing-house |	Dis-honored //
	[S]Bal. $10,000 ||	Check for $10,000 to payee |	Payee to his bank |	Presented through clearing-house |	Paid ||

The second deviational transaction is to be compared, also, with a sequence in institutional relation with the sequence comparable to the initial deviational transaction preceded by "Bal. $10,000." The comparison is to be made by substituting in the transaction-series its comparable sequence for the initial deviational transaction. In symbolic notation, the transaction-series, so modified, and its comparable sequence-series may be expressed as follows:

II C	[T]Bal. $10,000 || Note for $10,000 offered for discount | Accepted // Check for $10,500 to payee | Payee to his bank | Presented through clearing-house | Dishonored //
	[S]Bal. $10,000 || Note for $10,000 offered for discount | Accepted || Check for $10,500 to payee | Payee to his bank | Presented through clearing-house | Paid ||

The first comparison of the second deviational transaction with its second comparable sequence is made by substituting for the concluding terms of the transaction the correlative terms of the comparable sequence. The transaction, so modified, and its comparable sequence are, in symbolic notation, expressed as follows:

III A
^{T}Bal. $10,000 || Note for $10,000 offered for discount | Accepted // Check for $10,500 to payee | Payee to his bank | Presented through clearing-house | Paid //
^{S}Bal. $10,000 || Note for $10,000 offered for discount | Accepted || Check for $10,500 to payee | Payee to his bank | Presented through clearing-house | Paid ||

Obviously the terms to be compared are identical. A measurement of the degree of deviation is implicit in this statement.

The second comparison of the second deviational transaction with its second comparable sequence is made by substituting for the prior terms of the transaction the correlative terms of the comparable sequence. The transaction, in this instance, remains unmodified after such substitution. The transaction and its comparable sequence are, in symbolic notation, expressed as follows:

III B
^{T}Bal. $10,000 || Note for $10,000 offered for discount | Accepted // Check for $10,500 to payee | Payee to his bank | Presented through clearing-house | Dishonored //
^{S}Bal. $10,000 || Note for $10,000 offered for discount | Accepted || Check for $10,500 to payee | Payee to his bank | Presented through clearing-house | Paid ||

(3) The assumed transaction-series numbered (3) may, in symbolic notation, be expressed as follows:

^{T}Bal. $10,000 || Oral order for $500 | Dishonored //

It will be observed that it is concluded by an initial deviational transaction. That transaction is within the "extinguishment" subdivision of the field of investigation. It is comparable to the sequence which is expressed in symbolic notation as follows:

^{S}Bal. $10,000 || Counter check for $500 | Paid ||

The first comparison is made by substituting for the concluding terms of the transaction the correlative terms of the comparable sequence. The transaction, so modified, and its comparable sequence are, in symbolic notation, expressed as follows:

I A
^{T}Bal. $10,000 || Oral order for $500 | Paid //
^{S}Bal. $10,000 || Check for $500 | Paid ||

The degree of deviation should be measured in accordance with the rules hereafter stated.

The second comparison is made by substituting for the prior terms of the transaction the correlative terms of the comparable sequence. The transaction, so modified, and its comparable sequence are, in symbolic notation, expressed as follows:

I B { ^{T}Bal. $10,000 || Check for $500 | Dishonored //
^{S}Bal. $10,000 || Check for $500 | Paid ||

(4) The assumed transaction-series numbered (4) may, in symbolic notation, be expressed as follows:

^{T}Bal. $10,000 || Check for $1,000 to payee | Payee to his bank | Presented through clearing-house | Dishonored //

It will be observed that it is concluded by an initial deviational transaction. That transaction is within the "transfer" subdivision of the field of investigation. It is comparable to the sequence which is expressed in symbolic notation as follows:

^{S}Bal. $10,000 || Check for $1,000 to payee | Payee to his bank | Presented through clearing-house | Paid ||

The first comparison is made by substituting for the concluding terms of the transaction the correlative terms of the comparable sequence. The transaction, so modified, and its comparable sequence are, in symbolic notation, expressed as follows:

I A { ^{T}Bal. $10,000 || Check for $1,000 to payee | Payee to his bank | Presented through clearing-house | Paid //
^{S}Bal. $10,000 || Check for $1,000 to payee | Payee to his bank | Presented through clearing-house | Paid ||

Obviously the terms to be compared are identical. A measurement of the degree of deviation is implicit in this statement.

The second comparison is made by substituting for the prior terms of the transaction the correlative terms of the comparable sequence. The transaction, in this instance, remains unmodified after such substitution. The transaction and its comparable sequence are, in symbolic notation, expressed as follows:

I B { ^{T}Bal. $10,000 || Check for $1,000 to payee | Payee to his bank | Presented through clearing-house | Dishonored //
^{S}Bal. $10,000 || Check for $1,000 to payee | Payee to his bank | Presented through clearing-house | Paid ||

The method proposed for the measurement of degrees of deviation within the field of deposit currency will now be stated. There is observable within this field a high degree of correlation between those courses of behavior which are most profitable and those which are institutional. Profitableness may thus be considered a constant factor in banking institutional transactions.

There is also, because of the manner in which the abstraction, or institution, was derived, a high degree of correlation between those courses of behavior which frequently are followed and those which are institutional. So that a high frequency of occurrences may be considered also a constant factor in banking institutional transactions. It seems, then, not unreasonable to make the comparison in terms of these two factors: profitableness and familiarity.

Profitableness of a particular transaction is, it will be observed, a complex of four variables: gross return, joint cost, severable cost, losses. Given a perfected statistical method, and ideal conditions for its application, neither the joint cost of a particular transaction, nor in many cases its gross return, can be measured. Since the transaction and its comparable sequence are assumed to have a like conclusion, these factors are equal for each and may be disregarded. It need only be pointed out that since net profit of a particular transaction is the sum rather than the product of these four factors, any ratio composed of only the last two of them (severable cost, losses) for a particular transaction and its comparable sequence will indicate rather than express the ratio between the profitableness of the transaction and the profitableness of the comparable sequence.

A further analysis of these two factors can now be made. A transaction requires a certain expenditure of labor and materials to bring it to a successful conclusion (*i.e.*, to a conclusion conforming to the sequence). This may arbitrarily be called the efficiency of the transaction. This may be derived both for a successful transaction and its comparable sequence. But not all transactions, even those *otherwise* formally corresponding to a sequence, are in this sense successful. The ratio between the total number of transactions of a particular type (whether sequential or not) and the number of successful transactions of that type may be referred to as the certainty of such transactions. Since the unsuccessful transactions require approximately the same expenditure as the successful transactions, yet bring in no return, their cost must be borne by the successful transactions. Thus the severable cost of a transaction is equal to the product of its efficiency and certainty.

Similarly, what would be expressed as losses when dealing with a number of transactions are expressed as risks when dealing with a single transaction. A risk is simply an expression of the ratio between the number of transactions of a particular type in which a certain sort of loss occurs and the total number of transactions of that type. These risks may be classified in five main types. These can best be indicated by exemplification. Take the simple case of payment of a counter check. If the bank becomes involved in a dispute with its customer it may lose the amount of the check. This is called the risk of direct loss. It may have to expend money to prevent loss of the amount of the check. This is called the risk of collection expense. It may lose the good will of the customer or of others through being involved in dispute. This is called the risk of loss of good will. It may in the same way find its credit standing impaired. This is called the risk of loss of credit. Or, finally, if it becomes involved in litigation, it may find the judge and/or jury deciding not in accordance with the facts. This is called the juridical risk.

The risks incurred by the bank have been taken as exemplary. Like risks may be incurred by each actor in a transaction.

The following table recapitulates the "units" of measurement and is exemplary of the application of the method to the oral order appearing in one of the transaction-series which have been considered. The weighting of the several "units," it should be noted, is hypothetical.

		Oral Order	
		Factors of slight dissimilarity to the institution	Factors of gross dissimilarity to the institution
	Efficiency		5
	Certainty	5	
	Familiarity	5	
To the bank	Risk of direct loss	1	
	Risk of collection expense	1	
	Risk of injury to credit		1
	Risk of loss of good will	1	
	Juridical risk	1	
To the customer	Risk of direct loss	1	
	Risk of collection expense	1	
	Risk of injury to credit		1
	Risk of loss of good will		1
	Juridical risk	1	
	Total	17	8

By the application of the proposed methods of comparison and measurement to "the facts" of a decided case, the correlation between the decision and the measured degree of deviation between "the facts" and the institution can be stated. After the method has been applied to large numbers of cases in many fields it may be possible to state "laws" for some fields in terms of that correlation. Since the institution, if any, may be objectively determined and the degree of deviation between it and the particular transaction-series may be measured approximately, if such "laws" can be stated, their utility in prediction is apparent.

[15]

NEW YORK UNIVERSITY
LAW QUARTERLY REVIEW

VOL. XV | JANUARY, 1938 | No. 2

THROUGH TITLE TO CONTRACT AND A BIT BEYOND*

K. N. LLEWELLYN

THE law of Sales, as is well known, is in one phase part of the law of contract, in another phase part of the law of property.

KARL NICKERSON LLEWELLYN is Betts Professor of Jurisprudence at Columbia University. This paper is a corrected version of the paper originally printed in 3 LAW—A CENTURY OF PROGRESS (1937) 80 *ff*.

*References to "Act," "the Act," or to mere section numbers are to the Uniform Sales Act. References to "Williston" are to his SALES (2d ed. 1924).

A major indebtedness for help during the preparation of this paper (help not only in chasing or searching books, but in testing or suggesting ideas) runs to Henry Harfield, and especially to Soia Mentschikoff. Essays and research of other students, past and present, are noted where I am conscious of the debt; sometimes one absorbs, forgetting the source; and memory has a statute of limitations of its own. No less obvious is the obligation to Underhill Moore's thinking in the field, and, especially in the companion papers, to the most challenging material on our Sales law which I have seen in print: that from Nathan Isaacs' pen. The debt to Emma Corstvet's detailed critique and correction is not obvious, because its results have been worked into every portion of the paper.

I should make clear that this paper, unlike its companions, undertakes no exploration of unfamiliar material. It relies heavily on my CASES AND MATERIALS ON SALES (1930), seeking to put together and expand much that is suggested in scattered portions of that book. Its aim is exploration rather of the possibilities of reweighing and realignment of cases and an Act which have grown so familiar that their meaning pales. For this I have no apology to make. Year by year, I find cases and statutory sections already taught ten or fifteen times taking new color, new light, indeed new shape, if one can forget how they looked last year and read them as if they were new. One should not, indeed, rest content with familiar cases alone; but it is worth-while putting down the things that they have come to mean. And it is gratifying to discover the extent to which the Merchants' Association of N. Y. has been thinking along similar lines. See App. to the version of this paper printed 3 LAW—A CENTURY OF PROGRESS, 80, at 108 ff.; *infra* p. 206.

Another point needs note. I have tried, in dealing with the cases, to keep in mind place and time. But even crucial cases are of two sorts. There are those which, a century ago, settled a then moot point in apparently permanent fashion, and whose underlying policy is as solid now as then. There are others which rested on shifting sands of condition and of policy. Such an issue as warranty to consumer, for instance, is still in violent flux, and a case may be outdated even within a decade. On the other hand, Bramwell's announcement of buyer's option in 1859, or Blackburn's approach to risk of loss, is still prophetic. When, in this paper, doctrine spread over long time-stretches is compressed into a single doctrinal plane, that compression represents my *deliberate* judgment that the *particular* older cases concerned *deserve* to be treated as modern.

But I cannot say the same about the throwing together of cases from different jurisdictions. Occasionally such throwing together does represent deliberate judgment that the full backgrounds in the jurisdictions concerned are really and significantly alike. *Very* occasionally. More often, such throwing together represents acquiescence, for the moment, in the convention that there is *an* American law of Sales and contracts. All of us know that in any jurisdiction which has decided any point there has practically ceased to be an *American* common law on that

It is one thesis of this paper and its companions[1] that in both these phases our prevailing theory has come to overstress heavily the importance of *assent*, in Sales law, whether such theory be regarded as a tool for describing the results of the cases, or as a tool for guiding decision into wise channels, or both. It is a second thesis that the concepts in vogue in Sales law are repeatedly overbroad for intelligent use (so notably the concept Title, or Seller, or Purchase for Value); but that those concepts are at other times too narrow for intelligent use (so the American concept of Action for the Price).[2] The key both to perception and diagnosis of these

point; there is instead the common law of Minnesota or of Washington. The convention of the writers persists, I take it, partly for business reasons: single-state lawbooks have not the market that "national" lawbooks have. And partly for reasons of inertia: it just takes too much time to get the requisite background, state by state. Partly, however, the convention foots on fact: The common lake of American decisions *is* a place to pump from when there is no water in any particular jurisdiction. But that is no reason for following the convention without detailed examination of its justification in the particular instance. It may be an excuse, but a first-year student knows that excuse is not performance. The present paper sins on this point; it has not the excuse of ignorance of the sin; it offers instead a fighting position: it is devoted to a critique of general doctrine and approach, and so must rest on the type of material out of which general doctrine and approach have grown. For there is at least this common factor in our "common law": Ideas and approaches to problems cross state lines even when precedent on particular points does not. Indeed, a new *common* law of Sales may be in process of reëmergence, today, among the states—see *Warranty, II* (1937) 37 Col. L. Rev. 341, 381. But as appears in the text, it is destined to heavy subdivision and specialization in its application to persons.

If I were permitted, I should inscribe this essay, like its fellows, to Thomas Edward Scrutton—who for reasons of personality as well as circumstance has no such sin upon his scroll.

[1]*On Warranty of Quality and Society* (1936) 36 Col. L. Rev. 699, and 37 *id.*, 341, also revised under the title *Courts, Quality of Goods and A Credit Economy* and printed together with the third one, *Purchase for Value and the Course of Trade*, and this paper, in *Sales, Law and Society* (to appear).

[2]Title and Action for the Price will be discussed below. In the Act, Seller, as such, is opposed to Buyer, as such. Waite, *Retail Responsibility and Judicial Law Making* (1936) 34 Mich. L. Rev. 494, effectively challenges the lumping of all sellers, especially as to warranty of fitness in the case of food and drink, when he goes into study of the small retailer's peculiar position; and insists also on the consumer-buyer as a separate category. My own attack would be to broaden "food" into "articles for family—even factory—use" or the like, and to split "retailer" still further, into petty, and large (department store; chain store). See Note (1937) 37 Col. L. Rev. 77. But differences of judgment as to which categories may be significant do not alter our agreement on the more vital point: that the mere category "Seller" does not suffice to meet our needs. Isaacs' insistence on the marketing organization cuts into the "Seller" concept indirectly: In point of work done and ends sought and *business* (as distinct from legal) rights and duties, he sees Seller and sale merging into Principal and agency, etc. Isaacs, *Agents and Agencies* (1925) 3 Harv. Bus. Rev. 265; *Business Security and Legal Security* (1923) 37 Harv. L. Rev. 201. And peculiarly fruitful (compare my *Purchase for Value and the Course of Trade*) is his sustained demonstration that "Buyer" is a concept which no less needs subdivision of investigation, and often, in consequence, of rule. From the individual or family consumer who is Waite's concern, *supra*, Isaacs distinguishes

ills and to their cure lies, it will be argued, in examination of the fact-situations to which the concepts are applied and of the results of the application. It is a third thesis that again and again, in the history of Sales law, illuminating ideas have been worked out, only to be ignored, or jettisoned, or overwhelmed by less adequate ideology; they are not yet made into standard tools for systematic use, available and availed of whenever and wherever needed. It is time we took thought about such a misfortune and turned to the work of salvage, if Sales law and its relation both to contract law and to effective guidance of decision have any importance to our legal system.[3] The three papers together can only scratch the surface of these phenomena, for the latter pervade every aspect of the field which I have explored and signal their presence in every aspect which I have even visited on tour. The papers do, however, attempt to demonstrate the existence of the phenomena in sufficient quantity and variety to force a challenge, warrant a protest, and suggest the way for study and reform.[4]

Finally, the three papers represent a personal faith and an

The Dealer-Purchaser (1927) 1 U. of Cin. L. Rev. 373, and the industrial purchaser, *The Industrial Purchaser and the Sales Act* (1934) 34 Col. L. Rev. 262. Isaacs does not convince me that the Act requires change, as distinct from careful recanvassing, in all the points raised. *E.g.*, the "reliance" test of 15(1) seems to me to take care of preventing seller's liability where an industrial buyer lays down precise specifications. *Cf.* the division of the court in the borderline case of Dunbar Bros. v. Consolidated Iron-Steel Mfg. Co., 23 F. (2d) 416 (C.C.A. 2d, 1928). But Isaacs' hammer not only hits nails, but finds unsuspected nails to hit, of which not the least is this: The subdivision of *Seller* need not *match* the subdivision of *Buyer*. It will be noted that Isaacs' emphasis is on that outfit which distributes goods consumer-wards—whether it appear in the particular situation as "seller" or as assembler of raws or of partially manufactured articles or of completed articles made for its brand. On the various Warranty concepts, see the one companion paper; on subdividing Purchase for Value, the other. Also Isaacs, 8 Am. L. S. Rev. 424 (1936).

[3]Throughout the history of modern Sales doctrine (which can hardly be conceived as beginning before Mansfield) it has been contributing to and borrowing from the contract doctrine of the time being. Compare the effect of concurrent conditions on action for the price, *infra*, note 27. Throughout the same history it has been living whenever it chose in hermitlike isolation. Compare the rejection, in the Act, of the New York price rule—which was a *contract* rule. Until we learn the detailed history of both the neighborliness and its reverse, we shall remain ignorant of doctrine in both fields, and hampered in either developing or reforming it. For a beginning, *cf. Warranty* (1936), 36 Col. L. Rev. 701, 726, 731, 743; 37 *id.* 341, *passim*.

[4]There has also been some effort, in both companion papers, to inquire into what may be the reasons for things so unpleasant and perplexing; in that aspect those papers branch out into what may be considered sociology of law or the nature of legal thinking (at least in our system), and may raise the question how far similar things occur in other fields of our law. Here the analytical job is complex enough to force concentration on the results, as distinct from the causes of their being reached.

attempt to justify it—the faith: that a realist's interest in fact, and in the meaning of people to law and of law to people, in no measure impairs interest on his part for better law.[5] The present jobs

[5]I cannot understand the difficulty found by the realists' critics in perceiving this, unless it be that the more general programmatic or controversial writings obscure those writings which really test the realist pudding; to wit, the monographic work in a specialized area, which either paves the way for better law or presents some portion of a way out. That the misconception is prevalent, see Pound, *The Call for a Realist Jurisprudence* (1931) 44 HARV. L. REV. 697, 700: "Faithful portrayal of what courts and law makers and jurists do is not the whole task of a science of law. One of the conspicuous actualities of the legal order is the impossibility of divorcing what they do from the question what they ought to do or what they feel they ought to do," but especially the queer blindness or wilful perversity of his *The Future of Law* (1937) 47 YALE L. J. 1, in regard to the views of uncited and unnamed persons. E.g. (p. 2, italics mine): "In the same spirit *the realists of the moment,* as they call themselves, tell us that it is *all no more than* a matter of what those who wield the authority of political organized society *choose* to do. What they do is law because they do it. . . . All this *is a complete negation* [of something or other.] It *throws over* the ideas of the classical Roman jurists, as well as those of the classical jurists of the modern world, *and rejects the conception of a government ruling according to law.*" These are bold allegations to trumpet forth without evidence, when all those known at the moment to call themselves realists talk, write, and act in denial of "all no more than," and in denial of complete negation of anything other than the total *sufficiency* of any view of law which fails *to take account of* aberrant or non-regular official behavior.

More moderately: Fuller, *American Legal Realism* (1934) 82 U. OF PA. L. REV. 429, 461: ". . . the cleft between Is and Ought causes acute distress to the realist. He sets about resolutely to eliminate it. There are two ways in which this may be done. The Is may be compelled to conform to the Ought, or the Ought may be permitted to acquiesce in the Is. . . ." And at p. 452: "At the other extreme is the view that 'society' is the active principle and that 'law' is simply a function of this principle . . . Llewellyn seems to me to place himself in this class." Cohen, *Justice Holmes and the Nature of Law* (1931) 31 COL. L. REV. 352, 357: "Many, however, of those who, like Holmes, reject the old confusion between law and morality, ignore his cautious qualifications and profess to do away altogether with the normative point of view in law. They make law synonymous with what people actually do, i.e., with social behavior." Or at 360: "It is the essence of positivism to view the law exclusively as uniformities of existing behavior, in total disregard of any ideals as to what should be." There are other passages from all three of the above which indicate appreciation of the values, so heavily insisted on by realists, of trying to get at the facts of lawmen's interaction with laymen; all three have, indeed, themselves contributed much to such attempts. The misconception lies in conceiving that any one thinks facts are *all* that jurisprudence is concerned with, merely because he cries out for needed facts or in a particular preliminary study tries to report facts as objectively as possible; or that any one conceives that all law has to do is to *follow* society because in a *particular* instance under discussion the following of society is urged to be the adjustment needed. For instance, one could argue vigorously in favor of the sane rule allowing the holder of a check time to present it through regular banking channels as determined by banking practice in his own city, while inveighing against certain regular abuses in the affiliate practice of the same banks, and crying out for investigation of facts to give light on whether or not and when certification of a raised check should protect a bona fide holder to the extent of the apparent face amount. I should do all three.

For further instances of a misconception, *cf.* Kantorowicz, *Some Rationalism About Realism* (1934) 43 YALE L. J. 1240; Dickinson, *Legal Rules* (1931) 79 U. OF PA. L. REV. 833. Once acquired, the misconception tends to persist, though evidence accumulates against it. *Cf.* M. Cohen in 3 LAW, A CENTURY OF PROGRESS, where the status of realistic literature on problems of value and evaluation simply is not accurately reflected.

attempt their bit toward justifying the faith by building their suggestions on prior labor over facts and over how the law works out. The realist's credo is and has been that only such labor yields an effective attack on the problem of better law. I hold to that credo.

One caveat is vital. In an effort to get and stay close enough to typical facts to make discussion meaningful, I shall confine this paper to *mercantile* phases of Sales. The situations and results described and the judgments expressed lie primarily in the realm of the dealer-seller, and again primarily in the realm of dealer-to-dealer or of factorage transactions. They have no application to a farmer's horse trade, and almost none to the purchase by Mrs. Sweeney of a fountain pen or of a new oil burner. They do not touch the questions raised when a boardinghouse keeper turns her furniture over to her landlord for back rent just before the sheriff arrives with an attachment for the coal bill. All these and many other nonmercantile or hardly even semimercantile situations raise problems to which the "general" law of Sales *purports* to have been more or less adequately applied. I suspect that a closer examination of those "Sales" problems in which farmers, consumers, corner retailers other than chain stores, and the like other-than-major-mercantile types dominate the picture would turn up a series of interesting discrepancies, in patterns of outcome as well as in need, between some or all of such situations and the more purely mercantile ones. For the traditional lump-concept "Seller," in terms of which the Uniform Sales Act is cast, has lost working value not only in the measure in which sellers, and selling units, and business units which have sales units as adjuncts, have come to vary in complexity and power; but has lost value also as growing economic differentiation has channeled the activities and interests of significantly different types of seller (or buyer) into different lines. For example, the utter dominance of contract for sale over

For illustrations of fact-inquiries *accompanied by* conclusions on desirable change, see, in addition to various papers listed in (1931) 44 HARV. L. REV. 1222, 1257, such studies as Corstvet, *Inadequate Bookkeeping as a Factor in Business Failure* (1936) 45 YALE L. J. 1201; Feinsinger, *Observations on Judicial Administration of Divorce Law in Wisconsin* (1932) 8 WISC. L. REV. 27; Note, *Collusive and Consensual Divorce and the New York Anomaly* (1936) 36 COL. L. REV. 1121; Schechter, *Fog and Fiction in Trade Mark Protection*, 36 *id.* at 1; Phillips, *A Practical Method for the Determination of Business Fact* (1934), 82 U. OF PA. L. REV. 230. A multitude of such excellent monographic studies are appearing from all over the country. See notably CURRENT LEGAL PROBLEMS.

present sale is today not only largely limited to the mercantile phases of Sales law, but it is unequally developed in various of those mercantile phases.[6] In consequence, and in test of the thesis that the concepts basic to the "general law of Sales" are in many aspects not only too general but in their lines of generality poorly adjusted to the facts, I concentrate upon a single portion of the material, itself manifold enough: the mercantile.

* * *

What, then, are the problems with which it is the business of the mercantile law of Sales to cope? They turn chiefly about occasional hitches in the process known to economists as distribution (which includes assembling), to business-school men as marketing (which includes purchasing), to lawyers as formation and performance of contract (which includes sale; which includes also single deals, long-run deals, and legally queer running arrangements of various complexion[7]). A group of men have had a lawyer arrange a number of semimagical rituals of corporation-creating, by virtue of which a whole group can thenceforth be known as "*the* seller"; they have engaged some capital in a business enterprise. They make a series of bargains with other groups, somewhat similarly organized. The bargains include descriptions, general or in finespun precision, of goods to be delivered, often enough leaving much to be filled in later: "Specifications to follow." There are commonly indications of price, time, manner of delivery, manner

[6]On this, see the Warranty paper, Part II. The Introduction to my CASES AND MATERIALS, at xiv, improperly overgeneralizes its statement of the tendency (curiously enough, after carefully noting the distinction between mercantile and other cases anent "warranty"). Indeed, in discussing the waning importance of Sales law (Warranty, I, at 706) my argument should have been more explicitly confined to the mercantile aspects; for an excellent corrective, see the admirable collection of CASES AND MATERIALS by Bogert and Britton (1936), and note the degree to which the interesting problems they collect from the modern reports play around the farmer and the consumer.

Yet it needs noting that "conditional sales," which bulk ever larger in reported litigation, and promise to continue large in life, involve a consumer initially almost always in a *contract for sale* as to a chattel merely generically described, and also in a contract-after-delivery until the full price is paid. To Whiteside's figures, (which disregard this fact) (1930) 16 CORN. L. Q. 140, add Mentschikoff's (1936) 36 COL. L. REV. 706, n. 24. But at least the *selling* end of such deals is not only mercantile, but highly organized. See *Warranty, II* (1937) 37 COL. L. REV. 373 *ff.*, 396 *ff.*

Isaacs might properly urge against this division that "mercantile" is no unified or uniform category. It is not intended as such. It is intended to indicate the limits *outside* of which this paper does not attempt to go, in its conclusions.

[7]See *Warranty, II* (1937) 37 COL. L. REV. 375 *ff.*; also Note, 37 *id.* at 610.

of packaging, and the like. In most lines the delivery is agreed to be on credit; in some (notably agricultural produce and automobiles sold to dealers)[8] the seller insists on cash.

Let us take the case of one peculiarly significant type of hitch: *"The buyer" goes back on "his" bargain.* The question is whether "the seller" can recover the price, or only damages. The issue is real, narrow, and, under our law, important. But it is also, as we pose it technically, silly. To a silly issue no sane answer is possible. This one we currently pose thus: Has Title passed? and solve by locating a mythical—or should I say more accurately "mystical"? —essence known as Title, which is hung over the buyer's head *or* the seller's like a halo. Halos are, it appears, indivisible. And there is only one halo for buyer and seller to make out with. This does not, as our orthodox doctrine goes, require explanation. It simply is so.

Nature and Utility of the Title-Concept

Nobody ever saw a chattel's Title. Its location in Sales cases is not discovered, but created, often *ad hoc.* In real-property matters, to be sure, it is a meaningful concept, because a chain of documents is there for art to construe; it is possible, objectively and definitely, to determine and agree in the great run of cases just where title to a disputed piece of land lies. Not so in Sales disputes, if Title be treated as one fixed whole. The reason for this is clear, though neglected. But before discussing it, let it be remembered that we have in chattel matters availed ourselves of the mass of conceptual inventions already worked out in the law of real property only as one or another of them has been casually found and almost unlawfully detained.[9] Is there an unambiguous chain of documents

[8]"Dealers" in the legal sense, including wholesalers as well as retailers or retaileers.

[9]When the modern law of sales began, real-property lawyers were familiar with legal title as distinct from equitable title; maybe they knew the concept of equitable estate. They knew the mortgage, the equitable mortgage, and the mortgagor's persisting use-appreciation-risk-redemption interest. They knew the equitable charge. They had no hesitation in allowing a mortgagor "who did not have the property" to insure, yet Buller feels that a consignee of goods, to insure, must "have *the* property"; and "security-title" is a concept worked out most painfully in chattels, with muff upon muff after the ball had been thrown straight. The Act in Section 20(2) and 22 finally makes the analysis explicit. But the Act leaves us wondering about the nature of stoppage in transit, though realty models gave us legal powers of appointment, legal options on another's land, and innumerable "equities," as suggestions to work with. Again, after a contract to sell, the realty lawyers were

which would afford a firm base line? In the common law of trust receipts such a chain has been seen and seized on,[10] but then, repeatedly, with disregard of what the realty lawyer could offer as a tool to help the buyer out, to wit, the full interest of a mortgagor in possession. Elsewhere, as in the statutes requiring the original bill of sale to be indorsed, etc., when second-hand cars are sold, or in the shipment of goods under straight or order bill of lading, we let the chain-of-title evidence run into curious confusion with unseen, intangible intention.[11] We do not, I repeat, in chattel matters, lay hold on a firm objective basis for allocating title when we have one—nor have we consistently utilized or remodeled the available concepts about divided interests. The quarrel thus is, first, with the use of Title for purposes of decision as if the *location* of Title *were* determinable with certainty; and second, with the insistence on reaching for a single lump to solve all or most of the problems between seller and buyer—and even in regard to third parties.

Why is a one-lump Title not determinable with certainty in Sales cases? It is because such a Title is a static concept, a some-

familiar with enforceable rights in the prospective buyer, in equity, and with escrows at law; but working out "seller's effective appropriation, subject to a condition of payment," still bothers many common-law courts in the draft against order bill-of-lading cases. Nobody would doubt the power of an escrow-beneficiary to waive a noncompliance, but buyer's option after nonconforming shipment has been hard to grasp and is not explicit in the Act, save in cases like Secs. 7, 8, and 44, where the purpose seems to be rather to delimit than to affirm the option-power. The C. O. D. rule of 19(4) (2) is an almost perfect escrow-analogy. Good—but why stop with the one instance, *if* there appears point (*after due examination*) in generalizing?

Incidentally, the law of pledge had suggestions for Sales law. But the notions "one chattel, one owner" and of ownership as one single something withstood assault. *Cf.*, in comparison, the Notes in (1937) 37 Col. L. Rev. 621 and 630.

[10]Excellent on trust receipts is Vold, Sales (1931) 341-372. Considerable modifications in the common law are made by the Uniform Trust Receipts Act. *Cf.* n. 16.

[11]Cases on the effect of noncompliance with the statutes regulating motor sales (together with cases that have no perceptible bearing thereon) are collected in (1925) 37 A.L.R., 1465; (1928) 52 A.L.R. 701. On bills of lading in their effect between seller and buyer the cases are collected and analyzed in Note (1929) 29 Col. L. Rev. 1100, where an effort is made to clear up the confusion of doctrine. How effectively the ancient armor of "intention" can turn even the shafts of statute appears when courts return to presumptions of the Sales Act, Section 19, variety despite the absence of any clause on "intention to the contrary" in Section 20, and the express exception of cases within that section from the rule of Section 19(4) (2). There emerges a lesson for the statutory draftsman: A semicode like a uniform commercial act should contain *one general* clause permitting variation by prescribed means of agreement and, in the present state of American statutory construction, might do well to open any presumption or in-the-absence-of-agreement section with "Subject to Section X." But certainly rules intented to be ironclad should contain: "No agreement to the contrary shall be valid." Compare the companion *Warranty* paper (1937) 37 Col. L. Rev. 384 *ff*; and 3 Law, A Century of Progress, 109, *re* Federal Sales Bill, § 15; *infra*, p. 206, f.

thing which is conceived as continuing in somebody. Its type is the book or handkerchief or dog or house, lastingly owned. A pledgor is "owner" not only before and after the pledge, but also after redemption; so is one whose rights are subjected to a common-law lien. You know in such cases where you start from, you know whither to return; you have your base-point firm and fixed. From that base-point courts can work out the rights and powers making up the particular "special property," in terms of what and how much is needed; from that base-point courts can see how much *not* to give. There is no great occasion for confusion on the point of ownership. This is, I think, one reason why the law of chattel mortgage in some "title" states, or of chattel mortgagee in possession where title is held to pass on such possession, runs into difficulty: a lump-title is conceived to rest where, from the angle of recurring in due course to the original static situation, it does not belong.

But in Sales cases, no static concept is at home. The essence of the Sales transaction is dynamic. Lump-title fits only in that rare case in which our economy resembles that of three hundred years ago: where the whole transaction can be accomplished at one stroke, shifting possession along with title, no strings being left behind—as in cash purchase of an overcoat worn home. But the contract for sale on credit, the shifting of goods to market via a factor, the shipment against draft, the installment sale, the delivery or shipment on approval, the agreement to sell goods lying in warehouse under non-negotiable receipt—these are not one-stroke transactions. They involve, each one, a complicated *series* of actions of varying significance. They involve a period, often an extended period, during which matters are in temporary suspension or are in active flux between the parties; over considerable periods of time there is no such Title in *either* party as the static picture of Title suggests. Take non-commercial shipbuilding. Admit that the builder has much or most of what we know as ownership. Yet is he "*free* to use," if buyer's inspector is on the job, checking on what goes on?[12] Or if a possible action for specific delivery, or

[12]This much is certain: that in the conduct of a business the introduction of a check-up officer with access to books and records is felt by a debtor as a grievous strait jacket and by a creditors' committee as an important safeguard. And one

injunction against sale to another, is in the offing? Should the buyer who makes contract payments as building proceeds be regarded as bare of interest simply because the time has not yet come when the transaction will be wholly over and the vessel "his" and his alone? One needs no passing of Title to the vessel, plank by plank, nor does one need a vessel that is buyer's up to six feet from the keel, and seller's in what has been built since. One needs only, on the price and security side, a concept akin to equitable charge.[13] But I do not want to linger on one illustration. The important point is to see the seller-buyer relation, save where a single stroke severs it utterly, as dynamic movement to which the Whole-Title concept applies on *neither* side. What other meaning have such concepts as specification, assent of seller and assent of buyer to appropriation, lien, stoppage in transit, goods not readily remarketable, delay in delivery, installment, severability? Where the transaction proceeds in a series of lesser actions, often long-drawn-out, no static legal whole-hog concept can fit comfortably, unless some almost violently vital step in the series can be seen to shift the whole scene—as perhaps when a letter of acceptance drops into the mailbox. Such a violently vital step, in Sales transactions, is almost nonexistent. Even open shipment on credit remains subject to stoppage in transit—an idea which the United States Postal Regulations seem not to have been faced with when they entered court.[14] *De facto,* then, Sales questions move much along the motto of the most orthodox of modern economists: *Natura non facit saltum.* Which can be rendered: It takes legal fiat to give little facts huge meaning.

This has been felt, and partly responded to, in the Act. Security-title, with action for the price and with risk on buyer, is

hears that there is little need to resort to dirty work to discourage an outsider who gets a city contract but will not play the machine's game: one has only to inspect—be on hand, and *inspect.*

[13]See Note (1937) 37 Col. L. Rev. 621. Will Sales lawyers never learn that there are courts of equity? Or a law of Quasi-Contract? See Anderson in (1937) 21 Minn. L. Rev. 529.

[14]In the Acceptance cases, after Adams v. Lindsell had made its way. The reasoning and even the impulse on which the English cases rest fail in the light of our postal regulations. Yet the rule remains sound, if its functional basis be accepted: to wit, that *in a régime of revocable offers, a decent division of market risks* calls for sticking the offeree when he has moved into external action. For illuminating discussion, see Nussbaum, *Comparative Aspects of the Anglo-American Offer and Acceptance* (1936) 36 Col. L. Rev. 920.

provided for. Risk does not stay with title when there is undue delay in delivery, under Section 22. Under 43 (3) a seller may have passed title, yet have failed to complete his obligation if he does not procure the bailee's attornment to the buyer. (The Conditional Sales Act goes to some trouble to allocate rights, privileges, and powers between the parties while the deal is going on.) Section 49 allows warranty to survive acceptance of title; 47 (1) allows inspection-privilege to survive delivery; and so on.

All of which is excellent, so far as it goes; but no less insufficient than excellent. *It is insufficient not so much because it does not go far enough*—and indeed, it does not—*as because it fails to lay bare the true problems for visualization and for inquiry.* And *so,* for sound solution. The approach of prevailing Sales doctrine, before or apart from the Act and in it, is this: Unless cogent reason be shown to the contrary, the location of Title will govern every point which it can be made to govern. It will govern, between the parties, risk, action for the price, the applicable law in an interstate transaction, the place and time for measuring damages, the power to defeat the other party's interest, or to replevy, or to reject; it will govern, as against outsiders, leviability, rights against tort-feasors, infraction of criminal statutes about sales, incidence of taxation, power to insure. The burden is put upon any individual issue to show why it should be honored by being severed from the Title-lump in any particular, and given individualized treatment. Now this would be an admirable way to go at it if the Title concept (or other basic integrated concept used) had been tailored to fit the normal course of a *going or suspended situation during its flux or suspension.* But Title was not thus conceived, nor has its environment of buyers and sellers had material effect upon it. It remains, in the Sales field, an alien lump, undigested. It even interferes with the digestive process.

What is to be striven for, if it can be produced, is some other and different integrated base-line concept which does fit the normality of the seller-buyer relation. I greatly doubt that such a single concept can be produced; today I find too many kinds of seller in contact with too many kinds of buyer in too many kinds of transaction. But what I am clear on is that we *can* isolate *types,* either of transaction, or of party, or of issue, and get light on how better to deal with those *types*. The retailer, the individual consuming-purchaser, the dealer-purchaser, the industrial purchaser have already been suggested and somewhat studied in the literature. The conditional sale,[15] the trust receipt,[16] the letter of credit,[17] the open-term contract,[18] similarly. In a companion paper subdivision of purchase for value is attempted. These are immediate and worth-while lines of inquiry. One does not go far into any of them without coming on results that sparkle. They may dazzle but at least they urge on, and many of them will prove jewels of price.

I do not suggest the elimination of the Title-concept. It has its uses. But it should be made to serve merely as the general residuary clause. It should not give forth the norm for decision in each case when no cogent reason is shown to the contrary. Rather should it serve as a better-than-nothing, when inquiry has failed to reveal any other line of solution adapted to the problem in hand. Two further illustrations may make my meaning clear: (1) A statute penalizes "sale of liquor" within a state, and liquor is shipped in, C.O.D. I suppose that the statute could, if drawn with more astuteness, have penalized "delivery" of liquor within the state, or "transfer of possession" of liquor, or "collection of the price" of liquor. One would want to study carefully the lay practices, the decisions, and the personnel of the highest bench, before choosing or cumulating language for the purpose in any state. But no man can doubt the apparent intention of the statute, nor doubt that to a layman the statute seems evaded rather than avoided by the C.O.D. shipment. What reason is there for mak-

[15]So BOGERT, COMMENTARIES ON CONDITIONAL SALES (1924). And the less scholarly handbooks are numerous. Even a service has appeared.

[16]Vold's WOODWARD'S CASES ON SALES (1933) xxvii, *ff.*, cites papers by Dalzell Frederick, Hanna, Taylor, Vold. One can add GUTTERIDGE, LETTERS OF TRUST, the Uniform Trust Receipts Act, and on the latter the article by Bogert. See, more recently, Bacon's excellent *A Trust Receipt Transaction* (1936) 5 FORDHAM L. R., 17, 240. Djorup, *Uniform Trust Receipts Act with Annotations* (1936) 18 *Am. Acc. Bull.*, No. 3, 1-16. Financing "needs" on turned-in cars are raising lobbying problems.

[17]Work prior to FINKELSTEIN, LEGAL ASPECTS OF COMMERCIAL LETTERS OF CREDIT (1929), is cited there. See also Neidle and Bishop, *Commercial Letters of Credit* (1932) 32 COL. L. REV. 1; Thayer, *Irrevocable Credits in International Commerce: Their Legal Nature* (1936) 36 COL. L. REV. 1031; *Their Legal Effects* (1937) 37 *id.* 1326; GROSSMANN-DOERTH, DER ÜBERSEEKAUF (1930).

[18]Some of the literature is gathered in *Warranty, II* (1937) 37 COL. L. REV. 378, n. 96.

ing the matter turn on Title, when a substantial portion of the action sought to be prevented, and its effective nub, occurs within the state? (2) An ordinance levies a sales tax on goods sold within the city. The amount is small, but the public consciousness of being newly taxed is great. Shall goods shipped out of the city be held subject to the tax? I say the question is an open one of policy.[19] There is no point in making it turn on whether the article is a chair, of which that seen in the store is only a sample, but which is itself shipped from warehouse, or is a rug, and is the particular rug selected. There is no point in making it turn on whether the store does or does not happen to use its own delivery service in the buyer's community. The question is rather whether or not out-of-town shoppers will be scared off, and the city lose more by that than it gains if it taxes them. Even if one can reach no decision on that, a ruling which turned on the Title lines of the Act—wholly artificial lines, *as to the purpose in hand*—would be a nuisance to administer.

In the balance of the paper an effort will be made to show that in a number of nice issues between seller and buyer, on the mercantile side, Title works out, no less, either to obfuscate statement of the results of rather reasonable decisions, or to misguide decision. The Title-concept is not adapted by courts to the real field of Sales dispute; it is also too blunt to fit particular issues as they arise. The cut of its many facets is an old-fashioned one which fits few of the modern situations for which it is called upon as a touchstone. In a word, the Title-concept lumps so many policy decisions together that the same decision about Title, in two cases having similar facts, would repeatedly lead to unfortunate results in one or the other, according to the issue.[20] And the courts,

[19]There are four questions—each essentially an open one of policy for its appropriate tribunal: (1) Can a tax be constitutionally laid on negotiations not resulting in a civil-law *sale,* but resulting in a *contract* for sale? (2) Does a statute authorizing a city to lay a "sales tax" authorize taxing such a transaction? (3) Does the city's ordinance taxing "sales" within the city cover such a transaction? (4) If yes, to all of these, is there discretion in an administrator to rule to the contrary; and if not, who can challenge his ruling?

[20]Take a situation in which "something remains to be done" under Act 19(2) or its common-law equivalent. On their facts Sherwin v. Mudge, 127 Mass. 547 (1879), and Chenoweth Hardware Co. v. Gray, 104 Ala. 236, 15 So. 911 (1894), have distinct superficial similarity: "sale" of a stock in trade; price in the first case to turn on inventory; in the other, excess to remain the transferor's property if the inventory exceeded the debt owing the seller's uncle, the transferee. A tax

whether they talk Title or talk the precise issue, whether they shelter themselves under or disregard the Title-formulae, show in a surprising proportion of the cases a *feel* for the precise issue, for the narrow situation-type, for a fair portion of the relevant policy.[21] The necessary result of such a situation is that a rule on passage of Title, worked out commonly in a situation where its application fitted the issue well enough, is either (1) applied blindly to situations in which a different implication is concerned, with regrettable consequence,[22] or (2) is sleight-of-handed into inconsistent use in the new situation, to achieve a consequence deemed desirable.[23]

levy intervened during inventory in the first case, a creditor's levy during the other. Title held to have passed before levy in the second case; the contrary was held in the first. If one sympathizes with uncles and preferences, as against mere competing creditors, the cases give no difficulty in result. But I find difficulty in reconciling the tendency of the Chenoweth case with that of Smith v. Sparkman, 55 Miss. 649 (1878), and Pierce Oil Co. v. Carroll, 277 S.W. 220 (Tex. Civ. App. 1925) (bales of cotton "sold" for antecedent debt; before they were identified and made fully ready for delivery, another creditor's attachment intervened successfully), and Barton v. Trumbull, 226 Mich. 685, 198 N.W. 186 (1924) [where the purchaser had even made advances on price to get the lumber out, but Act, Section 19(5) was surprisingly and unfortunately held to protect an attaching creditor of seller]. As I do in reconciling the tendency of these last with such cases as Young v. Matthews, [1866] L.R. 2 C.P. 127 (1,300,000 bricks "sold" against a debt; "this said quantity" to be held; three clamps pointed out "*from* which" the delivery was to be made; Erle, C. J., repeats the evidence as *"all these* bricks!" and the "buyer" beats the trustee in bankruptcy). For full discussion, see Note (1937) 37 Col. L. Rev. 630.

These are hardly mercantile cases. Illustrations from the mercantile appear below. Compare the semimercantile case of Warrick v. Liddn, 230 Ala. 253, 160 So. 534 (1935), where the court avoids the statutory lien of a judgment by treating the interest of a pledgor of negotiable warehouse receipts as equitable, applies Sales Act rules to the sale of the pledgor's resulting "equity of redemption," finds the quantity "fixed" at 104 bales when the goods were to be weighed to ascertain the poundage, and so protects the buyer of the "equity" against the creditor. Head whirls, but result is sense.

[21]Similarly in New York warranty. See (1936) 36 Col. L. Rev. 699, 37 *id.* 341. Compare also Latty, Subsidiaries and Affiliated Corporations (1936). Radin, Moore, Oliphant, Tulin, Arnold, have, *e.g.*, given illustrations in other fields.

[22]See such cases as Seaver v. Lindsay Light, *infra,* note 35 or Levine v. Hochman, 273 S.W. 204 (Mo. App. 1925). The New York Merchants' Association even relies on the Seaver Case as support for its proposal to change the Sales Act, Sec. 58. See 3 Law, A Century of Progress, 111; *infra,* p. 206.

[23]See cases, notes 40-41, on destruction. Some judges not only understand but describe the process. So Cresswell in Gilmour v. Supple, 11 Moo. P.C. 551, 566, 14 Eng. Rep. 803, 809 (1858) (whom I take to be the Cresswell of the superb argument for the plaintiff in Bryans v. Nix): "It is impossible to examine the decisions on this subject without being struck by the ingenuity with which sellers have contended that the property in goods contracted for had, or had not, become vested in the buyers, according as it suited their interest; and buyers, or their representatives, have, with equal ingenuity, endeavored to show that they had, or had not, acquired the property in that for which they had contracted; and Judges have not unnaturally appeared anxious *to find reasons* for giving a judgment which seemed to them most consistent with natural justice. Under such circumstances, it cannot occasion much surprise if some of the numerous reported decisions have been made to depend upon very nice and subtle distinctions, and if some of them should not

Even the process of qualifying and distinguishing, but much more the two processes just noted, in their combination, throw into confusion any lines of *predictable* presuming about *Title*.[24] Yet the

appear altogether reconcilable with each other." But Cresswell does not see that the solution lies in refining and subdividing not rules about the property-concept, but the property-concept itself. Blackburn, in Martineau v. Kitching, L.R. 7 Q.B. 436 (1872), as he rejects Cockburn's ploughhand analysis of the case, reveals the finer type of judicial attitude: "As a general rule, *res perit domino* . . .; and when you can shew that the property passed the risk of loss, *prima facie*, is in the person in whom the property is. If, on the other hand, you go beyond that, and show that the risk attached to the one person or the other, it is a very strong argument for showing that the property was meant to be in him. But the two are not inseparable. . . . In the present case I think *all that is necessary to decide is, that the risk was not in the sellers.* When the first month had elapsed, and payment had been made, still the buyers had, from their express stipulation, a right to have the goods remain a month at the refiners' warehouse at the refiners' risk. Let us suppose that the refiners had become bankrupt. If in consequence of the risk being in the refiners . . . the property was still in the refiners, their assignees in bankruptcy would take the entire property, and the buyers, who had paid the approximate price, would be obliged to come in and prove, and get so many shillings in the pound as they might be able to prove for. That would be a monstrous hardship, and *in such a case as that I should be very much inclined to struggle very hard to find any legal reason* for saying that, though the risk remained in the sellers, yet the property had passed to the buyers as soon as they had made the payment." Here is clean, narrow-issue thinking, and clean recognition of what a court is for; also clean recognition that *reasons* for decision must be "legal." I read that to mean: They must be very close to the accepted authoritative tradition. Results are another matter. A good many of the courts have been getting results—while making "reasons" for later courts a bit harder to find.—The italics are mine, in both passages.

With Blackburn's expressed foreknowledge of his own reactions, compare the actual reactions of the Idaho court in Idaho Products Co. v. Bales, 36 Idaho 800, 214 Pac. 206 (1923). Contract, grower to produce buyer, for alfalfa hay in stack, "all of his strictly No. 1 merchantable"; delivery in stack or to the baler on the premises, buyer's option. To be paid as loaded at the ranch. Grower to insure; loss payable to buyer as its interest may appear. The grower labored in vain to get buyer to act, and then resold. The market rising, buyer sues for conversion. All that is necessary to decide the case is found in a few lines: The reasonableness of the time given to buyer to remove the hay was squarely submitted to the jury, and found against buyer. Contract or sale, this entitles the grower to rescission. But Budge, C.J., embarrassed between sense and Sales theory, actually perpetrated the argument that the insurance clause showed title *still* to be in the grower, since without title he could have no insurable interest—which does not make it easier when a case like that put by Blackburn next turns up.

[24]The procedure of apparent conformance to accepted rule can be accomplished only in two ways. Either the facts are squarely faced, and the inconsistency among the cases in applying the concept then becomes apparent, or the facts are manhandled, and the actual inconsistency in applying the concept is thereby concealed. The two courses lead equally into confusion. For in advising a client about action or litigation, or in facing a court in first instance or on appeal, we have as our tool kit (1) the seeming facts in hand and (2) the practice of the judges as recorded. Little else, unless it be a thing as yet too little studied to be standardized or even communicable: a *lawyer's* hunch. But if "the practice of the judges" in applying the concept is patently inconsistent, it amounts to no real *practice* on which prediction, and so guidance, can be based. Whereas if the facts will not remain stable in the judges' hands, no certainty that a single and consistent verbal formula will be uttered and "applied" can afford even that relative certainty of result which commercial lawyers have some reason to feel needful. (The interplay of rule and fact, and its relation to predictability, is examined by Jerome Frank in an overdrawn

courts in such cases are wrestling with a court's proper job: sound

but stimulating paper, *What Courts Do in Fact* (1932) 26 ILL. L. REV. 645, 761. It must always be remembered that Frank had his eye on the trial court in a dispute; not on counseling beforehand.)

The individual lawyer worth his salt attempts to escape this trouble (which most individual lawyers—and judges—as they look to precedent for guidance, much more feel than know) by almost subconscious hunching. He gets an idea from somewhere that one line of argument will get over, whereas another line may not, or will not. Or, if counseling, he sees shoals and breakers worth skirting, on certain points, if skirting is possible, because he does not trust too much the seeming state of judicial language. Why, he ordinarily finds it hard to tell. To some extent, this type of hunching is inevitable. It is much like the problem of lighting to a photographer, or of wind to a marksman. The photographer can use inventions testing and to some extent standardizing and charting the degree of light (as a physician can test hemoglobin rating against a standardized chart); but there is no chart to test the *incidence* of light. The marksman can find sights correctable for windage, and doubtless could transport a truckful of instruments for testing its velocity; but only his own hunch works in space between muzzle and target, or in time between trigger-pull and the bullet's arrival at (or not at) the mark. Apart from the *relative* simplicity of their technical problems, such persons have one tremendous advantage over the litigating or counseling lawyer: They have discovered what their problem is; and they are, and have persuaded others to be, at work on it. The lawyer has not been much concerned with demarcating where the area of lawyer's hunch begins, nor with the range and intensity of the hunch process in a lawyer's work. He is in a stage of technique in which a Steiglitz operating a pinhole-camera, or a Daniel Boone with bow and arrow, could indeed stand forth in glory and utterly transcend his medium—and be therein no less unique than glorious. I see no other adequate explanation for the unbelievable diversity in lawyer's adequacy, nor especially for the unbelievable prevalence of lawyer's inadequacy. For I believe the essential techniques to be not too complex for any person without mental handicap to master. I believe moderately workable teaching solutions to be also within the range of any persons who lack mental handicap, if pursued consistently over a period equivalent to what has led up to modern rifling, cartridge, and rifle-sight, or to modern photo-technical devices. I am thus led to believe that lawyers and law teachers have been tardy in studying their problem. More: I think they have been losing almost as much ground as they have been gaining. I give a single instance. The reports increasingly exclude even the points, much more the development, even in summary, of counsel's argument. Yet, for the training of lawyers, the arguments in, say, Bryans v. Nix, 4 M. & W. 775, 150 Eng. Rep. 1634 (Ex. 1839), are worth ten of the opinion. If counsel's argument were not a factor in the decision, moreover, the whole profession, save the judges, might as well abdicate advocacy. Yet such argument is only in the rarest cases even mentioned by writers as bearing on how a decision came about. And the factor of the leeway which is both due to and presupposed by counsel's argument, and of the probable effect of future argument within that leeway, is practically never touched on even in modernistic discussion of how cases *will* come out. This means that a known and necessary major factor of uncertainty in prediction has not yet even come in for serious study.

In the same way, but in an even more crucial area, that of judicial behavior itself, the problem has failed of study, as to how far and where *and why* judges continue blind use of inadequate concepts, how far they remodel such by finding useful qualifications or distinctions, how far they get results by distortions of the facts which leave the legal formulae seemingly unchanged. Once we are really awake to the area of unpredictability and to the types of variation that occur within it, we can set about the invention of what would correspond to light- and wind-gauges, and exposure or sight adjustments—and about testing out propositions about legal behavior which purport to correspond to any of these—and so somewhat to narrow the area of what is *de facto* becoming perhaps increasingly unpredictable, even while it continues *de jure* "certain."

I have noted elsewhere that the question of just where in law "certainty" needs to be approximated, is another neglected field of study. Pound's "*commercial* law and

solution as nearly as may be, of the case in hand, in terms of what will be sound solution of significantly similar cases. They move from facts and issue to result. I do not mean from the mere specific facts of the specific case, nor from the issue merely of "Is this judgment to stand?" I mean that they move from *types* of fact, and *types* of issue, felt, even when not expressly classified, in categories as narrow as seems necessary to get roughly adequate results in the cases. I hold that they ought to move thus. I hold that the Title-concept hinders them as often as it helps. Why, then, bother to insert the mythical Title into the reasoning? I find "no better reason than that it was so laid down in the time of" not the fourth Henry, but the third George. Holmes thought such a reason disgusting.

1. *Price or Damages*

When one returns to the buyer who goes back on his contract, and to the question whether the seller can have the price or must rest content with damages, one finds Title, as it operates in the decisions, a useless additional link in reasoning, and one often clumsy. The issue of the seller's remedy presents an instance. We pose it: price or damages? Posing it thus is, as has been said, essentially silly, because it distracts us from the true issue.

For consider: We live, for better or worse, in a bargain economy. If bargains, or any particular bargains, are to be enforced by courts at all,[25] Benefit of the Bargain is the sane standard for a

property" is silly, as to "the" former; though it does hold as to corporation procedures and much long-term finance. Indeed, such work as that of Frank, Dickinson, Fuller, and my own, seems hardly to have marked out the field for study. More satisfactory is such a sweet monograph as Goble's on a *single* unsettling phase of a *single* type of contract. (1937) 37 Col. L. Rev. 410. More good monographs, heeled with fact guided by sense and an ideal or two: in these lies the *immediate* future of Jurisprudence. After them, comes consolidation of their *net* meaning, in further general writing.

[25] I do not regard the dominance of bargain in our economy as even remotely justifying passive acceptance by court or other tribunal of the letter of an "agreement" merely because a "writing" turns up under that label. Those once moderately fungible legal persons, *A* and *B*, or *S* and *B*, have ceased to be at all fungible in fact; and the process of agreeing—which once implied not only meditation but room to choose and freedom within that room, not only choice but relatively conscious choice with some inkling of consequence—that process, thanks to differential uses of forms, differential character of the forms used, differential knowledge, power and bargaining skill in the "agreers," has also ceased to be fungible in fact. This means need for control, lest old rules based on Adam Smithian postulates be made tools of outrage. And the problem presses. For some phases, see my *Legal Institutions and Economics* (1925) 15 Am. Econ. Rev. 665; *What Price Contract* (1931) 40 Yale L. J. 704, 741 *et seq.* (the function of the law

court to enforce by. This has been challenged as to particular types of case; but the challenge, when applied to a deal between mercantile outfits who have bargained *on a moderately equal footing,* can hardly be maintained in the face of business men's accounting practices; consider their handling of "commitments" in internal administration of wares, supplies, personnel and planning, or in arrangement of their financing.[25a] Unambiguous contract—"acceptance" as a final point of closing a bilateral (moderately even) bargain, is indeed so sudden as to seem almost arbitrary; but the suddenness, with benefit of the closed bargain to be had at law, not only accords with expectation, but is convenient for both the courts and the parties to administer. One's quarrel runs rather to another point of doctrine: the insistence on such "acceptance" as the *sole* way of proving that a bargain has been closed.[25b] In any event, our policy is fixed in most cases in terms of purporting to award Benefit of the Bargain. I think the choice wise. But then decently admeasured damages are all a seller needs, and are just what a seller needs, when the mercantile buyer repudiates. It is, indeed, social wisdom for the rest of us to leave the selling house, in most cases which have not involved shipment to a distant point, to dispose of whatever goods may have come into existence or into his warehouse; that is its business, and the buyer's prospective

of consideration); Phillips, *A Lawyer's Approach to Commercial Arbitration* (1934) 44 YALE L. J. 31 (the business arbitrator's tendency to take the writing at its face); my *Warranty of Quality and Society* (1936) 36 COL. L. REV. 699, and especially (1937) 37 *id.* at 393-404 (the need, *today,* for controlling "agreement" expressions by stressing the-nature-of-the-case)—with which contrast the troubles of such stressing where it is uninformed or difficult or blind: Note (1928) 28 COL. L. REV. 65, and Note (1933) 42 YALE L. J. 782 (on the patterning of queer corporate-security devices); and the "rigid" periods of our pleading history. Pound's notion of "status" as a vital working tool of our law, SPIRIT OF THE COMMON LAW (1921) 28-31, Isaac's appreciation of cycles in the treatment of contract and contract-patterns, *The Standardizing of Contract* (1917) 27 YALE L. J. 34, and Demogue's views on "contracts of adhesion," *Fundamental Notions of Private Law* in MODERN FRENCH LEGAL PHILOSOPHY, 472 and 477, are all valuable contributions to the working out of the problem. No simple solution will do. While, as a challenge to the "how far" of *even quite legitimate contracting,* we have Fuller and Perdue, *The Reliance Element in Contract Damages* (1936-1937) 46 YALE L. J. 52, 373.

[25a]If you are a merchant merely, you cannot let your stock run out. Fail to fit or please your inquirer, and you have lost more than a single customer. If you are a manufacturer-merchant, you have a production-schedule, and have therefore to arrange both financing and selling. Not for nothing did Sombart see "accounting," in its slow and baby-like increasing grasp of the significant, as one of the vital factors in the growth of our Western capitalism.

[25b]Until roughly the War, the *Courts* escaped in this field queer doctrine which molded more than moulded as it aged. Since about 1925, however, Taught Doctrine is making itself felt. The results are not happy. But that calls for another paper.

inability has been already evidenced. To force such goods on the buyer, where they are reasonably marketable by the seller, is social waste; moreover, even a welshing buyer can properly ask that goods neither manufactured nor contracted for by the seller be not made up or acquired to his damage. On the other hand, shipment to a "buyer" at a distant point makes seller's resale burdensome in too many cases for comfort, and affords almost indecent leverage to a defaulting buyer, if he bargains for reduction of the price in return for his acceptance, whereas the merchant in the market of arrival is on the ground and can normally exercise better judgment in reselling than can the distant seller. This presents a case that tips the balance of social utility in favor of forcing title on the buyer. Yet, curiously, a line of cases has tended precisely here, under the semiprotection of Act, Section 19(5), to allow the buyer to repudiate title,[26] though in a contract for delivery f.o.b. seller's city he could not. Whatever one's views on who can best resell in the seller's home market, it is clear that, once proper goods have arrived in the buyer's city, the social balance tips against the buyer, and so in favor of allowing price recovery.

When, however, the selling outfit is remitted to damages, surely it needs reasonable time to dispose of goods, and needs some time doubly if the market continues to drop and weaken while it tries to; and it needs account taken of expenses incurred (as in reshipping or commissions), or else it needs account taken of the normal selling overhead in its line, if it uses its own organization to resell. None of these factual needs turns at all on whether or not Title has Passed, which is the basic legal criterion under Act, Section 63. But with our eyes firmly fixed on the nineteenth-century precedents about Goods Bargained and Sold,[27] and with Price making the seller

[26]*Cf.* WHITNEY, SALES (2d ed. 1934) 79, 80. The American Bar Association version of the Federal Sales Bill even hoped to incorporate this rule. Sec. 20(6). Why, I cannot fathom. The Merchants' Association rightly repudiates it.

[27]Not on the *ancient* precedents, reports Mentschikoff.

The original action for the price lay in debt, but without necessity for alleging performance by the seller, the theory being that the requirement of *quid pro quo* was satisfied by the seller's "grant" to the buyer of the right to sue in detinue. [Ames, *Parol Contracts Prior to Assumpsit* (1909) 3 ESSAYS IN ANGLO-AMERICAN LEGAL HISTORY 304, 312, and 313. See especially cases collected in note 1, p. 313.] With the development of assumpsit and the doctrine of mutual promises as consideration, the seller retained this right to the price until the development of the doctrine of conditions precedent and concurrent. "Plaintiff need not to aver the delivery of the cow, because it is promise for promise." (Nichols v. Raynbred.

whole (at buyer's cost, and sometimes at cost to the rest of us) wherever the seller happens by the accidents of Title-theory to be able to get the price—and there only!—we get our minds distracted from the real point, which is the working out of a sane law of Benefit of Bargain for such cases.[28]

Has this distraction come about because no man has yet conceived a sounder solution? It has not. New York had before the Sales Act worked out a somewhat persuasive answer by way of extending the action for the price, politely junking all regard for the technical requirements of the common counts by inventing an action for the price in special assumpsit. The solution was persuasive enough to have found favor with most American courts. It was, thereupon, deliberately rejected in the Act. It was rejected at least in good part because England had not happened to work it out, and because its introduction in New York had rested on exceedingly dubious legal reasoning.[29] But what real innovation

Hob. 89, 80 Eng. Rep. 238 (1615). *Cf.* also Strangborough v. Warner, 4 Leon 3, 74 Eng. Rep. 686 (1589); Whitcalfe v. Jones, Moore K. B. 595, 72 Eng. Rep. (1598-1599), and Anonymous, 1 Lev. 88, 84 Eng. Rep. 311 (1663). Conditions precedent are not finally established in the law until Thorpe v. Thorpe, 1 Ld. Raym. 662, 91 Eng. Rep. 1341 (1699), and Lock v. Wright, 8 Mod. 40, 88 Eng. Rep. 30 (1722), whereas the development of the notion of concurrency drags on until Mansfield's famous dictum in Kingston v. Preston, Loffts, 194, Doug. 659 (1773). —That a judge who could do that work, and that of Boone v. Eyre, had no opportunity to make clear, inside of "mercantile" cases, the difference between "warranty" in Sales and the same word in marine insurance, is a price the case-lawyer pays for judges' creation. I do not say the price is too high. I think it is not. *But I think it is reducible*—certainly, as a Federal Sales Bill pends.

28Note, however, that Fuller and Perdue, *supra* note 25, recanvass this "sane" base line; and make one ponder. Yet my guess is that they will modify, not shift, my base line. See also a lovely forthcoming paper by Malcolm Mason.

292 WILLISTON, SALES, gives the older New York rule (§ 563), and indicates the relative spread of its acceptance in American courts (§ 564). He follows with a defense of the Sales Act Choice, in Section 63(1), to which I probably do injustice. [§§ 565-573. See also Williston, *The Right of a Seller of Goods to Recover the Price* (1907) 20 HARV. L. REV. 363.] What that defense does not include is a careful canvass of the business and general economic bearings of the competing choices, nor a canvass of the procedural difficulties entailed in many states by providing two remedies mutually exclusive and "inconsistent in theory," nor a weighing of what type of damage admeasurement is needed to balance the effects of limiting recovery of the price, in the ordinary case, to the old common count situation. The sections on the buyer's damages would help a little, if their theory were carried over. (§§ 597-600.) For a different attack on the problem see Waite, *The Action for the Price* (1919) 17 MICH. L. REV. 283. 38 COL. L. REV. plans a Note on this.

Purely as a matter of construing language, one may note that Section 51 of the Sales Act could be made to open, together with 60 and 61, all needed remedies to the *seller*, wherever buyer's repudiation has not preceded seller's request that buyer take delivery, and perhaps even where it has. It remains for counsel to try out how far courts can be made to shift eyes from 63(1) to other sections. 63 does not state that it is exclusive. Nor would Fed. Sales Bill and Merchants' Assn. let

ever rested on anything but dubious legal reasoning? By the definition of innovation, real innovation on sound legal reasoning is impossible. The question must always be: Is the thing accomplished *worth-while enough to warrant revising* prior legal theory? In this instance, it was. Not that the New York solution was perfect. It was not. But it was reasonably good. It *allowed* a performing seller coverage against falling market while he resold, by letting him recover price less proceeds (though the selling overhead was lost from sight). It did not, however, *force* his resale, and thus allowed him to throw the goods onto the buyer's hands—which, as the Act recognizes,[30] is sound enough policy as to a set of false teeth or a batch of castings manufactured on unique specification, but is far from a satisfactory outcome in the run of mercantile cases. What made the older New York rule relatively satisfactory in practice was that a seller could, and would, put himself in funds more rapidly by resale than by a lawsuit; but that resale was not forced on him by considerations of safety while negotiations looking toward adjustment were still running their business course.[31] On paper, the allotment of remedies in the Act can be made persuasive enough (save for the relations of Sections 60 and 61).[32] In practice it is both harsh to the particular case and uneconomic to the

(63) be exclusive. See 3 LAW, A CENTURY OF PROGRESS III, *re* sec. 43 *ff.*; *infra*, p. 208 f.

[30]Act, Section 63(3).

[31]Eno, *Price Movement and Unstated Objections to Defective Performance of Sales Contracts* (1935) 46 YALE L. J. 782, and Note (1935) 35 COL. L. REV. 726, deal with other aspects of the law as it affects or hampers intelligent business adjustment of disputes on quality. See Appendix. Both have to do with what is in function a partial compensation for the initially unwise rule which holds a mercantile seller, as against a mercantile buyer, to the precise performance described in his agreement—a rule *not* applied, interestingly enough, to installment defects in their empowerment of cancellation. Act, § 45. To an uncommercial initial premise working against the seller is added a partially corrective and equally uncommercial set of rules on waiver by buyer, and on acceptance, which can work well enough as a balance weight where a buyer is ducking for extraneous reasons, but which can also work real injustice, and does, where the defects are material. The text deals with a similar maladjustment in function where the mercantile seller is offering adequate performance and it is the buyer who is kicking over.

Failure to diagnose who needs the court's help, and when, may explain the vagaries recorded in (1937) 37 COL. L. REV. 340, *ff.* Or even the failure of merchants to pull wholly workable results out of the muddle of circumstance. *E.g.*, the Merchants' Association's failure to urge introduction of substantial performance into domestic Sales law.

[32]I do not believe anybody will ever work out an intelligible theory of these two sections. Fortunately, such cases as D'Aprile v. Turner-Looker Co., 237 N. Y. 427, 147 N. E. 15 (1925), where the judges' aesthetics of the Act determine their votes, are rare indeed. The Merchants' Association moves vigorously to remove such doubt. See their proposed Sections 51, 52, 56 of the Federal Sales Bill.

community. And, in a falling market, the type case in which the buyer backs out, *the rules of the Act press the seller away from Adjustment and into a lawsuit.*[33] He is not safe in waiting to negotiate.

For be it noted that in pruning the older New York rule out of the law, our Act did more than merely choose between two base lines each of which was adequate after a fashion. The English model, in limiting the price action (normally) to the case where "title has passed" (and thus frequently forcing the seller to do its own redisposition, which is commonly good) is accompanied in English court administration by a leeway in damage admeasurement which leaves such admeasurement substantially true to its function; a leeway not nominal, but real; a discretion not merely available, but used. True, the language of the sections on buyer's damages for nondelivery and seller's for nonacceptance does not differ materially in either the English Sale of Goods Act or the American Sales Act, nor as between those Acts. What does differ is *practice of the courts.*[34] I suspect that such divergence in judicial practice was, if not foreseeable, at least so probable as to call for special wording in the American Act to make the bor-

[33]See Note (1935) 35 Col. L. Rev. 726. *Re* decent buyers, *cf.* Eno, *supra* note 31.

[34]The language of Sales of Goods Act, § 50(2)(3), on nonacceptance, is literally that of 51(2)(3) on nondelivery. That of Sales Act 64(2) on nonacceptance is that of S. G. A. § 50(2). But Sales Act 67(2), on nondelivery, amazingly uses "the loss" instead of "the estimated loss." Sales Act 67(3) and 64(3) correspond to the dot with each other. Both differ from the English Act. The latter speaks of damages "prima facie to be ascertained . . . " whereas the American Act substitutes "damages, in the absence of special circumstances showing proximate damages of a greater amount." Either this change is meaningless, or it deliberately attempts to narrow the English discretion. The case results accord with the latter alternative.

For the English application of discretion, buyers' actions under the equivalent language are thus as significant as sellers'. Sharpe v. Nosawa, [1917] 2 K. B. 814: on failure to ship c.i.f. from Japan or to forward documents diligently, buyer must be allowed time to consider—his duty being to buy on the same terms, if possible (which means room to try), or, if not possible, then to cover on the spot market. Clemens Horst Co. v. Biddell Bros., [1911] 1 K. B. 214; on nonacceptance, Hamilton, J., gave damages measured by contract price less the highest price sellers were able to get quoted when, after repudiation, they sought (which implies time) to resell on the same contractual terms. The House of Lords reduced this, following the Court of Appeal, to a shilling, [1912] A. C. 18: the sellers had failed to prove any substantial loss. This disregards the overhead cost of selling; which is not so good. Yet it looks not to any mechanical test, but to *loss*. "The same terms" is an excellent measurement device to *start* with, *if* one is allowed leeway to "consider"—and to try. Payzu, Ltd. v. Saunders, [1919] 2 K. B. 581: improper revocation of credit, and suit for nondelivery; defense that buyer should have covered at cash prices as offered by seller; buyer had the cash; judgment for £50 for "serious business inconvenience" affirmed. McCardie, J., had felt "no inclination to allow in a mercantile dispute an unhappy indulgence in far-fetched resentment."

rowed English price rule work here as well as it did at home. But, that apart, the present American judicial practice under the damage rules cries out for reform either of itself or of the statutory language. There is not only the strict "time and place where title was to have passed" line of damage-measurement, with its queer assumption that a market operates in frictionless instantaneity;[35] there is, beyond that, the insistence in a number of our states that when, on doubtful fact or law, no man can tell whether or not "title" will be held to have passed, a seller who is *ex hypothesi* in the right can yet be forced to elect his theory at his peril—a procedural barbarity.[36] The English model does not operate thus. I have not yet seen a modern English case in which a seller, in a case thus doubtful on location of title, was forced to his election at risk of upset;[37] or in which, without inquiry regarding business decency in the circumstances, a flat rule of precise time and place of agreed delivery was insisted on.

The problem is, I repeat: Why has our Sales law failed to *develop*, or even to *use*, serviceable discriminations and devices *after* they have been invented?

I concur with Fuller that conceptual or "doctrinal bridges"[38]

[35]Compare, for intelligent attack on the problem, such minority rulings as Cook Mfg. Co. v. Randall, 62 Iowa 244, 17 N. W. 507 (1883) (nondelivery of carriages at Cincinnati for the Des Moines market; place of expected resale taken as the measure); with which contrast Cahen v. Platt, 69 N. Y. 348 (1877) (glass c.i.f. Antwerp to New York; action for nonacceptance; damages to be measured as of Antwerp). Or again, with Seaver v. Lindsay Light Co., 233 N. Y. 273, 135 N. E. 329 (1922) (nondelivery on a contract c.i.f. Chicago to London, payment Chicago in advance: damages held to be measurable as of Chicago and time of breach), as developed by Standard Casing Co. v. California Casing Co., 233 N. Y. 413, 135 N. E. 834 (1922) (nondelivery of pigs' guts, f.o.b. San Francisco for New York: the California market held to govern damages); compare Perkins v. Minford, 235 N. Y. 301, 139 N. E. 276 (1923) (sugar f.o.b. Cuba for New York, *B* to furnish vessel and insure, cash against documents; *B* sues for nondelivery of part, the defect being discovered on arrival. The court followed the blind "place where title was to pass" rule, but qualified the *time* to be when *B* knew or should have known of the breach. This helps, some. But *time for covering* is not allowed). 2 WILLISTON, SALES (2d ed. 1924) 599, urges that the measurement of damages be at need dissociated from time and place of agreed passage of title. Wisely. The Act certainly leaves room for this. The trouble is only that its language gives no push to overcome judicial inertia. *Neither does the Federal Sales Bill.*

[36]See Clark's discussion in my CASES AND MATERIALS, 147 *ff.;* 38 COL. L. REV., Mar.

[37]A lovely example of the English practice in Stein, Forbes v. County Tailoring Co., 115 L. T. R. 215, 86 L. J. K. B. 448 (K. B. D. 1916). The plaintiff sellers had "sued *only* for the price." They were not entitled to price. So: judgment for the plaintiff—for *damages.*

[38]See Fuller, *American Legal Realism* (1934) 82 U. OF PA. L. REV. 429, 441. But Fuller is wrong in believing that I had "failed to mention" the effect of the chance order in which cases arise and the doctrinal effects of that chance order.

mightily further legal engineering. But here, on both the price side and the damages side, such bridges have come into existence—only to be later either ignored or dynamited.[39]

2. *Risk of Damage or Loss*

Let us turn to another typical hitch in the normal marketing process, in which again Title-reasoning deflects attention from the issue, and, again, despite clear indications of a wiser approach in cases more than half a century old. *Certain goods are damaged or destroyed.* The question is: Shall buyer or seller take the loss? Once more, the question bears procedurally on price: Must the buyer pay it; or if it has been paid, can he get it back? Again we make it turn normally on the location of the Title-halo. At times the reasoning of the cases, put together, verges on the ludicrous; if the parties have agreed where risk is to be, we use that to tell where Title is,[40] whereas we manage to learn from Title

On the contrary, in the same book he was reviewing, a section of the materials was arranged and annotated to develop the very point. PRÄJUDIZIENRECHT U. RECHTSPRECHUNG IN AMERIKA (1933) see especially II, 129, 134 *ff.*—Fuller's note 25, by the way, deserves prayerful attention by the student of case law in society.

[39] Of course, the careful seller or buyer whose organization contains some one aware of the difficulty can find the outline of an excellent and balanced solution in Garfield and Proctor Coal Co. v. Pennsylvania Coal and Coke Co., 199 Mass. 22, 84 N. E. 1020 (1908). Suggestions for pure pro-seller clauses can be found in Wales Adding Machine Co. v. Huver, 98 N. J. L. 910, 121 Atl. 621 (1923) with refinements on credit terms ably discussed in Havighurst, *Clauses in Sales Contracts Protecting the Seller Against Impairment of the Buyer's Credit* (1936) 20 MINN. L. REV. 367. But why should sane rules be limited to the use of the careful and informed who can afford to pay counsel who are also skillful and informed?

[40] 1 WILLISTON, SALES, 573 n., reasons thus, in full consonance with the tradition; see Blackburn, *supra* note 23. This has, at times, consequences that would have been distinctly undesired by the parties at the time of contracting, had they been foreseen. Business men do not ordinarily get specific about the location of Title. Indeed, when it comes to deliberate expression, as in standard forms, this absence of express "intention" on the whole lump seems to me wise. Whereas Isaacs is still wiser in indicating that since particular provisions (*e.g.*, f.o.b.) may induce courts to lump Title-passing in undesired ways, such matters as recoverability of price, risk of loss or deterioration, security to seller, should *each* be contracted for in specie; so also should excuse, credit limitation, inspection privilege, or other right or remedy of buyer or seller. Isaacs points a moral: that if one does not do each specific job with adequate specificity, he may find undesired consequences hung around his neck. On the reasoning from risk see also Rosenberg v. Buffum, 234 N. Y. 338, 137 N. E. 609 (1922). Contrast Stein, Forbes & Co. v. County Tailoring Co. 115 L. T. R. 215, 86 L. J. K. B. 448 (K. B. D. 1916), sheepskins c.i.f. N. Y. to London "net cash against documents on arrival of steamer." The issue is that of the Buffum case: price after nonacceptance. The reasoning runs the opposite way; it also disregards the insurance line of argument used later in the Marano case, n. 41; nor does it mention the "on arrival" clause, which so frequently affects American sea-shipment cases. The problem the case raises is: Are Sales Act 20(2) and 22(a) (both lacking in the English Statute) necessary, in order to bridge out of 63 into allowing recovery of the price? That problem arises from lumping all aspects of title into one, despite the prior invention and the carry-over into the

where to put the risk.[41]

But in any other contract than one envisaging a sale of goods we should, in solving a risk-problem, go to work very differently. We should ask first, of course, as we do now, whether or not any

Sale of Goods Act of the *ius disponendi* concept, and the clean indications in Miribita v. Imperial Ottoman Bank, 3 Ex. Div. 164 (C. A. 1878), of the extent to which shipment reserving *ius disponendi* passes effective rights to the buyer. Again, *this time in England*, a clarifying and useful intellectual invention has been junked. But we have done the same. *Cf. Warranty, II*, 375, n. 85, and citations, n. 23.

[41]So Cockburn in Martineau v. Kitching, [1872] L. R. 7 Q. B. 436. Smith v. Marano, 267 Pa. 107, 110 Atl. 94 (1920) illustrates the reasoning: c.i.f. shipment; customary insurance, not yet including war risk; sunk by submarine. *S* sues for price and recovers. The court's argument runs thus: the case turns on the point of "delivery." The cases show "property" to pass on shipment. Inclusion of insurance in price bars argument that *B* is to have "no interest" till arrival. (This is the concept lacking in Anderson v. Morice, 10 C. P. 58, [1874] described n. 53.) "The property" was retained for security only; hence the unforeseen and uninsured risk is on *B* under Sales Act 20(2) and 22. Now add Standard Casing Co. v. California Casing Co., 233 N. Y. 413, 135 N. E. 834 (1922), nondelivery of pigs' guts f.o.b. San Francisco, for New York, sight draft against bill of lading, inspection permitted on arrival. The reasoning is: from delivery for transit, to passage of title, to passage of risk, to completion of seller's performance on delivery for transit, to agreed place for such delivery as place of default, and so for measure of damages. The Marano case has no need to touch title, even to avoid 19(5); it would be enough that risk rests on the buyer by the insurance provision, and that the seller has done all he is required to do. The Standard Casing case unnecessarily decides a risk issue for purposes of becoming obscured by a mechanical device for measuring damages so that a commercially sane admeasurement of damages is excluded. In such a case as Skinner v. Griffiths, 80 Wash. 291, 141 Pac. 693 (1914), herring boxes to be delivered "f.o.b. scow Winslow or Seattle." and partially lost on the scow before time for loading aboard a barge in Seattle harbor had elapsed, the court sees the question as whether or not title passed when the boxes were delivered at the place and in the manner agreed upon, no stipulation having made inspection a condition precedent to the passing of title—and so renders a decision whose soundness no man can determine from the report. For any commercial man knows that "delivered f.o.b. scow Seattle" means job complete when goods are put aboard scow, if the delivery is intended *from a Seattle wharf*, but requires time for unloading, if the goods are to *come to Seattle by scow*. The opinion suggests that the latter was the fact, and, therefore, that the decision is unfortunate. If so, I submit that forgetting title would have helped mightily in reaching a wiser result; if not, that it would have helped no less in reaching a clearer one. Meanwhile, as indicated 3, Law, A Century of Progress, 109, the point of Federal Sales Bill, Sec. 33(3) [original Act, 46(3)] risks being imperiled by Sec. 21(3)—a situation unthinkable if sound analysis of Skinner v. Griffiths were the order of the day. See p. 207, *infra*.

It is not enough merely to avoid the Scylla of Title. What is needed is to chart the true course to the sane port. For instance, in Cundill v. Lewis, 245 N. Y. 383, 157 N. E. 502 (1927), we have a loss by theft. Camphor, identified, lies in a warehouse. Contract for sale, net cash in five days. Payment by *B* against a dedelivery order, March 21. Four days later, *B paid storage charges to the warehouseman, without asking attornment.* A nonnegotiable receipt was outstanding, in *S*'s hands, and called for "proper endorsement and surrender of this receipt" before delivery. The court allowed *B* to get the price back. It relied on no heavy nonsense about Title. It relied instead on Sales Act 43(3), which makes clear that the seller "has not fulfilled his obligation to deliver," when goods are in third-party hands, until attornment. Which is a good rule, and a pure contract rule. But the application of which to the particular case requires attention also to Act 22(b): where delivery is delayed through fault of seller or buyer, risk lies with the fault. This is another contract rule, and another good one, and in direct point to the issue of *risk*. And the problem of *risk* is the problem of *risk*, to be dealt with as such.

goods were clearly enough specified to the contract even to raise a question of risk. We should ask next after an express agreement. Lacking one, we should not go chasing haloes. We should, instead, ask whether or not the active party had done enough of what he agreed to do to earn his agreed reward. He agreed to ship goods of a certain description. Well, has he shipped? Or has anything supervened which makes it fair to throw risk on the buyer without the shipment?[42] He agreed to hold specified goods until call. Well, did he? He was under duty to let the buyer inspect on demand. Is it reasonable to disregard that duty, in view of the supervening destruction?[43] If he agreed to hold until call, who should carry the risk, pending call?[44] If he agreed

[42]Act. § 22(b). *Cf.* also n. 41.

[43]One of the most baffling concepts in the law of Sales is the "condition precedent to the passing of title," with "inspection" as its main exemplar, which sometimes obscures both this problem and that of the action for the price after rejection. In the System of the law of Sales, this concept is a halfhearted and two-faced counterpart of the circles-running-on-circles which were resorted to in later Ptolemaic astronomy to make an inadequate first premise fit *some* of the facts which that first premise could not handle unaided. The inadequate first premise here lies in the lumping for discussion of a conforming and of a nonconforming shipment, with "title passing subject to rescission on discovery." See *infra,* and my CASES AND MATERIALS at 393 *f.*, 401. The condition precedent to the passing of title (typically consisting of "inspection," but sometimes of "acceptance of title") has been repeatedly used in the same manner as has "reservation of title by taking the bill of lading to seller's order"; *i.e.*, it has been called upon, where the shipment did *not* conform, to work out proper pro-buyer results hard to achieve under the "title passes on shipment" analysis. (For an excellent analytical attack on the cases in the order bill-of-lading matter, see Note (1929) 29 COL. L. REV. 1100, *esp.* 1108 *ff.*) Apart from "sale on approval" cases and odd cases such as Agri. Mfg. Co. v. Atlantic Fertilizer Co., 129 Md. 42, 98 Atl. 365 (1916) (where it is, on one branch of the case, barely arguable that the agreement limited seller, in any lawsuit, to justifying his position by specific evidence which had become impossible to produce), the "condition precedent to sale" cases seem to bunch significantly around seller's nonconformity. There are, however, aberrations, and they appear sometimes in commercial transactions and at a point of real leverage. Compare Larkin v. Geisenheimer, 201. App. Div. 741, 195 N. Y. Supp. 577 (1922), in result, and its ideology as revived by Glass v. Misroch, 239 N. Y. 475, 147 N. E. 71 (1925): "The seller may not force the goods upon a buyer unwilling to receive them"—which is at utter odds with the effect of normal shipment under 19(4)(2) and 46(1). What is this magic of postponing the place of delivery, when sense calls precisely there. most of all, for the defaulting buyer to take the burden of redisposition? The Merchants' Association, as noted in n. 26, has here cut through "Assent" into sense. See their proposed excision of Rule 6 from the Federal Sales Bill, Sec. 20.

[44]Isaacs, *The Industrial Purchaser and the Sales Act* (1934) 34 COL. L. REV. 262, 269, regards Act 19(1), where specific goods are contracted about but are to be held pending order to ship, as hard on an industrial (and, I should add, no less on a commercial) buyer whose insurance does not cover goods in warehouses of others. The same holds where setting aside occurs postcontract, "with the implied assent of the buyer." Of course, insurance by seller for buyer's account is always possible. *Cf.* the facts of Berkshire Cotton Mfg. Co. v. Cohen, 236 N. Y. 364, 140 N. Y. 726 (1923). But it calls for a special clause. There would certainly be much to be said for a rule that, in mercantile cases, risk should not pass, though

to deliver at destination, and has not delivered, how has he earned his price?[45] In the conditional-sales situation, after delivery, we do think thus,[46] and the commercial cases which make sense work out to such results. But of what assistance is the Title-concept in the working out, *when the case is not clear in advance?* And why, having discovered that risk of loss or damage has problems of its own, do we not settle down to thinking those problems through, as such? If we should, the effects of the thinking would clarify our Sales law much. And the effects would not be limited to Sales.[47]

title-for-purposes-of-price did pass, unless *seller insured to cover buyer* during any period in which, under the contract, seller retains control and holds at buyer's disposal. A half step, in a special case, in this general direction is found in Act 46(3). Certainly Tarling v. Baxter, 6 B. & C. 360, 108 Eng. Rep. 484 (K.B. 1827), for all its value in advancing analysis, is without much bearing on the policy of such a situation. Compare Idaho Products Co. v. Bales, 36 Idaho 800, 214 Pac. 206 (1923), also a case of stacked hay, note 23. The Federal Sales Bill is a bit roughhewn, though sound in base line, on the matter. See Sec. 23(c) as proposed by the Merchants' Association. The problem is clear; seller needs price, and is entitled to it; and buyer is defaulting. Neither should a seller who knows a buyer is defaulting be put to risking further expense. *Yet* goods in S's control are not lightly to be lifted into B's risk, despite even Goble's lovely study in (1937) 37 Col. L. Rev. 410. Is there no compromise, via mercantile goods insured for account of whom it may concern—and, after request for authorization, at expense of buyer when it concerns him? The matter bothers me, as being one where Rules of Law (old *or* new) give too little *effective* guidance, even to counsel.—*Cf.* facts and Blackburn, in Martineau v. Kitching, L. R. 7 Q. B. 436 (1872).

[45]*Cf.* Hunter Bros. v. Kramer Bros., 71 Kan. 468, 80 Pac. 963 (1905). Why, when obligation to deliver is clear, must Title get in the way? Unperformed seller's obligation goes beyond risk to damages for nondelivery, and so includes all that Title can give, and more. The place of Title in such a picture is at points where goods which *are* delivered (or are specific) prove to show a defect in title. Act, Section 13.

[46]Cond. Sales Act, § 27. And Bogert's Commentary thereon.

[47]For example, the definite turning of attention to risk forces closer definition of what risk one is thinking of. Risk of loss may be one thing, risk of deterioration another. *Cf.* Sale of Goods Act, § 33. As risk of insolvency is one thing, and risk of dishonesty another. And the risks of unforeseen commercial or industrial difficulty deserve more attention than our cases on impossibility give. In The Common Law, Holmes marked out a line of prophetic thought: "The price paid in mercantile contracts generally excludes the construction that exceptional risks were intended to be assumed." P. 303. (Holmes can grow absurdly technical, and lose the thread of creation, as in those fraud cases where he finds "no contract," and thus no title even voidable. But when creative, he has never had a master.) The "subject to strikes . . . and other causes beyond the seller's control" clauses, which have become familiar, point in the same direction. I have seen no indication that their presence materially decreases the price paid, or is felt as a deprivation of extra insurance otherwise counted on by buyers. Isaacs, *Industrial Purchaser and the Sales Act* (1934) 34 Col. L. Rev. 262, at 270, points out that some buyers are beginning to balance (or overbalance) by their own forms of full pro-buyer clauses, but here, too, I lack evidence that such clauses affect the *price*. Leaving the matter to clauses does result, however, in *penalizing little* men where bigger outfits bargain out; and this is not wise lawmaking wherever the level either of factual expectation or of commercial decency is such as to make the clauses normally desirable. It is of interest that German law recognized most of our current seller's exemptions, without explicit clause. It is of double interest that the Scandinavian legislators,

So much at least is clear: In a bona fide commercial deal in process of execution, the fact that either party has insured goods which have become specific should of itself warrant recognition in that party of insurable interest; and, if the other party has not insured, should of itself determine risk *pro tanto*. What have the presumptions of Act, Section 19, to do with this, except for tradition or arbitrary fiat?[48]

though their general attack on commercial law distinctly followed the English model, found this phase of our contract-law too much to stomach, and incorporated the exemptions in their code. Anglo-American judges, however, including even Scrutton [Bourgeois v. Wilson, Holgate & Co., Ltd., 25 Com. Cas. 260 (1920)] are only beginning to feel their way into consonance with need and sense on the point. For in contract law such lumps as "promise," "consideration," and "legality" can distract attention from the fundamental issue quite as well as "Title" can in Sales. Note again the problem in intellectual history. Both the need and the technical road out (constructive conditions) are made clear by 1881, in a peculiarly famous book by a peculiarly famous judge—indeed, for him who cared to look, they had been made clear a century earlier by another judge of curiously similar personality. Holmes builds on Mansfield. The Great War brought up a series of drastic cases to point the moral. But "serious commercial difficulty," as a line of thinking about "excuse," goes down before the analogies derived from the "frustration" idea.

[48]Williston recognizes part of this: where there is an agreement between seller and buyer as to insuring for the benefit of one of them. I SALES, 695; also that risk and property may part company. § 302 *ff*. But it cannot be said that the idea of severing risk and Title appeals to him. Blackburn's clear-eyed approach to risk problems simply as such is classic, and repeated; it recurs in famous cases; *for all that, it is almost consistently disregarded*. In three wholly distinct types of situation he vigorously refused to be misled by arguments from title. Calcutta Co. v. De Mattos, 32 L. J. Q. B. 332, 33 L. J. Q. B. 214 (1863); Martineau v. Kitching, L. R. 70 B. 436 (1876); Anderson v. Morice, 10 C. P. 58 (1874): "It may be observed that risk and property generally go together [in the easy cases], and consequently in many of the cases, though the important point was, at whose risk is the thing, it is treated as if the sole question was, whose property is it? *In the present case, however, the real question was, whose risk was it?*" (Italics supplied.) I think, in this last, that there was a further step to take. See text p. 188, and notes 53 and 23 *supra*. But Blackburn's sharp, crisp analysis invigorates.

If legal dogmatics is a science, one is free to admire technique, even while challenging one or another premise. Indeed, one is free to admire *the lines of premise* chosen even while disagreeing with the *particular premise* chosen. Blackburn, Bramwell, and earlier, Mansfield, and later, the by-the-Law-of-England-crippled Scrutton, raise a question. Namely, this: if Mansfield (whatever intervened) could be followed by a Bramwell and a Blackburn, *and built on*—for they did that—then why is Scrutton sterile? I mean sterile in *result*. I feel this man to be the greatest commercial judge who ever sat in English-speaking countries. I think that clear. He outranks even Mansfield. You have only to read him. Yet he indulged "judicial self-limitation" when Mansfield would have rolled up his sleeves and gone to work. It may be that times had changed. Some of my students urge on me that an era of consolidation of law had proceeded to arrive. As in the American situation from 1890, say to now, among gentlemen who happen to be lawyers, or vice versa. But before my eyes remains this figure, Scrutton—who could have taught Bramwell and Blackburn, and who had courage that Mansfield never could have conceived, as well as a sensitivity to commerce which had no need of Mansfield's merchant-jury. An American revolter struggles like a diver in strange waters as he attempts to work out an understanding of why this genius in commercial law saw the better, and then bowed to the worse, as being *the Law of England*. But again; one is free to

A further and frequent hitch (as frequent as buyer's backing out) occurs when *the seller's performance is, in a material point, not up to his agreement.* In any other field than Sales, we should say without more ado: The buyer can either take it or leave it—with due qualification anent substantial performance.[49] And if he takes it, he can have his damages for the defect. But in Sales we are embarrassed. Our accepted, and even statutory, theory runs in terms of "appropriation" of *"the"* goods to *"the"* contract, and of "assent" thereto by the nonappropriating party—whole lump or none again, for both at once.[50] Let me not linger on the older theory of "offer in full satisfaction," duly accepted and performed, which the Act under the combined influence of contract theory and of sense is now rather successful in removing from the legal scene.[51] Let me rather recall three situations, all solved by most

admire technique! I think, also, one is free to admire sense of duty. For my part, I would give my one eye, and perhaps both, to have had Scrutton as chief on the Exchequer Bench between 1820 and 1860. Read Scrutton (William Harrar has studied his commercial opinions in an essay that cries for publication) and then read Parke, C. B., and the matter is plain.

May a "jurisprude" hazard an opinion which runs *pro sua domo?* I guess that Scrutton's sense of decency had been hamstrung by a tradition, derived I know not whence, that judges just stayed put. "I have said nothing about the results being just, because justice is not what we strive after in the Courts . . . if you mean by justice some moral standard which is not the law of England." This is a libel of Scrutton on Scrutton. He *did* strive after justice, and twist the law of England to that end. But it is even more a truth, because Scrutton felt that law to bind him with a singular bindingness and strove with all his strength to fight down any urge to alter it, unless he saw a loophole. This was not the tradition of the nineteenth century, through Bramwell and Blackburn. Nor had it been Mansfield's. Something happened, between; else Scrutton would have moved. Moved, despite the statute. The attitude of English judges toward the Factors Acts gave precedent enough. And Scrutton knew well how to use precedents with an Aye, when they had eyes, with a Nay, when they neighed. Hence: here is a gap in English legal history. The perfect exemplar of the man who ought to innovate grows curiously slow in innovation. "Trimming?" You do not know Scrutton. When Scrutton had prejudices, he voiced them and so got rid of them. No. Something which cripples judges has happened, rather recently, in the British Judicial System What? It is merely a symptom that the Court of Appeals has changed its doctrine, and now regards itself as "bound" by its own decisions—even when they are distinguishable. Taylor v. Oakes, 127 L. T. R. 267 (C. A. 1922) is one instance out of many.

[49]On substantial performance and Sales law see Note (1933) 33 Col. L. Rev. 1021; Note 1935) 35 *id.* at 726; n. 86, *infra.*

[50]Act, § 19, hallows the tradition. The acts of "appropriation" are almost always done by the seller. In contracts for sale, the buyer's assent is almost always "implied" because no buyer's representative is present. Difficulty arises when the buyer is present, as in tender at destination, when "refusal to accept title" may enter to complicate the picture. See note 43, *supra.* Where no "implied assent" of the non-acting party is found, the orthodox analysis proceeds on a basis akin to the orthodox law of offer and acceptance, but gets into confusion between technique and justice when it comes to interpreting the seller's "offer-in-breach-of-contract." See Note (1937) 37 Col. L. Rev. 610.

[51]Act, § 49. The saving of buyer's rights is introduced by "in the absence of

courts in rough, but interesting ways; all of which have, however, thrown Title-theory and Title-theorists into bafflement. On these points, decisions that are in fact consistent cannot be described as consistent, *via* the halo verbiage. They have to be described as contradictory, and some of them as wrong.[52] Which means that the theorists' misdescription is not only cumbersome and inaccurate, but (which is bad) may at any time mislead a further court.

3. *Destruction in Mid-Delivery*

Wheat, contracted to be delivered into a vessel, is in process of being loaded. Before delivery is complete, it is destroyed by tempest. Can the buyer, as against the recalcitrant insurer, exercise an option to call the delivery good *pro tanto,* collect his insurance, and so to mutual satisfaction pay off his uninsured seller?[53] Common sense answers: "Of course! Why the pother?" But the insurer argues that Title never reached the buyer; until delivery completed, he had not assented to any appropriation of "the goods";

express *or implied* agreement of the parties." Williston's text makes it clear that the words were intentional; which is, with respect, a little queer, since *implied* offer in full satisfaction was all that the worst common-law cases had argued. But the courts have paid little attention to the introductory clause—fortunately, in this case. More troublesome is the meaning of "other legal remedy" in the section. Even the draftsman deals with it primarily in terms of action for damages. Does it apply equally to power to cancel for material breach in an installment, or is it limited to the damagelike recoupment? If the former, one quarrels with inadequate phrasing; if the latter, with policy. See also 3 LAW, A CENTURY OF PROGRESS, 110, *re* Sec. 32, *infra*, p. 208; and the Warranty paper.

52Typical is 1 WILLISTON, SALES, 578-9, n., 580, n.

53Colonial Ins. Co. v. Adelaide Ins. Co., 12 A. C. 128 (P. C. 1886). Anderson v. Morice, 10 C.P. 58 (1874), was there distinguished on grounds on which that case had carefully tried to avoid resting, grounds too technical to satisfy or to give certainty as to the outcome of the next similar case. (I personally believe that on the point of insurable interest the Anderson case was overruled, and, on that point, will be confined to its *exact* facts.) Blackburn's opinion in the Anderson case is, however, notable for its explicit insistence that *risk* may pass with full loading of "the cargo" contracted for, even though "full property" may not have passed; and that the words "the cargo" contain no necessary magic about risk, since bag-by-bag passing of risk may be arranged, even without an explicit clause to that effect; and in taking risk rather than title as the crucial matter. What it overlooks is that risk was not the issue of the case, as it would have been in seller's suit for price, in which the buyer could properly insist on complete performance. The issue was *insurable interest;* and buyer's option to take an incomplete performance (plus his factual interest in the venture) affords an ample basis for recognizing such an insurable interest. More interesting still is Bramwell's concurrence—for it was Bramwell who sixteen years before had made the buyer's option clear.

Contrast such a case as Rochester and Oleopolis Oil Co. v. Hughey. 56 Pa. 322 (1867), where the issue was *really* risk; can seller recover the price of partially loaded oil, after its destruction, against his recalcitrant buyer? Held, and properly: no. Blackburn's ghost, finding these cases dealt with at large on the "issue" of property, will be remembering certain words of Carroll: "I said it very loud and clear. . . ."

and no man, after destruction, can by mere act of will take halo-Title to now nonexistent goods. On this last, I gather that Williston would agree in general with the insurer. The court did not. But Williston approves the case because property had passed to the extent of the *delivery*.[54] Precisely what the court thought it was holding when it affirmed a judgment by the insurer who had paid buyer, against a reinsurer, I have never been able to determine. What seems certain is that its remarks on *property* having passed were hardly more than desultory. The recurring nub of the opinion is that the case turned on *insurable interest*—thus advancing the analysis yards beyond that in *Anderson* v. *Morice*, which had itself already moved from *property* to *risk*.[55] Insurable interest is found because the vessel was under buyers' control, because buyers would have had to return the partial delivery or pay, and because seller could not without buyers' consent regain what had been put on board. The delivery vested property from time to time as loaded, and at the time of the loss the partial delivery was at buyers' risk. (!) Buyers' option to return did not prevent their having an insurable interest. Their "interest" was defeasible at *their* option.—That out of all this a modern writer should pick for emphasis only the passing reference to "property," which throws analysis not only back to Blackburn, but back beyond Blackburn's scrimmage line for a handsome loss, is hard to grasp. For all that is needed to avoid difficulty is to recognize that, as usual, the sum of interests which we know as Title is *divided* between buyer and seller during the process of loading, and to use the concep-

[54]Sales, § 277. VOLD, SALES, 200 *f.*, makes the Colonial Ins. case turn (as the court does in part) on the buyer's having chartered the vessel, delivery of the loaded portion "to the buyer" having occurred; and where this is not the case, insists that *nothing* passes to the buyer till the delivery to the carrier is complete, there being then nothing to show assent to piecemeal appropriation. The insurance aspects of these cases would seem to have since been covered by practice, and in the buyer's favor; else the matters would have been litigated into clarity—that is, in the United States. For England, see note 59 *infra*. Apart from the treatment in the texts cited, the treatment in the casebooks is significant. Lewis (1929) (an excellent job, his collection, though I do not like arrangement around the Act) quotes it purely on the question of "delivery," with a "but" to the *Rochester* case *et al.* 371, n. Williston and McCurdy (1932) quote it merely to distinguish the Anderson case. 190, n. VOLD'S WOODWARD (1933) gives the holding accurately: "an insurable interest." gives two of the three grounds adduced for distinguishing the Anderson case, and quotes an "insurable interest" sentence along with the property sentence. Bogert and Britton disregard the case. Llewellyn, in 1930, had only digested its facts and reasoning, and tends today toward repentance for not printing the report in full.

[55]See n. 47, and 53.

tual bridge thoughtfully provided by Bramwell as early as 1859 in *Langton* v. *Higgins*[56] and reasonably well rediscovered by Barnes Peacock in the case in hand, to wit: that the buyer has power to claim, if he will, a delivery still imperfect; but also power to reject if and when delivery proves imperfect or incomplete. And it is needed to see the question not as one of Title primarily, but in first instance as one of *contract.* Bramwell in that case had announced (though in Sales language) a principle broader than Sales, one, indeed, which many sections of the Act accept,[57] one which lines up a goodly body of cases that at first sight might seem mutually inconsistent, arrays them along lines not only of solid common sense but of broad, simple rule. Why should we discard such analysis? The task of law writing or legislation is to produce broad generalizations *which work out to satisfaction.* Failing that —and often as a preliminary to it—one needs differentiation. Neither is a sole solvent. Neither can justify itself, except in terms of fact and need. But one would have thought that, in the age of principle, such a principle would have been welcome. Perhaps it

[56](Ex. 1859) 4 H. & N. 204. "In all reason, when a vendee sends his ship, or cart, or cask, or bottle to the vendor, and he puts the article sold into it, that is a delivery to the vendee." This is the language that seems to have drawn the attention. The likening of bottles to ships (the "buyer's receptacle" idea) is enough to show that Bramwell was still groping. Bottles, sacks, boxes are one thing. Carts are another. Tank cars owned or leased by one party or the other are a third. But chartered vessels raise problems different from all three. Williston properly criticizes Bramwell for "finding" a "delivery" here. There was no real delivery. But the creative part of the opinion remains: "Suppose the oil of peppermint had been badly manufactured, I am not prepared to assent to the argument that the plaintiff [a buyer-financer-mortgagee] would not have had a power of rejection. *Again, suppose only a portion of the oil had been put into the bottles, inasmuch as the plaintiff was not bound to take a part only, would the property vest?* Aldridge v. Johnson is an authority on that point. It may be that the plaintiff would have the option of refusing to take a part only of the oil or of accepting it, but *that right is not inconsistent with the property vesting at his election.*" (Italics supplied.) It is a natural progression to carry this thinking from property forward into risk (which would work for the buyer), and again from risk forward into insurable interest (which would work for the buyer again.) Aldridge v. Johnson had well prepared the way. And appropriation at the buyer's option, ambiguous in that case, ought to have been perceived as unambiguous in Anderson v. Morice.

[57]The fundamental section is 11, coupled with 49. Other sections, especially those relating to quantity, presuppose 11 and 49, and somewhat limit the buyer's option: 7 and 8; 44 and 46(2) make special express repetition of the option. 46(3) does not. I read "promise" in 11(1) as including all the "duties" on the seller laid down in Sections 41-47, 13-16. Section 69(1) (c) seems to repeat 11, in favor of the buyer, on the condition side, adding a possible damage action; 69(1) (b) seems to repeat 49, first sentence; or else they conflict. 69(1) (d) makes the buyer's option clear, even when title is held to have passed, as the language of 69(4) and (5) ("elects to rescind the sale") reinforces. All of this becomes clearer in the wording of the proposed Federal Sales Bill. On the quasi-contractual aspects, see Anderson, *supra* note 13.

was, until it tangled with title-thinking. Title-thinking, Sales law viewed as property law,[58] possessed an intellectual vested inertia which even a sane and simple principle found it impossible to upset without due process of time. But English legislation (ignored by all American Sales scholars) saw sense, and did sense,[59] in the same year in which the Sales Act did not, in this particular: 1906. The story of the Factors Acts is parallel, as appears in the companion paper, *Purchase for Value*.

SELLER'S NONCONFORMING SHIPMENT

This leads into a second and broader disruption of the marketing process. Seller makes a patently nonconforming shipment and (to point the argument) it is no clerk's mistake, but principal's deliberation. Here orthodox theory runs into muddle, as is evidenced by almost any discussion, judicial or other, which one may pick up. If one is to think precisely, appropriation of "the goods" is out, wherever whatever goods are sent fail to conform to the contract description.[60] The best you can do is: "seller's *attempt* to appropriate *some* specific goods." Again, appropriation of anything "to *the* contract" is no less difficult to see, there being a deliberate breach—or shall I say defiance—of the contract obligation. Yet the bulk of the courts, and Williston in his first edition, have talked of appropriation by the seller to the contract, vesting title, but with power in the buyer to revest title on discovery of the breach.[61] This gives trouble, though the trouble is often more

[58]Even Vold's text and his WOODWARD'S CASES, and Bogert and Britton's cases, cling in arrangement and analysis essentially to this point of view. What does, I think, appear, is increasing *feel*, in the choice of cases, for significant facts and their influence—in which regard both collections are admirable—and, more hesitantly, a somewhat greater tendency to hammer on the seller's *contract* as needing examination before one turns to his acts of seeming appropriation.

[59]The MARINE INSURANCE ACT, 6 EDW. VII, § 7 reads:

"(1) A defeasible interest is insurable, as also is a contingent interest.

"(2) In particular, where the buyer of goods has insured them, he has an insurable interest, notwithstanding that he might, at his election, have rejected the goods, or treated them as at the seller's risk, by reason of the latter's delay in making delivery or otherwise." *Cf. also* § 14 (2). Is our case-law doctrine impervious to hints? Can scholars not recognize declaratory legislation? *Cf.* the Statute of Anne.

[60]Whether the "description" be by words of contract, words of representation, sample, blueprint, the nature of the case, or other line of implication. The FEDERAL SALES BILL, Sec. 16(4) and 17(d) attempts a not wholly complete clarification. I attempted one equally unsatisfactory in (1937) 37 COL. L. REV. 364, n. The need is clear.

[61]SALES (1st ed. 1909). §§ 473, 474. For typical judicial language: "If the goods are not up to the sample, the right to refuse them exists, which is, in effect, a rescission. The title passes upon delivery to the carrier, subject to this right, of which the pur-

aesthetic than practical. It raises difficulty on "the goods" side where goods that do not conform get into trouble on the way (nonconformity appearing rarely on their destruction, but appearing often enough on partial damage or on attempts by creditors to attach). It gives trouble where goods conform but documents do not, though no deterioration supervene (as when the documents in a c.i.f. contract misdescribe).[62] The concept gives trouble, on the "appropriation" side, in the case, say, of shipment by an improper route and destruction in transit. But the trouble which the theory, if really taken literally, would raise rarely becomes practical because, *as between buyer and seller,* courts simply, by one route or by another, avoid its application.[63] Moreover, in his second

chaser may avail himself or not." Kuppenheimer v. Wertheimer, 107 Mich. 77, 64 N. W. 952 (1895).

[62]Interesting instances in Gillespie Bros. v. Thompson Bros., 13 Ll. L. Rep. 519 (C. A. 1922); Finlay & Co. v. Kwik Hoo Tong, [1928] 2 K. B. 604. The same problem arises under any defect of quality, payment having been made against documents before arrival of the goods. Here blunt Title-analysis goes haywire. Compare 2 WILLISTON, SALES, 1237-8, n. Most of the cases there cited *act* sense. Thus the English cases, although their Act repudiates rescission for breach of warranty, permit rejection under a documentary contract when the goods prove, after documents have been taken up, to be noncomforming. This is sound law, under SALE OF GOODS ACT, Sections 11(1) (c) and 35, which deal only with acceptance of *goods.* It is necessary commercial sense. The best American case is Pierson v. Crooks, 115 N. Y. 539, 22 N. E. 349 (1889). Of course throwing back the goods and desire to sue for damages are rarely coupled, since commonly even defective goods will be taken on a rising market; but where the goods are flatly unusable, either a dealer-buyer or an industrial purchaser may need the action for nondelivery, and should not be deprived thereof by false analysis in terms of title having passed and of rescission being the sole available remedy. Williston here undercuts for documentary contracts the whole point of his remarks on nonconforming shipment. 1 SALES, 585, 587; 2 *id.* at 1237. The curious thing is—and it shows how firm a grip Title can take across a good Sales lawyer's eyes—that the technical way out is suggested in the note directly across the page, which speaks, anent a concealed defect in seed, of a delivery "conditional only. the contract to remain executory." Similarly, there can be payment that is tentative or conditional only, and documents in the buyer's hands which he can hold at option. having, indeed, power to transfer [as even a buyer without title has, under Section 20(4)] but which have been taken on a constructive contractual condition that there is no prejudice to buyer from acting on the seller's implicit assurance (by taking money against them, under the contract) that the goods will be found to conform both to documents and to contract. The courts hurdle the theoretical difficulty by talking rejection where necessary, and by giving incidental damages along with return of the price, even when talking rescission. See Note (1935) 35 COL. L. REV. 726.

[63]So, especially, where goods or shipment-manner run counter to the agreement, by insisting on seller's order bill of lading as reserving title, and so risk: compare Penniman v. Winder, 180 N. C. 73, 103 S. E. 908 (1920); and cases cited (1929) 29 COL. L. REV. 1100, 1102-3; or by finding a condition precedent to passing of title in some inspection clause: compare Wall Rice Milling Co. v. Continental Supply Co., 36 Utah, 121, 103 Pac. 242 (1909); and on both lines of operation compare note 43 *supra.* Less frequent is clean-cut reanalysis to meet the case of nonconforming goods, as in Libman v. Fox-Pioneer Scrap Iron Co., 175 Wisc. 485, 185 N. W. 551 (1921). The situation that would force reanalysis, to wit, rejection plus a nondelivery claim, is rather rarely presented.

edition, Williston observes cogently that there can be no wise implication of buyer's assent to a noncontract shipment (which applies equally whether it be non-contract as to kind, quality, manner, documents, insurance coverage, price demanded, what have you); and this is sense. But Williston proceeds to urge further that Title in such case will, therefore, not vest till buyer's acceptance: seller is perforce making a "new offer."[64] I think this an unnecessary and unfortunate addition. I cannot believe that the logical consequence would be applied by courts, in all their apparent implications—as, *e.g.*, that the seller's creditors, attaching before arrival, should defeat a buyer *who demands* the shipment.[65] Or that the seller itself, by virtue of its own breach, can

The courts' instinct has been somewhat less certain where claims over, for damage or destruction, were concerned (in the United States, especially against railroads) and the defense was skillfully presented that title at the time of the damage was essential to the claim, and that under Sales rules such title was not in the present plaintiff. So Kleinhans v. Canadian Pac. Ry. Co., 203 App. Div. 715, 196 N. Y. Supp. 862 (1922). The business reasoning (convenience of adjustment) and the general policy reasoning (speed and cheapness of adjustment) run here as in the cases on insurable interest, *supra*, especially notes 44, 47, to wit: Let whichever takes the loss as against the other be free to make the claim over. That the UNIFORM BILLS OF LADING ACT largely cures the situation, see Watts v. Norfolk So. R. R., 183 N. C. 12, 110 S. E. 582 (1922).

The North Carolina cases (collected by Leon Malman) present a fascinating study in the struggle of sound judicial instinct against technical stumbling blocks. (I leave the "Ry." in the titles as it came to me, although my own practice runs *contra*. There is real dramatic power in its repetitive impact.) "The other party is the only proper plaintiff" dominates the scene in Asheboro Mfg. Co. v. Ry., 149 N. C. 261, 62 S. E. 1091 (1908) (for a while the local leading case); Parker Buggy Corp. v. Ry., 152 N. C. 119, 67 S. E. 251 (1910); Elliott v. Ry., 155 N. C. 249, 71 S. E. 339 (1911); Ellington v. Ry., 170 N. C. 36, 86 S. E. 693 (1915). Restiveness of the court, and technical twisting to avoid technical defense, appear as early as Wilkins v. Ry., 160 N. C. 54, 75 S. E. 1090 (1912). In 1916 mercantile views begin to prevail: Meyers v. Ry., 171 N. C. 190, 88 S. E. 947 (1916) (where buyer's failure to get an order bill of lading properly indorsed is the ground of nonsuit). In Adylett v. Ry., 172 N. C. 47, 89 S. E. 1000 (1916), and Trading Co. v. Ry., 178 N. C. 175, 100 S. E. 316 (1919), a technical device appears which does the necessary work, even without statute: consignor's adjustment with consignee is made to amount to an "equitable assignment" of consignee's claim against the carrier. Then come the BILLS OF LADING ACT and the Watts case, *supra*. And in Anderson v. Express Co., 187 N. C. 171, 121 S. E. 354 (1924), the court holds almost a military review of its resources for keeping Sales rules from interfering with a suit against the carrier for loss, damage, or delay. For cases in other jurisdictions see (1929) 29 COL. L. REV. 1100, 1104-5.

[64] 1 SALES, 585, 587; and the implications of 2 *id.*, § 474. How the language on 587, so far as it deals with prior *"contract"* (as distinct from buyer's mere "order" or "offer"), is to be reconciled with ACT, Section 49, and WILLISTON, SALES, §§ 484a *ff.*, escapes me.

[65] On which point cases like Aldridge v. Johnson, 7 El. & Bl. 885, 119 Eng. Rep. 1476 (Q. B. 1857), and Langton v. Higgins, *supra*, with their semi-"delivery" aspect seem to me more persuasive than the type of case symbolized by Andrews v. Durant, 11 N. Y. 351 (1854). Had it been decided in any state lacking the Lanfear v. Sumner rule, Low v. Pew, 108 Mass. 347 (1871), would be a clean authority against

effectually stop and divert the shipment,[66] although the buyer be the named consignee, be still solvent, and be now claiming. Or that any acquiescence at all by the buyer in the noncontract mode of shipment per se throws title and so every risk in transit onto him.[67]

As in the preceding situation, what one has, in fact, is divided interest, with full Title in neither party. Again the situation is one essentially of contract and only incidentally one involving phases of property. Again the courts bunch decisions (even when not their reasoning) with sense. What the judges typically *do*, today, whatever they or the writers may *say* about it, *is to give the buyer power to take the shipment, if he wants it*: to take it moreover, as a defective performance *referable to the original agreement* and so entailing damages for the defect; *but to reject it if he pleases.*[68] Risk remaining in consequence on the seller; the price

the prevalence of the view I urge as likely to prevail in fact. Among modern cases, note the diverse tendencies evidenced by Procter & Gamble Co. v. Peter White Jr., Co., 233 N. Y. 97, 134 N. E. 849 (1922), and Craig Brokerage Co. v. Goddard Co., 92 Ind. App. 234, 175 N. E. 19 (1931). But let a *shipment* once get off to the buyer, without contract for delivery at destination, and the divergence in tendency would cease.

[66]*Cf.*, Lynch Davidson & Co. v. Denman Lumber Co., 270 S. W. 225 (Tex. Civ. App. 1925); Greenwood Grocery Co. v. Canadian Elevator Co., 72 S. C. 450, 52 S. E. 191 (1905) (in both cases *dicta*); and note *infra*. I read the nonrecovery by the buyer of certain cars, in the Procter & Gamble case, 233 N. Y. 97, 134 N. E. 849 (1922), as turning on absence of shipment to him. A more conventional and somewhat treacherous phrasing would be: absence of "delivery."

[67]See Lamborn v. Seggerman Bro., 240 N. Y. 118, 147 N. E. 607 (1925) (documentary contract for a 1,200 case carload of apples; delivery order covering 1,200 cases out of a 1,770-case carload paid for without objection; yet recovery by buyer of the price paid, after government had seized the carload).

[68]Often, but by no means always, almost the same treatment is accorded to nonshipment cases. Aldridge v. Johnson and Langton v. Higgins may once have stood on "buyer's receptacle" notions, though I doubt that that is their present-day meaning. But cases involving apparent present sale of misdescribed goods challenge attention hard to evade. A defective performance is there referred to a contract "performed" on seller's side when made. The buyer has been allowed to reject or rescind, one cannot tell which. Hawkins v. Pemberton, 51 N. Y. 198 (1872, Com. App.). The ACT permits him to rescind title-and-contract together. § 69(1) (d). That he can at his election keep the defective goods and have damages has not been doubted for a century.

Now, an exciting phase of these cases, shipment or nonshipment, is that Sales here contributes its bit toward exposing the inadequacies and exploding the fallacies that lie in certain phases of the orthodox theories of Offer and Acceptance, and of Consideration—at the same time showing that Contract, for all its huge value, is no full key to Sales problems; certainly not, in the present condition of accepted contract theory.

Let the facts of Powers v. Dodgson, 194 Mich. 133, 160 N. W. 432 (1917), serve as an illustration. Seller offered specific but absent wool. Buyer answered: "If there ain't over 300 lbs. [of fine wool in the lot] I will give you 25½ cents." Accepted. But there *were* over three hundred pounds of fine wool. At this point, I

remaining in consequence, during transit, still unearned. The orthodox theoretical difficulties involved in "the" goods and in appropriation to "the" contract the courts simply vault over. As well they may. For they are foolish difficulties; foolish, because once more they arise from seeking to locate an entire "title" in one single party as a key to solution, in a circumstance in which both sense and the cases demand recognition of first, divided interests (in fact, and so in law), and, second, of one particular typical line of division of interests, to wit: favoring interests (especially the chance of market gain) being allocated to the non-defaulting buyer; disfavoring interests (especially risks of loss or rejection, etc.) lying almost entirely in the contract-breaking seller.[69]

think it clear that (1) *B* has not in any normal sense assented to appropriation of anything as *against* himself; and (2) that whereas he can have the wool and damages, if he wants them, despite *S*'s most desperate efforts to get out, (3) he need not take the wool. As in the case of "sale on approval" (what obligation on the buyer's side?), the standard Law of Consideration goes into the discard. Here, either *S* is obligated (*e.g.*, to deliver on tender, or to procure any bailee's attornment) while *B* is not, or *B* is obligated without having received the explicitly bargained-for equivalent. Something, then, is wrong with orthodox theory of consideration or with the obvious outcome. I hold with the latter. The case itself I do not wish to discuss in detail here save for this: that it is a magnificent example of strong-arming a sound result out of an impossible given theory by rough and ready mayhem and surgery. ("How can Your Honor decide that way?" says counsel in one of the favorite and throat-chuckled yarns of Taft, C. J. The Court answers, "By main strength!") The Federal Sales Bill moves toward making this main strength statutory. Sec. 20(4)(2) "order or." Is case-law doctrine still impervious to hints?

Indeed, on the offer and acceptance side, the most frequent case runs in terms of an order to ship, followed by prompt shipment of goods which do not wholly conform. If buyer takes the goods and sues for nonconformity, any modern citizen unspoiled by the accepted pseudo-law of counteroffers and unilaterals would agree that such buyer should recover, for seller's failure to perform. If the defect was latent, even unilateralists would turn to some theory of "the passing of title" (to what? to *what?*) having been "called for," so as to work out a recovery for him. *Common-sense* contract theory would recognize in such a case that any shipment really referable to the offer was acceptance-and-breach together, and that the seller was bound though buyer was not—just as common-sense reading of the offer would recognize that it called, implicitly, *in the alternative,* for *either* a reasonably prompt shipment *or* a reasonably prompt promise to ship with reasonable dispatch. To explore the extent to which the cases conform to such common sense on this will require a paper in itself. It will appear. Meanwhile, it is obvious that wherever orthodox offer-and-acceptance doctrine is argued to the court, the court must either duck, squirm, manhandle the facts, or do injustice. PAGE, CASES ON CONTRACTS (1935), gathers what to a Sales lawyer is a surprising collection of decisions that do this last. One of the easiest outs is to treat notification of a shipment already made as if it had been a promise to ship in terms of the order. What makes the situation peculiarly interesting here is that when the nonconformity lies in words (such as disclaimers of warranty tagged onto bags of seed) the orthodox offer-and-acceptance doctrine may overwhelm Sales sense; just as when nonconformity to *prior* contract lies in a demand of excessive price before delivery, the "voluntary-payment" line of cases so often knocks on the head the statutory hope of SALES ACT, Section 49. But, as Kipling remarks, that is another story. See my forthcoming *Case-Law, Sense, and Contract Doctrine,* 47 YALE L. J.

[69] I owe to Bruno Schachner the idea that title has *lines and planes* of cleavage akin to those of crystals.

The orthodox theoretical difficulties arise, *inter alia,* from an antiquated overconcentration on the effect of consensual acts. It will be recalled what discomforts this approach entailed in the law of Offer and Acceptance, where it became necessary to meet difficult cases by ceasing to look for actual intent or consent, and turning instead to contract-without-agreement-in-fact in many situations in which an offeree had been reasonably misled by the offeror's expression. It will also be recalled that until theory cleanly accepted and articulated the "objective" standard of interpreting the offeror's expression[70]—*i.e.*, while courts were still *talking* "meeting of the minds" but trying to *do* "reasonable outcome in the case"—there was confusion of language and occasional very dubious decision.[71] It is argued here that that is one phase of the

The nub of this can be fitted somewhat into orthodox Sales terminology. We already know the concept "Security-title," which recognizes that some, or much, or most of Title can pass, leaving a limited body of rights behind. This concept one might call division of *Title*. Without explicitly *dividing* Title, moreover, we have already become grudgingly familiar with splitting from it such attributes as risk, or the power of stoppage, or lien. I propose that one might split with equal ease the concept "*pass*." Indeed, we are familiar with such splitting of the legal *process* of the passing. We differentiate consent of the seller from consent of the buyer, and either can come first, and either can be "implied." Can we not then go on to *recognize* the existing split in legal *effect* of their so-called "consents"—especially when those "consents" are at odds, or absent? To recognize that title can pass *as against* the seller, in these cases of nonconformity, without passing *as against* the buyer, would come moderately close to stating both sense and case results in traditional terms. It would not be wholly adequate phrasing. It would emphasize only one of the lines of cleavage. It would obscure the possibilities of a real contract analysis. It would fail to point such issues as leviability, and who can recover from a carrier, and when will a penal statute operate, and who can transfer to some type of purchaser for value. But it would help greatly. Indeed, on all the property phases, such phrasing would further materially the clean-cut introduction into Sales theory of that *inter partes* v. *third party* distinction which, though present here and there and everywhere in Sales doctrine, has yet to be organized and integrated there as it has been in Agency or in Bills and Notes. *Cf.* Note (1937), 37 Col. L. Rev. 630.

[70]Subject always, as Oliphant used to point out, to limitation by the offeree's *subjective* understanding, where *he* had facts that the ordinary reasonable man did not have, to see that the objective expression was not intended to convey all it seemed to say.

[71]The picture is presented by following Cook v. Oxley, 3 Term R. 653, 100 Eng. Rep. 785 (K. B. 1790), through the later reports. That case, in attitude, is pure "meeting-of-the-minds." Adams v. Lindsell, 1 Barn & Ald. 681, 106 Eng. Rep. 250 (K. B. 1818), is a beginning into "reasonable expectation"—though, on its exact facts, it seems obvious that it would today be differently decided, for the cricumstances of the offer-letter gave the offeree utterly no grounds of reasonable reliance. The curious case of Dickinson v. Dodds, 2 Ch. Div. 463 (1876), shows meeting-of-the-minds conceptions still at work, with results that, if they were frequent, would be really unsettling: What rumors about revocation is an offeree to trust, when he cannot reach his offeror?

One major place of true-consent views today is in the situation of the mistransmitted offer. But its revivification there occurs, I suspect, under peculiar stimulus. Ayer v. Western Union, 79 Me. 493, 10 Atl. 495 (1887), for instance, proceeds first upon a ruling that the telegraph company's clause of exemption from liability in its

present situation in Sales.[72] We still *talk* Title and *talk* Assent to lump-Appropriation. That still makes sense enough in the uncontroverted or the easy cases. But doctrine needs equipment to handle the hard cases, as well. In those hard cases the courts are departing in result from the accepted orthodox approach, without yet having (other than spasmodically) concepts and language proper *either to express or to guide* the departures. Indeed, in the Sales field, the courts are even in certain cases treating the Assent aspect as to be wholly disregarded, on one side or the other. Certain types of prior action, notably the formation of an agreement for sale, may put a seller or selling outfit into a position in which his or its later acts will be referred to his or its existing obligation, whether he likes it or not, and even though he expressly repudiates the reference in advance. In other words, the sovereign power of breach is here and there in process of being limited in American law; a line of specific performance *at law* is becoming noticeable in the decisions.[73]

contract with the offeror was *not* binding. When such clauses become binding upon the offeror, the Ayer case becomes troublesome, however strictly it may be in accord with modern "general contract theory" (concerning which see RESTATEMENT, CONTRACTS, § 23). The run of cases which are cited as rejecting its rule [COSTIGAN, CASES ON CONTRACTS (3d ed. 1934) 210] needs detailed study. How great a proportion of them are successful suits by an offeree against a telegraph company, under circumstances which would bar suit by an offeror, if the Ayer rule were followed blindly? And *must* the problem of recovery against an agency at fault tangle up the law of contract between the parties? See an excellent Note (1937) 37 COL. L. REV. 980.

[72]One phase only. For in the law of "express" warranty, the objective contract theory finds expression. Act, § 12. It really lies at the base of Section 15(1), and, in most cases, of 15(2). Indeed, it lies (as a theory) at the base of the bulk of the "presumption" rules in the Act. They *seek* less to lay down controlling rules than to standardize, on the basis of the most general practice discoverable, the probable meaning of the acts or words concerned, to most bargainors concerned, and to give effect to that meaning. Only subsidiarily, it seems to me, do they seek to solve for the parties problems about which parties would have had hardly a guess, or had two-wayed guesses, had the problems been presented to them at the time of dicker. And this, in my view, is the sound basic approach to regulative law about socially unobjectionable transactions which can be reasonably standardized, and where bargaining power is moderately balanced or fair dealing is the practice. At times a different approach is needed, as where an overdevelopment of automobile theft leads to new and noncustomary regulation of procedure in sales of second-hand cars, with possible effects even *inter partes*. See Notes (1925) 37 A. L. R. 1465 (1928) 52 A. L. R. 701. But all transactions must be conformed to the more necessary forms of policing.

[73]Waite, *loc. cit. supra* note 29, as does Williston, *The Right of a Seller of Goods to Recover the Price* (1907) 20 HARV. L. REV. 363 points out that that action is also in effect for specific performance, a fact that cannot really be obscured by tiddlywinking a Title onto or into the buyer, or refusing to. The *facts* are: a broken contract, in which the seller has done most of his part, and full recovery after buyer's repudiation; which means specific performance.

NONCONSENSUAL "ASSENT"

This a third situation brings out even more sharply: *Seller is behind in its running account with Buyer.* Seller agrees to ship described goods, their whole value or part of their value to be taken in partial settlement of the existing debt.[74] Seller repents of the agreement; it ships, but it ships taking the bill of lading to its own order, and carefully attaching a draft for invoice price. Courts are now recognizing power in the buyer to cut under Seller's manifest attempt at repudiation and to get the goods, despite the patent absence of assent to any appropriation except on condition of prior cash payment.[75] Similarly, cases are appearing which give literal effect to clauses on order forms announcing that "This order cannot be countermanded," and holding the buyer to the price even though he gets notice of his repudiation to the seller before "appropriation" has occurred.[76] These cases do not find

[74]In the cases about to be put, the debt was a *commercial* one, and the two parties had been in a *going* relation of which the transaction in dispute was but one incident. How important that going relation was becomes unmistakable in Rudin v. King-Richardson., 37 F. (2d) 637 (C. C. A. 7th, 1929). But not at all dissimilar is the letting down of the bars on "appropriation" which repeatedly appears (and repeatedly does not appear) where the buyer has financed the production (*e.g.*, in lumbering, canning, farming) or even where the matter is merely one of preferring one old creditor. General examination of cases of these two types indicates that the situation makes itself felt strongly enough to throw the application of orthodox Sales concepts almost into unpredictability, but not strongly enough to substitute for them any other line of predictability. Perhaps studies made state by state, with an eye to time sequence and the detail of the facts, would give more light. I doubt it. I suspect the uncertain results to indicate almost pure groping, because the situation is *seen* as Sales, but often *felt to be security* (almost always favored, in emotion) or preference in insolvency (as to which emotions divide according as the judge pictures the general creditors or some specific creditor as adversary). For excellent discussion see Notes (1937) 37 COL. L. REV. 621, 630. Compare the companion paper on *Purchase for Value.*

[75]Banik v. Chicago, M. & St. P. Ry., 147 Minn. 175, 179 N. W. 899 (1920). Has any one ever commented on the curious pro-buyer leaning of the Minnesota court through the years? To the cases collected in my CASES AND MATERIALS, Index by Jurisdiction, add Wilhelm Lubrication Co. v. Brattrud, 268 N. W. 634 (Minn. 1936) discussed in (1937) 37 COL. L. REV. 309.

Illustrating the trend noted in the text: J. L. Price Brokerage Co. v. Chicago, B. & J. R. Co., 199 S. W. 732 (Mo. App. 1917); Rudin v. King-Richardson Co., 311 Ill. 513, 143 N. E. 198 (1924). And *cf.* the Miribita case, *supra* note 40.

[76]Lewis v. Scoville, 94 Conn. 79, 108 Atl. 501 (1919). Renne v. Volk, 188 Wisc. 508, 205 N. W. 385 (1925), to the same effect, is seemingly repudiated in Knight & Bostwick v. Moore, 203 Wisc. 540, 234 N. W. 902 (1931). But in accord with the Lewis case: Jonesboro Compress Co. v. Mente & Co., 72 F. (2d) 3 (C. C. A. 8th, 1934). It will be noted that once a contracting has been accomplished, such clauses as that in the Wales case, note 39, produce the same effect *re* price as the no-countermand clauses. The latter flout both consideration doctrine and title doctrine; the former flout only the last. Yet parties are commonly regarded as in control of the remedies in their contracts, even though Act 63, contains no "unless otherwise agreed" clause; but the "day certain" clause shows that agreement is to do some controlling. *Cf Warranty, II* (1937) 37 COL. L. REV. 384 *ff.* and 393 *ff.*

favor with sales or contract theorists.[77]

Now I have no convictions on its being desirable to force all contracts into a base line of specific performance, or to force specific performance through in the particular situations just instanced, nor even in the case of the clause suggested in footnote 77. Indeed, in the first case put above, that of the running account, I question whether all the decisions fit comfortably with those phases of the modern law of order bills of lading which I believe more wise and useful than their contraries.[78] And in the second case put, that of the "irrevocable order," I grow doubtful indeed about the wisdom of any power of differentially favorable contracting being allowed to rest merely upon a printed form prepared by one party (a Concentrated Business party) and put out upon a Mere Consuming Individual.[79] But doubts on wisdom constitute no reason for refusing to face the facts. The facts are that these two last lines of decision do *point a trend.* They point a trend toward recognition in law of the realities and needs of a *going* relation. The going customer-supplier relation is a fact, and a fact for lawyers to take account of—as, *e.g.*, they have taken (in part) of the current account relation between customer and banker. Even a single bilateral sets up a going relation. The instinct of the courts

[77]Especially, not the cases overriding seller's repudiation. The Rudin case, with general citations to other cases, appears in two footnotes in WILLISTON AND McCURDY, CASES ON SALES (1932) 291, n., 331 n.; it appears in a footnote in Bogert and Britton, 459 *f.*, solely in relation to replevin and levy when an order document is outstanding, and there is no citation of, *e.g.*, the Banik, Price and Greenwood Grocery cases. Woodward in his second edition thought the case important, as I did. Vold's WOODWARD'S CASES prints the case, with annotations none too full, and no comment. Neither is there any comment in VOLD ON SALES. But see (1924) 24 COL. L. REV. 931; and on the Lewis case, (1920) 29 YALE L. J. 689.

I venture to predict that on the order document point—*i.e.*, replevin when an order document is outstanding—the Rudin case will not survive. But on the buyer's power point—as will be evidenced, *e.g.*, by replevying the document in the hands of seller's agent—it will march on, despite Sales theorists. I suspect the same fate to await the price-despite-repudiation contracts, once they get drawn in persuasive form. As a technician, I should like to see what would happen to something like this: "The price under this contract is agreed to be due at the expiration of the agreed credit term, calculated from the date when seller ships or offers to ship the goods; but should the buyer mail or otherwise communicate his intention to break the contract, the seller may cancel the credit term and declare the price due at once." *Cf.* Federal Sales Bill, Sec. 23(c)

[78]My doubts and suggestions appear in the companion paper on *Purchase for Value;* they were foreshadowed in the TRUST RECEIPTS ACT.

[79]Compare *supra,* note 25, and Warranty, Second Part. Bogert, Hale, N. Isaacs, M. Cohen, Pound, all have an eye to the problem. But it is still to be really canvassed. I think its real canvassing will revolutionize our ideas on Offer and Acceptance, Consideration, Statute of Frauds, and Integration—*inter alia.*

in frequently finding *modification* on facts which would not support *creation* of contract has been sound, though erratic; the judicial law of "waiver" is sane; it will repudiate straitjacket the American Law Institute *Restatement* attempts to give it in section 279. The law of consideration has a real function in the field of forming contract relationships, although there is plenty of overhauling to be done before our doctrine will accurately fill its function.[80] But the law of consideration, save for the antiholdup phases of the preexisting duty rule, has no place in regard to *modification* of an existing relationship. *Whether* to *start* relying and expecting is often enough an arm's length matter; but once you are relying and expecting, then adjustment, readjustment, are the other side of the reliance-coin. The law of accord and satisfaction, and substituted performance on its positive side, are a recognition of the facts of life; whereas Sales Act, section 49, is a recognition that such recognition should not open gate and door to the chiseler. Perhaps even more, the law of anticipatory repudiation shows—in most courts—appreciation of life's facts: that such law exists, either on the excuse side or on the side of active remedy, shows appreciation of what a going expectation-relation means; that an "election doctrine" can develop shows a groping not too unskillful for the true line of issue-drawing: how to keep a technically pure party from trading indecently upon the needed decencies.[81] This is not the place to discuss anticipatory breach at large, but it is worth observing again not only that the existence of the concept implies a *going* relation, but also that the election doctrine depends upon a real cousinship to specific performance. (The "offered breach" idea even parallels our "assent" problem.) The aggrieved has power to *keep* the going relation (legally) a *going* one—to refuse effect to a breach. Our cases, above, carry just this idea forward into the title phase. They do point a trend.

They point a trend away from inadequate theory; nay, a revolt against it. Revolts commonly exaggerate; revolts also, however, commonly have a point. Here the point is clear: when courts which have been conditioned to regard the power of breach as the order of nature come somewhat persistently to disregard that

[80]Llewellyn, *What Price Contract?* (1931) 40 YALE L. J. 704, esp. 741 *ff.*
[81]Note (1937) 37 COL. L. REV. 610.

power, then we need to recanvass our thinking both about the fact of power of breach in our legal system, and about the wisdom of our prior thinking on the subject. When courts *per*sistently (not *con*sistently) kick over any existing accepted theory, they may be wise or unwise, right or wrong.[82] But what is certain is that the theory which they persistently (whether or nor consistently) kick over *must* be wrong, if it purports to be law for those courts.

To sum up, what I see in the situation in hand is, first, a recognition-in-action of a clear working principle: "Buyer's option, on Seller's breach," even in cases that affront the policy of seller's order bill of lading, and of assent as dealt with in Act, Section 19; and even though the result drives counter to all supposed common-law tradition against specific performance.[83] That is worth pondering. Indeed, it has value in making clear that the question "Specific Performance at Law—where and when?" is not academic, but is raised by the decisions.

The immediate bearing on our inquiry is no less clear: The "mutual assent to appropriation" attack on certain typical mer-

[82]Fuller gives a beautiful illustration: put an animal in an enclosure too small or badly shaped to hold it comfortably and it will struggle to get out. You cannot predict the result; you *can* predict the struggle. Fuller, *supra* note 5, at 437. In a word: inadequate legal theory makes for *uncertainty* in the results of legal cases. In transaction-law at least, this is a heavy debit item.

[83]This discussion centers, it will be recalled, on *mercantile* transactions, and here. on mercantile cases involving *shipment*.

The phrasing in the text requires qualification along two major lines:

(1) It has only dubious application to the "deliverable state" cases when goods are still in seller's possession. See notes 44, 56. Note that such cases raise the point of buyer's *option* almost exclusively when the buyer either has financed production of the goods in question or is, as a creditor, on other grounds, attempting to secure a preference, *and*, in either case, when the seller has become insolvent, *and* when certain goods were originally or have later become specified to the contract. Such issues as price and risk test, of course, not buyer's option, but seller's right. The older common-law cases of financing-buyer against bona-fide-purchaser are under the Act to be settled under Section 25, which, on the facts of most of the common-law cases, would make a decided difference in result.

(2) The text also has only dubious application to cases where delivery is agreed to be at a point distant from the seller. The text ought, indeed, to apply without qualification to those cases and as soon as the seller tenders or offers delivery. It ought to apply in favor of seller, where the goods conform; in favor of buyer where they do not. But the seller seems to have full power to divert before the goods arrive at the agreed point. Between arrival-time and time of tender or offer, the situation is not clear. If, as in the normal c. i. f. contract, both shipment and tender of documents are required, the buyer's option as against the *seller* will operate from the time of shipment.

Cf. Federal Sales Bill § 20(5), and the Merchants' Association proposal to excise (6).

cantile Sales problems breaks down. That lump simply fails to work. Do we Sales lawyers then analyze the problem? On the contrary. We leap instead into unexamined, groping application of another, albeit smaller, lump: Buyer's Option. Perhaps because it has not been phrased for application, and tried out over the years to find its proper limits, it is applied blindly, without reference to those limits. For such limits it has, as the last set of cases put suggests. Even a principle announced by as keen a Sales judge as Bramwell at his best[84] does not escape the need for critique and for limitation.

CONCLUSION

Harboring a suspicion that Sales Theory could learn more from the law of contract than it has, and that the concepts in that field ("the seller," "purchase for value," and the like) need re-examination if Sales law is to be made an effective tool for the men who operate it or upon whom it operates, we have explored something of the mercantile phases of the field. The results indicate that Sales situations are more complex than one would suspect from reading merely about the Seller, the Buyer, and the Goods; but, especially, more complex than one would suspect from reading merely of Title and Assent. One gathers, again, a suspicion that sustained inquiry into, let us say, sale of farm produce, or sale to ultimate consumer, or sale to manufacturing consumer, would turn up equally interesting need for rethinking how our Sales law works. One thing stands out, to baffle: the way, for over a century, in which the ideology of Title and of other cumbersome lump-concepts has defied or overcome suggestions, from within the field or from without, which offered high utility. Much has indeed been done in the Act—of which the companion papers seek to give evidence. But as much and more remains to be done. The Federal Sales Bill, with the amendments proposed by the Merchants' Association of

[84]Bramwell epitomizes in himself the growth of Sales law in England, as Cowen (see the companion paper, Part II) epitomizes the warranty law of New York over an equal period. When Bramwell is *seeing,* he can see more prophetically even than Blackburn. But I do not recall ever seeing Blackburn in a commercial case as muddled as Bramwell was in Household Fire Ins. Co. v. Grant, 4 Ex. D. 216 (C. A. 1879). The point in which Bramwell sums up the century is in his magnificent ability, even when seeing straight in general, *to ignore his own prior insights.* Compare his opinion in Anderson v. Morice, 10 C. P. 58 (1874), with that in Langton v. Higgins.

New York, may prove a way out. It reached my desk too late for detailed discussion in this paper. It needs the addition, on the remedy side, of what is here suggested. It supplements, anticipates, and extends, with acumen and skill, many things which my students and I might (with luck) have later hit upon. But it also urges, things I believe to be, in part, not fully thought through. A second thing stands out no less: the curious slowness of this branch of mercantile law, which one might have conceived to be peculiarly close to life—its curious slowness to adjust its doctrine and conceptual equipment to its needs. There is a third thing: over the long haul, the amazing skill with which judges have managed to work their cases out, despite the inadequate equipment furnished them by theory. I do not reason from this that adequate theory is unnecessary. I reason merely that we *can* further fumble on without it. A judge experienced and skillful enough, a judge with flair, can make out reasonably well with any tools, however clumsy, and with any guideposts, however many-fingered. But ordinary judges and ordinary lawyers and young lawyers and law students will do better work if they are given better wherewithal than buttered mittens to sort and pick out those elusive peas known as wise decisions in cases involving Sales. Indeed, one can hope more. One can hope that a more exact equipment will make it possible not only to pick up the wise decisions more consistently, but to *cumulate* those wise decisions and the concepts and lines of analysis which grow out of them, instead of having them slither away again into the mass as so many of them have been doing these hundred years and more.

Appendix on Needed Amendments Not Already Included in the Federal Sales Bill

To present a criticism of a statute without at least attempting to propose a cure is to fall down on the hardest job faced by the legal reformer. An exercise in drafting has here the additional value of helping to determine whether a number of useful changes in theory cannot be worked out within the confines of traditional language. Piece-meal amending is, however, a thankless task. Thus it would require overhauling of the Act to distinguish among "sellers";

though it does not require overhauling of the entire set of title sections to make practically effective change in Act, Section 63.

Yet something useful could be done by easing up the damage rule in at least the case most important to safe and fair commercial adjustment of a nonacceptance. Thus one might add to Section 64 (with an equivalent addition to Section 67):

> "*Section* 64 (3) (b). Provided, however, that if the seller has resold within a time and on terms mercantilely reasonable in the circumstances, the net price received shall be taken as the market price. The burden is on the seller to establish that this proviso applies."

With this compare Federal Sales Bill, Merchants' Association amendment, Section 51, which aims more elaborately at a similar goal. Their proposed Section 55 (3) will limit itself, in practical effect, to the case where no goods have been specified.

Other amendments likewise looking toward the easing of adjustment, as well as toward simpler litigation and fairer disposition of litigation, are suggested by Eno and Pilpel.[85] To complete the picture they need addition:

Section 49 [modified from Eno, after consultation]

(2) (a). The buyer who, before demand for a formal statement, gives notice of objections, may set up in any subsequent litigation objections whose omission from his notice has not actually, reasonably, and materially misled the seller, unless his statement, together with the surrounding circumstances, indicates that the unstated or then unknown defects were not really material to the rejection. The burden of proving actual, reasonable, and material reliance on the statement, and immateriality of the unstated defect, is on the seller.

(b). The seller is entitled, on demand therefor, to a formal statement of all objections readily ascertainable by the buyer at the time of such demand. Such statement will bar the setting up in any subsequent litigation of any defect unmentioned whose existence was not already reasonably ascertainable by the seller. Failure to reply to the seller's demand with a formal statement of objections within a reasonable time will bar the setting up in any

[85](1934) 44 YALE L. J. 818, and in (1935) 35 COL. L. REV. 739.

subsequent litigation of all objections ***not specified prior to the receipt of such demand.*** [Suggested substitute: ***which would have been barred by their omission from a formal statement, of either rejection or rescission.***]

Section 44 (3). Where any or all of the goods delivered by the seller are [substantially?[86]] nonconforming, the buyer may reject them all, or he may reject any of the nonconforming goods and retain the rest; provided that he notifies the seller, within the reasonable time specified in Section 48, of what goods he will reject, which notification is irrevocable; and provided further that the saleability of the part rejected is not materially impaired by its severance from the remainder. The burden of proving such impairment shall be on the seller.

Section 69 (1) (c). Reject any or all of the goods, subject to the provisos of Section 44 (3), either

(i) by refusing to accept them or part thereof if the property therein has not passed, or

(ii) if the property has passed, by rescinding the transfer of title to the goods or part thereof, unless he knew of the breach of warranty when he accepted them.

Rejection in either of these two ways shall not impair the buyer's right to damages for the breach of warranty.

It may, I think, be fairly urged that Pilpel has here done a more inclusive job than the Merchants' Association did in Federal Sales Bill, Sec. 60 (1) (d).

The problems of appropriation by or after shipment can also be in fair part clarified:

[86]On substantial performance, I find that some such language as the following, working as a change in Act 11, so as to pervade the entire Act, lures me:

"Any promise or warranty, so far as concerns damages or recoupment operates subject to this act precisely in terms of the agreement made. So far as concerns rejection or rescission by the buyer, it is not the promise but the condition which controls. The seller's performance shall be deemed substantial and so to be in compliance with the condition resting on the seller whenever, disregarding any supervening change in the market, the delivery offered would reasonably have met the buyer's operating requirements and an appropriate reduction of the price would have served as adequate compensation to the buyer for failure of exact performance. In the case of goods sold for non-business consumption, even minor defects going to the taste of the buyer and in the case of any goods sold for use even minor defects going to efficiency of the operation of the goods and in the case of documentary sales or contracts to sell, even minor defects in the documents are presumed to negate substantial performance. The burden of proving substantiability of the performance rests in all cases with the seller, excepting that language written (not merely printed) into the documents or memorandum of agreement, such as '90 per cent delivery guaranteed' and the like makes full performance of the language by the seller a condition."

Section 19 (4) (2). Where pursuant to an order or a contract to sell the seller delivers or tenders goods to the buyer or, except in the cases provided for in the next rule or Section 20, where the seller so delivers them to a carrier or other bailee (whether named by the buyer or not) for the purpose of transmission to or holding for the buyer, this amounts to appropriation of the goods to the contract by the seller, or, in the case of an order, to acceptance thereof and also to such appropriation. Such appropriation is presumed to be unconditional and this presumption is applicable although by the terms of the contract the buyer is to pay the price before receiving delivery of the goods, whether or not the goods or the shipment are marked with the words: "collect on delivery" or their equivalent.

If such delivery or tender is referable to the order or to the contract to sell, but is not in full accordance therewith, the seller's appropriation is, at the buyer's option, effective as of the time when it was made; but the exercise of the option shall not impair any remedy to the buyer for breach of promise.

Appendix on the Federal Sales Bill and Merchants' Association Proposals

Section 5 (1). A statute of frauds on matters involving less than $500 is of dubious value. *Cf.* my *Materials,* 916 *ff.* The defendant's risks are small, in a mercantile case. The reason for the statute drops out of sight, in the petty case; and the larger limit fits closer to those houses and transactions which already have business machinery to ensure confirmation. Finally, the fifteen-cent can of goods with fifteen thousands of claimed damage escapes even a fifty-dollar limitation: it has been delivered and "accepted."

Section 12. No substantial performance rule for nondocumentary contracts appears. This is very queer. Compare n. 86.

Section 12 (3) (4). The Merchants' Association offers material improvements; but the last clause should read "no sale *or contract.*"

Sections 15 *ff.* 15 gets off on a right foot. 16 (4) is a material improvement. (See my *On Warranty of Quality, and Society, II*, 37 *Columbia L. Rev.* 341, 362 *ff.*, esp. n. 58.)

But 15 should cut out the word "implied" wherever it appears. "*There is a warranty*" is the only proper language. I should add: "The warranty herein provided is not subject to negation." See *On Warranty, ubi sup.*, at 383-388.

Since state statutes may be expected to take up occasional matters which need particular control, it is unwise to cut out "of any statute in that behalf" in the preamble of Section 16.

Section 20. It gains, mildly, in clarity by the proposed changes. The addition in Rule 4 (2) of "an order" to "a contract" is a notable forward step. The new Rule 5 fits convenience and sense. The excision of the original Rule 6 is, to my mind, essential to any intelligible purpose of the old, or of the modified, Rule 5.

Yet I regard my proposal *re* Sales Act, 19 (4) (2), as a most useful addition to anything thus far available in regard to the Federal Sales Bill. See p. 206, and n. 69.

Section 21 (3). I find it very difficult to grasp the shifting of risk under a cost-and-freight contract to the buyer (which I have no quarrel with) without provision for such notice of shipment as will enable the buyer to insure: see the proposed excision of Section 33 (3). This law professor thinks this particular combination proposed by the Merchants' Association to be distinctly unmerchantlike. He would regard an obligation to insure, for buyer's benefit, and at buyer's charge, as something to be meditated on with some seriousness.

Section 23 (c). Swell. And goes far to clarify the new price-action proposals.

The omitted Sections on Documents of Title. See the companion paper on *Purchase for Value and the Course of Trade.* In rough summation: "Value" and "Notice" have been whittled too thin. The nub *ought* to be: Is this a course-of-trade transaction? This would distinguish, *e.g.*, preferential transfer by Robinson of Jones's goods to Robinson's *banking* creditor from delivery by Robinson to Brown on credit, under the preëxisting mercantile contract. It would distinguish pledge of an order bill of lading from mortgage of an inventory. Certain sane lines of cleavage are indicated in the English Factors Acts, the Bulk Sales Acts, and the Trust Receipts Act. *"In the ordinary course of the transferor's business"* (*cf*. Sec. 5; Sales Act, 4) should be inserted into the definition of "Value."

Section 32. The Merchants' Association addition to (2) is bothersome in language: "if wilful and inexcusable" invites trouble. It also gets out of balance, as between seller and buyer. We still lack objective tests to guide practice in this field, but I would suggest such language as follows, as coming an inch or two closer to the mark:

> "Where goods are to be delivered in separate installments, to be separately paid for, material default in either any delivery or any payment justifies the opposing party in refusing to proceed. If, after such default, and on demand by the party aggrieved, the defaulting party fails to provide, promptly, reasonably satisfactory assurance and security against future material default, the aggrieved party may cancel and sue for damages for breach of the entire contract.
>
> "The burden is on the defaulting party to show that any default was not so material as to endanger confidence in later adequate performance; and that any assurance and security offered were adequate to overcome any uncertainty, reasonably induced by the default, about adequate future performance."

Section 33 (3). See *supra,* under Section 21 (3). 33 (3) needs deletion.

Section 39. Where the f.o.b. clause envisages destination, one needs a further clause arranging for reasonable time to receive. It could perhaps be done by an addition to (c) along some such lines as these:

> "and, if the place is the place of destination, until the buyer has been given a reasonable time to take delivery."

This is both case law and sense.

Section 43 *ff*. If the seller's remedy is to be worked out from Part IV, then Section 43 requires express extension by adding to (1): *"whether or not property in any goods has passed."* Otherwise hopeless ambiguity develops between Parts IV and V. With such an addition, the Merchants' Association proposals do an adequate job on seller's remedy. It is needed. See especially Section 51 (1) (b), as proposed. The proposed Section 55 (3) raises a worry or two; but can be handled by any lawyer, and so does not need to bother.

Sections 58-60. Here there is a real and grave defect. The buyer ought to be given the same power and freedom to cover which the seller needs. To limit him *prima facie* to the market at the time of repudiation and the contract place of delivery means only one thing: to wit, that the buyer's problem has not been fully envisaged in terms of what he can *do* about it. The rules proposed are sound enough *where no actual covering has occurred.* They need an addition, to facilitate both negotiation and mercantile coverage. Something like this:

> "A buyer who learns of a misdelivery or nondelivery may cover within a time and on terms mercantilely reasonable in the circumstances, and the net cost of cover shall be taken as the market price. The burden is on the buyer to establish mercantile reasonableness."

Given such a provision, a buyer can negotiate with his defaulting seller with no more fear of the market than afflicts any business man; nor is he met in court, later, by the need of doing more than showing businesslike action.

It is nice, but in strong contrast, to see the proposed 60 (7) giving the buyer just about this, if goods have been *mis*-delivered, instead of *non*-delivered. The conclusion is inescapable that the nondelivery situation has not been wholly thought through. For the intention to step up remedy, and to keep the buyer-seller relation in balance, is obvious.

The inclusion of damages, in the event of buyer's rescission, Section 60 (1) (d), is needed. One would have been glad to see damages also allowed to follow recoupment as in England.

The net effect is that the Federal Sales Bill, with the Merchants' Association proposals, is a notable forward step in our Sales law. Yet the Eno and Pilpel proposals, and my own, would fill out the harmony of needed reforms. *The remedy sections still need simplification.*

[16]

WILLISTON ON CONTRACTS

Revised Edition*

Walter Wheeler Cook†

THE first edition of Williston on Contracts appeared in 1920 and became at once the leading text upon the subject. The present writer reviewed that edition in another magazine.[1] Since 1920 much water has gone over the dam. For one thing, Professor Williston has acted as Reporter for the Restatement of Contracts of the American Law Institute. As Reporter he has had the theories and conclusions reached in the first edition subjected to the acute criticisms of other leading students of the law of Contracts who were employed by the Institute to advise in the drafting of the Restatement. Furthermore, in the interval between the appearance of the two editions a steadily increasing number of so-called—perhaps miscalled—'realists'[2] have been subjecting to critical analysis the presuppositions and modes of thought underlying the work of the men of Williston's generation. A review of the second edition ought therefore, among other things, to point out the extent to which the new edition has been influenced by these events, and an attempt to do so will here be made.

At the outset it should be noted that in preparing the present edition Professor Williston has had the aid of Professor George J. Thompson of Cornell University. The preface tells us that

> "while the detail of the preparation of the manuscript of this edition has been carried on chiefly by the associate au-

* A Treatise on the Law of Contracts. By Samuel Williston. Revised Edition. By Samuel Williston and George J. Thompson. New York: Baker, Voorhis & Co., 1936-38. Vol. I, pp. xix, 926; Vol. II, pp. xi, 927-1723; Vol. III, pp. xii, 1725-2579; Vol. IV, pp. xiii, 2581-3669; Vol. V, pp. xiv, 3671-4699; Vol. VI, pp. xiv, 4700-5726; Vol. VII, pp. iv, 5727-6703; Vol. VIII, pp. 6705-7725. $80.00.

† A.B., 1894, A.M., 1899, LL.M., 1901, Columbia; LL.D., 1929, Wisconsin; Professor of Law, Northwestern University. Author of Cases on Equity (2d ed., 1932); co-author with the late Professor Hinton of Cases on Pleading (1923).

1 Review (1920) 20 Col. L. Rev. 716; (1921) 21 Col. L. Rev. 395.

2 The so-called 'realists' do not constitute a 'school': they differ too much with each other. This is true even though their thories are subdivided under subheadings, such as "Skeptical Realism" and "Logical Positivist Realism": see Dean Pound's classification in Fifty Years of Jurisprudence (1938) 51 Harv. L. Rev. 777, 790-798. They have all, however, been influenced to a greater or less extent by currents of thought which are running today in all fields of intellectual endeavor: see the reviewer's introductory note to his paper on, 'Contracts' and the Conflict of Laws (1936) 31 Ill. L. Rev. 143, and the papers in the International Encyclopedia of Unified Science (1938) Vol. 1, No. 1: Encyclopedia of Unified Science, especially the paper of Charles W. Morris on 'Scientific Empiricism.' This latter term as used by Professor Morris comes nearer to describing the present writer's approach than any other single label, but as commonly used has misleading connotations. With this explanation, the word 'realist,' since it is so widely accepted by others, will be used at later points in the discussion to describe the general point of view in question.

thor, the author has himself undertaken the revision of certain subjects in which he was especially interested, and has personally examined every section of the manuscript and either collaborated in its production or approved its form."

Full responsibility for the final text is thus assumed by Professor Williston.

When the plans for the Restatement of the law were first announced by the American Law Institute, the program as outlined provided for treatises to accompany and explain the black-letter texts of the various Restatements. For reasons never fully made public but which can perhaps be guessed, the Institute soon abandoned the plan for these treatises, without which the Restatements have in the opinion of many lost much of whatever value they might otherwise have had. In the case of the Conflict of Laws the lack has been in part supplied by Professor Beale's three-volume treatise on that subject. This Treatise is printed in the form of a commentary on the Restatement of the Conflict of Laws, the numbering of its sections following that of the Restatement. In a similar way the present edition of Williston now partially supplies the lack of an official treatise explanatory of the Restatement of the law of Contracts. The preface to the present edition states that the authors have

> "made it a primary purpose in their undertaking to provide such an exposition of the decisions and reasons supporting the rules of the Restatement as might fairly take the place of the treatise which was originally planned as a part of the Institute's publication. To this end the presentation of the law in the revised treatise has been carefully collated with the Restatement, the various sections of which are referred to, wherever appropriate, throughout the text and notes. The distinctive contributions of the Restatement are pointed out and evaluated and the position of the Restatement on all controversial subjects defined and supported. In Volume VIII a table is provided to facilitate reference to the discussion of the respective sections of the Restatement of Contracts and of the Restatements of other subjects."

An addition which the practitioner will find of great utility is the volume of forms, which has been prepared by Edwin M. Bohm of the New York Bar. This volume has been "keyed to the preceding six volumes" in which the principles have been discussed, i. e., the forms have been given section numbers corresponding to those in the text. In order to facilitate the use of the forms without necessarily referring back to the other volumes, the volume containing them is separately and thoroughly indexed.

The first edition consisted of four volumes, containing a total of 4182 pages. The present edition consists of eight volumes, with a total of 7725 pages. The size of the treatise has therefore been almost doubled. The volume of forms alone accounts for nearly one thousand of the additional pages, and the eighth volume, which corresponds to the fourth volume of the first edition in that it contains the table of cases, index, etc., and no text, contains over a thousand pages as compared with approximately seven hundred in the corresponding volume of the first edition. This is in part due to the substantial increase in the number of cases cited: about 70,000 in the second edition as compared with (at a rough estimate) somewhat less than

60,000 in the first edition. It is also due to the greatly improved index, which occupies nearly though not quite twice as many pages as in the first edition, and carries on each page (because of smaller type) some ten additional lines of items.

To complete this survey of changes and additions, it may be noted that the binding of the present edition is decidedly more attractive than that of the first edition, and seems on the surface to promise greater durability.

A random sampling of the citation of cases has convinced the reviewer that not only have citations been added, but that the cases listed in the previous edition have been checked for relevancy, and the accuracy of citation thereby somewhat improved. That is to say, one is likely to find that a larger proportion of the cases are 'in point' or 'relevant' to the issue under discussion in the text. In saying this the present writer is aware that there is room for much difference of opinion as to when a case is 'in point' or 'relevant': the question is of course one of degree. And it is also true that when a work cites some 70,000 cases one cannot expect as careful analysis of the cases as in, say, a critical law review article: the writer of a large text must necessarily resolve doubts as to 'relevancy' in favor of inclusion rather than exclusion. Even so it would seem that cases which contain only the merest dicta should, if cited, be distinguished from those which can at least with some plausibility be considered 'in point.' The reviewer's random sampling indicates that this has not always been done. One example must suffice. In §211 the subject for discussion is, "how far intent to deliver must be accompanied by actual delivery" in order that a "formal contract" (under seal) may become effective. In note 3 on page 649 some twenty cases are cited for the proposition that "though generally the cases in the United States have not gone so far as the English decisions [in dispensing with 'actual delivery'], not a few courts have acquiesced in the principle that the manifest intention to create an immediate obligation is the only essential to delivery." A check of the cases cited shows that four of them are not cases of formal contracts at all and that what references there are to 'delivery' of 'formal' contracts are the merest dicta. The reviewer hastens to add that a score of eighty per cent of cases 'in point' is, as text books go, a fairly high one, and that the present work seems to be on a somewhat higher level in that respect than many of our comprehensive legal treatises.

Coming now to more fundamental matters, we may first inquire as to the influence of the learned author's experience in drafting the Restatement. To the reviewer it is clear that the effects of the criticisms of the Advisers can be discovered at many points in the revision. These appear particularly in connection with the analysis of fundamental terms. To show this we may compare two passages, one from the first and the other from the revised edition, both relating to whether there is any necessity for the "contemporaneous existence" of 'offer' and 'acceptance.' In the first edition we find the following passage:

> "It is of course true that *offer and acceptance must exist at the same time,* but the offer is not merely evidence of a state of mind; it is an element in the formation of a contract irrespective of the offerer's mental attitude, and may continue effective in spite of a change in that attitude. It is, therefore, unnecessary to resort to a fiction that the acceptance relates back, in order to support the validity of a contract made without practically simultaneous expressions of assent. It is the only accurate way to express the matter to say that *the offer continues till the acceptance,* rather than that the offer relates back to the acceptance. It is now well settled that an offer will continue in force subject to the limitations hereafter stated."[3]

In the revised edition, the matter is put as follows:

> "It is true that *offer and acceptance must exist at the same time,* and this necessity, as well as the supposed necessity of denying prolonged life to an offer, has sometimes been met by the fiction of a relation back of the acceptance to the offer. But the offer is not merely evidence of a state of mind; it is an element in the formation of a contract irrespective of the offeror's mental attitude, and may continue effective in spite of a change in that attitude. It is, therefore, unnecessary to resort to a fiction that the acceptance relates back, in order to support the validity of a contract made without practically simultaneous expressions of assent. The only accurate way to express the matter is to say that *the offeree's power of acceptance continues till the acceptance,* rather than that the acceptance relates back to the offer. It is now well settled that the effect of an offer continues in force subject to the limitations hereafter stated. *It is not the offer which continues but the power of acceptance which it confers on the offeree.*"[4]

It can hardly be denied that the second passage is better phrased than the first: it recognizes the distinction between factual 'offer' and resulting legal 'power.' To be sure, even now the terminology is less precise than is desirable: note the inconsistency of the statement in the passage last quoted, to the effect that *"the offer must exist"* at the same time as the acceptance, with the latter statement that *"it is not the offer which continues, but the power of acceptance which it confers upon the offeree."* This failure of the learned author to attain complete consistency in his analysis grows out of the fact that that analysis is not explicitly based upon the simple and fundamental distinction between the 'factual' elements of transactions and the resulting 'legal relations' attached by the law to these factual elements. The result is that the learned author has not clearly made up his mind, when he embarks on his discussion of the "duration of offers," whether the verbal symbol 'offer' denotes 'facts' or 'legal relations' attached by the law to the facts.

The effects of the author's failure to adopt an analysis based upon the fundamental distinction referred to appear throughout the work. For example, the opening sentence of Section 1 reads:

> "A contract is a promise, or set of promises, for the *breach of which* the law gives a remedy, or the *performance of which* the law in some way recognizes as a duty. (Italics supplied.)

At a later point in the same section the author tell us that

> "the meaning [of the word 'contract'] here adopted is that of customary legal usage and probably of scientific convenience also."

3 (1st ed.) Vol. I, p. 85. (Italics supplied.)

4 (2d ed.) Vol. I, p. 143. (Italics supplied.)

With this definition of 'contract' we need to correlate the author's definition of 'promise.' In Section 1-A this is given as follows:

> "A promise is an undertaking that something shall happen or that something shall not happen in the future."

From these definitions it follows logically that a 'breach of contract' must always be a 'breach of a promise,' or, put the other way around, that unless there is a 'breach of promise' there can be no 'breach of contract.' The same idea can of course be expressed by saying that the definition assumes that the 'legal duty' of performance is to carry out the factual 'promise' as made, and nothing more.

When this definition of 'contract' was first incorporated in a tentative draft of the Restatement, the present writer ventured to criticize it at the meeting of the American Law Institute, and to point out what he believed to be the desirability of distinguishing carefully between the 'factual events' (the promises) and the resulting 'legal relations' attached by the law to the promises.[5] Professor Williston replied that he felt "satisfied that to make the restatement in that form would make it unintelligible to a large part of the Bar and Bench and destroy its practical value."[6] It may be worth while, therefore, to note some of the difficulties to which the definition adopted logically leads.

As already stated, what the definition asserts in substance is that a 'breach of contract' is always a breach of (factual) promise; that the legal duty is simply to 'perform the promise': note the precise language — "breach of *which*"; "performance of *which*," i. e., of the promise or set of promises. Observe now what happens. In Section 1288 we are, consistently enough, told that

> "a breach of contract is a failure, without legal excuse, to *perform a promise* which forms the whole or part of the contract. (Italics supplied.)

Furthermore, we are told in Section 1296,

> "The fundamental idea of contractual duty is to perform that which has been promised . . . if, as must be assumed, a contract is properly defined as a binding promise or set of promises, there can logically be no breach of a promise [and so no breach of contract] until the terms or conditions qualifying the promise have been fulfilled. One who contracts to do a certain thing on a certain contingency or at a certain time does not and indeed *cannot break that promise until the contingency happens or the time arrives.*" (Italics supplied.)

It follows, we are also told in the same section, that "on principle" there should be no action for "anticipatory breach" of a contract, and the "prevalent doctrine in regard to bilateral contracts . . . commonly known as the doctrine of anticipatory breach asserts an exception to it," i. e., the "principle" that a breach of contract is necessarily a breach of promise.

Obviously this conclusion, which makes the whole of a well-recognized doctrine in Anglo-American law an anomalous exception to legal "principle," is a logical consequence—and nothing more—of the definition of a 'contract' adopted in Section 1. It re-

[5] See III Proceedings of the American Law Institute (1925) 167.

[6] Id. at 168.

sults from the initial failure to distinguish between factual promises and resulting legal obligations, and to note that the definition adopted involves a tacitly-made assumption that the two are coextensive in scope.

If one were to begin his discussion by carefully noting the distinction in question, he would be compelled to recognize at least the possibility that the scope of the resulting legal obligations may not be coextensive with that of the factual promises. He would therefore have to face squarely the question whether it is true in our legal system that the resulting legal obligations attached by the law to promises are identical in scope with those promises. They may be, but again they may not be: the matter must be determined not by a priori theorizing or by tacit assumptions but by observing the relevant phenomena, namely, the decisions of the courts.

A review is not the place in which to pursue this analysis into its detailed application to a discussion of contract law, and we must be content with a brief and more or less dogmatic statement, namely, that it seems to the reviewer to require only the slightest of observation to see that the phenomena of judicial decision in the field of contract law cannot be adequately described except in terms of the general statement that the legal obligations attached to promises by the law are not precisely coextensive with the promises themselves: the law has had a hand in molding them. Every case of a 'condition implied in law' or 'constructive condition' shows this: the factual promise in such cases is in terms unconditional; the resulting legal duty is conditional. Why? Because considerations of fairness so demand, as indeed the learned author himself admits in his discussion of 'constructive conditions.'[7]

The same thing may be said of the rules concerning the so-called "mutual dependency of the promises" in bilateral contracts. The promises as made are in terms independent; it is the resulting *legal duties of performance* that are mutually dependent. In other words, because of the "inherent justice of the situation" the courts have so molded the resulting legal obligations of performance as to make them mutually dependent, in spite of the non-dependent character of the promises.[8]

[7] The matter is discussed in §69, where *inter alia* it is said:

"It is settled law that whenever in a bilateral contract the completion of his performance by one party is peculiarly within his own knowledge, *a condition precedent is implied in fact* requiring him to notify the other party of his performance, as a requisite of holding the latter liable. A corresponding need for implication arises in the case of an offer requesting performance peculiarly within the knowledge of the offeree. . . . The contract is complete on the performance of the act but is *subject to a constructive condition* that if notice of the performance of the act is not given, or duly dispatched within a reasonable time by the promisee, he cannot impose a duty of immediate performance upon the promisor." (Italics supplied.)

[8] In §828 the learned author recognizes the truth of the statement in the text where he puts the matter as follows:

"The theory of mutual dependency of the promises in a bilateral contract is based on fundamental principles of justice, and if the court conceives of its action in enforcing such dependency as due not to the will of the parties but the inherent justice of the situation, there is no difficulty in so applying and molding the principle of failure of consideration as to protect the defendant without subjecting the plaintiff to the risk of unjust forfeiture. Therefore, promises will be regarded as *constructively dependent* whenever it is possible so to do." (Italics supplied.)

Furthermore, when one recalls the complex body of law developed by courts of equity in connection with contracts for the purchase and sale of land—the so-called 'law of vendor and purchaser'—one realizes still more clearly the inadequacy of a theory which gives the law nothing more to do than prescribe remedies for breach of the promises as made. The reference here of course is to the rules governing the rights of a purchaser who has not offered to perform on time ("Is time of the essence?," etc.); the rules governing the acquisition, transfer, and extinguishment of the purchaser's 'equity of purchase'; the rules governing foreclosure by the vendor; partial performance with abatement in price, etc., etc. To attempt to describe these in terms of merely enforcing promises as made seems to the reviewer to attempt the impossible.

It was perhaps only natural for Williston as a child of his age to adopt the premise he did. As we all know, the later years of the nineteenth century and the early years of the twentieth were those which emphasized "freedom of contract" and read that favored doctrine into the due process clause of the constitution. It was therefore to be expected that one whose thinking took shape under such a 'climate of opinion' would adopt as one of his fundamental premises the notion that the purpose of the law of contracts is to put pressure on people to do what they have promised to do: simply that and nothing more. That the adoption of this particular premise was tacitly made and without discussion of its validity was perhaps also to be expected.[9]

Another example of what seems to the reviewer a lack of adequate analysis of fundamental terms is found in Section 97, which is entitled "Place of Contract." Here the author falls a victim to the confused terminology usually found in writings on the Conflict of Laws in connection with discussions of the 'place of contracting' or place in which a contract is 'made.' No notice is taken of the ambiguities in the statement that the "place of contract" (the author's synonym for 'place of contracting' or 'place where the contract is made') is the

> "place where the *last act* necessary to the completion of the contract was done,—that is, where the contract first creates a legal obligation." (Italics supplied.)

Ignored is the fact that in important groups of cases, of which the life insurance contracts discussed below are examples, there is often a disagreement in the law of different states as to what is the "last act necessary to the com-

[9] "It often happens, therefore, that in criticizing a learned book . . . one's whole trouble is with the first chapter, or even with the first page. For it is there, at the very outset, where the author will probably be found to slip in his assumptions. Farther, the trouble is not with what the author does say, but with what he does not say. Also it is not with what he knows he has assumed, but with what he has unconsciously assumed." A. N. Whitehead, Science and the Modern World (1925) 34-35.

In the latter part of the nineteenth century and the early part of the present century our courts, guided by the same unwarranted assumption referred to in the text, began to enforce in equitable suits harsh provisions as to forfeiture in the vendor and purchaser cases. The result is that remedial legislation is now necessary: see Note (1938) 52 Harv. L. Rev. 129, discussing the inadequacy of the law developed by our courts and the statute proposed for enactment in New York by the New York Law Revision Commission.

pletion of the contract."[10] Furthermore, as is also usual with writers on the Conflict of Laws, cases which involve problems in that field and cases which involve purely intra-state situations are cited without noting that the problems in the two groups are quite distinct.[11] Finally, there is no discussion of why the "place of contract" is of legal importance, with the result that no reason is given for the 'last act' rule: we are simply told that that is the "universal principle."[12]

This brings us to a still more fundamental problem, namely, whether the so-called 'realistic' movement in American jurisprudence has influenced the learned author in the preparation of the revised edition. The answer is that it has not; that there is no evidence in the text that that movement has in any way commended itself to Professor Williston. At this point, therefore, this review might end. However, it seems to the present writer that the appearance of this new edition of a leading text, prepared along orthodox lines and using only orthodox techniques, makes it an opportune moment to appraise briefly those techniques in the light of the general assumptions of the newer movement referred to. To this the remainder of this review will be devoted, using the present work as an outstanding example of the orthodox techniques referred to.

The first and one of the most fundamental things about these techniques is an assumption that the legal universe is far simpler than the 'realist' believes it to be. Consider, for example, the following passage from the preface to the first edition, a passage which is equally applicable to the second:

> "The law of contracts suffers from a difficulty opposite to that which has hampered the development of the law of torts. That law grew up piecemeal and with limitations varying in different forms of action. Only in recent years has much effort been made to knit together with broad fundamental principles the various kinds of torts. The law of contracts, on the other hand, after starting with some degree of unity now tends from its very size to fall apart. The simplest applications of fundamental principles of contracts when found in an insurance policy or a contract of suretyship are often considered by writers on those topics as peculiarities of the law of insurance or of suretyship, controlled by no general rules. It therefore seems desirable to treat the subject of contracts as a whole and to show the wide range of application of its principles."

Reduced to its lowest terms the assumption is that in so far as the law of contracts "tends to fall apart," the result is one to be deplored, and counteracted if possible by treatises like the present, designed to show the "unity" of contract law. For example, if in dealing with life insurance contracts courts and writers take the type of transaction into account in reaching their decisions, they are thereby failing to apply the "fundamental principles of contracts" and asserting, at least by implication,

---

[10] See the discussion of the life insurance cases, infra, p. 512; and for a discussion of the 'last act' doctrine in general consult the reviewer's paper on 'Contracts' and the Conflict of Laws (1936) 31 Ill. L. Rev. 143, especially at pp. 158-162.

[11] An example is found in note 15 on p. 312, discussing the 'place of contract' where the contract is made by telephone. Compare the discussion in the paper cited in the preceding note, at p. 176.

[12] The arbitrary character of the 'last act' rule is discussed in the paper cited in note 10 above.

that the cases before them are "controlled by no general rules."

If one asks what justification the author gives for this assumption, the answer is that there is no discussion of it at all: it is merely assumed that the alleged "unity" does or at least should exist. The assumption is, of course, one which many at least of the so-called 'realists' would at once challenge. They would inquire what warrant there is for assuming, for example, that the formation of a life insurance contract must or should necessarily be governed by some "general principle of contracts" equally applicable to all other types of contract. They would inquire, where do such "principles" come from? Are they distilled from the decisions of the courts? If not, what is their source?

Perhaps the best way to bring this somewhat abstract discussion down to earth is to note how this fundamental postulate as to the "unity" of contract law and the "wide range of application of its principles" affects the learned author's treatment of concrete topics. More or less at random let us choose: (1) the treatment of the problem of 'consideration'; (2) the discussion of 'acceptance of offers,' with special reference to life insurance contracts.

1. *Consideration.* The problem of the 'consideration' necessary to 'make a simple contract binding' has possessed a peculiar fascination for legal writers, and much ink has been consumed in its discussion. Professor Williston reviews the leading theories in Sections 99-103. Underlying his whole discussion is the assumption that there is a single theory of 'consideration' for all 'unilateral' contracts, and another one for all 'bilateral' contracts: a single theory, that is, in the sense that it can be stated in a single comprehensive and at the same time brief form, valid for all types of contractual transactions. For bilateral contracts Williston's final formula is as follows:

> "Mutual promises in each of which the promisor undertakes some act or forbearance that will be, or apparently may be, detrimental to the promisor or beneficial to the promisee, and neither of which is void, are sufficient consideration for one another."[13]

Underlying the adoption of this formula is another assumption, namely, that the word 'consideration' is to be limited in meaning to "the exchange or price requested and received by the promisor for the promise." This is stated to be "undoubtedly the fundamental and as to most cases the generally accepted idea of consideration at the present time."[14]

The 'realists' will of course at once inquire whether these broad generalizations will 'account for' the 'law' as it is found in the decisions. From their point of view that is the acid test of the validity of any generalization. Let us therefore note some of the difficulties into which the generalizations in question lead. In the first place, the learned author is confronted by the fact that under his theory of 'consideration' both parties to a bilateral contract are 'bound' or neither is 'bound': note the following excerpt from Section 103E:

> "Total incapacity of one party to contract precludes his promise from sup-

13 Vol. I, §103F.

14 Vol. I, §100.

porting a return promise. For the same reason a promise in a bilateral agreement which is void for lack of a proper counter-promise to serve as consideration, is itself insufficient consideration, since it is not binding and is therefore valueless. The principle is ordinarily stated in *the axiom that in a bilateral agreement both promises must be binding or neither is binding.* In recent years in a few states this application of the law of consideration has sometimes been referred to as if based on some special requirement of 'mutuality,' but *no other doctrine than that of consideration is involved.*" (Italics supplied.)

In the notes to this passage the learned author quotes in support of his statements and with apparent approval the following passages from judicial opinions:

> "A promise is a good consideration for a promise. But no promise constitutes a consideration which is not obligatory upon the party promising. . . . Either all is a *nudum pactum* or else the one promise is as good as the other."

And immediately after the last excerpt the author states: "A [bilateral] contract must be obligatory upon both parties so that each may have an action upon it."

To be noted carefully is that the learned author emphasizes that no "special requirement of mutuality" is involved, but only the "doctrine of consideration." Now the interesting thing is that there are a number of well-recognized situations in which only one party to a bilateral agreement can maintain an action for breach of contract against the other. These are stated by the learned author as follows:

> "A bilateral agreement between an infant and an adult though voidable by the infant is binding upon the adult. So a promise made by an insane person (when promises made by such a person are voidable), or a promise of one who has been induced to enter into a bargain by fraud, or a promise unenforceable because within the Statute of Frauds and because the memorandum required by the Statute is signed by one party only, is sufficient to support a counter-promise. Indeed, though the statute is satisfied as to neither promise, the agreement is not a nullity. The same principle is involved where one promise only of a bilateral agreement is enforceable because of illegality."[17]

The introductory sentence to the section listing these cases states that:

> "A defense given by law to one promisor in a bilateral agreement will not prevent his promise from being sufficient consideration for the counterpromise."

If we ask why not, the answer is that:

> "The rule exemplified by these cases must be regarded as an exception to the general principles of consideration."[18]

In other words, the author's generalization fails to account for or to include large and important classes of cases: they therefore become "exceptions" to "principle."

Further study of the Treatise discloses that the case of the bilateral executory contract in which the infant can recover from the adult, although the adult cannot recover from the infant, is dealt with at a later point in a

15 Vol. I, p. 345, n. 5.

16 Vol. I, p. 345, n. 6.

17 Vol. I, §105. On the general problem see Oliphant, Mutuality of Obligation in Bilateral Contracts at Law—I (1925) 25 Col. L. Rev. 705; Williston, The Effect of One Void Promise in a Bilateral Agreement (1925) 25 Col. L. Rev. 857; Non-Binding Promises as Consideration (1926) 26 Col. L. Rev. 550; Oliphant, Mutuality of Obligation in Bilateral Contracts at Law—II (1928) 28 Col. L. Rev. 997.

18 Vol. I, p. 264.

somewhat different manner and an attempt made to harmonize the result with the author's general doctrine of consideration:

> "Most of the disputed questions in the law of infancy turn upon the legal meaning of the word 'voidable' as applied to an infant's acts. The natural meaning of the word imports a valid act which may be avoided, rather than an invalid act which may be confirmed, and the weight of authority as well as reason point in the same direction. Moreover, so far as executed transfers of property are concerned the authority of the decisions clearly supports this view. Thus the deed of an infant it is universally agreed transfers a title though the title is voidable. . . . As to executory contracts, a distinction sometimes has been taken, and the doctrine laid down that such bargains are wholly invalid until confirmed. This distinction has been severely criticized, and must be regarded as unfounded. . . . Now inasmuch as the performance of the contract by the infant or his liability for non-performance are wholly dependent upon his own choice until and unless he ratifies the contract after coming of age, it might seem accurate to say that there is until then no contract. But though the distinction is doubtless fine between no contract and a contract which the promisor may perform or not at his pleasure, it is of legal importance. . . . *If an infant's executory promise amounted to nothing until ratified, it is impossible to see how it could be consideration for the counter-promise of an adult, but that it is so was early and conclusively settled.* Again, the defense to an infant's promise can be taken advantage of only by special plea. If that promise were wholly without validity this practice is not defensible."[19] (Italics supplied.)

Thus instead of being looked upon as an exception to the doctrine of consideration, the rule that the infant can recover from the adult but not the adult from the infant is now treated as consistent with the doctrine, and we are told that the rule that the infant's executory promise is "consideration for the counterpromise of an adult . . . was early and conclusively settled." But in order to make this harmonize with the author's doctrine of consideration it becomes necessary to argue that the infant as well as the adult is bound by the contract, and so to draw the "fine distinction" between "no contract" and "a contract which the promisor may perform or not at his pleasure." With all deference to the learned author, the reviewer ventures to suggest that the alleged distinction does not exist. That is to say, if we translate "no contract" into its plain meaning *no contractual duty* and "a contract which the promisor may perform or not at his pleasure" into *a contractual duty which one may perform or not at his pleasure,* we discover that we are confronted with a legal duty which one can disregard with impunity: surely a contradiction in terms.

It may be added that the argument based upon the rule in modern pleading that infancy is an affirmative plea in confession and avoidance proves altogether too much. In the first place, prior to the Hilary Rules of 1834, a defense of infancy came in under the general issue of non-assumpsit. If the learned author's argument is valid, the change made by the Hilary Rules was one of substantive law and not merely of procedure. In the second place, under the Hilary Rules coverture as well as infancy had to be specially pleaded, and no longer came in under the general issue, yet no one ever ventured to

19 Vol. 1, §231.

suggest that in consequence a married woman's promise became 'voidable' instead of 'void.'[20]

There are still other classes of cases in which transactions are enforced as contracts although the learned author's doctrine of consideration is not complied with. One class consists of cases of so-called 'past' or 'executed' consideration. In these cases past events, i. e., events which happened before the 'promise' was made, have been treated by the courts as constituting 'consideration.' Under the learned author's theory, such cases are anomalous and constitute an exception to "principle," since nothing has been given in exchange for the promise. Accordingly we find in Section 142 the following:

> "In several classes of cases, however anomalously, a past consideration has been regarded formerly by the law as sufficient consideration, and at the present time in some of these classes at least, the early law still persists. These classes may be stated as follows, though the boundaries between the groups are not always distinctly marked:
>
> (1) Promises to pay a precedent debt;
>
> (2) Promises in consideration of some act previously done by the promisee at the request of the promisor;
>
> (3) Promises where past circumstances create a moral obligation on the part of the promisor to perform his promise. Under this head may be included cases of ratification and adoption of promises previously made for sufficient consideration but invalid when made for lack of authority or capacity. These groups may be separately considered."

"In some of these classes, at least, the early law still persists": indeed it does, and if this part of our law appears abnormal or "anomalous" it is because of the adoption of the super-generalization of the author, or some similar over-generalization. The same is true of the so-called "promissory estoppel" cases, in which many courts have held promises enforceable because of conduct not given in exchange for the promises but done in justifiable reliance thereon. The Restatement of Contracts, Section 90, has now given the weight of its approval to this development of our law. That section reads:

> "A promise which the promisor should reasonably expect to induce action or forbearance of a definite and substantial character on the part of the promisee and which does induce such action or forbearance is binding if injustice can be avoided only by enforcement of the promise."

To be noted is that the Restatement and Professor Williston group both the 'past consideration' and 'promissory estoppel' cases under the heading of "Promises Not Requiring Consideration." The implication seems to be that they are in some way "exceptional" or "anomalous": the only normal thing is that provided for by the rule concerning 'consideration.'

If now the interested reader—if there be one—asks how a so-called 'realist' might deal with the problem, the answer is perhaps somewhat as follows (the reviewer of course speaks only

[20] It should be kept in mind that a 'plea in confession and avoidance by way of excuse or justification' sets up affirmatively facts which taken with the plaintiff's facts show that the supposed right of action *never existed*, unless indeed the plaintiff can set up still other facts confessing and avoiding the legal effects of those in the plea. Furthermore, all rules of pleading of this kind are to be justified, if at all, on the ground of convenience and fairness in the distribution of the burden of getting the 'facts' before the court, and not as laying down rules of substantive law.

for himself): Presumably a 'realist' would first of all start with the assumption that the lawyer's universe is probably even more complex than that of the physical scientist, or at any rate that it is equally complex, and that while he is to seek for simplicity in his generalizations, he is always to be on his guard lest he over-simplify, especially at the outset. His motto would be, in the words of Whitehead: "Seek simplicity, but distrust it."[21] In the field under consideration he would be likely to suspect that a study of all the relevant phenomena of judicial decision would reveal that no single one-sentence formula could be expected to account for or describe accurately the results actually reached, or to serve as a really helpful guide in solving new problems. In any event, he would first survey the whole field and note the different types of fact-situation[22] involved, summarizing each as he went along by as simple a statement as seemed feasible; and only then, if at all, would he undertake to see to what extent a single general statement would apply to all the various types. In making his survey he would keep in mind that courts are always engaged in deciding concrete cases, not in writing treatises on 'consideration,' and that, whether they will or no, they are influenced in large part by "inarticulate major premises" derived from other fields than the law. In putting his generalizations into words he would endeavor to choose his vocabulary so far as possible in conformity with existing usage, provided always that consistency and clarity of expression were not unduly sacrificed in doing so.[23]

If one began with assumptions of this sort, what could he say? Obviously only the briefest outline of the results of such a procedure can be here given; details must be left to be filled in by readers who feel inclined to do so. The first thing, the reviewer believes, would be to take note of the fact that historically the term 'consideration' has not been confined to something given in exchange for a promise. In order to delimit the field under discussion, he might say that 'consideration' is a word which has been used in Anglo-American law to denote shifting and varying groups of factual events, the happening of any group of which has seemed to the courts to constitute a reason for treating a simple 'promise' as 'legally binding.' The word 'consideration' would thus *denote* —if one may use the technical terms of the logician—these varying groups of factual events, and *connote* that each one of them has the same net legal

21 A. N. Whitehead, The Concept of Nature (1928) 163.

22 Life insurance, fire insurance, suretyship, etc., etc. Any classification would necessarily be tentatively held and revised as the study proceeded.

23 At this point our hypothetical 'realist' might call attention to the fact that many of the words in our legal vocabulary are borrowed from every-day speech: 'consideration' and 'promise' are conspicuous examples; and that because of this there is an unfortunate tendency to read into these terms after they have become 'words of art' meanings which they have in popular language. It is in this way, he might point out, that the notion arises that a 'promise' in order to be a 'promise' must be communicated, and that a determination that a 'promise' can be made without communication is somehow or other 'anomalous.' He might therefore suggest that the choice of the word 'promise' was not entirely a fortunate one. Words like 'consideration,' 'unilateral' and 'bilateral,' etc., etc., might well be subjected to a similar analysis. In the text this has been suggested by setting off some of these terms with single quotation marks, thus warning the reader of possible ambiguities without indicating their source.

consequences of making a simple promise 'legally binding.'

An examination of these groups of factual events would show that while they cannot be summarized under a single formula, at least at first sight and perhaps not at all, they can be classified. In some cases the factual events in question happened prior to the making of the promise; in others, something was given in exchange for the 'promise'; in still others, the events occurred after the 'promise' was made. It would be found that these large groupings need subdivision; for example, in the cases in which a 'promise' is given in exchange for a 'promise,' it would be discovered that the learned author's formula would apply to some of the cases but not to all. Due recognition could thus be given to the fact that in holding an adult bound but not an infant, or the fraudulent person bound and not the one deceived, the courts were in the final analysis guided not by some far-reaching principle of 'consideration' such as that enunciated by the learned author, but by the social and economic policy involved in the particular type of case under consideration. This is not to say that in reaching their conclusions courts have ignored, or should ignore, relevant legal analogies which are summed up in generalizations of the kind under consideration. That the infant or deceived person is not bound, and that in most other bilateral contracts both persons are bound, should be duly noted before the economic or social policy of holding the other person in these groups of cases can be adequately considered. This does not mean, however, that if in the infancy and fraud cases the decision is to hold one person and not the other, the result is an "anomaly" or a violation of "sound principles" of consideration.

Similarly, in connection with 'past' or 'executed' consideration, it would be noted that although nothing is given in exchange for the promise in question, the happening in the past of certain specified events has commended itself to the courts as ample reason for holding the present promise legally effective. In this way the results actually reached by the courts would cease to be looked upon as necessarily 'anomalous,' and could be dealt with in language in keeping with historical usage. So also in the 'promissory estoppel' cases: these could be described as involving a modern extension of the meaning of 'consideration.' It is believed that such a treatment of the matter would be entirely in keeping with the historical development of the idea of 'consideration,' as indeed the learned author himself recognizes in the following passage:

> "It may fairly be argued that the fundamental basis of simple contracts historically was action in justifiable reliance on a promise—rather than the more modern notion of purchase of a promise for a price."[24]

[24] Vol. I, §139. The mode of procedure outlined in the text would also permit the well-known cases in equity, in which promises to convey land are enforced where the prospective grantee has taken possession and made substantial improvements, to be described in terms familiar to courts of equity, namely, that the making of the improvements is the 'consideration' which makes the promise binding: see for example, the opinion in Freeman v. Freeman, 43 N. Y. 34 (1870). It would also permit one to approve the reward cases, condemned by Williston (in §33A) as unsound, which give the offered reward to one who gave the in-

If it be asked what advantages an analysis of this kind would have over the more orthodox treatment exemplified in the Treatise, the answer briefly is that: (1) it would first of all recognize the complex character of the human relationships dealt with in the law of contracts; (2) it would thereby help to bring into the forefront of the discussion the social and economic problems involved; (3) it would not relegate to the category of 'exceptional' or 'anomalous' rules of law which deal sensibly with those problems; and (4) it would enable courts to deal more intelligently with new situations as these arise in a developing social and economic order.

2. *'Acceptance' of Offers.* This brings us to the second example which has been selected for discussion, namely, the learned author's treatment of 'acceptance' of 'offers' where contracts are made between parties who are at a distance from each other. The author's assumption, tacitly made, to be sure, but none the less obvious, is that in all cases of this kind, irrespective of the subject-matter of the contract, there is a single rule which determines when the acceptance, if it is a 'promise,' becomes binding. This assumption may be stated in another form, namely, that *where a 'promise' is asked for by the offer, the word 'promise' has the same meaning no matter what type of transaction may be involved.* More concretely, it follows from this assumption that, so far as the meaning of 'promise' is concerned, there is no difference, for example, between the formation of an executory contract for the purchase and sale of a house and the formation of a life insurance contract.

It will be well first to state as clearly as possible the learned author's theory on this point, and then to examine the 'law' as found in the cases. We begin with the author's theory as to when 'acceptance' is complete when the offer calls for a 'promise' rather than an 'act.' Fortunately on this point the text is quite clear and free from ambiguity. The following excerpts fairly represent, the reviewer believes, the author's views on the matter. The first excerpt is from Section 24, and reads:

> "A promise also seems to connote some communication from the promisor to the promisee. . . . The law, however, has enlarged this conception of a promise, by giving the same effect in some cases to *messages started on their way to the promisee* as to those which actually reach him." (Italics supplied.)

The second excerpt is from Section 70, which is headed: "Acceptance in a bilateral contract requires communication":

> "As has been seen the acceptance of a bilateral contract is not only a manifestation of assent to the proposition but is a giving of the return promise requested. To complete a contract, the offeror must always be given what he requests as the return for his promise and in an offer for a bilateral contract he requests either a promise in fact or an obligation in law. In order to complete a bilateral contract, therefore, on the former supposition *the offeree must in fact make a promise to the offeror, and a promise, as the offeree should reasonably understand, is something which involves, if not communication, at least attempted communication.* If

formation before learning of the offer, as well as those which divide the reward between a number of persons, each of whom acting independently contributed needed information. These latter cases Williston naturally regards as "difficult on principle" to support. See §74A.

an obligation in law is requested, the same thing will generally be true, since contractual obligations in law are imposed as a rule only when promises in fact are made." (Italics supplied.)

In Section 71, which bears the heading: "Acceptance in unilateral contracts where the offeree is promisor requires communication or its equivalent" the author, after pointing out that there are offers for unilateral contracts in which what is called for by way of acceptance is a 'promise,' goes on to say:

> "In this kind of unilateral contract, since the offer requests a promise, it is necessary that the acceptance should be communicated or that something which the law regards as equivalent to communication shall be made. The offer is like that of a bilateral contract in respect to the thing which it requests to be given."

To make his meaning still more clear the author appends the following note to Section 70:

> "It is sufficient authority for this statement to refer to the cases of contracts by correspondence. *Infra*, §75; see also *supra*, §24. These decisions on contracts by correspondence assume or decide that *it is necessary at least that a properly addressed acceptance shall be started towards the offeror.* The early case of Hallock v. Commercial Ins. Co., 26 N. J. L. (2 Dutch) 268, did indeed hold that any overt act by the offeree manifesting assent was sufficient whether it came to the offeror's knowledge and apparently whether it was intended to come to the offeror's knowledge or not, but this decision certainly goes too far." (Italics supplied.)

Note the learned author's language where, in referring to the insurance case cited, he says: "This decision certainly goes too far." Why does it go "too far?" Obviously, because it is in violation of a principle of "wide range of application" throughout contract law, which determines what is an 'acceptance' in the case of contracts involving correspondence where the offer calls for a 'promise' to be made by the offeree. Note that the case which "goes too far" is an insurance case. It will be well, therefore, to examine the law of insurance contracts as found in the cases. In order to simplify the discussion, only life insurance cases will be considered, since each type of insurance raises special problems demanding separate treatment. The first thing to note is that where an applicant for a life insurance policy pays his first premium to a local agent and signs his application

> "in legal terms . . . the applicant makes an offer . . . for the company's promise to insure him. More precisely, since the money paid to the local agent becomes the company's money, the applicant offers to extinguish the company's obligation (evidenced by the receipt) to repay this sum, in exchange for the company's insurance promise."[25]

The writer from whom the foregoing is quoted uses, quite correctly, the word 'promise' although the resulting contract is unilateral, since the offer calls for a 'promise' to be made by the company. In the life insurance cases, then, the problem is: when has the asked-for 'promise' been made?

An examination of the cases shows that the overwhelming weight of authority is that when the first premium has been paid at the time of the signing of the application and there is no explicit statement in the application as

[25] E.W. Patterson, The Delivery of a Life Insurance Policy (1919) 32 Harv. L. Rev. 198.

to what shall constitute an acceptance, a life insurance policy becomes effective at some moment before a "properly addressed acceptance" is "started towards the offeror" by being put into the mails. The authorities are collected by Professor Patterson in the article already quoted from above. He tells us:

> "In only two states, it seems, is the formation of the contract postponed until the delivery of the policy by the local agent to the applicant, and in those states, the conclusion is supported upon the theory that the insurer's acceptance of the applicant's offer must be actually communicated to the latter; not until then is a contract formed. On the other hand, the decided weight of authority is that the contract comes into existence before this final step takes place. Considerable uncertainty exists as to where the line of demarcation is to be drawn between that which is preliminary and inchoate, and that which is final. It is generally agreed that the contract is complete when the policy, duly executed, has reached the local agent, and that the beneficiary may recover the face amount of the policy if the *cestui que vie* dies at that time, if all conditions have been complied with, even though the policy is never delivered but is returned to the home office. In a number of instances, the courts have declared that the contract is made as soon as the policy, duly executed, is placed in the mails, addressed to the company's local or district agent, for delivery by the latter to the applicant. Indeed, judicial support is not wanting for the view that the contract is made as soon as the policy has been executed by the officials at the home office, and some courts seem to regard the contract as completed as soon as the application is approved."[26]

At a later point he adds:

> "It is important to note, however, that the foregoing decisions in which the contract was held to have been completed when the policy reached the local agent, or at some earlier stage in the process, represent *a distinct advance in legal doctrine beyond the ordinary contract-by-correspondence cases.*"[27] (Italics supplied.)

The present writer regrets that he cannot quote more extensively from Professor Patterson's illuminating discussion. Space permits of only the following additional excerpt:

> "The prevailing rule as to contracts by correspondence is thus a compromise. The same may be said of these life-insurance cases. Once it is conceded that the promise need not actually come to the consciousness of the promisee, the question, how far back in the sequence of events between the mental determination to accept and the delivery of the policy the decisive utterance is to be found, is to be answered with a view to the practical result attained."[28]

In reaching these results courts were clearly guided by practical considerations connected with the type of transaction in question. They were dealing with life insurance, "a desirable social habit"; the "company computes and charges a premium from the date of the application, as a rule, and hence, it is arguable, the risk should attach at the earliest possible moment.[29] Clearly, also, these life insurance cases do put "a considerable strain on accepted theories of contract," as Professor Patterson suggests, *if it is assumed that these theories apply to and are uniform for all types of transactions.* On the other hand, if that assumption is not made, all that need be said is that on the point in question the rules governing completion of contracts of

[26] Id. at 203-205.
[27] Id. at 207-208.

[28] Id. at 214.
[29] Id. at 214.

life insurance differ and very properly ought to differ from those in other branches of contract law because of the nature of the transaction involved.[30] If 'law' is thus discovered to be more complex than many have supposed, there is no need for alarm; the complexity in question is merely a reflection of the complexity of life itself.

The learned author's failure to give due recognition to this complexity of the law of contracts and his desire to show its unity has had one interesting result, namely, that by far the larger number of the cases cited by Professor Patterson on the point in question are not listed at all in Professor Williston's table of cases. Some are, but of these a number are referred to solely for another point. Here, then, as is of course true in all fields of work, the selection of data for consideration is guided by one's initial assumptions: what one does not expect to see he either does not see, or, if he 'sees' it at all, he passes it over in silence as unimportant or irrelevant. These initial assumptions are therefore of the highest importance, and if not wisely chosen are likely to result in an inadequate picture of that part of the universe under discussion.

The 'legal universe,' then, as some of the newer writers see it, is far more complex than that visualized by the more orthodox writers of whom Professor Williston is an example. It may be well to note in passing that this recognition of complexity is quite in keeping with the 'climate of opinion' in other fields of thought. Thus it is a commonplace in physical science that the world-picture of nineteenth century physics and chemistry was an enormous over-simplification. Compare, for example, a present day text on chemistry with one current in the days when the author of the present work, or the writer of this review, was in college. In the earlier text atoms were treated as indivisible units out of which an indestructible universe of matter was built. All atoms of any particular element were thought of as alike in size, in 'equivalent weight.' In the text of today, 'atoms' are treated as extremely complex structures. Indeed, the data are so confusing and new data are accumulating so fast that present-day science has not yet succeeded in building a completely satisfactory picture. Some things however seem to be clear: atoms are not only extremely complex, consisting of electrons, protons, neutrons, and other 'particles';[31]

[30] It is of course common today to insert in the application for life insurance a specific statement as to when the policy shall take effect. A common type is that which states that the policy shall not 'take effect' or 'become operative,' etc., until it is 'delivered' to the applicant. Even under such a stipulation it is necessary to keep in mind that one is dealing with a life insurance problem, and not merely with 'contracts.' Thus some courts have protected applicants by holding that the benefit of the stipulation has been 'waived' by the company, or that delivery to the local agent of the company, or a mailing of the policy to him, constitutes a 'delivery to the applicant': see the cases cited by Patterson, The Delivery of a Life Insurance Policy (1919) 33 Harv. L. Rev. 198, 219-222. It has even been held that such a stipulation is to be construed as applying only to a case in which the first premium is not paid at the time of the application: Fidelity Mutual Life Assn. v. Harris, 94 Tex. 25, 57 S. W. 635 (1900). For an interesting example of the efforts of the courts to give the insured a 'square deal' in spite of the wording of the application or policy, see Penn. Mutual Life Ins. Co. v. Forcier, 24 F. Supp. 851 (E. D. Mo. 1937).

[31] For a brief statement of some of the changes in the chemical field, see Frederick Barry, The Scientific Habit of Thought (1927) 128-139. The reviewer has discussed the general situation in science, with special reference to the study of law, in Scientific Method and the Law (1927) 15 The Johns Hopkins Alumni

but transmutation of the elements—that dream of the alchemists at which the nineteenth century scoffed—is today an everyday occurrence in the laboratory; and atoms of the same element may have varying 'equivalent weights.'[32] And so throughout physical science in general, including under that term biological science, we find the over-simplified theories of the late nineteenth century being replaced by others whose pattern recognizes the complexity of the universe in which we live. It is therefore not surprising that these currents of thought in other fields of intellectual endeavor have led a growing number of legal writers to the conviction that an attempt to summarize the phenomena of judicial decision in any field as wide as that of the law of contracts in terms of a relatively few principles of "wide application" is foredoomed to failure, since it cannot lead to either an adequate description of these phenomena or a set of 'principles' which will guide the courts in developing our law so that it will continually adapt itself to our changing civilization. Furthermore, it is also not surprising that these same currents of thought have also led this group of students to recognize clearly that the generalizations they formulate are not

> "fixed rules for deciding doubtful cases, but instrumentalities for their investigation, methods by which the net value of past experience is rendered available for the scrutiny of new perplexities."[33]

From all this it follows that legal 'principles' and 'rules' should not be formulated in terms so broad that it becomes difficult—as it is under orthodox techniques—to give due consideration to the types of social and economic problems involved and so to the 'inarticulate major premises' which in fact underlie the decisions of the courts.

Doubtless much of what is said above will not commend itself to most lawyers who were trained in the traditional techniques and ways of thinking of the legal profession.[34] That is to be expected, for although it may be true, as Mr. Justice Holmes once wrote, that "to have doubted one's own first principles is the mark of a civilized man,"[35] it is also true that to do so is exceedingly difficult for most of us, especially in our later years. Even so, it is the reviewer's belief that an attempt to estimate the long-time value of a work conceived and carried out along traditional lines must be made in terms of these newer and possibly more scientific points of view: hence the foregoing discussion. To be sure, time alone can tell whether adoption of the assumptions and tech-

Magazine, 213, reprinted in (1927) 13 A. B. A. Journal, 303; also in A Scientific Approach to the Study of Law, printed in (1937) Essays in Political Science in Honor of W. W. Willoughby, 200.

32 As the words in the text were being penned, the reviewer noted the following list of 'atomic particles' in the current number (Dec. 16, 1938) of the weekly magazine Science: "electrons, positrons, neutrons, neutrinos, deuterons, mesotrons *and all the rest.*" (Italics supplied.)

33 John Dewey, Human Nature and Conduct (1922) c. VIII The Nature of Principles.

34 Doubtless also the majority of them, because of unfamiliarity with the trend of thought in modern science, will not even understand precisely what is being said. It is an unfortunate fact that our institutions of higher learning are not giving their students an understanding of the 'scientific habit of thought' and its significance for all fields of intellectual endeavor; instead, they are primarily teaching their students the results of science as a new set of dogmas, to be accepted as 'the truth' about the world: see Barry, The Scientific Habit of Thought (1927) especially Part IV: Scientific Humanism.

35 O. W. Holmes, Collected Papers (1920) 307.

niques of the newer 'school of thought' will, as the reviewer believes, furnish the profession with a more useful set of tools with which to work.[36]

It will be seen that the foregoing criticism is primarily not of Professor Williston but of the orthodox techniques and traditional assumptions upon which he has relied. Given those assumptions and techniques it is difficult to see how anyone could turn out a better or more useful product than this revised and greatly improved edition of Williston on Contracts. For the lawyer, the law teacher, and the judge it is as indispensable in the field of contracts as Wigmore's Treatise is in that of evidence.

[36] The discussion in the text of the way in which a 'realist' might analyze problems in the field of contract law gives, of course, a greatly over-simplified picture of the process. It is necessarily, for lack of space, only a rough outline, and omits numerous qualifying details and explanations. It is hoped that in spite of this it will at least provoke further inquiry into the adequacy of orthodox techniques as well as into the validity of the criticisms directed against them. It it does this the purpose for which it was written will have been accomplished.

[17]

YALE LAW JOURNAL

Vol. XXXIII | MARCH, 1924 | No. 5

THE LOGICAL AND LEGAL BASES OF THE CONFLICT OF LAWS

WALTER WHEELER COOK

Time was when the students of the physical sciences sought to judge the truth or correctness of any particular statement about a particular physical thing,—plant, heavenly body, or case of chemical change—by assuming that they had already in hand "a general truth with which to compare the particular empirical occurrence." The assumption was, as John Dewey, from whom I am quoting, puts it, that the human "mind was already in possession of fixed truths, universal principles, preordained axioms" and that "only by their means could contingent, varying particular events be truly known."[1] So long as this assumption maintained its hold upon men's minds no real advance in physical science was possible. Modern science really began only when "men trusted themselves to embarking upon the uncertain sea of events and were willing to be instructed by changes in the concrete. Then antecedent principles were tentatively employed as methods for conducting observations and experiments, and for organizing special facts: as hypotheses."[2] In the field of the physical sciences, therefore, the deductive method of ascertaining the truth about nature has given way to what is called—perhaps with not entire accuracy—the inductive[3] method of modern science, in which the so-called "laws of nature" are reached by collecting data, i.e. by observing concrete phenomena, and then forming, by a process of "trial and error," generalizations which are merely useful tools by means of which we describe in mental shorthand

[1] John Dewey, *Human Nature and Conduct* (1922) 242.

[2] *Ibid.* 243.

[3] Schuppe, *Erkenntnistheorie* (1894) 52 ff; Montague, *On the Nature of Induction* (1906) 3 JOURNAL OF PHILOSOPHY, PSYCHOLOGY AND SCIENTIFIC METHOD, 281 ff; Morris R. Cohen, *The Subject Matter of Formal Logic* (1918) 15 JOURNAL OF PHILOSOPHY, PSYCHOLOGY AND SCIENTIFIC METHOD, 686-687.

as wide a range as possible of the observed physical phenomena, choosing that form of description which on the whole works most simply in the way of enabling us to describe past observations and to predict future observations.[4]

Upon the basis of this second, or experimental,[5] method the imposing structure of modern physical science has been erected; and the attempt to arrive at the truth about particular events by pure deduction from general principles assumed to be true has been definitely and finally abandoned.

In the field of the social sciences, the same development has more recently been going on. Much of the classical political economy began with the assumption that we were already in the possession of general truths about the nature of man. Starting with the economic man, motivated by a supposed "instinct of acquisitiveness" or desire for "gain" or to realize the "greatest pleasure," the "science" was developed deductively. As in other fields, the results were of little if any value. In recent times the method has been giving way to the experimental one of collecting economic facts and formulating general statements which will describe those facts as accurately and simply as possible.

It is interesting to note that in the field of law we find the same rivalry between the two methods of working, and that this is especially true in the conflict of laws. If we open Dicey's great work, we find that he tells us that the subject has been treated by two methods, which he describes respectively as the "theoretical method" and the "positive method"—which turn out upon examination to correspond exactly to the two methods described above. The "theoretical method," which has been followed chiefly by continental writers, maintains (I quote from Dicey) that "the fundamental principles of private international law can be ascertained by study and reflection, and that the soundness of the rules of law maintained, say in England, as to the extra-territorial recognition of rights, can be tested by their conformity to, or deviation from, such general principles." It follows that "the object of a writer on the conflict of laws is to discover the principles" of the subject, and "starting with some one principle . . . . to show how in accordance with the fundamental principle assumed by the writer as the basis of his system"[6] the specific rules for the decision of concrete cases are or should be reached by all countries.

[4] Karl Pearson, *The Grammar of Science* (1900) 112; Morris R. Cohen, *Mechanism and Causality in Physics* (1918) 15 JOURNAL OF PHILOSOPHY, PSYCHOLOGY AND SCIENTIFIC METHOD, 365. On the possibility of different ways of formulating "natural laws," each accurate but differing as to simplicity, see F. R. Moulton, *M. Henri Poincaré* (1912) 20 POPULAR ASTRONOMY, 11-12; and current works upon relativity theories, such as A. S. Eddington, *Space, Time and Gravitation* (1920).

[5] As to the meaning of "experimental" here, see John Dewey (1916) *Essays in Experimental Logic, passim.*

[6] Dicey, *The Conflict of Laws* (3d ed. 1922) 18.

As contrasted with this, the "positive method starts" (again I quote from Dicey) "from the fact that the rules for determining the conflict of laws are themselves 'laws' in the strict sense of that term, and that they derive their authority from the support of the sovereign in whose territory they are enforced."[7] As Dicey points out, this is the method followed by Story, and it is the one Dicey himself chose as the basis of his work. Its merit is that (to quote once again from Dicey) "it constantly impresses upon the minds both of writers and of readers the truth of the all-important doctrine that no maxim is a law unless it be part of the municipal law of some given country."[8]

It must however be noted that the writers of neither school have succeeded in adhering consistently to their main point of view. Thus, both Story and Dicey do at times, without being fully conscious of it, revert to the theoretical method which professedly they had abandoned; and on the other hand, no writer of the theoretical school has actually failed to spend a great deal of his time in examining the actual decisions of the country in which he lived and wrote.

So far as the theoretical method has influenced Anglo-American writers, it has done so chiefly in the form of "territorial" theories about law and legal rights. Such writers begin with reflecting upon and establishing to their own satisfaction the general or essential nature of law and legal rights. This leads them to certain general or fundamental principles, supposed to flow from the nature of law and legal rights as thus established. These fundamental principles take the form of general statements as to what,—in view of the essential nature of law and legal rights,—a state or country "can" and "cannot" do in the way of creating rights, duties, and other legal relations. They thus come to think that the conflict of laws "deals with the recognition and enforcement of foreign-created rights,"[9] or that it has to do with the application of law in space—back of which statements seems to be the assumption (also deduced from the nature of law and legal rights) that for every situation dealt with in the conflict of laws there is always some one and only one "law" which has "jurisdiction," i.e. power, to determine what legal consequences shall be attached to the given situation. They then proceed to determine on this basis what "law" has "jurisdiction" in each group of cases—torts, contracts, property, etc.—and take the position that no other "law" than this appropriate[10] or "proper" law[11]

---

[7] *Ibid.* 19.

[8] *Ibid.* 20.

[9] Beale, *Summary of the Conflict of Laws*, in 3 *Cases on the Conflict of Laws* (1902) 501.

[10] Beale, *op. cit. supra* note 9, sec. 41, p. 515:

"Rights being created by law alone, it is necessary in every case to determine the law by which a right is created. The creation of a personal obligation, which has no situs and results from some act of the party bound, is a matter for the law which has to do with those acts. A personal obligation, then, is created by the law of the place where the acts are done out of which the obligation arises. Where acts are done in one State by the procurement of a party who remains

has "jurisdiction." They also draw the conclusion that when a given right or other legal relation has been validly created by the appropriate law, its validity "cannot" be called into question anywhere.[12]

In the present discussion it is proposed, instead of following the *a priori* method, to adopt the procedure which has proved so fruitful in other fields of science, viz. to observe concrete phenomena first and to form generalizations afterwards. We shall therefore undertake to formulate general statements as to what the "law" of a given country "can" or "cannot" do in the way of attaching legal consequences to situations and transactions by observing what has actually been done. In making our observations we shall, however, find it necessary to focus our attention upon what courts have *done,* rather than upon the description they have given of the reasons for their action. Whatever generalizations we reach will therefore purport to be nothing more than an attempt to describe in as simple a way as possible the concrete judicial phenomena observed, and their "validity" will be measured by their effectiveness in accomplishing that purpose. In other words, they will be true in so far as they enable us to handle effectively the concrete materials with which we must deal.

For convenience, I shall start with so-called "jurisdiction" over crime, for here we find some striking illustrations of results of *a priori* thinking. We are told—the accuracy of the statement is not entirely clear—that at one period in the development of English law, a murderer could not be punished unless both the blow and the death took place in the county in which the prosecution was brought.[13] The difficulty seems

in another State, the acts being actually performed by an agent, the obligation is created by the law of the place where the agent acts."

Sec. 47, p. 517:

"A right having been created by the appropriate law, the recognition of its existence should follow everywhere. Thus an act valid where done cannot be called in question anywhere. And a right to land which has accrued will be recognized as valid though the territory is afterwards annexed to a country where the right could not be created. And so a body created as a corporation in one State must be recognized as such in another State. This is true even though the right so created is absolutely illegal in the other State. Thus, a polygamous or incestuous marriage contracted in a State where it is valid must be recognized as a legal status of that kind even in a State where it is illegal; though it need not be treated as a so-called "Christian" marriage would be. It is merely recognizing a foreign fact (sec. 4). This doctrine, though obvious, has not been universally recognized. And there is good authority for the doctrine that if the marriage is against universal notions of decency because between very near relatives it will not be recognized as a possibly legal marriage anywhere. A slave for the same reason must be recognized as such even in a free State. It is true that if a slave comes into a free State he cannot be restrained by his master; not because he ceases to be a slave, but because in such a State there is no right in a master to restrain a slave." *Cf.* Beale, *Treatise on the Conflict of Laws* (1916) 168-169.

[11] Minor, *Treatise on Conflict of Laws* (1901) seeks to find the "proper law" for each transaction, this being deemed to depend upon the "situs" of the "transaction."

[12] See passage quoted from Beale, *op. cit. supra* note 10.

[13] See discussion of the old law in *Commonwealth v. Macloon,* cited *infra,* note 16.

to have been connected with the fact that the early triers of fact answered of their own knowledge and without testimony of witnesses, and therefore could not know both who struck the blow and that the death had happened unless both events occurred in the county.[14] This rule was changed, or at least the doubt as to the law settled, by statute in the reign of Edward VI[15] so as to give jurisdiction to the county in which the death occurred. It is interesting to find this common-law rule, introduced originally apparently for purely practical reasons, later erected into an immutable "principle" of "jurisdiction," based on arguments as to the territorial nature of law. In *State v. Carter* (1859, N. J. Sup. Ct.) 3 Dutcher, 499, the blow was struck in New York; the death occurred in New Jersey. The decision of the New Jersey court was that that state had no jurisdiction, and could have none. The argument was that as no "act" of the accused took place in New Jersey, that state could not attach any legal consequences to the accused's conduct; that that must from the nature of things be done only by the state where the "act" took place. The court said:

> "Here no act is done in this state by the defendant. He sent no missile, or letter, or message, that operated as an act within this state. The coming of the party injured into this state afterwards was his own voluntary act, and in no way the act of the defendant. If the defendant is liable here at all, it must be solely because the deceased came and died here after he was injured. Can that, in the nature of things, make the defendant guilty of murder or manslaughter here? . . . . An act, to be criminal, must be alleged to be an offence against the sovereignty of the government. This is of the very essence of crime punishable by human law. How can an act done in one jurisdiction be an offence against the sovereignty of another? All the cases turn upon the question where the act was done. The person who does it may, when he does it, be within or without the jurisdiction, as by shooting or sending a letter across the border; but the act is not the less done within the jurisdiction because the person who does it stands without."

The thing which to the New Jersey court seemed impossible was accomplished by the Supreme Court of Massachusetts in *Commonwealth v. Macloon,*[16] where Massachusetts law was applied to a murderer where the death had occurred in Massachusetts although the blow was struck on a British merchant ship on the high seas. So far as I can discover, the validity, as distinguished from the expediency, of the action taken by the Massachusetts court has never been successfully challenged, either as a violation of international law or of the constitutional law of

---

[14] It seems that it was supposed the difficulty was surmounted by taking the dead body back into the county in which the blow was struck. See opinion in *Commonwealth v. Macloon*, cited, *infra*, note 16.

[15] (1548) 2 & 3 Edw. VI, c. 24.

[16] *Commonwealth v. Macloon* (1869) 101 Mass. 1. The fact that the decision in this case is based on a statute does not affect the argument as to the "power" of the *state*.

the state or nation.[17] If then, we base our generalizations as to the "jurisdiction,"—the power of a state or country to attach legal consequences to groups of fact—upon observations of what has been and is being done, we may, I think, conclude that a state or country, if it deems it wise to do so, can punish people on whom it can lay its hands for "acts" done in other states or countries, at least where some "result" of the act takes place within the state or country in which the prosecution is had.[18]

In the developed system of the criminal law in this country, it became the orthodox rule to deny "jurisdiction" to punish crime to the courts of the state in which the physical motion of the accused's body took place, unless also that motion "took effect" within the same state, i.e. unless the force set in motion by the actor came into contact with the person injured within the state. "Jurisdiction" to punish was given, on the other hand, to the state in which the actor's bodily movements "took effect," even though the physical motion, the "act" in that sense, of the accused, occurred in another state.[19] This result was sometimes expressed by the statement that the "act" was "in contemplation of law, done" in the state where it "took effect." The rule of law applied to define the crime was accordingly that of the state thus given "jurisdiction," for in the field of criminal law no one has ever supposed that a state or country ever enforced any law but its own.

The use of the word "jurisdiction" in stating this rule, coupled with notions previously referred to—as to the inherent nature of law and its territorial operations—similar to those expressed in *State v. Carter*,[20] are likely to lead a writer or judge who, consciously or unconsciously, is following the theoretical or *a priori* method, to the conclusion that only the state where the force comes into contact with the person injured can from the "nature of things" have "jurisdiction." They therefore proceed to deny "jurisdiction" to apply its law to the state in which the bodily movements of the actor took place.[21] If all that is meant by such statements is that according to existing rules of positive law the *courts* of the state in which the actor's bodily movements take place are not authorized to deal with the situation, well and good. But if, as is sometimes the case, this rule of positive law is interpreted as expressing some inherent or immutable principle limiting the "jurisdiction," i.e. the power, of the *state* concerned to authorize its courts to deal with the situation and apply its law to the offender, so that any attempt of the

[17] A number of the cases are collected in *State v. Hall*, cited *infra*, note 22.

[18] The word *power* as applied to a "sovereign" cannot mean *legal power*, for the sovereign is the law-giver and by hypothesis not subject to law. If international law exists as *law*, it necessarily means that states (in the international sense) are not really "sovereign" in the full sense of that term.

[19] May, *Criminal Law* (3d ed. 1905) secs. 79-80.

[20] (1859, N. J. Sup. Ct.) 3 Dutcher, 499.

[21] *United States v. Davis* (1837, C. C. D. Mass.) 2 Sumn. 482, Fed. Cas. No. 14, 932; and other cases cited by May, *op. cit. supra* note 19, at p. 82, note 3.

state so to do is necessarily void, I for one cannot follow the argument. The reason why I cannot is that I find states actually doing the supposedly impossible thing, and doing it without successful challenge by anyone.

Before examining cases in which the impossible has been accomplished, let us note the practical reasons why it has been attempted. In *State v. Hall*[22] the accused had stood on the North Carolina side of the state line and shot into Tennessee. The bullet struck and killed the deceased in Tennessee. It was held that in the absence of a statute the accused could not be punished in North Carolina, since "in legal contemplation" the "killing" took place in Tennessee. The court quoted with approval the following passage from an opinion in a Georgia case.[23]

> "Of course, the presence of the accused within this State is essential to make his act one which is done in this State; but the presence need not be actual. It may be constructive. The well established theory of the law is, that where one puts in force an agency for the commission of crime, he, in legal contemplation, accompanies the same to the point where it becomes effectual. Thus, a burglary may be committed by inserting into a building a hook, or other contrivance, by means of which goods are withdrawn therefrom; and there can be no doubt that, under these circumstances, the burglar, in legal contemplation, enters the building. So, if a man in the State of South Carolina criminally fires a ball into the State of Georgia, the law regards him as accompanying the ball, and as being represented by it, up to the point where it strikes."[23]

But in *State v. Hall*[24] the same court held that although Hall had been "constructively" absent from North Carolina and "present" in Tennessee at the time of the "killing,"—and, I am tempted to add, had "constructively returned" to North Carolina as soon as he had accomplished the purpose for which he constructively accompanied the bullet into Tennessee,—such constructive conduct did not make him a fugitive from justice so as to authorize his surrender to the authorities of Tennessee, as that required actual and not merely constructive presence and flight.

Fortunately courts have recognized that the absurd and socially bad result reached in these cases is not due to inherent lack of power on the part of our states, but merely to the operation of certain rules of positive law. They have therefore never, so far as I am aware, doubted the validity of legislation giving authority to punish to the courts of the state in which the accused was and in which he actually moved his body, even though the results of such bodily action take place beyond the territorial limits. As we all know, statutes are common which provide—I am quoting the substance of the New York law—that the courts of the state shall have power to punish anyone who "within the state commits any crime, *in whole or in part*." This was held in *People v.*

[22] (1894) 114 N. C. 909, 19 S. E. 602.

[23] *Simpson v. State* (1893) 92 Ga. 41, 43, 17 S. E. 984, 985.

[24] (1894) 115 N. C. 811, 20 S. E. 729.

Zayas[25] to authorize the punishment in New York of any who in that state made false pretenses but obtained the property in Pennsylvania. Speaking for the court, Mr. Justice Seabury said:

> "The reversal could be sustained upon either of two grounds, viz., first, that the acts alleged constitute a crime under the law of this state, or, second, that the acts alleged considered in connection with the law of the state where the crime was consummated, constitute a crime . . . . We are now called upon to determine upon which of these grounds our decision should rest, and I think that we should place our judgment in this case on the ground that the acts alleged constitute a crime under the law of this state without regard to the law prevailing in the state where the crime was consummated."[26]

For our present purposes, it is not material which view is taken. It is clear from the case, and from similar cases which can be cited,[27] that the state in which the human action takes place can if it so wishes authorize its courts to apply its criminal law to the situation, even though the results of the action in the way of injury to others occur outside the territorial limits. It is equally clear from our preceding discussion, that the state where the act takes effect can apply its law.

On the basis of actual observation of what courts have done and are doing, then, I think we may safely make the following generalization: Where A in state X sets a force in motion which injures B in state Y, and B goes to and as a result of the injury dies in state Z, either X, Y, or Z, if it can get its hands on A, can apply its own criminal law to the case. What each will do will depend solely upon its own positive law, common or statutory—and not upon any inherent principles of "jurisdiction" limiting its powers. Its choice therefore will have to be purely pragmatic—as to what, all things considered, it is desirable to do.

If we assume that none of the facts which go to make up the alleged crime—human action and results—took place in the state or country seeking to punish the actor, does that state or country necessarily, i.e. because of territorial limitations to which all "law" is subject, lack "jurisdiction"? Note that the question is not whether, according to the existing positive law in the state or country concerned, its *courts* are authorized to punish, but the broader one of the "jurisdiction" of the so-called "sovereign," the law-giver, to authorize its judicial and other officers to deal with the situation. It is perhaps a common notion in the Anglo-American countries that such inherent limitations do exist, and it may well be that some of the rules of our existing positive law have taken their present shape under the influence of such ideas.[28]

---

[25] (1916) 217 N. Y. 78, 111 N. E. 465.

[26] Cuddeback, J., concurred in the result but not in the reasoning.

[27] *People v. Botkin* (1901) 132 Calif. 231, 64 Pac. 286, is an example.

[28] See discussion in such cases as *State v. Knight* (1799, N. C.) 2 Haywood, 109; *Hanks v. State* (1882) 13 Tex. App. 208; and the quotations in the opinion in the latter case from Cooley, *Constitutional Limitations* (4th ed. 1883) 154-155. This was the view asserted by the United States in *Cutting's Case*, 2 Moore, *International Law Digest* (1906) 228.

Nevertheless, there seems to be no logical foundation for such a limitation. Suppose England were to enact a law providing that all persons who anywhere in the world commit what would if done in England amount to unlawful homicide, shall, if found in England, after due trial and conviction be separated from the rest of the community by being sent to jail, what—aside from some positive rule of international law, recognized as binding by the civilized nations—would interfere to prevent the carrying out of the law? Whether laws of this kind would be desirable or practicable is not the question—although much can be said and is being said by a number of continental writers in favor of such a system.[29] Aside from questions of practicability in execution, it seems to be in keeping with the idea that the object of the criminal law is not to satisfy the thirst for revenge but rather to protect society from persons whose overt conduct reveals dangerous and anti-social tendencies.[30] If, with Holmes, we say that "the prophecies of what courts will do in fact, and nothing more pretentious" are what we "mean by law,"[31] and, given a statute like that suggested above, we can prophecy that if X kills Y in China or anywhere else on the planet certain English officials—judges and others—will, if they can get hold of him, deal with him just as though he had done the killing in England, must we not say that English "law" applies to determine for England and English officials the legal consequences of acts and results, all of which happen abroad? Whether existing international law forbids such action by England is, I repeat, another question. I venture to suggest that a study of continental law and legal writing will reveal that there exists no consensus of opinion among the civilized nations of the world which forbids laws of the kind under discussion, and that very possibly when the matter does come up internationally, the rule will probably be settled in favor of recognizing the jurisdiction of countries to do this very thing if they so wish. It would seem that only a clinging to the crude and primitive idea that the sole object of the criminal law is "punishment" for an "offence" against the "sovereign" could lead to the opposite conclusion.[32] It seems also that

[29] See 2 Travers, *Le Droit Pénal International* (1920) 199 ff. The "cosmopolitan" principle has been accepted farthest by Austria, Italy, Norway and Russia, according to Meili, *Lehrbuch des Internationalen Strafrechts und Strafprozessrechts* (1910) 183. Grotius apparently was the first to advocate the principle. 2 *De Jure Belli et Pacis*, c. 20, sec. 40. Consult also 1 Binding, *Handbuch des Strafrechts* (1885) 379, note; 2 Carrara, *Programma del Corso di Diritto Criminale* (8th ed. 1897) 1040 ff.

[30] The protection may consist simply in segregating the "offender," or, where that seems practicable, in "reforming" him.

[31] Holmes, *Collected Legal Papers* (1920) 173. The word "courts" should include some other more or less similar officials.

[32] *Cf.* Holmes, *op. cit. supra* note 31, at p. 189, citing Havelock Ellis, *The Criminal* (1890) 41.

as a matter of fact some continental systems already go a long way toward embodying in their criminal jurisprudence this "cosmopolitan" theory of criminal justice.[33] Whether similar laws passed by American states would violate the "due process" clause is of course a still different question, upon which also no opinion is offered at this place, other than to say that apparently only a blind following of unsound territorial notions would lead to the conclusion of unconstitutionality as distinguished from social desirability.

Suppose now we put the same case of wrongful death, involving the three states X, Y, and Z and inquire first as to the powers of X, Y, and Z respectively to determine the legal consequences of the situation in the way of an action for wrongful death on behalf of B's dependents. Can there be any rational doubt that either X, Y, or Z can if it so wishes apply its law in determining the civil as well as the criminal liability of A? It would seem not. If this conclusion is sound, it becomes obvious that there is no universal or inherent principle of "jurisdiction" which can be used in testing the "validity," "soundness," or "correctness" of decisions by courts in X, Y, or Z, in which they choose one "law" rather than another as the basis for deciding a case of the kind under consideration. It is of course common to say that the "common-law" rule is, to apply the "law" of the place where the "act claimed to be a tort was committed."[34] This is usually interpreted to mean, the place where the force set in motion by the actor "took effect," i.e. first came into contact with the person or property injured, or "where the injury happened."[35] Note that the first form of statement gives to the word "act" an arbitrary and unnatural meaning, for it excludes as part of the "act" the physical motion of the actor's body and includes only a certain limited portion of the results of such action. In our hypothetical case of wrongful death involving the three states, the "act" would, according to this way of stating the rule, consist solely of the contact of the bullet with B's person in state Y and would not include A's bodily motion in X or the resulting death in Z. If we note that the alleged tort consists of the totality of all these physical events—a com-

[33] See note 29, *supra*.

[34] 3 Beale, *op. cit. supra* note 9, sec. 86. The language in the cases is not at all clear-cut. See *LeForest v. Tolman* (1875) 117 Mass. 109, one of the two cases cited by Professor Beale for his statement, in which "the injury sued for was done to the plaintiff in New Hampshire by a dog owned and kept by the defendant in Massachusetts." Gray, C. J., said: "The act which is the cause of the injury . . . . must be actionable or punishable by the law of the place in which it is done . . . . The wrong done . . . . consists not in the act of the master in owning or keeping or neglecting to restrain the dog, but in the act of the dog for which the master is responsible . . . . The injury for which the plaintiff seeks to recover having taken place in New Hampshire" [the New Hampshire law applies]. Note that nowhere does Gray, C. J., say expressly that the *master's act* took place in New Hampshire.

[35] *LeForest v. Tolman*, *supra* note 34.

plete statement would doubtless include A's state of mind when he acted in X—we see clearly and at once the arbitrary nature of the attempt to give "jurisdiction" solely to Y and to deny to X or Z *power* to determine whether or not this group of events shall as a whole give rise to a duty to compensate B's dependents. The "common-law" rule, however convenient it may be, thus appears for just what it is—simply a rule of positive law, having had its origin possibly, in part at least, in grounds of supposed logic, but to be defended to-day entirely on the basis of social convenience and practical expediency. Perhaps all that can be said for it is that it is at least as good as any other, and that as we already have it, we should stick to it.[36]

Suppose, in order to make our problem somewhat more concrete, we assume that state X has no wrongful death statute; that Y has a "penal" statute like that in Massachusetts;[37] and that Z has a compensatory statute like that in many states.[38] Suppose farther that the action—B's dependents against A—is brought in the courts of X. If our conclusions down to this point are sound, X has "jurisdiction" to apply its own "law" to the case, and is not bound to apply any other state's law. This does not mean, however, that it will necessarily apply the same rule that it would have applied to a purely domestic case, i.e. one in which all the facts—actions of A and resulting injury to and death of B—had occurred in X. For the court in X is confronted with a problem in the conflict of laws, and it may well choose the rule found in Y's law, or that found in Z's law. In fact, in cases of the kind under consideration, involving wrongful death, there is some authority for choosing the rule of the place where the death occurs, rather than where the bullet struck the deceased, the argument perhaps being that the "injury" to B's dependents, as distinguished from B, arises only upon the death.[39] Other cases apply the rule of the place where B receives the injury.[40] As either result is equally possible, so far as "jurisdic-

[36] Holmes, *op. cit. supra* note 31, at p. 239:

"Indeed precisely because I believe that the world would be just as well off if it lived under laws that differed from ours in many ways, and because I believe that the claim of our especial code to respect is simply that it exists, that it is the one to which we have become accustomed, and not that it represents an eternal principle, I am slow to consent to overruling a precedent, and think that our important duty is to see that the judicial duel shall be fought out in the accustomed way."

[37] By that statute damages are to be "assessed with reference to the degree of . . . . culpability," in amount not less than $500 and not more than $10,000. Mass. Rev. Laws, 1902, ch. 171, sec. 2, as amended by Laws, 1907, ch. 375, reprinted in *Loucks v. Standard Oil Co. of New York* (1918) 224 N. Y. 99, 120 N. E. 198.

[38] That is, damages are to be estimated according to actual loss inflicted on the dependents of the party killed.

[39] *Hoodmacher v. Lehigh Valley R. R.* (1907) 218 Pa. 21, 66 Atl. 975, criticized in (1907) 21 HARV. L. REV. 143, as "unsound" because "the real cause of action is the infliction of the injury"—whatever that may mean.

[40] *Rudiger v. Chicago, St. P. M. & O. Ry.* (1898) 94 Wis. 191, 68 N. W. 661, and (1907) 21 HARV. L. REV. 143.

tion" is concerned, we shall have to choose on some basis other than that of "power."

Suppose now that in our hypothetical case of the wrongful death, the action is not brought in X, Y, or Z, but in the courts of a fourth state, Q. The writers of the theoretical school have, as I have indicated, sought to answer this by picking out the one state having, according to their notions, power to deal with the case, and arguing that Q must "enforce" the "foreign right" created by the "law" of the state so chosen. If the views here set out are sound, Q's task is not so simple, for all three states, X, Y, and Z, have "jurisdiction." Which one shall Q choose, and why? Suppose in investigating the actual decisions we were to find that Q has chosen Y's rule, and that R has chosen Z's rule:[41] which decision would "on principle" be erroneous? Obviously, we can no longer turn the crank of the logical machine and produce the answer ready-made, for no single state has exclusive jurisdiction; there is no single foreign right to recognize and enforce.

Before proceeding farther, we must take note of an ambiguity in the word "law" involved in the question as usually asked: Shall Q apply X's "law," or Y's "law," or Z's "law"? This ambiguity is often overlooked. If, for example, we say that Q is to "apply the law of Z," do we mean that Q is to decide the case, with its factual elements involving X, Y, and Z, in exactly the same way that the courts of Z would decide it? That is, do we mean that the court in Q is to find out whether or not the courts of Z would give *these plaintiffs* (B's dependents) a judgment against *this defendant* (A) if the action had been brought there? That is of course just what some territorialists have said, for they deny to Q any "jurisdiction" to determine the legal consequences of events all of which have occurred beyond the territorial limits. To carry out their theory, they therefore are compelled to give to "law" the suggested meaning. Note the consequences of doing so: the court in Q is compelled to study the decisions of the courts in Z upon the conflict of laws, for, be it noted, a suit by B's dependents against A in the case supposed will wherever it is brought present a problem in the conflict of laws. If the court in Q were to examine Z's decisions on the conflict of laws--assuming Q had decided to apply Z's "law" applicable to this very case—it might well find that those decisions would say, "This case is governed by the 'law' of Y, since the injury and not the death is the cause of action." Q would therefore find itself sent on to Y. If now the word "law," in the statement quoted from the hypothetical opinion of the court in Z, again means that Z would decide the very case exactly as Y's courts would, it is logically conceiv-

[41] The word *rule* is substituted for the word *law* in the above statements, for, as I attempt to show more at length later, it is believed that the rule thus adopted by the forum from the foreign system of law is "enforced" as a rule of the "law" of the forum and not as foreign "law."

able that Q would find itself sent back by Y to Z, on the ground that the death happened there and that therefore Z's law should govern.

This of course is not what happens. The reason is that, probably without being fully conscious of the logic involved, Anglo-American courts have refused to adopt the *"renvoi."* The escape is actually due to a refusal to give to "law" the meaning that leads to these difficulties, i.e., a refusal to mean by it that Q is to decide the case exactly as Z would. Do courts really so refuse? If we examine carefully into judicial phenomena, I think we shall find that (except in a few cases to be noted later) they do, even if their loose language belies their action. What do they do? It seems that actually they content themselves with finding out what decision would be rendered by some foreign court (with whose state or country the facts are in part connected) in a suit similar to the one under consideration, but differing in one, for our purposes vitally important, respect, viz. that it involves for the foreign court a situation purely domestic, with no foreign element.

If this is what really happens, note the result: the court in Q would not, in the case supposed, inquire into the conflict of laws cases of X, or Y, or Z, but would content itself with finding out how each one of these states would decide a case involving a similar but (for it) purely domestic group of facts. Moreover, the court in Q as the result of such an inquiry would not know how X, or Y, or Z, would decide this case now before it, of B's dependents against A, i.e. it would be totally ignorant of whether there were or were not foreign-created rights for it to recognize and enforce. If it nevertheless gives the plaintiffs a judgment, can we accurately describe that action otherwise than by saying that the right so enforced is a right created by the law of Q and not a foreign-created right?

The view outlined may be stated as follows: the forum, when confronted by a case involving foreign elements, always applies its own law to the case, but in doing so adopts and enforces as its own law a rule of decision identical, or at least highly similar though not identical, in scope with a rule of decision found in the system of law in force in another state or country with which some or all of the foreign elements are connected, the rule so selected being in normal cases, and subject to the exceptions to be noted later, the rule of decision which the given foreign state or country would apply, not to this very group of facts now before court of the forum, but to a *similar but purely domestic group of facts involving for the foreign court no foreign element.* The rule thus incorporated into the law of the forum may for convenience be called the "domestic rule" of the foreign state, as distinguished from its rule applicable to cases involving foreign elements. The forum thus enforces not a foreign right but a right created by its own law.

The exceptions to the foregoing statement seem to fall into two classes. The first includes those cases in which the facts involved are all, from the point of view of the foreign state. purely domestic facts. Here the rule of decision adopted into its law by the forum is normally identical in scope with, or at least highly similar to, the rule of decision which the foreign state would apply to the very case before the forum. A simple example is an action in state X for an alleged tort committed wholly in state Y, the parties concerned being all citizens of and domiciled in state Y. The second class includes cases in which on grounds of practical expediency the forum decides to apply as its rule of decision the rule which the foreign court would have applied, not to a (for it) purely domestic case, but to this very case if it had been brought there. Obviously the rule so selected is the one indicated by the rules of the conflict of laws in force in the foreign state. An example is the case of *Ball v. Cross*.[42] Note, however, that even in these exceptional cases it is not the foreign "law" or "right" that is enforced, but that the law of the forum adopts as its law a rule of decision reaching the same, or at least a highly similar, result to that reached by the foreign law.

Professor Beale enunciates in the first part of his *Treatise on the Conflict of Laws* a territorial theory of law which, if I understand it, furnishes the logical basis for this position. He says:

> "If by the national law the validity of a contract depends upon the law of the place where the contract was made, then that law is applied for determining the validity of a contract made abroad, not because the foreign law has any force in the nation, nor because of any constraint exercised by an international principle, but because the national law determines the question of the validity of a contract by the *lex loci contractus*. If it were really a case of conflicting laws, and the foreign law prevailed in the case in question, the decision would be handed over bodily to the foreign law. By the national doctrine, the national law provides for a decision according to certain provisions of the foreign law; in the case considered, according to the foreign contract law. The provisions of this law having been proved as a fact, the question is solved by the national law, the foreign factor in the solution—i.e. the foreign contract law—being present as mere fact, one of the facts upon which the decision is to be based. To explain the territorial theory in other terms, all that has happened outside the territory, including the foreign laws which have in some way or other become involved in the problem, is regarded merely as fact to be considered by the national law in arriving at its decision, and to be given such weight in determining the decision as the national law may choose to give it."[43]

If I am right in my interpretation of this passage, the territorial theory set forth in it seems to be a thoroughly sound one, by which I mean merely that it is an accurate general description of what courts have done and are doing in dealing with cases in the conflict of laws.

The distinction between the commonly accepted view and that here set forth may be made clearer if we examine a case from the field of

[42] (1921) 231 N. Y. 329, 132 N. E. 106. See COMMENTS (1921) 31 YALE LAW JOURNAL, 191, for discussion of that case.

[43] Beale, *Treatise on the Conflict of Laws* (1916) 106.

contract law. From the abundance of illustrative material, let us select the familiar case of *Milliken v. Pratt.*[44] W, a married woman, domiciled in Massachusetts, in that state signed and gave to H, her husband, an offer addressed to P, offering to guarantee payment by H for goods to be sold by P to H. The offer was for a unilateral contract, the acceptance to be the shipment of the goods from Maine. H sent the latter by mail to P in Maine, who there received it and accepted by shipping the goods from that state. W was sued by P in Massachusetts. The usual way of stating the problem is, that by the "law" of Massachusetts W lacked capacity to bind herself by such an agreement, but that by the "law" of Maine she had capacity; and the result is usually stated in the same terms, viz. that the Massachusetts court held that as the contract was made in Maine, the "law" of Maine was to be applied in determining W's capacity to bind herself. That this is the usual way in which courts and writers describe such cases cannot be denied, and it will perhaps do well enough if we do not misinterpret it, although personally I hope some day to see a more accurate terminology come into general use. If I am right about it, properly interpreted this does not mean that Massachusetts recognized and enforced a "right created by the law of Maine." Statements that it did so of course are not wanting.[45]

First let us notice that the usual way of stating the problem cannot be taken literally. If the statement that "by the law of Massachusetts W lacked capacity to bind herself" means that by that law *this married woman W* lacked capacity to bind herself *by this transaction* to *this P in Maine,* we need go no farther; the case is decided for a Massachusetts court. The statement thus literally interpreted means that under Massachusetts law this defendant W is not bound to this plaintiff P; but that is just what we are trying to find out and by hypothesis do not know. If the statement means anything, it must therefore not be taken literally. *What we really start with is a knowledge of the Massachusetts law applicable not to this W but to another W, in a hypothetical case similar to this but differing in that all the facts are, so to speak, Massachusetts facts.* In other words, all we know is the Massachusetts "domestic rule," using that phrase in the sense already defined.

Is the statement—made, be it noted, in stating the problem raised by the case—that "by Maine law W had capacity to bind herself," to be interpreted differently? We may give it a literal meaning, but I venture to think that that is wrong, in the sense that it does not describe accurately what the Massachusetts court knew. Let us look at the facts. Did the Massachusetts court really know at the outset—when stating the problem for solution—what rights this plaintiff would have been recognized by the Maine courts as having against this defendant? Note

[44] (1878) 125 Mass. 374.

[45] *Cf.* 3 Beale, *op. cit. supra* note 9, at p. 540, sec. 87.

that for the Maine court as well as for the Massachusetts court this case presents a problem in the conflict of laws. Note also that merely by knowing that Maine has a statute "removing the disabilities of married women" we do not know how a Maine court would deal with a Massachusetts woman all of whose acts[46] took place in Massachusetts, even though her letter was read and acted upon by a Maine plaintiff in Maine. To know how a Maine court would decide *this very case* involves necessarily a study of the Maine rules as to the conflict of laws. I find no evidence that the Massachusetts court had such knowledge *either when it stated the problem before it or later when it decided the case.* I find no evidence that it ever tried to get it. The evidence as found in the opinion is collected in the note below.[47] Had the Massachusetts court embarked upon this arduous and perilous adventure (of trying to learn how the Maine court would treat this married woman domiciled in Massachusetts, and whose only actions were done there), it might have found—treating Maine for the moment as a name standing for any other state than Massachusetts—that the supreme court of the other state would say that its statute removing the disabilities of married women applied only to married women domiciled in its own state[48] or to married women entering into agreements while actually within the state, or that the capacity of a married

[46] "Acts" here means *actions* as distinguished from consequences or *results* of action.

[47] All that the report of the case gives is a statement of the Maine statute ("the contracts of any married woman, made for any lawful purpose, shall be valid and binding, and may be enforced in the same manner as if she were sole"), and the following: "The law of Maine authorized a married woman to bind herself by any contract as if she were unmarried . . . . The law of Massachusetts, as then existing, did not allow her to enter into a contract as surety or for the accommodation of her husband or of any third person," at p. 376. The Massachusetts court then cites as authority for these statements one and only one Maine case—*Mayo v. Hutchinson* (1869) 57 Me. 546. *That case was a purely domestic one,* raising no question of the applicability of the statute to cases involving foreign elements. It therefore furnishes no basis for a conclusion as to the Maine law applicable to W in the principal case. Similarly, in supporting its statement that the Massachusetts law did not at the time W acted allow "a married woman" to make a suretyship contract, the Massachusetts court cites a single case—*Nourse v. Henshaw* (1877) 123 Mass. 96. That also involved a purely domestic (Massachusetts) group of facts.

[48] The real question would be, shall the Maine statute be construed to cover: (1) only Maine married women (women domiciled in Maine); or (2) any woman actually acting in Maine; or (3) any woman so acting or who sends an agent (in the ordinary sense of that term) into Maine to act for her—see *Freeman's Appeal* (1897) 68 Conn. 533, 37 Atl. 420; or (4) all such and married women actually acting in other states who by post send offers to Maine which are received and read there and acted upon there? This list of possible interpretations is not exhaustive, but merely suggestive. Compare, for example, the variety of views as to the construction of statutes requiring the filing of chattel mortgages and conditional sale contracts and their application to contracts made in other states.

woman to contract is governed by the "law" of her domicile,[49] or some other "law."[50] Note that if, on finding that the cases in the other state said that the capacity of W was to be settled by the "law" of her domicile, the Massachusetts court were to interpret "law" to mean the rule which W's domicile (Massachusetts) would apply to *the very case*, it would become involved in a discussion of the interesting game of international lawn tennis known as the *"renvoi."*

If, as seems clearly to be the case, the Massachusetts court in fact contented itself with ascertaining the Maine "domestic rule," applicable to a purely Maine group of facts, it could not of course know whether by the law of Maine this defendant W was under a contractual duty to this plaintiff P or not, and so could not know whether there was a Maine-created right for it to enforce. What the Massachusetts court did in *Milliken v. Pratt*, what other courts have done in other cases in the conflict of laws, is of course purely a question of fact, to be ascertained, like any other fact, by observation. My observations lead me to believe that—except in the cases previously referred to—Anglo-American courts have contented themselves with ascertaining the "domestic rule" of the foreign country, and that they are likely to continue to do so for the reason that any other course will as a rule land them in endless difficulties. If my observations of fact have been accurate, must we not say that in *Milliken v. Pratt* all that the Massachusetts court did was to adopt as the Massachusetts law a rule of decision identical in scope with the Maine "domestic rule"? If so, it follows that we must say that it neither applied Maine "law" nor "recognized and enforced a Maine-created right," as such, and that what it did do was to apply to the case before it the Massachusetts law and so to enforce a Massachusetts-created right.

The difference between the two views is not merely one of words, as some perhaps may suppose. The two ways of stating the matter lead

---

[49] *First National Bank v. Shaw* (1902) 109 Tenn. 237, 70 S. W. 807, and cases cited in Lorenzen, *Cases on the Conflict of Laws* (1909) 231, note 2. In this Tennessee case the Tennessee married woman signed negotiable notes in that state, but they were negotiated and delivered in Ohio and payable in Ohio. The Tennessee court held that although the contract was "made" (consummated) in Ohio, the defendant's capacity was governed by the Tennessee "law." It is quite probable that the Massachusetts court would have decided *Milliken v. Pratt* the same way, had it not been for the fact that before the suit was brought the Massachusetts legislature had changed the Massachusetts "law" so that it was the same as the Maine "law." This change in the Massachusetts law was mentioned in the opinion and obviously played a large part in the actual decision.

[50] In *Poole v. Perkins* (1919) 126 Va. 331, 101 S. E. 240, the note in question was signed in Tennessee by a married woman domiciled there, but payable in Virginia. The forum was Virginia and all parties were domiciled there at the time of the action. *Held*, that the Virginia "law" (rule) governed, as that was the law which the "parties presumably intended to govern." *Cf. Burr v. Beckler* (1914) 264 Ill. 230, 106 N. E. 206; Ann. Cas. 1915 D, 1132; and see note on the general question in L. R. A. 1916 A, 1054.

to differences of result in the actual decision of cases. This is strikingly illustrated by the very recent case of *Guinness v. Miller* (1923, S. D. N. Y.) 291 Fed. 769, in which Judge Learned Hand adopted a view like that here advocated. The plaintiff in that case was a citizen suing to recover a debt owed by a German on a stated account payable in Germany in marks. The sole question was, whether the decree should be for the value in dollars of the marks when the account was stated, December 16, 1917, or for their value as of the date of the decree. In a remarkably illuminating opinion Judge Hand said:

"In the case of tort committed in a foreign jurisdiction it is pretty clear that the judgment should be based on the exchange at the time of the loss inflicted. In such cases we are familiar with the idea that his wrong imposes on the tort-feasor an obligation to indemnify his victim in money. A court of the sovereign where the tort occurs enforces this obligation in the money of that sovereign, regardless of its change in value, merely because those are the terms in which it is cast. When a court takes cognizance of a tort committed elsewhere, it is indeed sometimes said that it enforces the obligation arising under the law where the tort arises. And, if this were true, it would seem to follow that the obligation should be discharged in the money of the sovereign in whose territory the tort occurred, and that the proper rule would be to adopt the rate of exchange as of the time of the judgment.

"However, no court can enforce any law but that of its own sovereign, and, when a suitor comes to a jurisdiction foreign to the place of the tort, he can only invoke an obligation recognized by that sovereign. A foreign sovereign under civilized law imposes an obligation of its own as nearly homologous as possible to that arising in the place where the tort occurs. But since, apart from specific performance, such an obligation must be discharged in the money of that sovereign, none other being available, the obligation so created can only be measured in that medium. The form of the obligation must therefore be to indemnify the victim for his loss in terms of the money of the foreign sovereign, and that obligation necessarily speaks as of the time when it arose; that is, when the loss occurred. Hence a foreign court is as little concerned with the changes in the value of money in the territory where the tort arose as are the courts of that territory itself. Each court is enforcing a different obligation, imposed by different sovereigns, necessarily defined in the terms of its own money. . . . There is, in my judgment, no sound basis for distinction between torts and contracts to pay fixed sums of money. The confusion arises from the assumption that payment after the due date is performance. But that appears to be untrue. A promise to pay a sum at a given day is not a promise to pay then or later. When the promisor defaults, he fails to perform the only promise he has made, and his liability is as much a new creation of the law as though he had failed to deliver a chattel; or, if it be insisted that his liability is an alternative performance, still that performance is not to pay at any later time, but generally to indemnify the promisee, subject, of course, to the limitations imposed by law. That liability is, as it seems to me, quite analogous to the obligation to indemnify raised upon a tort, and the same reasoning should apply to it. A foreign sovereign will raise an equivalent obligation, but couched in terms of its own money, because that alone it has the power to secure.

"A different rule it is true might be applicable if specific performance were possible in such cases. No doubt a sovereign might insist upon the delivery of foreign money, if the occasion were proper. On obligations to pay money, this remedy does not, however, lie. All that can be done is to seize the promisor's property, and sell it, a procedure which can result only in domestic money. To take the exchange as of the period of the judgment or decree is, therefore, to adopt a rule applicable only to specific performance, in a case where specific performance is not exacted. Since the loss is to be indemnified in the money of the sovereign where the court sits, it has no alternative but to calculate it in terms of that money when the loss occurred, and to enforce its judgment, regardless of variations in its value between that time and the date of collection."

In quoting from Judge Hand's opinion it is not meant to endorse all that is said. The present writer does not believe that the conclusion he reached follows by some inevitable logic from the premise that the forum is enforcing a right created by its law and not a foreign right. It would be conceivable that the forum might on grounds of policy so mould its right that it would contract or expand as the rate of exchange varied. That would, however, be a less natural view. But if the forum is conceived to be enforcing a foreign right, it is believed that this means that the amount of the judgment in dollars *must* at all times correspond to the amount of marks which at the moment of entering judgment would be recovered in the courts of the foreign country whose "right" is being enforced. Otherwise, the so-called "foreign right" enforced by the forum differs in scope from the "right" enforced by the foreign court—and so could not be really a "foreign right."

In the conclusion that a court never enforces foreign rights but only rights created by its own law, I see nothing extraordinary. Indeed, if we examine into the meaning of the terms "law" and "right" as they are used by judges and lawyers, I think we shall conclude that this way of stating the matter is the only satisfactory way. For we as lawyers, like the physical scientists, are engaged in the study of objective physical phenomena. Instead of the behavior of electrons, atoms, or planets, however, we are dealing with the behavior of human beings.[51] As lawyers we are interested in knowing how certain officials of society—judges, legislators, and others—have behaved in the past, in order that we may make a prediction of their probable behavior in the future. Our statements of the "law" of a given country are therefore "true"

[51] That if we deal with individual atoms instead of with vast numbers of them, it may conceivably turn out to be just as difficult to predict the behavior of any particular atom as it is to prophesy how any given human being is going to act, see Morris R. Cohen, *Mechanism and Casuality in Physics* (1918) 15 JOURNAL OF PHILOSOPHY, PSYCHOLOGY AND SCIENTIFIC METHOD, 365, 378-379. Now that scientists are looking inside the atom, they find that the so-called "laws of physics" do not apply to the electron, and that it may be that the "old laws of nature" are merely "statistical averages." Bertrand Russell (1923) *The A B C of Atoms, passim;* and review of Russell's book in 37 THE NEW REPUBLIC, 209 (Jan. 16, 1924).

if they accurately and as simply as possible describe the past behavior and predict the future behavior of these societal agents. A statement, for example, that a certain "rule of law" is the "law of England" is therefore merely a more or less convenient shorthand way of saying that, on the basis of certain observations of past phenomena,[52] we predict certain future behavior of the appropriate English officials. So, a statement that by the law of New York A has under given circumstances "a right" and that B is under a correlative "duty" is a conventional way of asserting that, on the basis of certain past behavior of certain New York officials, we now predict that New York officials will behave in a certain way if specified events happen and the officials are set in motion in the appropriate way by the injured party.[53] "Right," "duty," and other names for legal relations are therefore not names of objects or entities which have an existence apart from the behavior of the officials in question, but merely terms by means of which we describe to each other what prophecies we make as to the probable occurrence of a certain sequence of events—the behavior of the officials.[54] We must, therefore, constantly resist the tendency to which we are all subject to reify, "thingify" or hypostatize "rights" and other "legal relations." If, as we are told by an eminent philosopher, "the tendency to think of relations and operations as *things* is one of the most common sources of philosophic error,"[55] it is equally true that the tendency to reify legal "rights" has been a fruitful source of confusion in the law. We must never forget, as Mr. Justice Holmes told us long ago, that,[56] "for legal purposes a right is only the hypostasis of a prophecy—the imagination of a substance supporting the fact that the public force will be brought to bear upon those who are said to contravene it—just as we talk of the force of gravitation accounting for the conduct of bodies in space. One phrase adds no more than the other to what we know without it."

[52] Decisions by judges; passage of statutes by legislators; etc. These phenomena may include past reactions of the particular judges to social, industrial, economic or ethical problems, not part of their activity in deciding cases.

[53] By "serving a summons and complaint" on B, bringing the case to trial, etc.

[54] To be entirely accurate we must add that the assertion that A has a "right" and B is under a "duty" is an assertion that not only the officials but also the members of the given political community are in the habit of reacting in certain ways to certain stimuli. It is because these habit-patterns exist that we can safely predict; and the total prediction must be as to the reaction of the vast majority of the inhabitants of the country as well as of the judges, or we cannot speak of law as "existing." If, for example, a majority of the community were not in the habit of acquiescing in the acts of the officials, there would be not law but the absence of law. This conduct of the rest of the community is commonly assumed and we devote our attention to the probable action of the officials. *Cf.* Underhill Moore, *The Rational Basis of Legal Institutions* (1923) 23 COL. L. REV. 609.

[55] Morris R. Cohen, *Communal Ghosts and Other Perils of Social Philosophers* (1919) 16 JOURNAL OF PHILOSOPHY, PSYCHOLOGY AND SCIENTIFIC METHOD, 673, 682.

[56] *Op. cit. supra* note 31, at p. 313.

Concretely, the assertion that in such a case as *Milliken v. Pratt* P has against A a "Maine right" to damages is merely a conventional way of prophesying that if P sues W in Maine and follows the correct procedure, the court there will give him a judgment, i.e. it is a prophecy that certain Maine officials will behave in a certain way. So the assertion that a Maine court "has enforced a Maine right" is merely a shorthand way of stating that the Maine officials have acted in the way predicted.[57] If now we say that a Massachusetts court will enforce a Maine right, the only meaning that can be given to the statement seems to be that we prophesy that the Massachusetts judicial officials will act in precisely the same way that the Maine officials would act if the case were presented to them. However, as we are prophesying what Massachusetts officials are going to do, the meaning we have given to "right" compels us to say that a Massachusetts right exists, identical in scope with the Maine right, and that the Massachusetts court is going to "enforce" this Massachusetts right. If so, do we not express what we mean in a simpler and more accurate way by saying that there is a Massachusetts right identical in scope with a Maine right, which statement on being translated means simply that we predict action by the Massachusetts officials precisely like that which would be taken by the Maine officials if the case were presented to them? Are we not justified in concluding, therefore, that the statement that the forum enforces a foreign right arises out of a failure to give the word right a definite meaning, and that when we do fix upon a meaning, we find the statement misleading and confusing?

Our conclusion then is, that if we say that in *Milliken v. Pratt* the Massachusetts court "enforced a Maine right," we mean, if indeed we mean anything definite, that the Massachusetts officials have acted *precisely* as the Maine officials would have acted had *the precise case* been presented to them. Note now the italicized words in the last sentence. Is it not true that in such cases as *Milliken v. Pratt,* and in the vast majority of conflict of laws cases, as I have tried to show above, we do not obtain or try to obtain the information necessary to make such a statement, and that the reason we do not is, that it would (except in cases where the facts involved were from the point of view of the foreign court purely domestic) compel us to ascertain the "law" of the foreign jurisdiction on the conflict of laws, and so would lead to endless difficulties? To this question it is believed there can be but one answer.[58]

---

[57] Where we cannot predict with any certainty, e.g., whenever we have a really new case, we say that the law is unsettled, or that whether there is or is not a right is doubtful. When the court later decides the new case, the court is said to have "made law." This means that it has given us new data upon the basis of which we believe that we are able to predict action in another case like the case just decided.

[58] *In re Tallmadge* (1919, Surro. Ct.) 109 Misc. 696, 181 N. Y. Supp. 336, rejects the *"renvoi"* theory in construing the provisions of the New York Decedent

It may perhaps be asked, is not the statement that a foreign right is enforced sufficiently accurate in the relatively simple cases where all the operative facts involved are connected with some one foreign state or country? It is from cases of this kind that the usual statement derives whatever plausibility it has. To test the matter, consider a tort wholly committed in Germany, the forum being New York. If we say New York is going to enforce a German right, this means at most that we predict that the New York officials are going to act *precisely* as the German officials would. If so, the New York officials at the time of entering the judgment ought to find out how many marks the plaintiff would at that moment recover if judgment were to be entered in a German court. Indeed, if we were to take our statement at its face, it might be argued that the New York judgment ought to be in marks! As we already know, this is not what the New York courts would do in such a case; it is not what other courts would do. The real problem is, what action may we expect the New York officials to take? Will they take any, and if so, how great will be the similarity of that action to that which the German officials would take? Our prediction about these things ought therefore to be cast in terms of New York and not of German "rights." The most practical and simple statement thus appears to be that the forum always "enforces rights" created by its own "law" and never "foreign law" or "foreign rights." Even in making this statement we must as always guard ourselves against thinking of our assertion that "rights" and other legal relations "exist" or have been "enforced" as more than a conventional way of describing past and predicting future behavior of human beings—officials and others.

Shall we, must we, say that there are as many "rights," all growing out of the one group of facts under consideration, as there are jurisdictions which will give the plaintiff relief? Since such an assertion is merely a shorthand way of making the prophecy that the appropriate persons, the officials, in each of these jurisdictions would re-act to the situation, if it were presented to them, so as to "give relief" to the plaintiff, there seems to be no other statement to make. Thus interpreted, the statement is not only not startling but plain common sense. To those accustomed to the more common way of putting the matter, this view doubtless will not at first commend itself, and will seem to be needlessly complex. Its validity, I must emphasize, will depend upon its value as a reasonably accurate, understandable and workable description of judicial phenomena as they have occurred in the past and as they are likely to occur again. To the holders of the traditional view that the earth was flat and that the sun went round the earth, the assertion that the earth was round and that it went round the sun seemed needlessly complex, but it won its way because it worked better and, all

Estate law, and properly so; and in doing so gives to "law" the meaning contended for in the present discussion.

things considered, really was the simpler view. So to-day, to one who has not carefully observed and attempted to piece together into a coherent whole the totality of observed phenomena in the field of physics and astronomy, the current theories of relativity seem unnecessarily artificial and complex; but, so far as I can discover, they are coming to be recognized as the best and on the whole the simplest way to organize the totality of our experiences with the physical world into a working system of concepts which accomplish the purpose for which they are created. The same thing is true of the modern conception of the atom as a complex structure of units of positive and negative electricity, as complicated at least as the solar system. On the fact of it this is a far more complex conception than that of the indivisible, indestructible atom of the older chemical theory, but in fact it is far simpler when the attempt is made to piece the chemists' universe together into a consistent whole. So in our problem, it is believed that the seemingly simple way of describing things which has been current proves upon consideration to lead to inconsistencies and complexities, and that what seems at first sight a more complex and less natural approach turns out in the end to bring us to the only true simplicity—an adequate description of observed phenomena in language as clear and accurate as possible.

Returning to the consideration of concrete cases: in the well-known case of *Slater v. Mexican National Railway*[59] it was held that no recovery could be had in the federal court for a wrongful death in a case where all the operative facts took place in Mexico, and by Mexican law the dependents of the deceased were to be compensated in an unusual way in a series of installments. In accounting for the decision, Mr. Justice Holmes, who wrote the prevailing opinion, said:[60]

"But when such a liability [for wrongful death] is enforced in a jurisdiction foreign to the place of the wrongful act, obviously that does not mean that the act in any degree is subject to the *lex fori*, with regard to either its quality or its consequences. On the other hand, it equally little means that the law of the place of the act is operative outside its own territory. The theory of the foreign suit is that although the act complained of was subject to no law having force in the forum, it gave rise to an obligation, an *obligatio*, which, like other obligations, follows the person, and may be enforced wherever the person may be found. *Stout v. Wood*, 1 Blackf. (Ind.) 71; *Dennick v. Railroad Co.*, 103 U. S. 11, 18. But as the only source of this obligation is the law of the place of the act, it follows that that law determines not merely

[59] (1904) 194 U. S. 120, 126, 24 Sup. Ct. 581, 582.

[60] The logic of the *obligatio* theory led Mr. Justice Holmes to dissent in *Atchison, T. & S. F. Ry. v. Sowers* (1909) 213 U. S. 55, 29 Sup. Ct. 397, a case which is a striking illustration of the practical importance of clarity in fundamental legal conceptions. Very possibly Mr. Justice Holmes' dissent in that case may have back of it a pragmatic basis which is obscured by the abstract *obligatio* theory. Adopting a different theory would have compelled him to bring that basis, if it existed, into the foreground of the discussion.

the existence of the obligation, *Smith v. Condry,* 1 How. 28, but equally determines its extent. It seems to us unjust to allow a plaintiff to come here absolutely depending on the foreign law for the foundation of his case, and yet to deny the defendant the benefit of whatever limitations on his liability that law would impose."

This way of stating the matter was followed by Judge Cardozo in *Loucks v. Standard Oil Co.*[61]

I do not mean to quarrel with the decision in either case, but the reasoning seems to me unsatisfactory. While Mr. Justice Holmes in the *Slater* case seems to be arguing deductively from his *obligatio* theory to the conclusion that the plaintiff can have no relief, it is believed that the real reason for the decision is contained in the statement that "it seems to us unjust to allow a plaintiff to come here absolutely depending on the foreign law for the foundation of the case, and yet to deny the defendant the benefit of whatever limitations on his liability that law would impose." In other words, the result in the case is reached if we say that the forum has no judicial machinery to enforce a right identical, or even similar, to the Mexican right, and that it would be unjust for the forum to create a right of a very different character. The decision thus appears not as an inevitable outcome from fixed premises (that the forum is enforcing an *obligatio* created by foreign law, and *must* inevitably take it or leave it, just as it is), but for what it is, and for what Mr. Justice Holmes undoubtedly knew it was—a practical result based upon the reasons of policy established in prior cases. This policy limits the creation of rights in cases of foreign torts to those which are if not identical with, at least highly similar to, the rights created by the foreign laws where the torts were committed.

In this connection I cannot forbear to quote Mr. Justice Holmes against himself, by recalling his statement already quoted, that "for legal purposes a right is only the hypostasis of a prophecy—the imagination of a substance supporting the fact that the public force will be brought to bear upon those who do things said to contravene it." According to this, the statement that by the law of Mexico an *obligatio* has arisen is merely a mode of making a prophecy of the action of the appropriate Mexican tribunal. If so, we are talking figuratively when we reify or hypostatize the *obligatio* and say that it "accompanies the person," or say, as did Judge Cardozo in the *Loucks* case, that

[61] *Supra* note 37. The case involved an action in New York for wrongful death in Massachusetts. The Massachusetts "law" was held to govern. Cardozo, J., writing the opinion of the court, said: "A foreign statute is not law in this state, but it gives rise to an obligation, which, if transitory, 'follows the person and may be enforced wherever the person may be found.' . . . 'No law can exist as such except the law of the land; but . . . . it is a principle of every civilized law that vested rights shall be protected.' . . . The plaintiff owns something, and we help him to get it. . . . We do this unless some sound reason of public policy makes it unwise for us to lend our aid." At p. 110, 120 N. E. at p. 201.

"the plaintiff owns *something* and we give *it* to him." The figurative language may or may not be a convenient way of stating a result; it cannot be the reason for the result. Moreover, in many cases we refuse to give relief although the foreign *obligatio* exists—witness the orthodox rule that an action for trespass to land is not transitory but local. Our refusal to do so is to be defended purely on grounds of practical expediency, and the rule in trespass is being broken down by statute[62] or judicial legislation for the reason that under the changed conditions of modern life judges and legislators seem to be coming to think that the opposite rule will give better social results. The statement that certain causes of action are "transitory" is therefore merely a shorthand way of stating that courts in other jurisdictions enforce similar rights created by their own systems of law, and nothing more.

It seems difficult to reconcile the result reached in *Jacobus v. Colgate*[63] with the *obligatio* theory. Here also the opinion was written by Judge Cardozo. The New York legislature had passed an act allowing actions in New York for trespass to foreign land. Did the act apply to actions brought after its passage but for trespasses committed before its passage, or only to future trespasses? It was contended that the statute merely changed the procedure for the enforcement of a right which already existed and so should be construed retroactively. Not so, said Judge Cardozo, for no "right of action" existed under New York law until the passage of the statute. The result seems sound, but I have difficulty with the learned judge's attempt to harmonize this result with the *obligatio* theory. He argues that:

> "Out of the foreign tort there once grew a right of action territorial and local, which our courts would not enforce. Out of the same tort there now grows a transitory right of action which our courts will enforce. The right of action has not merely been changed; so far as our law is concerned, it has been created. But the wrong, the violation of the primary right, which it redresses, is defined by the foreign law."

If we recall what we mean by "right," this way of stating it is hardly satisfactory. To assert that a foreign primary right exists (to have a person refrain from trespassing on land in the foreign state) is but a way to predict what courts in the given foreign state would do if the person asserted to be under the primary duty correlative to the right were to act in a certain way. When that person has acted in the way described, we can make the prophecy without the "if," at least so far as respects the trespasser.[64] This we do by saying that the one whose land

[62] The New York statute is given in *Jacobus v. Colgate*, cited *infra*, note 63.

[63] (1916) 217 N. Y. 235, 243, 111 N. E. 837, 840.

[64] There are other "ifs," e.g. if the injured party gets a summons properly served, and if he takes the other appropriate steps, etc., all of which must happen before we can expect action by the court called "entering a judgment." Of course the court will already have acted in conducting the trial, etc., all of which is a part of the predicted conduct.

has been trespassed upon has a (secondary) right to damages.[65] Clearly, if we know that a New York (secondary) right to damages is going to "come into existence" or be "created" if someone trespasses on foreign land, this means that we can before the trespass is committed make a prophecy with an "if" in it as to the probable action of the New York courts. If so, a New York primary right exists, for that is all we mean by that phrase.

On the *obligatio* theory, however, it seems that the plaintiff in *Jacobus v. Colgate* already owned "something," only previously New York had refused to give "it" to him; now because of the statute it is willing to do so; nothing has been created by New York law except a procedural method for enforcing the "foreign-created right." It is not surprising, therefore, to find the decision criticized as erroneous by a writer who is following the theory that courts recognize and enforce foreign-created rights, on the ground that the statute merely "gave a remedy for a right already existing."[66] Here again the two theories logically followed out give contrary results in the decisions of concrete cases. That they did not in the actual case is because Judge Cardozo's sound judicial instinct led him actually to refuse to follow the *obligatio* theory to its logical outcome.

Mr. Justice Holmes seems to have been led to his view by the notion, which I imagine is a common one, that a state or country cannot impose a duty on a person outside its territory, except perhaps in exceptional cases, such as where the person is a citizen of or domiciled in the state concerned. For example, in *Mulhall v. Fallon*[67] he says: "It is true that legislative power is territorial, and that no duties can be imposed by statute upon persons who are within the limits of another State." It is hoped that the preceding discussion has shown how erroneous this idea is. Only the slightest observation is needed to disclose the truth. A negligently fires a gun in New York and the bullet hits a man in New Jersey. Clearly New Jersey law can and does impose on A, no matter where he lives and of what state or country he is a citizen, a duty to pay damages to the injured person. This we have already discussed. A statement that A "constructively accompanied" the bullet on its flight into New Jersey is at most a clumsy and purely fictitious way of asserting this very power of New Jersey to subject A to a legal duty

---

[65] At one time the present writer indicated a doubt whether the conception that there was a duty to pay damages was a useful one. See Cook, *The Powers of Courts of Equity* (1915) 15 COL. L. REV. 36, 45. This doubt was long since dispelled. Here as elsewhere there is, of course, no absolute right or wrong about the matter, but purely a practical question of so forming our concept of duty as to have the most helpful mental tool to work with in handling our material.

[66] (1916) 29 HARV. L. REV. 875. The note suggests that possibly the actual result in *Jacobus v. Colgate, supra* note 63, might be supported on some other ground.

[67] (1900) 176 Mass. 266, 268, 57 N. E. 386, 387.

and nothing more. Some other relevant phenomena are collected in a note.[68]

The error of all such views lies, it seems, in confusing the "creation" of the right-duty relation with the problem of its "enforcement." Even though the party upon whom the duty is imposed is not within the territorial limits, we may be able, on the basis of past phenomena, to make a prediction as to how the officials will act if the one said to be under a duty is later "personally served" in the jurisdiction, or "property" belonging to him is "attached," or some other condition is satisfied. As by definition a duty exists when we can make the prediction, even with "ifs" in it, we may and I think do express this by saying that the duty "exists" but cannot or will not be "enforced" until "proper service" is had.[69] Much of the confusion in Anglo-American legal thinking goes back to Story's treatise. An examination of all that Story said will, it is believed, reveal that he at times sensed the actualities of the situation.[70]

I may be told that by sending the bullet into New Jersey A "submits" himself to the law of that state. This also seems to me a pure fiction. If we assume that the injured person goes to some other state and dies there, shall we say that the law of that third state can impose a duty on A to compensate the deceased person's dependents because A "submitted" to its laws? Does he "submit" to the laws of any state or

[68] The Massachusetts-New Hampshire dog case, cited note 34 *supra*, is another illustration; also, cases in which a person in one jurisdiction starts a fire which burns a building in a second jurisdiction, as in *Connecticut Valley Lumber Co. v. Maine Central R. R.* (1918) 78 N. H. 553, 103 Atl. 263. Consider also: X owns land in New York. By deed, in proper form, executed and delivered in New Jersey X conveys the land to Y. At the time, A is in Massachusetts; B in New Jersey; C in New York. A, B, and C are later sued by Y in New York for trespass to the land. Here the *situs* of the land is New York; all the "acts of conveyance," i.e. all the operative facts necessary to pass title to Y, take place in New Jersey. The forum is New York. Obviously New York law attached to the operative facts occurring in New Jersey: (1) a duty (owed to Y) on the part of A, in Massachusetts, to stay off the land; (2) a similar duty on the part of B, in New Jersey; (3) a similar duty on the part of C, in New York. But, if any other state allows action for trespass to foreign realty, its law also imposes similar duties.

[69] Note that continental countries have very different notions as to what is proper service; also that England by statute or rule of court has recently extended substituted service against absent defendants to cover many more types of cases. *Cf.* the American case of *Flexner v. Farson* (1919) 248 U. S. 289, 39 Sup. Ct. 97, with the recent Rule of Court in England authorizing substituted service upon non-resident natural persons doing business through agents in England. Dicey, *The Conflict of Laws* (3d ed. 1922) 246; (1923) 23 COL. L. REV. 793, 795. Compare also the Australian notions as to "jurisdiction" of Australian State courts to render judgments, as shown in the Service and Execution of Process Act, 1901-1912, reprinted in (1919) 28 YALE LAW JOURNAL, 441, 449.

[70] Compare (8th ed. 1883) sec. 7, p. 8, with sec. 306, p. 424. The latter passage recognizes in essence the validity of the views here contended for.

country into which the injured person may subsequently go? Does a criminal or a tort-feasor *submit* to the law when he commits a crime or a tort? Surely such statements are nothing but fictions invented to make the facts appear to fit an unworkable theory based upon inadequate observation and analysis of legal phenomena.

For lack of space I must refrain from discussing the significance of *Fauntleroy v. Lum*[71] in which the Supreme Court of the United States upheld the validity of a judgment rendered (after proper personal service) by the Supreme Court of Missouri, in which the latter court had attached to a purely Mississippi group of facts[72] legal consequences entirely at variance with the law of Mississippi; but it seems to me to have a bearing upon our problem. In saying this, I do not forget such cases as *New York Life Insurance Co. v. Head*,[73] and *New York Life Ins. Co. v. Dodge*,[74] which are of course to be explained as limitations on the power of American states to create rights, growing out of the due process clause as interpreted by the Supreme Court. As to whether the results reached in these latter cases are "sound," I express no opinion.[75]

My conclusion then is, that while, so long as we have the territorial organization of modern political society, the law of a given state or country can be *enforced* only within its territorial limits,[76] this does not mean that the law of that state or country cannot, except in certain exceptional cases, affect the legal relations of persons outside its limits. As we have seen, "law" is not a material phenomenon, which spreads out like a light wave until it reaches the territorial boundary and then stops. Whatever be the legal limitations upon the power of a state or country to affect the legal relations of persons anywhere in the world, they must be found in positive law of some kind—be the same international law or constitutional law, and do not inhere in the constitution of the legal universe. Whether international law imposes limitations and if so, what they are, can be determined only by observation. Personally, I

[71] (1908) 210 U. S. 230, 28 Sup. Ct. 641.

[72] An agreement was made in Mississippi between two citizens of that state resident there, to be performed there. The agreement was illegal and void by Mississippi law.

[73] (1914) 234 U. S. 149, 34 Sup. Ct. 879.

[74] (1918) 246 U. S. 357, 38 Sup. Ct. 337.

[75] Very possibly the result in these cases depends, as in some other "due process" cases, upon the fact that the members of the Supreme Court shared the notions about the necessary territorial limitations upon "law" which have been current and which it is here sought to show are erroneous. *Flexner v. Farson*, *supra* note 69, is possibly another example.

[76] The present territorial organization is of course not the only possible form, though probably most of us would regard it as the only convenient one. *Cf.* the situation after the Goths, Burgundians, Franks and Lombards had founded kingdoms in the countries formerly subject to Rome, as described in Story, *op. cit. supra* note 70, sec. 2a, at p. 3; 1 Savigny, *History of the Roman Law in the Middle Ages* (Cathcart's translation, 1829) ch. 3, pp. 99-104.

can find no consensus of opinion among civilized countries upon the matter under consideration; in fact, the utmost diversity of opinion seems to exist. I must, however, leave it to others more competent to speak to say whether my observations are in accord with the facts. Constitutional limitations exist, in the case of American states—the due process clause and the full faith and credit clause. Beyond these, I discover no limitations.

The fundamental point of the foregoing discussion may perhaps be expressed as follows: by far the larger number of the rules for the solution of cases involving the conflict of laws do not relate to the "power" or "jurisdiction" of the particular court or state to decide the case before it in a certain way. Cases involving power arise only where some limitation is imposed by some system of positive law—such as the federal constitution. Other limitations on power do not exist.

I shall probably be met with the statement that the view presented in the foregoing discussion is directly contrary to all that the courts have *said*, as distinguished from what they have *done*. To some extent this is true, although it is believed that that extent is not quite so great as imagined. To begin with, apparently few courts have directly said that they were enforcing a foreign-created right. Such expressions are found chiefly in texts. The language of the courts is usually that they are applying the foreign "law" to the case in hand. As I have pointed out, this expression is ambiguous and can be given an interpretation which will describe what the courts actually have done. That the courts have not *consciously* given it the other meaning (equivalent to saying that they are enforcing foreign-created rights) is clear from the fact that they do not in the typical cases go on to find what the foreign law applicable to the very controversy before them really is, but content themselves with ascertaining the foreign domestic rule. The truth is, most of the judges have never had time or taken the trouble to analyze very clearly just what they do mean. In view of the fact that the legal training of most of them did not include a study of these problems, and of the further fact that only a limited time can be devoted by a busy judge to the study of a single case, this is only natural. In the second place, even if the formulation here presented is novel, in the sense of departing from the language of the opinions, if it is true that the courts have actually done certain things, and that the usual way of describing these things is inaccurate and misleading, does it follow that we ought to continue to misdescribe the actual decisions because such has been the loose practice in the past? Surely progress in the science of the law consists in continually reformulating our generalizations so as to make them bring out more clearly just what the past phenomena described really are and just what we predict will happen in the future.[77]

[77] Note the beneficial effect of the re-formulation by law teachers of the rule as to "lack of mutuality" in specific performance, as shown in *Epstein v. Gluckin*

But, I may be asked, if the answer to conflict of laws cases cannot be deduced from certain pre-existing principles relating to "jurisdiction," how are they to be decided? The only answer that can be given, by the same methods actually used in deciding cases involving purely domestic torts, contracts, property, etc. The problem involved is that of legal thinking in general. It requires for its adequate discussion an inquiry into the technique of human reasoning in general and that of reasoning in the field of law in particular. It must be admitted that the "outrageous bit of nonsense"[78] that men think in syllogisms, that they solve the problems of life by deductive reasoning, has apparently ruled in law as well as in morals and theology. Actually, however, in law as in the natural sciences, practice has preceded theory, at least to a considerable extent, and conclusions have not actually been reached deductively. The reason for this is shown by recent investigations into human thinking. These investigations have convinced the leading students of logic that formal logic, the deductive syllogism, is always purely hypothetical reasoning and never of itself assures us of the factual truth of the conclusions reached.[79] Its content seems to be identical with pure mathematics, which, Bertrand Russell tells us, is "the science in which we never know what we are talking about nor whether what we are saying is true."[80] The actual process involved in settling a situation of doubt—a new case, if we are dealing with law—involves a comparison of the data of the new situation with the facts of a large number of prior situations which have been subsumed under a "rule" or "principle" within the terms of which it is thought the new situation may be brought. This comparison, if carried on intelligently, necessarily involves a consideration of the policy involved in the prior decisions and of the effects which those decisions have produced.[81]

(1922) 233 N. Y. 490, 135 N. E. 861. The work of Ames, Stone, and others showed that while saying one thing courts were actually doing another; the re-formulation was an attempt to get an accurate general description of the *decisions*. The result was to modify the current of decisions in New York. In the present discussion the attempt is to do for the fundamentals of the conflict of laws what these writers did for the more narrow field of mutuality.

[78] C. I. Lewis, New York Evening Post Literary Review, Feb. 4, 1923, reviewing H. B. Smith, *First Book in Logic*.

[79] Morris R. Cohen, *The Subject Matter of Formal Logic* (1918) 15 Journal of Philosophy, Psychology and Scientific Method, 673, and other discussions referred to in that article.

[80] Quoted in A. S. Eddington, *Space, Time, and Gravitation* (1920) 14.

[81] Any result reached is of course an experiment—merely a working solution, whose validity is to be tested by how it works. This is what is meant when modern students of logic tell us that "men think as a cat opens a gate—by trial and error," and that "even the mathematician . . . . presents finally in deductive form what he himself has arrived at after a dozen false starts and by continual emendation." C. I. Lewis, in the review cited *supra* note 78. An interesting and illuminating example of the continual redefining of a "middle term" in deciding new cases as they arise is found in the line of New York cases beginning with *Thomas v. Winchester* (1852) 6 N. Y. 397 and coming down to *MacPher-*

If the points in which the new situation resemble the older situations already dealt with are thought to be the qualities the existence of which were decisive in leading to the decisions in the prior cases, the new case will be put under the old rule or principle. In doing this, the rule or principle as it existed has not been applied; it has been extended to take in the new situation. In other words, however great the appearance of purely deductive reasoning may be, the real decision where a case presents novel elements consists in a re-defining of the middle term of the major and minor premises of the syllogism; that is, of the *construction* or *creation of premises* for the case in hand, which premises did not pre-exist. The statement of the premises of the deductive syllogism is therefore a statement of the conclusion which has been reached on other grounds, and not of the real reason for the decision. When once the premises have been thus constructed, the conclusion inevitably follows.[82]

This view does not lead to the discarding of all principles and rules, but quite the contrary. It demands them as tools with which to work; as tools without which we cannot work effectively. It does, however, make sure that they are used as tools and are not perverted to an apparently mechanical use. It points out that the use never can be really mechanical; that the danger in continuing to deceive ourselves into believing that we are merely "applying" the old rule or principle to "a new case" by purely deductive reasoning lies in the fact that as the real thought-process is thus obscured, we fail to realize that our choice is really being guided by considerations of social and economic policy or ethics, and so fail to take into consideration all the relevant facts of life required for a wise decision. We shall thus be guided by the "inarticulate major premise" of Mr. Justice Holmes, and that may be a premise which if dragged out into the light we should after examination decide to be unsound.[82]

In the field of the conflict of laws, it is unfortunately true that past judicial phenomena are so confused that the formulation of tools with which to work is vastly more difficult than in most fields of the law.

---

son v. Buick Motor Co. (1916) 217 N. Y. 382, 111 N. E. 1050. The statement in the opinion of Cardozo, J., in the latter case, that "the principle that the danger must be imminent does not change, but the things subject to the principle do change" is of course not true if taken literally, and contains within it a lingering trace of the traditional notions as to the efficacy of deductive logic. The words or symbols may not have changed; what they stand for has changed as each new case was decided. There is new wine in the old bottles, even though the labels remain unaltered.

[82] The traditional legal view in its clearest form is expressed in the article on *German Legal Philosophy* by John M. Zane in (1918) 16 MICH. L. REV. 287, at pp. 337-338, 345-348. It would be difficult to imagine a more complete misdescription of the actual process of deciding a case involving a new situation than the one presented by Mr. Zane, who ignores the modern studies of human reasoning to which reference has been made. Quite naturally he does not understand the realism of Mr. Justice Holmes.

This is due largely to the fact that when American courts first began to be confronted with cases involving the problem, there were so few phenomena in the way of decisions to describe that there could hardly be said to be well recognized principles and rules established by prior English decisions. Without adequate guides to go by, and confronted by the chaotic and conflicting views of continental writers as gathered together in Story's treatise, the courts of last resort in our states found themselves on a largely unchartered sea. For this reason a writer attempting to set forth the "American law" upon the conflict of laws is necessarily compelled more often than in any other field to choose between conflicting rules. In making a choice between such rules, it is obvious that here as elsewhere the basis must be a pragmatic one—of the effect of a decision one way or the other in giving a practical working rule.[83] In this connection it may be suggested that in many cases it makes little difference which rule is adopted, so long as it is reasonably simple and definite and after its adoption is not departed from in cases clearly falling within it.[84]

---

[83] The essence of this view was presented almost a generation ago by Mr. Justice Holmes in his two papers on *The Path of the Law* (1897) 10 HARV. L. REV. 457, *Collected Legal Papers*, 167, and *Law in Science and Science in Law* (1899) 12 HARV. L. REV. 443, *Collected Legal Papers*, 210. Compare the remarks of Holmes, *Collected Legal Papers*, 239:

> "I think it most important to remember whenever a doubtful case arises, with certain analogies on one side and other analogies on the other, that what is really before us is a conflict between two social desires, each of which seeks to extend its dominion over the case, and which both cannot have their way."

There is a fine chapter in Dewey, *Human Nature and Conduct* (1922) 238-247, on "The Nature of Principles," which can be made to apply to the lawyer's "law" as well as the "moral law" by substituting the word *law* for *morals*, and *legal* for *moral*, wherever the terms occur. It is the best and clearest statement of the matter of which the present writer is aware.

[84] Compare the passage from Holmes, *Collected Legal Papers* (1920) 239, cited *supra*, note 36.

Part III
Critique

[18]

March, 1934

University of Pennsylvania Law Review
And American Law Register
FOUNDED 1852

VOLUME 82 | MARCH, 1934 | No. 5

AMERICAN LEGAL REALISM

L. L. FULLER †

The realist movement in American legal thought [1] may be said to have reached its flower within the past five years. There were, to be sure, premonitions of it as early as the beginning of the present century. The realist himself likes to consider his movement as taking its origin in an address delivered by Justice Holmes in 1897.[2] As early as 1912 there existed a systematic formulation of the realist view, however little it may have been noticed.[3] These beginnings should suffice to confer at least a semblance of historical respectability on the realist movement. It is not a mere upstart without roots in the past. Yet it is only recently that the realist view has begun to fire the imaginations of legal scholars, that it has provoked men

† A. B. 1924, J. D. 1926, Stanford University; Professor of Law, Duke University; author of *Legal Fictions* (1931) 25 ILL. L. REV. 363, 513, 877, and of notes and book reviews in various legal journals.

[1] A good bibliography of American legal realism may be found in Llewellyn, *Some Realism about Realism* (1931) 44 HARV. L. REV. 1222, 1257-1259. It should, perhaps, be pointed out that American legal realism has no traceable connection with the neo-realist movement in American philosophy. On the contrary the adherents of legal realism have for the most part inclined to an epistemology which may be called idealistic in the modern acceptation of that term. This bent is particularly noticeable in Bingham, Cook, Frank and (with less consistency) in Llewellyn.

On the other hand legal realism has a close affinity with the various "descriptive" and "institutional" methods applied by American scholars during the past decade in economics, sociology and political science. In common with all these movements it has in recent years derived much from that philosophy of life known as behavioristic psychology.

[2] *The Path of the Law,* published in HOLMES, COLLECTED LEGAL PAPERS (1921) 167.

[3] Bingham, *What is the Law?* (1912) 11 MICH. L. REV. 1, 109. While one finds the core of the realist approach in these early articles of Bingham, it is hardly fair to class Bingham with the modern realist school. The principal difference between him and them, as I see it, consists in the fact that he does not, either expressly or impliedly, set up a principle of exclusion. He sought to broaden the field of the legal scholar's research, not to rule anything out of it. The relation between his approach and that of the more recent exponents of legal realism is analogous to that existing between the early experimental psychologists and modern behaviorists. The early experimentalists insisted that muscular reactions ought to be studied; the behaviorist insists that nothing else is worthy of study. Bingham insisted that we ought to observe what courts actually do without assuming that what they do corresponds exactly with what they say; the left-wingers of legal realism seem to assume that this neutral observation of official behavior constitutes the whole of legal science.

to concerted and sustained "vocal behavior",—that it has become, in a word, a movement.

Even yet the movement reveals rather conspicuously the defects of youth. It has lived so far largely by the process of discounting its own future. There have been manifestoes, programs for action. There have been discussions of the proper "approach",—conducted for the most part at a respectful distance from the problems to be approached. Recently there have appeared scattered applications of the approach. But we lack as yet a comprehensive work which will both describe and apply the methods of legal realism, which can serve both as an exposition of the approach and as an exemplification of it. We have nothing which could be compared, let us say, to Geny's four volume *Science et Technique* [4] which rounded off a movement for the reform of legal method in Europe.

The nearest approach to such a work is to be found in a book recently published by Professor Llewellyn.[5] It was this book which furnished the stimulus for the present article. Though the remarks which follow are intended as a critical evaluation of legal realism generally, attention will be chiefly centered on Llewellyn and the book just mentioned. There are several justifications for this course. As the realists themselves insist, there is no realist "school".[6] The movement represents a variety of points of view; it has its left and right wings. An attempt to criticize the movement as a whole within the limits of a law review article would break down under the weight of qualification required to take into account the divergencies in the views of particular realists. On the other hand, by centering attention on the work of a single individual we may secure a point of orientation from which the entire movement may be surveyed. There are, it seems to me, good reasons why Llewellyn is entitled to be regarded as the man most representative of the movement as a whole. In the first place, despite the contrary impression sometimes created by his impulsive literary style, he is not a radical. His realism is distinctly of the middle-of-the-road variety. Furthermore, he has written extensively and his writings constitute a more or less comprehensive exposition of the realist view. Finally, more than any other realist he has been willing to expose the premises which are implied in his approach. He is a "philosopher" in the sense that he has the intellectual temerity to reveal the hidden springs of his convictions,—at least most of the time.

---

[4] François Geny, SCIENCE ET TECHNIQUE EN DROIT PRIVÉ POSITIF (1913-1924).

[5] LLEWELLYN, PRÄJUDIZIENRECHT UND RECHTSPRECHUNG IN AMERIKA, EINE SPRUCHAUSWAHL MIT BESPRECHUNG (1933). A review of this book appears elsewhere in the present issue of this REVIEW. See page 551.

[6] Llewellyn, *supra* note 1, at 1254; Yntema, *The Rational Basis of Legal Science* (1931) 31 COL. L. REV. 925. If in the course of this article I occasionally slip and refer to the "realist school" the offended realist is invited to substitute the word "movement" for "school". He should, however, remember that most schools have been started by men who protested their innocence of any desire to sectarianize their teachings.

Professor Underhill Moore with his "institutional approach" has given the realist movement a significant, and in some respects symptomatic turn which deserves a place in any criticism of the movement. Though Llewellyn's writings betray a certain sympathy for the "institutional approach", Moore's contribution remains distinctive enough to require special treatment. Accordingly a section of this article will be devoted to an analysis of his studies.[7]

In what follows I make no claim to dispose of all the questions raised by the realist movement, nor even of all of those raised by the writings of Llewellyn and Moore.[8] I have, however, attempted to select for discussion those problems which seem most intimately involved in the movement as a whole. While, as I have indicated, attention throughout is directed primarily to Llewellyn's work (supplemented to some extent by Moore's studies), I think that most of what I have to say may be applied, with some qualifications and shifts of emphasis, to the position of other legal realists.

Legal Certainty

In one of the most interesting and penetrating portions of his recent book Llewellyn takes up the question of legal certainty.[9] He does not follow the example of those realists who attempt to ridicule this problem out of existence. For him the demand for certainty is something more than evidence of a childish petulance, unworthy of the twentieth century mind. Legal certainty is treated as a genuine social value, and the inquiry whether case law produces it is considered as having an important bearing on the merits of the system as a whole.

Llewellyn takes a needed distinction between: (1) predictability of judicial decision, and (2) the ready availability of the materials upon which prediction is based.[10] The first is a matter of legal certainty, the second a matter of legal "system". A body of law may be systematized to a very high degree—so that a lawyer can turn at once to the relevant section of a code,

[7] See *infra*, p. 453.

[8] The reader will find valuable and somewhat comprehensive criticisms of the realist movement in COHEN, LAW AND THE SOCIAL ORDER (1933) 198-247, 357-362 and *passim;* Dickinson, *Legal Rules: Their Function in the Process of Decision, Their Application and Elaboration* (1931) 79 U. OF PA. L. REV. 833, 1052; and Pound, *The Call for a Realist Jurisprudence* (1931) 44 HARV. L. REV. 697.

Llewellyn's answer to the criticism of Dean Pound, which he terms "realistic", seems to me the antithesis of realism. *Some Realism about Realism, supra* note 1. Llewellyn finds the refutation of Dean Pound's criticisms in the fact that (1) the realists have never expressed in so many words the implications which Pound drew from their writings, (2) when a realist reads his own articles he fails to discover these implications in them. It is interesting to speculate what things could be proved by this method. One could prove that the neo-realist movement in American philosophy is not interested in epistemology, that the New Testament does not in any essential contradict the Old. One could even prove that Dean Pound himself is innocent of the oft-repeated charge of Hegelianism.

[9] *Op. cit. supra* note 5, §§ 55-61.

[10] *Id.* § 60.

for example—without this implying certainty in the prediction of judicial action. On the other hand (and this *may* be a characteristic of case law), the materials on which prediction must be based may be scattered and difficult of access, without this implying that prediction, when finally arrived at, may not have a high degree of accuracy.

It is well to have these two notions explicitly separated. There is often a too ready assumption that "system" necessarily implies predictability, and that predictability is impossible without a highly developed "system". On the other hand, it seems to me that Llewellyn goes too far in assuming that the two are completely independent. Surely "system" has generally been something more than a mere indexing device having no connection with the process of decision. As a matter of fact is it not clear that an indexing system which was entirely dissociated from the judicial process would necessarily fail of its own limited purpose?

A more significant contribution to the problem of certainty is found in Llewellyn's distinction between certainty for the attorney and certainty for the layman. For the attorney certainty means predictability of judicial action. It is often assumed that the layman's interest here is identical with that of the lawyer. Llewellyn points out that this is not true. I translate his argument:

> So much for the lawyer. Incomparably more important seems to me to be the legal certainty which the layman demands. . . . It must not be forgotten that the ordinary layman guides his conduct not by *legal* norms but by *social* norms. Often these social norms are similar to those of the law. Seldom is correspondence complete. Legal rules can hardly serve as a guide to life. On the other hand the continuous reshaping and reformulation of social norms . . . does not cease because lawyers have set up legal rules. . . . Legal certainty in business and for the layman does not lie in the fact that an attorney can predict the outcome of a law suit. . . . This sort of calculability is not so important for the layman; it means for him only legal certainty in a particular piece of litigation. For him legal certainty consists rather in the fact that the transaction which he has entered, *if* it gets into litigation, will be adjudged as a prudent man (that is, a prudent *layman* in the particular circumstances) would have foreseen, if he had had in mind at the very beginning the unforeseen dispute.[11]

Legal certainty for the layman is not predictability of judicial decision, it is *congruence between legal rules and the ways of life.*[12]

[11] *Id.* § 58. (If the word "certainty" seems somewhat inappropriate to describe the notion here involved, it should be said that Llewellyn uses the German word *Sicherheit* which has a somewhat broader connotation than the word certainty and might have been translated here as "security".)

[12] The phraseology here is mine, not Llewellyn's. I say "congruence" instead of "correspondence" because I take it Llewellyn does not insist that legal rules be *formulated* in the same way as social norms but only that they have ultimately the same points of reference,—that they "come to the same thing in the end".

Furthermore, this kind of certainty cannot be achieved unless legal rules *change*. Congruence with lay ways demands a constant reshaping of legal rules, since social norms are continually changing.[13]

This distinction between lay certainty and lawyer's certainty seems to me to be most useful and I have no desire to comment on it, except to express a doubt whether "lay norms" are quite so definite and clear-cut as Llewellyn seems to assume and to suggest that the task of determining the congruence of law and the ways of life is not so simple as he seems to imply.[14]

There is, however, another point about legal certainty which Llewellyn does not discuss at any length, but which it seems to me deserves careful consideration. I mean the question, what will be the probable effect on legal certainty, *i. e.*, on "lawyer's legal certainty", of an adoption by courts of the approach recommended by the realist school? The realist school has generally evaded this question, not because it was embarrassed by it, but because it considered it unimportant. One realist tells us that the really enlightened and normal person takes a "positive delight in the hazardous, incalculable character of life", and regards "life's very insecurity" as its "most inviting aspect".[15] The implication seems to be that for the person free from psychic repression legal uncertainty, far from being a source of concern, is really a source of delight.

I have already pointed out that Llewellyn does not embrace this left-wing view. On the other hand, he seems somewhat hesitant to claim that his own approach will create greater certainty than that produced by the

---

[13] LLEWELLYN, *op. cit. supra* note 5, at 83. Llewellyn acknowledges that the two kinds of certainty (certainty for the layman and certainty for the lawyer) tend to coalesce, as it were, in those situations where every step of a business transaction is guided by legal counsel. Here lay certainty is a reflection of lawyer's certainty. Llewellyn adds this further observation: In those situations where lawyer guidance is customary there is no great danger of a lack of correspondence between legal rules and social norms. The legal profession is here forced to gain an insight into changing social relations. This collective insight of the profession will tend, in some measure at least, to keep law in step with life.

In the field of lawyer-guided transactions a kind of double safeguard exists. If there is a lack of correspondence between lay ways and the law this is rendered harmless through the guidance of the lawyer. There is not likely to be such a lack of correspondence because the legal profession here cannot be ignorant of the demands of life. Both of these safeguards are absent in the case of those transactions ordinarily undertaken without legal advice.

Llewellyn might have added that there is perhaps still another reason why a lack of correspondence between law and life is unlikely in the field of lawyer-guided transactions. Is it not possible that the conservative influence of the lawyer may have operated to retard social change in these fields?

This whole discussion recalls an observation of Ihering's, that Roman law was workable in spite of its technicality because of the omnipresence of the lawyer, whose services were open to all—gratis. Where legal counsel was not likely to be available (on the battle field, for example) various legal requirements were relaxed. GEIST DES RÖMISCHEN RECHTS (7th ed. 1923) II.2, 417.

[14] Underhill Moore's valiant attempt to determine the degree of this congruence in the field of banking law is evidence of the difficulties of the task. Moore and Sussman, *Legal and Institutional Methods Applied to the Debiting of Direct Discounts* (1931) 40 YALE L. J. 381, 555, 752, 928, 1055, 1219. In spite of the elaborateness of the method the results of this research seem to me to remain inconclusive.

[15] FRANK, LAW AND THE MODERN MIND (1930) 17.

method generally followed by courts.[16] In this it seems to me that he and the rest of the realist school have overlooked one of the strongest arguments against the traditional approach.

One of the chief characteristics of the traditional method is that it conceives of the area of the *legally relevant* as quite limited. Only certain types of argument, certain lines of reasoning, are "legal" in nature. Other arguments, other modes of reasoning may have relevance to the decision and may even be taken collaterally into account in deciding the case. But they remain "extra-legal" or "non-technical" considerations, mere (*sic*) arguments of "policy". They definitely occupy a humbler status than "legal" considerations. One of the chief services of the realist school has been to enlarge the field of the legally relevant and to invest "extra-legal" considerations with a species of respectability.[17] And it seems quite clear to me that this has also been a service to the cause of legal certainty.

The traditional method furnished the judge with a set of legal concepts and said to him, "These are the materials from which you are to build your decision. We realize that in reaching your decision you have been influenced by numerous considerations, many of which have nothing to do with these materials. We are willing to wink at that. But we insist on one condition: When you come to the actual work of construction, you must limit yourself to these materials." But suppose that by no amount of manipulation and ingenuity can the materials furnished be made to build the structure planned. What will happen then? Will the plan be revised? Or will the judge break through the taboo and get what he needs elsewhere? Here lies the source of a great deal of legal uncertainty. And here the uncertainty is directly attributable to the restraints imposed by the "traditional method".[18]

In a pamphlet which served as a sort of manifesto for the free law movement Kantorowicz drew an analogy between the "torture" which modern judges inflict on codes to wring from them the results they consider just and convenient, and the literal torture which judges in the middle ages inflicted on persons accused of crime.[19] There is a surprising parallel be-

[16] At the end of section 55 (*op. cit. supra* note 5) he asserts somewhat cautiously that the freer method of decision he advocates will produce a more "effective" legal certainty than the method generally followed. This is preceded by a statement that the freer method will not "endanger" legal certainty.

[17] It would, of course, be foolish to give the entire credit for this change in attitude to the realist school.

[18] Llewellyn has himself recognized this source of uncertainty in the "traditional method". In 1931 he wrote, "But a fair portion of present unpredictability is certainly attributable to the fact that the courts are using official formulas which fit, only part of the time, what the facts seem to call for. Sometimes the facts win, sometimes the formula." Llewellyn, *supra* note 1, at 1241, n. 45. The idea is also adumbrated in a note in his most recent work. *Op. cit. supra* note 5, at 77 n. 3. It is significant that the discussion of the point is in both instances relegated to a footnote.

[19] GNAEUS FLAVIUS (H. U. KANTOROWICZ), DER KAMPF UM DIE RECHTSWISSENSCHAFT (1906) 49.

tween the two phenomena. The middle ages feared and distrusted the judge, particularly the judge sitting in criminal cases. It was thought dangerous to give him much discretion. The law, expressing this common distrust of judges, permitted the conviction of a criminal only when guilt was proved in certain ways, principally by the confession. This was intended to provide a guaranty that no man should be convicted unless the proof of his guilt was clear and certain. This was the legal theory. The practice is more generally known. What actually happened was that the judge first made up his mind—on the basis of what was then "extra-legal" evidence—whether the accused was guilty. If the decision went against the accused he was put on the rack and compelled to give up, in the form of a confession, the legally acceptable evidence of his guilt.

The traditional conception of legal method imposes a like hypocrisy on the modern judge. Often his procedure is to decide the case first on the basis of "non-technical" considerations. Then armed, not with rack and wheel, but with the intellectual equivalents of those instruments of torture—fictions, analogies, "theories",—he proceeds to wring from his code or other body of doctrine the legally acceptable basis for his decision. The medieval institution of torture was eliminated by the simple expedient of permitting the judge more freedom in passing on the sufficiency of evidence. The intellectual torture which our courts inflict on legal doctrine will be obviated when we have brought ourselves to the point where we are willing to accept as sufficient justification for a decision the "non-technical" considerations which really motivated it.

This millenium, when it arrives, will bring not only a humanitarian reform in our treatment of legal doctrine, but also, I feel sure, greater certainty in the prediction of judicial action. For there are hazards involved in the procedure of putting legal doctrine on the rack which were not involved in the medieval institution. Legal doctrine can sometimes be very stubborn. It may hold its lips tight in spite of all our efforts and ingenuity. Furthermore the modern judge, unlike his medieval predecessor, has the unpleasant duty of spreading on the public record a written description of the process of torture itself. This puts something of a damper on the intellectual inquisition. And all of these things add to the uncertainties of the process.

In the usual course in personal property the student is introduced to certain cases which are intended to develop a concept of "possession",—usually with especial reference to the law of wild animals. He studies the case of the harpooned whale, the case of the intercepted fox hunt, and many others.[26] After the "doctrines" involved in these cases have been

[26] I think it could be demonstrated that more money is spent by the law schools of the United States in teaching the juristic aspects of fox-hunting than is spent in the actual pursuit of that ancient and worthy sport itself.

thoroughly digested the instructor puts a series of hypothetical cases—on an ascending scale of temptation, as it were—to test the student's fidelity to the legal doctrine he has absorbed. A great favorite is this case. Two men, *A* and *B*, happen to be hunting in the same swamp. Neither is aware of the other's presence. *A* shoots a duck; it lands in the arms of the surprised *B*. Whose duck is it? I used to put this case to my classes and I generally found a fairly even split of opinion. One group—those who stood steadfast for "legal principle"—were sure it was *B's* duck because he alone had the requisite Power to Control. The other group were sure it was *A's* duck, and, though they were less articulate about their reasons, they intimated a doubt as to *B's* Intent to Possess. After this discussion had gone on for some time, I used to make it a practice to say, "Suppose you knew no law and had never read the cases in the casebook. Whose duck would you say it was?" Immediately there was a subsidence of feelings and argument gave way to complete unanimity. It was *A's* duck. Why? *Because he shot him.*

Now I am not arguing that this is a proper kind of reason, legal or "extra-legal", to assign for a decision, though with some elaboration I think it might be expanded into a respectable argument for the decision in favor of *A*. Nor am I urging inarticulate intuition as a proper basis for judicial decision. What I am trying to say is that from the standpoint of legal certainty no rationalization at all may be better than a poor rationalization. Legal scholars are, of course, generally aware that there is danger in hasty systematization. But it is usually assumed that this danger consists merely in the possibility that "system" may work hardship in the individual case. It is ordinarily supposed that even bad "system" will at least carry the compensating advantage of greater certainty.[21] This assumption is demonstrably false. In the illustration I have given "legal theory", far from producing certainty, destroyed a certainty and uniformity which was already present. And in how many fields of the law is this not true?

When lawyers gather informally and argue about the probable outcome of a case pending before a court, about what does their argument usually turn? (I am supposing a case outside the field of public law, a case without any marked "political" complexion.) Do they argue about the judge's conception of proper business policy, about his social philosophy, about how he would decide the case if he were a layman? They may, but they are not likely to. More often their argument will turn on this kind of

---

[21] This assumption is made in most of the discussions of the various RESTATEMENTS of the American Law Institute. Professor Havighurst has pointed out that a RESTATEMENT may bring about uncertainty when it produces a stress in the judicial process such as is described above. Havighurst, *The Restatement of the Law of Contracts* (1933) 27 ILL. L. REV. 910, 917.

question: Will the judge take a "technical" view, or will he yield to "non-technical" considerations? This is the source of their uncertainty.[22]

Perhaps I can sum up my discussion with a simile. If you put an animal in too small an enclosure you may rely on it that he will make a violent effort to escape. There is no way of predicting whether he will succeed in this effort, or where he will go if he breaks out. If you put him in a larger enclosure you may be reasonably sure that he will be content to stay inside the enclosure. And if you study your animal's habits closely, you will be able to follow his movements within the enclosure and discover regularities in them. What we need, as I see it, is a larger grazing area for judges. The realists are bringing this about, and they ought to realize that in doing so they are making the judge a more tractable and predictable animal.

The traditional method places a stigma on "non-technical" considerations. This tends to produce uncertainty for a reason which I have attempted to demonstrate, namely, that we have no way of predicting when the judge will break through the taboo imposed on him. It also tends to produce uncertainty in another way. It prevents these "non-technical" considerations from being talked and written about. It prevents their possible rationalization and systematization.

In our metropolitan centers the work of trial judges is frequently specialized. One judge will hear only criminal cases, another domestic relations cases, *etc.* From time to time it will be necessary to transfer a judge to a class of cases he is not in the habit of trying. This generally produces some consternation among attorneys practicing in the court. They know they are in for a period of legal uncertainty. This may, of course, be due to the judge's ignorance of legal doctrine. More often it is due to his ignorance of the glosses practice has put on legal doctrine. Often there is no way for him to learn of these glosses—these compromises that law has made with life—except to retrace the experience of his predecessors. He finds by the method of trial and error what needs to be read between the lines. Meanwhile litigants receive arbitrary treatment and legal certainty suffers. Now a legal method, such as the realist school proposes, which would recognize these glosses and compromises as falling within the province of legal science would tend to eliminate this source of uncertainty. If these things were written and talked about the judge might not have to acquire them in the uncertain and painful way he does. Not only that. If these things were openly discussed we should be in a position to attempt a rational and critical evaluation of them. Out of this evaluation would come greater certainty and greater justice for litigants.

[22] Of course, I realize that this sort of question would still exist, though to a less extent, under a more liberal and realistic conception of legal method. For example, in the interpretation of requirements of formality there is always room for difference of opinion as to how strictly a requirement should be applied.

Of course, I realize that there will always remain a fringe of practice which will not get into books. There are many reasons why this is so. But the fact remains that many things are not talked about and do not get into books for the rather prudish reason that they are not supposed to be "law", —though it is admitted they have a tremendous influence on judicial decision. The absence of these things from books, the fact that they must be "picked up", introduces an element of uncertainty in the law which might, in part at least, be remedied by the general adoption of a more liberal conception of the province of legal science.

Case Law v. Code Law

The American legal realist, though in obvious conflict with his environment, enjoys an advantage usually denied to revolters against things as they are. He is fundamentally satisfied with the "system" under which he lives. The Anglo-American system of case law is entirely to his liking. It fits into his pragmatic conception of legal method. Whatever evils it may seem to display are due not to the system itself but to perversions of it, to the ogre Conceptualism which has taken possession of it.[23] Perhaps this affinity for case law explains why the American legal realist has displayed so little interest in European legal speculation. European realists and near realists—men like Ihering, Geny, Duguit, Ehrlich, Wurzel, Bozi, Sternberg, Kantorowicz, and Radbruch—for the most part go unnoticed in this country.

It would require no elaborate demonstration to show that the realist's assumption of the superiority of the American case system has generally been based on no actual investigation of the workings of case law as compared with code law. The "pragmatism" which intuitively prefers the case method exhausts itself in the preference,—it is not applied to determine whether the preference has any empirical justification. This *a priori* pragmatism is not found in Llewellyn's recent book. Partly because the nature of his task demanded it, and partly because his own inquiring temperament led him in that direction, he attempts here something new in the literature of realism: a painstaking examination of the way case law actually operates. He begins by raising an issue of fundamental importance. I translate his own phrasing of the question. "How does it come about that a system of law which develops out of fortuitously selected cases can develop in a way that is tolerable from a political or social point of view? Why does not such a legal system become a planless, orderless chaos of doctrine?" [24]

[23] It has even been suggested that the deficiencies of case law are traceable to "a wave of continental learning [which at one time] swept over England, leaving a thick deposit of its obscurant abstractions, . . ." Oliphant, *A Return to* Stare Decisis (1928) 6 AM. L. SCHOOL REV. 215, 221. Later in America the process was repeated and "Great cargoes of continental speculations were imported and thrown in to make the dikes of the old abstractions hold." *Ibid.* In this way the pristine pragmatism of our Anglo-Saxon fathers was debauched, and our law became abstract and conceptual.

[24] *Op. cit. supra* note 5, at 98.

Under our precedent system courts do not regard themselves as free to anticipate the need for legal rules; they manufacture rules *ad hoc* only, for the particular case in litigation. But what issues will get into litigation? This depends on the interest of individual litigants, and there is, therefore, no way of predicting or controlling the kind of questions which will be the subject of adjudication. In consequence it might appear inevitable that our case law would be spotty and incomplete. A developing field of business practice may be in urgent need of legal direction and control, yet the purely fortuitous circumstance that no individual happens to have an interest in litigation may bring it about that no cases are decided in the field and in consequence no "law" is made.

Now as a matter of fact we know that things do not work out quite as badly as this theory would make it appear. Where legal direction is needed it is generally forthcoming. There are hiatuses in our law, to be sure, but they are neither so numerous nor so extensive as one might be led to suppose in view of the apparently planless way in which our law grows. In spite of its dependence on the past, in spite of the lack of conscious direction over its growth, our system of case law has generally proved itself capable of meeting new social conditions. How does this come about?

Llewellyn solves this problem in a way one might have anticipated. Litigation is not purely a matter of chance and individual interest. Litigation arises out of conflict. Conflict in turn arises in those fields of social activity where growth is taking place, where the relative strength of interest-groups is changing. Things are so arranged that where changing social practice demands new law individual interest will see to it that suits will be brought which will furnish a substratum for the elaboration of the needed doctrine. There is happily a kind of automatic correlation between the interest of the individual litigant and the social need for new law.

That there is an element of truth in Llewellyn's solution of this problem is pretty obvious. It is equally obvious that the solution is partial and incomplete. The correlation between the interest of the individual litigant and the interest of society in legal development—like the correlation assumed by classical economics between the individual economic interest and the common good—is unfortunately far from complete. It is scarcely necessary to demonstrate that our courts' piece-meal and backward-looking system of legislating frequently proves inadequate to meet the need for legal control in fields where social practices are changing rapidly. There are many reasons why this should be so. If the growth in social practice is at all rapid it is likely that with our crowded court calendars case law cannot keep up with it. Again, though the change in social life may involve the interests of whole sections of the population, the pecuniary interest of any individual may be so slight as to make litigation (or at least appeal to the upper courts) impracticable.[25]

I do not for a moment believe that Llewellyn meant to assert any complete and nature-given coincidence between the interest of the individual litigant and the social need for new law. Perhaps he would recognize the need for the qualifications suggested here. But if that is so it must be confessed that his own treatment of the subject leaves too much to inference and presents, at most, intimations of the darker side of case law.

After proving that case law will, or is likely to, grow to meet new social conditions, Llewellyn points out that there are things which may operate to prevent that growth from being a healthy one. Often a whole field of law is influenced permanently by the particular turn taken by the first case arising in the field. This case may have carried a certain factual and ethical complexion which was actually the determinative element in its decision. The court in deciding it, however, may lay down a categorical rule which subsequently becomes divorced from the particular circumstances of its first utterance and controls perhaps hundreds of cases which from an ethical or "factual" viewpoint are quite different from the first and "critical" case. There is an even more sinister possibility. Organized interest-groups, aware of the importance of such critical cases, may see to it that these cases "come up in the right way". Thus by the expenditure of a little money and

---

[25] An example of this is to be found in the field of what is called "industrial insurance". The history of regular life insurance, on the other hand, justifies pretty well Llewellyn's optimism concerning the ability of case law to deal with new situations. A whole new field of social practice grew up with life insurance and, as was inevitable, all sorts of abuses grew up with it. *A priori* one might argue that this is the kind of situation case law is not adequate to meet. Yet we know that, in general, the courts saw that the problem of life insurance was really a *new* problem, and they remade the law to fit this new field. They refused to apply in this new field the supposedly fundamental principles of contract, tort and agency law—not, to be sure, without causing some distress to the student writers of law review notes.

The history of standard life insurance is repeating itself, so far as social practice is concerned, in what is called "industrial insurance". Industrial insurance is written in small amounts (say $100 to $500). Premiums are collected weekly. The policy is issued without a medical examination, though not without warranties concerning the health of the insured sufficiently inclusive to make most of the policies issued void if these warranties were taken literally. It is no exaggeration to say that the abuses which have arisen out of this type of insurance are appalling. Many of the policies are so worded as to bind the companies to practically nothing. Not infrequently a large portion of the premium is paid for disability insurance which *is cancellable at any time by the company*. Of course, the practice is not as bad as these provisions might imply. But it is bad enough. And all of these social abuses are growing up without judicial curb. Why? For the very obvious reason that the amounts involved are too small to attract lawyers to undertake litigation. The man of moderate means, who takes out regular life insurance, has been freed from abuses of this sort by the courts—even if the courts have had to hurt the juristic sensibilities of legal theorists in order to do it. But the poor man remains a victim of the rapaciousness of the less responsible insurance companies. Is not the general indifference toward his plight in some part the product of our faith in the capacity of case law to take care of new problems? We think in terms of case law, and *we assume that the need for statutory reform is not really pressing until it makes itself manifest in the decisions.*

effort at the right time the whole future development of a field of law may be influenced.[26]

Llewellyn fails to mention another element of contingency in the growth of case law which it seems to me is necessary to complete the picture. I refer to the fact that it is a matter of chance *in what order* cases will arise, and what the *doctrinal* connection will be between the cases which do arise and those already decided. Just as a whole field of law may be influenced by the accidental *presence* of a particular case at a particular stage of its development, so a whole field of law may be influenced by the accidental *absence* of a decision which might serve as a sort of *doctrinal bridge* between existing rules and needed new law.

The case of *Shuey v. United States*[27] decided that the published offer of a reward might be effectively revoked by an announcement given equal publicity. Pollock in his treatise on contracts admits the reasonableness of the decision but adds the remark that it "seems a rather strong piece of judicial legislation".[28] Why this? Because previous decisions had declared that a revocation takes effect only when "communicated". This revocation had not been "communicated" since it had never come to the knowledge of the claimant of the reward. Now suppose that there had intervened between these previous decisions and the case of *Shuey v. United States* a case in which a letter of revocation had been promptly delivered at the place of business of the offeree and had been allowed to remain unopened on his desk. Without much question a court would have held that such a revocation was "communicated" so soon as the offeree had had a fair opportunity to become familiar with it. And had such a case existed before the *Shuey* case is it likely that anyone would have regarded that decision as a "strong piece of judicial legislation"? Pollock's attitude was influenced by the purely fortuitous circumstance that there did not exist a case which could operate to carry his mind, without shock, from the older cases to the decision in the *Shuey* case.

The possibility that a doctrinal bridge may be lacking represents, then, an additional element of fortuity in the development of case law, operating to make the litigant's rights depend on the chronological order in which his case comes up. Furthermore it is an element which is especially likely to be operative in fields where social practice is changing rapidly. Social practice may change so rapidly that by the time cases actually get into litigation

---

[26] LLEWELLYN, *op. cit. supra* note 5, at 100. This notion of the "critical" case is obviously realism of the right-wing variety. It assumes that the "vocal behavior" of courts has a significant influence over the judicial process. Llewellyn has elsewhere declared that the position on which some realists verge, that "rules" have no influence over judges at all, escapes his understanding. Llewellyn, *supra* note 1, at 1241 n. 46.

[27] 92 U. S. 73 (1875).

[28] PRINCIPLES OF CONTRACT (4th ed. 1885) *20.

they are so far removed from what the court is familiar with that the court is left without any intellectual conduit to carry it from the old to the new.

It may be argued that the need for "doctrinal bridges" is not a peculiar fault of the case system, and that the whole thing can be reduced to a psychological truism, that men's minds hesitate at making violent jumps. This may be so, but I think it can be shown that this native intellectual skittishness of man is aggravated by the methods of reasoning necessitated in a system of case law. Under a code courts are, of course, faced with the same problem that faces our common-law courts, that of deciding cases which do not fall within existing doctrine. But the procedure under code law is generally to bring the unforeseen situation within some very general provision of the code, vague enough not to interfere with the proper decision of the case and just definite enough to appear to give the court some support. Where a large number of such general provisions are available, as they are in most codes, "doctrinal bridges" are not necessary. The statute itself will carry you anywhere you want to go. The doctrinal bridge becomes important in a system of code law where a somewhat specific provision is gradually extended to cover situations not originally comprehended within it. Here the order in which cases come up is important, and if the cases which lie just beyond the literal meaning of the section arise first, the process of extension will be accelerated. In a system of case law we have, for the most part, nothing corresponding to the catch-all provisions found in codes. Of course, one will find laid down in the cases some rather broad and general principles, but their apparent scope is generally limited by being given a point of reference in the particular case at hand. Such general principles as we have in case law lack the authoritative force which backs a statutory enactment. They are apt to be relegated to Austin's field of "positive morality". They are not quite law. The full force of precedent applies only to the particular decision. All this means that the doctrinal bridge will necessarily play a more important rôle in case law than it does under a code. And, as I attempted to show, it is an alogical, fortuitous factor.

Incidentally this whole discussion gives point to a statement once made by Ihering which would probably be disturbing to the orthodoxy of most realists.[29] The statement was that Roman law was great because it was built upon a system of "case law" which did not discriminate between real and hypothetical cases. The jurisconsults gave answer to all cases put to them, without inquiring whether they were real. This gave a continuity to the body of doctrine which they developed which cannot exist where only "real" cases are dealt with.

---

[29] GEIST DES RÖMISCHEN RECHTS (4th ed. 1858) II.2, 385-386.

Legal Rules and the Nature of Concepts

An attitude of scepticism toward rules has characterized the realist movement from the beginning. This scepticism rests on two closely related grounds. The first lies in a conviction that "reality" is a thing too complex, tumultuous, and vital to be kept in a straight-jacket of rules. I shall deal with this aspect of the realist's scepticism later under the heading *Law and Society*. The other ground for his distrust of rules lies not so much in a belief in the impossibility of the task imposed on rules as in a belief in the essential impotence of rules themselves. Rules are made up of concepts, and concepts are but the shadowy figments of our own minds, wholly unworthy of the simple faith the conceptualist places in them. It is with this aspect of the realist's scepticism that we are here concerned.[30]

The realist movement has done an immense service to American legal science in inculcating in it a healthy fear of such very real demons as Reified Abstractions, Omnibus Concepts, and Metaphors Masquerading as Facts.[31] One seldom encounters a law review article today of the type so common ten years ago, in which the writer starts with an inquiry into the "nature" of some legal concept and ends by deducing all sorts of important consequences from the supposed inner nature of the concept,—without more than a passing reference to the practical effects of his conclusions, and then with an air of condescension, as if to compliment the facts for showing good judgment in conforming to his theories. The outstanding foe of this sort of verbal trifling has been Professor Cook. There can be no doubt that his influence, and that of other realists like him, has been in the main beneficent.

On the other hand, it seems to me that we are now in danger of carrying the crusade against "conceptualism" too far. American legal science gives evidence that it is on the verge of making an orthodoxy of the sterile and uninspired behavioristic philosophy which has worked such havoc in the other social sciences. Professor Cohen has been warning against this danger for a long time, and one only wishes his warnings had a more discernible effect. There is so much breadth of learning and sound sense in what he has written that I hesitate to attempt any supplementation of it. Nevertheless I think I may contribute something in the matter of diagnosing the disease.[32]

---

[30] Valuable criticisms of the realist's attitude toward rules will be found in COHEN, *op. cit. supra* note 8, and Dickinson, *supra* note 8. Dickinson is not merely critical, but presents a carefully thought-out theory of his own in which he makes use of so much of the realist theory as he considers acceptable.

[31] I have attempted a contribution toward the cause myself. See Fuller, *Legal Fictions* (1930-1931) 25 ILL. L. REV. 363, 513, 877.

[32] In the matter of diagnosis I feel I enjoy an advantage over Professor Cohen. I have suffered from the disease myself. In my discussion of the "fictitious" nature of classes (in the article cited *supra* note 31, at 877, 884) there is exemplified the same erroneous assumption concerning the use of concepts in thinking that is found in Berkeley, Llewellyn and Wurzel.

Professor Cohen calls the rule-phobia of the left-wing legal realist "nominalism".[33] Now one gets into all sorts of difficulties if one attempts to explain just what is meant by nominalism in the ontological sense. This is not the place to enter into that problem.[34] Let us, therefore, use the word nominalism frankly as a term of opprobrium, as meaning a *too* distrustful attitude toward universals and abstractions. Now what is the cause of this attitude? This is the question which has not been sufficiently examined. We can never rid a man of a disease of thought until we know how and why he succumbed to it. As I see it, the realist's nominalism generally arises from an error of psychology. This error may be stated as the belief that the individual in his own private thinking does not employ universals and abstractions and that these things are only convenient devices for the communication of ideas. It is the notion that in the internal economy of the mind only "things" are dealt with, and that abstractions and concepts are simply packages of these "things" bundled together,—for export purposes, as it were.

Nominalism is usually defined as the belief that universals exist only in the mind of the individual. So far as the origin of the nominalist attitude is concerned it seems to me that this inverts the thing. Nominalism starts with the assumption that in the mind of the individual universals have no place, that they are only a sort of social convention making language possible.

Confirmation for this theory of the psychological genesis of nominalism is found in the fact that Berkeley, certainly the greatest nominalist who ever lived, begins his *Principles of Human Knowledge* with an inquiry into the processes of thought in the mind of the individual.[35] The conclusion reached on the basis of this psychological investigation—that abstractions cannot be "conceived" and are mere conveniences of language—is then made the basis for his whole philosophy.

While our legal realists have vied with Berkeley in the extremes to which they have carried the nominalistic attitude, their distaste for "philosophic" discussions has generally led them to neglect any statement of the basis for this attitude. It is, therefore, fortunate that in his recent book Llewellyn has undertaken to discuss in some detail the problem of the nature of concepts and rules. His discussion seems to me to reveal the fact that

[33] *Op. cit. supra* note 8, at 208-247.

[34] Modern epistemologists, incidentally, have developed a very neat device for dodging the problem. It is no longer asserted that concepts and relations "exist", but it is firmly insisted that they do have "subsistence". But what is "subsistence"? Why, that is the kind of existence that things like concepts and relations have!

[35] *Introduction* §§ 1-25. *Cf.* ". . . if the nominalistic logic is good it should lead us, as it led Berkeley, to deny that there can be any universal ideas in the mind." COHEN, *op. cit. supra* note 8, at 210. As I have indicated, this statement seems to me to reverse the process by which the nominalistic attitude develops.

his fundamental error, like Berkeley's, is a psychological one. I translate a passage from his book:

> To speak of "*applying* the rule" is to use a misleading expression. Rather you either *fill the rule out,* or *put limits on it.* You can only "apply" the rule *after* you have first either included or excluded the case at hand. . . .
>
> Let us assume a case not involving any doubt, but a case nevertheless which would never have occurred to any one at the time the rule in question was established. In spite of this let us assume it to be a case which everyone, after considering it and the rule, would acknowledge would *have* to be governed by the rule. Now I claim there is here no real "interpretation" of the rule. Even here there is an enlargement, a reformulation, an importation of something new into the rule. For the rule consists of a series, a complex of word-symbols. In itself a symbol is nothing. A symbol is, however, a means of pointing to things or thought-constructs.[36] In so far as things were *demonstrably* aimed at in the original use of a symbol, the symbol has from the beginning content. Every symbol, however, has to an uncertain degree something which we may call *latent content,* a capacity for expansion, as it were, which, though partly equivocal and unforeseeable, is also in part unequivocal and foreseeable. Some things that are new, some things that have hitherto not been thought of, are nevertheless perceived, so soon as they are considered, to fall at once into the already established category. . . . In our hypothetical case every lawyer would make the same extension. When he does that and does it at once *he does not note the extension.* It appears to him as if the case had always lain within this category, as if it had always been consciously intended that this case should belong to the category. In spite of this he has, though unconsciously, extended the category . . . the legislator could not have *intended* the inclusion of this case *in concreto,* the case was by hypothesis not yet thought of.[37]

The assumption concerning the psychological nature of concepts which underlies this discussion is, I think, demonstrably false. Suppose a legislator

[36] Llewellyn uses the word *Gedankengebilde* which, in an effort to be fair, I have translated as "thought-constructs", though it might have been translated as "mental images".

[37] *Op. cit. supra* note 5, at 72-74. Llewellyn's discussion rather closely parallels Wurzel's treatment of "projection". WURZEL, DAS JURISTISCHE DENKEN (2d ed. 1924), translated in THE SCIENCE OF LEGAL METHOD (1921) 298-428.

A similar notion, that in the *Urerlebnis* of the inner soul the mind is freed from the shackles of categories and logic, is expressed in the following passage: ". . . of the many things which have been said as to the mystery of the judicial process, the most salient is that decision is reached after an emotive experience in which principles and logic play a secondary part. The function of juristic logic and the principles which it employs seems to be like that of language, to describe the event which has already transpired. These considerations must reveal to us the impotence of general principles to control decision. Vague because of their generality, they mean nothing save what they suggest in the organized experience of the one who thinks them, and, because of their vagueness, they only remotely compel the organization of that experience." Yntema, *The Hornbook Method and the Conflict of Laws* (1928) 37 YALE L. J. 468, 480. The reader will observe that the nominalist view ("the impotence of general principles to control decision") is here based on an hypothesis concerning the inner processes of thought.

enacts that it shall be a crime for anyone "to carry concealed on his person any dangerous weapon." After the statute is passed someone invents a machine, no larger than a fountain pen, capable of throwing a "death ray". Is such a machine included? Obviously, yes. It falls within the "latent content" of the symbol. But does the inclusion of this new machine under the concept "dangerous weapon" *change* or *enlarge* the concept? Yes, says Llewellyn, because the legislator could not have intended to include it at the time he enacted this statute since it was not then in existence. But what *did* the legislator intend *"in concreto"*? Why are we forced to conclude that his intent cannot extend to something not yet in existence? Would Llewellyn contend that the "actual intent" of our legislator could not extend to revolvers of the ordinary type manufactured after the statute was passed? Is it impossible for a man to "intend" a gift to unborn children? Perhaps Llewellyn has in mind the fact that it would be impossible for the legislator to "visualize" the non-existent object when he enacted his statute. But is a man's intent coextensive with the mental images which accompany it? Would it be impossible for a legislator to prohibit the sale of stock in any company organized to manufacture a perpetual motion machine unless he could visualize the machine? In the case of our "dangerous weapon" statute would the accident that there popped into the mind of the legislator the picture of a Colt revolver mean that his intent excluded Smith & Wesson revolvers? No one would contend that. We should have to say, he intended the class "revolvers". But if he can intend the class "revolvers", why not the class "dangerous weapons"? The fallacy underlying Llewellyn's whole discussion is the assumption that thinking must be directed toward particular "things", when as a matter of fact, it may be, and generally is, directed toward classes or universals.

The old notion that the application of a concept involves merely an extraction of something already implicit within it is misleading, though it presents in a metaphorical way one aspect of the truth.[38] Exactly the same thing can be said of Llewellyn's notion that *any* application to "new" situations, however obvious, effects a "change" in the concept.[39] Indeed, both notions, in so far as they are false, rest on the same error, namely, a hypostatization of the "concept". The old notion treated the concept as an opaque

[38] A very readable and interesting refutation of the notion that concepts in some way or other "develop" new meanings out of themselves will be found in 1 JAMES, PRINCIPLES OF PSYCHOLOGY (1890) 464-468. Needless to say James does not find it necessary to embrace the notion that any "new" application of a concept is a change in it.

[39] The grain of truth contained in Llewellyn's statement consists in the fact that the application of a concept usually involves a mental operation on the part of the person making the application which did not occur in the mind of the man who first used the concept. If you say, "Man is a wonderful being", and I say, "That statement includes Beethoven", I am making an application of the concept "man" which probably did not "occur" to you; something has happened in my brain which did not happen in yours. But that does not mean that I am *changing* your concept of "man". See 1 JAMES, *op. cit. supra* note 38, at 472.

container with all sorts of unknown contents in its interior waiting to be extracted. In Llewellyn's view the concept is—for the individual who uses it—a sort of show case with its contents hung neatly in a row ready to be inventoried at a glance. The fact is that from the standpoint of individual psychology the concept is not a container or "thing" at all, but an activity of the conceiving mind. The "thingifying" comes about when we convert this mental activity into logical terms. It may be that this process of converting a dynamic activity into a static "thing" necessarily involves some distortion. But there is no need to increase the amount of this distortion by the gratuitous assumption that intent and thinking *must* be directed toward "things", and cannot be directed toward classes.[40]

We shall have gone a long way toward ending the controversy concerning "nominalism" if we can secure recognition for the plain fact that the inner mental experience of the individual, however precious and ineffable it may be, is "conceptual". The issue will at least be clarified if we recognize with James that we have available to us "a perfectly satisfactory decision of the nominalistic and conceptualistic controversy, so far as it touches psychology", and that "We must decide in favor of the conceptualists".[41]

The legal realist is emphatically of those James called "tough-minded". He loves "things",—things that are concrete, tangible, *anschaulich.* In Llewellyn's own words, the realists "want law to deal, they themselves want to deal, with things, with people, with tangibles, with *definite* tangibles, and *observable* relations between definite tangibles—not with words alone; when law deals with words, they want the words to represent tangibles which can be got at beneath the words, and observable relations between those tangibles".[42] Now this intellectual bias, for it *is* a bias, has its value in a science which has suffered for centuries from an unbridled pseudo-rationalism. But like all biases the realist's peculiar bias may sometimes lead him astray. He should remember that not all significant facts are "concrete". He needs to be reminded that the love of the tangible and concrete, like other human loves, may sometimes, when thwarted, fabricate its own object.

Do the Proposals of the Realist School Relate Solely to Method?

The proponents of the realist approach have left an ambiguity in their position which, I think, ought to be removed. Do they propose a different kind of law, or only a different way of talking about law?

---

[40] The difficulty of expressing adequately the principles which we employ in our inner thinking is produced, not by the fact that our inner processes of thought do not employ concepts, but, as Dickinson points out (*supra* note 8, at 1064), by the fact that we often employ in our private thinking concepts and thought-units which do not correspond exactly to those implicit in ordinary language. The difficulty is increased by the fact that these unnamed concepts are peculiarly evanescent. We cannot always call them back at will for purposes of comparison and clarification.

[41] 1 JAMES, *op. cit. supra* note 38, at 472.

[42] Llewellyn, *supra* note 1, at 1223.

On the rare occasions when the realist discusses this question he seems to say something like this: "I am not a philosopher. I have no interest in developing a scheme of ethical values. My only interest lies in seeing that the judicial process is accurately described, that it is recognized for what it actually is. My interest is, therefore, primarily methodological, though it is obvious that good method has a social value of its own. If the judge recognizes what he is really doing, he is less apt to be led astray by delusions as to what he is doing."

On the other hand the enthusiasm for his position which the realist displays seems hard to understand if this disclaimer of any interest in ethics is accepted at its face value. When a man talks with all the zeal of the most ardent social reformer it is difficult to assume that his interest is limited to methodology. When the realist ridicules the "vocal behavior" of courts as an unimportant by-product of the judicial process it is hard to believe that his energies are concentrated on changing this "vocal behavior" and that he has no desire to change anything else.

This ambiguity in the position of the realist ought to be removed. Removing it would clarify discussion. It might have an even more important effect. It might reveal that the realist school—though free from evil intent, of course—has been guilty of the crime of misbranding its intellectual wares. For I strongly suspect that the realist movement has not been so free of "philosophic" pretensions as its proponents would have us believe. Certainly I am not inclined to take seriously Llewellyn's occasional disclaimers that his own approach involves any distinctive ethical bias.[43]

The Relation of Law and Society

One of the fundamental problems which any social philosophy must face may be stated in a somewhat vague way as the problem of the relation between law and society,—or, if one prefers, of the relation of Law to Life.[44] Many of the problems of ethical philosophy, in whatever terms they may have been expressed, will be found to center about this relationship. The most imposing legal philosophies will often disclose themselves as involving fundamentally nothing more than a bias concerning this relation,—a bias in favor of "law", or in favor of "society".

A study of Llewellyn's writings [45] convinces me that he has reached his own solution of this problem. In discussing his solution one is under

[43] "I make no effort here to indicate either the proper rule, or the proper action on any legal subject." *A Realistic Jurisprudence—The Next Step* (1930) 30 Col. L. Rev. 431, at 463. "When the matter of *program* [*i. e.*, of the realists] *in the normative aspect* is raised, the answer is: *there is none.*" Llewellyn, *supra* note 1, at 1254.

[44] Geny's distinction between the *donné* and the *construit* states in a somewhat different form the fundamental relation involved here and has the advantage that its terms are freer from metaphorical contamination than those employed in the text. 4 Geny, *op. cit. supra* note 4, c. 3. However, for present purposes, I have preferred to use the more common terms.

[45] In the discussion which follows I draw freely from all of Llewellyn's writings, particularly from the Bramble Bush (1930).

the embarrassment that Llewellyn nowhere makes as distinct and explicit an avowal as one might wish of the social philosophy which it implies. The difficulty is increased by his failure to put his own view in its historical perspective by indicating its relation to the thought of other writers.[46] There is, therefore, of necessity some conjecture in the account I am about to give, and I warn the reader that it is possible I have misinterpreted his views.

I shall begin by quoting a series of statements which will furnish the background for what I have to say:

> "Law and the law official are not therefore in any real sense what *makes* order in society. For them society is given and order is given because society is given.[47] . . . The law then, the interference of officials in disputes, appears as the means of dealing with disputes which do not otherwise get settled. Not as *making* order, but as *maintaining* order when it has gotten out of order.[48] . . . By and large the *basic order* of our society, and for that matter in any society, *is not produced by law*.[49] . . . Law plays only upon the fringes." [50]

Certainly the emphasis is here placed on the "society" side of the relation. Law, the principle of conscious guidance, is relegated to the back-

---

[46] The citation of authorities is so often a form of intellectual exhibitionism that one hesitates to criticize a man who is free from this ostentation. Yet it does seem to me that Llewellyn errs too far in the opposite direction. I am particularly distressed at the absence of reference to that great pioneer among "realists", Rudolph von Ihering. There are a number of places in Llewellyn's writings where Ihering's views almost intrude themselves. Llewellyn seems sometimes to imply that prior to American legal realism it had never occurred to anyone to question the "ideology" of the law, or to inquire whether it coincided with the real motivation of legal rules. Yet most of Ihering's life was devoted to ferreting out the social reality concealed behind the "ideology" of the Roman Law. In addition to refusing to accept the conventional formulations of the law at their face value, Ihering also pointed out that there are frequently regularities of judicial behavior ("latent rules" he called them) which do not appear in the rules talked and written about,—something which Llewellyn regards as a particularly esoteric discovery of American realism. I. IHERING, *op. cit. supra* note 13, at § 3; *cf.* Llewellyn, *supra* note 43, at 439 n. 9. Llewellyn speaks of norms (*Sollsätze*) taking on the appearance of affirmations of fact (*Seinsätze*). *Op. cit. supra* note 5, at 89. There is no reference to Ihering's penetrating discussion of the phenomenon. III.1 IHERING, *op. cit. supra* note 13, at 311-326. Beginning on page 96 of the same book Llewellyn discusses the creation of new legal institutions, and describes the process by which existing institutions are diverted to new purposes. A good part of his article, *What Price Contract?* (1931) 40 YALE L. J. 704, is devoted to the same topic. In neither case is there any reference to Ihering's famous discussion of the problem. II.2 IHERING, *op. cit. supra* note 13, at 334-352, 504-537; III.1 *ibid.*, at 281-301. The reader will find portions of Ihering's treatment translated in my article *Legal Fictions, supra* note 31, at 533-535.

While I am on this subject I should like to take notice of Llewellyn's interpretation of Ihering's theory of interests as an attempt to remove legal science still further from reality than it already was under the notion of substantive rights. Llewellyn, *supra* note 43, at 441. This interpretation is, in my opinion, nothing short of perverse.

[47] BRAMBLE BUSH (1930) 12.

[48] *Id.* at 13.

[49] *Id.* at 112.

[50] *Id.* at 113.

ground, and becomes a kind of midwife called in occasionally to assist the processes of nature, but having no hand in the act of creation itself.[51]

I do not contend, of course, that Llewellyn denies altogether any creative rôle to law. Though he emphasizes the "power of society over courts", he admits that there is another side to the thing which occasionally manifests itself: "the power of courts over society".[52] He recognizes that sometimes even a single legal decision may shape the growth of an institution,[53] and that men "often do orient the action which they take *apart from* litigation" on the basis of legal rules.[54] Llewellyn himself, then, qualifies the broad statements I have quoted previously. It cannot be asserted that he does not see the whole picture. What I fear is that he may suffer from a species of color blindness which causes him to see one part of the picture with especial vividness while the rest fades into an indistinct background. The aspect of the relation of law and society which he constantly chooses for categorical assertion is "the power of society over courts". The qualifications come later, too late to restore a proper balance of emphasis.

This bias on the side of "society" is evidenced in many parts of Llewellyn's work. It is illustrated in his theory that case law will, in a more or less automatic fashion, develop in those places where social change demands it.[55] It is found in his conception of the "pathological case" as the case "so exceptional that the normal ways of society afford . . . no solid basis for deciding [it] . . . "[56] The implication is that the ordinary, "non-pathological" case can and should find its regulation in the "normal ways of society". The same attitude is found in his discussion of legal certainty. "Layman's legal certainty" is identified with the congruence of law and social norms, and it is assumed, not only that law should generally conform to the "ways of life", but that these ways afford a substantial basis for judicial decision.[57]

This emphasis on the society side of the relation is also found in Llewellyn's constant insistence that the legal scholar's first task must be to master in its last detail the whole pattern of human behavior before he attempts to prescribe regulations for it. This insistence that "value judgments" be postponed until we have traced out exhaustively the whole labyrinth of social norms certainly involves itself a "value judgment", how-

---

[51] Dean Pound has pointed out the similarity between the "juristic pessimism" which the realist movement seems to imply and the views of the historical school and the positivists. Pound, *supra* note 8, at 703.

[52] BRAMBLE BUSH (1930) 55.

[53] *Ibid.*

[54] *Id.* at 54.

[55] LLEWELLYN, *op. cit. supra* note 5, at 98.

[56] *Id.* at 82. BRAMBLE BUSH (1930) 54.

[57] LLEWELLYN, *op. cit. supra* note 5, at 81.

ever much Llewellyn may protest the rigid exclusion of "ought" from his approach. If I tell a sculptor that he must spend twenty years investigating the physical and chemical structure of the clay used in modelling before he takes up the study of modelling itself, it will hardly do for me to say I am not teaching sculpture. I shall be judged by the effects of my instructions. The man who has spent most of his life studying clay will be a different kind of sculptor from the man who has devoted more of his time to the art of modelling. There is no *a priori* reason for supposing he will be a better sculptor. If I assume he will be, it must be because of some notion I have concerning the relative importance of clay and modelling in the process of sculpturing.[58]

If I have to choose someone to draft a statute regulating the banking business I may put a high value on a knowledge of banking practice. I may regard as the ideal man for the task the man who knows the practices of the banking world so thoroughly that he can predict with certainty the psychological reactions which the sight of a postdated check will invoke in any banking employee, from messenger boy to president. I may prefer him to a man who, though less familiar with the behavior of bank employees, has spent his life studying the history and theory of banks and banking law, and many hours in arm-chair reflection on the possible ways of organizing and controlling the banking business. I am entitled to my preference. But I am not entitled to escape responsibility for it by saying it involves no "value judgment", no philosophy of what ought to be.

I do not deny that Llewellyn's bias for the society side of the relation may answer to a real need in our law. Lawyers have been too prone to think of society as mere clay in the hands of the "Law". Our courts too often talk as if their task were merely to cut channels, largely after a design of their own fancy, through which the waters of life are expected to flow inertly and complaisantly. To this conception Llewellyn offers a needed antidote. But it is wise to remember that antidotes can be administered too liberally, and that in the case at hand there is danger we may escape one simplification only to fall victims to another.

There are two extreme, and therefore simple, ways of conceiving of the relation of law and society. "Law" can be conceived of as the active principle operating to shape an inert element "society". This is the view toward which the imperative school tends, and it is the view tacitly assumed by most legal writers not of a particularly philosophic turn of mind.

[58] In his Cases and Materials on Sales (1930) xv. n. 3, Llewellyn expresses regret that his book errs "in rarely reaching beyond business practice in the evaluation of legal rules." His defense is that "time for building a wider foundation for judgment has been lacking." This frankness is commendable, and one can only hope that it means that the man who devotes more of his time to "evaluation" and less of it to the investigation of business practice may look forward to being greeted by the realist as a valued co-worker whose efforts supplement his own.

At the other extreme is the view that "society" is the active principle and that "law" is simply a function of this principle. This is the view toward which Maine, Savigny, Ehrlich and Duguit tend. Llewellyn seems to me to place himself in this class, though his closest affinity is with the last two mentioned.

These are the extreme views. Each of them has a value,—as a corrective of the other. Indeed it is often difficult to say whether the emphasis made by a given writer is intended to convey his conception of an ultimate truth, or is intended simply to restore a balance which he considers to have been disturbed by extremists on the other side. But fighting fire with fire is always attended by hazards. We avoid the difficulties which arise from these extreme simplistic positions if we recognize frankly that the relation is one of mutual action and reaction. In the relation of law and society neither element is wholly determinative, neither wholly determined. This intermediate view seems to me to represent the position of such scholars as Ihering, Pound, Geny, Stammler and Cohen.

In dealing with this problem we can employ with advantage Cohen's principle of polarity.[59] Law and Society are polar categories. Though we are under the necessity of opposing them to one another we must recognize that each implies the other. If we deny one, the other becomes meaningless. We may picture Law and Society as the two blades of a pair of scissors. If we watch only one blade we may conclude it does all the cutting. Savigny kept his eye on the Society blade and came virtually to deny the existence of the Law blade. With him even the most technical lawyer's law was a kind of glorified folk-way.[60] Austin kept his eye on the Law blade and found little occasion in a book of over a thousand pages to discuss the mere "positive morality" which social norms represent. Blackstone shifted his eye from one blade to the other and gave us the confused account in which, on the one hand, he bases the common law on custom, and, on the other, informs us that the authoritative statement of this custom is to be found only in court decisions. As if to add to the confusion, he then lays down rules for determining when a custom should be recognized by the law.[61] We avoid all these difficulties by the simple expedient of recognizing that both blades cut, and that neither can cut without the other.

[59] See COHEN, REASON AND NATURE (1931) 165 *et seq.*

[60] Incidentally it is interesting to note that Savigny's problem here is much the same as that which Llewellyn attempts to dispose of with his notion of the "pathological case". Both start with the assumption that law ought to conform to folk-ways. Both are embarrassed by "technical lawyer's law". What shall we do with it? We not only have it, we also obviously need it. Yet it threatens the theory. Savigny's solution of the dilemma was to attempt a specious reconciliation of the fact with the theory. Llewellyn's solution is to isolate the fact so that it may not contaminate the theory as a whole.

[61] 1 BL. COMM. *38-92. See Bentham's strictures, A COMMENT ON THE COMMENTARIES (1928) 186 *et seq.*

By saying that we avoid difficulties by adopting the "polar" view of the relation of law and society, I do not mean to imply that the adoption of this view renders the problem a simple one. On the contrary, the advantage of this view lies precisely in the fact that it reveals the difficulties which exist and enables us to prepare to meet them. This view makes it clear that the problem of the relation of law and society is not the sort of issue which can be "solved" by some "theory" and then passed over. It is, to use Radin's suggestive phrase, one of the "permanent problems of the law". But while we may not have disposed of the question, we shall at least have divested it of a specious simplicity which is itself the source of endless difficulty.

The "Institutional Approach" of Underhill Moore

What these difficulties are becomes apparent when an attempt is made to apply in a practical way a simplistic conception of the relation of law and society. One of the most recent and most thorough-going attempts to do this is to be found in Underhill Moore's "institutional approach". Professor Moore starts with the question, What actually controls judicial decisions? The judge moves in a complex environment—moral, intellectual, and physical—and his decisions may be regarded as reactions to that environment. But of the numberless factors of this environment, which are the most significant? The traditional theory supposed, or pretended to suppose, that the judge was influenced solely by a segment of his intellectual environment, that represented by "law" and legal theory. This view is no longer tenable. We now realize that rules are impotent to exercise any real control over the judicial process. Even when they seem to chart a definite course (which is seldom because of their vagueness) frequent judicial aberrations from the charted course remind us that there must be other, more significant factors in the judge's environment. Professor Moore then sets about to discover what these more significant factors are. One item after another is rejected. Common sense rejects the assumption that the physical environment has any very important, or at least measurable, influence over judicial decisions. A poorly ventilated court room may conceivably affect the judicial process,—but this is a remote and conjectural possibility. The notion that prevailing philosophic notions, conceptions of the good life, may have any very great influence is rejected because these things are matters of "intuition" and are therefore incapable of scientific treatment. The search for some ultimately determinative element begins to look futile. But let us not give up hope. There is one constant in our shifting firmament. We still have the "institutional patterns of behavior" which prevail in the community. We know that "men's actions move along the well-cut channels or straggling ruts of habits,"—this is, indeed, "the conclusion of the philosopher, the psychologist and the common man." These folk-ways, these institutional patterns of behavior, become then, like "the sun, the tides, the rain, one of the constant factors among the welter of variables." Can we not assume that the judicial process is controlled by them, that judicial decisions turn ultimately on the institutional or non-institutional character of the litigants' behavior?[62]

Professor Moore does not rest content with enunciating a theory; he proceeds to test his theory in practice. Do the decisions actually reveal that judges are primarily controlled by the patterns of behavior which prevail in the community? To determine this three cases were selected for study. All three related to the same point of banking law. Two cases (from New York and Pennsylvania) decided the point in one way;[63] the other case (from South Carolina) decided it in another way.[64] Can we explain this difference as arising, not from a different conception of "law", not from a different philosophy of life or from other such imponderables, but from an *observable* difference in the banking practices of South Carolina as compared with those of New York and Pennsylvania? An elaborate investigation was undertaken to answer this question.[65]

Now before undertaking such an investigation, one has to consider at least four questions. How do you ascertain what social institutions exist, or, to use Moore's own phrase, how do you go about "ethnologizing a particular present day culture"? How do you extract out of the social institutions so ascertained a norm of decision? Can you be sure that the courts will be familiar with existing social institutions and will extract from them the same norm of decision that you do? Can you be sure that the courts will

---

[62] This paragraph is intended to summarize the arguments found in *Rational Basis of Legal Institutions* (1923) 23 COL. L. REV. 609, and *An Institutional Approach to the Law of Commercial Banking* (1929) 38 YALE L. J. 703.

It may be objected at this point that Moore's study is not pertinent to the present inquiry because he clearly disclaims any intent to say what law ought to be. He does not say how courts *ought* to decide cases; he only describes how they *must* decide them. It would be easy to answer this objection by pointing out that it is no unheard of thing for moralists to present their Utopias as necessities, their "oughts" as "musts". But let us give Professor Moore the benefit of the doubt and assume that he is not a preacher disguised as a scientist. His study still remains pertinent to our discussion. Moore is at least disposing of other people's "oughts" whether he is setting up one of his own or not. If courts *must* decide cases by a reference to prevailing behavior patterns, then those who argue that they ought to decide them on some other basis are wasting their breath. For this reason the ethical philosopher cannot avoid bringing Moore into his discussions, however little Moore may feel inclined to return the compliment.

[63] Delano v. Equitable Trust Co., 110 Misc. 704, 181 N. Y. Supp. 852 (1920); Goldstein v. Jefferson Title & Trust Co., 95 Pa. Super. 167 (1928).

[64] Callahan v. Bank of Anderson, 69 S. C. 374, 48 S. E. 293 (1904).

[65] Moore and Sussman, *supra* note 14, a total of 145 pages. The method succeeded in explaining the South Carolina decision, and Moore therefore concludes that "the study probably justifies the inference of a causal relation" between judicial decisions and the institutional or deviational character of the litigants' behavior. *Id.* at 1249. Aside from the question whether the ability to explain a single decision is a very impressive demonstration of the validity of a method, it is interesting to observe that the South Carolina case was decided by an equally divided court. So while Moore succeeded in explaining why two of the judges voted to affirm the decision of the lower court, he has yet to explain why the other two members of the court voted the other way.

necessarily regard the norm of decision implied in a given social institution as the best one? Moore's study involves an answer to each of these questions and, it seems to me, in each case the answer which he gives is erroneous.

First of all, how do you go about determining what social institutions, what folk-ways, exist? Professor Moore's answer is that you simply observe the way people behave. If you are investigating banking practice with reference to notes, you send an investigator into the cage of the note teller to make a record of what he does. Or, you put a hypothetical situation to an experienced banker and ask him how he would conduct himself in such a case. The emphasis is on behavior. The purpose back of that behavior, the rationalizations and intellectual activity which accompany it are ignored.

This, it seems to me, constitutes the fundamental fallacy of the "institutional approach" of Moore—the assumption that the significance of institutions is exhausted in behavior. In an early article he writes, "To say that a legal institution,—private property, the federal government of the United States, Columbia University,—exists is to say that a group of persons is doing something, is acting in some way." [66] Now many people would say that a legal institution consists not of actions, but of attitudes of mind to which actions merely give external expression. This view is rejected by Moore on the ground, I take it, that these attitudes of mind are usually simply rationalizations of the behavior which they accompany, and are therefore the effect of the behavior, not the cause of it. *Now it is quite true that this is often the case.* But the truth here happens to be complex, and it is also true that behavior is, at least sometimes, the expression of mental attitudes. This fact is enough to vitiate any purely "behavioristic" approach to social institutions.

Bankers were never asked by Professor Moore's investigators what they were trying to accomplish, or why they acted as they did. They were only "observed", or were asked to state how they would react to certain situations selected by Professor Moore and phrased in his own language. The fallacy of this procedure becomes apparent when we realize that it is impossible to define what the "situation" is to which the banker reacts unless we know what is going on in his mind. We observe that a banker, whose customer's note is due and unpaid, refrains from charging the amount of the note against the customer's checking account until the consent of the customer has been obtained. What is the situation which called forth this reaction? Moore defines the situation entirely in terms of "observables". Was the note secured? How did the note come into the hands of the bank? Had the note just come due, or had it been overdue for some time? Yet from the standpoint of the banker, these were perhaps the least significant elements in the situation. The most significant factor from the standpoint of the

[66] Moore, *supra* note 62, at 609.

banker may have been the fact that the customer's default on the note was obviously due to an oversight, or the fact that the customer was a man of good credit standing, or some other fact not stated in Moore's hypothetical "situation".

The realists regard as one of the fundamental fallacies of the traditional method its assumption that the judge reacts only to those facts of the case which are visible through the prism of legal theory. In truth, the judge's decision represents a reaction to the whole situation, including many facts which from the standpoint of legal theory are irrelevant. The realist condemns the traditional method for its mistaken assumption that you can limit the influence of facts to those tagged as legally relevant, and for the corollary assumption that it is profitable to discuss the solution of controversies on the basis of textbook outlines of the facts. Yet precisely the same fallacy, if it is a fallacy, is contained in Moore's approach. He adopts toward bankers the same attitude the traditional theory adopts toward judges,—a procedure which could only be justified on the doubtful assumption that bankers possess less complicated personalities than judges. He assumes that there are principles guiding the practice of banking which one can discover merely by asking a banker how he would react in certain skeletonized "situations".[67] He seems aware of the temerity of this procedure and of the need for justifying it for he is at pains to report that the answers which bankers gave to his questions were "stated with the positive assurance with which are given descriptions of the way everyday situations are met."[68] This may seem to prove that he had accurately stated the "situations" to which bankers react, but I think that this inference is wholly without justification. If some earnest sociologist were to attempt a "scientific" investigation into the folk-ways of lawyers, and were to ask one hundred unselected lawyers, "Can a man who has rescinded a contract, sue on it?" I suspect that most of his answers would be in the negative and would be given with "positive assurance". The "positive assurance" would exist precisely because the lawyer was asked about a skeletonized, "conceptual" situation. If he were put a series of actual cases his assurance would probably diminish to the vanishing point. Professor Moore asked his bankers if, when a customer's note was due, they charged the note against his account without authority from him. They gave, for the most part, ready answers. Would the answers have been so ready if the situation had been filled out with such

[67] For the purpose of making clear my own attitude, I should say that I do not share unqualifiedly the realist's antipathy toward skeletonized cases. I think such cases have both a dialectic and a pedagogical utility. But the "skeletonizing" of cases is a delicate business, and necessarily anticipates the analysis which will be applied to the simplified situation. This means that when you "skeletonize" situations for bankers you have to do so with reference to the principles on which bankers act in the conduct of their business. This is what Moore made no attempt to do.

[68] Moore and Sussman, *supra* note 14, at 759.

pertinent facts as the credit standing of the customer, the availability or non-availability of legal advice inside the bank, the apparent reason for the customer's default (oversight, insolvency, temporary stringency, *etc.*) and the purpose for which the account was being used? And if not, does the uniformity of the banker's reactions to skeletonized fact situations represent a really significant "institution"?

An uncritical adherence to the behavioristic approach leads to another erroneous assumption, that norms of decision may be extracted directly from regularities of behavior, and that where you have a definite "behavior pattern" you necessarily have a correspondingly definite norm of decision. Now this is demonstrably untrue. It may be the practice of department stores generally to accept goods returned by customers. This behavior pattern may be exemplified in literally thousands of instances. But what norm of decision is implied in this practice? The department store, we shall assume, refuses to accept goods returned by the customer and the customer sues. Now we cannot decide this case simply by referring to the existence of a pattern of behavior. The mere fact that people habitually act in certain ways in certain situations is not itself a criterion on the basis of which lawsuits may be decided. If a folk-way is relevant to decision, it must be because it has a "normative" aspect.[69] But we cannot discover this normative aspect

[69] Moore does not attempt to extract a norm of decision directly out of the behavior patterns which his investigation uncovered. This would have been impossible in view of the behavioristic method pursued in charting these patterns. Nevertheless it is obvious that sooner or later it will be necessary to bridge the gap between plain brute fact and sentiments and attitudes which alone can serve as a basis for judicial decision. It is interesting to note how and where Moore makes this transition. His investigation disclosed that the behavior involved in all three cases was "non-institutional"—a result which he had anticipated. Yet obviously this cannot explain why one case was decided in one way and the other two cases in another. This disparity is to be explained by the fact that there was a difference in the *degree* in which the behavior involved deviated from the *nearest institutional pattern*. *Id.* at 1219. Now two questions arise. What is the nearest institutional pattern? One might have expected that Professor Moore would begin at this point to treat his bank tellers as something other than automata, and he might inquire what patterns *they* would be most likely to regard as offering a precedent for their behavior. But no, our bank tellers remain mere habit complexes, and the "nearest institutional pattern" is determined without any reference to their possible mental processes by a mechanical procedure akin to matching samples of cloth. We are now ready to measure the degree of deviation. One might suppose that the same "objective", mathematical method would have been preserved in dealing with this problem. But instead we find that Professor Moore has suddenly endowed his bank tellers with brains, and they are now assumed to act purposively and intelligently. We measure the "degree of deviation" by asking such questions as whether the actual conduct of the parties was as efficient a device for doing business as the institutional pattern, whether it was such a deviation as would be likely to arouse resentment on account of its unfairness—in short, by asking whether the departure was "reasonable" under the circumstances. In the end, then, Moore's method turns out to involve the same intangible elements which are involved in the more conventional approach. The only difference is that in determining "reasonableness" under his method you are forced to take as your standard of comparison what the charts reveal as the nearest institutional pattern of behavior. But after all this limitation is more apparent than real, since the basis on which comparison is made remains vague enough to afford sufficient leeway for the active legal imagination.

by a mere statistical investigation, by inquiring, in the case I have supposed, how many times department stores have accepted returned goods. We have to discover whether this practice is merely a matter of accommodation ("the customer is always right"), or has established an attitude of expectancy, a sentiment of "ought", which can serve as a norm of decision. The interesting thing is that we can get the most light on this normative aspect of the practice from the way in which the department store acts in what Professor Moore calls "deviational" cases, for example, where the customer's dissatisfaction with the goods is patently unreasonable. The essence of an "institution" will generally be found, not in "behavior", but in mental attitudes, *and frequently the nature of these attitudes is revealed and defined only in "non-institutional" situations. Often it is the observation of behavior in the unusual case which gives definiteness to the contour of an institution.*

So soon as we abandon the attempt to stick to a purely behavioristic approach, and begin to take into account the intellectual processes which accompany and guide behavior, we see at once the absurdity of the view that the law should (or does) simply take over social institutions as a ready-made norm of decision. We see that our note teller's patterns of behavior may be shaped, not by an invisible psychological force which confines him to some "straggling rut of habit", but by his own imperfect notions of the law, so that to take over his patterns of behavior as a norm of decision is simply to put the judicial ermine on the bank teller and to substitute second-hand knowledge and rumor for the researches of judge and counsel. We see also that "law" and "institutional patterns of behavior" often derive from a common emotional and intellectual source—for example, from current conceptions of business expediency and social justice.[70] For assistance in

Moore's method requires us to answer three questions: (1) what institutional patterns of behavior exist? (2) which of the institutional patterns does the actual behavior of the parties most nearly resemble? (3) how much does the actual conduct of the parties deviate from this pattern? Moore attempts to answer the first two questions on a purely behavioristic basis. In answering the third question the behavioristic approach is abandoned. Moore's study does not, then achieve "objectivity" through the total elimination of "rational" and "intuitive" elements. All it achieves is a postponement of these elements. What is accomplished by that postponement remains unexplained.

Professor Moore has performed a valuable service in calling attention to the need for an actual investigation of lay practices where they are relevant to judicial decision. Courts too often glibly and erroneously assume that they know what these practices are. But Moore's method, as I see it, is fatally defective in its assumption that these practices can profitably be divorced from their "rational" background.

[70] The South Carolina deviation from the rule obtaining in Pennsylvania and New York might conceivably have been explained on the basis of Southern business *mores*. My own experience in the South would lead me to believe that the Southerner does not typically regard the debtor-creditor relationship in the impersonal, "business-like" way it is regarded in the North. It is a personal relation, involving a duty of consideration not only of debtor toward creditor, but of creditor toward debtor. This makes it understandable why a Southern judge would feel a resentment toward a banker who suddenly began turning down his customer's checks, after allowing his note to remain overdue without action for a considerable

understanding these intangibles we shall be forced to call back the "brilliant intuitionalists" whom Professor Moore so cavalierly dismissed at the beginning of his study.

Professor Moore claims for his method that it corresponds to the method actually employed by courts, whether they are aware of that fact or not. This necessarily assumes that courts are familiar with the behavior patterns of the community. For the culture patterns of life inside the bank teller's cage can influence the judge only if he knows of them. Yet there seems a certain temerity in the assumption that the justices of the Supreme Court of South Carolina (whose biographies incidentally reveal no practical banking experience [71]) already knew what Moore's investigators took months to learn. Moore meets this point only by saying that the judge's "attitudes and ideas are molded by a cultural matrix whose patterns are engraved by frequency. Put in another way, if the court [the judge?] is not conditioned by frequent contact with the behavior itself, it is conditioned by verbal behavior which will be found, on last analysis, to be causally related to the patterns or institutions." [72] I am not quite sure that I understand this. It seems to mean that the judge in the contacts of daily life will inevitably hear turns of expression which, in some subtle way, will convey to him an insight into what note tellers are doing about debiting direct discounts. But it is hard to believe Professor Moore meant anything quite so preposterous as that. In view of the uncertainty of his meaning, perhaps it would be best to let this point go without refutation.

Let us, then, grant Professor Moore his point about the "cultural matrix", even if we remain a little obscure as to what it is we are granting. Let us assume that there exists a definite pattern of behavior, that the court knows of it, and that the court has been able to extract from it a norm of decision. Still it by no means follows, as Moore seems to assume, that the court will or should regard the norm so obtained as the most desirable basis of decision. Obviously where a court disapproves the end toward which a social practice is directed, it may refuse to accept the practice as a norm of decision. A court may decline to enforce a gambling debt, though it be

---

period. Professor Moore would, of course, scoff at any such explanation as resting on "intuition". But is any more "intuition" involved in this explanation than is involved in his assumption that, in some mysterious way, judges know or "sense" the institutional patterns of behavior prevailing in their communities? But then this assumption probably represents an example of the "qualitative subjective judgment" which Moore admits is involved in his method; it cannot be mere "intuition" for that is presumably excluded from his approach.

[71] See Brooks, South Carolina Bench and Bar (1908) for biographical sketches of the four justices involved. Incidentally there is nothing in the biographies of the two dissenting judges which would explain why the cultural matrix failed to make an impress on them.

[72] Moore and Sussman, *supra* note 14, at 1219.

admitted that the norms of society call for the payment of such debts. Courts exercise at least a veto power over folk-ways. This qualification of the "institutional method" is so obvious that we would be unfair if we did not assume that the proponents of the method had it tacitly in mind. Let us turn to a less obvious point. Does the institutional method remain valid in those situations where the court regards as innocent the purpose which the parties are attempting to achieve? I think not. To accept the "institutional approach" uncritically even in these cases is to overlook the fact that a court may refuse to conform to a folk-way, not because it disapproves of the object toward which it is directed, but because it considers it ill-adapted to achieve that object. It is to ignore the possibility that a court may undertake to reshape a "behavior pattern" to assist it in reaching its own end. If it were true, for example, that laymen generally regarded the ceremony of "shaking on it" as creating a binding contract, it would not follow that a court would have to accept this ceremony as a valid legal formality if it considered that it offered insufficient safeguards against the dangers which legal formalities are supposed to avert.[73] *The law has always to weigh against the advantages of conforming to life, the advantages of reshaping and clarifying life,* bearing always in mind that its attempts to reshape life may miscarry, or may cost more than they achieve.[74]

Llewellyn does not, I think, carry the behavioristic view as far as it is carried by Moore. He recognizes a qualification on the "institutional approach" which Moore apparently does not—that in many cases law, instead of merely conforming to folk-ways, actually shapes and controls them. Nevertheless he is not, I think, entirely free from the erroneous assumptions found in Moore's study. I have already expressed the view that he is guilty of at least an error in emphasis. Furthermore there seems to run through his writings the assumption that "law" is only a kind of surrogate for missing folk-ways. In terms of the figure of the scissors, the Law blade only comes into operation when for some reason the Society blade is unable to cut by itself. Indeed, the situation where "the normal ways of society afford . . . no solid basis" of decision and where, accordingly, we must resort to the

---

[73] Our courts probably made a mistake in following lay practice in the "liberalization" of the requirement of a seal. In this way they frittered away, perhaps irretrievably, a valuable social practice.

[74] Ihering speaks of the close relation which existed between law and business in ancient Rome. He goes on to say, "The intimacy of the relation between legal science and business redounded to the benefit of both. To the benefit of business, because the lawyer had his hand constantly on its pulse and knew what it needed and how it could be helped. To the benefit of jurisprudence because, without denying in any material respect the demands of business, it could bring business into that form which was, from the legal standpoint, the most desirable one." IHERING, *op. cit. supra* note 13, at 418. American "institutionalists" should, I think, ponder the last sentence, to see whether it may not describe a desideratum they have fallen into the habit of overlooking.

"law" for solution is quite frankly labelled "pathological".[75] This, it seems to me, clearly implies a behavioristic ethics.

The Emotional Foundations of Realism

The positivistic and behavioristic ethical philosophy of Llewellyn and Moore is found in other realists. In fact it may be said to constitute a strong undercurrent of the realist movement as a whole. Duguit's "positivism", which is another kind of realism, has led him to a similar position. Why should this be? Why should realism, which starts out as a reform movement, carry in its loins this essentially reactionary principle? I think the paradox is explainable.

It is well to remember that the difference between the realist and the "conceptualist" is not so much a matter of specific beliefs as it is of mental constitutions. The conceptualist is not naïve enough to suppose that his principles always realize themselves in practice. Indeed, since he is usually a practical man, he is apt to be more familiar with the specific ways in which life fails to conform to the rules imposed on it than the more philosophic realist. It is not, then, that the conceptualist is ignorant of the discrepancy between Is and Ought. He is simply undisturbed by it.

On the other hand, the cleft between Is and Ought causes acute distress to the realist. He sets about resolutely to eliminate it. There are two ways in which this may be done. The Is may be compelled to conform to the Ought, or the Ought may be permitted to acquiesce in the Is. There are enormous difficulties in the first course. Life resists our attempts to subject it to rules; the muddy flow of Being sweeps contemptuously over the barriers ot our Ought. There is something even more disheartening. We find it impossible to say exactly what it is we wish life to conform to, what our Ought is. Life laughs at our rules, and even our rules betray us by refusing to reveal their nature to us. The easier course beckons temptingly, to let the Ought acquiesce in the Is, to let law surrender to life.

The realist ends in ambiguity. About one thing he is clear. The disgraceful discrepancy between life and rules must be eliminated. But he is not sure whether his prescription is to force life into conformity with a new, more carefully drawn set of rules, or to permit rules to give way to life. This ambiguity is found in what is perhaps the most ancient formulation of legal realism: *Regula est, quae rem quae est breviter enarrat. Non ex*

[75] LLEWELLYN, *loc. cit. supra* note 56. The attitude of Moore and Llewellyn toward the problem of the relation of law and society may perhaps reveal the distortion which comes from viewing the law from the perspective of one specialty; in their case, commercial law. It is doubtful whether it would occur to a specialist in torts or criminal law to urge a greater *conformity* of law to folk-ways, though such a person would probably go along with Moore and Llewellyn in urging the *relevance* of folk-ways in those fields.

regula ius sumatur, sed ex jure quod est regula fiat.[76] *Don't get your law from rules, but get your rules from the law that is.* Is this merely a methodological caution, warning us that paper rules often fail to express adequately the principles actually in force? Or does it mean that principles really have no force, and we must get our rules from the "law" of life itself? The clarity of the realist position has not increased perceptibly since the time of Paulus. The modern realist is still not clear in his own mind whether he objects to "conceptualism" because it fails to achieve an accurate formulation of its principles, or because it pretends to proceed according to principle at all.

[76] Paulus in Dig. 50, 17, *De diversis regulis*, 1.

May, 1931

University of Pennsylvania Law Review
And American Law Register

FOUNDED 1852

Published Monthly, November to June, by the University of Pennsylvania Law School, at 34th and Chestnut Streets, Philadelphia, Pa.

VOL. 79 MAY, 1931 No. 7

LEGAL RULES: THEIR FUNCTION IN THE PROCESS OF DECISION *

JOHN DICKINSON

The part law plays in the process of adjudication has been obscured by Montesquieu's classic stereotype of the judicial function.[1] For orthodox believers in the separation of powers the judge who does his duty is an automaton; what decides the case must be the law itself in the sense of known public rules which the judge applies with machine-like precision.[2] At the same time it has been customary to assume that these rules are all somehow so related into a rational system that any rule which is needed can be deduced from others by a process of logic; with the result that the decision of cases turns out not to require from beginning to end the intervention of human choice, but on the contrary to be dictated throughout by sheer legal necessity.

Lawyers are seldom philosophers enough to formulate or even be fully aware of such deeply basic presuppositions of their

---

*The substance of this article was presented at the Round-Table on Jurisprudence and Public Law at the annual meeting of the American Political Science Association at Cleveland, Ohio, December, 1930.

[1] MONTESQUIEU, DE L'ESPRIT DES LOIS, bk. II, c. 6.

[2] For an exposition of this view see Alexander Hamilton in THE FEDERALIST (1789) No. 78, "The judiciary," he says, "can take no active resolution whatever." For other illustrations see Dickinson, *The Law Behind Law* (1929) 29 COL. L. REV. 113, 115, especially notes 7-10 inclusive.

thought. The ideal of a complete and perfectly logical system of legal rules has survived because for the most part it has remained implicit in conventional habits of legal analysis instead of projecting itself into conscious belief. So far as it did emerge, it long found congenial company, and confirmation by analogy, in the contemporary assumption of Newtonian science that the physical universe was governed by a body of natural laws whose interactions dictated with rigorous determinism the occurrence of each least event in space and time.[3]

The most spectacular crisis in intellectual history since Darwin's *Origin of Species* has come with the challenge which Einstein and the modern physicists have flung down to the Newtonian conception of nature. Like its Darwinian predecessor this more recent crisis has sent waves of repercussion into other fields of thought; and arriving within the domain of jurisprudence, the impact has struck amidships not merely the idea of law as a system of logically connected rules, but even the more fundamental idea of rules as controlling factors in the process of decision.[4] It may be suspected that this particular direction of the impact has not been altogether due to unguided operation of the analogy from Einstein.

The revolt against the idea of law as a complete and coherent system has come significantly from teachers in American law-schools, whose daily ritual is to demonstrate by the "case-system" a coherence sometimes more suppositional than real; the rigor of the task has turned some of the hierophants into unbelievers. The further fact that teachers under the case-system are concerned exclusively with decisions of appellate courts, and almost always

---

[3] DEWEY, THE QUEST FOR CERTAINTY (1929) 201. The notion that nature in its entirety is governed by absolute laws and that every phenomenon is capable of explanation by such laws was first definitely formulated and strongly insisted upon by the Stoics. See quotation from Alexander of Aphrodisias in E. MEYERSON, L'EXPLICATION DANS LES SCIENCES, v. I, 112, quoted from NOURRISSON, DE LA LIBERTÉ ET DU HAZARD, ESSAI SUR ALEXANDRE D'APHRODISIAS (1870) 260. It is significant that it was also the Stoics who developed the conception of a body of absolute natural laws governing men's jural and social relations.

[4] For a recent exposition of this view which has attracted much attention see FRANK, LAW AND THE MODERN MIND (1930), and the Book Review by Professor Francis H. Bohlen (1931) 79 U. OF PA. L. REV. 822, to which I am indebted throughout this article.

on dubious and mooted points, has invoked the still deeper scepticism which presumes to doubt even the existence of rules of law as ordinarily understood.[5]

The effect of this sceptical movement in recent jurisprudence has been altogether beneficial insofar as it helps dispel the Montesquieu phantasy that rules of law dictate completely the outcome of the decisional process. The actual decision of any litigated controversy results almost always from the determination of numerous issues, on many of which there is not, and on some of which there cannot ever be, a controlling rule of law. Judicial discretion thus inevitably plays its part, and a large and important one, in the administration of what we call justice according to law.[6] This has been too much overlooked by traditional theory, with the result that insufficient attention has been paid to the discretionary aspect of the judicial process. Insofar as this discretionary element is duly recognized, the result is to emphasize the inexorably authoritarian character of government, even in the performance of its most purely legalistic function.

The fact that legal rules do not always dictate the decisions of cases does not, however, mean that they may not have influence, and sometimes a controlling one, in the process of decision. Sceptics who minimize the influence of such rules often seem only disappointed absolutists, who expected the traditional theory of legal determinism to work out to the bitter limit of its clock-work logic, and on finding it play them false, react into an opposite extreme of naïve unwillingness to recognize the less absolute, but none the less relatively effective, way in which legal rules do their

---

[5] Bingham, *What is the Law?* (1912) 11 MICH. L. REV. 109; Bingham, *Legal Philosophy and the Law* (1914) 9 ILL. L. REV. 96.

[6] This is obscured by conceiving of the gross result of governmental action taken with respect to an individual in a particular case as "law" in the way in which Professor Llewellyn, for example, seems to conceive it in the following statement: "More often than not administrative action is, to the layman affected, the last expression of the law on the case. In such a situation I think it highly useful to regard it as the law of the case." Llewellyn, *A Realistic Jurisprudence* (1930) 30 COL. L. REV. 431, 455. The administrative, or even judicial, action taken with respect to a given individual always represents the component of a number of factors of which "law" is only one if the term "law" is to be preserved so as to have any distinction from the activity of government in general.

work, holding an impossibly exalted view of certainty, they insist on all or none.

The form which the sceptical doctrine currently takes is that legal rules are a device for producing certainty, and as such are open to censure on two grounds: *first,* because they are ineffective, in that they do not eliminate discretion; *second,* because the proposed end itself is an illusory fetish. The attack on the ability of rules to produce certainty is not ordinarily based on actual analysis of the manner in which they function in the process of decision, but is usually content to parallel the line of attack of the new physics on the supposed certainty of scientific "laws of nature". The latter attack seems to have shattered the notion of a body of eternal and immutable rules dictating the happening of every occurrence in space and time;[7] but it has by no means caused scientists of the new school to believe that they can carry forward the work of science without continuing as before to formulate and employ scientific "laws".[8] Rather the new theory emphasizes the importance of such laws as tools of scientific procedure, even though cosmic validity has to be denied to them as patterns of absolute truth.

It is difficult to see what other bearing this development can have in the field of jurisprudence than to confirm by analogy the abandonment of the now discredited theory of absolute self-existent "natural laws";[9] certainly a rule of positive law devised by authority to meet a current need, and subject constantly to the possibility of revision or repeal, would seem precisely such a tentative "pragmatic" formulation as the new theory supposes scientific laws to be. To employ such rules in the process of decision carries no implication of belief in the attainment of an absolute metaphysical certainty.[10]

The analogy of the new conception of scientific laws has not, however, been developed by the progressive jurists toward the outcome just suggested. Instead, their imagination has been caught

---

[7] DEWEY, *op. cit. supra* note 3, at 205-9.

[8] Blumer, *Science without Concepts* (1931) 36 AM. J. OF SOCIOLOGY 515.

[9] DEWEY, *op. cit. supra* note 3, at 211; Dickinson, *op. cit. supra* note 1, at 20-5.

[10] See *infra* note 12.

by the resemblance between the new conception of a law of nature as "a formula for the prediction of the probability of an observable occurrence",[11] and Mr. Justice Holmes' fruitful suggestion that from a certain point of view jural law also is only a prediction of how future cases will be decided.[12] This analogy has fathered a far-flung demand for revision of the concept of jural law. Law, it is urged, consists of whatever will lead to better prophecy of how cases will be decided. We have noted, however, that decisions often depend largely on discretionary elements; henceforward whatever will aid in predicting how such discretion will be exercised is to be brought under the rubric of "law". Thus, if it can be anticipated on the basis of past knowledge that a police magistrate will exercise his discretion in accordance with the wishes of a particular politician, this fact, or knowledge of it, it is not quite clear which, becomes apparently a part of the "law" applicable to a case coming before that magistrate;[13] similarly "law" must include such a fact as that in jurisdictions where justices of the peace rely for their fees on amounts collected from defendants, there is likelihood that such officials will give judgments for plaintiffs. In short anything of which knowledge is useful to an attorney in deciding how to act in his client's interest is to be labelled "law".[14] The comprehensiveness of the result is startling to per-

[11] DEWEY, *op. cit. supra* note 3, at 206.

[12] "The prophecies of what the courts will do in fact and nothing more pretentious, are what I mean by law." HOLMES, COLLECTED LEGAL PAPERS (1921) 173.

[13] "The peculiar traits, disposition, biases and habits of the particular judge will then often determine what he decides to be the law. . . . If the personality of the judge is the pivotal factor in law administration, then law may vary with the personality of the judge who happens to pass on any given case." FRANK, *op. cit. supra* note 4, at 111.

[14] Speaking of the action of a tax official Professor Llewellyn says: "If the official's decision is adverse and erroneous, I should include as a subtraction from my effective legal rights, if I proceeded to get a reversal, the ill will and subsequent trouble I might incur at the hands of that official; as a part of the law, if I won; and its predictability as a determining part of the law if I decided not to fight." Llewellyn, *op. cit. supra* note 6, at 456. In other words law is accountable for the entire gross result of what happens in any given case, and since it is a prediction, it includes all that may go into that result. Turned about, a right does not exist at law except insofar as it is absolutely certain to be realized in fact. Here surely "law" and absolute certainty are identified more closely than by traditional theory, which admits that law does not always work out into fact.

sons accustomed to more conservative terminology, and there has consequently arisen a war about words in which for the moment the progressive dialectic is largely consuming itself.[15]

There seems no reason why the term "law" should not be expanded to include any and every kind of knowledge which is admittedly useful to lawyers and judges and law-teachers and law-students, unless it should seem desirable to preserve the word for a narrower use,—*i. e.*, unless there is possible advantage in maintaining a certain precision in the use of the term, thus making verbal distinctions more convenient between thought-units which sooner or later it may be desirable to contrast. For example, it may become desirable to keep distinct for purposes of discussion the fact of Judge *A's* known animosity to Lawyer *X*, and the fact that there is a rule of law which in a given instance the judge's animosity led him to disregard. If both the animosity and the rule are equally "law", it becomes difficult to state the situation in appropriate terms, or to find any proper standard for criticising the behavior of the judge.[16]

I

Whether the term "law" is expanded to include all that may shed light on future decisions, or is limited to mean rules of decision in distinction from discretionary elements which may enter into the making of decisions, the important thing from a practical point of view is to understand the way in which the rule-element and the discretion-element interact and coalesce in the

[15] Professor Llewellyn apparently suggests at one point, *ibid.* 431, that the term "law" should perhaps be abandoned as covering too many different kinds of things. This is an argument which has already been brought against the use of the term "sovereignty" and many other central concepts of legal and political thinking. To adopt the suggestion would mean the abandonment of some of our most familiar and focal, and therefore most useful, tools of thought.

[16] The problem of what actual consequences result from the application or attempted application of a rule of law includes as one of its aspects the question of the degree and kind of resistance which such application meets and the resulting question of how far such resistance deflects the actual results of the rule from its intended result. If the law is taken according to Professor Llewellyn's terminology (*op. cit. supra* note 6, at 459) as the actual results of the rule in action, if as he says: "Rules in the realm of action are what they do," it is difficult to see how the foregoing problems can be clearly faced. If the perverted result is taken as the "law", how can there ever be a perversion of law?

decisional process. This question is central even on the view that law is only an apparatus for predicting the outcome of future cases. The way in which we can predict how a judge will decide an issue on which a rule of law exists is after all different from the way in which we can anticipate from observed past uniformities how a muscle will react when brought into contact with an electric current. In the case of the muscle, prediction does not have to assume that the muscle will react with conscious intent to conform to a rule formulating its proper behavior under the circumstances. That is, however, precisely what a judge can and must in most cases be expected to do. Hence in predicting how a case will be decided, it is not merely pertinent to know the social, economic, political, psychological, physiological and other pressures operating unconsciously on the person of the deciding magistrate,[17] but also to know the rule of decision, if any, which exists for a case of the kind in question; for, if this be known, a fairly safe prediction may often be hazarded as to the judge's decisional behavior without knowledge at all of the more esoteric factors above enumerated. A rule of law is thus not a descriptive generalization of all the factors which influence the outcome of a case, but rather a formulation of a special and active kind of influence which operates on the mind of the judge and through that medium affects the outcome.

A rule of law, insofar as it is a prediction, is accordingly a prediction in a different sense from that in which a scientific law is a prediction of what will happen if two chemical elements are combined, or if a body with a certain mass and speed meets another body with a certain other mass and speed. Failure to give weight to this distinction is observable in much of the insistence of the newer jurisprudence that "law is what judges do, not what they say".[18] Understood in its proper technical meaning the statement

[17] Schroeder, *The Psychologic Study of Judicial Opinions* (1918) 6 CALIF. L. REV. 89. Haines, *General Observations on the Effect of Personal, Political and Economic Inflences in the Decisions of Judges* (1922) 17 ILL. L. REV. 96.

[18] This point, recently re-emphasized by Judge Cuthbert W. Pound (N. Y. Bar Ass'n Bull., Sept., 1929, 279, 282-83), has been insisted on by many of the more recent writers: Oliphant, *A Return to Stare Decisis* (1928) 6 AM. L. SCHOOL REV. 215 *et seq.*; Yntema, *The Hornbook Method and the Conflict of Laws* (1928) 37 YALE L. J. 468, 480; FRANK, *op. cit. supra* note 4, at 148 *et seq.*

is unexceptionable; but often it seems to carry the suggestion that by studying how past judges have acted we can predict the behavior of future judges in precisely the same scientific way in which a study of the past behavior of chemical reagents enables us to forecast their future reactions.[19] While it is true that a study of the decisional behavior of past judges can be expected to shed light on what their successors will do, this is for the most part dependably so only to the extent that judges follow rules and precedents, or in other words make a deliberate effort to imitate their predecessors. Resemblance based upon such deliberate and conscious imitation is fundamentally unlike the automatic repetition of like reactions in the behavior of physical bodies under like circumstances; for it operates indirectly through the mental understanding which the later judge has of what the earlier judge has done. It is therefore not simply a case of an act of an earlier judge repeating itself inevitably in the act of a successor, as one chemical reaction repeats another.[20] If the repetition were in this sense automatic,

[19] "An answer to these questions must . . . lead us to the opinion that the personality of the judge is the pivotal factor. Where then is the hope for complete uniformity, certainty, continuity of law? It is gone except to the extent that judges will all have substantially identical mental and emotional habits." FRANK, *op. cit. supra* note 4, at 133. So Professor W. W. Cook: "We as lawyers, like the physical scientists, are engaged in the study of objective physical phenomena. Instead of the behavior of electrons, atoms or planets we are dealing with the behavior of human beings. As lawyers we are interested in knowing how certain officials of society—judges, legislators, and others—have behaved in the past, in order that we may make a prediction of their probable behavior in the future." Cook, *The Logical and Legal Bases of the Conflict of Laws* (1924) 33 YALE L. J. 457, 475, quoted in FRANK, *op. cit. supra* note 4, at 129.

[20] "To call a decision the behavior of the judge is to confuse physically organic with social-teleologic categories. We usually mean by the behavior of the judge those physical acts which are connected with his organism. Doubtless the judge's organism functions when he speaks or writes; and we believe that it conditions his individual thinking, though precisely how, we do not know. But the legal effect of a judicial decision is altogether different from the physical effects of what is properly the judge's behavior. The latter is something in a physical *continuum* and it operates from point to point in time and space. But a legal decision relates situations remote in time and space through a purely logical connection. The logical relation involved in the question whether a given state of affairs can be subsumed under a rule laid down in a given decision, is a non-temporal one. As a social event, also, a legal decision does not operate on the pattern of physical causation. Whether, for instance, one on whom a decision is legally binding will actually obey it or not depends on an independent judgment and will. The decision orders me to pay, but I may decide not to, and it is not at all certain that the order of the court will be physically enforced." Cohen, *Justice Holmes and the Nature of Law* (1931) 31 COL. L. REV. 352, 365.

it would not be misleading to say that all we need to know for prediction is what past judges have done, for the connection between the past and future acts would lie in a set of common determining causes observable only through the resulting acts, and would not run through the medium and influence of words on the mind of the later actor. However it is precisely through the medium of words that the influence of past decisions does operate as a determining cause of future ones. The likeness of the future decision to the past decision is not involuntary repetition, but a deliberate imitated likeness resulting from the influence of the earlier decision on the thought processes of the later judge; and that influence operates almost altogether through the medium of verbal communication.[21] In this sense the form of words through which earlier decisions are transmitted to the minds of later judges becomes a factor of the highest importance.

Even, therefore, if we take our stand on the common law doctrine, addressed to a wholly different problem, that a case is "authority" only for what it actually decides,[22] and not for the words used in the opinion, it seems clear that a legal rule based purely on what judges have done and not on what they have said must itself be reduced to, and take the form of, language before it can enter as a factor into the decision of later cases. The forces which operate to produce a given chemical reaction under certain circumstances will produce the same reaction if the circumstances are repeated, irrespective of whether or not they have meanwhile been translated into a scientific formula. A legal rule however is not this sort of shorthand expression for relentless forces which thus operate irrespective of it, but is itself an independent active

[21] Professor Llewellyn notes that the effectuation of the purpose of "legal rules in the accepted sense of the term," or what he calls "official rules", "must be sought by means of verbal formulation. . . . Our officials move to a great extent on the stimulus, and in the light, of verbally formulated rules. In part, moreover verbal formulations . . . are an inherently essential tool of communication in a complex society; they are peculiarly important in a society which depends upon written records to maintain continuity of practice." Llewellyn, *op. cit. supra* note 6, at 451.

[22] Mr. Frank and those who think like him are apparently led by the common law verbal formula that a case is "law" to the conclusion that the act of deciding a case is the same thing as "making a law", with the result that the law made is law for that case and for no other case. FRANK, *op. cit. supra* note 4, at 137.

force. Whether the rule is based on the mere facts and results of past decisions, or whether it also takes account of the reasons which judges have put in words for those decisions, it is equally under the necessity of depending for its operation on being translated into a verbal formula.

The attitude of the newer psychology toward the function and importance of words is an aspect of current science which juristic progressives neglect in this connection in favor of analogies drawn exclusively from the physical sciences. Their position seems to be that since words are often instruments of loose thinking, and have characteristics which prevent them from attaining the accuracy of scientific symbols, legal thinking must be emancipated from "verbalism" by escaping from words to "facts".[23] Recent psychological investigations, however, have only served to fortify the long familiar belief that thinking is almost wholly synonymous with the language process.[24] It is therefore no more a disparagement of the influence of legal rules to admit that they are "forms of words" than to say that their formation and application involve acts of thought. The extreme behaviorist himself admits the importance of words by promoting thought itself to the status of "laryngeal behavior".[25] Even, therefore, if we insist on conceiving the behavior of a judge under the influence of a verbal rule as on a par with the reaction of a muscle to the stimulus of an electric current,[26] it becomes all the more important

[23] For an attack on "verbalism", based on the theories of C. K. Ogden and others that primitive "word magic" persists insofar as modern thought is dependent on language, see FRANK, *op. cit. supra* note 4, at 57 *et seq.*, 84 *et seq.* Similarly Dean Leon Green has argued that the possibility of developing a true science of law is retarded because lawyers have not risen above the "word-level". *The Duty Problem in Negligence Cases* (1928) 28 COL. L. REV. 1014.

[24] See especially LORIMER, THE GROWTH OF REASON (1929) *passim*. In contrast with the writers cited in the preceding note the trend of thought represented by Lorimer regards verbal thinking as the necessary medium of the higher intellectual processes. "Verbal processes (spoken or silent) supply the dominant systems of all typically human intellectual life." (*Ibid.* 71.) "Once established as an important mode of social control and mental life, words become both the trellis and the tendrils of human culture; they are the support of civilization and undergo constant revision and refinement in every new field of experience." (*Ibid.* 78.) See also RIBOT, THE EVOLUTION OF GENERAL IDEAS (1899); DELACROIX, LA LANGAGE ET LA PENSÉE (1924).

[25] WATSON, BEHAVIORISM (1925) 190 *et seq.*

[26] WATSON, PSYCHOLOGY FROM THE STANDPOINT OF A BEHAVIORIST (1919) 331 *et seq.*

to understand the way in which the form of words called a "rule" causes him to react.

Here it is necessary to guard against an apparently widespread misunderstanding. In distinguishing between the influence of rules on the one hand and discretionary elements on the other in the processes of judicial thinking, we are, of course, not dealing with separate physical entities interacting on one another mechanically. The discretion-element and the rule-element, when both are operative, are but moments in a single decisional process. This does not, however, mean that for understanding the process it may not be convenient to distinguish the two elements in our thinking about them in the same way that even so satisfactorily modern a philosopher as Dewey finds it continually desirable to distinguish between the element of *datum* and the element of intellectual effort in the thought process, wherein neither functions without the other.[27] In the same way the legal rules with which a judge is familiar exert an influence on his progress toward the decision of a case which can be intellectually marked off for discussion from the operation of concurrent influences more purely private to himself, and therefore designated as discretionary.[28] These discretionary influences may in various ways affect and qualify the influence exerted by the rule, as we shall see later; but that only adds another reason for distinguishing the two.

II

The view that law is a prophecy of what will be decided has the weakness of emphasizing exclusively the outside spectator's

[27] DEWEY, *op. cit. supra* note 3, at 123-124, 147-149, 164-165, and *passim*.

[28] Speaking of the distinction between "law" and "discretion" Mr. Frank says: "Words have an emotive value, and to say that part of what a judge does is 'not-law' or 'non-legal' is to create the impression that part of the judge's conduct is tinged with impropriety." Therefore, apparently on the ground that it would be improper for anything done by a judge to be "not-law", Mr. Frank assigns that it is impossible to distinguish "what Pound calls law and what he calls not law" (*i. e.*, discretion). "They are so thoroughly intermingled that it is impossible to divide them; nothing but false attitudes can be engendered by labelling either of these components as if it were not a necessary, and therefore desirable, part of the processes of law." FRANK, *op. cit. supra* note 4, at 141. It would, however, appear that the possibility of distinguishing two objects of reflection is an altogether different question from the question whether one of the two is necessary or desirable.

point of view—the point of view of the advocate or client who is interested in reading the future,—and consequently of ignoring the point of view of the judge through whose active agency the future is to be transmuted into fact. It is submitted that the sound way to anticipate a future decision is to attempt to put oneself in the place of the judge or judges who will actually make the decision. The judge will find himself confronted with one or more legal rules applicable, or conceivably applicable, to the case before him. For him these rules cannot be conceived as mere rules of prediction. He is not interested in predicting what he himself is about to do. The standpoint of prediction is that of the observer; the judge's attitude towards the rule is that it is a guide or mandate for action,[29] bidding him consider certain aspects of a case and not others, and reach one decision or another according as certain factors are or are not present. Only by thus visualizing the judge as he stands in the presence of the rules which will help him to decide, can an outsider undertake to make accurate forecast of what decision will be reached. From this standpoint, what judges have done in the past becomes only indirectly of importance for purposes of prediction; because what they have done will influence the decision only insofar as formulated into a rule which the judge regards himself as bound to follow, and which therefore, to a greater or less extent, limits and focuses his discretion.[30]

There seems a certain confusion about what is meant by saying that a judge in deciding a case "feels bound" to permit rules of law to influence his decision, or in other words, that he regards such rules as "authoritative". There is no reason for understanding this to mean that the judge takes a mystical view of the suprem-

---

[29] Professor Llewellyn says that "rules of law in the accepted sense" are not eliminated from his conception of the workings of the judicial process. They are "rules of authoritative *ought*, addressed to officials, telling officials what officials ought to do." Llewellyn, *op. cit. supra* note 6, at 449.

[30] Cook seems inferentially to recognize this where he says: "The case is by hypothesis new. This means there is no compelling reason of pure logic which forces the judge to apply one of the competing rules urged on him by opposing counsel." Cook, *Scientific Method and the Law* (1927) 13 A. B. A. J. 303, at 308. This must mean that if there are such things as "old" cases the judge in such a case may be forced by the compelling reason of logic to apply an existing rule.

acy of legal rules, or treats them with any superstitious reverence.[31] All that it signifies is that he accepts the working assumption of every system of law that a certain amount of uniformity between decisions on similar points is socially desirable, since otherwise men would not attempt to have a legal system at all, but would be satisfied to entrust themselves to the purely discretionary authority of an oriental *cadi*.[32] Assuming the desirability of aiming at some uniformity, the only practical way to secure it is for different judges to recognize and abide by an obligation to bring their decisions into unison by giving effect in those decisions to the same legal formula or rule. In all this one need see nothing superstitious or mystical, although mystery and superstition doubtless had their part in starting the process,[33] as they had in starting other processes during early stages of human history; under present conditions the objective is merely the practical one of getting decisions made in a way which will somewhat restrict the purely personal and incalculable reactions of individual judges by causing them to give controlling influence to considerations which have to a certain extent been standardized for all judges in the jurisdiction.

---

[31] "The Law—a body of rules apparently devised for infalliby determining what is right and what is wrong and for deciding who should be punished for misdeeds—inevitably becomes a partial substitute for the Father-as-Infallible-Judge. That is, the desire persists in grown men to recapture, through a rediscovery of a father, a childish, completely controllable universe, and that desire seeks satisfaction in a partial, unconscious, anthropomorphizing of Law, in ascribing to the Law some of the characteristics of the child's Father-Judge. The childish longing is an important element in the explanation of the absurdly unrealistic notion that law is, or can be made, entirely certain and definitely predictable." FRANK, *op. cit. supra* note 4, at 18. See also *ibid.* 196-203, 267.

[32] Mr. Frank's theory is in fact an argument for reversion to the *cadi*. He says: "The honest, well-trained judge with the completest possible knowledge of the character of his powers and of his own prejudices and weaknesses is the best guaranty of justice. Efforts to eliminate the personality of the judge are doomed to failure. The correct course is to recognize the necessary existence of this personal element and to act accordingly. Indeed, as Ehrlich puts it, this personal element 'should not be tolerated as something unavoidable but should be gladly welcomed. For the one important *desideratum* is that his (the judge's) personality must be great enough to be properly instrusted with such functions.' The central problem of adequate administration of justice is 'how to organize the judiciary so as to give plenty of scope to strong personalities.'" FRANK, *op. cit. supra* note 4, at 138.

[33] See Dickinson, *Social Order and Political Authority* (1929) 23 AM. POL. SCI. REV. 605-608.

One of the objections brought against legal rules is that actually they do not have this result; that in fact the judge reaches his decisions on the basis of his personal reaction towards a case as a whole in its individual uniqueness, and then simply casts about and finds one or another of the forms of words called legal rules which he can attach to his conclusion for the purpose of rationalizing it.[34] This argument against the effectiveness of legal rules is much in the mouth of law-school teachers. The reason why it appeals to them is not far to seek. It is approximately true when applied to decisions of appellate courts which establish creative precedents, and these are precisely the decisions which find their way into "case-books". Here a court in deciding a new case to which one or more rules seem applicable with equal plausibility purports to bring the case under one rule rather than another, and it is quite true in such instances that it is not a rule of law but some non-legal consideration which ultimately accounts for the decision. This type of case, however, by no means exhausts or even fairly represents the operation of legal rules, and even in cases of this type the influence of rules has often a somewhat larger part than at first sight appears.

There is, however, a large and important class of cases in which it is not too much to say that the outcome is in fact directly dictated by a legal rule without the intervention of judicial discre-

[34] It is no doubt true that frequently the mind of the judge may be made up as to what decision to reach before consciously searching for legal grounds upon which to base the decision. That this is uniformly the case, however, as suggested by Mr. Frank and other recent writers (FRANK, *op. cit. supra* note 4, at 100 *et seq.*), can hardly be accepted. Even where the judge thus comes to a conclusion in gross before consciously seeking reasons, it is highly likely that his conclusion has been reached in part upon the basis of legal rules whose influence upon his mental process has become automatic. It would not seem sound to assume as so many anti-rationalistic modern writers do, that a conclusion must be reached for no reasons at all and that reasons are merely tacked on to it afterwards. It is quite true that in balancing the applicability of various possible grounds of decision a judge may ultimately be determined by a flash of insight, "a hunch" (Hutcheson, *The Judgment Intuitive: The Function of "the Hunch" in Judicial Decisions* (1929) 14 CORN. L. Q. 274); but this process is not unknown to practitioners of mathematical reasoning (POINCARÉ, SCIENCE ET METHODE (1912) 50 *et seq.*) and by no means implies that previous generalizations have not been at work in striking the balance which is registered by the intuition. Mr. Frank recognizes this when he says that "rules and principles of law are one class of stimuli which make a judge feel that he should try to justify one conclusion rather than another." FRANK, *op. cit. supra* note 4, at 104.

tion in the smallest degree. Suppose for example that a purported will is offered for probate which bears the signature of but one witness in a jurisdiction where two are required by the statute. The rule of law which requires that the witnesses shall be two operates with the deadly inevitability of a guillotine to decide the question of probate. Similarly where land is claimed under a deed from a married woman not signed by her husband, in a jurisdiction where the law requires the husband to join in the deed. The automatic operation of direct specific rules of law of this character is seldom sufficiently brought home to professional teachers of law and students in law-schools. It does not always appear from a study of litigation, because cases where the rule thus leaves absolutely no doubt are seldom litigated. But this does not mean that the automatic operation of legal rules in situations of this kind is not of the utmost importance from the standpoint of the value of law as an agency of social order. It is one of the great preventives of litigation. It enables counsel to advise their clients with an assurance which does not need to be tested by resort to the courts in every instance. It operates with equal value in another way. Clean-cut and specific rules make it possible for men to accomplish in their business dealings the legal results they intend without the necessity of constant recourse to the courts to resolve doubts. Thus it is well established that a deed expressed in certain words and executed, acknowledged and recorded in a certain way will have the legal effect of transferring land from one person to another without having to be adjudicated. Similarly a check will serve to transfer a right to money in such a way that no doubt will arise about the validity of the transfer. These results are made possible by the practically automatic operation of legal rules which are so simple and specific that legal scholars do not ordinarily find them interesting.

Where the bar is reasonably well educated, cases which reach the stage of litigation are all cases presenting a substantial element of doubt. This doubt is not necessarily, however, as to the legal rule or rules applicable; often the rule is clear, but doubt exists as to the facts of the situation to which it is sought to be applied. This is true of perhaps the largest number of controversies litigated in *nisi prius* courts which are not carried forward into courts of appeal. Thus the rule is clear that if an individual requests another to supply him with specific goods at a certain price and the other agrees to do so, and in accordance with the agreement does supply the goods, the former is legally bound to pay the agreed price. There may, however, be doubt as to the facts of a given case,—doubt, that is, whether the defendant did actually request the plaintiff to supply the goods, or whether the plaintiff did actually supply them. The decision of the case will turn on the conclusion reached as to what happened between the parties. The case is accordingly one which may well be taken into court, but it comes there not because of any uncertainty in the applicable rule, but solely because of uncertainty about the facts. Such a case will almost never get beyond a lower court except on a point of evidence or procedure; and therefore the vast mass of litigation of this character is seldom impressed on the attention of teachers who teach from case-books. The conditions of their work invite them, unless consciously vigilant, to overlook the obvious.

In a third variety of cases, which includes most of those decided by appellate courts, the issues are relatively more complex. They involve the application not of a single rule, but of a number of rules. In these cases the part played by any particular rule in determining the decision is less mechanical than in those hitherto considered. Any one rule may dictate or aid in determining the decision of a particular issue which will affect the ultimate decision of the case as a whole without necessarily determining it. Thus a legal rule applicable to one issue frequently operates merely to determine whether or not there are other issues in the case which are entitled to determination. For example there is a New Jersey rule that whether or not certain kinds of fraud afford ground for dissolving a marriage depends on whether or not the marriage was consummated.[35] Here the rule requires that the fact of non-

---

[35] Ysern v. Horter, 91 N. J. Eq. 189, 110 Atl. 31 (1920); Dooley v. Dooley, 93 N. J. Eq. 22, 115 Atl. 268 (1921).

consummation must be established before it becomes important to determine whether or not fraud of the character in question has been committed. Only if the marriage has been consummated is the fraud material. Similarly in actions against carriers, where the plaintiff has taken a bill of lading with a clause exempting the carrier from liability, the legal rule allowing or denying effect to such an exemption stands guard at the outset of the case to determine whether or not the issues relating to the cause and nature of the damage are entitled to influence the decision.

In cases of any complexity it may thus be said that legal rules, even if of a highly specific character, operate on the decision mainly by determining whether or not any issues, and if so which ones, remain to be decided in order to reach an ultimate decision of the case,—operate, that is by guiding the attention of the adjudicating official to certain particular issues rather than others, and by making his ultimate decision of the case as a whole meet the test of consistency with the decisions which are determined or influenced by the pertinent rules as to these particular issues. In the absence of rules, the attention of the official would be free to wander at large over the manifold elements of the case so that the ultimate decision might be reached on the basis of any factor or factors which for the time being loomed largest to the judge's mind. The operation of rules is to make certain factors the primary elements before the judge's attention, and to push other considerations into the background until he has reached conclusions on those which the rules single out as primary.[36] It thus helps him to decide without making the ultimate decision for him; it supplies a structure for his thought to follow, it draws a sketch map for him of the way into and through a case.

[36] Mr. Frank, *op. cit. supra* note 4, at 127n., 135n., and writers who have the same point of view seem to think it impossible that the mind in reaching a conclusion can be influenced by general propositions, but only by specific facts which appeal to them as relevant. There would seem to be no proper ground for this assumption. It might be significant to ask why an individual regards a specific fact as relevant? If he thinks reflectively, *i. e.*, if he thinks at all, does he not regard a fact as relevant precisely for reasons which bring the specific fact under a generalization? This is aptly and amply pointed out by Morris Cohen in his recent article, *op. cit. supra* note 20, at 361.

III

The degree in which the ultimate decision of a case will be controlled by legal rules depends in part on this matter of the relative complexity of the case, *i. e.*, the number and mutual relation of the various applicable rules, and in part on the character of the rules themselves, *i. e.*, on their relative definiteness or vagueness, and their closeness or remoteness of application to the fact-situations to which they are sought to be applied.

Where a case is complex enough to involve a considerable number of rules, the relation between these may be such that once the fact-situation is settled, they will practically dictate the decision. Take, for example, the case of a person who has been injured while riding on a railroad train. He holds a ticket to a station at which the train is scheduled to stop. The ticket contains a clause exempting the carrier from liability for negligence. The injury occurs through the breaking of an axle which the carrier cannot prove to have ever been tested. However, the plaintiff at the time of the injury was riding on an outside platform of the car. The legal rules applicable to these facts are so related and connected in their operation that once the facts are established the rules up to a certain point practically dictate the result. The exemption from liability is ineffective. Therefore if the plaintiff has grounds for action he can recover. Failure by a carrier to cause equipment to be tested constitutes want of care for which it is liable to a passenger. However, a person riding in a part of the train where he had no right to be without authorization from the carrier is not entitled to the duty of care which the carrier owes to passengers. The decision will therefore turn on the question of whether or not any train official permitted the plaintiff to ride on the platform. If no one employed by the company saw the plaintiff on the platform, so that there is no question of such authorization, the case is decided; if the plaintiff was so observed, the question arises as to whether the employee was authorized by the carrier to give such permission and whether his conduct amounted to giving permission. The legal "rules" as to what will amount to such authority, and what conduct by an authorized agent will confer such permission, are of broader and looser scope than the other rules involved, and their "application" to the facts therefore leaves larger leeway for discretion in the manner which remains to be discussed below.

There is another class of cases where the rules involved do not thus fit into a sequence guiding the conclusions of fact toward a decision, but where one rule which seems applicable to certain facts in the case is capable of sustaining a result at variance with another rule which may conceivably apply to the same or other facts. Thus the earlier Married Women's Property Acts did not expressly confer on a married woman the right to sue her husband. However, they provided that a married woman should enjoy her separate property free from interference or control by her husband. Suppose that under such a statute a husband collected rents which had accrued on property belonging to his wife. Clearly this would amount to a violation of a legal right of the wife under the statute. Did this provision of the statute, in order that it might be given effect, operate to confer on the wife a power to sue the husband, although the statute did not expressly amend the common law rule in this respect? Whenever a fact-situation thus creates possibility of conflict between two rules of law, the opportunity arises for a *creative precedent*,—for a decision, that is, which will make a new rule of law to cover a doubtful case. The creation of such a new rule involves something more than is usually involved in the application of existing rules; it involves choice and balance between the rules themselves by an exercise of legislative discretion.

Choice and balance, however, are frequently involved even in the application of existing rules. This is what was meant above by saying that the extent to which a rule governs a decision depends not merely on the nature of the case and the number of rules involved, but also on the nature of the rule itself and particularly on its relative definiteness or vagueness. Thus in the case already considered of the rule requiring two witnesses to a will, no choice or balance between opposing considerations is involved in applying the rule to an instrument bearing only one signature besides that of the testator. Not merely is the rule specific, but the case to which it is to be applied is such as to fall squarely within it. There are cases, however, where doubt may arise as to the application of even such a highly specific rule. For example a will may on its face bear the signature of two witnesses, thus apparently satisfying the rule, but doubt may be raised as to the genuineness of one of the signatures, or as to whether or not it was duly affixed in the presence of the testator as required by law. Such cases illustrate that issues may have to be decided by conclusions as to both facts and law before it can be determined whether even a highly specific rule has been complied with, though in the great majority of cases the application of the rule is practically automatic and no such questions arise.

Many legal rules, however, are not thus specific; on the contrary they are expressed in forms of words which on examination permit considerable latitude as to what may or may not be included within them. The most familiar example is the basic rule of negligence law that liability results from failure to employ "due care under the circumstances". Obviously "due care under the circumstances" is a concept which leaves wide leeway to the agency applying it to a specific case. In "applying" a rule of this character composed of terms so broad that they have been referred to as "India rubber concepts", the decision of the adjudicating agency is substantially a discretionary act, determined, inside the limits of the broadest possible meaning of the rule, by the interplay of a mass of subjective influences, prejudices, pre-conceptions, of which the adjudicating officer himself can be expected to give no complete or adequate account, and of which he is probably in the normal case not even aware.[37] But the decision is not determined completely by such imponderables. The imponderables themselves are at least confined to those which can be suggested, however remotely, by the idea of "due care"; and in the midst of their protoplasmic incertitude emerge firmer structures of crystallized social opinion, as, for example, that a person crossing a crowded street must look about him, and certainly ought not to read a book

[37] For the character of decisions on points of this kind and the nature of the elements entering into them, see Bohlen, *Mixed Questions of Law and Fact* (1924) 72 U. OF PA. L. REV. 111.

as he goes. Such crystallized judgments, when present, are not subjective; what is subjective, however, is the degree of influence which any such consideration will have on the adjudicating officer in any particular case. They are the material for a possible rule of law, and may actually be on the way to becoming such a rule, as has happened, for example in the case of the so-called "stop, look, and listen rule" which in some jurisdictions precludes recovery by one who has failed to stop, look, and listen before crossing a railroad track. Here a consideration which might otherwise merely influence the mind of the tribunal if it chose to be influenced, has become a rule of law because the tribunal has come to feel authoritatively bound not merely to give weight to it, but to allow it determining effect on the decision.

The degree to which legal rules are elastic depends on the elasticity of the words in which they are formulated, and hence on the extent to which the meaning of given terms has become particularized in legal usage. There is a rule, for example, that a person must be "accepted" as a guest at a hotel before the hotel-keeper incurs the special liability which the law imposes in favor of guests. What acts or acquiescences by a hotel-keeper will amount to "acceptance"? The contour of the concept is shadowy. This indefiniteness of contour characterizes even concepts which at first sight appear to be delimited with a fair measure of precision. Take the familiar rule of negotiable instruments law that a promissory note must be expressed to be payable in "money". It would seem that the term "money" is sufficiently specific to indicate its content with precision; but the number of cases which have been litigated discloses the room for doubt which remains as to whether or not certain media of payment fall within the legal meaning of "money".[38]

In all these instances the determination of whether or not to treat a given state of facts as included within the terms of a rule, where the meaning of those terms is not sufficiently narrowed

---

[38] Burton v. Brooks, 25 Ark. 215 (1868); Chambers v. George, 5 Litt. (Ky. 1824) 335; Lampton v. Haggard, 3 T. B. Mon. (Ky. 1826) 149; Farwell v. Kennett, 7 Mo. 595 (1842); Cockrill v. Kirkpatrick, 9 Mo. 688 (1846); Thompson v. Sloan, 23 Wend. (N. Y. 1840) 71; Chrysler v. Renois, 43 N. Y. 209 (1870); Taylor v. Neblett, 4 Heisk. 491 (Tenn. 1871).

to indicate the case as specifically included, involves that kind of choice between possible considerations uncontrolled by any authoritative determining factor which we have called discretion. Once the decision has been made, however, as to whether or not a given state of facts falls within a rule, it will, so far as treated as a precedent, establish what amounts to a subordinate rule that for the future a state of facts of that kind is to be included under the rule. This is what happened, for example, in the case of the "stop, look, and listen rule" above referred to, and this is the way in which the structure of the law is gradually built up from precedent to precedent, so that each more general rule ramifies with the multiplication of decided cases into an ever larger number of more specific rules of inclusion and exclusion.[30] Of course, where a rule is expressed in extremely broad terms, like the rule of "due care", so that the fact-situations presented for possible inclusion vary infinitely from case to case, it follows that for the larger number of possible situations no subordinate rules develop because of the infrequency of the recurrence of any particular situation. Where this is true, we say that each situation is left to be decided on its own "facts", which means that it must be decided, within the rationally possible outside limits of the rule, by discretion uncontrolled by any factor recognized as authoritatively decisive.

In all these ways the opportunity for discretion to influence decisions is very great, as was emphasized at the outset of this paper, and the controlling influence of rules is correspondingly narrowed. A still further enlargement of the field of discretionary influence results from the necessary power of the adjudicating tribunal to determine the "facts" of a case, or in other words to reach a conclusion as to what happened between the parties, before going on to decide the legal consequences to be attached to those facts. Obviously if the parties acted in a certain way, the case may fall within the scope of one rule, while if they acted in a different way, a different rule will apply. For example, if the tribunal reaches the conclusion that as a matter of fact a steam-

---

[30] For the growth of law through the successive singling out of new facts as having legal pertinence see DICKINSON, ADMINISTRATIVE JUSTICE AND THE SUPREMACY OF LAW (1927) 202-5.

ship company has not been in the habit of permitting deckhands on its steamboats to accept goods for shipment, the rights of a shipper leaving goods in the custody of a deckhand will not be covered by the legal rules prescribing the relations between shipper and carrier. Similarly in a case where it is claimed that a deed was given as a mortgage, if the court finds as a fact that the grantor's intention was to give a deed and not a mortgage, the case is excluded from the operation of rules applying to mortgages. This power of finding the facts confers on the adjudicating agency a wide area of discretion in many types of cases to determine whether legal rules of one tenor, or others of opposite tenor, shall apply to the determination of the case. There can be no doubt that occasionally courts employ this power of finding the facts to evade the necessity of applying a legal rule to a case to which it would otherwise be applicable, and to that extent the effectiveness of any rule in controlling the action of courts and in facilitating the prediction of decisions may be seriously impaired.[40]

IV

The question of how far a rule, which is a general proposition, can control particular states of fact, and how far particulars inevitably escape such subsumption, is an aspect of the fundamental problem of the relation between "particular" and "general"[41] in human thought. The result of what has so far been said is substantially that the operation of legal rules in determining decisions of particular cases is subject to the same limitations as the application to specific facts of any generalizations which are employed as a basis for reasoning towards conclusions from those facts. Jurists of the sceptical school are correct in pointing out

[40] This point is very heavily relied on by FRANK, *op. cit. supra* note 4, at 134-135, also 127n. and is noted by Llewellyn, *op. cit. supra* note 6, at 450.

[41] I adhere to this mode of expression because it usefully points out an important distinction in the terms in which that distinction has customarily been expressed. It is desirable to note, however, that recent thinkers have pointed out that "general" and "particular" are relative terms with reference to one another and that any given item of experience includes both particular and general according as attention is concentrated on one or another aspect of it. HALDANE, THE REIGN OF RELATIVITY (1921) 47-48. Because of this fact Whitehead regards "universal" and "particular" as misleading in their suggestion. WHITEHEAD, PROCESS AND REALITY (1929) 76.

that legal rules enjoy no advantage in this respect over other rules. The essential difference between a rule of law and a non-legal rule is not, however, in this matter of its operation in the reasoning process, but rather in the peculiarity that it commands acceptance by the adjudicating agency as a basis for reasoning, while in other fields of thinking there is greater subjective freedom to pick and choose between possible variant rules. It is a presupposition of a system of law that a legal tribunal feels and must feel a sense of obligation to employ in the decision of litigated controversies those applicable rules which happen to be stamped as authoritatively legal, irrespective of whether the tribunal agrees with them, and whether or not it would employ them if they were not so authoritative.[42] Only an appellate court will exercise its power to decide a case in disregard of a rule which it feels has once been accepted as authoritative, and in the rare cases where the power is exercised, it must be for reasons far stronger than would cause the disregard of commonly accepted general propositions in some other field of thought.[43]

One primary source of confusion in the position of the sceptics is that they fail to distinguish between two separate problems,—between this problem of acceptance by the courts of particular rules as authoritative to the exclusion of other possible

[42] "A rule, that is become settled law, is binding on the courts, and is to be followed. 1 W. Bl. 181; 1 Eden 250; 7 Bing. 279, 280; 3 Ves. 529; 7 Ves. 199; 1 Russ. 423; 3 Russ. 35; 1 Sch. and Lef. 5. And a rule, that is become settled law, is to be followed, although some possible inconvenience may grow from a strict observance from it, 4 M. & S. 352; or although it is not 'bottomed in reason,' 7 Durn. and E. 415; or a satisfactory reason for it is wanting, 8 Bing. 536, 537, 557; or although the principle of the rule appears to be doubtful, 14 Ves. 449; 16 Ves. 196, 197; or although both the principle and the policy of the rule may be questioned, 3 Russ. 435; or although in some cases it may be productive of hardship and oppression, 1 Durn. & E. 8; 7 Bing. 280; 2 Ves. Jun. 426; or although it has been objected to and lamented by great authority, 2 Younge and J. 623." Ram, The Science of Legal Judgment (2d Am. ed. 1871) 83-84.

[43] An illustration of the duty of courts to apply an existing rule of law even though they may disagree with it, and even though the purpose for which the rule was adopted has disappeared, is given by Max Radin in the case of the statutes adopted in many Western states which granted a bounty for coyotes' scalps. "The ultimate purpose was unquestionably that of extirpating coyotes, or, at any rate, of reducing them in number. It turned out that coyote farms were established and coyotes bred in order to collect the bounty. Yet the statute was so nearly determinate that it took little color from this remoter result, and it would have been an unlawful violation of duty for a court to disregard the sharp limitations of the statutory extensibility." Radin, *Statutory Interpretation* (1930) 43 Harv. L. Rev. 863, 879n.

rules, and the quite different problem of the extent to which rules, even if accepted as authoritative, can and do determine particular decisions. The adherence of courts to authoritative rules is for the obvious practical purpose of securing some degree of uniformity between decisions with certainty. The position of the sceptics seem to be that this effort is misdirected because rules do not actually dictate decisions.[44] Since in addition to the rule an element of discretion often turns out to be necessary, they conclude that rules are superfluous and that decisions should be committed to discretion entirely. This clearly amounts to more than an attack on the acceptance of legal rules as authoritative, since the argument for abandoning the authority of rules goes on a ground which in effect denies the value of all reasoning from rules. Any use of rules involves reasoning from supposed uniformities; and if uniformities are in fact fictitious, all reasoning which proceeds by resort to rules must be unsound.[45] If on the other hand rules in spite of their limitations supply a valid element in the reasoning

---

[44] "What, with unfortunately few exceptions, judges have failed to see is that in a sense all legal rules, precepts, concepts, standards—all generalized statements of law are fictions." FRANK, *op. cit. supra* note 4, at 167.

[45] It is a natural consequence of Mr. Frank's general position that he would not have a judge in deciding a particular case seek for a rule of decision which will be applicable to other cases (*op. cit. supra* note 4, at 153-154). He feels that any ground of decision which is applicable beyond the particular case will not afford a just ground for deciding that case since it will necessarily disregard some of the unique features of the case. Here once more we are thrown back upon the question whether an intelligent decision on any particular state of facts can be reached without reference to considerations which reach beyond that particular state of facts. One reason why the modern writers object to the application in a later case of the ground laid down in an earlier case as the ground of decision for that case is apparently because they take what seems an impossibly exalted view of precedent. Thus Frank writes, "The rules which a judge announces when publishing his decision are intelligible only if one can relive the judge's unique experience while he was trying that case,—which, of course, cannot be done. One cannot even approximate that experience as long as opinions take the form of abstract rules applied to facts formally described. . . . You are not really applying his decision as a precedent in another case unless you can say that, having relived his experience in the earlier case you believe that he would have thought his decision applicable to the facts of the latter case." *Ibid.* 150. These sentences in effect deny the possibility of reasoning from general propositions since they imply that no rule which governs one set of particulars can be employed as a precedent to govern another set of particulars unless both sets of particulars are absolutely identical in the minutest details. It is precisely the function of any generalization to be applicable to different sets of particulars which may differ from one another in many respects. Generalization is a rough medium of approximation, and therein consists its usefulness if its function is properly understood.

process, then there is at least no inherent objection to consciously accepting, as lawyers and judges do, certain rules to the exclusion of others as a basis for reasoning toward legal decisions.

The reason why the sceptical school so strongly object to the fact that courts in reaching their decisions employ rules which are stamped as authoritative appears to be primarily because this method is not followed by modern thought in other fields than the adjudication of legal controversies, and particularly because it is not followed in scientific thinking.[46] The modern scientist when called upon to solve a problem does not feel obliged to reason from any particular propositions because they bear the *imprimatur* of authority. Time was, in the history of science, when the contrary was true; when the scientist felt bound to reach conclusions, irrespective of what the facts might show, which were in accordance with settled and authoritative propositions [47] in the same way that a judge feels bound to reach his decision of a case in accordance with settled legal rules. It is clear that in the case of science the abandonment of this procedure was essential to progress, and that so long as it persisted it made any real science impossible. Under the influence of analogy progressive jurists assume that what has been good for science must be good also for law,[48] and that the abandonment of reasoning from legal rules will make possible a corresponding advance in the administration of justice. This conclusion involves failure to note the difference between the objectives of scientific thinking and the nature of the problems to which it addresses itself, as contrasted with the judicial thinking which is directed toward deciding litigated controversies in accordance with law. The distinction is fundamental. It needs to be

---

[46] FRANK, *op. cit. supra* note 4, at 82-83, 285-288.

[47] An interesting illustration of this attitude is the story recounted by Myerson (L'EXPLICATION DANS LES SCIENCES, v. I, 119) of Father Scheiner who reported his discovery of sun-spots to the provincial of his order and was told by the latter that such a thing could not be. "I have read," said the latter, "my entire Aristotle several times and I can assure you that I never found there anything of the sort. Go, my Son, calm yourself and be sure that it is defects in your lenses or in your eyes which you take for spots in the sun."

[48] "There is danger in the assumption that legal science resembles physical science to such a degree that methods which have proved successful on the one hand necessarily will be valid when applied to the other." Goodhart, *Law and the State* (1931) 47 L. Q. REV. 118, 138.

elaborated in view of the fact that most of the attention which has recently been given to questions connected with human thought-processes has been in relation to scientific thinking, and that conclusions reached in connection with scientific thinking have been unreflectingly transferred and applied to judicial thinking.[49]

Some of the confusion between scientific thinking and the judicial thinking which is directed towards deciding controversies has no doubt been promoted by the insistence of Dewey and his followers that the objective of scientific thought is action,—is to inform human beings what to do.[50] Clearly the objective of judicial thinking is also action, in the sense that it aims to inform the judge how to act with reference to the case before him. From this point of view the objectives of the two types of thought seem superficially the same. But on analysis there becomes apparent an essential difference which was set in clearer relief by the older conception of scientific thinking. According to the older form of statement, the object of scientific thinking is not to inform an actor how to act, but rather to describe what will happen if a given situation is left undisturbed, or is disturbed in a particular way. Dewey's conception does not affect the validity of this conception,—it merely adds to it by emphasizing why men may wish to know what will happen. Since it is true that men are dominantly interested in what will happen because they may wish to adapt their conduct to the future situation, it is to this extent true that men's ultimate interest in action stimulates and to a certain extent may be said to account for scientific thought. It remains true, however, that scientific thought itself is not directly concerned, and indeed, so far as it is scientific, is not concerned at all, with how men may choose to act in view of the situation disclosed by science; it stops with disclosing the situation.

The aim of science may therefore still be accurately described as discovery. The scientific procedure of discovery rests on the assumption that, given identical conditions, what has happened

[49] See, *e. g.*, Rueff, From the Physical to the Social Sciences (1929). In the introduction (xxviii) Professor Oliphant states "there is no difference in the nature of the subject matter of law or of any other social science, as contrasted with physics, for example, which precludes a like rigid scientific pursuit."

[50] Dewey, *op. cit. supra* note 3, at 104-105, and *passim*.

once will happen invariably. Scientific thought, therefore, concerns itself with analyzing and classifying the elements of given fact-situations and determining their relations to one another for the purpose of acquiring ability to predict the relations between these elements if recurring in a future situation. This procedure involves the same basic thought-processes which are also involved in the procedure of judicial thinking,—the isolation of identities, their formulation in general propositions, and the application of these propositions to specific situations. Here, however, the resemblance ends.[51] The aim of science being discovery, its concern with its general formulations is primarily to test them for their conformity to future situations. The interest of the scientist in a scientific "law" is to determine the degree of accuracy with which it turns out to describe a future case,[52] and if possible to supersede it with a new generalization which will make possible a description having a higher degree of accuracy. In a sense therefore the generalization is created with the idea of being overthrown; it is created with specific understanding that its application to future cases shall be for the purpose of testing its validity. Each specific case thus controls the generalization; each future happening supplies a standard to which a scientific proposition must conform at the risk of being rejected for some other proposition which will state the observed facts more closely.

---

[51] Of course in cases when there is doubt as to what the rule of law *is*, then under a system of law which adopts the doctrine of precedent it is necessary to "discover" the rule from past adjudications. The method of doing this seemed to Hammond and Bishop, and apparently still seems to Llewellyn and Cook, the same method as that whereby scientific laws are discovered. Legal rules seem to Llewellyn discoveries of what "is". Thus he writes: "Real rules . . . are descriptive, not prescriptive, except insofar as there may be occasionally implied that the courts ought to continue in their practices. Real rules, if I had my way with words, would by legal scientists be called the practices of the courts, and not rules at all. . . . Factual terms. No more. . . . They are on the level of *isness* and not of *oughtness*. . . . Their intent and effort is to describe." . . . Llewellyn, *op. cit. supra* note 6, at 448. It is important to note, however, that a legal rule, even though derived by generalization from what has been done, is not a rule of "isness" because it either may or may not be applied in the next case, *i. e.,* the case for which the rule is sought, depending on the volition of the judge. There is thus no possibility as in the case of a scientific rule of testing the "correctness" of the rule by seeing whether the instant case conforms to it. In other words the uniformity between cases is an imitated, not a scientific or physically necessitated, uniformity.

[52] DEWEY, *op. cit. supra* note 3, at 205 *et seq.*

This whole procedure is radically different in intent and method from the kind of reasoning which is directed toward deciding controversies by the application of law. Once more the distinction can best be explained by recourse to older conceptions, in this instance the long-established distinction between scientific and so-called "normative" thinking.[53] The decision of controversies by recourse to authoritative rules is an instance of normative thinking. The goal of normative thinking is not discovery; the judge who is called on to decide whether or not to award damages to a plaintiff is not, like the scientist, engaged in the discovery of new truth, or in adding to the sum total of human knowledge. The judge does not employ the case before him as a means of testing the validity of the rules which he employs in reasoning towards his decision. The whole theory of decision according to law is that the rules are to govern the case, and not, like scientific laws, to be governed by it.[54] Normative thinking rests on the assumption that it is socially beneficial that action shall be taken which is in accordance with a rule primarily because it is in conformity to observed fact, and the reason for applying the rule raises a different issue which is not for the moment in question.

In the case of a scientific rule, the problem of applying the rule and the problem of testing its "correctness" are substantially one and the same problem, since "correctness" means only conformity to observed fact and the reason for applying the rule in scientific experiment is primarily to determine its conformity to fact. In the case of a normative rule, on the other hand, the problems are distinct. The reason for applying the rule is not directly or immediately concerned with determining its "correctness". This is not the task of ordinary judicial thinking, which is concerned with deciding in accordance with rules because they happen to be the established rules, but is the task of what, for the purpose of emphasizing the distinction, may be called "construc-

[53] Cohen, *op. cit. supra* note 20, at 358; see also Dickinson, *op. cit. supra* note 1, at 285, 289 *et seq.* 1 GÉNY, SCIENCE ET TECHNIQUE EN DROIT PRIVÉ POSITIF (1914) 179-181.

[54] "There is a real danger for the stability of our law if it comes to be believed that the contingency of rules of law is of the same nature as the contingency of the laws of mechanics, physics or chemistry." A. KOCOUREK, AN INTRODUCTION TO THE SCIENCE OF LAW (1930) 209.

tive juristic thought," which is concerned with the criticism and formulation of rules.[55] This constructive thought must at one time or another be performed by practically all judges in dealing with difficult or unprovided cases,—*i. e.*, cases not falling clearly under an existing rule; but it does not form the principal function of *nisi prius* judges, or even of appellate courts except in connection with new and difficult cases. It is, however, an essential factor in the judicial process, and as such can only be understood in connection and contrast with the more usual type of normative thinking which is concerned with the application of rules.

The term "correctness" has a different meaning when applied to a scientific and to a normative rule. Normative rules, which are statements that in certain kinds of fact-situations certain action is to be taken, are not statements that any fact-situations will occur, and therefore cannot be tested by conformity between actual and predicted occurrence. What we mean by saying that they are correct is that the action which they prescribe will produce a result which for one reason or another we regard as the result that ought to be produced in contrast with other results which are physically capable of being produced.[56] To determine the correctness of a rule in this sense, a double process is necessary. There must first be determined the fact-consequences which the application of the rule can be expected to produce; secondly there must be determined whether this result should be regarded as desirable.

The determination of the consequences which may be expected to follow from the fact of applying a normative rule involves, like

---

[55] See *ibid.* 43; but Kocourek apparently confines his attention to the criticism of rules enacted by legislatures. The same type of criticisms is of course applicable to judge-made rules.

[56] Llewellyn's interest in descriptive rules, which are generalized statements of the past action taken by courts and officials, as contrasted with rules which are verbal commands to officials, turns out in the last analysis to be only an interest in causing the verbal rule to be altered so as to produce the result desired by giving the right command to the officials. Thus he says: "Since the ultimate effectuation of a purpose is in terms of action, of behavior, the verbal formulation to be an efficient tool must be such as will produce the behavior desired. This turns on the relevant prevailing practices and attitudes of the relevant processes." Llewellyn, *op. cit. supra* note 6, at 452. Again he says that the draftsman of a statutory rule "must so shape it as to induce its application". *Ibid.*

other "scientific" determinations, simply the possibility of establishing connections between past observed and future observable facts. The difference between the establishment of such connections in the field where legal rules operate,—*i. e.*, the field of social relations,—on the one hand, and in the fields of physics and chemistry on the other hand, is a difference in the nature of the subject-matter and not in the basic character of the problem. It has frequently been pointed out that the subject-matter of social relations, because of the infinitely greater complexity of the facts which compose them, the greater number of interconnections between these facts, the vaguer and less determinate way in which identical facts or types of facts can be isolated, and above all because of the impossibility of controlled experiment, presents vastly greater difficulties for the formulation of generalized statements of relations between causes and consequences than is true in such sciences as physics and chemistry where the inquirer is solely concerned with relations between such relatively simple and controllable facts as weight, size, shape, and motion.[57] It has, therefore, seemed to many that the effort to establish scientific generalizations which shall formulate connections between relevant social facts with anything approximating the accuracy of generalizations in the field of the natural sciences is doomed from the outset to failure because of these differences, and that generalizations are only possible for the trivial and the obvious. However, modern social science is for the moment busy with the development of various statistical and other measuring devices which it is hoped may result in making possible generalizations which will have some degree of accuracy. The possibility of developing such generalizations is of the highest interest to legal thinkers insofar as it is desirable for purposes of constructive legal thought to estimate the fact-consequences of the application of rules of law, and, in this country especially, many progressive legal thinkers are for the moment directing their whole attention to it. This work deserves to be done, if for no other reason than to determine the limits beyond which it may ultimately be found impracticable to

---

[57] 1 GÉNY, *op. cit. supra* note 51, at 172-179.

estimate the results of law by other than old-fashioned rule-of-thumb methods. One unfortunate consequence, however, is that the concentration of many legal scholars on work of this character tends not merely to withdraw their attention from other essential aspects of legal thinking, but even leads them to deny the existence of these other aspects of what is after all a single problem. The result is that they tend to conceive legal thinking exclusively in terms of scientific thinking, with the consequence of confusing and obscuring the ways in which science can be of real service to law.

After the fact-consequences of applying a legal rule have been estimated by methods of observation, either scientific or rule-of-thumb, a further step still remains for the determination of the "correctness" of the rule. This involves the determination of whether or not the predictable fact-consequences are desired or desirable. Whether they are desired is a fact-question insofar as it concerns, for example, whether they are desired by the parties to the controversy, or by the opinion of particular groups in the community. The ultimate question, however, is whether they are desired by the judge or other agency responsible for making the decision, and this is in substance the question of whether in the eyes of that agency they are desirable. Here we are once more confronted with a question which calls for normative thinking by the judge or the legal scholar who undertakes to criticize the rule. Whether or not the consequences of a rule are desirable is not a question which can be ultimately decided by the mere scientific determination of connection between cause and consequence. To assume that it can be so decided is to assume, as Dewey and some other recent thinkers apparently do, that the desires of human beings are ultimately uniform and that disagreements are due simply to confusion or ignorance as to proper methods for attaining those desires. Only from this standpoint can it be taken for granted, as Dewey and others seem to take for granted, that science by disclosing the consequences of a rule of conduct affords a test of its desirability. Science may indicate the method of attaining the object of a desire, but if ultimate desires differ, mere predictions of fact, which is all that science has to offer, cannot decide between them. A more sophisticated view, which recognizes that there can be other differences than differences as to fact-relations, must leave room for the solution of such differences by other methods than appeals to fact. The only resort in such cases is to norms of value, and it is by reference to such norms that the decision must ultimately be made as to whether or not a legal rule having certain predictable consequences is a desirable rule.[58] The normative thinking which is involved in making such a decision differs in one important respect from that which is involved in the simpler task of applying an established legal rule to the decision of a controversy. In the application of a rule of law, the rule itself supplies the norm; in testing a rule for desirability, after determining what its fact-consequences will be, the norm must be some generalization which is found outside of and above the law, and which therefore is not vested with the sanction of authority which is attached to legal rules.

In view of the present direction of interest of many legal scholars, it seems desirable to point out that the relative importance of predicting the probable factual consequences of a legal rule is not always as great as it is now generally assumed to be. There are, of course, certain rules whose social consequences are properly regarded as the most important factor in determining their validity so that the determination of these consequences becomes of the highest importance. This is true, for example, of the rules which govern the liability of employers for injuries to their employees,—the so-called fellow-servant rule, the rule of assumption of risk, and the like. The effect of these rules in imposing difficulties in the way of recovery by injured workmen produced a definite consequence on an entire social class which had a positive bearing of the most significant kind on the question of the

[58] "The idea of a normative science cannot be replaced by the idea of pure technique, of a practical art. For technique tells us that if we wish to achieve one or another result we must employ such or such means; but it does not tell us to aim at one objective rather than another. Normative science on the contrary has as its characteristic the fact that it is addressed to free will, that is to say to the human capacity to choose between different possible acts, in order to fix the determination of such choice by means of its rules." Norero, *La Philosophie de Wundt* (1908) 16 REVUE DE METAPHYSIQUE ET DE MORALE 214-243, quoted in 1 GÉNY, *op. cit. supra* note 51, at 68n.

desirability of the rule. However, there are many legal rules to which such widespread social consequences cannot be traced, and of which it is hard to estimate the consequences to others than the parties immediately affected in the relatively infrequent cases to which the rules apply. Take for example the question of whether or not a finder of a lost article who has had repairs or improvements made to the article shall be entitled to recover the value of the improvements from the owner after the latter reclaims the article.[59] It is clear that the consequences of allowing such a recovery would be to throw a possible burden on the owner of lost property. Social consequences, however, there would seem to be none. In such a case the question of the correctness of the rule is accordingly limited to the immediate value judgment presented by the rule itself without the necessity of any elaborate intermediate observational process. The same thing is true in connection with the rule that a woman who has lived with a man under the belief that she is his wife is not entitled to recover the value of her services on learning that he has a wife living.[60] In cases of this character the rule itself raises at once the question of the comparative value of the opposing interests involved and that question has to be faced directly without the aid of data supplied by statistical procedure. Such procedure is of assistance only in the case of rules which have definite and widespread social implications.

It thus appears, in summary of what has been said, that legal rules at various times form elements in a number of different types of thought-processes. In the simplest and commonest case where they are employed by a lawyer in advising a client or by a court in deciding a litigated case, the process of reasoning is concerned simply with the question of whether a given fact-situation falls within the rule,—whether the rule is to be applied to the fact-situation in question for the purpose of determining, or aiding to determine, the decision of the case. In the second place, legal rules form elements in the process of constructive legal thinking, *i. e.*, of determining whether or not a rule which is admitted to apply authorita-

[59] Chase v. Corcoran, 106 Mass. 286 (1871); STORY, BAILMENTS (2d ed. 1840) 391; 2 KENT COMM. (Holmes's ed. 1873) 256.

[60] Cooper v. Cooper, 147 Mass. 370, 17 N. E. 892 (1888).

tively to a given situation, is the rule which ought to apply in contrast with other conceivable rules. In this procedure of constructive legal thought the rule figures in two types of processes. On the one hand it figures in a process of scientific reasoning to determine what will be the fact-consequences of its application; on the other it figures in a process of comparison with some norm of value to determine whether or not these consequences are desirable, *i. e.*, whether they are consequences which ought to be brought about through the action of the state. If it should be determined that the application of a rule to a particular type of case will have consequences which for one reason or another are regarded as undesirable, this result, if reached by a private jurist, may lead to advocacy of the repeal or amendment of the rule; if reached by a court of last resort in the exercise of its judicial function, it may bring about an abandonment of the rule or a narrowing of it so as to exclude from its operation the particular case in question.

Usually all these different processes go on together and at one and the same time. This is particularly true in the unofficial thinking of legal scholars who are primarily interested not in advising clients but in discussion and criticism of the legal system. It is also true of the thinking of courts in dealing with cases which do not fall squarely under an established rule and in the thinking of courts of last resort when presented with the argument that an established rule should be abandoned or narrowed. Inevitably where the different processes thus go on at the same time they are not kept formally distinct. The natural tendency toward economy of effort leads to their combination in a single process. The part which each different process plays is taken for granted and in most instances is well understood and leads to no confusion. On the other hand the result is sometimes to generate confusion in the thought of speculative jurists through undue concentration of attention upon a single phase of the process.[61] This is what seems to have occurred in the thinking of some recent progressive jurists with the result that a mass of confusing theory has originated which needs to be cleared away by a reiteration of the elementary

[61] This has been noted by Llewellyn, *op. cit. supra* note 6, at 439.

and the obvious before sound progress can be made towards considering the technique of legal thinking in the application and elaboration of law. The whole argument of this paper has been concerned with this emphasis on the obvious for the purpose of brushing aside false issues and misleading lines of approach. Only after this has been done does it become possible to proceed to the consideration of the central question of the way in which the application and elaboration of rules are affected by considerations of logic on the one hand and by discretionary considerations of policy, taste, and value judgments on the other.

[20]

SOME RATIONALISM ABOUT REALISM

HERMANN KANTOROWICZ†

IT should be stressed from the outset that this article is meant as a criticism and is therefore directed exclusively against those sides of the realist movement in American jurisprudence which are open to criticism. I do not intend to give a comprehensive picture of the whole movement, nor do I minimize the admirable achievements of the realists, especially in the field of research. Moreover, I do not deny that my remarks can be criticized on the ground that the realists teach the contrary of what I say they teach. It is indeed one of their weak points that it is possible to find in their writings contradictions of many of their assertions. It will therefore be necessary to give a number of literal quotations in order to prove my criticism, but I know and admit that I could give other quotations to the contrary. These contradictions are to be found in the same author, often even in the same article, still more often in different authors. For the realist movement—and this is another difficulty for the critic—does not form a school or a party; it has no caucus, no boss, no platform, no slogans. It suffices to name some of the adherents in order to realize that one can not expect them to agree. Their senior is the "great dissenter," Oliver Wendell Holmes, and among his followers there are such different personalities as Bingham, Clark, Cook, Frank, Llewellyn, Oliphant, Moore, Patterson, Radin and Yntema.[1] But nevertheless they agree in two fundamental postulates, one, a substantive postulate regarding the nature of the law, the other, a formal postulate regarding the nature of legal science. It is these fundamental theories alone which I wish to discuss here.

The substantive theory is that the law is not a body of rules but of facts; the formal theory, that legal science is not a rational but an empirical science. I do not assert that these theories are simply untrue; I shall try to show that they are exaggerations of the truth. But the truth is not original. The nucleus of the substantive theory was developed by a Franco-German movement which produced the free law doctrine;

†Professor of Law, formerly at Kiel University (Germany), now at The New School for Social Research, New York. This article is in substance the same as that read in Professor K. N. Llewellyn's Seminar, Columbia University, in April, 1934.

1. For a bibliography of Legal Realism see Llewellyn, *Some Realism about Realism* (1931) 44 HARV. L. REV. 1222, 1257-1259, with additions in 1 LLEWELLYN, PRAEJUDIZIENRECHT UND RECHTSPRECHUNG IN AMERIKA (Leipzig 1933) 120 *et seq;* 2 *id.* 350. See the excellent historical survey in Auburtin, *Amerikanische Rechtsauffassung und die Neueren Amerikanischen Theorien der Rechtssoziologie und des Rechtssocialismus* (1932) 3 ZEITSCHRIFT FÜR AUSLÄNDISCHES ÖFFENTLICHES RECHT UND VÖLKERRECHT 529-567.

the nucleus of the formal theory, by a German-American movement known as the sociological school of law.[2]

The free law doctrine teaches (if we may sum up an elaborate system in a few words): The traditional sources of the law, the "formal" law, statutes and precedents, have gaps which must be filled up, must be filled up with law if the decision is to be a judicial decision, and this law must have a general character if equality before the law is to be maintained; the gap-filling material must therefore consist of rules, rules of law. These are "free" law in the sense that they are not formal law: they have not been formalized but are still in a state of transition like bills, principles of policy, business customs, inarticulate convictions, emotional preferences. Many of them are formulated for the purpose of a concrete judicial decision by the courts, acting within their discretion, through acts of will and value-judgments, and constitute therefore judge-made law. Their validity is far less than that of the formal law and sometimes nil, but their practical importance is even greater, because, where the formal law is clear and complete, litigation is not likely to occur. This free law thesis has been exaggerated by those realists who teach that law consists of judicial decisions alone, and therefore of facts.

The sociological school of law teaches that the law must be interpreted according to its aims, that these aims are to be found in its (desirable) effects on social (including economic) life, and that therefore the law cannot be understood nor applied without the aid of a sociological (including economic) study of social reality. This sociological thesis has been exaggerated by those realists who teach that legal science is itself a sociological, and therefore an empirical science.

Both schools have their fountain-head in Rudolf Jhering.[3] The free law school was developed in France by Geny and his many followers, in Germany (and Austria) by men like Ehrlich, Fuchs, Kohler, Mayer, Radbruch, Sternberg, and Zitelmann. It apparently has no adherents in this country.

The sociological movement has been headed in Germany by Ehrlich, Heck, Hedemann, Nussbaum and the greatest of sociologists, Max Weber; in America by Mr. Justice Brandeis, Mr. Justice Cardozo and Dean Pound. The writer has himself had a certain share in both movements.[4]

---

2. The most complete bibliography (and history) of both movements is to be found in GÉNY, MÉTHODES D'INTERPRÉTATION ET SOURCES EN DROIT PRIVÉ POSITIF (2d ed. 1919), with additions in GURVITCH, LE TEMPS PRÉSENT ET L'IDÉE DU DROIT SOCIAL (1931) 213-295.

3. KANTOROWICZ, AUS DER VORGESCHICHTE DER FREIRECHTSLEHRE (Mannheim 1925) 38 *et seq.*

4. *Cf.* TAT UND SCHULD (Zürich 1933) 25 *et seq.* with bibliography (since 1906). The

But for the realist exaggerations he is not responsible, although he has sometimes been praised for them.[5] It is disagreeable enough for a man to have to pay alimony for his own illegitimate issue; but he cannot be expected to pay for other men's bastards, and like it.

Returning to the American counterparts of these two schools of legal thought, let us examine two of these exaggerations, as found in the assertions of the American realists, and point out the strange consequences to which their treatment of both the substantive and the formal theories must lead. Here again, however, it must be admitted that statements of opposite tenor are to be encountered, and even emphasized, in the writings of certain realists, especially in those of Llewellyn,[6] who notwithstanding his radical bearing, belongs to the moderate group of the movement.[7] These other statements are to the effect that the law is not exclusively a body of judicial decisions, but also a body of rules, and that legal science is not only a sociological, but also a rational science. However, these moderate views scarcely any one will dispute; they were comparatively new thirty years ago, but are now accepted almost universally—in theory, though not in practice.

The realist movement owes its astonishing growth to the radical theories stated above. These are the doctrines which threaten the quiet progress of science. It cannot, therefore, be considered unfair if I restrict my criticism to the radical theories of the realist movement; other critics such as Adler, Cohen, Dickinson, Fuller, Goodhart and Dean Pound have done more or less the same.[8] It is for the realists themselves to avoid such unilateral criticism in the future by changing their "vocal behavior," as they would call it. They should abandon these radical views, confine themselves to voicing their moderate doctrines, and continue, by all means, their excellent research work which does not presuppose their untenable postulates and does not clash with their tenable ones.

The Nature of the Law According to the Realists

In setting forth the realists' concept of the nature of law, let us adduce a number of typical quotations:

---

article most easily available for American readers is Kantorowicz, *Legal Science—a Summary of its Methodology* (1928) 28 Col. L. Rev. 679, with footnotes by E. W. Patterson.

5. Llewellyn, *The Constitution as an Institution* (1943) 34 Col. L. Rev. 1, 10; Book Review (1934) 43 Yale L. J. 516.

6. See Llewellyn, *supra* note 1, at 1241.

7. Fuller, *American Legal Realism* (1934) 82 U. of Pa. L. Rev. 429, 433, 441 n. 26, 450, 460.

8. Adler, *Law and the Modern Mind: A Symposium* (1931) 31 Col. L. Rev. 82, 91; Cohen, Law and the Social Order (1933) 198 *et seq*, 357 *et seq;* Dickinson, *Legal Rules*

"I use the phrase 'the law' in the sense of sequences of external facts and their concrete legal consequences through the concrete operation of governmental machinery."[9]

"This past behavior of the judges can be described in terms of certain generalizations which we call rules and principles of law."[10]

"Rules, whether stated by judges or others, whether in statutes, opinions or text-books by learned authors, are not the Law, but are only some among many of the sources to which judges go in making the law of the cases tried before them . . . The law, therefore, consists of decisions, not of rules. If so, then, whenever a judge decides a case he is making law."[11]

"What these officials [the officials of the law] *do about disputes is, to my mind, the law itself."*[12]

". . . the theory that rules decide cases seems for a century to have fooled not only library-ridden recluses, but judges."[13]

"To say that a legal institution,—private property, the federal government of the United States, Columbia University,—exists is to say that a group of persons is doing something, is acting in some way."[14]

The realists' conception of the Law, their substantive thesis, is therefore: the Law is not a body of rules, not an Ought, but a factual reality. It is the real behavior of certain people, especially of the officials of the Law, more especially of the judges who make the Law through their decisions, which, therefore, constitutes the Law.

Before we criticize this theory, one logical observation may be permitted. The discussion, by all means, must not degenerate into a fruitless logomachy—one man understanding by law, this, and another desirous of understanding something else. This question is far more than a terminological dispute. It has momentous consequences. Whatever we define as "law" must be the chief subject among those which the "law" schools teach, or ought to teach; whatever we define as "law" must be the topic, or the chief topic, of the science of "law"; and whatever, in an American discussion, is defined as "law" must be in harmony with positive American Law insofar as it uses the expression "law." Now, for instance, the judge charges a jury on questions of law, not of fact; the error in fact sometimes excuses, the error in law does not;

(1931) 79 U. OF PA. L. REV. 833, 1052; Fuller, *supra* note 7, at 429 *et seq.;* Goodhart, *Some American Interpretations of Law,* in JENNINGS, MODERN THEORIES OF LAW (1933) 1; Pound, *The Call for a Realist Jurisprudence* (1931) 44 HARV. L. REV. 697.

9. Bingham, *What is the Law?* (1912) 11 MICH. L. REV. 109, n. 29. Obviously Bingham defines "the law" by the concept of "legal."

10. Cook, *Scientific Method and the Law* (1927) 13 A. B. A. J. 303, 308.

11. FRANK, LAW AND THE MODERN MIND (1930) 127-128.

12. LLEWELLYN, THE BRAMBLE BUSH (1930) 3. Italics are those of the author quoted.

13. Llewellyn, *supra* note 5, at 7.

14. Moore, *The Rational Basis of Legal Institutions* (1923) 23 COL. L. REV. 609.

appellate jurisdiction is not the same over law as it is over fact. This alone should suffice to show that in the interpretation of American law, and for that matter of European law also, we must distinguish between law and facts. For this reason alone a theory which ignores this distinction by calling only factual behavior "law" breaks down at the outset. But then, how can we explain the commission of such an elementary mistake by distinguished jurists?

The explanation is that it is based on extrajural dogmas, on erroneous assumptions, not about the law but about the philosophy of law. It is, therefore, based mostly on unconscious *prejudices*, six of which may be pointed out. Fortunately, we can illustrate this connection between the theory and the underlying prejudices by means of literal quotations from Llewellyn, who is as outspoken in his premises as we have seen him to be in his conclusions. The illustrations are confined to the writings of a single author, in view of the indubitable fact that Mr. Llewellyn is considered the most representative among American realists. It ought, however, to be pointed out, that the same views could be traced in the writings of other realists, especially in those of Joseph W. Bingham, Jerome Frank, and Max Radin.

1.

"If rules decided cases, one judge would be as good as another, provided only the rules had been adduced before him."[15]

This displays the formalistic prejudice, which, by the way, is common also to many critics of realism. It is a prejudice to believe that the Law consists of nothing but formal law handed down by tradition, and it is fatal to overlook those rules which a judge must form whenever the formal law has a gap. Of course, only the best judges, only lawyers who know more than law, who have thoroughly studied, not only experienced, real economic and social life, its effects and its needs, are capable of conceiving and formulating the proper rules for the concrete cases. One should not object that this would be a task solely for the judge's discretion. Discretion is not opposed to rules, as is usually said; it is an intuitive way of finding rules: those "inarticulate major premises," which must be general if they are to be *major* premises, and which must be rules of law if they are to serve as major premises for *judicial* decisions.

2.

"An inch from the eye is a portion of the Text; the whole living world behind is 'covered' by it . . . It is institutions which validate the Words, not the Words which validate the institutions . . . To study the Words of a Document . . . is to invite inattention to either [governmental] effects or needs."[16]

15. Llewellyn, *supra* note 5, at 7.

16. Llewellyn, *supra* note 5, at 17, 35.

Here we are faced by the verbalistic prejudice: it is erroneous to believe that the law is the wording of the Law, still more erroneous to believe that it is the printed document. This prejudice overlooks the fact that only the *meaning* of the Law counts in the decision. But every interpretation, however free and audacious, must be at least compatible with the text, with one of its possible meanings. Here lies the great significance of the language technique as a means of interpreting the wording of statutes and decisions. The frequent attacks on words are therefore unjustified. Whatever the relation of thought to language may be, words are indispensable tools for fixing and communicating legal ideas; even an attack on words must be couched in words. If I myself have rejected the old conception of legal science as that of a *Wortwissenschaft,* I have meant that the words of the Law must not be considered in the way the professional word scholar, the philologist, considers them. The philologist interprets them as they were subjectively meant, the lawyer as carrying an objective meaning which must be construed by highly technical means. This meaning can remain unaltered even if the words are changed—many rules of English law have been translated from law-French without essential alterations of their meanings and vice versa—and this shows that the subject-matter with which the lawyer deals is not words but their meanings.

3.

"If rules decided cases, law stood still . . . whereas growth and change of law were as striking in nineteenth—and twentieth—century America as they have ever been. . . . At the beginning of a code experiment, intent of the language has a clear and proper bearing on men's actions. . . . The words are thus—at the beginning—best read in terms of the legislative history. . . . But even here, intent cannot rule purely. Some cases have *not* been put in the debate. Resort must then be had to language and circumstance, to 'obvious' rather than to real intent."[17]

This is what may be called the historical prejudice. To the historian, of course, the Law is an historical act; its meaning is the original, the "real" intent of the makers of the statute or of the drafters of the decision, and therefore unchangeable like everything that is past. To the jurist the Law is the objective meaning of statute or opinion, that which the legislator or the judge would have meant if he had been able to fit his meaning into the whole body of the Law. As Mr. Justice Holmes has said: "We do not inquire what the legislator meant; we ask only what the statute means." That which we call the "life" of the Law, its constant adaptation to constantly changing social conditions, is due to this objective method more than to anything else.

17. Llewellyn, *supra* note 5, at 7, 12-13. *Cf.* HOLMES, COLLECTED LEGAL PAPERS (1921) 207.

4.

"Let us assume a case not involving any doubt, but a case nevertheless which would never have occurred to anyone at the time the rule in question was established. . . . The legislator could not have *intended* the inclusion of this case *in concreto;* the case was by hypothesis not yet thought of."[18]

This introduces the nominalistic prejudice (in the philosophical meaning of the term). The nominalist overlooks the fact that the language of the legislator, like most language, is chiefly related to classes of things, not to individual objects. With the same right, one could oppose the application of any statute because it speaks of persons, and the litigating persons were not yet born when the statute was enacted.

5.

"The existence of an institution lies first of all and last of all in the fact that people do behave in certain patterns a, b and c. . . . Every living constitution is an institution; it *lives* only so far as that is true."[19]

Here we have the sociological prejudice. It is not true that social phenomena can be studied by themselves without regard for the rules that govern them. Gray has given a brilliant example: "Suppose King, Lords and Commons should meet in one chamber and vote together, an order passed by them would not be obeyed by the English people." The pure sociologist could not explain this phenomenon. In the same way we may ask: Which is the institution with which Llewellyn identifies the Constitution of the United States? Is it Columbia University? Or some speakeasy? Certainly not, but the Congress is one of them. Why? Only because it acts more or less according to the rules of the Constitution. No constitutional institution can be singled out among all other institutions except against the background of the rules of the Constituion.

The sociological bias is particularly prevalent among constitutionalists who are obviously dazzled by the frequent contrast between the legal and the factual aspect of the state and the immensely greater interest attached to the latter. But I challenge any sociologist to describe, for instance, the difference between sovereign and non-sovereign states and between states and municipalities in terms of power, size, population or other factual elements. The first attempt would evince the futility of any such effort.

6.

Of the last prejudice, the professional one, examples have already

18. Correctly translated by Fuller, *supra* note 7, at 445, from the German of 1 LLEWELLYN, *op. cit. supra* note 1, at 72, 74.

19. Llewellyn, *supra* note 5, at 17. *Cf.* GRAY, THE NATURE AND SOURCES OF THE LAW (2d ed. 1921) 76.

been given. The realists constantly speak of the Law as the behaviour chiefly of the judges. Why chiefly of these? Because the judges are the persons whom the attorney has professionally—directly or indirectly—to handle; and the realists are attorneys, or have been attorneys, or else they are trainers of attorneys. But f we are to speak as real realists, not as mere legalists, the behavior of every normal layman, of everybody standing in any normal jural relation to anybody else, is infinitely more important; for the great majority of these jural relations never come before the courts. We now understand why the realists, instead of focusing their attention upon the invisible certainty of the law in the normal cases, are obsessed by the obvious uncertainty of the law in the few contested cases. If they were more conscious of the logical distinctions between the legal and the sociological approach they would give full credit to the latter method and would accordingly be more interested in those phenomena which influence and shape the whole body of society, not only the functions of one important organ of it, the courts of law.

The Nature of Legal Science According to the Realists

As shedding light upon the realists' conception of the nature of legal science, the following quotations are significant:

"The prophecies of what the courts will do in fact, and nothing more pretentious, are what I mean by the law."[20]

". . . lawyers, like the physical scientists, are engaged in the study of objective physical phenomena. . . . As lawyers we are interested in knowing how certain officials of society—judges, legislators, and others—have behaved in the past, in order that we may make a prediction of their probable behavior in the future."[21]

The realists "want law to deal, they themselves want to deal, with things, with people, with tangibles, with *definite* tangibles, and *observable* relations

20. Holmes, *The Path of the Law* (1897) 10 HARV. L. REV. 457, 461, reprinted in HOLMES, *op. cit. supra* note 17, at 173. This dictum of Mr. Justice Holmes could also have been quoted *supra*, p. 000 of the text, as he does not distinguish between the Law and the Science of the Law. *Cf. id.* 10 HARV. L. REV. at 458, HOLMES, *op. cit. supra*, at 168: "The primary rights and duties with which jurisprudence busies itself again are nothing but prophecies." If this were true, the prophecy and the prophecied event would be the same. *Cf.* also, Bingham, *supra* note 9, at 11, 12: "His [the lawyer's] essential business is to predict these future sequences accurately . . . it is a field for scientific study analogous to the field of any other science. . . . [When the word law is used in the sense of 'studying law' or 'the law of property'] the speaker or writer consciously or unconsciously indicates by it causal relations of occurrences external to the mind of the observer and their governmental consequences, past or potential."

21. Cook, *The Logical and Legal Basis of the Conflict of Laws* (1924) 33 YALE L. J. 475. *Cf.* also, Oliphant, *A Return to Stare Decisis* (1928) 14 A. B. A. J. 159: "Not the judges' opinions, but which way they decide cases will be the dominant subject matter of any truly scientific study of law."

between definite tangibles—not with words alone; when law deals with words, they want the words to represent tangibles which can be got at beneath the words, and observable relations between those tangibles."[22]

"The 'normative' conception of legal science . . . precludes the objective narration of conventional legal principles by confusing law and ethics . . ."[23]

According to these quotations, then, legal science is not a rational and normative science which tries to transform the given law into a more or less consistent system of rules. To the realists, legal science is empirical, the method of which is observation; the purpose, foretelling effects; the model, natural science. This naturalistic thesis clashes with the oldest teachings of logic as well as with modern conceptions of methodology. It is based upon confusion of categories. It will suffice to point out six of these confusions.

First of all, the realists confuse *natural* and *cultural* science. Natural science deals only with real events governed by laws of nature. Even if it should prove to be true that these laws were nothing but statistical averages, they would always remain inviolable in the sense that facts can never contradict them, since they would then cease to be laws of "nature." At the same time the harmony of observed facts with the laws of nature provides a test for the reality of the facts. But cultural sciences deal with human actions and are governed by laws of men, and these actions can be either lawful or unlawful. Indeed, they are very often unlawful, and it is precisely the existence of unlawful acts which makes legal science necessary; it alone allows us to judge unlawful acts and this presupposes the knowledge of how they *ought* to have been. But these unlawful acts are quite as real as the lawful acts. For this reason a natural science which knows nothing of "unlawful" and, therefore, of unreal acts, nor of unreal and, therefore, of "unlawful" acts, can teach us nothing decisive. Ours is a science which must learn to distinguish between lawful and unlawful acts, which must be able to judge the unlawful ones and therefore must previously know the unreal acts which *ought* to have been real. The natural science which a realist should study is that part of astronomy which might teach us how the stars ought to move, and how they move and whenever they choose to violate the laws of celestial mechanics. Unfortunately, such a branch of astronomy has not been developed, and if a person actually developed it, he would probably look to legal science for guidance, not vice versa.

Secondly, the realists confuse *explanation* and *justification*. If legal science were an empirical science, its chief method would be explanation through cause and effect. If it were a rational and normative science,

22. Llewellyn, *supra* note 1, at 1223.

23. Yntema, *The Rational Basis of Legal Science* (1931) 31 Col. L. Rev. 925, 945.

its chief category would be justification through reason and consequence. Now let us approach the courts in a realistic attitude and ask which of these methods they in fact apply, for the actions of courts must be an application of legal science to a concrete question. Must a court refuse to apply a clearly worded statute if it fails to understand its historical causes or the intentions of the legislators, on the ground that a judgment based on such a statute cannot be scientifically explained? Not at all. The question chiefly interesting the judge is whether the decision he wants to give can be justified as a consequence of the particular statute, or at least as being compatible with its consequences. And what about an appellate court which has to pass on an absurd decision of the trial judge, explainable, and only explainable, by the fact that the judge was intoxicated or insane? Must his decision be upheld on the ground that it has been explained and therefore satisfies legal science? On the contrary, it will be reversed because it cannot be reasonably justified by law, and this is the only question which interests the appellate court. Genetic explanation and normative justification must be kept apart—this is one of the most important lessons of modern epistomology. It may be sense or nonsense to explain with Jerome Frank that the "childish' desire to attribute inviolable certainty to the law is caused by a "father complex"—in any case the truth or untruth of that alleged attribution is quite independent of its psycho-analytic or any other genetic explanation. Of course, the genetic method may be used as a tool in the service of the normative method and vice versa.

The third confusion is between *law* and *ethics*. This is the reproach which the realists make to the classical, normative conception. But their misgivings are entirely due to their own mistake, their confusion of legal with moral norms. The former demand some external behavior and can be complied with whatever may be the motives. The latter always take into account the motive—for instance, a selfish or altruistic aim.

Fourthly, the realists fail to distinguish between *realities* and their *meaning*. Llewellyn wishes to restrict legal science to "observable" and even "tangible" facts. Now the essential relations in law are never observable; for instance, at the same moment that a man dies in an accident without having made his will, his new born child may have become a rich man by having inherited the deceased's property without anybody knowing it. Nothing in this important legal change is in any way observable—and so it is everywhere in law. It is the *meaning* of observable realities with which the lawyer is concerned, but meanings are not observable, still less tangible. It is the *history* of law which is interested in observable and unobservable facts, and much of the research work of the Realists is indeed nothing but contemporary American legal history. This is one of the legal sciences and a very respectable science at that, especially if it is approached in a true sociological spirit, so that not only contemporary American facts, but also the general problem of law as conditioned by its social background is taken into consideration. But this is not the legal science of which we are speaking, the legal science which the law schools teach and which the future lawyer must learn —if for no other purpose than to influence the judge.

The fifth confusion is between the *concept* and one of the *elements* which compose the concept. If, as Mr. Justice Holmes says and all the realists repeat (as if they wished to advertise the one theory of the great judge and jurist which one would prefer not to find in his work), the law is what courts of law do, one could also say: religion is what the churches preach; science is what the universities teach; medicine is what the doctor prescribes; art is what the artist produces; and shoes are what the shoemaker makes. All this is placing the cart before the horse. One cannot define church without religion, university without science, doctor without medicine, artist without art, shoemaker without shoe, and courts of law without law. The law is not what the courts administer but the courts are the institutions which administer the law. For this reason alone can it be foretold what the courts will do. In so far as the lawyer knows the law, and in so far as the judge will follow the law, the lawyer will be able to foretell what the judge will do. The other sources of the judge's decision are in great part unknown and always will be unknown.

The last confusion is that between *cases* and *case law*. The realist movement could start and progress only in a case law country because there indeed the law seems to be a heap of decisions, and therefore a body of facts. But the cases themselves are not binding; they are not the case law; only the rationes decidendi are binding. These are—according to the controversal theory which here, of course, cannot be discussed—not the factual reasons adduced by the judge, which are only psychological facts, often based on self deception, or otherwise subject to suspicion. They are the principles from which the decisions ought to have flowed, the principles by which alone the decisions could be justified. These rationes decidendi therefore cannot simply be arrived at by an inductive process; they must be construed through purposive interpretation, they must be generalized and fitted into the whole body of the Law, which is more or less a system.[24] The system into which these

24. If the Realists object to the idea of a "system" they are thinking of a "rational" system in the strict sense of the term, and in this, of course, the writer concurs. The whole free-law movement has always emphasized that the "system" which legal science tries to erect is permeated with many emotional and volitional elements.

rationes decidendi are assimilated is the case law, and therefore something very different from a mere fact that could be the object of an empirical research. But even if it were nothing else, it would lose its meaning if there were not behind it the rule of stare decisis, whatever its limits and authority may be. Accordingly, the whole temple of case law is founded upon a rule and not upon a fact. Those who deny that rules are binding can hardly admit the binding force of precedents, which they profess to worship. Thus they destroy the Law itself.

Reductio ad Absurdum

Let us finally endeavor to know the realists by their fruits. We may first consider the startling consequences of the substantive thesis: that there is no law outside the decisions. Undecided cases could not be decided, since the respective human actions would be outside the range of the law. But every case was at one time undecided To violate a new statute would not mean breaking the "law", nor could new statutes be interpreted, since there would be no science of law to interpret them if this science dealt with decision alone. But every statute was once a new statute. The same holds true of such parts of an old statute concerning which there are contradictory decisions. Here the decision cannot be foretold and therefore, where scientific treatment would be most necessary, it would be impossible. Certain rules which have never come before the courts. nor ever could come, would cease to be law. For instance, the rule of the Constitution that the President must be 35 years of age could not be law, and it would, therefore, not be unconstitutional to make Colonel Lindbergh President. It is futile to answer that such rules are merely sources of law. They are not "sources" in the factual sense because no decisions have flowed from them. And if one means by calling them "sources" that decisions *ought* to be drawn from them, one does nothing else but recognize them as rules of law. Establishment of rules by legislation would be practically useless; it would not change the jurisprudence of the courts since they are not determined by rules, or are so determined only to a small extent. The legislator, if he is not to be considered a "ruler," would be a liar: "murder is punishable by death" would mean that it is in truth punished by death. But we know that many murderers are not, because the murderers have not been caught or convicted. Why should we have learned men to decide the cases? Whatever the courts decide is the law. This may be tolerable today, because the judges have learned how they ought to decide; but a realist should not insist on their legal training. Why not staff the Supreme Court with nine generals? Surely they would know how to enforce their decisions, such a Court would "work," and that is all a realist ought to demand.

Equally startling are the consequences of the formal theory: that the objective of legal science must be to foretell future behavior. Dissenting opinions would always be contrary to legal science, and consciously so since the dissenting judge himself knows beforehand that the prevailing opinion will be different. True, sometimes he foresees that in the future his opinion will be adopted by the Court, and then according to the formal theory both opinions would be in harmony with legal science, the dissenting as well as the prevailing. Charging a jury would involve telling it what it is about to do. This seems rather superfluous. The proper study of the law student would be the behavior of individual judges; such a study would be not only farcical but also useless. Every new generation of students would have to be taught the psychology of a new batch of judges. An essential feature of this law study of the future would be the art of bribing judges.[25] In such a case the appellate court would be in a strange position. It would be compelled to say: it was foreseeable that the judge of the first instance would be bribed; his decision therefore corresponds to realistic legal science, and accordingly must be upheld. The most important task of the law schools would be to teach which citizens are going to abide by the law and which of them are going to break it. But the law schools cannot compete with inquiry offices and detective bureaus. It is their task to turn out men like Mr. Justice Holmes, not like Mr. Sherlock Holmes.

Conclusion

This article has been for the most part critical; but as was said at the beginning, that does not mean that I do not cordially appreciate the merits of the realist movement. American readers need hardly be reminded in detail what these merits are. I would merely state, with the deepest sympathy, that American realists have begun to do what European free law jurists and legal sociologists have promised to do. We Europeans have, most of us, only tuned our instruments, they have played them. Even their exaggerations have had the wholesome effect of giving a sensational touch to the movement which perhaps was necessary in order to arouse general attention. But sound methods without a sound

25. This reminds the author that many years ago he had a Russian student who was the star of Freiburg University, and especially brilliant in Roman law. He was pressed to join the faculty, but for some reason or other was forced to accept the modest post of an attorney in a Russian provincial town. After some years he wrote the writer a letter, complaining: "What is the use of all my Roman law now? The only important thing for me to know now is which of the judges can be 'fixed' and if he can't, how to 'fix' the witnesses."

[21]

PRAGMATIC INSTRUMENTALISM IN TWENTIETH CENTURY AMERICAN LEGAL THOUGHT—A SYNTHESIS AND CRITIQUE OF OUR DOMINANT GENERAL THEORY ABOUT LAW AND ITS USE

Robert S. Summers†

TABLE OF CONTENTS

---

† McRoberts Research Professor of Law, Cornell Law School. B.S. 1955, University of Oregon; LL.B. 1959, Harvard University.

This Article is a condensed version of features of a book that will appear in German and Dutch in 1981 and, as revised, in English in 1982. Parts of this work appeared in abbreviated form in R. Summers, *Naive Instrumentalism and the Law,* in Law, Morality, and Society—Essays in Honour of H.L.A. Hart (P. Hacker & J. Raz eds. 1977) and Summers, *Professor Fuller's Jurisprudence and America's Dominant Philosophy of Law,* 92 Harv. L. Rev. 433 (1978).

I have lectured on the subject of this Article at the University of Sydney, the University of Basel, the University of Louvain, and at Cornell University, Boston University and the University of Oregon. On January 28, 1981, I presented a Faculty Research Seminar at Cornell Law School on several of the topics treated here. In each of the foregoing instances, I profited from discussions that followed and I wish to record my indebtedness to participants.

Several students at Cornell Law School have provided valuable assistance in the course of my work on the subject of this Article. I wish, in particular, to record my gratitude to Erik M. Jensen '79, Leigh B. Kelley '80, Michael M. Horowitz '82, Anne Willis Reed '81, and Joseph T. Rotondo '81.

I am especially indebted to David B. Lyons, Professor of Law and Philosophy at Cornell University for valuable commentary at various stages in the evolution of this work and to Professor Russell Osgood of Cornell Law School for several useful suggestions. I also wish to thank Ms. Genie Hurme who patiently and cheerfully typed many revisions of the manuscript.

INTRODUCTION

Between 1881 when Oliver Wendell Holmes published *The Common Law*[1] and the 1930s, a dramatic reorientation in American legal thought occurred. Philosophical pragmatism, sociological jurisprudence, and certain tenets of legal realism coalesced to form America's only indigenous theory of law. During the middle decades of this century, this body of ideas was our most influential theory of law in jurisprudential circles, in the faculties of major law schools, and in important realms of bench and bar. Many of its tenets continue to prevail today.

This theory of law remains unfinished. It is more a body of general directions of thought than a fully developed set of views

[1] O. W. HOLMES, THE COMMON LAW (1881).

completely worked out in all major respects. Yet some of its tenets were the subject of extensive development, and, in my opinion, its substance and range qualify it as a full-fledged and distinctive jurisprudential tradition alongside such European predecessors as analytical positivism and natural law philosophy.

If America's special contribution fell short because it was undeveloped and errant in important ways, the same can be said of the other theories as well. Overall, our contribution did represent a salutary development. Moreover, it remains to this day a fertile stimulus to further theorizing of a kind likely to figure in that ultimate ideal of most jurisprudential thinkers: the perfect general theory of law and its use. In my view, a perfect theory must of necessity draw upon not only what is best in analytical positivism and natural law philosophy, but also what is best in pragmatic instrumentalist thought.

I

Pragmatic Instrumentalism

A. *The Name and the Theorists*

It is important to give the legal theory under study a name. I have chosen to call it "pragmatic instrumentalism." This phrase is cumbersome, yet more descriptively apt than any other.

The theory is instrumentalist in four related yet distinguishable ways. First, it views law not as a set of general axioms or conceptions from which legal personnel may formally derive particular decisions, but as a body of practical tools for serving specific substantive goals. Second, it conceives law not as an autonomous and self-sufficient system, but as merely a means to achieve external goals that are derived from sources outside the law, including the dictates of democratic processes and the "policy sciences." Third, it assumes that a particular use of law cannot be a self-justifying "end in itself." Uses of law can be justified only by reference to whatever values they fulfill. Finally, the law is considered to serve generally instrumental values rather than intrinsic ones. That is, law's function is to satisfy democratically expressed wants and interests, whatever they may be (within constitutional limits).

Does it add anything to say that instrumentalism is also "pragmatic"? After all, viewing law as essentially instrumental is itself pragmatic. Moreover, a theory of value largely devoid of intrinsic goods is open-ended, allowing wide scope for pragmatic modification of the law's goals over time. The adjective "pragmatic," nonetheless, is not redundant. It designates features of the theory that are not implicit in the term "instrumentalism," some of which are pragmatic in either lay or philosophical senses.

First, the theory is pragmatic in its emphasis on the primacy of context in arriving at law's ends and means, stressing time, place, circumstance, and particular wants and interests rather than ideology, abstract theory, principle, and an *a priori* normative view of the "nature of things."

Furthermore, the theory treats the law "in action." It is concerned not only with the general nature of law as social means but also with law as it is actually used, and with the practical differences that law's uses make. This focus extends beyond law's external effects to the workings of its internal processes—the operation of its complex implementive technology. Thus, the theory necessarily addresses official legal personnel, their roles as "social engineers," and the technical skill they must deploy in those roles. More than any other theory of law, pragmatic instrumentalism is concerned with the effectiveness of legal action.

Another pragmatic feature of the theory is that it conceives of reality as something essentially for human use, which may be readily altered through human action. Social reality—including the law's own machinery—is relatively malleable.

A strong experimental strain runs through this theory: uses of law must be experimental, especially given the rapidity of social change. A pragmatic method of trial and error is appropriate. As evidence of law's successes and failures accumulates, we must modify the law accordingly.

In the foregoing ways, then, "pragmatic instrumentalism" is a descriptively apt name for the general theory of law under study here. Although it is new, I believe the introduction of some such name is long overdue.[2]

---

[2] Some readers may think that I am merely introducing a new name, "pragmatic instrumentalism," for a body of ideas that has long had a name—legal realism. My first response is simply that this is not so. "Legal realism" is an expression that has been used most often to refer to the work of a group of thinkers the bulk of whose writings appeared in the 1920s and the 1930s. *See generally* Llewellyn, *Some Realism About Realism—Responding to Dean Pound,* 44 HARV. L. REV. 1222 (1931). Among the leaders of this group were Karl Llewellyn, Jerome Frank, and Walter Wheeler Cook. The phrase "legal realism" has not regularly been used to refer to the general coalescence of pragmatism, sociological jurisprudence, and legal realism that is the subject of this study. If I am right about this, and, of course, conventional usage in such matters is never wholly consistent, then it is not true that the body of ideas I am addressing has long had the name "legal realism."

But even though "legal realism" is today sometimes used more widely to encompass the entire body of ideas, there are compelling reasons to cease this practice and to use instead the name "pragmatic instrumentalism" or some other suitable name. First, the practice of continuing with both a wide use (all the ideas) and a narrow use (the ideas mainly of Llewellyn,

The classical pragmatic instrumentalists, except for Gray and Cohen, were all contemporaries for about two full decades. They include:

John Chipman Gray	1839-1915
Oliver Wendell Holmes, Jr.	1841-1935
John Dewey	1859-1952
Roscoe Pound	1870-1964
Walter Wheeler Cook	1873-1943
Joseph Walter Bingham	1878-1973
W. Underhill Moore	1879-1949
Herman Oliphant	1884-1939
Jerome Frank	1889-1957
Karl N. Llewellyn	1893-1962
Felix S. Cohen	1907-1953

This list is not exhaustive. Many readers will see what seem to be significant omissions. Only the principal progenitors and enough others are included to provide substance to the rise and continuity of the general movement in legal thought singled out here for study.

These thinkers were all lawyers, law professors, or judges, except Dewey, the only professional philosopher. Dewey wrote several essays on law, however, and his general philosophy influenced most instrumentalists.

Frank, Cook, et al.) only invites confusion, especially if this involves use of a name for the whole that in its more common meaning is associated only with a part. Second, using "legal realism" in a wide sense invites the impression that the earlier theorists—who are not the ones most commonly designated by this phrase—were mere precursors of the main event. Yet Holmes, Gray, Pound and Dewey were not mere precursors. The work of these earlier thinkers was seminal. It may be true that such paradigm realists (in the narrow sense) as Llewellyn, Frank, and Cook seem closest to us today in time, but this proves nothing. One must be wary of treating the past as a mere backward extension of the present. Third, some tenets of legal realism (in the narrow sense) do not form part of the general directions of thought considered here. These tenets, the more extreme kind, were not as influential. They include, for example, a radical value skepticism and an emphasis on non-rational and even irrational factors in the judicial process (*e.g.*, "gastronomic jurisprudence"). Fourth, the term "legal realism" has misleading philosophical connotations. Most of the pragmatic instrumentalists were not realists in traditional philosophical usage. They did not hold that general or abstract words name independent and unitary entities that "exist" outside the mind. They might, of course, be called "realists" in literary parlance, for they were concerned with fidelity to real life and with accurate representation of life. Finally, the expression "pragmatic instrumentalism" is, for the reasons given in the text, a descriptively appropriate name. I might add that it is not my invention. Dewey sometimes used it, although for a somewhat different purpose, and glimmerings of it appear in Llewellyn's work. *See, e.g.*, J. DEWEY, THE QUEST FOR CERTAINTY 37 (1929); Llewellyn, *A Realistic Jurisprudence—The Next Step,* 30 COLUM. L. REV. 431, 447 n.12, 454 (1930). The words "instrumentalist" and "instrumentalism" in this Article refer to the tenets of pragmatic instrumentalism.

Of course, these thinkers did not hold identical views. Pioneers, even in the same general directions of thought, seldom do. Some of them were skeptics about reason, at least in their theoretical moments, while Dewey had great faith in the power of reason, or at least his own empiricist view of it. Several of these thinkers actually attacked each other in print. A few changed their views significantly over time. For example, the earlier writings of Pound, Frank, and Llewellyn more fully qualify them as pragmatic instrumentalists than do their later ones. There were also important differences in the sophistication of these thinkers. Yet all joined in the same general directions of thought about law. Even the well known polemic between Pound and Llewellyn[3] was really an "inside" affair.

The thinkers I have listed did significant original or critical work, or otherwise shared in the rise of instrumentalism before the beginning of World War II. Although more than half lived and worked past 1950, I will not treat that part of their work done after 1940. By then the coalescence of general directions of thought was more or less complete, and in "full flower." These ideas dominated legal thinking during the middle decades of this century.

B. *Origins of the Theory*

A systematic inquiry into the origins of pragmatic instrumentalism would itself call for a book-length study. For introductory purposes it will be enough merely to provide a sketch. A rough but useful distinction may be drawn between reactive and affirmative influences. Pragmatic instrumentalism was partly a reaction to certain conditions in the world of American law during the last part of the nineteenth and the early part of the twentieth centuries. I will begin with these.

Holmes, Dewey, Pound, and other pragmatic instrumentalists reacted critically to what they perceived to be "formalism" in judicial reasoning, in legal education, and in legal theory. They did not subject the precise nature of formalism to detailed inquiry. No simple definition of formalism can be adequate, for the distinction between a formalistic and a non-formalistic view really breaks down into a vari-

[3] *See* Llewellyn, *supra* note 2; Pound, *The Call for a Realist Jurisprudence*, 44 HARV. L. REV. 697 (1931). Llewellyn's overall place is illuminatingly treated in W. TWINING, KARL LLEWELLYN AND THE REALIST MOVEMENT (1973).

ety of possible contrasts, with the meaning of "formalism" and its derivatives varying in different contexts.[4]

[4] Consider this table of examples:

CONTRASTS OF FORMALISTIC AND NON-FORMALISTIC VIEWS

CONTEXT	FORMALISTIC VIEW	NON-FORMALISTIC VIEW
1. ambit of legal creativity and legal change	scope narrow; law is like a static and closed logical system	scope wide; law is like a dynamic and open framework
2. judicial power to make law	due to separation of powers, judges may only discover, declare, and apply the law as it already exists	judges have power to make law, and regularly do so, covertly as well as overtly
3. Responsibility of Supreme Court to test constitutionality of legislation	responsibility broad; legislation at least presumptively invalid if conflicts with literal text of constitutional phrase	responsibility narrow; legislation presumptively valid
4. whether there is a single "perfect" form of law as a solution to each problem	always one "true rule," ascertainable by reason; laws of governance are thus similar to universal laws of nature	plurality of plausible forms of law for the usual problem
5. considerations relevant in lawmaking	coherence, harmony, and consistency with existing law	social facts and existing wants and interests
6. tests for identifying valid forms of law	whether law is traceable to an authoritative source	whether law has defensible substantive content
7. nature of reality of valid law	general rules "in books"	predictable law "in action"
8. structure of valid law within a field	reducible to a unitary general theory, as in science	pluralistic and irreducible
9. correct statement of valid law	susceptible to statement only in a limited number of abstract and wide generalizations	susceptible to statement only in many concrete and narrow generalizations
10. interpretation and application of case law	words of opinion and their "logic" control	judge's action in light of facts controls

In due course, I will consider instrumentalist reactions to the varieties of formalism. It is enough for now to illustrate two of the most common types. These thinkers singled out as formalists such legal educators as Christopher C. Langdell, Dean of Harvard Law School from 1870 to 1895, and Joseph H. Beale, Professor at Harvard Law School from 1890 to 1938. Langdell claimed, for example, that an "irrevocable" offer to enter into a contract was simply a "legal impossibility." In his view, the inherent logic of the concept of an offer dictated that it must always be revocable at will, regardless of whether the offeror had induced reasonable reliance on the part of the offeree.[5] Similarly, Beale proclaimed that varied issues in the field of conflict of laws were governed by a conception of domicile that was, in his view, being perfected as a unitary conception in the course of our law's evolution. According to Beale, once the domicile of the party or parties was determined, certain legal consequences always followed automatically, even in cases as diverse as those involving the right to vote, choice of law for divorce, and jurisdiction to tax.[6] Pragmatic instrumentalists repudiated such formalism, and contended that existing law should be extended or elaborated not in light of the supposed inherent logic of its concepts or "perfect" unitary conceptions, but in light of policy goals derived from prevailing wants and interests.[7]

Formalism was not confined to legal educators; judges were guilty of it, too. Oliver Wendell Holmes and Roscoe Pound, two of the leading pragmatic instrumentalists, were particularly vigorous in their condemnation of those judges of the federal and state supreme courts who invalidated social legislation partly on the ground that the

Table (Continued)

11. interpretation and application of written law	authoritative language and "logic" of the concepts expressed controls	goals of lawmaker infuse the language and these together control
12. elaboration and extension of existing law	"logic" of existing concepts controls	"policy" controls

[5] C. LANGDELL, A SUMMARY OF THE LAW OF CONTRACTS § 178 (2d ed. 1880). Langdell, of course, takes a different view if the offer is a binding option.

[6] 1 J. BEALE, A TREATISE ON THE CONFLICT OF LAWS 92-94 (1935). Beale seems to have come to this viewpoint early. *See* Beale, *Residence and Domicil,* 4 IOWA L. BULL. 3 (1918).

[7] *See, e.g.* W. COOK, THE LOGICAL AND LEGAL BASES OF THE CONFLICTS OF LAWS 196-97 (1942); Holmes, Book Review, 14 AM. L. REV. 233, 233-34 (1880). For Cook's general description of formalist legal education as late as 1927, see Cook, *Scientific Method and the Law,* 13 A.B.A.J. 303, 307-08 (1927).

"logic" of such very general constitutional conceptions as liberty of contract and substantive due process dictated that outcome.[8]

Pragmatic instrumentalism, however, was much more than a reaction against formalism. It was also a reaction against substantive ideas underlying formalism such as laissez-faire theories of government and judicial conservatism. Moreover, instrumentalism was born of affirmative influences. Some of these were jurisprudential. Pound, for example, borrowed from Rudolf Von Ihering's conception of law as a means to accepted ends.[9] By the close of the nineteenth century, some of Jeremy Bentham's work on the uses of law for social improvement had become well-known in America.[10] Much pragmatic instrumentalism was Benthamite in spirit. Of the leading theorists only Holmes was not a reformer.

The reform effort within American politics known as the Progressive Movement (1890-1920) was another affirmative influence.[11] Several leading instrumentalists were themselves progressives, including Dewey and the young Pound. And although later figures such as Llewellyn, Oliphant, and Frank were not yet of mature age during the heyday of Progressivism (1895-1915), it is very likely that they would have joined up had they been. The Progressives were not radical socialists, but they believed that democracy had been corrupted and political power concentrated in big corporations, trusts, and political bosses, that the voting franchise should be extended, especially to women, that industry needed to be regulated, that poverty and old age hardship must be relieved, that workers needed protection, and that natural resources must be conserved.[12]

The Progressives and their forebears were partly responsible for numerous laws purporting to achieve Progressive aims, including the Sherman Act,[13] the Pure Food and Drug Act,[14] and the 17th amend-

---

[8] *See, e.g.*, Lochner v. New York, 198 U.S. 45, 76 (1904) (Holmes, J., dissenting); Pound, *Law in Books and Law in Action*, 44 AM. L. REV. 12, 16 (1910); Pound, *Liberty of Contract*, 18 YALE L.J. 454, 457, 480 (1909). For an unusual view of Holmes, classifying him as a formalist, see G. GILMORE, THE AGES OF AMERICAN LAW 48-56 (1977).

[9] R. VON IHERING, LAW AS A MEANS TO AN END (1877, Eng. trans. 1914). Pound regularly drew on Von Ihering's work. *See, e.g.*, Pound, *Mechanical Jurisprudence*, 8 COLUM. L. REV. 605, 610 (1908).

[10] *See, e.g.*, J. BENTHAM, WORKS OF J. BENTHAM (J. Bowring ed. 1843).

[11] *See generally* R. HOFSTADTER, THE AGE OF REFORM (1955).

[12] *See, e.g.*, W. LAFEBER & R. POLENBERG, THE AMERICAN CENTURY 37-48 (1975). *Cf.* C. STROUT, THE PRAGMATIC REVOLT IN AMERICAN HISTORY: CARL BECKER & CHARLES BEARD (1958).

[13] Sherman Act, ch. 647, 26 Stat. 209 (1890).

[14] Pure Food and Drug Act, ch. 3915, 34 Stat. 768 (1906).

ment[15] providing for popular election of senators. It is hardly surprising that pragmatic instrumentalism in legal theory took root during the Progressive Era. If the Progressives themselves had articulated a theory of law, it almost certainly would have been instrumentalist, pragmatic, and mindful of social change. Moreover, the very force of the Progressive example—extensive resort to law as a tool to serve social goals—led legal theorists to conceive of law in the same terms and to repudiate the formalistic, static, and conservative conceptions of law's nature so influential in many quarters at the end of the nineteenth century.

The scientific ethos of the day influenced terminology and permeated basic conceptions. All instrumentalists wrote and spoke of "scientific" lawmaking and administration. Holmes said "an ideal system of law should draw its postulates and its legislative justification from science."[16] These thinkers viewed uses of law as hypotheses to be tested experimentally in the laboratory of social experience. They called for empirical research on the effects of law. Fields as diverse as behaviorist psychology, biology, and physics provided models. Thus, for example, many of these theorists conceived of law as overt action—observable official behavior. One can see a striking parallel between Darwin's earlier rejection of the use of static categories to classify evolving species and the instrumentalists' rejection of the use of formalistic judicial method in a changing society. The overthrow of Newtonian physics, with its model of a comprehensive deductive system of natural laws, appears to have led some of the new legal theorists to reject a similar model for civic law and to substitute as a theory of law predictions of official behavior.

Another major factor in the rise of instrumentalist thinking within the law was the technological advance of the late nineteenth and early twentieth centuries. In many respects this new technology was even more visible than that developed during the Industrial Revolution; it spread beyond the factory gates and transformed the very social setting in which people conducted daily life. The period from 1880 to 1920 saw the development of the automobile, the electric light, the telephone, a whole new range of business machines, and the airplane. This reinforced the instrumentalist view that by his own effort, man could transform the social order. Instrumentalist writings are filled with analogies and metaphors that relate law and government to "instruments," "tools," "machines," and even "engines."

---

[15] U.S. CONST. amend. XVII.

[16] O. W. HOLMES, *Learning and Science*, in COLLECTED LEGAL PAPERS 138, 139 (1920).

These thinkers viewed law as a technology, legal personnel as "social engineers," and law's uses as "social engineering."

Certainly the most important intellectual influence on the founders of pragmatic instrumentalist legal theory was the philosophy of pragmatism, a body of thought that ramified into many fields. Charles S. Peirce (1839-1914) and William James (1842-1910) were the principal progenitors.[17] John Dewey was a leading pragmatist philosopher, and a legal theorist only secondarily.[18] Naturally, he imported pragmatist tenets into his legal theory, including some that were largely of his own making.

The pragmatists were themselves anti-formalist. James, for instance, stressed that theorists should turn "away from abstraction . . . , from verbal solutions, from bad a priori reasons, from fixed principles, closed systems, and pretended absolutes and origins."[19] Instead, they should look "towards last things, fruits, consequences, facts."[20]

James also profoundly influenced the value theory in instrumentalist legal thinking. He held that the social order should endeavor to maximize the satisfaction of wants and interests of the time.[21] Similarly, Dewey stressed that laws are social means—instruments of progress. He rejected Spencer's social Darwinism. More than any other philosopher, he was responsible for the optimism in the newly evolving theory of law.[22]

The "pragmatic method," James wrote, was concerned with the "ways in which existing realities may be changed."[23] Because society is constantly changing, needs for law regularly arise. On the pragmatist view, lawmakers will find that reality, including the machinery of the law, is relatively malleable and thus adaptable to man's own ends.[24] In lawmaking, moreover, context—not ideology—is to govern substantive content. Indeed, questions of value that arise in the process can be reduced very largely to questions of fact.[25]

To the pragmatists, solutions to legal problems would have to be specific, and above all, plural. Given the nature of knowledge and the

---

[17] *See generally* COLLECTED PAPERS OF CHARLES SANDERS PEIRCE (1931-58); THE WRITINGS OF WILLIAM JAMES (J. McDermott ed. 1967).

[18] *See generally* M. THOMAS, JOHN DEWEY: A CENTENNIAL BIBLIOGRAPHY (1962).

[19] W. JAMES, *supra* note 17, at 376, 379.

[20] *Id.* at 380 (emphasis omitted).

[21] *See* W. JAMES, *supra* note 17, at 610, 617, 623.

[22] *See, e.g.*, Dewey, *Progress*, 26 ETHICS 311 (1916).

[23] W. JAMES, *supra* note 17, at 380.

[24] *See* H. THAYER, MEANING AND ACTION: A CRITICAL HISTORY OF PRAGMATISM 426-27 (1968).

[25] *See* text accompanying notes 65-67 *infra*.

nature of social reality, particularly its changing character, lawmakers cannot be certain of the efficacy of particular uses of law. Hence such uses must be "experimental."

Dewey stated that "the task of philosophy is to clarify men's ideas as to the social and moral strifes of their own day. Its aim is to become so far as is humanly possible an organ for dealing with those conflicts."[26] He called for "use of scientific method in investigation and of the engineering mind in the invention and projection of far-reaching social plans."[27] To this end, Dewey developed an influential "new logic"—not a logic of demonstration in the tradition of logical theorizing, but a logic of inquiry, particularly into the likely consequences of social decisions and actions.[28]

Probably the most widely accepted tenet in pragmatic instrumentalist legal theory passed under the name of the "prediction theory" of law. On this view, first set forth by Holmes,[29] laws are nothing but predictions of what officials will do. Although developments in physics presumably help account for the reception of this theory, it is not difficult to identify pragmatist influence as well. Both Peirce and James espoused "predictive" conceptions of meaning and truth. They wrote that the true significance of any concept is found in its consequences.[30]

As we will see,[31] most instrumentalists held that the success of a use of law should be judged by its effects. This "efficacy" criterion also had antecedents in pragmatist philosophy.[32]

---

[26] J. DEWEY, RECONSTRUCTION IN PHILOSOPHY 26 (1920).

[27] J. DEWEY, LIBERALISM AND SOCIAL ACTION 73 (1935).

[28] *See* J. DEWEY, ESSAYS IN EXPERIMENTAL LOGIC (1916); J. DEWEY, HOW WE THINK (1910); J. DEWEY, LOGIC: THE THEORY OF INQUIRY (1938); J. DEWEY, STUDIES IN LOGICAL THEORY (1903).

[29] *See* Holmes, *The Path of the Law,* 10 HARV. L. REV. 457, 457 (1897); Holmes, Book Review, 6 AM. L. REV. 723, 724 (1872).

[30] *See generally* Fisch, *Justice Holmes, The Prediction Theory of Law,* 39 J. PHILOSOPHY 85 (1942).

[31] *See* section XI *infra.*

[32] Many tenets and corollaries of pragmatic instrumentalism must be traced out and pieced together from the diverse writings of a number of thinkers. Those who wish to study a legal theory can usually be directed to single volume works that articulate and draw together most of the leading ideas. Thus, a student of analytical positivism may read John Austin's *Lectures on Jurisprudence* (5th ed. 1885), Hans Kelsen's *General Theory of Law and State* (1945) or H. L. A. Hart's *The Concept of Law* (1961). Not a single comparable treatise or textbook of general theory exists for pragmatic instrumentalism. (Pound's five volume treatise, *Jurisprudence* (1959), is too diffuse and eclectic to qualify). Two substantial articles published 40 years apart, however, each contain nearly all of the leading ideas of pragmatic instrumentalism: Holmes, *The Path of Law, supra* note 29; Cohen, *The Problems of a Functional Jurisprudence,* 1 MOD. L. REV. 5 (1937).

C. *Importance of Pragmatic Instrumentalism*

The study of general ideas can be justified simply as the pursuit of knowledge and understanding. The study of general ideas that relate to law is even easier to justify, because uses of law affect daily life, and general ideas influence how law is used. General theory about law is not a mere plaything of academic scribblers, with no meaning for men of action.[33] Officials and ordinary citizens are guided by such theory whether or not they acknowledge as much.[34] Judges, for example, have their own conceptions about the scope and force of precedent, about the appropriate court-legislature relation, about statutory interpretation, about what kind of an argument can be a good one, about what values appropriately shape law's goals, and so on. These are not merely technical matters. They are necessarily informed by general ideas—by theory.

In the same vein, the law is a form of social reality, the shape and content of which is determined in part by what those subject to it believe to be its nature and uses. How citizens conceive of law must—if their conceptions are widely enough agreed upon—affect what the law actually is or becomes. If, for example, citizens and legislators come to believe that good law is whatever the majority wants, then they will be less likely to subject actual and proposed law to independent rational scrutiny in light of basic values such as justice, liberty, or equality. As one thinker has put it, "[I]n human affairs [even] what men mistakenly accept as real tends, by the very act of their acceptance, to become real."[35]

In my view, pragmatic instrumentalism will be recorded as America's only indigenous general theory of law. It was also our most influential legal theory during the middle decades of this century. This is not to say that it ousted all others, or that all its tenets were equally accepted, or even that every one of its tenets commanded a majority in all quarters. It is at least to say, however, that its influence in America exceeded that of any other general body of thought about the law. Certainly it dwarfed analytical positivism as well as Catholic and secular natural law philosophies. Indeed, many tenets of pragmatic instrumentalism prevail today.

---

[33] *Cf.* J. Keynes, The General Theory of Employment Interest and Money 383 (1935).

[34] As Pound once remarked, men of affairs should be "conscious of a philosophy of law, and examine its tenets scientifically instead of taking for granted a naive philosophy while disclaiming all philosophical ideas." Pound, *The Philosophy of Law in America*, 7 Archiv fur Rechts und Wirtschaftphilosophie [A.F.R.U.W.] 213, 214 (1913).

[35] Fuller, *Positivism and Fidelity to Law—A Reply to Professor Hart*, 71 Harv. L. Rev. 630, 631 (1958).

In this Article I will identify, draw together, and discuss the leading general directions of thought that made up pragmatic instrumentalist theory. My effort will not be primarily historical, however, nor will it be a series of studies of the contributions of individual thinkers. Rather, my focus will be more aggregative in nature.[36] The reader should be warned that I will not dwell at any length on most of the specific virtues of pragmatic instrumentalism. Indeed, in the rest of this Article I will offer mainly evaluative commentary and demonstrate the fertility and suggestiveness of instrumentalist thought. In so doing, I will draw upon the writings of leading critics of pragmatic instrumentalism, including Lon Fuller, Morris Cohen, and John Dickinson.

II

Value Theory

A theory of value is normative. It sets forth what ought to be, not what actually is occurring. The central elements of a theory of value are twofold: notions of the right and good, and principles for resolving conflicts between particular forms of these conceptions. A theory of value provides a general and systematic account of these elements and their inter-relations. Thus, although it may be consistent or inconsistent with a particular political program, it is not to be identified with any such program.

A general theory of law may or may not explicitly incorporate value theoretic tenets. In the analytical positivism of the Austrian jurist Hans Kelsen, for example, one does not encounter an explicit theory of value.[37] The English theorist, Jeremy Bentham, however, was both a legal positivist and a leading progenitor of a value theory utilitarian in tenor.[38]

---

[36] This orientation and emphasis will disappoint and dismay some of the foxes. Most lawyers, in their professional moments, tend to be of an analyzing rather than a synthesizing bent. With the rise and dominance of analytic philosophy in this century, the foxes have been having their day among legal theorists. Thus, there is perhaps even more reason for me to assume the stance of the hedgehog here. I may invoke the authority of both Archilochus and Erasmus: "The fox knows many things, but the hedgehog knows one great thing," (fragment 103); "The Fox has many tricks, and the hedgehog has only one, but that is the best of all," (fragment 85) (*quoted in* I. Berlin, The Hedgehog and the Fox 1 (1953)). Of course, in his labors, the hedgehog cannot dispense with all foxiness.

[37] *See generally* H. Kelsen, General Theory of Law and State (1945); Kelsen, *The Pure Theory of Law*, 50 Law Q. Rev. 474 (1934).

[38] J. Bentham, *A Fragment on Government*, in Works of Jeremy Bentham, *supra* note 10, at 221, 289-90; J. Bentham, The Principles of Morals and Legislation (1948).

A general theory of law that does not address issues of value is, in my opinion, fundamentally incomplete. The law is not a mere formal receptacle. It includes substantive content. Insofar as law is consciously made and applied, its content is necessarily determined by values. These values show themselves in the reasons that lawmakers, judges, and other officials give for what they do, and in the very formulations of the law itself. Values figure not only in the making and application of law; they necessarily figure in its evaluation and criticism as well. It may be said that in a free and otherwise well-ordered society the life of the law has not been either logic or experience but vigilant critical scrutiny.

The pragmatic instrumentalists addressed basic issues of value. To begin with, many of them insisted on distinguishing sharply between the law as it ought to be and the law as it actually happens to be.[39] In this, they followed the English jurists Bentham and John Austin.[40] Several became value skeptics, however, and thus in varying ways and degrees denied the very possibility of a genuine value theory.[41] But most of the leading instrumentalists should not be classed as value skeptics. They followed not only Bentham and Austin but also the American pragmatist philosophers in subscribing to a theory of value that may be characterized as utilitarian, quantitative, conventionalist, and majoritarian. This is not to say that the instrumentalists systematically developed a full-fledged theory of value for use by legislators, judges, and other legal actors. Several value theoretic themes recur either explicitly or implicitly in the writings of most of the leading figures. Only two of those themes can be considered here.

A. *Maximal Satisfaction of Wants and Interests*

Most pragmatic instrumentalists believed that values in general and the goals of rules and other legal precepts in particular must derive from prevailing wants and interests. The views of the pragmatist philosopher William James were widely shared:

> Take any demand, however slight, which any creature, however weak may make. Ought it not, for its own sole sake, to be

[39] *See, e.g.*, J. Gray, The Nature and Sources of the Law 94 (1st ed. 1909); Holmes, *supra* note 29, at 2-3; Llewellyn, *supra* note 2, at 1236.

[40] *See* J. Bentham, *A Fragment on Government,* in Works of Jeremy Bentham, *supra* note 10; J. Bentham, The Principles of Morals and Legislation, *supra* note 38; J. Austin, The Province of Jurisprudence Determined (H. L. A. Hart ed. 1954).

[41] J. Frank, Law and the Modern Mind (1930); Moore, *Rational Basis of Legal Institutions,* 23 Colum. L. Rev. 609, 612 (1923).

satisfied? If not, prove why not. The only possible kind of proof you could adduce would be the exhibition of another creature who should make a demand that ran the other way. The only possible reason there can be why any phenomenon ought to exist is that such a phenomenon actually is desired.

. . . .

Since everything which is demanded is by that fact a good, must not the guiding principle for ethical philosophy (since all demands conjointly cannot be satisfied in this poor world) be simply to satisfy at all times as many demands as we can? That act must be the best act, accordingly, which makes for the best whole, in the sense of awakening the least sum of dissatisfactions. In the causistic scale, therefore, those ideals must be written highest which prevail at the least cost, or by whose realization the least possible number of other ideals are destroyed.[42]

On the foregoing view, we are to take wants and interests of individuals as they are expressed, and we are not to distinguish between them in qualitative terms; one interest is intrinsically as good as any other. The interests of individuals, of course, may conflict. How then are such conflicts to be resolved? We are to adopt one basic utilitarian injunction: maximize the realization of as many interests of individuals as possible. In light of this directive, particular interests can be evaluated, though only in quantitative terms. The pursuit of interest A should be chosen over conflicting interest B if (1) the pursuit of A will on its own terms be more successful, and (2) the pursuit of A will interfere less with the satisfaction of other interests. This is an essentially conventionalist view. We are to take the worth of existing interests for granted, at least if it can be assumed that the public endorses them, or that their fulfillment will serve other acknowledged interests. The true province of reasoned evaluation of matters legal, therefore, was assumed to be confined largely to the aptness of means to ends.[43]

Many pragmatic instrumentalists, including Oliver Wendell Holmes, Jr.,[44] Roscoe Pound,[45] John Dewey,[46] John Chipman

---

[42] W. JAMES, *supra* note 17, at 617, 623 (emphasis omitted).

[43] Dewey even argued that we should abandon the notion that anything can be a general "end in itself," and therefore valuable in its own right. J. DEWEY, RECONSTRUCTION IN PHILOSOPHY 163, 186 (1920); J. DEWEY, THEORY OF VALUATION 43 (1939).

[44] *See* Abrams v. United States, 250 U.S. 616, 630 (1919) (Holmes, J., dissenting); O. W. HOLMES, *supra* note 1, at 41; 1 HOLMES-POLLOCK LETTERS 163 (M. Howe ed. 1941); Holmes, *Law in Science and Science in Law*, 12 HARV. L. REV. 443, 460-61 (1899).

[45] *See* Pound, *Legislation as a Social Function*, 18 AM. J. SOC. 755, 763-65 (1918); Pound, *supra* note 34, pt. 2 at 385, 398-99.

[46] *See, e.g.*, J. DEWEY, THE QUEST FOR CERTAINTY 254-86 (1929); J. DEWEY, THEORY OF THE MORAL LIFE 98-101 (1960).

Gray,[47] Walter Wheeler Cook,[48] and Herman Oliphant,[49] wrote in their theoretical moments as though they subscribed to the kind of value theory that James expressed. Most of them adopted the terminology of "satisfying wants" or "serving interests." This in itself proves nothing. Such ways of speaking and writing might merely have been linguistic common currency that ultimately translated into independent and qualitative ideas of value rather than into the theory James set forth. But there is considerable evidence that most of these thinkers usually subscribed to James's general view. This is not to say that they sought to develop devices for systematically measuring interests, or that they prescribed overtly calculational analysis. In determining interests to be served, they seemed ready to rely mainly on the outcomes of duly reformed democratic processes and on rough and ready judicial judgment.

One aspect of the value theory of these thinkers was especially salutary. It purported to exalt the interests of the many above those of the few. In this respect, instrumentalist legal theory joined forces with the Progressive Movement. The Progressives were dedicated to rooting out undemocratic concentrations of power in politics, in the economy, and in American society at large. They believed that judges, legislators, and other officials ought not to be tools of the monied classes or of political bosses, but should serve the populace as a whole.

But other aspects of the kind of value theory expressed by James and his followers have long been the object of philosophical criticism.[50] Since this is not the place for yet another philosophical critique of utilitarianism, I will instead recount some of the reactions of American legal theorists. Among these, Lon Fuller was foremost.[51] He did not believe that the mere existence of interests, even when backed by wide popular acclaim, justifies legal intervention on their behalf. Rather, he held that such interests must be subject to *qualitative* tests—to the scrutiny of reason in light of substantive notions of right and good. He insisted on the primacy of reason with respect to *goals* as well as means.[52]

Majoritarianism, of course, is an imperfect index of maximally realizable interests, and representative democracy often is promis-

---

[47] J. GRAY, THE NATURE AND SOURCES OF LAW 12-26, 307 (2d ed. 1921).

[48] Cook generally followed Dewey. *See, e.g.*, Cook, *Walter Wheeler Cook*, in MY PHILOSOPHY OF LAW 49, 62-64 (1941).

[49] *See* Oliphant, *Current Discussions of Legal Methodology*, 7 A.B.A.J. 241 (1921).

[50] Thus, among other things, there has been a long tradition of criticism of utilitarianism. *See, e.g.*, A. QUINTON, UTILITARIAN ETHICS 82-105 (1973).

[51] *See generally* Summers, *Professor Fuller's Jurisprudence and America's Dominant Philosophy of Law*, 92 HARV. L. REV. 433 (1978).

[52] *See, e.g.*, L. FULLER, THE LAW IN QUEST OF ITSELF 88-95 (1940).

cuous. It can accommodate virtually any interest, whether bad or good. All it asks is that enough people subscribe. Moreover, it institutionalizes a colossal and irresponsible excuse that legislators, judges, and other legal actors may invoke to try to justify abdicating their duty to bring reason to bear—namely, that matters may always be "appropriately settled by vote," whatever the dictates of reason.

Critics like Fuller who insist on making every effort to accommodate reason within democratic process presuppose objective criteria by which interests can be evaluated qualitatively, rather than just quantitatively. To these thinkers, reason has something to work on and with beyond the instrumentalist maximization criterion. Thus the ancient issue of the relative validity of objective and subjective theories of value arises, an issue that cannot be addressed systematically here.

Some instrumentalists assumed that objective criteria for qualitative evaluation of interests are ultimately silent, empty, or easily stalemated and thus would call the majoritarian principle into play as the only tie-breaker. In contrast, Fuller contended that on most issues the weight of reason is clearly and heavily on one side.[53] He and other critics called upon instrumentalists to look more closely at evaluative disputes and see for themselves whether the only thing having any initial appeal is the fact that more people happen to want A rather than B. A closer look, they argued, leads one to construct and reflect upon the arguments for and against the interests expressed in A and B. They concluded that any such process will show that it is simply not the case, as James thought, that "the only possible reason there can be why any phenomenon ought to exist is that such a phenomenon actually is desired."[54]

Thus, even in the context of democratic processes the objective resolution of issues by reason is one alternative to the value theoretic notions embraced by many instrumentalists. This is not to say that anyone today has worked out a satisfactory general theory of value for use in the law, although there have been valiant efforts of late.[55] Nor is it to say that reasoned analysis is always easy or readily determinant. Even Fuller did not hold that reason rules all or ought to rule all. He acknowledged that "[w]e know in advance that we cannot reach our goal of a social order founded solely on reason. But we know equally well that it is impossible to set in advance a stopping place short of our goal beyond which all effort will be in vain."[56] It is

---

53 *See generally* Fuller, *Reason and Fiat in Case Law*, 59 HARV. L. REV. 376 (1946). *See also* Fuller, Book Review, 9 U. CHI. L. REV. 759, 760 (1942).

54 W. JAMES, *supra* note 17, at 617.

55 *See, e.g.*, R. DWORKIN, TAKING RIGHTS SERIOUSLY (1978).

56 L. FULLER, *supra* note 52, at 110.

sobering to contrast this remark with Holmes's deference to the "wants of the crowd" and Holmes's general skepticism about moral "preferences," which he viewed as "more or less arbitrary . . . Do you like sugar in your coffee or don't you?"[57]

Furthermore, the Constitution itself can be cited by critics of quantitative value theory to support the proposition that our society actually has recognized and institutionalized qualitative standards of reason both in matters of process and substantive outcome. As Fuller stressed, the Constitution provides guarantees of deliberateness in the processes of making and applying law that evince far more of a commitment to reason than does the principle of majority rule itself.[58] Moreover, citizens have certain substantive rights under the Constitution that cannot be violated or compromised even when this would satisfy a greater number of wants. It is hard to see how a consistent instrumentalist value theory could rationally accommodate these constraints. It would not do to say that enforcing such rights tends to promote the greatest satisfaction of wants and interests in the long run, for that simply does not seem to be true.

The gulf between the value theoretic tenets of many instrumentalists and "objectivist" critics is vast. Its main significance, at least for the actual course and tenor of legal practice, probably lies in its effects on dispositions and propensities. For example, those who see a greater qualitative role for reason in evaluative matters will be less willing to resolve differences by immediate resort to the principle of majority rule inside the body politic and the judicial conference room. Instead they will try harder and longer to work out conflicts of wants and interests through reason and, more importantly, try harder to articulate reasoned justifications for what finally is done in the name of law.

It must be said that one encounters in the writings of some instrumentalists an extreme value skepticism that might be interpreted as a repudiation even of the limited role for reasoned justification that I have allowed instrumentalist theory here. Holmes sometimes seemed an extreme subjectivist,[59] and Frank, at least before the war,[60] dismissed efforts at all reasoned justification as "rationalization."[61] Bingham believed that judges could dispense with opinion writing.[62] Even Llewellyn in his early years despaired that reason

---

[57] 1 Holmes-Pollock Letters, *supra* note 44, at 105.
[58] Fuller, *Jurisprudence,* 13 Encyclopedia Britannica 149, 152 (1965).
[59] 1 Holmes-Pollock Letters, *supra* note 44, at 105.
[60] J. Frank, *supra* note 41, at 27-32, 100-06.
[61] *See also* Oliphant, *A Return to Stare Decisis,* 14 A.B.A.J. 71, 159 (1928).
[62] *See* Bingham, *Joseph Walter Bingham,* in My Philosophy of Law 13 (1941).

lacks inherent force.[63] Yet an extreme value skepticism is not a necessary corollary of any of the general directions of instrumentalist thought. Nor can it be said that such skepticism was a widely shared tenet in legal circles beyond a few of the thinkers under study here. Hence I have chosen not to consider it a tenet of pragmatic instrumentalism.[64]

B. *An Empirical Approach*

A related facet of pragmatic instrumentalist value theory was its strong empirical flavor.[65] These thinkers held or assumed that questions of value arising in the course of making and implementing law are largely reducible to questions of fact. Their empirical approach might be elaborated in the following general way. The job of legislators, judges, and other legal actors is to devise and administer law and thereby resolve or alleviate concrete problems. Legal actors begin with some facts suggesting a problem. They then ascertain the existing interests involved in the problem. The interests, including those that emerge from any conflict, ultimately are translated into goals that might be pursued to resolve the problem. Of course, facts about the more specific nature of the problem must be determined, and available legal means must be identified.

On this analysis, what these means are is essentially a factual matter, as are differences between these means. Factual estimates must be made about the efficacy of alternative means and about likely further consequences and side effects. Factual estimates about which means would serve what interests most fully enter into the analysis. Once all these facts and estimates are in, the choices of legal actors are essentially dictated by factual considerations, many of which are determinable by scientific method.

The foregoing summary is faithful to much instrumentalist thinking. Dewey explicitly and systematically formulated his legal empiricism along these lines.[66] His approach was but an application of a more general "instrumental" theory of logic and value that he worked out over some time, and which appears to have been highly influential.[67]

---

[63] For an extended account see Purcell, *American Jurisprudence Between the Wars: Legal Realism and the Crisis of Democratic Theory*, 75 Am. Hist. Rev. 424 (1969).

[64] Aspects of another tenet of instrumentalist value theory closely related to maximal satisfaction of wants and interests—that law, legal decisions, and legal actions are to be judged by their consequences or effects—will be treated in section XI *infra*.

[65] *See* text accompanying notes 44-49 *supra* and notes 66 & 67 infra.

[66] Dewey, *Logical Method and Law*, 10 Cornell L.Q. 17 (1924).

[67] *See generally* works cited at note 28 *supra*.

The seemingly all-encompassing empiricism of these thinkers was to some extent a healthy reaction to past excesses. For example, Christopher Langdell, Dean of the Harvard Law School from 1870 to 1895, conceived of law as consisting solely of materials "contained in printed books."[68] Yet law must be applied to fact, and in judicial processes there is a constant interaction between the applicable law and the facts of the case. As late as the first decade of this century, Roscoe Pound had to call attention to the excessively technical procedures of American courts that frequently kept them from resolving disputes on the basis of their factual merits.[69] Furthermore, courts of the day hardly recognized what lawyers now call "legislative facts"—the essential factual premises of legal rules. Indeed, it was not until 1908 that the "Brandeis brief" was born—an appellate brief that recited general social facts relevant to the issues of rule-making before a court.[70] Even legislatures were relatively unconcerned with legislative facts. Through the first half of this century, state legislatures rarely conducted systematic factual inquiries. Although Congress regularly conducted "investigations," the art of legislative fact-finding remained relatively primitive until quite recent times.

But the law also constantly raises issues about what *ought* to be done, and these cannot, even under the foregoing "empirical approach," be reduced simply to issues of fact. In this respect the instrumentalists went too far. Even Karl Llewellyn, one of the most sophisticated, stood ready to try to convert value questions into wholly factual ones, a tendency evident in his work on the Uniform Commercial Code. For example, in the law of warranties in sales of goods he provided that a warranty of fitness of goods for a particular purpose may be excluded by trade usage. Yet he stated that the usage had to be one that is "currently observed by the great majority of decent dealers, even though dissidents ready to cut corners do not agree."[71] It should be clear that not even Llewellyn can reduce the ultimate question for decision in a particular case to one of pure fact in this way. What is to count as "decent dealing"? As "not decent"? No amount of factual evidence of trade usage can answer such questions.[72]

---

[68] Langdell, *Teaching Law as a Science, reprinted in* 21 AM. L. REV. 123, 123 (1887); Langdell, Speech at Harvard Law School (Nov. 5, 1887), *reprinted in* 3 LAW Q. REV. 123, 124 (1887).

[69] Pound, *The Causes of Popular Dissatisfaction with the Administration of Justice*, 40 AM. L. REV. 729, 738-39, 742-47 (1906).

[70] *See, e.g.*, Muller v. Oregon, 208 U.S. 412 (1908).

[71] U.C.C. § 1-205 (Official Comment 5).

[72] Among other important value theoretic tenets of pragmatic instrumentalism not considered here are (1) that in making practical decisions the concrete and the particular, rather than

III

Means and Goals

That law is, in essence, a means, and only a means, to goals derived from sources outside the law, was perhaps the most characteristic tenet of pragmatic instrumentalism. Oddly, these thinkers did not treat this fundamental tenet at all fully. Their general instrumentalist orientation, however, is itself fertilely suggestive, and marks a deep difference between their theory and that of many European, including British, analytical positivists.[73]

A. *Law as a Social Instrument*

Virtually all the classical instrumentalists believed that law is an instrument to serve ends. Oliphant's view is representative. He wrote in 1930:

> A century ago, Jeremy Bentham saw law not as an ultimate but merely as a means to an end and argued that it should be scientifically exploited as such. . . . Then came the pragmatism of James and the instrumental logic of Dewey, with the result that we are beginning to catch up with Bentham. Liberals now venture to talk of law as a means to an end. . . . [M]any are eager to stop talking and begin studying law as a means to present ends. . . .[74]

This very view was an obvious advance over certain earlier notions Some formalists tended to assume that law is a self-justifying body of precepts to be discovered by reason[75] and applied in light of the "logic" of the language expressing these precepts.[76] To an instrumentalist, a legal precept cannot be self-justifying. To justify having a form of law, it is at least necessary to inquire into its ends and its effects. Does it maximize present wants and interests? By apposite and defensible means? If so, this use of law is justified. In addition, the law does not consist of precepts that may be applied formalistically. Rather, law must be applied in light of its substantive ends.

---

the abstract and the general, have primacy; and (2) that the law as it is can and should be sharply distinguished from the law as it ought to be.

[73] Even in this day one encounters articles and books in the analytical positivist tradition that systematically neglect the elemental fact that particular forms of law exist to serve particular goals. Such writings, for example, inquire whether a precept at hand is a rule or merely a principle, whether it imposes a duty or confers a power, whether it is a member of this system or that system, but they do not inquire whether it embodies or reflects a means-goal hypothesis, and if so what the nature of that hypothesis is.

[74] Oliphant, *The New Legal Education,* 131 Nation 493, 495 (1930).

[75] *See, e.g.*, 1 Works of Rufus Choate 436 (S. Brown ed. 1862). *See also* Lochner v. New York, 198 U.S. 45, 53 (1904) (Peckham, J.).

[76] *See, e.g.*, C. Langdell, *supra* note 5.

It is not too much to say that the instrumentalists reconceptualized the nature of law. For them law was essentially a set of means to be used to serve social goals derived from conventional wants and interests.[77] Yet Holmes, Pound, and nearly all the other leading pragmatic instrumentalists failed to carry matters of theory much further. With the principal exception of Dewey, these thinkers theorized little about the general nature and relationship of ends and means in legal ordering.

B. *Law's Goals and Structures*

The theorists of pragmatic instrumentalism did not come to grips with the nature of law's goals and goal structures. In this they were not alone; most adherents of the theory of analytical positivism, for example, also neglected this subject. Yet the goals of law constitute a remarkably fertile and complex field for study. Although in this Article I can only indicate in a general way how these matters might be carried beyond the instrumentalists' fundamental reconceptualization of the nature of law, it will still be possible for the reader to see that most of what follows could be accommodated within a more sophisticated pragmatic instrumentalism. There are few, if any, inherent inconsistencies between instrumentalist theory and what will be offered here.

We have already seen[78] that for most leading instrumentalists the primary tenet of value theory was that law should attempt to maximize the realization of existing interests. Of course this qualifies as a meaningful goal for law only at the most abstract level. Within a society, the interests of the people translate into a number of basic goals that are more or less continuous and pervasive. These include not only goals of traditional legal concern such as preserving order and securing evenhanded administration, but also goals having to do with such matters as the promotion of community health and reinforcement of the family.[79] Of course many other goals that society will want the law to pursue will be far less fundamental.

After a rule or other law is formulated, it still may be difficult to determine the goals that should be attributed to it. This is so for two reasons. First, the lawmaker may not have explicitly incorporated the goals that determine the law's content in the law itself. This often

---

[77] This instrumentalist revolution occurred in America several decades after the one on the Continent led by Rudolph Von Ihering. *See* R. Von Ihering, *supra* note 9.

[78] *See* text accompanying notes 44-49 *supra*.

[79] Law's fundamental goals, particularly those of natural legal concern, call for extended treatment and are beyond the scope of this Article.

occurs in part because intelligible forms of law can ordinarily be formulated without incorporating goals. Intended goals, however, may be ascertained from available evidence in records of legislative bodies, in court opinions, in proceedings of administrative agencies, and the like. Even when not ascertainable, there may still be accepted types of argument for attributing goals to law. Second, the various goals that could be attributed to a form of law are usually ones that have come into conflict in the course of constructing the law. The emerging law is often the result of complex reconciliations, and this may make it difficult to map the extent to which various goals figured in the process.

Rules and other legal precepts characteristically have more than one goal. It is commonly possible to differentiate several goal levels along a means-end continuum of ascending generality, in which the realization of a low-level goal explicitly formulated in the law serves higher-level goals, usually not so formulated. Thus, we may usually attribute to a rule or other precept directing behavior one or more "immediate" goals, one or more "intermediate" goals, and one or more "higher-level" or "ultimate" goals.

Consider, for example, a law requiring private parties to register handguns with the police. In terms of the foregoing analysis, we might distinguish at least the following different goals: "registration of all privately owned handguns" (immediate); "deterrence and control of violence with firearms" (intermediate); and "general community peace" (ultimate). The nature of these goals and the relations between them are such that they cannot be reduced to one and the same goal. We can imagine ways of serving the immediate goals that do not also serve the intermediate goal. For example, if the public knows that more prosecutorial resources are needed to reduce handgun violence, and these are not provided, then registration of handguns, the immediate goal served, may have little or no deterrent effect on their use, the intermediate goal. Although realization of the immediate goal may actually serve the intermediate one, so might realization of many other imaginable immediate goals. For example, handgun violence might be deterred by increasing penalties.[80]

At least on the second and third of the three goal levels, one can usually identify a number of possible goals. Indeed, this will usually be the case even for a single precept. Consider, for example, the

[80] Of course, one cannot draw such distinctions between the types of goals of a single law in the abstract. They can only be drawn in relation to a specific law and a scale or continuum appropriate to it. Thus, one must begin with the immediate goal and trace out how the pursuit of this lowest-level goal would in turn serve higher goals along the appropriate means-end continuum.

ultimate goals for the hypothetical firearm-registration law. These might consist of community peace, facilitation of economic activity, the intrinsic good of preserving life, and enhancement of freedom of movement. Furthermore, aside from affirmative goals, lawmakers understand that almost any law has its costs in the form of expense, time, trouble, and the sacrifice of conflicting values. Lawmakers will therefore pursue the goal of minimizing such costs, too.

Thus, there usually will be no simple, single goal for a legal precept. The goals of a given precept form a goal "constellation" or "synthesis" that usually reflects some effort to accommodate conflicts in an optimal way. Only the most naive pragmatic instrumentalist would have denied these truths but even the most sophisticated did not address them, and much work remains.

C. *Should Law Be Described Merely as a Means?*

With few exceptions, the instrumentalists wrote as if rules and other legal precepts are to be described merely as a means. Thus Pound remarked, "Law is a means, not an end,"[81] and "the life of the law is in its enforcement."[82] Llewellyn, characterizing the group of which he claimed to be a member, added: "They view rules, they view law, as means to ends; as only means to ends; as having meaning only insofar as they are means to ends."[83]

One way to interpret writers like Pound and Llewellyn is to say that they believed a description of a particular form of law can be essentially complete even if it includes no account of, or reference to, its intermediate or ultimate goals. This mode of describing any particular form of law may be called *technological.* A description of a particular form of law in this mode goes only into such things as the wording of the law, its behavioral directives, if any, its sanctions or other implementive devices, and the like. A description of this kind may sometimes imply particular intermediate or ultimate goals, but more often it will be quite ambiguous in this respect, and will say nothing about the priority of any conflicting goals.

As an alternative to technological descriptions, one may claim that a description of a particular form of law is essentially incomplete if it does not include *some* account of, or reference to, its intermediate or ultimate goals. According to this view, a form of law is a "means-goal" complex; it incorporates *teleological* content.

---

[81] Pound, *The Need of a Sociological Jurisprudence,* 29 GREEN BAG 607, 612 (1907).

[82] Pound, *The Scope and Purpose of Sociological Jurisprudence,* 25 HARV. L. REV. 489, 514 (1912).

[83] Llewellyn, *Some Realism About Realism—Responding to Dean Pound, supra* note 2, at 1223.

Which of these descriptive modes, the technological or the teleological, is more faithful to the reality of law? Several arguments favor the teleological. It must be said that although many or even most instrumentalists might ultimately have agreed with this view, they did not confront the issue explicitly. Yet they were, after all, antiformalist. In proclaiming that "law is merely a means" the instrumentalists may only have meant that no particular form of law can be self-sufficient or self-justifying—that a form of law exists only to serve goals and is to be judged accordingly.

Still, the temptation to describe particular forms of law in the technological mode is powerful and recurrent among lawyers. Instrumentalists did adopt general slogans that are technological in tone, such as "law is merely a means." Moreover, some of them did undertake to describe particular forms of law solely in terms of generalities about what officials were doing, not what they were trying to do.[84] But it would be more natural for a full-fledged instrumentalist to insist that an essentially complete description of a particular form of law must include some account of or reference to its goals.

Three arguments favor teleological descriptions—characterizations which reveal particular forms of law as complexes of means and goals. First, it is frequently not possible to separate and distinguish means from goal without artificiality. Legal means may not be readily understandable, even as means, unless brought into relation with relevant goals. Consider, for example, the elaborate system of government transfer payments in modern societies. These are embodied in complex forms of law. One cannot adequately grasp the particular forms of law involved without taking account of what they are for—to relieve poverty, lessen inflation, equalize wealth, enhance liberty, or whatever. A particular form of law will vary depending upon which such goals are primarily at work. Thus, an essentially complete description of any such form of law requires an account of these goals.

Similarly, legal means may be constituents of a goal to such a degree that the abstract goal, standing alone, is not very meaningful. A society may proclaim the goal of equalizing wealth. Until a mode of equalization is prescribed, however, the goal remains abstract, indeterminate, and not very meaningful. This familiar interdependence of means and goal further supports the characterization of particular forms of law as means-goal complexes.[85]

---

[84] *See, e.g.*, Moore & Sussman, *Legal and Institutional Methods Applied to the Debiting of Direct Discounts*, 40 YALE L.J. 381 (1931).

[85] The preceding remarks follow Fuller to some extent. *See generally* L. FULLER, THE LAW IN QUEST OF ITSELF (1940); Fuller, *supra* note 35.

Second, descriptions of law that take account of or refer to goals are more faithful to the reality of law as a human artifact than are merely technological descriptions. We generally understand legal precepts as characteristically designed to serve goals and thus as phenomena adapted, at least to some extent, to those goals. This should hardly surprise anyone, least of all pragmatic instrumentalists. We make laws to accomplish ends. Thus, if a form of law is so ill adapted to its goals that it cannot reliably serve them, we are inclined at least to say it is much less a form of law and, sometimes even to say it is not law at all. Of course, this does not mean that to be law a given precept must be highly effective or that it must serve a good goal. And it is not to rule out, in the case of a totally functionless law, the appropriateness of saying: "This law is useless." Rather, when we think of law we ordinarily have in mind something that is at least minimally effective for its purpose. And the usual phenomena of law that we confront in daily life is, in fact, thus effective. This reinforces the appropriateness of *describing* particular forms of law in terms that take account of or refer to relevant goals.

The third argument for a teleological view derives its force from the requirements of an interpretive method that effectively implements the goals of particular forms of law. Indeed, the argument ought to have appealed to instrumentalists, for they generally subscribed to "goal-oriented" interpretation. In general, the language of a legal precept cannot be appropriately interpreted if divorced from all conceptions of the goals that this precept is to serve. Such language is not self-defining for legal purposes, and the authoritative goals it is meant to serve may not even be stated in this language. Yet these goals may dictate a different interpretation from that which the ordinary lay meaning of the language would suggest. Hence, one must infuse the language with relevant intermediate or ultimate goals in order to determine what the language means for legal purposes. When applying the law to particular circumstances, one can never determine what a legal precept means without considering its purposes. In this view, a particular form of law, considered as a whole, is a complex of means and goals.

The descriptive accuracy of the teleological view could be thought to depend on whether we really do generally interpret law in our system by reference to its goals. Interpreters might choose to ignore even reliable evidence of goals not explicitly incorporated in the law itself. But in fact, goal-oriented interpretation is widespread, and even if it were not it still would not follow that particular forms of law can be properly interpreted apart from the purposes they are to serve. It would follow instead that those who interpret law are in the dark about their responsibility. Their presumptive responsibility is to interpret law to serve goals. This can only be done by keeping goals in view.

Perhaps a brief example will reinforce this argument. Suppose an ordinance says only that "No vehicles shall be taken into public parks." The goals that this language is to implement (found in city council meeting records) are to keep down noise and enhance park safety. Without reference to these goals, a person who interpreted the language solely in light of the ordinary dictionary meaning of the words would be very likely to conclude that bringing a World War II jeep into the park and placing it on a concrete slab as a memorial qualifies as taking a "vehicle" into the park and therefore is a prohibited act. But in light of the goals that a "purposive" interpreter should resort to in order to infuse "vehicle" with appropriate meaning, the jeep would not offend the ordinance.[86]

D. *Relations Between Means and Goals in Effective Thought*

Although pragmatic instrumentalists saw law as a means to goals, all but Dewey and Cook (whom Dewey influenced on this point[87]) were generally silent about the subtle and complex relations between means and goals in effective legal thought. Many assumed or claimed that problems of legal ordering are essentially divisible into two distinct stages: setting goals and devising means. A few were quite explicit. Moore, for example, held that "A rational or logical process is directed towards an end chosen before the process is begun. The process is judging that certain means will tend to that end."[88] On this, Lon Fuller also had much to teach naive instrumentalists. He thought that a view like Moore's inaccurately portrayed the actual thinking of legal actors, and that it is not *possible* to think effectively about means and goals in this way.[89] Of course, when starting to think about a problem, a legal actor may profitably formulate some rather general and tentative goals. By stubbornly holding to these, he might even occasionally invent new legal means. But in law, the proverb that "where there is a will, there is a way" is false, or at least narrowly limited. Moreover, some delimitation of means at the outset is usually necessary to liberate the creative spirit and sharpen judgment. Otherwise, one is likely to flounder in generalities.

[86] *See* Fuller, *supra* note 35, at 662-64; Hart, *Positivism and the Separation of Law and Morals*, 71 HARV. L. REV. 593, 607 (1958).

[87] *See* J. DEWEY, THEORY OF VALUATION (1939); Cook, *supra* note 48, at 59-65.

[88] Moore, *supra* note 41, at 612.

[89] *See* L. FULLER, ANATOMY OF THE LAW 36-39 (1968); Fuller, *American Legal Philosophy at Mid-Century*, 6 J. LEGAL EDUC. 457, 473-81 (1954); Fuller, Means and Ends (1960) (unpublished manuscript on file with the author).

In the course of thinking about a problem, one must bring goals and means into relation. Goals acquire power to orient and discipline analysis when conceived in relation to available means. It is seldom possible to define a social objective meaningfully apart from all means of realizing it. Instrumentalists tended to assume that setting goals is relatively straightforward; the act of setting the goal goes far to determine means. But means also delimit and help determine goals. Indeed, the time is not ripe for a faithful description of society's commitment to, say, the goal of "equal treatment" until after it has settled upon the means of defining and administering the goal. In effective thought, goals and means interact. Goals tentatively point to means. Means then indicate some reformulation of goals. This interactive process continues until the thinker adopts a means-goal hypothesis, or abandons goals because acceptable means are unavailable.

In the course of lawmaking and law administration, a specific means-goal complex or hypothesis is the usual object of evaluation, not goal alone or means alone. The desirability of a goal depends not only on any intrinsic worth it may have. Its attractiveness depends also on any "means deficit"—the likely costs of serving it, including goal sacrifices, sacrifices of means that could serve other goals, and economic costs. It depends also on any "means surplus"—likely collateral gains from a projected means. Thus, goals must be viewed and means considered, in clusters. It follows that problems of means are not merely technical and factual; they too inevitably call for evaluative judgment.

Most of what is said in this section is addressed to omissions or naive corollaries, implicit or assumed, in the instrumentalist tenet that law consists of means to ends. A sophisticated instrumentalism could readily accommodate nearly all of the foregoing critical reactions.

Perhaps the most fundamental pragmatic instrumentalist tenets are the ones we have so far considered: the notion that law should maximize existing interests; the view that questions of value will prove to be largely reducible to matters of fact; and the basic conception of law as social means. We now turn to other elements of the theory dealing with lawmaking (Section IV), with the criteria accepted within our system for identifying precepts as valid law (Sections V and VI), and with the interpretation and application of valid law (Section VII).

IV

Change, Science, and the Creation of Law

Formalists generally viewed the law as a relatively closed system of conceptions and axioms from which judges and others could deduce resolutions of almost any issue.[90] In their view there was little need, let alone scope, for creating new law. Pragmatic instrumentalists, on the other hand, saw great potential for the effective use of law. Thus, they envisioned vast scope for legislators, judges, and other authorized legal actors to make wholly new law as well as to modify existing law. To them, social change was the major stimulus of legal change. Although some legal change would have to be brought about by legislators, these thinkers proclaimed that judges not only may interpret and apply pre-existing law, but may create law as well. The instrumentalists believed in scientific method and were the first to champion the relevance of empirical research to lawmaking of all kinds.

A. *The Creation of Law—Methodology*

Insofar as formalists and conservative theorists at the turn of the century did recognize proposals for genuinely new law, they often assumed that these proposals should be judged primarily by how well they meshed with existing law. Consistency, analogy, coherence, harmony, and symmetry were their main tests of soundness.[91] The pragmatic instrumentalists rejected this view. They did not look to the past and ask: Is this proposal consistent with X? Analogous to Y? Harmonious with Z? Rather, they looked forward and asked: What can now be done to alter the future? What substantive goals, derived from popular wants and interests, are relevant? What rules or other precepts are required to further them? Thus, the new theorists subscribed to a *substantive* means-goal rationality. Today, it may be difficult to believe that theorists could ever have thought differently about law. Yet in its time, this was a signal advance, especially in regard to the judicial role.

It was part of the creed of these thinkers that lawmakers must turn to social science to ascertain facts relevant to the creation and modification of law. At this time, the social sciences had not yet accumulated a store of knowledge which lawmakers could use. Accordingly, lawmakers usually had to commission an inquiry in regard to each problem as it arose. Several kinds of inquiry might be required for any given problem.

---

[90] Pound conceived the formalist position in precisely these terms. *See generally* Pound, *Mechanical Jurisprudence*, 8 COLUM. L. REV. 605 (1908).

[91] *See, e.g.*, J. BEALE, *supra* note 6; C. LANGDELL, *supra* note 5. *See also* Lochner v. New York, 193 U.S. 45, 52 (1904) (Peckham, J.) (existing law widely requires liberty of contract); 1 R. CHOATE, *supra* note 75, at 436.

First, lawmakers had to find facts about the nature and extent of the problem knocking on the law's door. What were the effects of a monopoly practice on economic efficiency? What kinds of official corruption were commonplace? How many women employees were being worked beyond a forty-five hour week? What impure foods and drugs were finding their ways onto the market? In all such inquiries, the lawmaker also had to determine the social effects of these events and states of affairs. What, for example, were the effects of long hours on the health of a woman and her family? Holmes and Pound were among the first to advocate the use of social science methods in such inquiries. In a famous essay, Holmes urged the use of statistics, economics, and science generally.[92] Pound stated that

> [t]he main problem to which sociological jurists are addressing themselves today [1912] is to enable and to compel law-making, and also interpretation and application of legal rules, to take more account, and more intelligent account, of the social facts upon which law must proceed and to which it is to be applied.[93]

Second, it was assumed that lawmakers must ascertain the causes of economic inefficiency, of official corruption, of excessive hours of labor, of practices that led to impure food and drugs entering commerce. Better yet, if social science methods were to be applied most faithfully, the very laws of social causation, which account for the occurrence of such states of affairs, and in turn their effects, would have to be scientifically formulated. A law of social causation would take the general form: "If certain conditions are satisfied, then certain effects will invariably occur or will occur with some specified degree of frequency." With knowledge of such laws, legislators would be in a better position to identify the "pressure points"[94] to which they could best direct their energies to prevent or remedy these occurrences and states of affairs. Also, with knowledge of such laws of causation, legislators could predict the social effects that would occur depending on the legal means deployed.

Third, science could help determine alternative legal means for coping with problems, and could even help construct such means by discovering or adapting technology. What if criminal penalties were used against monopolies? Or private treble damage actions? What new inventions in the fields of health and safety might be introduced and legally prescribed to cope with the effects of long hours for women? Should something more radical be attempted? John Dewey's

---

[92] *See* Holmes, *The Path of the Law*, *supra* note 29, at 467.

[93] Pound, *supra* note 82, at 512-13.

[94] *See* Cohen, *Field Theory and Judicial Logic*, 59 YALE L.J. 238, 252 (1950).

"logic of inquiry"—rather than demonstration—was viewed by some as suggesting fruitful ways to ascertain the likely consequences of using alternative means. Several of these thinkers, notably Oliphant, Bingham, Cook, and Moore, were particularly interested in how varying the legal means might produce desired consequences.[95] Indeed, some appear to have assumed that over time it would be possible to construct laws of legal causation similar to laws of social causation in which antecedent variables include the use of legal means. On this view, it would be possible to state that "If legal means X were used in circumstances Y, results Z would be expectable."

Armed with these tools, lawmakers could be truly scientific. They could invoke laws of social and legal causation to predict the likely efficacy of alternative legal means, determine costs and benefits, choose the preferred means, and implement them. Pragmatic instrumentalists generally prescribed this approach not only for legislators but for courts, too.

Once new law was made by legislature or court, the instrumentalists urged that social methods be continuously applied to monitor and evaluate whether the law was working out as envisioned. Fact-finding of this nature would prove useful in deciding whether to modify or perhaps even abandon the current law. Pound stressed that "[t]he compromises and adjustments that will achieve the largest securing of social interests with the least sacrifice, must be sought through a process of trial and error."[96] Holmes and many others wrote of uses of law as "experiments" and of society as a legal "laboratory." Holmes even viewed the Constitution in this spirit; "It is an experiment, as all life is an experiment."[97]

Instrumentalist trumpeting for vast infusions of empirical research into legislative and judicial processes of lawmaking was much needed in its time. At the turn of the century, our courts were regularly striking down social legislation, apparently in ignorance of social facts behind it.[98] Today it has become a truism that knowledge of social facts is essential to sound lawmaking.

---

[95] *See, e.g.*, Bingham, *What Is the Law?* 11 MICH. L. REV.. 1, 9-11 (1912); Cook, *Scientific Method and the Law*, 13 A.B.A.J. 303, 308 (1927); Moore & Callahan, *Law and Learning Theory*, 53 Yale L.J. 1, 3 (1943); Oliphant, *Facts, Opinions, and Value-Judgments*, 10 TEXAS L. REV. 127, 137 (1938).

[96] Pound, *Jurisprudence*, in HISTORY AND PROSPECTS OF THE SOCIAL SCIENCES 444-72 (H. Barnes ed. 1925).

[97] Abrams v. United States, 250 U.S. 616, 630 (1919). *See also* Truax v. Corrigan, 257 U.S. 312, 344 (1921) (Holmes, J., dissenting) ("There is nothing that I more deprecate than the use of the Fourteenth Amendment beyond the absolute compulsion of its words to prevent the making of social experiments . . . in the insulated chambers afforded by the several States. . . . ").

[98] *See generally* Pound, *Liberty of Contract*, 18 YALE L.J. 454, 480 (1909); Pound, *Law in Books and Law in Action*, 44 AM. L. REV. 12, 16 (1910).

B. *Excesses and Myopias*

Pragmatic instrumentalists overstated, perhaps understandably, the need for systematic scientific inquiry into social facts in lawmaking. Some important problems call for little or no inquiry beyond what is already known. Sometimes the main problem before a legislature is simply to state and codify a widely held moral tenet. This is true, for example, of many aspects of promulgating a criminal code. The problem may be that of codifying widely accepted case law and customary business practices in a new commercial code, formulating widely accepted norms for contract law, adopting a fair and efficient set of procedural rules, or specifying formalities for the valid exercise of private power to enter into contracts, make wills, or set up secured transactions. In all such instances, empirical research may either be largely irrelevant or relevant but of so little consequence that its cost would easily exceed its value.

Even when social science research is relevant and useful it frequently need not take so ambitious a form as the formulation of laws of social or legal causation. Commonly, the research will take the form of information gathering, as when a legislative body inquires into how many employers employ women beyond a forty-hour week, when it sends out inspectors to determine the living conditions in housing subject to rent control, or when it inquires into average prices of necessaries to determine the sufficiency of existing welfare payment levels.

Similarly, research to determine the success of a means-goal hypothesis may in some circumstances call for nothing very ambitious or systematic. For example, a new system prescribed in regulations for coordinating aircraft over large cities will either be followed by a reduction in accidents and near misses or it will not.

Furthermore, not all problems of lawmaking must be approached in accordance with the instrumentalists' one basic method: ascertaining the problem, determining its causes, and deploying legal means to operate directly on those causes or "pressure points." Frequently it is enough for the lawmaker to address the effects directly, without inquiring into causes at all. This is true, for example, of many legal programs for the distribution of such substantive social benefits as education, welfare, and the like. If lawmakers want basic literacy and minimum subsistence for all, they may simply raise the tax dollars and proceed accordingly. They need not worry much about why literacy would fall without public schools or why people would starve without food.

Pragmatic instrumentalists were unduly optimistic about what social science can contribute to sound lawmaking. We have already seen that once the facts are in, important questions of value always remain for the lawmaker to confront.[99] These theorists were wrong to assume that science can determine our ends as well as identify our means.[100] Rather, the lawmaker must compare and evaluate alternative means-goal hypotheses in some qualitative way. An ultimate judgment must be made in light of reasons. The force of such reasons depends not only upon empirical facts available in the decisional context, but also upon principles and ideas of what is good, right, and appropriate, beyond mere de facto wants and interests. A few instrumentalists, Pound included, sometimes wrote as if they believed that social sciences could generate not just findings of social fact but their own "normative" theories of value as well—theories peculiarly relevant to lawmaking.[101] This, too, was deeply misconceived. The social sciences do not each have a "normative side"—a theory of value—that is also the special scientific province of each discipline. No doubt the findings of these disciplines may interact with general notions of value which are not the province of any special discipline, and thereby give rise to policy recommendations.[102] These recommendations might or might not accord with existing wants and interests.

Nearly all of the pragmatic instrumentalists greatly underestimated the methodological and other limitations of social science. These limitations are especially acute insofar as the objective is to establish laws of social or legal causation so that legislators may predict the effects of uses of legal means to cope with problems. As early as 1927, the philosopher Morris R. Cohen wrote illuminatingly on the difficulties that plague efforts to establish causal laws in social affairs.[103] He set forth the following procedure for determining a causal law in most natural sciences: first identify all possible variables that one may hypothesize to be causes of the event or state of affairs in question; isolate each variable while holding the others constant, and determine whether the event or state of affairs in question nonetheless occurs; repeat this process for each of the variables and plausible combinations thereof; and, finally, formulate a statement of the variable or variables that turn out to be causal.

---

[99] *See* text accompanying notes 70-72 *supra*.

[100] *See, e.g.*, Holmes, *Law in Science and Science in Law*, *supra* note 44, at 462.

[101] *See, e.g.*, Pound, *supra* note 81, at 609, 615; Pound, *Enforcement of Law*, 10 GREEN BAG 401, 403 (1908). *See also* Oliphant, *supra* note 95, at 137-38.

[102] *See* Summers & Kelley, *Economists' Reasons for Common Law Decisions—A Preliminary Inquiry*, 1 OXFORD J. LEGAL STUDIES 213 (1981).

[103] *See* M. COHEN, *Law and the Scientific Method*, in LAW AND THE SOCIAL ORDER 184-87 (1933); Cohen, *The Social Sciences and the Natural Sciences*, in THE SOCIAL SCIENCES AND THEIR INTERRELATIONS 437 (W. Ogburn ed. 1927), *reprinted in part in* READINGS IN JURISPRUDENCE 724-47 (J. Hall. ed. 1938).

Cohen stressed that this procedure is not as applicable to social affairs as it is to nature. It is more difficult in social research to identify all possible causal variables. There are also special problems of access. For example, a relevant variable may consist of motives and reasons behind individual or group action, yet reliable evidence of these may be hard to find. In addition, the variables tend to be far more diverse, and thus less susceptible to definition and to measurement in a common unit. As a result, we cannot tell how much of a variable, or combination of variables, will be required to bring about an event or state.[104] Moreover, some antecedent variables may be "opposed" to other variables. For example, an economic motive may be pitted against a religious one. If we cannot measure these, we cannot know how much of one variable would counteract another. Furthermore, it is less easy to isolate the possible effect of a single variable, that is, less easy to vary one at a time. As Cohen put it, social situations are networks in which one cannot alter a single variable without affecting a great many others. Finally, it is rarely possible to repeat the sequence of events over and over again to determine the possible causal efficacy of each variable under consideration.

According to Cohen, all these factors drastically limit the availability of many kinds of social knowledge. He thought the inability to repeat sequences a factor specially worthy of note. Societies simply cannot afford to repeat phenomena such as famines, depressions, or deaths, etc. Social norms and taboos would bar the repetition of other sequences, for example, those invading privacy or the integrity of the person. Other phenomena that serve as variables are often in their nature not repeatable, for instance unique historical episodes.

Although these and other difficulties plague social science research, they should not be taken as a counsel of despair. As already noted, much fact-finding for purposes of lawmaking does not require the formulation of laws of social causation of any kind. Moreover, even when controlled experimentation and inquiry are not possible, simulations, field experiments, and statistical information and other analyses of data can provide important information and insight.[105]

---

[104] Consider, for example, the range of relatively unmeasurable variables listed below, all of which might be antecedent to a given event or state, the "cause" of which is to be determined: (1) varied motives, desires, ends of individual or groups; (2) varied motives, desires, ends of individuals or groups combined with any of a vast variety of possible means at their disposal; (3) varied traits of individuals or groups; (4) varied social structures; (5) varied legal structures; (6) varied social history; (7) varied natural events.

Indeed, today some philosophers of social scientific inquiry are not so pessimistic as Cohen.[106]

V

Criteria of Legal Validity I—Law as Official Action

One of the basic notions required to understand the nature of a system of law is that of legal validity. At any given time a society will have a very wide variety of social standards and norms, and people must be able to tell which are legal and which are non-legal. Where there are purported modifications of previously existing law, people will need to know whether past or present law controls. The validity of any additions to existing law will have to be determined. Then too, there will be proposed changes in the law and it will be important to be able to tell whether a proposal would be legal. When conflicts arise between what would otherwise be independently valid legal rules, for instance between a duly enacted statute and a court decision, there must also be some method of determining which law governs.

In all the foregoing and still other important types of instances the issue is one of legal validity: What is the *valid* rule or precept? Note that issues of validity do not necessarily address whether the precepts involved are good or bad. Indeed, as we will see, the controlling standards of validity accepted within a given society *may* be ones that determine validity without regard to the goodness of particular precepts.

Issues of validity are often distinguished too sharply from issues of interpretation and application of admittedly valid law. Questions of validity are themselves to be resolved by reference to law—standards and techniques for determining what is and what is not valid law. This law governing issues of validity may take a variety of forms, and itself calls for interpretation.

The literature of pragmatic instrumentalism includes two basic and not wholly compatible accounts of the nature of the law governing issues of validity in our legal order: (1) any rule or other precept acted upon or laid down by an authorized official is valid, and (2) valid law consists of predictions of what courts will do.

A. *The Validity of Law as Determined by Prior Official Action*

One basic task of the legal theorist is to provide a general descriptive account of the practices followed in our system for the identifica-

---

[105] *See* E. Nagel, The Structure of Science 456-59 (1961).

[106] For a more optimistic assessment, and for the view that Cohen's model of scientific method is unduly restrictive, see generally R. Rudner, Philosophy of Social Science (1966).

tion of valid law. This account would set forth the standards operative within our system for differentiating what is valid from what is not valid law.

Most pragmatic instrumentalists implicitly or explicitly took the view that a given precept is valid in our system if and only if the relevant highest court or other appropriate official has acted upon it or laid it down.[107] On this view, then, "the law" is not a "brooding omnipresence in the sky";[108] rather, it is whatever judges act upon or lay down as law. Of course, prior judicial action might diverge from prior official text or statements laying down standards for determining what precepts are legally valid; in that event, instrumentalists held that the later judicial action controlled.[109] Indeed, it seems to have been widely thought that provisions of the Constitution limiting the kinds of law Congress or state legislatures can validly create are merely whatever the courts make of them.[110] Similarly, if a statute required two witnesses for a valid will but the courts later required only one, the court actions would control as to validity.[111]

This simple doctrine is infelicitous in the following important way. To the extent that these thinkers held that judicial deeds always control prior official words laying down tests of validity, we are left with no independent standards by which to determine whether what judges consider to be valid law is itself in accord with legal tests of validity. Yet our very concept of a standard of validity generally requires that the standard be independent in this way. We subscribe to a system in which the rule of law prevails to some considerable degree. This means, among other things, that citizens are not meant to wait until a court speaks before they can know their legal rights. Generally, they are to have the means of ascertaining these rights in advance. Tests of validity operative in advance of final court action provide these means.

It misdescribes our system to say that judges have general authority to "bootstrap" their actions into legally valid status. As H. L. A.

---

107 *See, e.g.*, J. FRANK, *supra* note 41, at 124-26; J. GRAY, *supra* note 47, at 84-112; K. LLEWELYN, THE BRAMBLE BUSH 3, 5 (1930); Bingham, *supra* note 95, at 11; Cook, *The Logical and Legal Basis of Conflict of Laws,* 33 YALE L.J. 457, 460 (1924).

108 Southern Pac. Co. v. Jensen, 244 U.S. 205, 222 (1917).

109 *See, e.g.*, J. FRANK, *supra* note 41, at 124-28; J. GRAY, *supra* note 47, at 84-112, 309; Llewellyn, *A Realistic Jurisprudence—The Next Step, supra* note 2, at 455-56.

110 Thus, even a Chief Justice of the Supreme Court, Charles Evans Hughes, said "We are under a Constitution, but the Constitution is whatever the judges say it is." Speech by Charles Evans Hughes (May 3, 1907), *reprinted in* THE JUDICIAL PROCESS 501 (R. Aldisert ed. 1976). For extended and perceptive analysis of this viewpoint, see H. L. A. HART, THE CONCEPT OF LAW 138-43 (1961).

111 One may easily think the foregoing a surprising view of the priority between constitutional text or statute on the one hand, and subsequent judicial action on the other.

Hart has noted, this is true even though their decisions may be legally final.[112] If in resolving issues of validity judges are "bound" by something, then that something must be external to whatever it is that they are doing. They cannot at the time of acting be "bound" by their own immediate acts. It must remain possible that even judges could resolve issues of validity mistakenly. Yet if whatever judges do is *ipso facto* valid, then they can never be mistaken. And in our system, informed citizens, lawyers, and officials recognize that judges can be mistaken, for they not uncommonly criticize judicial acts when contrary to independent standards for identifying valid law. Moreover, through our processes of appellate review for error (and other corrective devices) we officially recognize that judges can be mistaken. Indeed, sometimes courts themselves invalidate long-established courses of judicial decision as never having been the true law.

In no modern legal system is it true that the standards and techniques for determining valid law are reducible merely to whatever it is that judges do. The reality is that these systems preserve a fundamental distinction between judicial action in accord with standards and techniques for determining valid law, on the one hand, and judicial action not in accord with such standards on the other. Certainly our own system has always embodied tests for determining valid law that are independent of what judges ultimately do.[113] A theory of legal validity that provides no place for such independent standards is *conceptually* inadequate. It simply lacks the categories required to take account of the reality of the relevant social practices.

I now turn to a second issue. Judicial actions and past official texts specifying tests of validity commonly do not diverge. At least in these circumstances, instrumentalists often wrote as if they were content with the notion that standards of valid law must consist of prior official pronouncements: valid law is whatever an authorized official has duly laid down or acted upon. This test, however, looks solely to the *source* of the law in question. Nothing inherent in the nature of law requires that tests of legal validity take exclusively the form of source-based criteria. Such criteria make no place at all for the fact that a legal system may resolve issues of validity partly upon the basis of the substantive *content* of the precept in question—upon the substantive reasons that figure in its content. In our own legal system many issues of validity are resolved not only by reference to the authority of the source of law in question, but also by reference to such substantive

[112] *See* H. L. A. HART, *supra* note 110, at 138-44.

[113] Of course, this is not to say that for every issue of validity that arises, there must be or is a determinate independent test of validity.

considerations. Hence, in this regard the instrumentalists' "source-based" theory of validity is simply descriptively awry. Whether a statute is valid may depend on its substantive content and not just whether it emanated from an authoritative source, namely the elected legislature. For example, a legitimately promulgated statute may be constitutionally invalid because it discriminates against an ethnic group.[114]

Analogously, a court precedent within a common law field can be invalid. If judged solely by a source-based test, however, it would seem to follow that such a precedent must necessarily be valid law. But it is familiar to lawyers in our system that we not uncommonly regard a precedent as no longer "good law"—meaning thereby that if the precedent were cited to a court, that court would not follow it. Our courts have power to overrule bad case law, and stand ready to do so. But an actual overruling is not required before lawyers and others may appropriately regard a precedent as bad law—as no longer valid. Difficult borderline cases of validity may arise, of course, but not all cases are near the borderline. Now, just what kind of test of validity is at work when we proceed to identify case law as bad and thus not valid? The test must be partly one of substantive content. Bad case law that is perceived to be no longer valid is simply law without sufficient reasoned justification.

Judges recognize various forms of custom as valid law in our system, too. Yet in so doing, judges consider whether the customs are unreasonable or unconscionable and this must surely count as a "test of content" rather than as merely a test of authoritative origin. There is a further difficulty of a different kind with regard to custom in the theory of those who would claim that its status as valid law depends on its authoritative origin. Usually there are no determinate authoritative originators of custom. Whether such custom be a course of past dealing, a usage of trade, or a general social practice, typically no determinable person in authority lays it down. It just grows up.

It might be thought that source-based tests of the validity of custom still apply, for a custom does not become valid law until a court later recognizes it as such. But this is not consistent with our actual law-identifying practices. Lawyers and others regularly identify customs as law, on their own footing, in advance of official stamps of validity.

In deciding cases of first impression, in fashioning new law to replace overruled law, in choosing between conflicting precedents,

---

[114] Of course, the courts might choose to ignore even explicit substantive criteria of validity in our Constitution, even for long periods; the past is not without amazing instances of this.

and in rounding out a statute or otherwise engaging in legitimate creative interpretation, judges make what is considered valid law. But it would misdescribe the facts to say that in our system this law is valid *merely* because authorized judges have made it. It is valid, too, because it has justified substantive content—because it has a sufficient ingredient of reason. Mere source-based criteria of legal validity do not take account of the actual play of such considerations of substantive content within our system. Instead, they divorce validity from content.

It follows that the general descriptive account of legal validity to which many instrumentalists subscribed was, in an important sense, formalistic. It looked to the exercise of formal authority and entirely neglected substantive content. This is a paradox, for as we have seen, the instrumentalists were virulently anti-formalist in their views. The paradox can be explained, if not resolved, however. Some of these thinkers were reacting, in an undiscriminating way, to certain unenlightened and highly conservative decisions of judges on the Supreme Court and on the highest courts of the various states. Holmes, Pound, and others viewed such judges as overly enamored with Abstract Reason.[115] These theorists, wishing to disassociate themselves, may have repudiated tests of validity that are content oriented in favor of source-based tests in which authoritative origins rather than substantive content control what counts as the law. Of course, in seeking to curb excesses of the day these thinkers were abandoning (perhaps unconsciously) the task of *describing* the criteria of validity at work in the system. Moreover, these thinkers were highly science-minded. It was natural for them to want to conceive of the legal validity of a rule or other precept as a matter of ascertainable brute fact—as something determinable solely by empirical evidence of concrete historical events like promulgation or decision. A mere source-based test of valid law also allowed them (or so they thought) to draw a sharp distinction between valid law and general moral principles, a distinction several of them were keen to insist on, again partly as a way of combatting excesses. Finally, a source-based criterion of legal validity, though itself formalist, does not necessarily entail that *bête noire* of instrumentalism, formalist interpretation and application of the law after it is once identified as valid.

Still, in its time, the instrumentalist effort to describe tests of valid law in terms of whatever has been laid down or acted upon by an

---

[115] See, for example, Professor Howe's discussion of Holmes's reaction to views such as those of Chief Justice Rufus Choate. Howe, *The Positivism of Mr. Justice Holmes*, 64 HARV. L. REV. 529, 538 (1951). See also Gray's critique of Blackstone and Carter. J. GRAY, *supra* note 47, at 219-40.

official may not have been wholly devoid of virtue, even though inaccurate. When Holmes, for example, stressed that valid law is something man-made rather than a brooding omnipresence in the sky, he was, among other things, reminding judges and others that the quality of the law is something for which they have responsibility.[116] These thinkers also unmasked judicial conservatism partly by stressing that under very general constitutional provisions the law is necessarily to some extent whatever the judges say it is.[117]

B. *Prescribing Criteria of Validity—A Task for Legal Theorists?*

Another basic task that legal theorists may undertake is normative rather than descriptive. For example, theorists may recommend that a society, where that choice is a real one for existing officials, generally opt for source-based criteria for identifying law as valid in a system of law, for content-oriented criteria, or for some other kind of criteria.

Some of the critics of pragmatic instrumentalism actually interpreted the instrumentalists to be recommending source-based criteria ("valid law is whatever officials have acted on or laid down") and not simply to be describing the criteria at work in the system. Fuller condemned exclusively source-based criteria. He found them formal and fiat-oriented and likely to breed a "law is law formalism" in which lawyers, judges, and others feel compelled to confine their arguments on the law's evolving content merely to points that have already been endorsed by some official. He thought that the worth of arguments in court should depend mainly on their intrinsic merits, and not just on whatever "authoritativeness" they might have.[118]

C. *What the Law Truly Identified as Valid Encompasses*

Even if a legal theorist has provided a satisfactory description of the standards of validity that officials and others use to identify rules and other precepts as valid law, it does not follow that he has also provided an account of what the law so identified encompasses. For example, according to the tests of valid law in our own system, certain judge-made precepts—common law concepts—are valid. But what does this law consist of? Is it merely the words in opinions—the law in books—or does it also encompass "the law in action"? Assume that the law in books is that a plaintiff who has been contributorily negligent may not recover. If factfinders regularly return verdicts in plain-

[116] *See, e.g.*, Holmes, *The Path of the Law*, *supra* note 29, at 467.

[117] *See* Pound, *supra* note 8, *passim*.

[118] *See, e.g.*, Holmes, *The Path of the Law*, *supra* note 29, at 467.

tiffs' favor in the face of evidence of their negligence, even though instructed that such negligence is a complete bar, is not the law in action really a principle of comparative negligence, and thus different from the law in books?

Certain formalists, at the turn of the century and later, held that valid law is to be found solely in books.[119] The instrumentalists, on the other hand, held that the law identified as valid must be construed in light of the law in action. Pound's essay, *The Law in Books and the Law in Action,*[120] was pathbreaking. He claimed that the law in books is frequently not the same as the law in action, and that a truly realistic and scientific approach must take account of any differences. Llewellyn, among others, insisted that these differences must be studied by means of "an observational science, of objective character."[121]

On this view, then, truly scientific "descriptions" of the law are not confined merely to general recitals of the law in books. For law is far more than words on paper. It at least includes what courts are *currently doing in the name of law.* Felix Cohen, for example, asserted that "legal rules are simply formulae *describing* uniformities of judicial decision."[122]

In their zeal thus *to be realistic* and scientific, many instrumentalists assumed that any form of law is always ultimately reducible to empirical fact—to generalizations about the actual behavior of officials. As Kelsen stressed, however, the law cannot consist just of descriptive generalizations about behavioral regularities. Law is inherently normative; it specifies that something *ought* to be done in given circumstances, and thus generates authoritative reasons (although not necessarily conclusive ones) for deciding legal issues one way rather than another. To portray law only as empirical fact is to distort its normative nature.[123]

If we seek to reduce law merely to official behavior patterns we not only lose sight of law's normative character, we render utterly irrelevant any inquiry into whether these behavior patterns are consistent with the law in books. Just because the "law in action" and the "law in books" may differ, it hardly follows that the law in action is necessarily the valid law. What a court or other official does that departs from the law in books may indicate that the law in books is sub

---

[119] *See, e.g.*, Langdell, *supra* note 68.

[120] Pound, *Law in Books and Law in Action, supra* note 98, at 12.

[121] Llewellyn, *The Theory of Legal "Science,"* 20 N.C.L. Rev. 1, 6 (1941).

[122] Cohen, *Transcendental Nonsense and the Functional Approach,* 35 Colum. L. Rev. 809, 847 (1935) (emphasis added).

[123] H. Kelsen, *supra* note 37, at 162.

silentio undergoing change, as in the comparative negligence example. But it may simply reflect a mistaken conception of the law. Whether what the court does is a mistake or a change in the law, of course, makes all the difference. The possibility that the law in action is a mistake must not be foreclosed by recasting our conception of what the law identified as valid encompasses to include only whatever the courts are doing, as some instrumentalists assumed. Valid law consists of the law in action only insofar as it is not a mistaken departure from the law in books.

Moreover, if we seek to reduce the law to what officials actually do we render irrelevant any inquiry into their *reasons* for doing what they do. It is at least possible to state in some way what officials do without going into their reasons. In failing to go into reasons, we make it more difficult to determine whether what they are doing really is consistent with any applicable law because we deprive ourselves of officials' own efforts to link their behavior up with the law through the mediating phenomena of reasons. But of far greater importance, we simply deprive reasoned argument of its true role in the judicial process. Valid law becomes just what judges do, not what they ought to do in light of reason, including any light in the form of applicable precedent or other law. It is true that what a judge does might be a response to reasons urged upon him. But then again, it might not be, and if not, this circumstance would be utterly irrelevant because, in the end, "the law" would consist of whatever it was that the judge actually *did* in that particular case. In adopting any such overall behavioristic position, as Henry M. Hart aptly put it, "we have not only negated the capacity of our officials to take thought, and by thinking change their action; we have nullified our own title to try to persuade them to do so."[124]

In the final analysis, a radically behaviorist reduction of law is significantly self-defeating anyway. It frequently is impossible to characterize the nature of what a person (including a judge) is doing without any reference to that person's reasons for so acting. Moreover, even when the person's behavior alone is generally intelligible in some way without reference to his reasons, a knowledge of those reasons will commonly cast further important light on the nature of that behavior. In sum, without reference to reasons, we frequently could not provide a reliable account of just what a judge *is doing*.

Thus, there are risks for those who would dwell indiscriminately on a distinction between the law in books and the law in action. They may wind up in the deadly bog of behavioralism. A number of

---

[124] Hart, *Holmes's Positivism—An Addendum*, 64 HARV. L. REV. 929, 934 (1951).

instrumentalists did just this. But if I am right, my critique of this behavioralist turn in instrumentalist thought also applies more generally to legal behavioralism whatever its source. Thus it applies as well to the behavioralist strains in contemporary economics and sociobiology as applied to law.[125]

VI

Criteria of Legal Validity II—Law as Prediction

There is a deep, though not unresolvable, ambivalence in pragmatic instrumentalist criteria of legal validity. As indicated in the last section, many of these thinkers held that the primary standard of validity actually operative in our system is that a rule or other precept is valid law if laid down or acted upon by authorized officials. Yet many of these same theorists also believed that in our system law consists of *predictions* "of the incidence of the public force through the instrumentality of the courts."[126] These two formulations are not identical. A rule might be valid under the former, but not under the latter, and vice versa. Instrumentalists generally were not mindful of this ambivalence.

In this section, I will treat the predictive theory merely as a theory of legal validity, although it ramifies into various other important views which cannot be considered here.

A. *The Predictive Theory*

Oliver Wendell Holmes wrote in 1897:

> People want to know under what circumstances and how far they will run the risk of coming up against what is so much stronger than themselves, and hence it becomes a business to find out when this danger is to be feared. The object of our study, then, is prediction, the prediction of the incidence of the public force through the instrumentality of the courts.[127]

The above passage is probably the most influential in the history of American legal thought.[128]

---

[125] Some modern economic analysis of law is behavioralist, at least in the sense that it ignores the reasons judges give for what they do. *See, e.g.*, R. Posner, Economic Analysis of Law (2d ed. 1979). The same is true of some sociobiological analysis. *See, e.g.*, Hirshleifer, *Evolutionary Models in Economics and Law: Cooperation Versus Conflict Strategy, to be published* in 4 Research in L. & Econ. (1982).

[126] Holmes, *The Path of the Law*, *supra* note 29, at 457.

[127] *Id.*

[128] Actually, Holmes had adumbrated his theory as early as 1872. *See* Holmes, Book Review, *supra* note 29.

At least two forms of predictivism must be distinguished, a mild form and a robust one. According to the former, valid law consists of a rule or other precept that in the generality of cases is *likely* to prevail, given the applicable constitutional, statutory, customary, or judge-made law. Holmes himself sometimes put the matter in these terms.[129] This version of predictivism may be considered mild in two respects. The lawyer is predicting not some particular outcome, but a precept that is likely to prevail in the generality of cases. Further, the lawyer uses only pre-existing law as the basis for his predictions. It may be doubted that this should even be called a predictivist theory, for the lawyer appears to be doing no more than identifying and applying the law.

Many apparent followers of Holmes, however, frequently wrote as if they subscribed to a more robust form of predictivism. According to this version, valid law consists of a predicted judicial or other official action in a particular case.[130] Moreover, the lawyer who is predicting the outcome is to base his prediction not only on pre-existing rules but also on such factors as past instances of judicial behavior, the stimuli of the raw facts of the case at hand, ideologies and personal values of the judges, their social backgrounds, and the like.[131] It was not always clear whether the robust predictivists viewed themselves as describing actual tests of validity in our system, or prescribing the use of such tests.

B. *Deficiencies of Robust Predictivism*

Robust predictivism poses several problems. First, there are methodological issues which these predictivists did not resolve satisfactorily. Apparently under the influence of analogies from science,

---

[129] Thus, Holmes once wrote, "The only question for the lawyer is, how will the judges act? Any motive for their action, be it constitution, statute, custom or precedent, which can be relied upon as likely in the generality of cases to prevail, is worthy of consideration as one of the sources of law . . . . " Holmes, Book Review, *supra* note 29, at 724.

[130] *See, e.g.*, Bingham, *Joseph Walter Bingham,* in MY PHILOSOPHY OF LAW, *supra* note 48, at 5, 12:

> [W]hen a lawyer tells his client that if he wishes to devise his land, "the law is" that witnesses must sign his will, does he not thereby mean to indicate that if the will is not thus executed, the courts will hold it invalid? The lawyer is not stating any rule as the law; he is predicting the governmental consequences of a particular case—the case of his client's will, executed so or otherwise.

See also J. FRANK, *supra* note 41, at 118-47; Cohen, *supra* note 122, at 845-46; Cook, *supra* note 95, at 308; Moore & Hope, *An Institutional Approach to the Law of Commercial Banking,* 38 YALE L.J. 703, 703-04 (1929).

[131] *See, e.g.*, Bingham, *Legal Philosophy and the Law,* 9 ILL. L. REV. 98, 109 (1913); Cohen, *supra* note 122; Cook, *supra* note 95, at 308-09; Llewellyn, *A Realistic Jurisprudence—The Next Step, supra* note 2, at 447-57; Moore & Hope, *supra* note 130; Oliphant, *supra* note 61, at 159-61.

many of these thinkers assumed that past instances of judicial behavior alone could serve lawyers as bases of prediction, in the same way that past instances of muscular reaction in response to electrical impulses serve scientists as bases of prediction. John Dickinson attacked this analogy, and pointed out that judicial reaction to past judicial behavior is unlike the "automatic repetition of like reactions in the behavior of physical bodies."[132] Rather, the judicial response to past behavior "operates indirectly through the mental understanding which the later judge has of what the earlier judge has done."[133] This can occur only through the medium of words characterizing the past judge's actions, not simply through past behavior. Moreover, it will not occur unless the later judge believes in following precedent—the described behavior of past judges—and believes the past behavior to be "close enough" to bring a precedent into play. But how is the predicting lawyer to know who the judges of his case will be, let alone reliably determine their views on the doctrine of precedent in general and in relation to the particular case at hand? As Kelsen noted, it would be "impossible to submit the judge to such an investigation before he has announced his decision. No sociological jurist has ever thought of such a foolish enterprise."[134]

Second, many of these thinkers assumed that a robust predictivism provides, or substitutes for, standards by which lawyers and judges can identify "the law": Valid law takes the form of a particular predicted decision, and the criterion for determining the validity of such a decision as law (as far as we can know the law in advance) is simply that it is the decision that the court is predicted to render. But what if the prediction turns out in fact to be in error and the judge decides differently? Some of these thinkers seem to have assumed that the law ultimately is whatever the court actually does.[135] If so, however, the prediction can only be an approximation of valid law—a stab at what the law will be—the best that we can do if we are to know the law at all in advance. Again, we are left with no ultimate criterion of law's validity that is independent of what the court actually does. Thus there is little or no point in asking whether a court action *accords with* the law. In a sense, predictivism of this sort simply cannot supply a criterion of legal validity.[136]

---

[132] Dickinson, *Legal Rules—Their Function in the Process of Decision*, 79 U. PA. L. REV. 833, 838-43 (1931).

[133] *Id.*

[134] H. KELSEN, *supra* note 37, at 173.

[135] *See, e.g.*, J. FRANK, *supra* note 41, at 46; Bingham, *supra* note 130, at 13-14.

[136] Alternatively, one might hold that if the court ultimately acts in a way contrary to predicted law, the latter remains valid. This would provide an independent criterion of sorts for determining validity of court action. Still, no pragmatic instrumentalist expressed this view.

Robust predictivism even fails as a general descriptive theory of what a good lawyer does when he identifies, interprets, and applies law, and advises his clients accordingly. Commonly, a lawyer will not proceed in the fashion of a weather forecaster, identifying the prospective decision makers, gathering data about those decision makers and about how they have acted in the past, and then, in light of the facts at hand, predicting which way these decision makers will jump on those facts. Rather, a lawyer will commonly "practice by the book." That is, he will identify applicable law (by reference to independent criteria of valid law) and then interpret and apply this to the facts of the client's case, all in accord with generally accepted interpretational and applicational technique. It would be a distortion to characterize this as a process of prediction. Lawyers are not weather forecasters. Indeed, it is possible for a lawyer to practice law for very long periods of time without predicting in any robust way that a judge will do anything.

The view that lawyers are essentially robust predictors of how individuals with power over the use of state force will act can subtly and unhappily influence lawyers' perceptions of their roles. Indeed, under this view, the lawyer's essential role is to forecast, to manage, and even to seek to control the exercise of state power. A lawyer is merely someone knowledgeable about state power—one who has "power skills." This is an impoverished perception of the lawyer's role, even granting that it is an advance over the formalist view that a lawyer is someone specially adept at the logical elaboration of concepts. As Lon Fuller stressed,[137] an additional and far more important part of the lawyer's role is that of designing, structuring, and choosing between frameworks for human interaction—frameworks within which private parties and also government functionaries can realize goals. Lawyers are experts in structure, and are knowledgeable about principles for ordering human relations. They regularly play important roles in the design and creation of interactional structures, many of which, like voluntary arbitration or arrangements in which each party has a power of cancellation, do not even contemplate that state power will be exercised in the event of a breakdown.

Moreover, the conception of the lawyer implicit in robust predictivism does not specifically provide for the work of lawyers in deciding how state power *ought* to be exercised, what the law ought to be, and whether existing law is good or bad. The lawyer engaged in these efforts is not stepping out of his role; he is performing it.

Of course, the effort that lawyers often make to predict what a particular judge will decide may have real utility. Sometimes the law

[137] *See* Fuller & Randall, *Professional Responsibility: Report of the Joint Conference*, 44 A.B.A.J. 1159, 1161-62 (1958).

confers broad discretion, is unclear, or is even conflicting. Here there is diminished scope for genuine divergence between the law (identifiable as valid by criteria independent of judicial action) and that action itself. In these instances the lawyer may be especially concerned with trying to predict which way the judge will jump. But in my view, far more often the law is relatively determinate and determinable in light of relevant standards of validity and accepted interpretational technique, although this is not to say the law is easy to determine, or that particular determinations will always be uncontroversial. Robust predictivists who failed to see this lacked perspective, and consequently overstated the function of predicting decisions.

Where there is room for genuine divergence between determinate law independently identified as valid and judicial action, predictivism could not be credible unless divergence were commonplace and the divergent course of the courts were itself taken to be the law. But my impression is that divergence is not commonplace, and that judges try hard to follow determinate law that has been identified independently as valid by reference to general criteria accepted by judges and others. As argued earlier,[138] the American system simply does not accept the general view that whatever judges say is valid, regardless of how the law reads.

This is not to say there are no genuine divergences. To determine just how narrow the foothold might be for a robust predictivism derived from such divergence it would be necessary to consider first the explanations that might account for the relatively small proportion of instances of genuine divergence. Such a project is beyond the scope of this Article.

VII

Methods for Interpreting and Applying Valid Law

Modern legal theorists have traditionally made more of the problems of specifying criteria for determining legal validity[139] than of the problems of interpreting and applying law actually identified as valid. But issues of validity that arise in the daily workings of a legal system sometimes merge into issues of interpretation or application. Moreover, the number of issues of interpretation and application arising over admittedly valid law vastly exceeds the issues about the validity of law itself.

---

[138] *See* text accompanying notes 107-10 *supra*.

[139] *See* §§ V and VI *supra*.

By the turn of the century, formalism and related vices were common in the interpretation and application of valid law. Methodological formalism itself took a variety of forms. The instrumentalists attacked these vigorously. Holmes, for example, reminded judges that "the life of the law has not been logic but experience."[140] Pound railed at the "mechanical jurisprudence" of the judiciary.[141] Llewellyn criticized the "formal style" and proclaimed the essential indeterminacy of all forms of law.[142] Frank joined in, ridiculing "Euclidean legal thinking."[143] These theorists agreed more on their negations than on their affirmations; few devoted much effort to constructing an alternative methodology. Still, their critique of formalist legal method may be their most important single achievement. It does not logically follow, however, that an improved legal method is necessarily a good thing. The legal personnel within a system may, for example, eschew formalistic techniques and interpret and apply law in a sophisticated instrumentalist fashion; yet the goals of the law and their implementive content could even be evil.

The instrumentalists were so successful in their attacks on formalist legal method that much of what I will now present as theirs is sure to seem not just familiar but banal to the well-trained lawyer of today. Although I will only treat their views on common law method, these views also apply, *mutatis mutandis,* to constitutional, statutory, and other forms of written law. Many of these theorists, of course, were reacting as vigorously to formalism in constitutional law and in statutory interpretation as they were to formalism in common law method.

A. *Legal Method*

Numerous issues of legal method have been the subject of discussion in jurisprudential literature: how far can judges appropriately reason from the "logic" of legal concepts to resolve issues? How authoritative are mere verbal formulations in precedent? In legal thinking, which has primacy: specific facts, things, and effects, or unitary general conceptions? May judges make law? How comprehen-

---

140 O. W. Holmes, *supra* note 1, at 1.

141 *See, e.g.*, Pound, *supra* note 90.

142 K. Llewellyn, *supra* note 107, at 67-72; Llewellyn, *Legal Tradition and Social Science Method—A Realist's Critique,* in Essays on Research in the Social Sciences 89, 106 n.8 (1931). It appears that it was not until his later period that Llewellyn regularly referred to this in his writing as a "formal style." *See, e.g.*, K. Llewellyn, The Common Law Tradition—Deciding Appeals 38 (1960).

143 Frank, *Mr. Justice Holmes and Non-Euclidean Legal Thinking,* 17 Cornell L.Q. 568, 572-79 (1932). *See also* J. Frank, *supra* note 41, chs. 3-7; Cook, *supra* note 107, at 457-60; Oliphant, *supra* note 61, at 160.

sive is the pre-existing law? All of these issues occupied the instrumentalists.

The corpus of the common law, as distinguished from specific precedents, may be viewed as a source of authority for a judicial decision. Formalist judges sought to reason from the "logic" of basic legal concepts pervading the common law. I have devised an example of such reasoning and have exaggerated its formalistic feature in order to make it as communicative as possible. (Yet the example is based on actual court opinions dealing with the type of problem involved.)[144] Consider the following judicial opinion:

> The issue before us is whether a child born with permanent injury attributable to the defendant's negligence during pregnancy may recover compensation for the injury. We hold that the child cannot recover such damages. The legal right to be awarded damages presupposes that the person against whom redress is sought violated a legal right of the injured. But a legal right can be violated only if that right is possessed by the injured party at the time of its alleged violation. By definition, the only entity that can possess legal rights is a legal person. Thus, one can violate a legal right of a party only if that party was a legal person at the time of the alleged violation of the right. But it is plain that only an entity that can have legal duties can possess legal rights, for in the law the concepts of right and duty are universally reciprocal and symmetrical; the one necessarily attends the other. An unborn child cannot have legal duties. Therefore, one cannot violate a legal right of one who was an unborn child at the time of the alleged violation. The plaintiff, therefore, has no legal right to be awarded damages because there were no legal rights possessed by him that defendant violated.

Note that most of this "argumentation" takes the form of a miniature essay on certain very abstract legal concepts such as "legal person," "right," and "duty." The crucial steps are buried within all the deduction. "Inherent" meanings and conceptual harmony and symmetry are at the fore, not substantive considerations of community policy.

One can well imagine a rather angry dissenting judge responding:

> What does it really matter that the unborn child had no legal duties? He can still have legal rights, for we as judges can alter these concepts as we desire to serve useful goals. If the majority insists on maintaining the right-duty symmetry, then call what the

---

144 *See, e.g.*, Allaire v. St. Luke's Hosp., 184 Ill. 359, 56 N.E. 638 (1900).

> child had something else, say an "imperfect right." The majority assumes that logic somehow tells us how to decide this case. But this is an abuse of logic. Indeed, it is arid conceptualism and mechanical jurisprudence at their very worst. The true issue has to do with a new type of tort claim. Here we have a negligently caused injury. I fail to see why this in itself should not be controlling.

Instrumentalist legal theorists applauded dissents of this kind. Law, they said, is not a formal system. Some instrumentalists went further, believing that more than a misguided notion about the logic of system-wide concepts was at work in such cases. Thus Holmes remarked, "Behind the logical form [of such decisions] lies a judgment as to the relative worth and importance of competing legislative grounds, often an inarticulate and unconscious judgment, it is true, and yet the very root and nerve of the whole proceeding."[145]

More common were opinions in which "formalistic" judges invoked over-generalized statements of case law as "authority" on which to decide cases.[146] Instrumentalists condemned this loose view because it made too much of the formulated words in the prior opinion or too much of the general form of a rule or precept articulated in the opinion. These critics asserted that general statements in prior opinions must be read against the facts of the cases involved and in light of what the judges actually decided, rather than what they *say* they are deciding; that narrow generalizations are the only reliable authority; and that such generalities must not, in any event, extend beyond the type of fact pattern implicated in the dispute before the court.[147]

Llewellyn, in particular, argued that it is not possible to determine what a common law case stands for in a vacuum or in the abstract. One must first relate it to other cases because they "color the language, the technical terms, used in the opinion."[148] But more important, other related cases, actual and hypothetical, "give you the wherewithal to find which of the facts are significant."[149] Only after comparing, contrasting, and distinguishing related cases can the lawyer determine what the opinion at hand stands for.

As a corollary, the instrumentalists insisted that when a later court chose not to follow a prior decision of which it appeared to

---

[145] Holmes, *supra* note 29, at 466.

[146] For important early examples of American over-generalizations, see Green, *Illinois Negligence Law*, 39 Ill. L. Rev. 36, 116, 197 (1944).

[147] *See* K. Llewellyn, *supra* note 107, at 34-68; Llewellyn, *A Realistic Jurisprudence—The Next Step*, *supra* note 2, at 431; Oliphant, *supra* note 61, at 71, 159 *passim*.

[148] K. Llewellyn, *supra* note 107, at 43.

[149] *Id.*

approve, the court should distinguish the prior case on substantive rather than formal grounds. That is, the court should single out factual differences that make it justifiable for the court not to follow the prior case. Mere formal distinctions are insufficient for distinguishing precedent, because they are simply distinctions without differences.

Above all, Holmes and his followers stressed in legal analysis the primacy of facts rather than words and of ends rather than "logic":

> We must think things not words, or at least we must constantly translate our words into facts for which they stand, if we are to keep to the real and true. I sometimes tell students that the law schools pursue an inspirational combined with a logical method, that is, the postulates are taken for granted upon authority without inquiry into their worth, and then logic is used as the only tool to develop the results. It is a necessary method for the purpose of teaching dogma. But inasmuch as the real justification of a rule of law, if there be one, is that it helps to bring about a social end which we desire, it is no less necessary that those who make and develop the law should have those ends articulately in their minds.[150]

The pragmatic instrumentalists also criticized the tendency of judges, when they *were* inclined to change the common law, to resort to what lawyers call legal fiction. For example, some courts were influenced to enforce a promise solely on the ground that the plaintiff justifiably relied on it. But because the law had not yet fully accepted reliance as an independent basis of promissory obligation, these courts simply refused to recognize this ground and instead proclaimed that in these cases there was "consideration"—an already accepted ground of obligation. Instrumentalists repudiated decisions in which judges paid homage through fiction to the form of case law doctrine while changing its substance. Judges should not appear to leave the law entirely intact when they are in fact significantly extending it. Moreover, fictions tend to come home to roost; a later court might fail to see what had been going on and, in our example, take the requirement of consideration seriously and deny recovery, even when the plaintiff had justifiably relied.[151]

The instrumentalists similarly argued that judges should explicitly address whether a precedent should be overruled. Instead of invoking remote analogies, judges should also openly confront the problem of what law should be made when there is no applicable

---

[150] Holmes, *Law in Science and Science in Law, supra* note 44, at 460.

[151] For an actual sequence of cases of this nature, see Siegel v. Spear & Co., 234 N.Y. 479, 138 N.E. 414 (1923); Comfort v. McCorkle, 149 Misc. 826, 268 N.Y.S. 192 (Sup. Ct. 1933).

precedent. In a realistic light rather than in terms of a formal separation of powers, it is evident that judges can and do make law.[152] Moreover, in normative terms, there are varieties of law that judges are as well suited to make as are legislatures—indeed, better suited.

One further methodological issue may be noted. With the rapid growth of case law, judges in the twentieth century increasingly found themselves confronted with conflicting lines of precedent converging upon the case at hand.[153] How were they to decide? Some of the responses to this dilemma took on a formalistic aura: decide in accord with the oldest precedents, decide in accord with whichever precedent commanded unanimity at the time, or the like. The instrumentalists objected. In their view, when judges confront a plethora of conflicting precedents, they should simply make choices in light of community policy.

B. *Two Criticisms*

There were two major deficiencies in the common law methodology of most instrumentalists. The first is understandable, the second a puzzle.

A number of instrumentalists (though not Holmes, Gray, or Pound) were what are sometimes called rule skeptics.[154] In reacting against formal deductive methods of reasoning from abstract conceptions, these thinkers advanced several skeptical theses: in every litigated common law case the judges always have a choice, no matter how "clear" the applicable precedent is; there is never a single right answer to a litigated question; there is no such thing as a genuine legal objectivity in the common law; and precedent is necessarily indeterminate because the materials themselves are, among other things, simply too fluid or too remote and indirect in their bearing.

As John Dickinson[155] and others were quick to point out, however, the rule skeptics had over-reacted. They left little place for our

---

[152] These points were fully made in an influential book widely read during the rise of instrumentalism. *See* A. Bentley, The Process of Government (1908). *See also* John Dewey & A. Bentley: A Philosophical Correspondence, 1932-1951 (S. Ratner & J. Altman eds. 1964); J. Paul, The Legal Realism of Jerome N. Frank 18 (1959).

[153] *See generally* Gilmore, *Legal Realism—Its Cause and Cure,* 70 Yale L.J. 1037 (1961).

[154] *See* W. Rumble, American Legal Realism: Skepticism, Reform and the Judicial Process 58-106 (1968). Most rule skeptics did not deny the existence of legal rules. They only denied that they were "*the* heavily operative factor in producing court decisions." Llewellyn, *Some Realism about Realism—Responding to Dean Pound, supra* note 2, at 1237 (emphasis in original).

[155] *See generally* Dickinson, *supra* note 132, at 833; Dickinson, *Legal Rules—Their Application and Elaboration,* 79 U. Pa. L. Rev. 1052 (1931).

widely used notions of "a correct application of the law" and its conceptually parasitic counterpart, "a mistaken application of the law." Many rules have a core of content that is quite settled and determinate. Both trial judges and appellate judges sometimes err in formulating and applying valid law. If there were never any right answers these occurrences would not be possible. Of course, to say that often there are single right answers is not to say that there always are, that judges always come up with them, that they are never controversial, or that law school casebooks include many cases in which there are such answers!

The other fundamental flaw in instrumentalist writings on common law method was that they simply did not make a sufficient place for the play of substantive reasons in working with and creating or modifying precedents. Substantive reasons cannot be dismissed as something necessarily metaphysical. There are three main types of substantive reasons at work in the law. Countless examples of such reasons can be found throughout case reports, reports on the legislative history of statutes and the legal literature generally. These are (1) "goal reasons"—reasons of substance that derive their justificatory force from the fact that, at the time they are given, the decisions they purport to justify can be predicted (sufficiently), to have effects that serve a good social goal; (2) "rightness reasons"—reasons of substance that derive their force not from predicted goal-serving effects, but from the way in which the decision that is justified accords with a norm of rightness applied to a party's actions or to a state of affairs resulting from those actions; and (3) "institutional reasons"—reasons of either of the two foregoing kinds that are tied to a specific institutional role or process and derive their force from the way in which the decision would serve goals or accord with norms of rightness peculiarly applicable to actions or participants in institutional settings. In what follows I will mean by "reason" one or more of the above three types.[156]

The instrumentalists failed to accord a proper place to substantive reason in the common law in a number of ways. To begin with, some of these thinkers did not, as we have seen, give the doctrine of precedent its due. Their rule skepticism left insufficient room for the notion of binding precedent. This may have been partly because they tended to view following precedent merely as a form of following authority for its own sake. Yet to cite a precedent is itself to give a

---

[156] *See* Summers, *Two Types of Substantive Reasons: The Core of a Theory of Common Law Justification*, 63 CORNELL L. REV. 707, 716-24 (1978).

reason, and when the reason has justificatory force the reason may derive from (1) the force of the reasons of substance behind the precedent itself and (2) the force of the general rationales, themselves reasons of substance, behind the practice of following precedent.

Further, in their zeal to expose formalistic jurisprudence in all its forms, instrumentalists tended to abandon the common law wholesale as a source of countless reasons of substance already recognized to some degree in some or all branches of the common law. Common law opinions include many passages employing reasons of substance that transcend the cases at hand and apply not merely by analogy but directly to issues to be decided. Only recently, and largely as a result of the perceptive and imaginative work of Professor Ronald Dworkin, have we become fully conscious of the extent to which this is so.[157]

In addition, most instrumentalists considered direct judicial resort to ordinary justificatory raw material—reasons of substance—to be an activity extrinsic to law and thus something extra-legal.[158] These thinkers were all too preoccupied with distinctions between "law" and "policy," as if the latter, which substantive reason encompasses, were somehow essentially extrinsic to law.[159] "Policy," however, is not something extra-legal. The regular resort to substantive reason is necessarily a part of the common law itself; it can even be said to have *primacy* in the common law.[160]

There are some apparent paradoxes here. I will close this section with a modest effort to resolve them. Many pragmatic instrumentalists talked and wrote about "policy" and even "justice," and it would seem natural that they would find a place for substantive reason within the law itself, or at least that they would not view appeals to substantive reason as necessarily extra-legal. As I have demonstrated, however, the general value theory of leading instrumentalists was relatively anemic; it made little place for qualitative considerations of policy or justice. As an unusually general theory, it lacked determinativeness in particular cases. Indeed, a few of these thinkers were highly skeptical of the validity of more particular notions of value for the resolution of specific issues.

It is also true that most of the instrumentalists were reformers. Some were even zealous reformers. Could these reformers deny a

---

[157] *See generally* R. DWORKIN, *supra* note 55, at 14-130.

[158] Indeed, many of them assumed that the law could be described without reference to the reasons of substance that figure in the law. *See* text accompanying notes 121-22 *supra*.

[159] This was even true of Pound. *See* Pound, *The Theory of Judicial Decision,* 36 HARV. L. REV. 940, 947 (1923).

[160] This primacy argument has been developed at length elsewhere. *See* Summers, *supra* note 156, at 730-33.

major role for the play of reasoned justification within the common law? Yes. Zeal for reform and faith in reasoned justification are not at all the same or even closely related. Reformers may even think it is enough that people generally *want* reforms for their own quite personal ends, and that public, reasoned justification is therefore superfluous or unnecessary. Belief in democracy can foster and reinforce this view, for in a democracy majority vote is the ultimate fall back; it controls regardless of how much rationality informs and enlightens the vote.

Although instrumentalists criticized formalists for not being sufficiently mindful of means and goals, it does not follow that these critics were committed to a large role for reason. Goals might be taken as more or less *given* and reason confined solely to means. Indeed, they may have thought that only the "factual" means-end relation can be a true subject of science.[161]

In the four preceding sections I have addressed instrumentalist views on lawmaking, the identification of valid law, and its interpretation and application. These topics concern the content and structure of the law, and have traditionally been at the core of legal theory. I now turn to topics relating to the function of law in daily life: the law's implementive machinery (Section VIII); the nature and role of officials (Section IX); the importance of coercion, force, and direct action in law (Section X); and the criteria for judging the success of a use of law (Section XI). Although not fully developed, these ideas were unmistakably important in instrumentalist theory.

VIII

Law's Implementive Machinery

According to the instrumentalists, law, in essence, consists of *means*—primarily means that direct and forbid behavior. But these primary means are not self implementing. Their implementation requires machinery and calls for "social engineering."

A. *An Inventory of Law's Resources*

Pragmatic instrumentalists almost uniformly assumed that the law is a kind of machine technology to be used by social engineers to serve goals. Pound led the way:

> [I] am content to see in legal history the record of a continually wider recognizing and satisfying of human wants or claims or

161 Or so many of these thinkers assumed. *See, e.g.*, Cook, *The Possibilities of Social Study as a Science*, in Essays on Research in the Social Sciences, 27, 47-48 (1931).

> desires through social control; a more embracing and more effective securing of social interests; a continually more complete and effective elimination of waste and precluding of friction in human enjoyment of the goods of existence—in short, a continually more efficacious social engineering.[162]

Llewellyn wrote that "the trend of the most fruitful thinking about law has run steadily toward regarding law as an engine (a heterogeneous multitude of engines)."[163] He also asserted:

> [L]aw operates under the principle of scarcity. The energy available for social regulation at any time and place is limited. . . . Because of this fact, control by law takes on the aspect of engineering. We require . . . to invent such machinery as, with least waste, least cost and least unwanted by-products, will give most nearly the desired result.[164]

To the leading instrumentalists, judges were prominent social engineers. Adjudicative processes and administrative agencies were important forms of implementive machinery. The workings of the criminal law provided a preferred model of law's general modus operandi. But Pound stressed that "[s]ocial engineering may not expect to meet all its problems with the same machinery. Its tasks are as varied as life and the complex problems of a complex social order call for a complicated mechanism and a variety of legal implements."[165]

We do not have an adequate general account of the varieties of legal resources to this day. It is important to provide at least a sketch here, by way of filling a basic gap in instrumentalist theory. The sketch to follow will of necessity be largely my own, but it is faithful to instrumentalist thinking. It will indicate the varied and complex nature of law's vast machinery, and thus will reveal in broad outlines how much more there is to law's resources than courts and adjudicative procedures. It will also help explain why it was so tempting, at least for those instrumentalists who had some sense of the totality of law's resources, to think of law as an elaborate machine technology. It will help clear up some misconceptions, including ones that plagued the instrumentalists. For example, it will reveal the inadequacy of any

---

[162] R. Pound, An Introduction to the Philosophy of Law 47 (rev. ed. 1955). *See also* Dewey, *supra* note 22, at 318-19.

[163] Llewellyn, *A Realist Jurisprudence—The Next Step*, *supra* note 2, at 464. "Machine" metaphors are common in the literature. *See, e.g.*, Cohen, *supra* note 32, at 6 ("mechanisms"); Cook, *Substance and Procedure in the Conflict of Laws*, 42 Yale L.J. 333, 358 (1933) ("tools").

[164] Llewellyn, *The Effects of Legal Institutions on Economics*, 15 Am. Econ. Rev. 665, 666 (1925).

[165] *See* Pound, *supra* note 159, at 956.

conception of law's resources that is modeled mainly on the criminal law. Indeed, law does not function in any single standard way.

We may begin by introducing the idea of a *primary* legal precept. Such a precept directs its addressee to behave in a given way or otherwise specifies a legal relation. It may originate in an explicit formulation or it may be constructed from the past behavior patterns of officials or private individuals. It may take the form of a rule, a general order, a principle, or a maxim. It may be constitutional, statutory, judicial, administrative, or private in origin. It may impose a duty, grant a liberty, confer a power, specify a feature of a process, structure an institution, and more. It may reflect such diverse concerns as the prevention of crime, the regulation of health or highway safety, or reinforcement of the family. The nature of primary precepts is a complex topic; whole essays have been devoted to the subject.

When primary precepts fulfill their goals to any degree, the law's implementive machinery is almost always somehow at work. Of fundamental importance in that machinery are *auxiliary* legal precepts.[166] These are designed to implement primary precepts, and are in this sense auxiliary to them. For example, a law imposing a new duty to respect privacy would be a primary precept, but new authorization to enjoin the invasion of privacy would be auxiliary, and so on.

Still another basic type of implementive legal resource consists of institutions, agencies, and other recognized *entities*. Courts, juries, legislatures, and administrative bodies of many kinds are familiar examples. These complex legal entities are built up out of other resources, including legal precepts. A frequent problem for the social engineer is that of deciding whether to create a new entity or to confer further powers and responsibilities on existing ones.

Institutions, agencies, and other legal entities typically operate via regularized *processes*. It is within and by means of such processes, both formal and informal, that such bodies make, administer, and enforce legal precepts.

Beyond precepts, institutions, and processes, the law's implementive technology includes a vast inventory of remedies, sanctions, and other specific implementive devices of varying degrees of complexity.[167]

---

[166] Bentham himself introduced this concept. *See* J. BENTHAM, BENTHAM'S POLITICAL THOUGHT 165-66 (B. Pareck ed. 1973).

[167] It will be sufficient here merely to list some of these devices: (1) threats and actuality of punishment; (2) incentives, rewards, and other inducements; (3) symbolic denunciations in laws and official pronouncements; (4) state propaganda; (5) continuous official or semi-official supervision; (6) threats and actuality of adverse publicity; (7) grants, denials, revocations, etc.,

All the main types of *implementive resources* identified so far may be relatively legal in nature. But many resources that are deployable for legal purposes are not in this way relatively legal. Manpower and scientific technology are examples. Law without personnel would be impossible. Indeed, a complex division of labor involving many varieties of specialized personnel is one of the salient features of a modern legal system.[168] Similarly, many legal programs would be impossible without scientific technology. A legally prescribed flood control program, for example, is not possible without flood control devices. Deployable but not otherwise legal resources also include general knowledge of human motivation (and much else), materials including equipment and the like, the media, and even language itself.

Some resources, then, may be characterized as relatively legal, while others are not relatively legal in nature but still deployable by social engineers. Beyond these two classes of resources is a third class on which social engineers may merely capitalize. For example, the draftsman of a penal code can capitalize on the strong moral aversions of a people to enhance the efficacy of a penal code. Similarly, the draftsman of a divorce law may capitalize on the influences of religious organizations within the society. Public opinion is also illustrative; a program to regulate the quality of manufactured foods may empower an official to threaten manufacturers with public disclosure of failures—disclosure that will turn people away from their products. The existence of private associations in certain lines of business and trade can be capitalized on in various ways, such as providing a means of communicating new laws.

When law is used, personnel combine the foregoing resources to devise and bring into operation a *functional legal unit.* A functional legal unit typically includes at least one primary precept and one or more auxiliary ones. As already stated, a primary precept directs its addressee to behave in a given way, or otherwise specifies a legal relation. An auxiliary rule is one designed to implement a primary one. To these are added other resources, such as manpower and technology, to organize a program for implementive action. The result is a functional legal unit.

---

of licenses and licensing; (8) official periodic inspections; (9) regular conferences and other means; (10) taxes, tax exemptions, deductions etc.; (11) grants subject to conditions; (12) rationing devices; (13) conditions facilitating exchange, *e.g.*, legal tender, weights and measures, gap-filler laws; (14) recognized incidents of ownership, and of specialty instruments like stocks and bonds; (15) validation and invalidation, and other forms of nullity; (16) status dissolution or modification, *e.g.*, divorce, bankruptcy discharges; (17) publicity provided facilities, *e.g.*, communications and transportation; (18) state distribution of welfare, in money or in kind; (19) court and agency remedies and orders, and threats of resort thereto.

[168] *See* section IX *infra.*

But law's implementive machinery is even more complex. A functional legal unit also typically serves as part of an *implementive technique*—a legal modus operandi. Even an isolated stop sign on a lonely prairie is part of a complex overall modus operandi for the deployment of law to serve goals—in this instance, a general regulatory scheme to facilitate road safety and traffic flow.

According to one traditional model the only basic type of implementive technique is penal in nature. The emphasis on state coercion and direct official action in instrumentalist thought indicates that these thinkers did not really free themselves from this model.[169] But there is more than one basic modus operandi. Social engineers design, organize, and combine legal resources into a wider variety of implementive techniques. Most technique designs in modern use may be classified as one of five main types:

> (1) A *private arranging type*—one that, as implemented, encourages the formation of private arrangements and facilitates their aims. Private contracts comprise one type of private arrangement. The law authorizes these, sets forth how they are to be made, facilitates their consummation and their administration, permits certain forms of self-help, and provides for other remedies in event of breakdown. In this technique, the fundamental duties of the parties to the arrangement are largely voluntarily incurred rather than imposed by officials.
>
> (2) A *grievance remedial type*—one that, as implemented, confers private rights and provides remedies for their infringement in civil courts. Unlike private arrangements, the basic duties are imposed by officials. But the choice of whether to do anything about breaches of duty is generally left to private parties.
>
> (3) A *distributive type*—one that, as implemented, distributes public goods and services to specified classes of people. Legal ordering providing for public health, education, welfare, and highways is illustrative. This technique calls for the imposition of taxes or other burdens in order that the benefits may be conferred.
>
> (4) A *regulatory type*—one that, as implemented, sets standards for specific classes of people and regulates their behavior through licensing or some other device. Radio and television broadcasting, food and drug manufacture, hazardous employment, etc., may be subject to such regulation, as may activities such as education, which are conducted by publicly owned bodies.

---

169 *See* section X *infra*.

(5) A *penal type*—one that, as implemented, prohibits behavior as criminal, and punishes its occurrence.[170]

Primary rules and other precepts that direct their addressees to behave in specified ways also may be classified as private arranging, grievance remedial, distributive, regulatory, or penal in origin. Such forms of law are ultimately implemented by appropriate techniques of the foregoing five basic types which incorporate various auxiliary resources. Considerable variety of design within each basic type is possible.

There are various forms of overlap between types of implementive techniques. There is overlap as to goals potentially served. Dispute settlement, for example, is a general goal that all five types serve. In addition, "distributive" techniques may be used in part for regulatory purposes. Thus, grants of money may be conditioned on acting in accord with regulations, and so forth. There is usually overlap in the resources deployed and sometimes even in the manner of deployment. For example, courts play roles in all the basic types. Notwithstanding this overlap, each basic type retains independent significance, for such significance does not require mutual exclusivity.

This completes the inventory of all the basic elements of law's technology. A use of law of any significant degree of complexity, then, may be analyzed in terms of its: (1) goals; (2) means-goal hypotheses; (3) primary precepts; (4) auxiliary precepts; (5) institutions, agencies or other entities; (6) processes; (7) implementive devices; (8) functional legal units; (9) overall implementive techniques and technique designs.

As Leon Green and others have stressed, the general implementive technology of the law is not static.[171] Social engineers regularly discover and devise new legal inventions and refine old ones. During the first four decades of this century, which saw the rise of pragmatic instrumentalism, there was a vast growth in American legal technology. This growth encompassed both the rise of the regulatory state beginning with the Progressive Era, and the elaborate welfare state constructions of the New Deal.

B. *The Fallacy of Unlimited Malleability*

It is not possible within limitations of space to offer a systematic assessment of all the technological themes in pragmatic instrumentalism. Accordingly, I will now single out only one, albeit a leading one.

---

[170] *See* Summers, *The Technique Element in Law*, 59 CALIF. L. REV. 733, 736-45 (1971).

[171] Green, *Leon Green*, in MY PHILOSOPHY OF LAW, *supra* note 48, at 129, 137-40.

This one might be called the "malleability" thesis. Perhaps because machine technologies are often highly adaptable, many instrumentalists tended to assume that the law's varied and complex resources must be similarly malleable.[172] Indeed, some appeared to go quite overboard.[173] One neo-instrumentalist generalized that "[n]ature doesn't present us with anything. . . . We have to slice nature as we do cheese, in the ways that suit our convenience and our specific practical purposes."[174]

An alternative view is that there is an "inner order" of things to be ascertained and taken into account. This view dates back to the ancient Greeks.[175] Fuller is the modern American legal theorist who has sought to develop this rival view most fully. He believed that neither the "materials" from which law is made nor the law's implementive machinery is infinitely pliable. He claimed that lawmakers must work with "basic forms of social order," including legislation,

---

[172] This was one of the most distinctive legacies of pragmatist philosophy. *See generally* H. THAYER, *supra* note 24, at 426-27.

[173] Oliphant, *supra* note 74, at 494.

[174] McDougal, *Fuller v. The American Legal Realists: An Intervention*, 50 YALE L.J. 827, 832 (1941).

[175] Thus, in the pseudo-Platonic dialogue *Minos*, we encounter this exchange:

> Socrates: And do doctors on their part, in their treatises on health, write what they accept as real?
> Com: Yes.
> Soc. Then these treatises of the doctors are medical, and medical laws.
> Com. Medical, to be sure.
> Soc. And are agricultural treatises likewise agricultural laws?
> Com. Yes.
> Soc. And whose are the treatises and accepted rules about garden work?
> Com. Gardeners.
> Soc. So these are our gardening laws.
> Com. Yes.
> Soc. Of people who know how to control gardens?
> Com. Certainly . . .
> Soc. And whose are the treatises and accepted rules about the confection of tasty dishes?
> Com. Cooks.
> Soc. Then there are laws of cookery?
> Com. Of cookery.
> Soc. Of people who know, it would seem, how to control the confection of tasty dishes?
> Com. Yes . . .
> Soc. Very well; and now, whose are the treatises and accepted rules about the government of a state? Of the people who know how to control states are they not?
> Com. I agree. . . .
> Soc. Then we rightly admitted that law is discovery of reality?
> Com. So it appears. . . .

Plato, *Minos*, 8 LOEB CLASSICAL LIBRARY 403 (W. Lamb trans. 1927).

adjudication, mediation, markets, contracts, elections, and managerial direction. He held that these forms are relatively few in number and have an inner integrity of their own that is to some extent "there" to be discovered. These forms are not, in his view, all-purpose tools of unlimited pliability. They have distinctive uses and limits, and their successful use requires careful choice.[176] Fuller warned pragmatic instrumentalists against neglecting the distinctive integrity of particular forms of social order. For example, social engineers may pay a heavy price for unduly "mixing" two different forms such as mediation and adjudication. A judge who tries first to mediate a dispute, thereby learning the facts of the case, and then later seeks to determine the facts as a judge not only may fail as a factfinder, but might also forfeit some degree of impartiality and taint the process. Similarly, assigning adjudicators "polycentric" tasks calling for managerial control of diverse yet interdependent factors not only puts the achievement of those tasks at risk, but compromises the integrity of adjudication as well. In Fuller's view, those concerned with the law must discover and master distinct "segments" of reality if they are to take advantage of relevant regularities in the effort to further group life.

IX

The Nature and Role of Personnel

Plainly, people must make the law and staff its implementive machinery. As will be seen, a surprising range of important types of tasks must usually be performed in order to create a legal precept and translate it into practice. The social engineers assigned to these tasks include a wide variety of public officials, private parties (non-corporate and corporate), and various bodies of citizens participating in group actions such as voting, jury service, and the like.

The pragmatic instrumentalists generally stressed the importance of what might be called the "personnel element" in a legal system. Unlike many of their jurisprudential predecessors in America and in Europe, they did not conceive of a legal system solely in terms of structures, processes, and precepts. Most of these thinkers assumed that officials, rather than private parties, have the primary roles

---

[176] In one of his most famous essays, widely circulated privately in the 1950s and 1960s and published in its entirety only posthumously, Fuller explored the compulsions necessarily contained in adjudicative ordering. *See* Fuller, *The Forms and Limits of Adjudication*, 92 Harv. L. Rev. 353 (1978). In a well known book, he dealt similarly with legislation and managerial direction. *See* L. Fuller, The Morality of Law (rev. ed. 1969).

within the division of legal labor in our own system. As the young Llewellyn put it, "what these officials do about disputes is, to my mind, the law itself."[177] And by "officials," instrumentalists usually meant only judges.

In my view, on the other hand, private parties actually have more significance within the division of legal labor in our system than do officials. Of course, whether this is so is largely an empirical question, and it is not possible to marshal the evidence here. It should be possible, however, to instill skepticism about the primacy of officials, and thus place their roles in more satisfactory perspective. This inquiry is critical to our understanding of how law works, a concern of central importance to the pragmatic instrumentalists.

First, it is necessary to explore in broad outlines the nature of our division of legal labor. To provide even a very general account of this division, it is necessary to identify at the outset the types of legal tasks that must be performed to translate rules into practice to serve goals. Earlier, five basic legal techniques were introduced: private arranging, grievance remedial, distributive, regulatory, and penal.[178] In order to create and translate a rule into practice via any one of these five modes, a number of creative and implementive tasks must be performed by officials or private parties, or both. That is, law must be brought into being and put to use through a dynamic sequence of events. I will now outline my own tentative theory of "legal tasks." The tasks that must be performed to create and implement law are numerous, and they vary to some extent between the basic technique types referred to above. It is not necessary to explore all this variety here; it will be enough to provide an abstract listing of the essential tasks common to all five techniques. These are, in their usual chronological sequence:

(1) Setting goals and creating primary and auxiliary rules and other legal precepts;
(2) Selecting the basic implementive technique;
(3) Setting up new organizations, entities, or structures, or modifying existing ones as needed;
(4) Providing any personnel, material goods, scientific technology, or other wherewithal required to implement law;

---

[177] K. LLEWELLYN, *supra* note 107, at 3. *See also* J. FRANK, *supra* note 41, at 46 *passim*; J. GRAY, *supra* note 47, at 84-125 *passim*; Bingham, *supra* note 130, at 17-18 *passim*; Cohen, *supra* note 32, at 9-18 *passim*; Holmes, *supra* note 29, at 457 *passim*. Llewellyn, much later, recanted. *See* K. LLEWELLYN, THE BRAMBLE BUSH 8-9 (rev. ed. 1950).

[178] *See* text accompanying note 170 *supra*.

(5) Communicating or rendering accessible the content of relevant law to the persons it addresses, and specifying what difference, if any, it is to make if these persons fail to adhere to the law;
(6) Assuring that persons who wish voluntarily to fulfill duties or exercise rights under applicable precepts will have the capabilities to do so;
(7) Providing encouragement, persuasion, incentives, or coercion in advance to induce persons not otherwise so disposed to fulfill duties or exercise rights;
(8) Allocating power both to officials and private parties to take initiatives to see that obligatory law is carried out;
(9) Monitoring how well persons fulfill duties or exercise rights;
(10) Providing for the resolution of, and resolving disputes about, *facts* when necessary to determine the existence and scope of rights and duties;
(11) Providing for the resolution of, and resolving disputes about, applicable *law* when necessary to determine the existence and scope of rights and duties;
(12) Taking any action ultimately required to fulfill duties, including the imposition of sanctions, official acts themselves in fulfillment of the duties, or the like.

Of course, the specific tasks needed to create and translate a primary precept into practice will vary depending on the goals of the primary precept and the implementive technique involved. Moreover, some tasks may overlap, or occur "out of sequence." For example, the creation of law may merge with authoritative resolution of disputed issues of law, as happens in novel common law cases. Sophisticated social engineers are aware that some tasks themselves call for complex social ordering. The distribution of a new benefit such as public health care, for instance, may require an entirely new distributional agency with both supervisory and operational personnel.

Who performs these various implementive tasks? The participants include judges, legislators, administrative officials and agencies, private individuals, private entities, and sometimes, as in elections, very large segments of the society acting as a group. Pragmatic instrumentalists viewed only judges as the primary functionaries in this division, but their preoccupation with courts was unjustified. It is not possible to discuss here all the tasks that private parties perform either exclusively or with officials. But it is possible to inject considerable skepticism about the "primacy" of the judges and other officials.

Let us begin with the initial tasks that personnel must confront in any sequence for the creation and implementation of law. Who sets goals for uses of law, and who creates the law?

In a libertarian, individualistic democracy with a relatively free market economy, most goals for the various legal precepts in force are not set by officials. Most of "the law" takes the form of private arrangements among private individuals and entities; thus most goals for contracts, property transfers, wills, corporate arrangements, and employment relations, to name a few fields, are set by the private parties and entities involved—not by officials acting for the public. Yet these goals are *legal*, because the corresponding precepts have the force of law between the parties. Even in a large democracy with its vast bureaucracies, these "private" legal goals are far more numerous than those the officialdom sets for statutes, regulations, case law rulings, and the like.

Actually, even the goals formally set by officials are often more faithfully represented as goals "writ large" of individuals or specific classes of individuals than as general goals espoused by all or even a majority of the society. For example, even such a seemingly "official" goal of a collective bargaining statute as "equality of employer-employee bargaining power" translates into something like "we employees want more say over our wages and working conditions, *qua* employees." As the instrumentalists themselves held, the needs and wants of private individuals and groups are the primary sources of goals for law.[179]

Who makes the law? Again, private parties, both corporate and noncorporate, loom large. Commonly they are either the exclusive lawmakers, or major partners in the lawmaking enterprise. In a private arranging technique, for instance, these parties are by far the dominant lawmakers. Every month they enter into hundreds of thousands of contracts, employment relations, property transfers, wills, partnerships, trusts, and leases, all of which have the force of law. In a grievance remedial technique, it is often assumed that the lawmakers consist solely of officials, but much of this law is judge-made common law and therefore is culled largely from perceptions of common sense and morality, both of which derive primarily from the citizenry. It must not be forgotten that private parties—the litigants—participate directly in the lawmaking activities of courts. Furthermore, the overwhelming majority of disputed grievances are settled out of court pursuant to private arrangements that, again, have the force of law. In the distributive technique it is true that much of the law concerned with public benefits is officially made, but private parties in the form of interest groups exert powerful influence on the content of this law in

[179] *See, e.g.*, Pound, *Interests of Personalty*, 28 HARV. L. REV. 343 (1915).

a democracy like ours. In the regulatory technique much law is also profoundly shaped and influenced by private parties participating in rulemaking and in adjudicative proceedings before administrative agencies and courts. In the penal technique state and federal legislatures pass laws, but not without hearings in which private parties often participate extensively, and the statutes themselves usually undergo many a gloss in court proceedings in which private parties participate as defendants.

Beyond goalsetting and lawmaking, the first basic tasks in our overall implementive sequence, it would be possible to demonstrate the large role of private parties in performing the second basic task in the typical implementive sequence, choice of the technique itself, in the third, setting up any needed new entities, and so on through all the remaining tasks in the sequence. But such a demonstration should be unnecessary.

For those who are not yet sufficiently skeptical of the pragmatic instrumentalists' view of the primacy of officials over private parties in our overall division of legal labor, two further general points may be made. First, when goals are finally realized, this is far more commonly attributable to voluntary self-administration than to official administration. The vast bulk of the law addresses private parties and private entities. Daily, private parties apply law to themselves: traffic laws, safety laws, laws entitling them to public benefits, property-boundary laws, penal laws, and on and on. In addition, virtually all of the vast domain of privately created law such as contracts, property arrangements, wills, corporate and other organizational norms is largely administered and applied by its private addressees.

Second, of the five basic technique types, the role of the officialdom is largest in the penal technique. One might even think that there, officials do everything. In truth, private parties probably play larger roles than do officials. Indeed, when the penal technique does not work, this is more often attributable to the inaction of private parties. For example, parties may fail to report violations; refuse to give evidence, or render themselves anonymous or unavailable; decline to "press charges"; refuse to convict when serving as jurors; decline to vote for reelection of vigorous prosecutors; refuse as employers or peers to help rehabilitate offenders, and so on.

An implicit corollary of the instrumentalist doctrine of the primacy of officials is that a legal system functions more or less in a simple top-to-bottom fashion; officials on top are assumed to exercise social control over citizens on the bottom. This simple model fits very little in our law fully. As already indicated, most law is self-imposed, not imposed from above. This is most clearly true of customary, contractual, and other forms of consensual law.

The fallacy of officialism is also partly responsible for the distorted relationship in much instrumentalist thinking between law made by officials and law made by private parties. As already indicated, law made by officials is quantitatively smaller, not larger, than privately created law. Moreover, much officially created law is auxiliary to private law. It exists to *facilitate* the creation and implementation of private law and private choice generally. Even that exemplar of official law, the criminal code, exists mainly to help keep harmful persons out of the way of those who are going about their business—to prevent prospective wrongdoers from interfering with the ordinary conduct of daily life.

The officialism fallacy may also help account for instrumentalist neglect of the informal side of law's techniques. The formal sequences within any of law's techniques rarely proceed through all projected stages, and even when they do officials do not serve at every step as the prime movers.

Even when disputes arise over the application or administration of law, it is unusual that they are resolved through official decision by formal processes. Thus, relatively few claimed torts and breaches of contract become the subject of court judgments; only a small proportion of alleged regulatory infractions become the subject of formal orders of regulatory bodies or courts. The same is true of disputed claims to public benefits such as welfare payments and accident compensation, and of disputes over tax liability. Criminal cases are seldom tried. Instead, most matters are settled informally. Moreover, in settlement processes, private parties will often be the prime movers, with or without lawyer help. Indeed, in many fields of law, the power to take initiative to put an official process for applying law in motion is left largely in the hands of private parties.

X

Coercion, Force, and Direct Official Action

When officials and others use law to serve goals, they may resort to coercion, force, direct action, or a combination of these. What is the place of these elements in a legal system? Most pragmatic instrumentalists held or assumed that the law's efficacy is attributable to the use of coercion and force. They also assumed that law's typical ways of serving goals are direct rather than indirect.

A. *Coercion and Force*

Holmes,[180] Gray,[181] Dewey,[182] and Felix Cohen,[183] in particular, stressed the role of coercion and force. In their view, when an ordinary daily use of law is effective, this will be due largely to the state's capacity and willingness to use, or its actual use of, coercion and force. Pound reinforced this view, remarking frequently that "the life of the law is in its enforcement."[184] Some differences between coercion and force should be noted at the outset. Coercion may be roughly defined as a *threat* of significant adverse action. These thinkers sometimes used "force" as a synonym for "coercion." But they also used "force" in another sense that differentiates it from "coercion." In this other sense, an official may use force without *threatening* adverse consequences, as when he forcibly takes a reluctant drunk off the street. Force need not involve physical action against the person, however. An official may also use coercion without resorting to force, as when he merely threatens a potential trespasser who then moves on. And coercion need not involve threats of force. It may, for example, involve threatened withdrawal of financial support.[185]

In my view, the instrumentalists' emphasis on coercion and force probably had no salutary effect whatsoever. Coercion and force have always been prominent in the history of thought about law. Although some theorists of the nineteenth century may have erroneously identified law with "reason" or "morals" and the like, they did not, as a practical matter, disregard likely actions of officials in power. Without evidence of such disregard, it is hard to justify the instrumentalists' emphasis on coercion and force as a corrective to possible extremism of the day.

The actual place of coercion and force in the workings of law within a particular system is, of course, an empirical question. A legal system may rely more heavily on coercion and force at one time than at another, or more heavily in some areas than in others. Still, I will try to offer some useful tentative generalities.

In the law, coercion and force are most commonly encountered in the working clothes of sanctions (although some sanctions involve neither coercion nor force). There are many forms of law, however,

---

[180] *See* Holmes, *The Path of the Law, supra* note 29, at 457-62.

[181] *See* J. Gray, *supra* note 47, at 12, 101, 116.

[182] *See* Dewey, *Force and Coercion,* 26 Int'l J. Ethics 359 (1916); Dewey, *Force, Violence and Law,* 5 New Republic 295 (1916).

[183] *See* Cohen, *supra* note 32, at 21.

[184] Pound, *supra* note 82, at 514.

[185] *See generally* Oberdiek, *The Role of Sanctions and Coercion in Understanding Law and Legal Systems,* 21 Am. J. Juris. 71 (1976).

that citizens or officials may depart from without incurring liability to a sanction and which do not otherwise bring coercion or force into play. For example, the legal effect of failure to follow rules that merely confer legal power on a private party is generally some form of *nullity* such as an invalid contract, not a sanction. In such a case no one is deprived of possible contract benefits as a sanction for untoward behavior. Or consider an example from the distributive type of technique, a statute providing social security benefits for persons over age sixty-five. Such a law merely defines eligibility. If a person fails to qualify because not yet sixty-five, he is simply ineligible rather than subject to authorized punishment or other sanction.

The efficacy of a particular precept may depend mainly upon educational effort, a reward or other incentive, symbolic deployment of a legal form, publicity, continuous supervision, a public signal, recognition of a status or an entity, and so on. It is not obvious that these implementive devices and mechanisms are necessarily coercive or involve the use of force. Yet many rules that depend upon such devices and mechanisms are nonetheless reasonably effective.

It is at least possible that not just particular rules but a whole system of law may function without organized sanctions. In fact, this is true of our system of international law. Similarly, we may imagine a municipal legal system without sanctions. The efficacy of such a system might depend upon social criticism, inducements, rewards, or the like. Coercion and force in the form of legal sanctions are at least not conceptually necessary features of law. Yet some instrumentalists disagreed. Felix Cohen, for example, thought that law could be "functionally meaningful" only as an act of state force: "[Functionalism] leads to a definition of legal concepts, rules, and institutions in terms of judicial decisions or other acts of state-force. Whatever cannot be so translated is functionally meaningless."[186]

But, it may be asked, is not the everyday efficacy of law generally attributable to the state's standing willingness to use, and its actual use (when necessary), of coercion and force to back up legal duties and directives? In my view an affirmative answer to this is not obviously compelled. It is possible to build an impressive case showing that, in our legal system citizens comply with most duties and directives mainly because of their perception that they *ought* so to behave, and not because of legal coercion or force.[187] The obligations of custom and contract, as we have seen, are by and large self-imposed and self-applied. Although the issue is empirical, the evidence would most

[186] Cohen, *supra* note 32, at 8 (footnote omitted).

[187] Again, Lon Fuller took this view. *See* Summers, *supra* note 51, at 445-47.

likely reveal that the average adult citizen seldom thinks of committing a crime of any seriousness; he takes the leading norms of penal law for granted and behaves consistently with them. Thus not even the fulfillment of the duties imposed by the criminal law—that seemingly most coercive form of law—can be attributed mainly to coercion and force. The same is true of most common-law duties. There are no deep discrepancies between most such duties and general community notions of what is fitting and just. This is true, too, of duties imposed by many statutes and regulations.

Another way to achieve perspective on the true role of coercion and force in accounting for law's efficacy is to return to the sequence of implementive legal tasks introduced earlier.[188] In many uses of law in the American legal order, most if not all implementive work is accomplished when all tasks are fulfilled up through task six—securing citizen capacity to carry out duties or follow directives. At this point the citizens will, assuming performance of the relevant tasks, know what the law expects of them, and will be in a position to fulfill the law's goals. For many citizens this will be enough; the law will mobilize various influences that channel their activity effectively. Few disputes will arise, and when they do it will be at a later stage after the activity has occurred. Many instrumentalists neglected law's channeling tasks, for they were preoccupied with its dispute-settling tasks and the role of courts.[189]

Much channeling of great importance to the social order occurs daily, and without coercion or force figuring prominently in it. Frequently those responsible for the law's implementation must confront task seven—provision of effective incentives. Yet it is probable that citizens are moved most often not by threats or actual uses of coercion or force, but by a sense of obligation, generalized respect for law, fear of criticism, habit and tradition, perception of self interest, recognition of common interest, or by encouragement, persuasion, and other incentives. Of course, it must be admitted that coercion is the only incentive that will work for some addressees of the law at this stage.

In assessing the true place of coercion and force, it is also important to bear in mind that normally these sanctions cannot come into play unless behavioral obligations and directives are involved. As already suggested, however, much law does not impose behavioral obligations or consist of behavioral directives. Distributive law is illustrative. A large part, though not all, of such law provides: "Here

---

[188] *See* section IX.

[189] *See, e.g.*, J. GRAY, *supra* note 47, at 84-125; Gray, *Some Definitions and Questions in Jurisprudence*, 6 HARV. L. REV. 21, 23-24 (1892). *See also* K. LLEWELLYN, *supra* note 107 *passim*.

is a benefit. Come and get it, if you qualify." Furthermore, much law simply confers liberties and powers to be exercised by the individual at will. To coerce the exercise of most liberties and powers would be to destroy their essential character. Rather, the major implementive problems for law of this kind are those of fostering regard for such liberties and powers, and of eliciting the positive responses—creative performances—that they are designed to facilitate. Coercion and force would often nullify rather than nurture such responses.

Once the law's overall implementive sequence has run up to task twelve—taking ultimate implementive action—it will usually be necessary to coerce or to use force, for by that stage a citizen's duty will be clear and by hypothesis he will be refusing to fulfill it. At this stage our legal order could not dispense with powers to use coercion and force. Certainly, the tax system is dependent to some degree on these powers. Prisons, police, and the like appear to be a pragmatic necessity for some small proportion of the population. Although countless daily interactions and exchanges occur without state coercion or force playing a role, some resort to these powers is required to reallocate certain losses that occur such as tort and contract claims. And of course, some citizens would not go along wth regulatory programs if the regulators had no ultimate power to coerce or use force. But although such cases are significant, they are far from the whole story. Of the totality of public and private goals realized to some extent through law on any given day, only a small proportion probably owe anything to official coercion or force.

It is important to distinguish the inherent credibility of the state's monopoly on lawful coercion and force from the incidence of actual resort to official power. Ours is a tolerably well-ordered society.[190] It would appear that the credibility of the state's monopoly does not regularly enter into the daily calculations of ordinary adult citizens. When a society is not tolerably well ordered, however, the contrary is more likely.

So far, I have concentrated on the role of coercion and force in accounting for the general efficacy of laws addressed primarily to ordinary citizens. Yet many laws are addressed primarily to officials: rules of jurisdiction and procedure applicable to legislators, courts, administrative agencies; rules defining the duties of officials; rules limiting official power to affect private citizens, and so on. These laws may be constitutional, statutory, or unwritten in form. In our system, many of these laws are rather closely observed. Is this because, as

[190] By "tolerably well ordered," I do not mean an order attributable to the omnipresence of state power but a set of relations the citizens themselves internalize and consider themselves responsible for.

many instrumentalists would have us believe, our officials fear sanctions, or are coerced in some way?

This too, is an empirical question, but the answer seems fairly clear. Frequently no legal sanction or official coercion will be in the offing, because the rules do not provide for such. A judge who exceeds his jurisdiction, for example, will not be subject to official sanction. Furthermore, as H. L. A. Hart has stressed, most officials generally accept and abide by laws applicable to them in their official capacities, as common public standards of official behavior.[191] They also stand ready to condemn those of their colleagues who do not abide by the rules. The prospect of such criticism no doubt induces some to follow the rules when they might not otherwise. Presumably there are still other explanations for compliance not attributable to coercion or force.

It is important to offer these correctives to the instrumentalist view that our law functions mainly through coercion and force. If law is identified only with state coercion and force it may prove more difficult to secure citizen cooperation in voluntarily upholding it (those parts that deserve to be upheld). Cooperation is dependent mainly upon a widely disseminated understanding that there are affirmative reasons of substance for following most forms of law. To dwell on coercion and force is to neglect these reasons.

B. *Directness of Official Action*

The pragmatic instrumentalist theory that the efficacy of law is essentially dependent on the power of officials to coerce and to use force has a natural corollary: when officials do act they typically take some form of direct action. For example, a police officer's direct efforts to stop a person from committing a crime, the direct action of a regulatory official to confiscate bad food and thus stop it from reaching the market, direct action of a traffic officer to coordinate traffic flow, and so on. Such direct action frequently involves official resort to coercion or the use of force. The "direct action" thesis in instrumentalist writings is more implicit than explicit, but is evident nonetheless.[192] Of course, nothing in instrumentalist theory necessarily requires that legal means be predominantly or even typically direct.

Instrumentalists would have done well to heed Jeremy Bentham's essay *Of Indirect Means of Preventing Crimes.*[193] Addressing himself

---

[191] *See, e.g.*, H. L. A. HART, *supra* note 110, at 109-14.

[192] *See, e.g.*, J. GRAY, *supra* note 47, at 12, 101, 116; Dewey, *Force, Violence and Law*, *supra* note 182, at 295; Holmes, *supra* note 29 *passim*.

[193] J. BENTHAM, *Of Indirect Means of Preventing Crimes*, in 1 WORKS OF JEREMY BENTHAM, *supra* note 10, at 533-80.

almost solely to the penal technique, Bentham postulated that the law's various modes of implementation are not predominantly direct. At least on the surface, the criminal law appears to provide the richest source of illustrations in our law of goals that are served by direct rather than indirect means. If it turns out that the means of implementing the ultimate goals of even the criminal law are largely indirect, this finding will go far to refute those instrumentalists who assume that legal action typically is direct.[194]

According to Bentham, "direct" legal means include both coercive threats of punishment operating at the moment of choice and actual uses of force. Bentham assumed that all other relevant legal means are indirect. A partial list of those other, indirect means, most of which Bentham cited, includes: (1) removal of "bad examples," *e.g.* eliminating violence from public entertainment; (2) deprivation of tools of misbehavior, *e.g.* firearm controls; (3) withholding knowledge required for misbehavior, *e.g.*, keeping secret the movement of valuables through the mails; (4) diversion of dangerous desires, *e.g.*, providing potential delinquents with public amusements to occupy them and to serve as outlets for aggression; (5) removal of open temptations, *e.g.*, counseling people to lock vehicles; (6) improvement of the capacity of potential victims to protect themselves, *e.g.*, encouraging technology for thief-proof locks and alarm systems; (7) reduction of access to judgment-impairing drink and drugs, *e.g.*, regulating liquor consumption; (8) provision of peaceful alternatives to violent self help, *e.g.*, making courts available for redress of grievances; (9) encouragement of public criticism of wrongdoing, *e.g.*, publicizing convictions and naming the parties involved; (10) reinforcement of specific values behind prohibitions, and strengthening dispositions not to engage in wrongful conduct, *e.g.*, providing moral education as part of general education; and (11) cultivation of general benevolence, *e.g.*, through education.

On a lower level of generality—a level of greater goal variety and particularity—I have found that it is possible to identify other more substantive contrasts between direct and indirect legal means. Most of these contrasts can be drawn not only within the criminal law, but in other fields as well.

One important contrast is between coercing a person to act or refrain (direct) and inducing him to do so voluntarily through incen-

---

[194] Of course, law may be used directly and indirectly at the same time. Moreover, a use of law may involve use of direct means to serve one goal, and indirect means to serve another related goal. Thus, while a use of law to provide education is a direct means to the goal of securing basic literacy, it is also an indirect means, when compared with threats of punishment, to crime control.

tives, rewards, etc. (indirect). Thus, instead of coercing private lenders to observe set ceilings on interest rates chargeable for loans, the state might, through publicity given to interest rates charged by competitors, encourage more competition between lenders, with the incentive consisting of larger shares of the total loan business for those with the lowest competitive interest rate.

A second contrast is between "treating the symptom" (direct) and "removing the cause" (indirect). For example, instead of forcibly jailing a public drunk each time he becomes a nuisance (direct), the state might induce him when he is sober to enter a hospital for a "cure" (indirect).[195] Of course, "causes" can be approached directly, too, but note that in this contrast the "direct" action is addressed to the objectionable behavior itself with a view to its immediate termination, whereas the "indirect" action focuses on underlying causes of the overall behavior pattern.

A third contrast is between providing a benefit, facility, or the like (direct) and maximizing the conditions under which people are able to provide such resources for themselves (indirect). For instance, instead of guaranteeing minimum material well being through welfare payments, the state might provide tax incentives for people to save for hard times, make job information available, prohibit job discrimination, and so on.

A fourth contrast is between direct and indirect imposition of burdens. For example, a tax or fine may be imposed directly on A, but A may eventually (indirectly) be able to pass it on to B.

A fifth contrast is that between burdens fixed in specie and generalized obligations. If the state wants to increase its resources for state use, for instance, it may adopt a rule to take specific property away from individuals (direct), but it might achieve the same result by imposing a general tax that forces owners to sell the property to pay the tax (indirect).

A final contrast is between using a means that allows officials to take action without going through legal processes (direct) and requiring officials to go through duly constituted processes before they act (indirect). For example, instead of invoking emergency powers and acting directly to stop people en masse from traveling during a time of peril, officials might take an individualized approach and stop movement only after they have secured specific detention orders.

---

[195] This might serve still other goals directly, as well.

Thus, in my view it is well, and perhaps a prerequisite to optimal use of law, to be aware of possibilities for indirect goal subservience. Many goals may be more effectively served by indirect means. Some are not readily achievable or not achievable at all through direct means. For example, a legal system cannot guarantee self-realization or happiness of citizens directly—it can only seek to secure conditions in which goals are realized. Even when law can contribute directly to the achievement of certain goals, an indirect contribution might be more effective, as in the foregoing array of indirect means of crime control.

Furthermore, direct means actually may be too effective, and thus do more harm than good. If so, indirect means may be preferable. Direct prohibition of liquor consumption is perhaps the best illustration of such "overkill." Similarly, the state may choose to use indirect rather than direct means because the latter are too paternalistic. Followers of John Stuart Mill might oppose direct uses of law to forbid smoking or direct uses of law to require drivers to wear seat belts, yet still favor laws against making cigarettes or laws requiring that cars have seat belts. Or the state might lack the substantive standards or bureaucratic means to set wages in private employment and therefore confine its efforts to setting up and policing systems of collective bargaining.

Moreover, what is politically acceptable at a given time may depend on whether an indirect rather than a direct use of law is involved. Thus, although a political party might not rally enough support for wage controls on unions (direct), it may be able to secure legislation imposing sanctions against employers who make excessive wage settlements (indirect). It should be plain that in some societies, direct official taking of property would be politically unacceptable, while a confiscatory tax with the same ultimate effect would be more palatable. Similarly, it may be more acceptable for governments to redistribute income through "free" state services (indirect) than through money payments to particular beneficiaries from tax revenues (direct). Indirect means can be more economical, too. Thus a tax deduction (indirect) usually costs less to administer than direct payments.

Finally, as Bentham noted, indirect means may be more gentle. Certainly educative and persuasive methods of disposing people to behave well are more gentle than is criminal punishment.

The implementive resources of the law, then, should and do include many devices that may be deployed indirectly rather than directly. It cannot be assumed that in our own system we rely more heavily on direct means than on indirect means.

XI

JUDGING THE SUCCESS OF A USE OF LAW

After law is created, used to serve projected goals, and after sufficient time has passed, it is natural for the pragmatic instrumentalist to inquire whether this use of law has been successful. For this, he needs some kind of criterion of success.

Among instrumentalists it became an article of faith that officials and the public must judge a use of law by its substantive "effects"—by the extent to which its effects served goals set at the outset. Thus Roscoe Pound, in his famous essay on the scope and purpose of sociological jurisprudence, wrote that we should "study . . . the actual social effects of legal institutions and legal doctrines . . . , [the end of which] is to make effort more effective in achieving the purposes of law."[196] Walter Wheeler Cook emphasized:

> the worth or value of a given rule of law can be determined only by finding out how it works, that is, by ascertaining, so far as that can be done, whether it promotes or retards the attainment of desired ends. If this is to be done, quite clearly we must know what at any given period these ends are and also whether the means selected, the given rules of law, are indeed adapted to securing them.[197]

The formalists, to whom the pragmatic instrumentalists were reacting in part, appeared to ignore law's effects. Their orientation was largely retrospective. In using law, their primary concern was to achieve consistency and harmony with the past; "logical" elaboration of preexisting doctrine was their basic tool. The orientation of instrumentalists to the future and its improvement was therefore a considerable advance. But their "efficacy criterion" of legal success was not free of difficulties, and to this day, it has received little systematic critical attention.

A. *The Complex Evaluative Nature of Efficacy Judgments*

Instrumentalists generally believed that to judge the success of a use of law, it is necessary only to identify its effects and measure them on some kind of scale. In the grip of a rampant empiricism, most of these thinkers assumed that all facts relevant to the application of this criterion of success must be determinable through observation, and

---

[196] Pound, *supra* note 82, at 513-15 (footnotes omitted).

[197] Cook, *supra* note 95, at 308. For similar views, see Cohen, *supra* note 32, at 18-24; Dewey, *John Dewey*, in MY PHILOSOPHY OF LAW, *supra* note 48, at 82-85; Llewellyn, *supra* note 2, at 1237; Moore, *Underhill Moore*, in MY PHILOSOPHY OF LAW, *supra* note 48, at 206-07.

that the ultimate judgment about success or failure therefore must be essentially empirical rather than evaluative. In my view, the truth is far more complex. The ultimate question is whether the use of law being judged is *sufficiently* effective, and an answer to this calls for the exercise of evaluative judgment.

For present purposes, it will be useful to think of the effectiveness per se of a use of law in relation to an imaginary scale on which complete effectiveness in the form of total "victory" over the problem is registered at the top of the scale (a state of affairs rarely achievable or rarely desirable as a goal), and complete ineffectiveness is registered at the bottom of the scale. Of course, whether a use of law is *sufficiently* effective to be successful is to some extent a function of the absolute level of effectiveness on such a scale. It would be absurd to judge as successful a totally ineffective use of law, and similarly absurd to judge as unsuccessful a totally effective one. Likewise, the regularity of any level of effectiveness would be relevant to determining whether a use of law is sufficiently effective. But because these factual matters are not the whole story, the actual level of effectiveness on such a scale for a given use of law may be one thing, and the determination of whether that use is sufficiently effective to be successful quite another. Thus, to judge the effectiveness of a given use of law, two separate questions must be addressed: (1) What level of effectiveness did it achieve? (2) What level of effectiveness is sufficient for it to be judged a success?

It is possible that even a low level of effectiveness, judged absolutely, may nonetheless count as sufficiently effective and successful. How is this so? First, in some fields, because of special difficulties of detection, as in the crime of incest, or of proof, as in the crime of rape, relatively little (here in the form of actual convictions) may be achieved. Even so, given such special difficulties, the uses of law involved may be judged sufficiently effective. Similarly, the intrinsic nature of a task might make it exceedingly difficult to achieve by any use of law, and especially by a coercive use. This would be true, for example, of tasks such as those of inspiring attitudes of charity or tolerance. As to these, considerable ineffectiveness might still count as sufficient and therefore successful.

Second, the state of affairs to be achieved may be one that can generally be brought about through law only indirectly, with substantial ineffectiveness more or less inevitable. Happy marriages are an example. Age requirements for valid marriages comprise one indirect means we use to pursue this end. These requirements tend, but only tend, to make for more mature judgments in the choice of spouses; yet even a high divorce rate would not signify that age requirements are insufficiently effective. Because it would be unwise for the law to prescribe particular marital matches or otherwise proceed directly, the law must proceed indirectly and therefore quite contingently.

Third, those who use law may deliberately choose a limited means for cost reasons. A society, for example, might decline to set up an independent review bureaucracy in order to combat problems of official abuse of power because it would be too costly. Instead, the society might choose to rely solely on private tort actions to protect against official abuse of power, yet this limited means might fail significantly to reduce abuses such as police brutality. Still, this use of law might be adjudged sufficiently effective and thus successful, given the costs society is willing to incur.

Fourth, legislators or judges may deliberately choose to adopt limited means because more effective ones would involve unacceptable sacrifices of other important goals. Considerations of liberty and humaneness, for example, might lead a society to choose to fight crime with one arm behind its back. The resulting shortfall in crime control should not necessarily be judged insufficiently effective.

Fifth, even considerable ineffectiveness in the short run does not necessarily imply long run ineffectiveness. For example, it might turn out that affirmative action programs designed to remedy racial imbalances fail badly in the short run but take hold in the long run. Or a country might only gradually embrace a set of norms like those in the International Convention on Human Rights. Some uses of law simply require time to take effect. When this is so, a relatively low level of effectiveness may still be viewed as sufficient, given the required time interval.

Thus, in all these cases more is involved in judging legal success than simply determining actual effects and plotting them on some kind of scale. Rather, the issue becomes one of sufficiency of effects in relation to such factors as the difficulties of realizing the goals, the amenability of the goals to direct means, the extent to which resources are allocated to the problem, the conflicting goals that are affected, and the time interval required for the use of law to "take hold." Whether a given use of law is sufficiently effective, as judged in relation to such considerations, is therefore a complex evaluative question. And it must not be thought that these considerations come into play only rarely. On the contrary, most are normally at work to some degree any time law is used.

It might be objected that the foregoing analysis illegitimately preserves an evaluative issue about the sufficiency of effectiveness beyond the initial stage of goal formulation; if goals are formulated in the first place not in absolute terms (*i.e.*, the top end of an effectiveness scale) but are adjusted downward in light of the bearing of such factors as difficulty of fulfillment, amenability to direct means and the like, then, once the facts about effectiveness level are known at the stage when success is to be judged, the remaining judgment as to efficacy will be wholly factual and non-evaluative.

But whatever the virtues of trying to set goals initially not in terms of total or absolute "victory" over a problem, but rather, in relation to the difficulty of the task, its amenability to direct means, and so on, we can rarely foreclose all evaluative questions at the final stage when facts are in and success or failure is to be judged. For it is not until then that we will have the fullest possible factual picture of the importance of such factors, and thus it is not until success or failure is to be judged that *sufficiency* of efficacy can itself be most realistically measured. It is this very judgment that is inescapably evaluative. Even if all evaluative issues as to what is sufficiently effective could appropriately be resolved at the initial goal formulation stage, this early determination would inevitably lend any final judgment of efficacy an *overall* evaluative character, no matter how exclusively factual the final judgment actually is. That is, to judge a use of law as effective in this way would also be to say that it is sufficiently effective, given the earlier resolution of "sufficiency" issues.

B. *Further Difficulties in Applying an Efficacy Criterion*

Instrumentalist thinkers varied greatly in the degree of their sophistication about the practical and other difficulties of applying an efficacy criterion. Most of them were unaware of these difficulties or did not take them very seriously,[198] yet the problems can be considerable, for even the simplest uses of law.

The very idea of an "object" of an efficacy judgment is at least problematic. What is to count as a "use of law" for purposes of judging efficacy? The meaning of this phrase may range from a single official action applying a rule in a particular case to the entire workings of, say, the penal technique. It would be inappropriate to confine the object of an efficacy judgment to some arbitrarily specified use of legal resources within this range. In practice, legal actors must make efficacy judgments about uses of law that fall across the whole range of uses, small and large, brief and lengthy. Thus, any functional unit of legal resources can be the object of an efficacy judgment, although care must be taken to see that such an object is not artificially separated from related resources.[199]

---

[198] *See, e.g.*, Bingham, *supra* note 95; Cook, *supra* note 95.

[199] It would be artificial, for example, to try to judge the effectiveness of a duty-imposing precept apart from the implementive resources devoted to it. The relevant goals are goals of the

Another problem is that the relevant goals may not be readily ascertainable for judging whether a use of law is sufficiently effective. It is one thing to attribute goals to a single precept, although this too, can be problematic. It is quite another to attribute goals to a use of law for judging efficacy. A use of law combines precepts with other legal resources into a functional unit, and it is to this complex unit that goals usually must be attributed.

The goals considered depend on the nature of the use of law to be judged. If the judgment is about a functional unit consisting only of a judicial decision within a given legal framework, for example, the goals will usually be less numerous and varied, and their identification easier, than if the judgment is about some larger use of law such as regulatory control of air pollution from stationary and mobile sources.

The goals relevant to judging efficacy also depend on how the intentions of legal actors limit what is relevant. As has been shown, it is important to separate three levels of "end result" goals, at least for uses of law that impose behavioral duties.[200] These levels can be distinguished along an ascending means-end continuum in which the realization of lower level goals, often explicitly formulated in the law, serves higher level goals, often not so formulated. Thus, for most uses of law we may identify one or more immediate goals, intermediate goals, and ultimate goals. Returning to an earlier example, consider a law requiring private handgun owners to register their ownership with the police. We might distinguish at least the following different goals for this law: registration of all privately owned handguns (immediate), deterrence and control of firearm violence (intermediate), general community peace (ultimate).

Note that just because a use of law serves an immediate goal well, it does not follow that its ultimate goal will be well served. Thus, even if all handguns were registered, firearm violence might nonetheless increase. It should be evident, therefore, that efficacy judgments must be framed with goal multiplicity in mind. A given efficacy judgment might read: "The law is effective as to immediate goals, but ineffective, or of limited efficacy, as to one or more intermediate or ultimate level goals."

Often, however, we will not know just what goal possibilities the lawmakers had in mind, or which goals of several a majority espoused. Standard legislative or other sources may be of little help. It may be necessary to review a variety of sources to have a sufficient

---

whole entity, not just the part, and effects cannot meaningfully be attributed to parts in isolation.

[200] *See* text accompanying notes 79-81 *supra*.

basis for determining intermediate or ultimate goals for a use of law. Where relevant law is a mix of statute, regulation, and court action, as is often the case, the whole mix must be considered. Moreover, goals can change over time even though the relevant law remains the same. A goal statement may prove over-general or vacuous. Or it may be that no single goal can be considered authoritative. In such a case, efficacy must be judged in relation to a posited goal.

Goal statements are often formulable in different ways: as general or specific, as more or less concrete, as time bound or not, etc. By manipulating goal formulations it is possible to convert inefficacy into efficacy or vice versa. For example, a goal statement for a use of law imposing a charitable tax contribution may purport to make people more charitable, or it might be interpreted only to call for coercive collection of a sum of money to be used for charitable purposes. If the latter, this use of law could be judged effective. If the former, only little might be achieved because the extent to which law can coerce charitableness is inherently limited. Thus, much depends on what goal formulations are fairly attributable to a particular use of law.

Sometimes what appears on the surface to be a goal will turn out not to be upon analysis. In tort law, for example, deterrence of unduly risky activities is always a natural candidate for goal status. But some torts do not involve this goal. The tort of "ultrahazardous" activity, for example, might be viewed more accurately as a kind of tax on a course of conduct. Similarly, many uses of law confer liberties or benefits. If individuals do not avail themselves of these advantages, it does not necessarily follow that a goal has not been met. It is not a goal that a given percentage of liberty or right exercises take place.

Once various goals are identified it often will be evident they conflict, and that the lawmaker does not desire substantial fulfillment of a particular goal but only the relative maximization of a number of goals. The interrelations of conflicting goals can thus inject considerable complexity into the process. Beyond problems of defining proper objects of efficacy judgments and problems of defining goals, a third basic difficulty in judging efficacy remains: determining the actual effects of uses of law.

The conditions that must be satisfied in order to make efficacy judgments are most often met with respect to the *immediate* effects that correspond to the immediate goals of a use of law. For example, an immediate goal of one important branch of law is to provide a compensatory judicial remedy for breach of contract if the aggrieved party seeks it. When a breach occurs and a remedy is sought, it will often be easily determinable whether the court granted a remedy and what remedy it gave. If a remedy was granted, then we may say that in light of this immediate effect of the use of relevant law, the immediate goal of providing a compensatory remedy was effectively realized.[201]

Other examples of more or less ascertainable immediate effects of a use of law may be cited from any of law's five basic techniques. For example, one immediate goal of a regulatory use of law might be that all car drivers possess a minimum knowledge of traffic laws. By prescribing examinations as a prerequisite for licensing, the immediate effects of a law requiring knowledge could be ascertained. Similarly, a distributive use of law might have as its immediate goal providing basic subsistence payments to qualified persons who apply. By comparing payments with applicants' qualifications, it would be possible to determine whether the immediate effect of this use of law was to provide the desired payments.

Immediate effects that correspond to immediate goals, however, differ in kind from the effects corresponding to intermediate and ultimate goals. As already indicated, immediate effects can occur without triggering intermediate and ultimate effects. The ready determinability of immediate effects may be relatively insignificant to an understanding of the efficacy of the law with regard to higher goals. Immediate effects may turn out to be merely mechanical; they merely may be necessary steps in a sequence of projected effects in which intermediate and ultimate effects must occur before the law can be judged sufficiently effective. These further effects may be difficult or impossible to ascertain. For example, one intermediate or ultimate goal of liability for breach of contract is to facilitate efficient reallocation of resources when the transaction breaks down. The degree to which granting a remedy (immediate effect) serves this further goal may be difficult to determine. Similarly, whether a law is effective in requiring drivers to possess knowledge of traffic rules may be ascertainable, but whether this law in turn significantly enhances safety (intermediate or ultimate goal), may be quite indeterminable. Although it may be easy to determine whether eligible welfare recipients get paid (immediate goal), it may be less easy to ascertain whether these payments actually nurture the minimum health and well being of recipients (intermediate or ultimate goal).

Determining intermediate and ultimate effects, and the degree of regularity thereof, may be difficult for a variety of reasons familiar to social scientists. The "effects" might have occurred in any event, caused by non-legal factors simultaneously at work. It may be impos-

---

[201] Notice, though, that this might be a rather hollow form of goal realization, for the defendant might be judgment-proof. Notice, too, that we have said nothing about whether the remedy is adequate.

sible to make comparative studies or whatever is required to sort out what is genuinely causal. Such studies might be impossible or exceedingly difficult to do because society will not permit costly or otherwise objectionable social experiments, because comparable social conditions may not exist, because the factors involved are too intangible or too difficult to measure, and so on.

In sum, the pragmatic instrumentalist social engineers who thought it relatively easy to determine the effects of a use of law were naively optimistic. The object of an efficacy judgment—a use of law—is rarely self defining. Goals for a use of law may not be readily specifiable. The actual isolation and description of effects genuinely attributable to this use may be speculative. Such difficulties are often compounded when the goals and effects under study are intermediate or ultimate in character.

C. *Efficacy as a Criterion of Success*

Even if an efficacy criterion could be readily and easily applied, it would not necessarily follow that it would be a satisfactory general criterion for judging the success of a use of law. Those who invoke an efficacy test might construe it narrowly to require inquiry only into whether the use of law being judged actually fulfills goals set at the outset. Among the technologically minded instrumentalists there may even have been some disposition to construe the criterion narrowly in this way.[202]

So construed, the criterion is deficient in several ways. First, it neglects the goodness or badness of the means used. Legal means may themselves be bad, and this badness may also infect the quality of the goals realized. Second, a merely technological focus fails to subject to scrutiny the goals originally set. A genuine criterion of *success* cannot take the desirability of these for granted. Even if means are effective and not objectionable, and even if original goals are good, we still may not have genuine legal success. Unanticipated bad effects may occur with the result that the use of law brings more harm than good. Third, a technological criterion ignores the effects that a use of law may have in influencing the general patterns of wants and desires within the society. Of course, these effects, too, may be good or bad. For example, the uses of law to structure and order an economic system may foster commercialism and materialism.

Thus, at its worst, a technological criterion of legal success allows legal actors and citizens to judge a use of law successful even though

[202] *See, e.g.*, Pound, *supra* note 82; Llewellyn, *supra* note 2. *See also* K. LLEWELLYN, *supra* note 107, at 79-80.

the means selected and the original goals are bad, the outcome is one that does more harm than good in the circumstances, and the ultimate effects on general patterns of wants and desires is unwholesome.

Although no pragmatic instrumentalist appears to have unqualifiedly subscribed to a merely technological criterion of legal success, many stated their criterion without addressing any of the foregoing issues. Moreover, the emphasis on means in instrumentalism, and its conventionalist value theory ("whatever the crowd wants," as Holmes put it),[203] was congenial to such a narrow criterion. A use of law could prove to be a highly effective means for satisfying antecedent wants and interests, yet be subject to objections on all of the various grounds just considered.

Furthermore, an efficacy criterion is myopic in two quite special ways. First, as a consequentialist criterion, it presupposes that values can be realized only through uses of law that are *causal*—uses that serve goals through cause-effect sequences. Only if these occur can there be legal success. But values can also be realized when law is used in ways that simply *accord with* norms of right behavior. Law is regularly used to resolve disputes, for example, but actual dispute settlements are not all that is of concern here. We also want settlements to accord with what is right. Such a relationship is not just some additional kind of effect. To illustrate: much law is concerned with "doing justice and equity" between the parties after the fact in light of rightness norms such as "act in good faith," "take care for others," "keep your word," "give others their just due," and "deal honestly." The accordance of judicial or other legal decisions with such norms in light of the facts of the case is not causal, for it does not depend on the occurrence of decisional effects. Rather, it depends on the relation between the decision and the way that rightness norms apply to the past interaction of the parties. Hence, the pragmatic instrumentalist slogan "judge legal success in terms of effects," takes no account of the accordance of a decision with rightness norms in a particular case as a distinctive form of legal success.[204]

An efficacy criterion is myopic in another way; it makes no special place for effects that may occur *in the course of law's workings* prior to or apart from any end result. These effects may implicate rule-of-law values such as certainty, predictability, reliability, and even-handedness; division of legal labor values such as democratic control, efficiency of specialization, and distinctive competency; process values such as notice and opportunity for fair participation in

---

[203] 1 HOLMES-POLLOCK LETTERS, *supra* note 44, at 163.

[204] *See generally* Summers, *supra* note 156, at 718-22, 764-82.

a legal process.[205] All these are important values, and in the course of law's workings they may not be realized even though antecedent substantive goals are. Sometimes such substantive goals can be realized only at the price of sacrificing these other types of values.

Conclusion

Some might deny that pragmatic instrumentalism constitutes a theory of law.[206] By all standards, however, this body of tenets qualifies as a general theory about law and its use. It incorporated a sufficiently wide range of tenets, and although many of its tenets were not the subject of extensive development, at least the general directions of thought were reasonably clear. Some of its tenets were evaluative, some analytical, and some empirical. But such diversity is rooted in the nature of the subject. Did the tenets lack sufficient thematic unity? Pragmatic instrumentalism is not without its general unifying themes—ones that range over or inter-relate many, if not most, of its tenets. The notion of law as an instrument to serve social goals was one of these. The scientific and technological ethos was another, as was the primacy of personnel, particularly the judiciary. Some facet of pragmatist philosophy underlay nearly every tenet. It must be admitted that there was no one root idea from which all else developed, but this is true of other legal theories as well.

Many Europeans have tended to dismiss American legal theory as merely derivative. They have worked within the continental natural law tradition or within the analytical positivist tradition, mainly Viennese or British. But pragmatic instrumentalism cannot be dismissed as merely derivative. Rather, it is a distinctive tradition in its own right. With its utilitarian and therefore consequentialist value theory, its orientation to the social sciences, and its technological emphasis, for example, no one could reasonably characterize it as in the natural law tradition. At the same time, it can hardly be considered merely another version of analytical positivism. Pragmatic instrumentalism incorporated a general theory of value. It viewed law as a human artifact, not as a mere inert datum on which analysts might ply their trade. It viewed law as a means to goals—as a social instrument—and it conceived legal theory to be concerned with the general uses of law as well as with its nature. It was antiformal, and was occupied—even preoccupied—with issues of legal method, particularly with regard to judging.

---

[205] *See generally* Summers, *Evaluating and Improving Legal Processes—A Plea for "Process Values,"* 60 Cornell L. Rev. 1 (1974).

[206] *See, e.g.*, W. Twining, *supra* note 3, at 375.

Not only is pragmatic instrumentalism a distinctive tradition within Western legal theory, it is also largely indigenous to the United States.[207] Further, many American lawyers who assumed themselves to be uninfluenced by jurisprudence simply were wrong. Many tenets of pragmatic instrumentalism dominated the American legal scene at least during the middle decades of this century. Some tenets were profoundly influential, and continue to be so now. This is true in particular of instrumentalist legal method. I cannot go into the evidence of instrumentalist influence here, but if I am wrong about the extent of it, I am in good company, including that of Gilmore,[208] and Llewellyn himself.[209]

It is too soon to attempt a definitive account of this influence. It is also premature to offer an overall assessment of the theory. Nonetheless, I have indicated some ways in which this body of thought was, in my opinion, errant. It neglected and distorted law's normative nature. It was utilitarian and therefore failed to subject goals and means to independent qualitative scrutiny (including the scrutiny of "rightness" concepts and principles). It was excessively means-minded. It incorporated exclusively source-based criteria of legal validity. It overestimated the freedom judges have, under the law, to decide cases as they wish. It oversimplified complex matters, including the nature and relations of means and goals, the techniques of the law, and the determination of law's effects. Yet many of these deficiencies can be remedied.

At the same time, there is much to welcome in pragmatic instrumentalist thought. Its spirit was humanistic and democratic—law was viewed as organized society's chief means of altering the future in the interest of social improvement. It opened up whole new branches of legal theory, including law's complex goal structures, the interactions of means and goals, and law's implementive technology. It brought technological rationalism and empiricism into the law. It introduced a concern for law's social effects. It provided a telling critique of formalistic legal method. It stressed the significance of legal personnel. And more.

In addition to these substantive contributions, there are methodological lessons, too. Perhaps the most important one to be learned from a study of pragmatic instrumentalism is that legal theory is something more than a branch of philosophy, more than applied

---

[207] This is not to say that there have been no instrumentalists or functionalists elsewhere. *See, e.g.*, R. Von Ihering, *supra* note 9.

[208] *See* G. Gilmore, *supra* note 8 *passim*.

[209] *See* K. Llewellyn, The Common Law Tradition, *supra* note 142, at 3-178.

social science, and more than just an exercise in the history of ideas. Legal theory cannot safely draw its models from any one discipline. If it was wrong for Llewellyn (and his like) to rail as he did at the philosophers, it was also wrong for him to embrace the scientists in the way he did. Legal theory has a kind of autonomy of its own. Law will not, without distortion, yield in some wholesale fashion to the analytical perspectives and methods of any one discipline.[210]

In 1957, H. L. A. Hart wrote that he had formed the belief that within analytical jurisprudence, inquiry had come to a "premature standstill."[211] In his view, much more could be done. Subsequent events have proven him right.[212]

At mid-century in the United States, pragmatic instrumentalist thought had come to a premature standstill. I have sought in this Article to indicate several of the more fertile yet relatively untilled domains. It is likely that some, perhaps much, further instrumentalist work will be done. Ultimately, however, I suspect that the perfect theory of law will not take the form of a duly revised and elaborated pragmatic instrumentalism. Rather, it will be a more inclusive theory that partakes of the best in each of the three great traditions. And even at that, this perfect theory will not be equally applicable to all societies.

---

[210] But for a somewhat different view, see Summers, *The New Analytical Jurists*, 49 N.Y.U. L. Rev. 861 (1966); R. Dworkin, The Philosophy of Law (1977).

[211] Hart, *Analytical Jurisprudence in Mid-Twentieth Century: A Reply to Professor Bodenheimer*, 105 U. Pa. L. Rev. 953, 957 (1957).

[212] In large measure it was Hart himself who not only showed the way but undertook the primary labors. See, for example, H. L. A. Hart, *supra* note 110, and the bibliography of his many other illuminating articles and books in Law, Morality, and Society—Essays in Honour of H. L. A. Hart (P. Hacker & J. Raz eds. 1977).

Name Index

www.ingramcontent.com/pod-product-compliance
Lightning Source LLC
LaVergne TN
LVHW102107300926
849161LV00014B/3069